WORKING LIVES

Essays in Canadian Working-Class History

Craig Heron is one of Canada's leading labour historians. His latest work draws together fifteen of his new and previously published essays on working-class life in Canada and covers a wide range of issues, including politics, culture, gender, wage-earning, and union organization. A timely contribution to the evolving field of labour in Canada, this cohesive collection analyses the daily experiences of people working across Canada over more than two hundred years.

Honest in its depictions of the historical complexities of daily life, *Working Lives* raises issues in the writing of Canadian working-class history, especially "working-class realism," and how it is eventually inscribed into Canada's public history. Thoughtfully reflecting on the ways in which workers interact with the past, Heron discusses the important role that historians and museums play in remembering the adversity and milestones experienced by Canada's working class.

CRAIG HERON is a professor emeritus in the Department of History at York University and author of *Working Steel: The Early Years in Canada, 1883–1935*, also published by University of Toronto Press.

Working Lives

Essays in Canadian Working-Class History

CRAIG HERON

UNIVERSITY OF TORONTO PRESS
Toronto Buffalo London

Toronto Buffalo London
utorontopress.com

ISBN 978-1-4875-0325-3 (cloth)
ISBN 978-1-4875-2251-3 (paper)

Library and Archives Canada Cataloguing in Publication

Heron, Craig, author
Working lives : essays in Canadian working-class history / Craig Heron.

Includes bibliographical references.
ISBN 978-1-4875-0325-3 (hardcover) ISBN 978-1-4875-2251-3 (softcover)

1. Working class – Canada – History. 2. Social history – Canada. I. Title.

HD8104.H47 2018 305.5′620971 C2018-903306-1

University of Toronto Press acknowledges the financial assistance to its publishing program of the Canada Council for the Arts and the Ontario Arts Council, an agency of the Government of Ontario.

Canada Council for the Arts
Conseil des Arts du Canada

Funded by the Government of Canada
Financé par le gouvernement du Canada

Contents

Part Four: A Gendered World

Part Five: Doing History

Introduction

"Apologies are no longer necessary when setting out to write the history of Canadian workers." That was the opening line of my PhD dissertation completed in 1981.[1] It is a sentence brimming with the cocky confidence of a young scholar in a dynamic new field of study that was exploding with energy, creativity, and ambition. I had been caught up in an intellectual wave that was sweeping over the historical profession in Canada and elsewhere. We had boundless optimism that workers would finally find their rightful place in history.

More than three decades later, while my focus and analytical lenses have shifted over time, I continue to believe that working-class Canadians deserve to have their history taken seriously and have tried to make a small contribution to the large project of exploring their past. I wrote a few books, but also several essays that appeared in scattered publications or, in some cases, remained buried in file folders. It now seems time to assemble some of these fragments in one place to make them more accessible and to let them speak together about some large themes in the working-class history of Canada. With two exceptions, I have chosen those that try to open up the widest panoramic analyses, rather than focusing primarily on one community.[2]

The essays included here were written over more than three decades. It would be misleading to suggest that they emerged in any logical order according to some master plan. It would be just as misleading to present myself an isolated writer locked away in my study churning out polished papers. Each essay took shape as part of a much more collective process of discussion and debate among relatively small groups of people with shared intellectual and political interests. I was fortunate to find myself in a long series of such groupings, sometimes distinct, often overlapping. Sometimes I was drawn into an existing group; sometimes I took the initiative to bring such a group together. Some were short-lived; some continue to the present. Sometimes their discussions inspired me to put pen to paper; sometimes I spearheaded an effort to put some of the discussions on paper; other times I was coaxed into joining some collective writing project. What I wrote was always shaped by the collective ruminations in each of these settings.

The starting point was undoubtedly the Centre for the Study of Social History at the University of Warwick in Coventry, UK, where I spent a year working on an MA in Comparative Labour History in 1975–6. In my previous work as an undergraduate and graduate student at the University of Toronto, I had developed an interest in the history of working people, not only because I came from a working-class family, but more because I had been inspired by New Left politics, which by the early 1970s was belatedly coming to terms with the working class.[3] The Centre at Warwick had been founded in the late 1960s by probably the most famous historian of the British working class, E.P. Thompson, and, although he had left long before 1975, the place still had a small staff of excellent labour and social historians and a considerable number of highly motivated graduate students interested in working-class history. The small, intense Master's program there, which mixed British, US, and Canadian students, gave me an opportunity to read about and discuss the exciting new work appearing in British and US working-class history, and to attend lively research seminars featuring a cavalcade of some of the United Kingdom's most prominent social historians. That exhilarating experience began my intellectual formation in the "new" labour history, which emphasized above all the patterns of active resistance and rebellion by workers in capitalist society. The British scholarship, however, tended to complicate the story of class mobilization with greater emphasis on the divisions within the working class and the constraints on radicalism and militancy (a debate raged, for example, about the "aristocracy of labour,"[4] which generally did not appear in North American labour history). My first scholarly articles drew heavily on what I learned in the English Midlands, notably "Labourism and the Canadian Working Class," which attempted to delineate a specifically working-class liberalism in Canadian politics that paralleled what was emerging in Britain in the same period. It is included here.[5]

It was clear to me that I was entering a field that was being profoundly reshaped and reconceptualized. On returning to Canada in

1976, I began a PhD in History at Dalhousie University, where a handful of faculty and several MA and PhD students coalesced into a community of engaged labour historians. The galvanizing force that was turning a small east-coast history department into a hotbed of radical history was Greg Kealey, hired only two years earlier. In the department's bi-weekly North American Seminar, professors and students presented unpublished papers and draft dissertation chapters, which invariably faced rigorous, challenging critiques. More informally, those of us interested in working-class history got inspiration from the works of E.P. Thompson, Eric Hobsbawm, Herbert Gutman, David Montgomery, and, in some cases, Sheila Rowbotham and Alice Kessler-Harris, but also from Karl Marx. Indeed, an unabashed historical materialism ran freely among many of us, and one winter several of us worked our way slowly through volume 1 of Marx's *Capital*. Class formation and the class struggle were at the centre of our analytical universe. We were particularly interested in the structures of class society, and, as part of our dissertation work, each of us researched and dug deep into the history of capitalist development in various industries in Canada, alongside our research on the workers who toiled there (admittedly, we felt we had to do this economic history because of the dearth of writing on industrial history on Canadian library shelves). We were wary, however, of crude, reductionist Marxism that simply saw class experience as a direct, unmediated reflection of the material base of society, and spent a lot of time looking across the Atlantic to the debates among sophisticated English Marxists.[6] Many of us were also inspired by new currents of feminist writing, which we juggled a bit awkwardly with our Marxism.[7]

We also reached out to a new interdisciplinary network of radical scholars in Canada known as the Political Economy Network, which began meeting around the same time within Canada's annual Learned Societies conferences. The common ground was a materialist analysis, although we historians often grumbled that, in searching for a homegrown radicalism, some of the Canadian political economists focused more on trade and investment than on the class struggle, and tended to ignore the working class or to emphasize its passive victimization.[8]

This blending of the new labour history and historical materialism shaped my dissertation on working-class life in early-twentieth-century Hamilton, Ontario (completed in 1981), and remained a central feature of my writing for many years after. With its emphasis on broad structural transformations in Canadian economic life and the capitalist visioning that lay behind them, the essay "On the Job in Canada," which was the introduction to the collection of essays that Bob Storey and I co-edited in 1986, resonates with those influences, with its sweeping overview of changing "social structures of accumulation."[9]

Our little "school" of labour historians in Halifax was also linked to national and international networks of like-minded historians. A new Committee on Canadian Labour History (CCLH), founded in 1971, had Dalhousie's Greg Kealey on its executive. He also edited the new journal that the committee launched in 1976, *Labour/Le Travailleur* (renamed *Labour/Le Travail* in 1984). Each spring we all trooped off to the Canadian Historical Association meetings and met other labour historians at the CCLH-sponsored sessions, where we presented papers and discussed new research in the field. It was here that we became aware of a growing division within Canadian labour and working-class history, roughly between the younger historians with a Marxist bent and an interest in the early encounters between workers and capitalists and a slightly older group with a more social-democratic perspective and a somewhat greater interest in the mid-twentieth-century experience of workers and their social movements. One senior historian characterized this standoff as E.P. Thompson versus the (then deceased) Canadian labour economist Harold Logan. It was in large part a debate about what to study – whether to focus on relatively modern, bureaucratized industrial relations and labour politics, or to broaden out to explore a more complex working-class "culture." At another, more political level, it was a disagreement about the modern potential of the working class as an engine of social change. With their roots in the New Left, the so-called culturalists were looking back into history for evidence of the radical potential of working-class resistance. The social democrats viewed these young radicals as romantics who did not understand the practical, not revolutionary dimensions of the modern labour movement and the working class more generally. Although my training at Warwick had left me slightly sceptical of easy essentialist assumptions about working people, I had no doubts that the writings of the "culturalists" offered far more potential.[10] There was no overt split, and all participants in the rapidly growing field basked in the greater attention that labour history was enjoying within Canadian historical writing.[11]

Some of us were also drawn into special conferences organized through the CCLH, which stimulated fascinating discussion and reflection. The article on labourism began as a paper at a symposium on the Winnipeg General Strike in 1983. I also joined large numbers of Canadian labour historians at two other international conferences in Wales and Australia in 1987 and 1988.[12] By that point several of us were also trekking off to Wayne State University in Detroit each fall to join US labour historians in stimulating discussions at the annual North American Labor History Conferences.

A few years later, it was in these national networks that I developed the project to produce a collection of regionally based essays on the "workers' revolt" in Canada at the end of the First World War. The aim was to bring together in one volume the insights of new scholarship on the widespread militancy and radicalism of that period that had been emerging from younger scholars over the previous decade and that had been making clear how widespread this upsurge of working-class resistance had been. That group of contributors corresponded with each other about common themes and met a few times to discuss the direction of the project. For that book, I co-authored with Myer Siemiatycki the article "The Great War, the State, and Working-Class Canada," which reviewed the rapidly changing forms of state intervention on the home front during the First World War, and wrote an overview essay on the predominant features of the revolt, reprinted here as "Contours of a Workers' Revolt."[13]

Local circles of discussion and debate continued to be just as important. Soon after moving back to Toronto in 1981, I was recruited, along with a few other young historians, into an incipient discussion group made up initially of graduates students in sociology at the University of Toronto interested in labour topics. We called ourselves the Labour Studies Research Group.[14] For much of the next decade, a dedicated band of about a dozen young scholars met monthly to read and discuss chapters and articles and to read new books on labour. We were particularly interested in the new subfield devoted to studying the labour process in capitalist society, initially inspired by the work of Harry Braverman. His book *Labor and Monopoly Capital* became the centrepiece of an increasingly sophisticated, international, interdisciplinary debate about management, technology, and workers.[15] We were centrally interested in the relations of production, where class and class conflict were central, but, in our discussions, where gender and ethnicity were also in play. Each of us was working on a research project that involved close examination of the changing nature of work in particular industries.[16] These issues figured prominently in a series of regional gatherings that ran through the 1970s and 1980s first known as the Blue-Collar Work Conferences and eventually renamed the Workers and Their

Communities Conferences, where young academics hoped to present their research and engage in discussion with interested workers (few of whom showed up). Many of us in the Labour Studies Research Group presented papers there, and I coordinated the last of these events at York University in 1989.[17]

I had addressed some of these questions in my dissertation on the changing nature of work in Hamilton's factories, but now drew on the insights of the labour-process literature for a new monograph on Canada's first steelworkers.[18] Bob Storey and I also brought together a collection of essays to showcase new Canadian research on the dynamics of the labour process across time. Since Bob was also working on the Hamilton steel industry in a later period from mine, we also co-authored an essay for that book, "Work and Struggle in the Canadian Steel Industry," which traced the emergence of mass-production steel-making and the efforts of steelworkers to assert their own needs and concerns, culminating ambiguously in the consolidation of the postwar collective-bargaining regime.

Through the 1980s, I was also part of a different network in Toronto. Since my teaching appointment at York University, starting in 1983, was primarily in the new Labour Studies Program in the Division of Social Science, I had to take a deep plunge into the vast literature of the well-established field of industrial relations. It was that teaching that prompted me to agree to James Lorimer's request for a short history of the Canadian labour movement, which, now in its third edition, continues to find space in a variety of academic and non-academic educational contexts.[19] I was quickly drawn to newer political economists whose work touched on industrial relations, especially those who worked on the state. In the inevitable overlap of these circles, many of these people were active in the Political Economy Network. Two specific projects helped to focus my thinking. The first was a large off-campus discussion group of sundry radical social scientists (I think I was the only historian), which began meeting monthly to discuss their unpublished papers on labour relations. Then a year-long Advanced Research Seminar at York in 1988–9 brought together a fascinating group of scholars interested in labour and the law. Since I had been asked to write an afterword for a collection of essays on workers and the state in Nova Scotia, I used the seminar as an opportunity to develop an overview article, published as "Male Wage-Earners and the Canadian State," a reflection on the many levels at which workers interacted with the state, voluntarily and through coercion.[20]

The convener of the York Advanced Research Seminar, Paul Craven, soon took on a new project that required the active participation of several labour historians. The Ontario Historical Studies Series wanted to include a volume on working-class history in the province, and Paul agreed to pull together a volume of original essays on the nineteenth-century experience. I undertook to explore what had happened to factory workers in the First Industrial Revolution. I built on much that I had previously done on the labour process, but had to move further back in time. I used this as an opportunity to explore the international literature on industrialization and to try to clarify the peculiarities of the Canadian experience. I learned a lot from the research of other participants in the project. Like the book on the workers' revolt, this project involved collective discussion of the overall project and collective critiques of each other's essays. The result was an impressive volume of social history. [21]

In the early 1990s the intense discussions of the labour process within capitalist society seemed increasingly relevant, as technological and managerial change swept through Canadian workplaces. When a flurry of debate began to develop about the length of the working day,[22] I decided to launch a study of the struggles to win more time away from paid work since the nineteenth century. The previously unpublished essay included here, entitled "Arguing about Idleness," presented my first exploration of the debates about reducing work time.

By this point, I was enjoying my cross-appointment to the York Department of History, home to so many outstanding scholars in many fields, including a large number of first-rate graduate students. In 1995 a number of colleagues from diverse fields of study in the department came together to present papers in a one-day colloquium, "Spectacle, Monument, and Memory," covering everything from Roman gladiators to Spanish bull fighters to Halloween.[23] The organizers wanted something on labour, and, since I had just begun a new project on issues of time, work, and leisure, I decided to turn my attention to the history of Canada's Labour Day. My research assistant at the outset of that project, Steve Penfold, soon became my co-author, and a decade later a book-length study finally appeared.[24] In the meantime, I had been invited to give talks on Labour Day to several different audiences, one of which, delivered in Sydney, Nova Scotia, is included in this collection as "Into the Streets." This project marked a turn in my work towards greater attention to cultural forms and representations within working-class life.

Most of this work had put male wage-earners in the foreground. But, after years of close contact with feminists, participation in many International Women's Day marches, and immersion in plenty of feminist literature, I had always been conscious of the need to integrate gender. A single chapter in my dissertation on female wage-earners would eventually blossom into a much more complex discussion of the experience of working-class women at home, in the workforce, and in their social lives in several chapters of my 2015 book on working-class Hamilton. Part of that story is reproduced here in slightly different form as "Working Girls." Gender did not mean simply women, however. In the late 1990s, a few of my graduate students and I decided to start a reading group on the exciting new field in the history of masculinities. We soon drew in a handful of other graduate students and faculty, and in monthly meetings worked our way through a long shelf of books and articles. Those discussions, generally held leisurely over Italian food, gave me a grounding to write a long paper that I presented at the North American Labor History Conference at Wayne State University in Detroit in 2002. With strong memories of growing up as a working-class male, I wanted to move beyond the preoccupation of so much of this new branch of gender history with middle-class men and to build on the still limited literature on working-class masculinities by looking at the city I had studied most intensively, Hamilton, and in the period that had always held my attention, 1890–1940. Shortly thereafter, a call for papers on working-class subjectivities from the journal *International Labor and Working-Class History* eventually convinced me to split the paper into two. One part was published there, and is reproduced here as "Boys Will Be Boys."[25]

Since the late 1980s, I had been active outside regular academic channels in helping to launch a popular centre for workers' history and culture. It opened in 1996 as the Ontario Workers' Arts and Heritage Centre (Ontario was dropped a few years later – hence WAHC). As a member (and for a few years as co-chair) of the board of directors, I was centrally involved in the organizational life of the Centre, but, like a few other professors sympathetic to labour, I also undertook to curate some exhibitions. One of those became "Booze: Work, Pleasure, and Controversy," which opened in 1998. Developing that project with artists, designers, researchers, unionists, and sundry others was a new experience that challenged and stimulated me immensely. When it became clear that the catalogue for the exhibition that I had planned was not going to be possible, I decided to produce a short illustrated history of drinking in Canada. The topic took hold of me, however, and grew into the more substantial book published in 2003 as *Booze: A Distilled History*. For me, the history of drinking was central to working-class history, and I included a lengthy section on how workers and their unions struggled with the issues around the Demon Rum and prohibition. I have extracted that passage, "Labour and Liquor" to be included here.

While that project gave me new insights into the use of the visual in historical analysis, I had actually been working with photographic images since my days as a graduate student, when I had helped to produce a pictorial history of Hamilton's working people through the Labour Studies Program at McMaster University, coordinated by Wayne Roberts.[26] I drafted the introduction to that book and, over the years, presented a few talks on visual history. But mostly I participated in the selection and use of images in several exhibitions at the Workers' Arts and Heritage Centre and then included many in my last three published monographs. The essay included here, "Workers in the Camera's Eye," contains my thoughts on the main issues in the relationship between photography and the Canadian working class.

By 2000 my work with WAHC was part of a two-decade-long experience of working in the world of museums, historic sites, historical societies, and other venues for the public programming of history, including three years as vice-chair of the Ontario Heritage Foundation, as well as giving lectures to several union audiences. I had had many opportunities to reflect on the challenges of presenting the past in all these non-academic settings through less scholarly formats and had learned a great deal from many creative workers in public history. I had also helped to launch an annual workshop held the day before the start of the Canadian Historical Association meetings to bring together labour historians with local unionists and community activists, where academics and non-academics could share research and insights in a less rigid format than the typical academic meeting. So I decided to publish some reflections, "The Labour Historian and Public History," in the hopes of encouraging more serious discussion of the interface between academic and public history.

In 2007 I became president of the Canadian Historical Association and, as is the custom, was expected to present a presidential address two years later. It seemed like an appropriate moment to reflect on the evolution of my thinking about working-class history and to link three decades of reading, researching, and writing to my own working-class background. It would be hard to imagine a better setting for such a presentation, since I had rarely missed a CHA meeting in thirty years and had learned so much from faculty and graduate students who had presented there over the years. The result was an essay that is reproduced here as "The Relevance of Class."

It would be easy to look back on all that hopping back and forth between different arenas with distinct agendas and orientations as the meanderings of a flighty dilettante. But there was nothing superficial about these engagements; they were intense, demanding, and mutually reinforcing, each adding another dimension to my deepening knowledge and evolving intellectual imagination. I also found some of the same people crossing back and forth with me – in particular, Bettina Bradbury, Paul Craven, Harry Glasbeek, Franca Iacovetta, Greg Kealey, Lynn Marks, Ian McKay, Jim Naylor, Steve Penfold, Ian Radforth, Bob Storey, Eric Tucker, and Jeremy Webber. The essays collected here, then, are products of discussions among a generation of engaged scholars who, for the most part, began to come into their own in the 1980s and 1990s. Yet they also stand alone as my own contributions within those circles. Several of them are efforts at synthesis – the changing political economy of work across the nineteenth and twentieth centuries, the specific experience of the industrial revolution in Canada, the nature of working-class resistance across the country after the First World War, the evolving relationship of workers to the state, the labour movement's struggles with the Demon Rum, and the impact of photography. Others have a narrower focus but retain a broad frame of analysis – on Canadian steelworkers, shorter worktime, Labourist politics, Labour Day revellers, and the "boys" and "working girls" of Hamilton.

Throughout there is an insistence that the material basis of workers' lives is fundamental in setting constraints and limits, but that they have nonetheless found diverse ways to assert their own needs and concerns. While I continue to be fascinated by transnational patterns of workers' struggles for survival and rights, I have always remained interested in the specific ways in which workers interacted with the state formation that emerged in Canada, experiences that often differentiated them from their counterpart inside other nation states (including the United States). Over time, my focus has shifted away from the waged workplace to households and neighbourhoods where workers turned to their families and their other associational networks to make a decent life for themselves.

Across time, the theoretical underpinnings of these essays have also evolved from a sensitive, empirically based Marxism to a great commitment to "intersectionality" among class, gender, and race/ethnicity. As I insist in "The Relevance of Class," the material, "structural" life of the working class is still central, but it is also inseparable from the dynamics of gender and race/ethnicity. It is also now essential to recognize the variation in consciousness among workers about the material situations in which they find themselves.[27] As I argue in that essay, the caution or boldness of their actions has depended historically on the economic, political, and cultural context and the resources available for mobilization. This is what I like to call "working-class realism."

It would be harder now to be as unapologetic about studying the working class as I was in 1981. There are even suggestions that the field is in decline, that it failed to rethink its persistent materialist analytic framework. Certainly, those of us who were present at the creation of the field of Canadian labour history in the mid-1970s have had to live with legitimate criticisms of gaps and silences we too often ignored. We were generally too insensitive to race and the colonialism that sustained racial oppression, to the distinct experience of visible minorities, and to socially marginalized Indigenous communities, whose history does not easily fit into our Marxist paradigms. Yet, recognizing these limitations is not to deny how many scholars of labour history have evolved and adapted in ways that integrate these critiques. Moreover, the field is far from moribund. Many more scholars across many disciplines have joined the process of reclaiming the workers' story, though they often do so beyond the old boundaries of labour history – particularly, the waged workplace and the various workers' movements – to touch on households, ethnic organizations, welfare programs, and so much more.

The essays collected here offer readers with varying intellectual and political interests some guideposts for thinking about workers' experience in Canada in the past and, arguably, in the present. They offer some long-range perspectives on the issues confronting workers in the early twenty-first century. I hope they will continue to remind Canadians that the inequities of class experience, and working-class challenges to them, have always been central to the way that our country operates.

Notes

1 W. Craig Heron, "Working-Class Hamilton, 1895–1930" (PhD dissertation, Dalhousie University), xiv.

2 Many of my published essays dealt with Hamilton, and, for the most part, found their way into my latest monograph, *Lunch-Bucket Lives: Remaking the Workers' City* (Toronto: Between the Lines 2015).

3 Ian Milligan, *Rebel Youth: 1960s Labour Unrest, Young Workers, and New Leftists in English Canada* (Vancouver: UBC Press 2014).

4 See, for example, Eric Hobsbawm, "Debating the Labour Aristocracy," in *Worlds of Labour: Further Studies in the History of Labour* (London: Weidenfeld and Nicolson 1984), 214–26; and "The Aristocracy of Labour Reconsidered," ibid., 227–51.

5 The Warwick influence is also evident in "The Crisis of the Craftsman: Hamilton Metal Workers in the Early Twentieth Century," *Labour/Le Travailleur* 6 (Autumn 1980), 7–48.

6 For example, E.P. Thompson, *The Poverty of Theory and Other Essays* (London: Merlin Press 1978); Perry Anderson, *Arguments within English Marxism* (London: Verso 1980).

7 For example, Sheila Rowbotham, *Hidden from History: 300 Years of Women's Oppression and the Fight against It* (London: Pluton Press 1977); Barbara Taylor, *Eve and the New Jerusalem: Socialism and Feminism in the Nineteenth Century* (New York: Pantheon Books 1983).

8 For a particularly troubling effort at writing Canadian labour history from this perspective, see Daniel Drache, "The Formation and Fragmentation of the Canadian Working Class: 1820–1920," *SPE* 15 (Fall 1984), 43–89. For a bibliography of the kind of work that was being produced in this network, see Daniel Drache and Wallace Clement, eds., *The New Practical Guide to Canadian Political Economy* (Toronto: James Lorimer and Company 1985).

9 Craig Heron and Robert Storey, eds., *On the Job: Confronting the Labour Process in Canada* (Montreal and Kingston: McGill-Queen's University Press 1986).

10 The debates generated a long series of articles, including: Bryan D. Palmer, "Working-Class Canada: Recent Historical Writing," *Queen's Quarterly* 1979–80; Gregory S. Kealey, "Labour and Working-Class History: Prospects in the 1980s," *L/LT* 7 (Spring 1981), 67–94; David Bercuson, "Through the Looking Glass of Culture: An Essay on the New Labour History and Working-Class Culture in Recent Canadian Historical Writing," ibid., 95–112; Kenneth McNaught, "E.P. Thompson versus Harold Logan: Writing about Labour and the Left in the 1970s," *CHR* 62, no. 2 (June 1981), 141–68; Desmond Morton, "E.P. Thompson dans les arpents de neiges: Les historiens canadiens anglais et la classe ourvrière," *RHAF* 37, no. 2 (1983), 165–84; Bryan D. Palmer, "Listening to History Rather Than Historians: Reflections on Working-Class History," *SPE* 20 (Summer 1986), 47–80;

Desmond Morton, "Some Millenial Relections on the State of Canadian Labour History," *L/LT* 46 (Fall 2000), 11–36. For reviews of these debates, see James Naylor, "Working-Class History in English Canada in the 1980s: An Assessment," *Acadiensis* 19, no. 1 (Autumn 1989), 157–69; Joanne Burgess, "Exploring the Limited Identities of Canadian Labour: Recent Trends in English-Canada and in Quebec," *International Journal of Canadian Studies*, 1990; Bryan D. Palmer, "Canada," in Joan Allen, Alan Campbell, and John McIlroy, eds., *Histories of Labour: National and International Perspectives* (Pontypool, Wales: Merlin Press 2010), 196–230.

11 See, for example, Ramsay Cook, "The Making of Canadian Working Class History," *Historical Reflections* 10 (1983), 127–42. In 1994 I contributed a bibliographic essay on working-class history to Doug Owram, ed., *Canadian History: A Reader's Guide, Volume Two: Confederation to the Present* (Toronto: University of Toronto Press 1994), which revealed how the field had expanded.

12 The paper I gave in Wales, "Canada's Second Industrial Revolution," an overview of the new wave of industrialization that hit the country at the close of the nineteenth century, was then published in a volume of essays comparing working-class experience in Canada and Wales: Deian Hopkin and Gregory S. Kealey, eds., *Class, Community, and the Labour Movement: Wales and Canada, 1890–1930* (Aberystwyth: Llafur/Committee on Canadian Labour History 1989).

13 Craig Heron, ed., *The Workers' Revolt in Canada, 1917–1925* (Toronto: University of Toronto Press 1998).

14 At some point in the 1990s, the name was informally changed to the Toronto Labour Studies Group. The membership of the group gradually shifted towards a predominance of historians, both professors and graduate students, and has continued to have rigorous discussions down to the present.

15 Harry Braverman, *Labor and Monopoly Capital: The Degradation of Work in the Twentieth Century* (New York: Monthly Review Press 1974).

16 The books that came out of that intense process of discussion included: Ian Radforth, *Bushworkers and Bosses: A Social History of the Northern Ontario Logging Industry, 1900–1980* (Toronto: University of Toronto Press 1985); Charlene Gannage, *Double Day, Double Bind: Women Garment Workers* (Toronto: Women's Press 1986); Ruth Frager, *Sweatshop Strife: Class, Ethnicity, and Gender in the Jewish Labour Movement of Toronto, 1900–1939* (Toronto: University of Toronto Press 1992); Franca Iacovetta, *Such Hardworking People: Italian Immigrants in Postwar Toronto* (Toronto: University of Toronto Press 1992); Ester Reiter, *Making Fast Food: From*

the Frying Pan into the Fryer (Montreal and Kingston: McGill-Queen's University Press 1996); Kathryn McPherson, *Bedside Matters: The Transformation of Canadian Nursing, 1900–1990* (Toronto: Oxford University Press 1996).

17 The last of these conferences met in 1988 at York University.

18 Craig Heron, *Working in Steel: The Early Years in Canada, 1883–1935* (Toronto: McClelland and Stewart, 1988).

19 Craig Heron, *The Canadian Labour Movement: A Short History* (Toronto: James Lorimer 1989, 1996, 2011).

20 In 1994 I was invited to join some of the same people in presenting to a symposium marking the 75th anniversary of the Ontario Department of Labour, for which I wrote "The Ontario Department of Labour and Class Relations in Ontario before World War Two" (which was never published).

21 Paul Craven, ed., *Labouring Lives: Work and Workers in Nineteenth-Century Ontario* (Toronto: University of Toronto Press 1995).

22 E.g., Ontario Task Force on Hours of Work and Overtime, *Working Times: Report of the Ontario Task Force on Hours of Work and Overtime* ([Toronto]: Ontario Task Force on Hours of Work and Overtime 1987); Advisory Group on Working Time and the Distribution of Work, *Report* ([Ottawa]: Advisory Group on Working Time and the Distribution of Work 1994).

23 Many of the papers presented were published in a special edition of *HS/SH* 29, no. 58 (1996).

24 Craig Heron and Steve Penfold, *The Workers' Festival: A History of Labour Day in Canada* (Toronto: University of Toronto Press 1995).

25 The other half of the original paper appeared as Craig Heron, "The Boys and Their Booze: Masculinities and Public Drinking in Working-Class Hamilton, 1890–1946," *CHR* 86, no. 3 (September 2005), 411–52.

26 Craig Heron, Shea Hoffmitz, Wayne Roberts, and Robert Storey, *All That Our Hands Have Done: A Pictorial History of the Hamilton Workers* (Oakville: Mosaic Press 1981).

27 I explore these themes more extensively in *Lunch-Bucket Lives.*

Acknowledgments

I am grateful to Mathieu Brulé, Jonathan McQuarrie, Ian Radforth, Jason Russell, and John Van West for helpful comments on the Introduction.

Chapters 1 and 3 were co-authored with Robert Storey and chapter 5 with Myer Siemiatycki. Chapters 4, 6, and 13 have not been previously published. The other chapters are reprinted from the following publications:

Chapters 1 and 3: Craig Heron and Robert Storey, eds., *On the Job: Confronting the Labour Process in Canada* (Montreal and Kingston: McGill-Queen's University Press 1987), 3–46, 210–44.

Chapter 2: Paul Craven, ed., *Labouring Lives: Work and Workers in Nineteenth-Century Ontario* (Toronto: University of Toronto Press 1995), 479–590.

Chapter 5: Craig Heron, *Booze: A Distilled History* (Toronto: Between the Lines 2003), 213–32.

Chapter 7: *Labour/Le Travail* 13 (Spring 1984), 45–75.

Chapters 8 and 9: Craig Heron, ed., *The Workers' Revolt in Canada, 1917–1925* (Toronto: University of Toronto Press 1998), 11–42, 268–304.

Chapter 10: Craig Heron, *Lunch-Bucket Lives: Remaking the Workers' City* (Toronto: Between the Lines 2015) (in part).

Chapter 11: *International Labor and Working-Class History* 69 (Spring 2006), 6–34.

Chapter 12: Michael Earle, ed., *Workers and the State in Twentieth-Century Nova Scotia* (Fredericton: Acadiensis Press 1989), 241–64.

Chapter 14: *Labour/Le Travail* 45 (Spring 2000), 171–97.

Chapter 15: *Journal of the Canadian Historical Association*, 2009, 27–56.

Abbreviations

AHR	*American Historical Review*
ARCS	*American Review of Canadian Studies*
BHR	*Business History Review*
CD	*Canadian Dimension*
CDP	*Contemporary Drug Problems*
CES	*Canadian Ethnic Studies*
CGJ	*Canadian Geographical Journal*
CHAAR	*Canadian Historical Association Annual Report*
CHR	*Canadian Historical Review*
CIHR	*Canadian Institute for Historical Microreproductions*
CJE	*Cambridge Journal of Economics*
CJEPS	*Canadian Journal of Economics and Political Science*
CJS	*Canadian Journal of Sociology*
CRSA	*Canadian Review of Sociology and Anthropology*
CWS	*Canadian Woman Studies*
FS	*Feminist Studies*
HP	*Canadian Historical Association, Historical Papers*
HOP	*History of Photography*
HSE	*Historical Studies in Education*
HS/SH	*Histoire social/Social History*
HW	*History Workshop*
ILWCH	*International Labor and Working-Class History*
IRSH	*International Review of Social History*
JAH	*Journal of American History*
JCAH	*Journal of Canadian Art History*
JCHA	*Journal of the Canadian Historical Association*

JCS	*Journal of Canadian Studies*
JEH	*Journal of Economic History*
JHG	*Journal of Historical Geography*
JPC	*Journal of Popular Culture*
JSH	*Journal of Social History*
JUH	*Journal of Urban History*
LH	*Labor History*
L/LT	*Labour/Le Travail*
MHB	*Material History Bulletin*
MHR	*Material History Review*
NLR	*New Left Review*
OH	*Ontario History*
PF	*Prairie Forum*
PH	*Public Historian*
RHAF	*Revue d'histoire de l'Amérique française*
RHR	*Radical History Review*
RI/IR	*Relations industrielle/Industrial Relations*
RRPE	*Review of Radical Political Economics*
RHAF	*Revue d'histoire de l' Amérique française*
SH	*Social History*
SHR	*Sport History Review*
SPE	*Studies in Political Economy*
UHR	*Urban History Review*

PART ONE

On the Job

Chapter One

On the Job in Canada

Industrial capitalism produces many different work experiences. On any given day, Canadian workers arrive on the job in such a huge variety of workplaces that we might well ask whether all these jobs have anything in common. Is it possible to generalize about such a diversity of human experience? We believe it is. The kaleidoscope of specific occupations should not blind us to some consistent patterns in the world of work in Canada. In the following pages we outline the main themes in the evolution of labour processes in Canada and highlight the central dynamics in the changing nature of work.

At the core of this analysis is the impact of working for wages – selling one's ability to labour to employers who view that labour-power as a factor of production to be used as intensively and cheaply as possible in their process of capital accumulation. All labour processes involve the application of certain instruments to raw materials to produce goods or services that have use value. But in capitalist labour processes, those goods or services also have an exchange value, and in their production a capitalist hopes to generate surplus value. The amount of surplus that can be extracted from the labour process depends ultimately on the degree of control capitalists hold over how their workers apply tools and machines to their tasks. Workers, however, tend to have their own notions about the fairness and equity that should apply to their wages and their experience on the job. Thus, a "frontier of control" results from the ongoing process of initiative and resistance between workers and their bosses. While this set of relationships is rooted in the private realm of capital accumulation, its essential ingredients have been

Printers at Toronto Lithograph Company. City of Toronto Archives, file 1137, item 0001 transplanted into apparently non-profit sectors, like schools, hospitals, and other branches of public service. Selling one's labour-power has now become broadly similar in all jobs in the capitalist labour market.

The complex class relationships that emerge when workers and employers confront each other this way – the managerial policies, the strikes, the labour legislation – contain a second crucial dimension, a sex/gender system often called "patriarchy," which predates capitalism but which persists in new forms within capitalist society. Women have always experienced class differently from men. They have lived and worked within confining patriarchal definitions of their primary responsibility for domestic labour, which has left most women in the household and which has shaped their participation in the wage-labour market. Similarly, though on a more limited scale, capitalist social relations have incorporated pre-existing discrimination against racial and ethnic groups, so that Chinese or Italian or Portuguese newcomers have been drawn into the Canadian labour force on different terms from their Anglo-Celtic workmates. To understand the changing nature of work in Canada, then, it is necessary to account for the specific forces of capitalist development that gave most workplaces their essential shape, as well as the differences that gender and race or ethnicity could make.

The general shape of labour processes in Canada has evolved through changes in what has been termed "the social structures of accumulation,"[1] that is, the specific, shifting configurations of economic activity, class formations and conflicts, and state intervention that mark off specific stages of capitalist development. The Canadian economy that provided the jobs has taken its particular texture from two parallel sets of productive activity. First, from the beginning of the European settlement, resource extraction for external markets in France, Britain, and finally the United States has been crucial – initially fish and furs, later agricultural, forest, and mineral products. These industries have had their own erratic pace of growth and decline, special requirements for labour and technology (often quite primitive until well into the twentieth century), and frequently a high degree of seasonality in production. From the mid-nineteenth century onward, however, a second, quite different path of development emerged as indigenous capitalists began to industrialize in order to supply the varied needs of a growing domestic population in British North America, especially the expanding numbers of commercial farmers. With help from the Canadian state's tariff policies, the cities and towns of southern Ontario, Quebec, and, for a few decades, the Maritimes created a highly industrialized economy with a wide range of manufacturing industries, technological sophistication, and a steady demand for an occupationally diverse workforce. The initial link between these two relatively distinct sectors of resource extraction and manufacturing was the railway, which spread quickly through the countryside in the 1850s and across the barren wastes in subsequent decades as the best means of moving resources to market, but which also continued to stimulate new industrial development. These long ribbons of steel remained the main arteries of the Canadian economy for more than a century, meeting the outside commercial world in the bustling Canadian ports on the Atlantic, the St Lawrence, and the Pacific.

These broad sweeps of development fell into five roughly defined periods – the first ending around 1840, the second lasting to the 1890s, the third to the Second World War, the fourth down to the mid-1970s, and the fifth since that point. There was no firm dividing line between each of these stages. Each was preceded by a transitional phase precipitated by an economic crisis – in the 1840s, 1890s, 1930s, and 1970s – during which established relationships in the workplace and the marketplace were shaken up and slowly reconstituted on new terms. While each period was distinguished by new structures, institutions, and forms of struggle, there were enough lags and continuities that by the late twentieth century we still found in Canada a residue of much earlier eras in firm size, technology, labour markets, and organization of workers and employers. We will consider the distinctive characteristics of each of these periods in turn.

Independent Commodity Production to 1840

In the two centuries before 1840, the most visible economic activities in New France and British North America were the gathering and shipping out of natural resources for European markets – primarily fish, furs, wheat, and timber. Yet for most of that period, the great majority of European settlers in what was to become Canada lived and worked in family units of independent commodity producers on the margins of the commercial capitalist economy. In tiny communities scattered along the Atlantic coast, families cooperated in catching and curing the fish; and throughout the colonies, farm families hacked away at the dense forests to clear space for their simple crops and then to live off the land. Most families provided for their own needs and had only relatively limited contact with the market when they sold or bartered any surplus production or took short-term employment in order to pay off debts or to buy the few necessities they could not produce themselves. Only in the 1840s were many farmers beginning to sow substantially more acres of wheat to be sold as a cash crop for export. In many of these same communities of "producers" were handfuls of self-employed artisans – blacksmiths, stonemasons, shoemakers, tailors, and the like – whose handicraft production serviced small, local markets. Compelled to cope with a harsh natural environment, isolated by poor transportation routes, and facing highly unstable European markets for their staple goods, few of these independent commodity producers could be expected to take the bit of capitalist entrepreneurship; in many respects their mode of living and working resembled that of European peasant-proprietors.[2]

Labour in and around the households of independent commodity producers was varied and demanding. A gender division of labour sent men into the fields, into the artisanal workshops, or out in the boats while the women stayed behind to mind the children, tend the kitchen gardens and livestock, and prepare a wide range of commodities for domestic consumption – food, clothing, soap, candles, medicines, and much more. The survival of independent commodity production units depended on the success of this female labour. Marriages, in fact, were highly practical arrangements before which the women's skills and abilities would be assessed, and widowers wasted little time in finding new wives to perform the crucial domestic tasks. The division of labour was never so rigid as to keep women out of the fields or workshops if their help was needed, and, despite the husband/father's legal status as patriarchal head of household and his right to participate in a wider public life, the hard physical labour demanded of both men and women produced a kind of economic partnership between the sexes. In general, there was a sense of all family members contributing their labour to their mutual support, with the household as the organizing base of the family's communal work. Cooperative, unwaged work might also involve the wider community, as in the celebrated "bees" organized for clearing new land, building a barn, or husking corn.[3]

The primary tensions in a society of independent commodity producers pitted farming and fishing families against merchants who marketed their wheat and fish and held them in the thrall of debt; against speculative, absentee, or seigneurial landowners who restricted easy access to the land or skimmed off some of their meagre surplus; and against the various "family compacts" whose oppressive control of the colonial state and administration of land policies seemed to hamper the producers' independence and material well-being. The rights and grievances of these producers echoed through the insurrections of 1837–8 in Upper and Lower Canada, in the farmers' agitations in Prince Edward Island, and in the Nova Scotia reform movement in the same period.[4]

Wage labour was certainly not unknown in these pre-industrial societies. In the first half of the nineteenth century, the western Canadian fur trade, the logging industry, and canal construction all required hired men, largely drawn from French-Canadian farm families and the growing pool of impoverished Irish immigrants. Domestic servants, farm labourers, seamen, and skilled craftsmen, like shipwrights and iron workers, also worked for wages. Most of these wage-earners had a close, direct relationship with their employers, characterized by a kind of paternalism and typically codified in individual contracts of employment, or indentures, which were made legally enforceable through British statutes or colonial legislation like the 1848 Master and Servant Act in Canada West. By the 1830s and 1840s, however, some of the skilled workers had begun to form local craft unions and to mount bitter strikes, like journeymen printers' battles with William Lyon Mackenzie and George Brown in Toronto. And, even more dramatically, Irish canal labourers adapted their Old Country secret societies to new purposes and confronted their contractors in violent battles, which for the first time brought the state's military might to bear in support of employers. Yet both on the canals and in the lumber camps, the lines of class identification were normally weaker than ethnic solidarities, as Irishmen spilled the blood of French Canadians or divided against each other in age-old feuds between Cork and Connaught. In any case, much of the wage labour in all these pre-industrial workplaces involved only short-term or seasonal absence from family farms or fishing villages, and few workers expected to remain wage-earners for life. Independent farming, fishing, or craftsmanship remained the ideal as well as the reality for most British North Americans.[5]

The modes and social relations of independent commodity production would change somewhat as more and more farmers turned to commercial agriculture, but the old patterns remained remarkably resilient in Canada. Not only did agriculturalists and rural dwellers, living and working in family units with little hired help, remain numerically predominant until well into the twentieth century, but significant pockets of population continued to survive on the basis of subsistence agriculture and part-time employment, notably in Atlantic Canada, parts of Quebec, eastern and northern Ontario, northern stretches of the Prairies, and the interior of British Columbia. Not until after the Second World War did Canada see a steep decline in this "semi-proletarianized" rural population.[6]

The Rise of Industrial Capitalism, 1840 to 1890

By 1850, a transformation was under way which would propel British North America into the industrial capitalist age. The colonial merchants' concerns about an efficient transportation network to compete with American exporters led to the construction of hundreds of miles of railway lines. These in turn opened up wider markets for local producers and stimulated a new demand for railway equipment. At the same time, as wheat farmers became more oriented to cash crops, a larger domestic market opened up for consumer goods like agricultural implements, stoves, and textiles. In this golden age of capitalist entrepreneurship, master artisans expanded their workshops, merchant industrialists set up new factories, transportation companies erected production facilities of major proportions, and new coal mines opened on the east and west coasts to produce fuel for the new age of steam power. At first this new industrial activity developed in the chill breezes of free trade, but when the American market disappeared behind high tariff walls, Canadian businessmen evolved a development strategy based on a protected manufacturing sector serving a large domestic population of agriculturalists. In 1879 the federal government tied the package together as a "National Policy" of high-tariff protection for industry, railway building across the Prairies, and promotion of immigration. The result was a brief burst of accelerated industrialization in the 1880s, widely dispersed across the Maritimes, Quebec, and Ontario. Throughout the last quarter of the nineteenth century, however, the economy continued to suffer from overproduction, business failures, unemployment, and out-migration of population. Only at the turn of the century did the National-Policy formula begin to work.[7]

In order for industrial capitalism to take hold in Canada, the uncertain labour market of the early nineteenth century had to be altered. A rapid increase in immigration helped, especially after the Irish famine of the late 1840s, but equally important was the disappearance of easily accessible land, which would leave new immigrants and farmers' children with little choice but to seek wage labour. By the 1850s, that process was producing a workforce of primarily full-time wage-earners. Moreover, many of the new immigrants were experienced industrial workers, especially skilled men, who left Britain or the United States intending to take up similar work in Canada. These workers brought with them a familiarity with existing work practices and a legacy of workplace struggle that were soon incorporated into colonial industry.[8]

The symbol of the new era was the smoke stack belching into the colonial skies from steamships, railway locomotives, and industrial enterprises in the major cities. Yet, however dramatic and eye-catching, the new steam powered machinery should not overshadow even more important changes in workplace organization and relationships. Jobs were changing, as employers set out to break down skills into more narrowly specialized tasks performed by less skilled, lower-paid workers, like the hundreds of women and children who found their way into textile, footwear, tobacco, and food-processing factories. As often as possible, these new operatives would handle new machinery intended to speed up their tasks; but in the late nineteenth century, technology in most industries remained relatively primitive, and mechanization was quite uneven across the industrial landscape. In some sectors, like clothing, production processes combined some centralization under the manufacturer's roof with outwork in homes or contract shops. In many cases, however, craftsmen's skills could not be diluted much at all, and employers had to hire large numbers of them to run lathes in railway shops, set type in newspaper offices, "puddle" iron at iron works, or extract coal from the ground. The use of subcontractors, the harsh discipline of iron-fisted foremen, and the widespread adoption of piecework to goad workers to higher levels of production suggest the importance of human relationships on the job, rather than machine-paced work rhythms.[9]

At the same time, the growing separation of work and home was arousing a new concern. Many employers joined campaigns to reshape working-class behaviour outside the workplace by stamping out the erratic habits of pre-industrial working life and inculcating new norms of sobriety, industry, punctuality, and self-discipline. These moral reformers took aim at working-class leisure patterns, especially the consumption of the "demon rum" and the desecration of the sabbath. In a similar vein, they created new institutions to implant a stricter industrial discipline in the hearts and minds of the urban poor – "houses of industry" for the desperately poor, penitentiaries and sundry other penal institutions for workers who turned to crime, and, most important, public schools to teach future workers "system, order, punctuality, and good conduct." A new work ethic was being forged for the industrial capitalist age.[10]

The emerging working class responded to this new work environment in many diverse ways. Perhaps the most important involved adapting domestic life to a reliance on wages as sole income. As in the pre-industrial past, families continued to operate as tiny collectivities of mutual support, but no longer produced their own subsistence in and around the household. Now sons and daughters would often join their fathers in the paid workforce outside the home, and all wages would be pooled. Married women now normally stayed home to care for the young and old and to perform the still labour-intensive tasks of feeding and clothing the family's wage-earners. Only a crisis like death, illness, or injury of the male head of household would send his wife or widow back out to work for wages. The working-class home thus became the mechanism for workers' survival in an economy based on wage labour, as well as the refuelling station for labour-power needed in capitalist industry.[11]

This new separation of work and home, of waged and unwaged labour, had particular implications for women, as the gender division of labour became much more sharply defined. Women participated in the paid labour market only when their primary responsibilities in the home would permit, normally only between school and marriage, and their transiency in that predominantly male work world shaped their treatment by employers and male workers. They were offered only the least skilled jobs, were paid at half the wage rates of men, and seldom found support from male workers for adjusting that inequality. They were also recruited into jobs designated as "women's work" – usually some transference into capitalist production of traditionally female tasks in the household, such as food and clothing production or nurturing and service. The largest number of women wage-earners entered domestic service, while many others worked in textile mills, garment shops, confectionery plants, and the like, or as poorly paid teachers and nurses. In the working-class home, women still performed essentially the same work, but in contrast to the households of independent commodity producers, they were now dependent for their survival on the wages of the family wage-earners, who were most often men. The rise of industrial capitalism had not created the oppressive patriarchal ideology and division of labour, which obviously predated it by centuries, but it had incorporated pre-capitalist gender divisions in such a way as to change the social relations of production by separating the privatized, unpaid, "feminine," domestic sphere from the public, waged, "masculine" sphere. Along with this distinction came a "cult of domesticity" that suffused the life-style of middle-class families and those working-class families struggling for a meagre level of decency and respectability in an insecure environment. Working-class men who supported this ghettoization of women and the ideal of the "family wage" were undoubtedly attempting to shore up working-class living standards against erosion by low wages, but they were also defending an element of male privilege and masculine identity in which the paid work world was steeped. In the class-conscious rhetoric of the times, they were protecting their "manhood."[12]

Inside industry itself, the workers most frequently contesting the emerging work relationships were the skilled men, who retained the shop-floor autonomy, power, and pride to sustain an aggressive craft-union movement, first organized on a local basis and ultimately linked up in continental ("international") organizations. By the turn of the century, many of these groups of workers had consolidated their hard-won workplace customs and routines into detailed union codes of rules and regulations, which they struggled to have accepted in contracts with employers, in the first attempt to establish a "rule of law" within Canadian industry. Yet their job control was never secure from employers' challenges, and industrial conflict flared up repeatedly wherever craftsmen still retained a significant role in the production process.[13]

These late nineteenth-century craftsmen have occupied centre stage in much of the writing on the workplace in this period.[14] Much attention has been focused on the workers' control that these men exercised on the job. Many writers in Canada and elsewhere who have studied them, however, have been struck by their narrow defence of exclusivist craft interests, at the expense of the less skilled.[15] In Britain an extensive literature has grown up concerning whether or not these skilled men composed an "aristocracy of labour,"[16] while in the United States new research has pointed to their roles as subcontractors who hired and supervised subordinate workers for their own profit.[17] Similar work on skilled workers' relations with women workers has revealed their anxiety to return the "working girls" to the domestic sphere, where they would pose less threat to their jobs, their craft status, and their masculinity.[18] These workers were even more aggressive in trying to drive out Asian workers, especially in British Columbia.[19]

Yet the story does not end there. Canadian historians in particular have drawn our attention to the larger vision of the craftsman, who criticized the dominant tendencies of the period towards consolidation of industry and degradation of the worker and his or her job. It was these men who provided the compelling rhetoric about the "nobility of labour" in the Nine-Hours movement in the 1870s and even more dramatically in the all-inclusive Knights of Labor (and the Provincial Workmen's Association in Nova Scotia) in the 1880s. In these movements, craft pride was transformed into working-class consciousness and assertiveness.[20] There was undoubtedly a deep ambivalence in the activities of these craftsmen that produced a craft, race, and gender exclusivism on the one hand, and a wider social criticism and leadership of generalized working-class interests on the other. This dilemma exemplifies the fragmentation that industrial capitalism was creating among workers, constantly forcing them onto the defensive against erosion of their workplace traditions, living standards, and sense of human dignity.

In any case, it was craftsmen's struggles that brought the Canadian state into a new phase in mediating work relations. In the early years of industrialization, the state had assisted capitalist employers by supporting workplace discipline with the force of law and permitting them to drag their workers into court to punish disobedience or insubordination. In the 1870s, however, the state legalized trade unions and their limited rights to picket; and by the 1880s, it was legislating some minimum standards of employment in mines and factories, primarily to protect women and children. The federal government even met the challenge of industrial militancy and radical rhetoric from the Knights of Labor by appointing a large Royal Commission on the Relations of Labour and Capital in 1886. The Commission travelled about the country hearing evidence on the new modes and relations of work, but its report produced nothing more concrete than the establishment of Labour Day as an annual holiday. The heavy hand of state repression in support of employers was never completely lifted, however; rigid legal constraints and ready use of military force to intervene in strikes remained effective curbs on working-class resistance.[21]

In this first phase of industrialization, then, entrepreneurs had begun to assemble the necessary workforce, to instil the appropriate work discipline, to attempt to cheapen the costs of production by subdividing labour into lower-paid, less skilled fragments, and to mechanize wherever possible. By the 1890s the results were ambiguous. In some industries, like textiles, complex machinery clattered away with relatively low skill requirements. Many others, however, were only part way along such a path of transformation. The small, unstable Canadian market made economies of scale difficult, and many of the more skilled workers had banded together to resist any degradation of their labour. Industrial capitalism, in fact, seemed so novel and alien that the Knights of Labor, as well as the massive farmers' movements of the period,[22] could still pose alternative visions of a more cooperative, humane future. It was nonetheless clear that half a century of industrial development had thoroughly altered the role and place of women within the workplace, largely excluding them from any control over the shape of the public work world, which was primarily a terrain contested by men.

The Consolidation of Monopoly Capitalism, 1890 to 1940

A whole new industrial age dawned at the close of the nineteenth century. In an unprecedented wave of economic expansion, thousands of new Prairie farmers pushed wheat to the top of the export list, while the forest industries struggled to keep up with the apparently insatiable demands of the United States for newsprint. New mining operations for hitherto neglected minerals – nickel, copper, lead, zinc, gold, silver – dotted the landscape of northern Ontario and Quebec and the interior of British Columbia. Vast new construction projects were launched, notably two more railways to the West Coast. Manufacturing expanded dramatically behind tariff walls, as completely new industries appeared – steel, auto, chemicals, pulp and paper, meatpacking, and electrical goods. A more tight-knit national bourgeoisie (centred in Montreal and Toronto) was pulling together the decentralized regional fragments into a more integrated national economy, which would eventually gut the Maritimes of much of its industrial life and restrict the development of northern and western Canada to a resource hinterland. Yet it was a highly fragile structure, which threatened to collapse on a regular basis. Boom periods in the first decade of the century, the First World War years, and the late 1920s were separated by deep troughs of depression just before the war, in the first half of the 1920s, and, most tragically, through the entire decade of the 1930s. These wild fluctuations in the business cycle would put serious pressure on industrialists to cut costs in order to survive and on workers to cope with their employers' aggression and the disciplining power of unemployment.[23]

Presiding over most sectors of the Canadian economy were huge new corporations, both home-grown giants like Dominion Cottons, Massey Harris, and the Steel Company of Canada, and new American branch firms like the Ford Motor Company and Canadian Westinghouse.[24] Within their far-flung corporate empires, the pressing need for centralized coordination of production and the competitive pressures of much larger markets prompted a new concern for more direct control over operating costs. The development of cost accounting was part of a new movement towards "systematic management" within commerce and industry (introduced much earlier by the railway corporations), which produced a new group of professional managers. Cutting production costs, especially labour, became a central concern.[25]

One result was the deployment of more sophisticated technology, driven by more flexible power sources like electricity and gasoline and reaching a kind of apotheosis in the assembly line in Henry Ford's Canadian and US auto plants. Massive mechanization transformed almost every industry, and by the 1920s a far larger percentage of the workforce were machine-operators than in the late nineteenth century. This time technological change had a qualitative difference from the first "industrial revolution": it incorporated much more scientific research (and more scientists) in solving production problems, and, in contrast to the informal experimentation by craftsmen on the shop floor (characteristic of the earlier phase of industrialization), it was carried on in research laboratories directly connected to major corporations, especially in new industries like chemicals and electrical goods.[26]

At the same time, many firms experimented with new, more centralized, more cost-conscious, and more authoritarian managerial systems, in order to move effective control of the labour process from the shop floor to the front office. The most famous hand-servant of these efficiency-conscious employers was Frederick Winslow Taylor, father of so-called scientific management (or Taylorism), whose staff invaded the shop floor armed with stop watches to measure the "scientifically" precise time required to complete a specific task and to gather up workers' shop-floor know-how, which could then be reorganized and parcelled out from the central planning and scheduling office. Incentive-wage payments would then encourage workers to keep up to management's production standards. There were Taylorist experiments in Canada, notably at the CPR's Angus Shops in Montreal, but recent studies have concluded that the actual impact of Taylor's own complex managerial package on North American industry was limited. Often, a great deal of latitude was still left with foremen and superintendents who, despite centralized employment offices, managed to control hiring and promotion and built departmental empires based on harsh supervision and favouritism. Workers consequently lived in constant fear of dismissal on a whim or in response to any "trouble-making" (like union organizing). Most employers nonetheless took their cue from Taylor's advice to wrench as much independent decision making about the pace and form of production as possible away from workers on the job and to centralize control over the labour process in managerial hands. Within this loose consensus, they simply adopted whatever managerial devices suited their particular situation.[27]

Owners and managers of Canadian corporations found they had greater flexibility for their workplace experiments as a result of a huge new pool of labour created by the massive immigrant wave of the early twentieth century that arrived in large part because of the promotional work of the federal government. Many of these newcomers had travelled from peasant villages in southern and eastern Europe, China, and Japan, and like their predecessors a century earlier, never intended to remain full-time workers. Some were earning cash in order to establish themselves on Prairie homesteads or in small retail businesses within their ethnic communities in Canada. Many others lived a frugal life in crowded urban boarding houses or work-camp bunkhouses in order to send their savings back to their families in the old country and then to return home themselves. Canadian employers thus assembled a shifting, heterogeneous, polyglot workforce, arranged in a stratified hierarchy with the non-Anglo-Celtic newcomers at the bottom in the dirtiest, heaviest, worst-paid manual jobs. Ethnic tensions had divided English, Irish, and French workers at many points in the nineteenth century, but the problem was magnified enormously by the proliferation of new ethnic and racial groups in a context of capitalist manipulation to undermine wages and erode skills. Even for the immigrants who eventually stayed in Canada as workers, the cultural gulf separating them from their Anglo-Celtic workmates would last at least until the Second World War.[28]

The great expansion of the managerial function had a further fragmenting effect on the workforce. Office staffs swelled to unprecedented proportions to handle the flood of paperwork generated by this transformation of the "means of administration." Small armies of predominantly female clerical workers soon emerged to give the Canadian working class a whole new complexion and to open up another wide rift, this time between blue- and white-collar workers. Within the new offices there were, nevertheless, strong parallels with the organization of work in factories – fragmentation of the well-rounded clerk's job into specialized tasks and mechanization of many of them with typewriters, adding machines, dictaphones, and data-processing equipment.[29]

The reshaping of labour processes in Canada with widespread mechanization, subdivision of labour, and centralization of management spelled the death of craft-dominated modes of production, but the process was more complicated than most popular notions of deskilling have suggested. We should be clear about our point of comparison. The late nineteenth-century workshop was not a static Never Never Land of custom and tradition. It was an incessant battleground between workers and their employers over workplace control in which many craftsmen had already lost much ground in several industries. The skilled workers who remained, especially in the all-important metal trades, were wage-earners who, for all their continuing craft autonomy, were working in a considerably altered context from the self-employed artisan of old. In the early twentieth century, many more skills were undermined or diluted, though by no means all of them. Some skilled workers simply had the variety of their tasks reduced while retaining high levels of technical competence in their jobs – some iron moulders and most garment cutters, for example. Some new skills appeared, like those of linotype operators and tool and die makers.[30] Perhaps most important, a new, more occupationally homogeneous workforce of "semi-skilled" machine-operators emerged with ambiguous skill attributes. Workers filling these jobs required less training than the old craft apprenticeships and lacked the all-round knowledge of the whole production process. But they were given more responsibility at the centre of the production process than the old-time day-labourers (whose usefulness for brute labour was declining with widespread mechanization). The "semi-skilled" jobs could be complex enough to require some care, attention, and familiarity with the work in order to perform quickly and effectively. By the end of the First World War, many employers were anxious to reduce the turnover of such workers and to keep them steadily at their jobs. Some of these workers would eventually use their enhanced importance in the production process as the basis for building industrial unions.[31] "Deskilling," it seems, was not as straightforward a process as many capitalists hoped (and as many theorists have assumed).

On the whole, workers greeted the new work world of monopoly capitalism with suspicion and hostility. Many of them kept their distance from the new jobs in mines and mills by quitting frequently and moving on, or, in the case of women and immigrants, returning home. Widespread labour turnover meant that within one year a man might have jobs in a steel mill, a construction camp, a coal mine, and a farmer's wheat field, while in the same period a woman might move from wrapping candy in a confectionery plant, to running a machine in a knitting mill, to folding sheets in a laundry, to cleaning someone else's house. Employers increasingly saw this informal, individualized form of resistance as a problem that required renewed efforts to encourage workers to stay on the job.[32]

Yet at the same time, many workers made a stand to defend familiar workplace routines and to demand living wages. Although under relentless attack, craft unionism hung on and surged up with renewed vigour during the First World War. Many of the less skilled were also organizing into all-inclusive industrial unions – radical centres like the Industrial Workers of the World (IWW) and the One Big Union (OBU), as well as one-industry organizations of miners, railway workers, textile workers, steelworkers, meatpackers, and others. Corporate employers had no room for unions in their industrial autocracies and strove to drive out those in existence and to keep out any newcomers. Besides firing and blacklisting union activists and breaking strikes with professional scabs, companies were beginning, by the First World War, to provide programs of corporate welfare – recreation programs, insurance and pension plans, profit-sharing schemes, and industrial councils – to promote loyalty and commitment to the firm. Successive explosions of industrial conflict nonetheless rocked the work world of early twentieth-century Canada. Detailed studies of pre-war strikes in southern Ontario and the Maritimes have revealed how often workers were battling over their right to some control within the labour process. The war years intensified these conflicts by giving workers steady employment at high wages. This was a more secure base from which to fight back and unleashed a powerful rhetoric of democracy and public service that workers could turn into a demand for "industrial democracy."[33]

The climax came in 1919, when almost 3.5 million working days were lost through 459 strikes, highlighted by the general strike in Winnipeg. The confrontation between labour and capital was also extending into politics, where vigorous labour parties were chalking up impressive victories in municipal and provincial elections by the end of the war.

A central political demand connected the industrial and political struggles: the eight-hour day. During the spring and summer of 1919, a hastily assembled Royal Commission on Industrial Relations observed the intensity of Canadian workers' revolt and their remarkable solidarity in hearings across the country. In some cases, such as the Cape Breton coalfields, the postwar industrial conflict was convincing workers to contest the entire structure of ownership and control in their industry.[34]

All of the momentum of workers' industrial and political challenge, however, was crushed in the early 1920s by the combined impact of a severe depression and an employers' anti-union offensive.[35] Except for construction and a few small pockets like printing, craft unionism would never revive, its basis permanently eroded by the transformation of work processes. The first industrial unions were also largely destroyed, but they would reappear sporadically in the inter-war period – first, in the late 1920s and early 1930s under Communist leadership, and then, in the late 1930s, under the inspiration of the American Congress of Industrial Organizations (CIO). By the beginning of the Second World War, however, these unions had made few inroads into Canadian industry. Generally, employers continued to control their workplaces unbridled by the presence of any formal worker presence.[36] It was an age of authoritarian, repressive management that old-timers still recall with a shudder of fear and resentment.[37]

Women workers played a marginal role in these workplace confrontations,[38] largely because of their short spell in the paid workforce between school and marriage, their isolation in female job ghettoes, and the reluctance of their unionized male workmates to devote much energy to helping them organize.[39] Their resistance tended most often to be informal (quitting and moving on), and by the 1920s their intolerance for one form of wage labour – domestic service – had forced middle- and upper-class employers to end their reliance on live-in servants and to begin the mechanization of housework. In their own homes, working-class wives and mothers were still the domestic managers they had been since industrial capitalism had first brought about the separation of work and home. Preparing their families to meet the rhythms of work in the factories, mines, and offices was still an extremely labour-intensive process. Mass marketing of ready-made clothing and processed food like bakery bread and canned goods had slightly reduced some of the domestic labour, as had the installation of running water, gas, and electricity. But the vast majority of Canadian households remained technological backwaters until the Second

World War, and women were still confined to this sphere for most of their lives.[40]

The opening decades of the twentieth century were also a period in which the Canadian state significantly expanded its role in workplace relations. In response to pressure from the labour movement, the federal government and several provincial administrations opened labour departments to monitor workplace relations. They gradually made a few additions to the statute books that required employers to meet some minimal employment standards, most particularly workers' compensation for industrial accidents and minimum wages for women. Typically these measures did no more than stabilize and routinize existing workplace relations. Far more important, however, were the state's efforts to curb workers' militancy. Troops were sent into strike situations even more frequently than in the past and almost invariably provoked violent responses. The courts hammered away at union security and freely granted employers a new weapon, the injunction. The most vigorous use of state repression was probably in Winnipeg in 1919, where the federal government intervened decisively by arresting and deporting strike leaders. The most famous form of state intervention, however, combined the twin goals of meeting enough of workers' demands to encourage legitimation of the industrial system and imposing the iron heel of repression. In 1907, the young William Lyon Mackenzie King drafted a new piece of federal legislation, the Industrial Disputes Investigation Act (IDIA), which prohibited strikes and lockouts in specified industries until a conciliation board had met and reported. Experience soon proved that the so-called cooling-out period did more damage to unions than to employers. Although the act was declared unconstitutional in 1923, its key features would remain a cornerstone of the Canadian state's industrial-relations policies throughout the twentieth century.[41]

Workers' resistance to the terms and conditions of employment and the frequently violent industrial conflict flared up most often when the reserve army of potential strikebreakers was smaller, when the process of industrial transformation was accelerated, and when a dramatic crisis like the war had disrupted normal social relationships. Throughout the period, sporadic industrial trench warfare raged more quietly on the shop floor out of the public eye, as small groups of workers and their bosses confronted each other daily along the "frontier of control" over managerial initiatives to alter or speed up work processes.[42] Yet there was another parallel pattern of worker-management relations that was more evident during periods of severe unemployment or following major defeats on the picket lines or at the ballot box. Many writers have used the term "consent" for a form of working-class consciousness that seemed to reveal a willingness to accept workers' subordination in industry. With thousands of immigrants flooding in to compete for jobs, with blacklists, spies, and company police at work, and with iron-willed magistrates ready to clamp down on troublemakers, it is easy to see how "consent" was actually fear, insecurity, and an unwillingness to rock the boat in the face of economic and political coercion. The corporate paternalism of welfare plans and favouritism in hiring and promotion could help condition workers to accept the coercive framework of their working lives more equably.[43] That consciousness and behaviour could be evoked more indirectly as well. Many workers absorbed appealing ideologies that encouraged quiescence or class collaboration – social Catholicism among Quebec workers, protectionist, jingoist Toryism among southern Ontario factory hands, and Maritime Rights activism in the East, for example.[44] Whatever the source, habits of deference had settled in among many Canadian workers by the 1930s, especially among those who clung to their jobs.

In the forty years before the Second World War, then, the labour process in Canada had been reshaped in fundamental ways. Large new corporate employers, struggling with an uncertain economic environment, had undertaken to restructure their workplaces with new technology and more centralized, authoritarian managerial systems that would wrest control of the labour process from workers on the job, especially from skilled workers and their unions. In the process they had produced new occupational categories and a new, ethnically stratified workforce. But they had also locked horns with many angry, resentful workers. With the help of a sympathetic state, the employers had driven out most craft unions and prevented consolidation of industrial unions; and they believed they had won more solid control over their production processes. By the end of the period, however, the seeds of future conflicts had been sown. During the depression of the 1930s, the workforce had stabilized somewhat, as immigration dried up and workers settled into scarce jobs. They had made a greater commitment to the industries in which they worked, but deeply resented the poor wages and the arbitrary tyranny of front-line supervisors. It was a workforce, which, although no longer maintaining formal control mechanisms in the workplace, often had substantial informal power and autonomy on the job as a result of the unevenness and ambiguity of the deskilling process and the effective leverage of so many semi-skilled workers. Workers could also draw some strength from the increased interdependence of production units within corporate consolidations, which a determined group of workers in one unit could disrupt. Canadian capitalists, it seems, had not delivered a knock-out blow to the workplace power of the Canadian working class; they had merely changed the battlefield. Primarily it was the overstocked labour market in so many of the inter-war years that prevented workers from mounting any more substantial challenges. Another world war would bring a remarkable transformation in workplace relations.

The Challenge of Industrial Democracy, 1940 to the 1970s

A fourth period in the evolution of capitalist labour processes in Canada began to take shape during the Second World War and stretched over the next four decades. In contrast to preceding periods, it was marked by almost unbroken prosperity until the onset of a serious international economic crisis in the 1970s. The prosperity provided the basis for a huge expansion of the service sector, where most of the new jobs were emerging by the end of the period. Within that long phase of high output and relatively full employment, however, some major restructuring of the Canadian economy took place. The protected national market for manufactured goods was slowly dismantled to conform to the new patterns of international free trade, inspired by the postwar General Agreements on Tariffs and Trade (GATT). In the new "international division of labour," many industries like electrical goods and clothing began to wither away in the face of cheaper Third World competition. At the same time, American industry, hungry for natural resources, penetrated Canada more aggressively in search of oil, forest products, and minerals. In both manufacturing and resource extraction, continental economic integration had resulted in a staggering increase in American ownership by the 1960s. In this new economic environment, the state played a much more active role in promoting economic development and attempting to stabilize business cycles with the new fiscal and monetary tools of Keynesianism. The collaboration of capitalists, politicians, and state bureaucrats over which C.D. Howe presided during the Second World War continued and expanded in postwar decades. Eventually, however, the Ottawa mandarins discovered that the regulatory tools of one nation state were feeble instruments in a context where industrial development and economic relations were dominated by a new institution – the multinational/transnational corporation, with branches and widely diversified investments around the globe.[45]

A third major technological revolution accompanied this economic expansion. Elaborate new machines replaced old manual techniques in most major resource industries like forestry, mining, fishing, and agriculture in particular.[46] Manufacturing and communications companies similarly introduced sophisticated new technologies, while in the transportation sector, diesel replaced steam power on trains and mechanized loading and unloading devices transformed the country's ports.[47] As in the past, the trend of all this mechanization was to cut costs by replacing workers and speeding up work processes. But what distinguished this period from the two previous "industrial revolutions" was the effort to automate work – to find machines that would run themselves. The key to this transformation became the computer, which was large, bulky, and expensive when first developed during the Second World War, but which became infinitely more flexible with the insertion of the microchip in the 1970s. Computerized technology began rapidly replacing human labour in manufacturing, communications, service industries (like banks, supermarkets, gas stations), and, most dramatically, in offices, where clerical workers from accountants to filing clerks have found their traditional jobs disappearing.[48]

As in previous phases of technological change, displacement of workers by computers has been accompanied by deskilling – word-processor pools are a striking example – and some reskilling, although most studies suggest that those learning the new skills in computer application are not the largely female labour being displaced. Even more important, however, is the ability of the new technology to control the workforce more effectively, both by setting the pace of production and by monitoring the performance of operators of word processors, cash registers, lathes, and other machines with more precision than F.W. Taylor could ever have dreamed of.[49] The lingering economic recession of the early 1980s slowed the spread of this "technical control" of the labour process into workplaces,[50] but the wave of the future was clear.

The workforce assembled in this technologically more sophisticated economy had some important new dimensions. The traditionally large, flexible pool of underemployed, "semi-proletarianized" Canadian farm dwellers declined drastically after the Second World War as farmers' children left for the city in unprecedented numbers.[51] Immigrants continued to flow in from southern Europe and the Caribbean to find jobs in sectors where muscle power was still in demand, especially in construction and domestic service; yet immigration also brought many professionals from eastern Europe and Asia.[52] In general, the workforce used in this new phase of economic development was much better educated, and a demand grew for technically trained personnel, usually with college or university degrees: engineers, research scientists, computer analysts, and other members of the so-called new working class.[53]

An important shift in employment patterns was the much greater use of female labour, including for the first time rising numbers of married women. Labour shortages during the Second World War had enabled many women to breach some of the bastions of exclusively male work in various versions of "Rosie the Riveter," but they had been promptly sent home at the end of the war. By the 1960s, however, larger numbers of women, including married women, were working more-or-less full time in the burgeoning female job ghettoes in offices and service-sector enterprises. Working-class families were now keeping their teenagers in school longer, while their mothers took over the role of secondary wage-earners. For most families this transition was made easier by the emergence of consumer services like take-out food and by the accessibility of new gadgets for mechanizing housework, from automatic washers and dryers to electric floor polishers. But for women it created the new burden of the "double day" – a shift in the factory, office, or store, followed by continuing responsibility for most domestic labour in the family home.[54]

No change in the workplace was more striking, however, than the unionization of hundreds of thousands of Canadian workers after 1940. The war provided the catalyst, although the seeds had been sown in the 1930s in the many struggles of unemployed workers and the first efforts at building industrial unions under the umbrella of the CIO. By the outbreak of the war, these unions had established only a tenuous toehold in a few sectors like steel, auto, textiles, clothing, and coal mining, but within two years, full employment and labour shortages had strengthened the organizers' hands. A strike wave, which reached a new peak of militancy in 1943, was propelled by workers' resentments at the wage freeze imposed by the Mackenzie King government, the continuing tyrannies of shop-floor management, and provincial and federal governments' reluctance to force employers to sit down at the bargaining table with recognized unions.[55]

Moreover, as in the First World War, workers seized on the wartime rhetoric of combating fascist tyranny and began to demand more democracy in the workplace. Employers fought back with a new flurry of corporate welfare, especially company unions and industrial councils. They also attacked as "totalitarian" the labour movement's connections with Canada's resurgent social-democratic party, the Cooperative Commonwealth Federation (CCF). But in Ottawa, a shrewd prime minister watched with more astuteness the CCF's incredible rise to the top of the public opinion polls in 1943 and the party's near victory in the Ontario provincial election the same year. Frustrations built up at the point of production were once again spilling over into the realm of electoral politics. In an effort to stave off the erosion of its political base, the King government moved sharply to the left. A new commitment to establishing a minimal social-security net for workers brought unemployment insurance, children's allowances, and promises of much more, with the result that for the first time, workers' complete dependence on their employers for income had been partially relieved. At the same time, the Cabinet enacted an order in council, PC 1003, that provided for the recognition of unions, compulsory collective bargaining, and close state supervision of industrial relations, along with the old IDIA compulsory conciliation procedures. This temporary wartime measure became a permanent fixture of the industrial-relations landscape at the federal and provincial levels in the late 1940s, but only after thousands of Canadian workers in virtually every major industrial sector had won their employers' grudging recognition of their unions in the biggest strike wave in Canadian history. Long, bitter disputes tied up auto plants, steel mills, rubber plants, packing houses, railways, and many other workplaces between 1945 and 1947; in most cases workers won the right to have their unions negotiate for them and to have employers deduct union dues from their pay cheques.[56]

The victory that Canadian workers won from their bosses in almost all mass-production, resource-extractive, and transportation industries, and which the state then proceeded to recognize in its postwar labour legislation, was an ambiguous legacy. On the one hand, workers established regular procedures for collectively negotiating their wages and for protecting their organizations' right to exist. They were thus able to achieve higher wages and shorter hours (the forty-hour week finally arrived in the 1950s) and in general to ensure for themselves and their families a vastly better standard of living – indeed, a whole new style of life based on suburban homes, family cars, and sundry consumer goods. On the job, collective agreements now demanded new standards of fairness and equity from front-line supervisors that reduced competition and division between workers. Seniority clauses and grievance procedures prevented foremen and superintendents from promoting favourites or dismissing workers on whim. A "rule of law" had finally arrived inside many workplaces. Postwar bargaining also included efforts to simplify and standardize wage rates across whole industries. Overall, the greatest beneficiaries were probably the minority ethnic and racial groups within the workforce who had suffered the worst abuses in the pre-war industrial regime.

On the other hand, limitations on this new collective power of workers were severe. According to the wide-ranging "management rights" clause in most collective agreements, employers still held onto control over the power to run their businesses, organize their production processes, and discipline their workers. Although in practice, four decades of negotiation and grievance arbitration would impinge somewhat on untrammelled employer control, the success of industrial democracy clearly did not mean a return to the workplace control mechanisms of nineteenth-century craftsmen. Moreover, the state imposed strict legal constraints on trade-union activity, forbidding strikes during the conciliation process and during the lifetime of the collective agreement, and broke working-class solidarity by banning sympathy strikes. Union officials were, therefore, cast in the role of policemen over their membership to keep them within legal bounds. Finally, the resolution of conflict on the shop floor was pushed into grievance procedures modelled on the legal system which were thus handled primarily by lawyers or other trained staff rather than by workers themselves. In many instances the procedure was painfully slow, insensitive, expensive, and ineffective in meeting workers' concerns.[57]

This much-discussed postwar "compromise" was not an inevitable outcome of bureaucratization, but a product of a particular period of struggle in which the state intervened decisively to contain and fragment a burgeoning movement of working-class militancy and solidarity. At the same moment the state joined employers and the media in whipping up a cold-war hysteria, which broke the momentum of all progressive movements and set the stage for the expulsion of many seasoned Communist trade-union leaders (and in a few cases, whole unions) from the Canadian labour movement. The potential for widening and deepening the working-class challenge to its subordination within the capitalist workplace was thus never allowed to reach fruition.[58]

For nearly two decades, the postwar institutionalization of industrial relations worked more or less as intended, confining most industrial conflict to relatively safe bureaucratic channels.[59] In the mid-1960s, however, the system began to break down. An explosion of strikes that extended into the mid-1970s shattered the relative calm. Illegal "wildcat" strikes, rejections of negotiated contracts, and internal challenges to union leadership were signs that the tensions arising from employers' freedom to speed up and innovate and from the emerging problem of rapid inflation in an increasingly unstable world economy were boiling over. This new militancy was also inspired by a blossoming youth culture that celebrated personal freedom and self-expression. The same factors were producing more turbulence on the shop floor, particularly increased labour turnover, absenteeism, and sabotage. This continuing ferment testified to the persistent autonomy of informal work groups, both from complete subordination to management and from the union leadership that collaborated in the collective-bargaining process. In some regions, the country's new social-democratic party, the New Democratic Party, gathered some momentum from this industrial unrest.[60]

Some of the same resentments at the bureaucratic insensitivity of a highly centralized management and at deteriorating wages brought a new set of actors into the industrial-relations system: public-sector workers. After a cautious process of turning the old government employees' associations into effective bargaining agents, and eventually into full-fledged unions, these workers convinced provincial and federal governments to enact legislation granting them most of the same rights to organize and bargain collectively that so many blue-collar workers had won in the 1940s, although often with tighter restrictions on their freedom to strike. The state's role in the industrial-relations system thus shifted abruptly from external mediator to central participant. By the mid-1970s, public-sector unions were negotiating for virtually all state employees and included almost 40 per cent of all union membership in Canada.[61] Para-public sectors like schools and hospitals also found the professionals on their staff – nurses, teachers, professors, librarians, technicians – turning into militant unionists. Their employers' attempts to cope with funding crises by more rigid application of private-sector managerial practices and resistance to salary increases threatened these workers' image of their status as professionals.[62] In fact, at the peak of strike activity in the early 1970s, it was workers from government offices, schools, and hospitals whom the media featured most prominently on the picket lines. Significantly, women workers figured more conspicuously in the struggles of the 1970s – a sign both of the impact of the emerging feminist movement and of women's increasing commitment to full-time employment.[63]

By the beginning of the 1980s, then, union organization in Canada had grown to a level where nearly two non-agricultural workers in every five were union members and almost three in every five were covered by union contracts, in sharp contrast to the United States, where union membership has been steadily declining.[64] Canadian workers had also developed an international reputation for combativeness – second only to Italy in proneness to strike. Yet that militancy has remained fragmented by related problems: the tight strictures of collective-bargaining legislation, which structured negotiations on a factory-by-factory basis and forbade sympathy strikes; and the persistent caution of a top union leadership that was more accustomed to bureaucratic manoeuvring than to mass mobilization and was legitimately concerned about safeguarding the existence of its organizations. Only in Quebec, where francophone nationalism and Marxism infused the labour movement, did workers connect up their individual workplace battles in a "Common Front," and even there the unity was largely limited to the public sector.[65] The repressive function of the postwar "compromise" helped to constrain and divide workers.

At the same time, not only were trade unionists divided from each other, but the much more numerous unorganized workers were left completely outside this industrial battle zone. These workers continued to find jobs in a "secondary" labour market, where small, more peripheral, or more labour-intensive enterprises demanded few skills, paid low wages, guaranteed little or no job security, and were run in the no-nonsense, authoritarian style of earlier capitalist management. It was here that we found Canada's many working poor – most particularly women and the new racial and ethnic minorities, who, as in the past, found themselves at the bottom of the occupational hierarchy, and whose vulnerability made them extremely difficult to organize. More skilled workers in the "primary" sector were often reluctant to try, but, contrary to the assumptions of some theorists of labour-market segmentation, they did not show complete indifference: the existing minimum-wage requirements, however inadequate, found their way onto the statute books largely because the labour movement demanded them. The rapid growth of part-time work in the 1980s (and beyond) suggested that this work experience in the secondary labour market was not about to disappear.[66]

The Counterattack since 1975

Whatever the divisions within the Canadian working class, employers, politicians, and state officials had been concerned for nearly twenty years that Canada's bureaucratized system of industrial relations had not succeeded in keeping workers on the job or in curbing their demands, especially for higher wages. By the end of the 1960s, the era of free collective bargaining and the "rule of law" in the workplace was unravelling in the face of renewed worker militancy and economic recession, both of which combined with increasing foreign competition to cut heavily into profit margins. After the federal state failed to win union leaders' voluntary consent to a restricted incomes policy, it imposed compulsory wage controls on all workers between 1975 and 1978 and on public-sector workers in the early 1980s. Most provincial administrations followed suit. Governments also used frequent back-to-work legislation and even jailed labour leaders in a pattern of disrupting legal collective-bargaining procedures that has been accurately called "permanent exceptionalism."[67] Some provincial jurisdictions, moreover, enacted legislation to weaken the rights of trade unions to organize and bargain.

Simultaneously, the Canadian state was aggressively promoting new forms of consultation between workers and their bosses that bypassed the collective-bargaining process and encouraged non-confrontational negotiation of problems. A new national Labour Market and Productivity Centre appeared early in 1984, with the federal government's blessing. Special committees in the workplace to discuss occupational health and safety and technological change had also been encouraged. "Quality of Working Life" schemes promoted by federal and provincial agencies ostensibly offered workers more interesting and challenging work through such measures as job rotation, job enrichment, "quality circles" to discuss quality control and productivity, and the formation of semi-autonomous work groups. Yet, like their predecessors – company unionism and industrial councils – these schemes tended, in practice, to be devices for reorganizing the workplace and intensifying work with the consent of the worker. In the context of stiffer international competition and pressures to adopt the latest technologies, a relatively small number of employers found these schemes effective. Many more turned to another device promoted by the Canadian state for the same purpose: profit sharing.[68] The goal of state intervention after 1975 had been primarily to help shore up the faltering Canadian capitalist system by restricting or suspending workers' hard-won rights to bargain collectively over the terms of their employment and to convince workers to accept some curtailment of their immediate material interests. Only in the context of the economic crash of the early 1980s, when official unemployment rates passed 12 per cent nationally (or probably closer to 20 per cent if "discouraged" workers were counted), did this strategy seem to work. However, a resurgence of strikes and union organizing – which hit anti-labour bastions like Eaton's – suggested that the long-term outcome was not clear.[69]

The postwar "compromise" had thus come unstuck. The industrial-relations system created in the 1940s to guarantee both stability in the work world and the continued subordination of workers to employers proved incapable of meeting the seismic shocks of technological change, mass unionization, and international economic crisis. On the job, workers had to confront the redesigning and intensification of production processes, which their employers pushed forward relentlessly in an effort to survive in a restructured economy. One result was one of the highest rates of industrial accident and disease in the Western world.[70] At the same time, workers found their formal organizations of resistance mired in bureaucracy and legal restraint. They also found an international inflationary spiral eating away at their real wages and the state moving in to coax them, and if necessary to compel them, to accept less in the name of economic recovery for their employers' firms. By the early 1980s, it was clear that Canadian industrial relations had entered a new phase – probably dating from the imposition of wage and price controls in 1975 – in which workers' power at the point of production was once again under attack.

Notes

1 David M. Gordon, Richard Edwards, and Michael Reich, *Segmented Work, Divided Workers: The Historical Transformation of Labor in the United States* (Cambridge: Cambridge University Press 1982), 9.

2 R.C. Harris and John Warkentin, *Canada before Confederation* (New York: Oxford University Press 1974); C. Grant Head, *Eighteenth Century Newfoundland: A Geographer' s Perspective* (Toronto: McClelland and Stewart

1976); Steven Antler, "The Capitalist Underdevelopment of Nineteenth-Century Newfoundland," in Robert J. Brym and R. James Sacouman, eds., *Underdevelopment and Social Movements in Atlantic Canada* (Toronto: New Hogtown Press 1979), 179–202; Gerald Sider, "The Ties That Bind: Culture and Agriculture, Property and Propriety in the Newfoundland Fishery," *Social History* 5, no. 1 (January 1980): 1–39; Peter Neary and Patrick O'Flaherty, eds., *By Great Waters: A Newfoundland and Labrador Anthology* (Toronto: University of Toronto Press 1974), 42–60; Andrew Hill Clark, *Three Centuries and the Isand: A Historical Geography of Settlement and Agriculture in Prince Edward Island, Canada* (Toronto: University of Toronto Press 1959); Robert Leslie Jones, *History of Agriculture in Ontario, 1613–1880* (Toronto: University of Toronto Press 1946), 1–174; Leo Johnson, *History of the County of Ontario, 1615–1875* (Whitby: Corporation of the County of Ontario 1973), 1–171; Leo Johnson, "Independent Commodity Production: Mode of Production or Capitalist Class Formation?" *SPE* 6 (Autumn 1981), 93–112; Douglas McCalla, "The Wheat Staple and Upper Canadian Development," *HP* 1978, 43–6; Allan Greer, "Fur Trade Labour and Lower Canadian Agrarian Structures," ibid., 1981, 197–214; Allan Greer, "Wage Labour and the Transition to Capitalism: A Critique of Pentland," *LLT* 15 (Spring 1985), 7–22; Allan Greer, *Peasant, Lord, and Merchant: Rural Society in Three Quebec Parishes* (Toronto: University of Toronto Press 1985); Graeme Wynn, *Timber Colony: A Historical Geography of Early Nineteenth Century New Brunswick* (Toronto: University of Toronto Press 1981), 11–86; Edwin C. Guillet, *Pioneer Arts and Crafts* (Toronto: University of Toronto Press 1968); Michael S. Cross, ed., *The Workingman in the Nineteenth Century* (Toronto: Oxford University Press 1973), 17–31.

3 Beth Light and Alison Prentice, eds., *Pioneers and Gentlewomen of British North America, 1713–1867* (Toronto: New Hogtown Press 1980); David Gagan, "'The Prose of Life': Literary Reflections on the Family, Individual Experience and Social Structure in Nineteenth Century Canada," *JSH* 9, no. 3 (Spring 1976), 367–81; Rosemary R. Ball, "'A Perfect Farmer's Wife': Women in 19th-Century Rural Ontario," *Canada: A Magazine* 1975, 3–21; Leo Johnson, "The Political Economy of Women in the 19th Century," in Janice Acton et al., eds., *Women at Work: Ontario, 1850–1930* (Toronto: Women's Press 1974), 13–32; Louise A. Tilly and Joan W. Scott, *Women, Work, and the Family* (New York: Routledge 1978); Guillet, *Pioneer Arts and Crafts.*

4 Johnson, *History of the County of Ontario*; Michael S. Cross, "1837: The Necessary Failure," in Cross and Gregory S. Kealey, eds., *Readings in Canadian Social History, Volume 2: Pre-Industrial Canada, 1760–1849* (Toronto: McClelland and Stewart 1982), 141–58; Lillian Gates, "The Decided Policy

of William Lyon Mackenzie," *CHR* 40 (1959), 185–208; Fernand Ouellet, "Les insurrections de 1837–38: Un phénomène social," *HS/SH* 2 (November 1968), 54–84; Colin Read, *The Rising in Western Upper Canada: The Duncombe Revolt and After* (Toronto: University of Toronto Press 1982); Errol Sharpe, *A People' s History of Prince Edward Island* (Toronto: Steel Rail Publications 1976), 73–6; J. Murray Beck, *Joseph Howe, Volume 1: Conservative Reformer, 1804–1848* (Montreal and Kingston: McGill-Queen's University Press 1982).

5 H. Clare Pentland, *Labour and Capital in Canada, 1650–1860* (Toronto: James Lorimer 1981), 1–60; Donald MacKay, *The Lumberjacks* (Toronto: McGraw-Hill Ryerson 1978); Wynn, *Timber Colony*, 11–86; Judith Fingard, *Jack in Port: Sailortowns in Eastern Canada* (Toronto: University of Toronto Press 1982); Greer, "Fur Trade Labour"; Peter Russell, "Wage Labour Rates in Upper Canada, 1818–1840," *HS/SH* 16, no. 3 (May 1983): 61–70; Eugene Forsey, *Trade Unions in Canada, 1812–1902* (Toronto: University of Toronto Press 1982), 9–31; Sally Zerker, *The Rise and Fall of the Toronto Typographical Union, 1832–1972: A Case Study in Foreign Domination* (Toronto: University of Toronto Press 1982), 3–49; G.S. Kealey, "Work Control, the Labour Process, and Nineteenth-Century Canadian Printers," in Craig Heron and Robert Storey, eds., *On the Job: Confronting the Labour Process in Canada* (Montreal and Kingston: McGill-Queen's University Press 1986), 75–101; Catherine Vance, "Early Trade Unionism in Quebec: The Carpenters and Joiners General Strike of 1833–1834," *Marxist Quarterly* 3 (1962), 26–42; William T. Wylie, "Poverty, Distress, and Disease: Labour and the Construction of the Rideau Canal, 1826–1836," *L/LT* 11 (Spring 1983): 7–30; Ruth Bleasdale, "Class Conflict on the Canals of Upper Canada in the 1840s," ibid., 7 (Spring 1981), 9–40; H.C. Pentland, "The Lachine Strike of 1843," *CHR* 29, no. 3 (September 1948), 255–77; Michael S. Cross, "The Shiners' War: Social Violence in the Ottawa Valley in the 1830s," ibid., 54, no. 1 (March 1973), 1–26; Bryan D. Palmer, *Working Class Experience: The Rise and Reconstitution of Canadian Labour, 1800–1980* (Toronto: Butterworth 1983), 1–55.

6 James Sacouman, "Semi-Proletarianization and Rural Underdevelopment in the Maritimes," *CRSA* 17 (1980), 232–45; Leo Johnson, "Precapitalist Economic Formations and the Capitalist Labour Market in Canada, 1911–71," in James E. Curtis and William G. Scott, eds., *Social Stratification: Canada* (Scarborough: Prentice Hall 1979), 89–104.

7 Pentland, *Labour and Capital*, 130–75; John McCallum, *Unequal Beginnings: Agriculture and Economic Development in Quebec and Ontario until 1870* (Toronto: University of Toronto Press 1980); Paul Craven and Tom Traves, "Canadian Railways as Manufacturers, 1850–1880," *HP* 1983, 254–81; Gregory S. Kealey, *Toronto Workers Respond to Industrial Capitalism,*

1867–1892 (Toronto: University of Toronto Press 1980), 3–34; Thomas William Acheson, "The Social Origins of Canadian Industrialism: A Study of the Structure of Entrepreneurship" (PhD dissertation, University of Toronto 1971); L.D. McCann, "The Mercantile-Industrial Transition of the Metal Towns of Pictou County, 1860–1931, *Acadiensis* 10, no. 2 (Spring 1981), 29–64; Robert Babcock, "Economic Development in Portland (Me.) and Saint John (N.B.) during the Age of Iron and Steam, 1860–1914," *American Review of Canadian Studies* 9 (1979), 1–37; Ian McKay, "Capital and Labour in the Halifax Baking and Confectionery Industry in the Last Half of the Nineteenth Century," *L/LT* 3 (1978), 63–108; Glenn Williams, *Not For Export: Towards a Political Economy of Canada' s Arrested Industrialization* (Toronto: McClelland and Stewart 1983).

8 Leo Johnson, "Land Policy, Population Growth, and Social Structure in the Home District, 1793–1851," *OH* 58 (1971), 41–60; Gary Teeple, "Land, Labour, and Capital in Pre-Confederation Canada," in Teeple, ed., *Capitalism and the National Question in Canada* (Toronto: University of Toronto Press 1972), 43–66; H.C. Pentland, "The Development of a Capitalist Labour Market in Canada," *CJEPS* 25, no. 4 (November 1959), 450–61; Del Muise, "The Making of an Industrial Community: Cape Breton Coal Towns, 1867–1900," in Don Macgillivray and Bryan Tennyson, eds., *Cape Breton Historical Essays* (Sydney: College of Cape Breton Press 1980), 76–94.

9 Joanne Burgess, "L'industrie de la chaussure à Montréal, 1840–1870: Le passage de l'artisanat à la fabrique," *RHAF* 31, no. 2 (January 1977), 187–210; Bettina Bradbury, "Women and Wage Labour in a Period of Transition: Montreal, 1861–1881," *HS/SH* 17, no. 33 (May 1984), 115–31; Susan Mann Trofimenkoff, "One Hundred and Two Muffled Voices: Canada's Industrial Women in the 1880s," *Atlantis* 3 (1978), 66–82; Kealey, *Toronto Workers*, 37–97; Bryan D. Palmer, *A Culture in Conflict: Skilled Workers and Industrial Capitalism in Hamilton, Ontario, 1860–1914* (Montreal and Kingston: McGill-Queen's University Press 1979), 71–96; McKay, "Capital and Labour"; Paul Craven and Tom Traves, "Dimensions of Paternalism: Discipline and Culture in Canadian Railway Operations in the 1850s," in Heron and Storey, eds., *On the Job*, 47–74; David Russell, "Fines, Piece Work, Factory Morality, and Blackholes: Factory Discipline in Nineteenth Century Montreal," *The Register* 3, no. 1 (March 1982), 83–101; Gregory S. Kealey, ed., *Canada Investigates Industrialism: The Royal Commission on the Relations of Labor and Capital, 1889* (Toronto: University of Toronto Press 1973); Raphael Samuel, "Workshop of the World: Steam Power and Hand Technology in Mid-Victorian Britain," *History Workshop* 3 (Spring 1977), 6–72.

10 Pentland, *Labour and Capital*, 176–99; Stephen A. Speisman, "Munificent Parsons and Municipal Parsimony: Voluntary vs Public Poor Relief in Nineteenth Century Toronto," *OH* 65 (1973), 33–49; Joey Noble, "'Classifying the Poor': Toronto Charities, 1850–1880," *SPE* 2 (Autumn 1979), 109–28; Alison Prentice, *The School Promoters: Education and Social Class in Mid-Nineteenth Century Upper Canada* (Toronto: McClelland and Stewart 1977); J.M. Beattie, *Attitudes towards Crime and Punishment in Upper Canada, 1830–1850* (Toronto: University of Toronto, Centre of Criminology 1977); Graeme Decarie, "Something Old, Something New ...: Aspects of Prohibitionism in Ontario in the 1890s," in Donald Swainson, ed., *Oliver Mowat' s Ontario* (Toronto: Macmillan 1972), 154–71; E.P. Thompson, "Time, Work Discipline, and Industrial Capitalism," *Past and Present* 38 (1967) 56–97; Daniel T. Rodgers, *The Work Ethic in Industrial America, 1850–1920* (Chicago: University of Chicago Press 1974).

11 Bettina Bradbury, "The Family Economy and Work in an Industrializing City: Montreal in the 1870s," *HP* 1979, 71–96; Bettina Bradbury, "Fragmented Family: Family Strategies in the Face of Death, Illness and Poverty, Montreal, 1860–1885," in Joy Parr, ed., *Childhood and Family in Canadian History* (Toronto: McClelland and Stewart 1982), 109–28; Jane Humphries, "Class Struggle and the Persistence of the Working Class Family," *CJE* 1, no. 3 (September 1978), 241–58; Bruce Curtis, "Capital, the State, and the Origins of the Working-Class Household," in Bonnie Fox, ed., *Hidden in the Household: Women's Domestic Labour under Capitalism* (Toronto: Women's Press 1980), 101–34. See also Gita Sen, "The Sexual Division of Labour and the Working-Class Family: Towards a Conceptual Synthesis of Class Relations and the Subordination of Women," *RRPE* 12, no. 2 (July 1980), 76–86.

12 D. Suzanne Cross, "The Neglected Majority: The Changing Role of Women in 19th Century Montreal," in Susan Mann Trofimenkoff and Alison Prentice, eds., *The Neglected Majority: Essays in Canadian Women's History* (Toronto: McClelland and Stewart 1977), 66–86; Trofimenkoff, "One Hundred and Two Muffled Voices"; Bradbury, "Family Economy"; Heidi Hartmann, "Capitalism, Patriarchy, and Job Segregation by Sex," *Signs* 1, no. 3 (Spring 1976), 137–69; Michele Barrett, *Women's Oppression Today: Problems in Marxist-Feminist Analysis* (London: Verso 1980), 152–86; Barbara Welter, "The Cult of True Womanhood," *American Quarterly* 18, no. 2 (Summer 1966), 151–74. A growing body of literature is beginning to grapple with the connections between work experience and working-class masculinity. See, in particular, Cynthia Cockburn, *Brothers: Male Dominance and Technological Change* (London: Pluto Press 1983); Paul Willis, *Learning*

to Labour: How Working Class Kids Get Working Class Jobs (London: Gower 1977); Paul Willis, "Shop Floor Culture, Masculinity, and the Wage Form," in John Clarke, Chas Critcher, and Richard Johnson, eds., *Working-Class Culture: Studies in History and Theory* (London: Hutchinson 1979), 185–98; Andrew Tolson, *The Limits of Masculinity* (London: Tavistock Publications 1977); Paul Hoch, *White Hero, Black Beast: Racism, Sexism and the Mask of Masculinity* (London: Pluto 1979); Stan Gray, "Sharing the Shop Floor," *CD* 18, no. 2 (June 1984), 17–32.

13 Forsey, *Trade Unions*; Kealey, *Toronto Workers*; Palmer, *Culture in Conflict*, and *Working-Class Experience*, 60–135; Robert Storey, "Industrialization in Canada: The Emergence of the Hamilton Working Class, 1850–1870s" (MA thesis, Dalhousie University 1975).

14 Kealey, *Toronto Workers*, 64–97; Palmer, *Culture in Conflict*, 71–96; Ian McKay, "Workers' Control in Springhill, 1882–1927" (paper presented to the Canadian Historical Association 1981); David Montgomery, *Workers' Control in America: Studies in the History of Work, Technology, and Labor Struggles* (New York: Cambridge University Press 1979), 9–31.

15 McKay, "Capital and Labour"; Craig Heron, "The Crisis of the Craftsman: Hamilton Metal Workers in the Early Twentieth Century," *LLT* 6 (Autumn 1980), 7–48.

16 For a good review of the debate, see John Field, "British Historians and the Concept of the Labor Aristocracy," *RHR* 19 (Winter 1978–9), 61–85.

17 Dan Clawson, *Bureaucracy and the Labor Process: The Transformation of U.S. Industry, 1860–1920* (New York: Monthly Review Press 1980), 71–125.

18 Ruth Frager, "No Proper Deal: Women and the Canadian Labour Movement, 1870–1940," in Linda Briskin and Linda Yantz, eds., *Union Sisters: Women in the Labour Movement* (Toronto: Women's Press 1983), 44–64; Barbara Taylor, "'The Men Are as Bad as Their Masters …': Socialism, Feminism and Sexual Antagonism in the London Tailoring Trade in the Early 1830s," *Feminist Studies 5* (1979), 7–40; Ruth Milkman, "Organizing the Sexual Division of Labor: Historical Perspectives on 'Women's Work' and the American Labor Movement," *Socialist Review* 49 (January–February 1980), 95–150.

19 W. Peter Ward, *White Canada Forever: Popular Attitudes and Public Policy toward Orientals in British Columbia* (Montreal and Kingston: McGill-Queen's University Press 1978); Paul Phillips, *No Power Greater: A Century of Labour in British Columbia* (Vancouver: BC Federation of Labour / Boag Foundation 1967).

20 Kealey, *Toronto Workers*, 124–290; Palmer, *Culture in Conflict*, 125–98; Gregory S. Kealey and Bryan D. Palmer, *Dreaming of What Might Be:*

The Knights of Labor in Ontario, 1880–1900 (New York: Cambridge University Press 1983); John Battye, "The Nine-Hour Pioneers: The Genesis of the Canadian Labour Movement," *L/LT* 4 (1979), 25–56; Steven Langdon, *The Emergence of the Canadian Working Class Movement, 1845–1875* (Toronto: New Hogtown Press 1975); Craig Heron, "Labourism and the Canadian Working Class," *L/LT* 13 (Spring 1984), 45–76.

21 Paul Craven, "The Law of Master and Servant in Mid-Nineteenth-Century Ontario," in David H. Flaherty, ed., *Essays in the History of Canadian Law* (Toronto: University of Toronto Press 1981), 1, 175–211; Paul Craven, "Workers' Conspiracies in Toronto, 1854–72: A Re-Examination," *L/LT* 14 (Fall 1984), 49–72 ; Craven and Traves, "Dimensions of Paternalism"; Fingard, *Jack in Port*, 140–93; Kealey, *Toronto Workers*, 124–53; James C. Cameron and F.J.L. Young, *The Status of Trade Unions in Canada* (Kingston: Queen's University, Department of Industrial Relations 1960), 24–9 ; Kealey, ed., *Canada Investigates Industrialism*, ix–xxvii; Desmond Morton, "Taking on the Grand Trunk: The Locomotive Engineers Strike of 1876–7," *L/LT* 2 (1977), 5–34, Desmond Morton, "Aid to the Civil Power: The Canadian Militia in Support of Social Order, 1867–1914," *CHR* 51 (1970), 407–25.

22 L.A. Wood, *A History of Farmers' Movements in Canada* (Toronto: University of Toronto Press 1975), 13–155; Russell Hann, *Farmers Confront Industrialism: Some Historical Perspectives on Ontario Agrarian Movements* (Toronto: New Hogtown Press 1975).

23 Williams, *Not For Export*; Kenneth Buckley, *Capital Formation in Canada, 1896–1930* (Toronto: University of Toronto Press 1955); Tom Naylor, *The History of Canadian Business, 1867–1914, Volume 2: Industrial Development* (Toronto: James Lorimer 1975); Joseph Smucker, *Industrialization in Canada* (Scarborough: Prentice-Hall 1980); T.W. Acheson, "The National Policy and the Industrialization of the Maritimes," *Acadiensis* 1, no. 2 (Spring 1972), 3–28; David Frank, "The Cape Breton Coal Industry and the Rise and Fall of the British Empire Steel Corporation," ibid., 7, no. 1 (Autumn 1977), 3–34; James D. Frost, "The 'Nationalization' of the Bank of Nova Scotia, 1880–1910," ibid., 12, no. 1 (Autumn 1982): 3–38; Michael Bliss, *A Canadian Millionaire: The Life and Business Times of Sir Joseph Flavelle, Bart., 1858–1939* (Toronto: Macmillan 1978); James R. Struthers, *No Fault of Their Own: Unemployment and the Canadian Welfare State, 1914–1941* (Toronto: University of Toronto Press 1983).

24 Abram Ernest Epp, "Co-operation among Capitalists: The Canadian Merger Movement, 1909–1913" (PhD dissertation, Johns Hopkins University 1973); J.C. Weldon, "Consolidations in Canadian Industry,

1900–1948," in L.A. Skeoch, ed., *Restrictive Trade Practices in Canada* (Toronto: McClelland and Stewart 1966); Tom Traves, *The State and Enterprise: Canadian Manufacturers and the Federal Government, 1917–1931* (Toronto: University of Toronto Press 1979), 73–100; Mira Wilkins, *The Emergence of Multinational Enterprise: American Business Abroad from the Colonial Era to 1914* (Cambridge, Mass.: Harvard University Press 1970); Herbert Marshall et al., *Canadian-American Industry: A Study in International Investment* (Toronto: McClelland and Stewart 1976).

25 Graham S. Lowe, "The Rise of Modern Management in Canada," *CD* 14, no. 3 (December 1979), 32–8; Joseph A. Litterer, "Systematic Management: The Search for Order and Integration," *BHR* 35, no. 4 (Winter 1961), 461–76; Bryan D. Palmer, "Class, Conception, and Conflict: The Thrust for Efficiency, Managerial Views of Labor, and the Working Class Rebellion, 1903–1922," *RRPE* 7, no. 2 (July 1975), 31–49; Daniel Nelson, *Managers and Workers: Origins of the New Factory System in the United States, 1880–1920* (Madison: University of Wisconsin Press 1975); Alfred D. Chandler, Jr, *The Visible Hand: The Managerial Revolution in American Business* (Cambridge, Mass.: Belknap Press 1977).

26 Richard Edwards, *Contested Terrain: The Transformation of the Workplace in the Twentieth Century* (New York: Basic Books 1979), 111–29; W. Craig Heron, "Working-Class Hamilton, 1895–1930" (PhD dissertation, Dalhousie University 1981), 193–287; Craig Heron and Robert Storey, "Work and Struggle in the Canadian Steel Industry, 1900–1950," in this volume; Stephen Meyer III, *The Five-Dollar Day: Labor Management and Social Control in the Ford Motor Company, 1908–1921* (Albany: State University of New York Press 1981); David F. Noble, *America By Design: Science, Technology, and the Rise of Corporate Capitalism* (New York: Knopf 1977); David Albury and Joseph Schwartz, *Partial Progress: The Politics of Science and Technology* (London: Pluto 1982).

27 Palmer, "Class, Conception, and Conflict"; Nelson, *Managers and Workers*, 55–78; Craig Heron and Bryan D. Palmer, "Through the Prism of the Strike: Industrial Conflict in Southern Ontario, 1901–14," *CHR* 58 (1977), 430–4; Heron, "Crisis of the Craftsman"; Heron and Storey, "Work and Struggle."

28 Cross, "Shiners' War"; Bleasdale, "Class Conflict"; J.I. Cooper, "The Quebec Ship Labourers' Benevolent Society," *CHR* 30 (1949), 336–43; Donald Avery, *"Dangerous Foreigners": European Immigrant Workers and Labour Radicalism in Canada, 1896–1932* (Toronto: McClelland and Stewart 1979); Jorgen Dahlie and Tissa Fernando, eds., *Ethnicity, Power and Politics in Canada* (Toronto: Methuen 1981); Edmund Bradwin, *The Bunkhouse Man* (Toronto: University of Toronto Press 1972); Robert F. Harney, "Montreal's

King of Italian Labour: A Case Study of Padronism," *L/LT* 4 (1979), 57–84; N.F. Dreisziger et al., *Struggle and Hope: The Hungarian-Canadian Experience* (Toronto: McClelland and Stewart 1982); Harry Con et al., *From China to Canada: A History of the Chinese Communities in Canada* (Toronto: McClelland and Stewart 1982); Ward, *White Canada Forever.*

29 Graham Lowe, "Class, Job, and Gender in the Canadian Office," *L/LT* 10 (Autumn 1982), 11–38, and "Mechanization, Feminization, and Managerial Control in the Early Twentieth-Century Canadian Office," in Heron and Storey, eds., *On the Job*, 177–209; Margery W. Davies, *Woman' s Place Is at the Typewriter: Office Work and Office Workers, 1870–1930* (Philadelphia: Temple University Press 1982).

30 Heron, "Crisis of the Craftsman"; Kealey, "Work Control"; Wayne Roberts, "Artisans, Aristocrats, and Handymen: Politics and Unionism among Toronto Skilled Building Trades Workers, 1896–1914," *L/LT* 1 (1976), 92–121. See also William Lazonick, "Industrial Relations and Technical Change: The Case of the Self-Acting Mule," *CJE* 3, no. 3 (September1979): 231–62; Jonathan Zeitlin, "Craft Control and the Division of Labour: Engineers and Compositors in Britain, 1890–1930," ibid., 263–74; Wayne Lewchuk, "The British Motor Vehicle Industry: The Roots of Decline, 1896–1982," in Bernard Elbaum and William Lazonick, eds., *The Decline of the British Economy* (Oxford: Clarendon 1986).

31 See Heron and Storey, "Work and Struggle," for a specific example of this process. Andrew L. Friedman has argued that managers actually encourage what he calls "responsible autonomy" on the job as part of their strategy of control; see *Industry and Labour: Class Struggle at Work and Monopoly Capitalism* (London: Macmillan 1977).

32 Heron and Storey, "Work and Struggle"; Heron, "Working-Class Hamilton"; Meyer, *Five-Dollar Day.*

33 Heron and Palmer, "Prism of the Strike"; Ian McKay, "Strikes in the Maritimes, 1901–1914," *Acadiensis* 13, no. 1 (Autumn 1983), 3–46 ; McKay, "Workers' Control in Springhill"; Stuart Marshall Jamieson, *Times of Trouble: Labour Unrest and Industrial Conflict in Canada, 1900–66* (Ottawa: Task Force on Labour Relations 1968), 62–157; A. Ross McCormack, *Reformers, Rebels, and Revolutionaries: The Western Canadian Radical Movement, 1899–1919* (Toronto: University of Toronto Press 1977); David J. Bercuson, *Fools and Wise Men: The Rise and Fall of the One Big Union* (Toronto: McGraw-Hill Ryerson 1978); Larry Peterson, "The One Big Union in International Perspective: Revolutionary Industrial Unionism, 1900–1925," *L/LT* 7 (Spring 1981), 41–66; Paul MacEwan, *Miners and Steelworkers: Labour in Cape Breton* (Toronto: Samuel Stevens Hakkert and

Company 1976), 3–150; David Frank, "The Cape Breton Coal Miners, 1917–1926" (PhD dissertation, Dalhousie University 1979); Jacques Rouillard, *Les travailleurs du coton au Québec, 1900–1915* (Montreal: Les Presses de l'Université du Québec 1974); Phillips, *No Power Greater*; Charles Allen Seager, "A Proletariat in Wild Rose Country: The Alberta Coal Miners, 1905–1945" (PhD dissertation, York University 1981); Heron, "Working-Class Hamilton."

34 Gregory S. Kealey, "1919: The Canadian Labour Revolt, " *L/LT* 13 (Spring 1984), 11–44; Heron, "Labourism"; David Jay Bercuson, *Confrontation at Winnipeg: Labour, Industrial Relations, and the General Strike* (Montreal and Kingston: McGill-Queen's University Press 1974); Norman Penner, ed., *Winnipeg, 1919: The Strikers' Own History of the Winnipeg General Strike* (Toronto: James Lewis and Samuel 1973); Nolan Reilly, "The General Strike in Amherst, Nova Scotia, 1919," *Acadiensis* 9, no. 2 (Spring 1980), 56–77; Frank, "Cape Breton Miners"; Seager, "Proletariat"; Brian F. Hogan, *Cobalt: Year of the Strike, 1919* (Cobalt: Highway Book Shop n.d.); Craig Heron and George de Zwaan, "Industrial Unionism in Eastern Ontario: Gananoque, 1918–21," *OH* 77, no. 3 (September 1985), 159–82.

35 Jamieson, *Times of Trouble*, 192–213.

36 Ibid., 214–75; Irving Abella, *Nationalism, Communism, and Canadian Labour: The CIO, the Communist Party, and the Canadian Congress of Labour, 1935–1956* (Toronto: University of Toronto Press 1973); S.D. Hanson, "Estevan 1931," in Irving Abella, ed., *On Strike: Six Key Labour Struggles in Canada, 1919–1949* (Toronto: James Lorimer 1974), 33–78; Desmond Morton, "Aid to the Civil Power: The Stratford Strike of 1933," ibid., 79–92; Abella, "Oshawa 1937," ibid., 93–128; Evelyn Dumas, *The Bitter Thirties in Quebec* (Montreal: Black Rose Books 1975); Terry Copp, ed., *Industrial Unionism in Kitchener, 1937–47* (Elora, ON: Cumnock Press 1976); Terry Copp, "The Rise of Industrial Unions in Montreal, 1935–45," *RI / IR* 37 (1982), 843–75; Ralph Ellis, "The Unionization of a Mill Town: Cornwall in 1936," *The Register* 2, no. 1 (March 1981), 83–101; Gloria Montero, ed., *We Stood Together: First-Hand Accounts of Dramatic Events in Canada's Labour Past* (Toronto: James Lorimer 1979), 1–68; Robert Storey, "Workers, Unions, and Steel: The Shaping of the Hamilton Working Class, 1935–1948" (PhD dissertation, University of Toronto 1981); John Manley, "Organizing the Unorganized: Communists and the Struggle for Industrial Unionism in the Canadian Automobile Industry, 1922–1936" (paper presented to the Canadian Historical Association 1981); Wayne Roberts, ed ., *Organizing Westinghouse: Alf Ready's Story* (Hamilton: Labour Studies Program, McMaster University 1980).

37 Storey, "Workers, Unions, and Steel"; Raymond Houlahan, "A History of Collective Bargaining in Local 200, UAW" (MA thesis, University of Windsor 1963); Roberts, *Organizing Westinghouse* and *Baptism of a Union: Stelco Strike of 1946* (Hamilton: Labour Studies Program, McMaster University 1981).

38 For evidence of sporadic women's militancy, see Frager, "No Proper Deal"; Joan Sangster, "The 1907 Bell Telephone Strike: Organizing Women Workers," *L/LT* 3 (1978), 109–30; Wayne Roberts, *Honest Womanhood: Feminism, Femininity, and Class Consciousness among Toronto Working Woman, 1893 to 1914* (Toronto: New Hogtown Press 1976); Star Rosenthal, "Union Maids: Organized Women Workers in Vancouver, 1900–1915," *BC Studies* 41 (Spring 1979), 36–55; Catherine McLeod, "Women in Production: The Toronto Dressmakers' Strike of 1931," in Acton et al., eds., *Women at Work*, 309–30.

39 Veronica Strong-Boag, "The Girl of the New Day: Canadian Working Women of the 1920s," *L/LT* 4 (1979), 131–64; Frager, "No Proper Deal"; Marie Campbell, "Sexism in British Columbia Trade Unions, 1900–1920," in Barbara Latham and Cathy Kess, eds., *In Her Own Right: Selected Essays on Women's History in B.C.* (Victoria: Camosun College 1980), 167–86.

40 Veronica Strong-Boag, "Keeping House in God's Country: Canadian Women at Work in the Home," in Heron and Storey, eds., *On the Job*, 124–51 ; Genevieve Leslie, "Domestic Service in Canada, 1880–1920," in Acton et al., eds., *Women at Work*, 71–126 ; Susan Strasser, *Never Done: A History of American Housework* (New York: Pantheon Books 1982); Jane Synge, "Young Working Class Women in Early 20th Century Hamilton – Their Work and Family Lives," in A.H. Turritin, ed., *Proceedings of the Workshop Conference on Blue-Collar Workers and Their Communities …* (Toronto: York University 1976), 137–45; Gail Cuthbert Brandt, "'Weaving It Together': Life Cycle and the Industrial Experience of Female Cotton Workers in Quebec, 1910–1950," *L/LT* 7 (1981), 113–26.

41 Michael J. Piva, "The Workmen's Compensation Movement in Ontario," *OH* 67 (1975), 39–56; Veronica Strong-Boag, "Working Women and the State: The Case of Canada, 1889–1945," *Atlantis* 6, no. 2 (Spring 1981), 1–9; Linda S. Bohnen, "Women Workers in Ontario: A Socio-Legal History," *University of Toronto Faculty of Law Review* 31 (1973), 45–74; Heron and Palmer, "Prism of the Strike"; McKay, "Strikes in the Maritimes"; Don Macgillivray, "Military Aid to the Civil Power: The Cape Breton Experience in the 1920s," *Acadiensis* 3, no. 2 (1974), 45–64; Paul Craven, *"An Impartial Umpire": Industrial Relations and the Canadian State, 1900–1911* (Toronto: University of Toronto Press 1980).

42 The classic American studies are Stanley B . Mathewson, *Restriction of Output among Unorganized Workers* (New York: Viking Press 1931); Donald Roy, "Banana Time: Job Satisfaction and Informal Interaction,'" *Human Organization* 18, no. 4 (Winter 1959), 158–68; Donald Roy, "Quota Restriction and Goldbricking in a Machine Shop," *American Journal of Sociology* 57, no. 5 (March 1952), 427–42.

43 Robert Storey, "Unionization versus Corporate Welfare: The 'Dofasco Way,'" *L/LT* 12 (Autumn 1983), 7–42.

44 Jacques Rouillard, *Les syndicats nationaux au Québec de 1900 à 1930* (Quebec: Les Presses de l'Université Laval 1979); Alfred Charpentier, *Cinquante ans d'action ouvrière* (Quebec: Les Presses de l'Université Laval 1971); Heron, "Working-Class Hamilton," 490–584; Ernest R. Forbes, *The Maritime Rights Movement, 1919–1927: A Study in Canadian Regionalism* (Montreal and Kingston: McGill-Queen's University Press 1979).

45 Paul Phillips and Stephen Watson, "From Mobilization to Continentalism: The Canadian Economy in the Post-Depression Period," in Michael S. Cross and Gregory S. Kealey, eds., *Readings in Canadian Social History, Volume 5: Modern Canada, 1930–1980s* (Toronto: McClelland and Stewart 1984), 20–45; Wallace Clement, *Continental Corporate Power: Economic Linkages between Canada and the United States* (Toronto: McClelland and Stewart 1977); Patricia Marchak, *In Whose Interests: An Essay on Multinational Corporations in a Canadian Context* (Toronto: McClelland and Stewart 1979); Robert Bothwell and William Kilbourn, *C.D . Howe: A Biography* (Toronto: McClelland and Stewart 1979); Reginald Whitaker, *The Government Party: Organizing and Financing the Liberal Party of Canada, 1930–58* (Toronto: University of Toronto Press 1977), 165–215; David Wolfe, "Economic Growth and Foreign Investment," *JCS* 13 (Spring 1978), 3–20; Barry Bluestone and Bennett Harrison, *The Deindustrialization of America: Plant Closings, Community Abandonment, and the Dismantling of Basic Industry* (New York: Basic Books 1982); Folker Frobel, Jurgen Heinrichs, and Otto Kreye, *The New International Division of Labour* (Cambridge, Mass.: Cambridge University Press 1980).

46 Ian Radforth, "Logging Pulpwood in Northern Ontario," in Heron and Storey, eds., *On the Job*, 245–80; Patricia Marchak, *Green Gold: The British Columbia Forest Industry* (Vancouver: UBC Press 1983); Wallace Clement, *Hardrock Mining: Industrial Relations and Technological Changes at INCO* (Toronto: McClelland and Stewart 1981); Rick Williams, "Inshore Fishermen, Unionization, and the Struggle against Underdevelopment Today," in Brym and Sacouman, eds., *Underdevelopment and Social Movements*, 161–75.

47 David F. Noble, *Forces of Production: A Social History of Industrial Automation* (New York: Knopf 1984); Sin Tze Ker, "Technological Change in the Canadian Iron and Steel Mills Industry, 1946–1969" (PhD dissertation, University of Manitoba 1972); Zerker, *Rise and Fall,* 253–77; Elaine Bernard, *The Long Distance Feeling: A History of the Telecommunications Workers' Union* (Vancouver: New Star Books 1982), 152–72; Joe Davidson and John Deverell, *Joe Davidson* (Toronto: James Lorimer 1978), 121–51; Rosemary Speirs, "Technological Change and the Railway Unions, 1945–1972" (PhD dissertation, University of Toronto 1974); John Bellamy Foster, "On the Waterfront: Longshoring in Canada," in Heron and Storey, eds., *On the Job,* 281–308.

48 Heather Menzies, *Computers on the Job: Surviving Canada's Microcomputer Revolution* (Toronto: James Lorimer 1982).

49 Ibid.; Heather Menzies, *Women and the Chip: Case Studies of the Effects of Informatics on Employment in Canada* (Toronto: Institute for Research on Public Policy 1981); Bernard, *Long Distance Feeling*; Marchak, *Green Gold*; Noble, *Forces of Production*; Philip Kraft, "The Industrialization of Computer Programming: From Programming to Software Production," in Andrew Zimbalist, ed., *Case Studies on the Labour Process* (New York: Monthly Review Press 1979), 18–50; Evelyn Nakano Glenn and Roslyn L. Feldberg, "Proletarianizing Clerical Work: Technology and Organizational Control in the Office," ibid., 51–72.

50 Peter Dungan, "Mass Unemployment and Technological Change in the 1980s – What Are the Prospects?" *Labour Relations News*, September 1983.

51 Johnson, "Precapitalist Economic Formations"; Radforth, "Logging Pulpwood."

52 Freda Hawkins, *Canada and Immigration: Public Policy and Public Concern* (Montreal and Kingston: McGill-Queen's University 1983); Grace M. Anderson and David Higgs, *A Future to Inherit: The Portuguese Communities of Canada* (Toronto: McClelland and Stewart 1976); Con et al., *From China to Canada*, 204–67; Makeda Silvera, *Silenced: Talks with Working Class West Indian Women about Their Lives and Struggles as Domestic Workers in Canada* (Toronto: Williams-Wallace 1983).

53 Paul Axelrod, "Higher Education, Utilitarianism, and the Acquisitive Society: Canada, 1930–1980," in Cross and Kealey, *Modern Canada*, 179–205; Serge Mallet, *Essays on the New Working Class* (St Louis: Telos Press 1975); Charles Derber, ed., *Professionals as Workers: Mental Labour in Advanced Capitalism* (Boston: G.K. Hall 1982).

54 Ruth Roach Pierson, *Canadian Women and the Second World War* (Ottawa: Canadian Historical Association 1983); Pat and Hugh Armstrong, *The*

Double Ghetto: Canadian Women and Their Segregated Work (Toronto: McClelland and Stewart 1978; Pat and Hugh Armstrong, *A Working Majority: What Women Must Do for Pay* (Ottawa: Canadian Advisory Council on the Status of Women 1983); Pat Armstrong, *Labour Pains: Women' s Work in Crisis* (Toronto: Women's Press 1984); Patricia Connelly, *Last Hired, First Fired: Women and the Canadian Work Force* (Toronto: Women's Press 1978); Paul and Erin Phillips, *Women and Work: Inequality in the Labour Market* (Toronto: James Lorimer 1983); Meg Luxton, *More Than a Labour of Love: Three Generations of Women's Work in the Home* (Toronto: Women's Press 1980); Julie White, *Women and Part-Time Work* (Ottawa: Canadian Advisory Council on the Status of Women 1983).

55 Jamieson, *Times of Trouble*, 276–94; Storey, "Workers, Unions, and Steel"; Laurel Sefton McDowell, *"Remember Kirkland Lake": The Gold Miners' Strike of 1941–42* (Toronto: University of Toronto Press 1983); Laurel Sefton McDowell, "The Formation of the Canadian Industrial Relations System during World War Two," *L/LT* 3 (1978), 175–96; Laurel Sefton McDowell, "The 1943 Steel Strike against Wartime Wage Controls," ibid., 10 (Autumn 1982): 65–85; Montero, *We Stood Together*, 47–112; Roberts, *Organizing Westinghouse.*

56 J.L. Granatstein, *Canada' s War: The Politics of the Mackenzie King Government, 1939–1945* (Toronto: Oxford University Press 1975), 249–93; Whitaker, *Government Party*, 132–64; Dennis Guest, *The Emergence of Social Security in Canada* (Vancouver: UBC Press 1980), 101–38; Carl Cuneo, "State, Class, and Reserve Labour: The Case of the 1941 Canadian Unemployment Insurance Act," *CRSA* 16 (1979): 47–70; McDowell, "Formation"; David A. Wolfe, "The Rise and Demise of the Keynesian Era in Canada: Economic Policy, 1930–1982," in Cross and Kealey, eds., *Modern Canada*, 46–78; Jamieson, *Times of Trouble*, 295–342; Storey, "Workers, Unions, and Steel"; David Moulton, "Windsor 1945," in Abella, *On Strike*, 129–62; Daniel Coates, "Organized Labour and Politics in Canada: The Development of a National Labour Code" (PhD dissertation, Cornell University 1973).

57 Heron and Storey, "Work and Struggle"; Don Wells, "Autoworkers on the Firing Line," in Heron and Storey, eds., *On the Job*, 327–52; David Brody, *Workers in Industrial America: Essays on the Twentieth Century Struggle* (New York: Oxford University Press 1980), 173–214; George Lipsitz, *Class and Culture in Cold War America: "A Rainbow at Midnight"* (New York: Praeger 1981); Leo Panitch and Donald Swartz, "Towards Permanent Exceptionalism: Coercion and Consent in Canadian Industrial Relations,"

L/LT 13 (Spring 1984), 133–57; Seymour Faber, "Rank and File Insurgency: The State and the Unions," *Our Generation* 11, no. 4 (Winter 1976), 38–43.

58 Abella, *Nationalism, Communism, and Canadian Labour*, 66–167; Jerry Lembke, "The International Woodworkers of America in B.C., 1942–1951," *LLT* 6 (Autumn 1980), 113–48; John Stanton, *Life and Death of the Canadian Seamen' s Union, 1936–1949* (Toronto: Steel Rail 1978); Merrily Weisbord, *The Strangest Dream* (Toronto: Lester and Orpen Dennys 1983).

59 Jamieson, *Times of Trouble*, 344–94. There were, nonetheless, some extremely bitter strikes in the 1950s; see, for example, Guy Belanger, "La grève de Murdochville (1957)," *L/LT* 8–9 (Autumn 1981–Spring 1982), 103–36.

60 Jamieson, *Times of Trouble*, 395–451; Myrna Kostash, *Long Way from Home: The Story of the Sixties Generation in Canada* (Toronto: James Lorimer 1980); J.H.G. Crispo and H.W. Arthurs, "Industrial Unrest in Canada: A Diagnosis of Recent Experience," *RI/IR* 23 (1968), 237–64; Brody, *Workers in Industrial America*, 204–8; Wells, "Autoworkers"; Walter Johnson, ed., *Working in Canada* (Montreal: Black Rose Books 1975) and *The Trade Unions and the State* (Montreal: Black Rose Books 1978); J.A. Frank, "The 'Ingredients' in Violent Labour Conflicts: Patterns in Four Case Studies," *L/LT* I2 (Autumn 1983), 87–112; E.G. Fisher, "Strike Activity and Wildcat Strikes in British Columbia, 1945–1975," *RI/IR* 37 (1982), 284–301. See also the several studies done for the Task Force on Labour Relations, especially Maxwell Flood, *Wildcat Strike in Lake City* (Ottawa: Task Force on Industrial Relations 1968). On the NDP, see Desmond Morton, *NDP: The Dream of Power* (Toronto: Hakkert 1974).

61 Allen Ponak, "Public Sector Collective Bargaining," in John Anderson and Morley Gunderson, eds., *Union-Management Relations in Canada* (Don Mills: Addison-Wesley 1982), 343–78; Davidson and Deverell, *Joe Davidson*; Anthony Thompson, "The Nova Scotia Civil Service Association, 1956–1967," *Acadiensis* 12, no. 2 (Spring 1983), 81–105; Montero, *We Stood Together*, 183–204; Bruce McLean, *"A Union amongst Government Employees": A History of the B.C. Government Employees' Union, 1919–1979* (Vancouver: BC Government Employees Union 1979); Joe Rose, "Growth Patterns of Public Sector Unions," in Gene Swimmer and Mark Thompson, eds., *Public Sector Labour Relations – Will It Survive the '80s?* (Ottawa 1983).

62 Mark Thompson, "Collective Bargaining by Professionals," in Anderson and Gunderson, *Union-Management Relations*, 379–97; Derber, *Professionals as Workers.*

63 Julie White, *Women and Unions* (Ottawa: Canadian Advisory Council on the Status of Women 1980); Briskin and Yantz, *Union Sisters;* Heather Jon Maroney, "Feminism at Work," *NLR* 141 (September–October 1983), 51–71.

64 Bradley Dow, "The Labour Movement and Trade Unionism: Summary Outline," in W.D. Wood and Pradeep Kumar, eds., *The Current Industrial Relations Scene in Canada, 1982* (Kingston: Industrial Relations Centre, Queen's University 1982), 201–65.
65 Carla Lipsig-Mumme, "Quebec Unions and the State: Conflict and Dependence," *SPE* 3 (Spring 1980), 119–46; Jean Boivin, "Labour Relations in Quebec," in Anderson and Gunderson, *Union-Management Relations*, 422–56.
66 The literature on segmented labour markets is voluminous. For a recent statement, see Gordon et al., *Segmented Work, Divided Workers*. For a critique of this perspective, see Jill Rubery, "Structured Labour Markets, Worker Organization, and Low Pay," *CJE* 2, no. 1 (March 1978), 17–36.
67 Panitch and Swartz, "Towards Permanent Exceptionalism"; John Deverell, "The Ontario Hospital Dispute, 1980–81," *SPE* 9 (Fall 1982), 179–90; Wolfe, "Rise and Demise"; Allan M. Maslove and Gene Swimmer, *Wage Controls in Canada, 1975–78: A Study in Public Decision Making* (Montreal: Institute for Research on Public Policy 1980); Peter Warrian and David Wolfe, *Trade Unions and Inflation* (Ottawa 1982).
68 Vivienne Walters, "Occupational Health and Safety Legislation in Ontario: An Analysis of Its Origins and Content," *CRSA* 21 (1984), 413–34; Donald Swartz, "New Forms of Worker Participation: A Critique of Quality of Working Life," *SPE* 5 (Spring 1981), 55–78; Charles Hechsher, "Worker Participation and Management Control," *Journal of Social Reconstruction* 1, no. 1 (1980), 77–102; Don Wells, *Squeeze Play: Quality of Working Life Programmes and the Attack on Labour* (Ottawa 1984); *Globe and Mail*, 20 October 1983, 32; 10 December 1983, 22; 28 December 1983, 8; 3 January 1984, 37; 27 January 1984, 1; 17 January 1984, 4; 16 February 1984, 10; 6 March 1984, 8; 24 March 1984, 9.
69 On the industrial situation in the 1980s, see the special issue of *SPE* 11 (Summer 1983).
70 Charles E. Reasons, Lois L. Ross, and Craig Paterson, *Assault on the Worker: Occupational Health and Safety in Canada* (Toronto: Butterworths 1981).

Chapter Two

Ontario's First Factory Workers

The night sky had only begun to pale into grey as Ottawa's bakers shuffled into the bake shops to begin work at five in the morning on 4 May 1888. In the next hour, the first light of a gloomy dawn fell over hundreds of men and boys trudging along the river under a light drizzle to get to their jobs in the city's lumber mills and woodworking factories by six o'clock. An hour later, men arrived at Thomas McKay's flour mill to start milling, just as women turned up at Woodburn's print shop to begin their bookbinding work. The numerous milliners and dressmakers heading for Crawford Ross's shop could wait somewhat longer for a break in the weather before presenting themselves for work at 8:30. A half dozen government commissioners got a more leisurely start on the day when, at 2 p.m., they convened the first Ottawa hearings of the Dominion government's Royal Commission on the Relations of Labour and Capital, popularly known as the "Labour Commission." Over the next two days the commissioners nonetheless put in long hours listening to testimony from industrialists, craftworkers, female wage-earners, and young boys of twelve and thirteen from all these Ottawa workplaces and several more. This was the end of their tour across urban industrial Ontario, which in thirty-eight days of testimony had already revealed the remarkable industrial transformation the region had undergone. In their long hearings the commissioners had heard many different versions of this story. The wide range of experience revealed in Ottawa was typical of the unevenness and diversity laid before them across the province.[1]

Coming at the end of some five decades of industrial innovation and on the eve of the great early twentieth-century leap into "mass

Moulders at Massey Manufacturing, Toronto, 1884.
Ontario Agricultural Museum

production," the Labour Commission's deliberations are a particularly useful benchmark of Ontario's First Industrial Revolution. Yet they do not stand alone. The 1880s witnessed a remarkable proliferation of investigations into the work world of the province's industrial wage-earners – two other federal royal commissions, detailed annual reports from the statistical staff of the provincial Bureau of Industries and from the new factory inspectors, reports in business journals, articles in daily newspapers, and increasingly voluminous writing by the leaders of wage-earners' organizations. The centre of attention in all this poking and prodding into the world of wage labour was the factory system, a mode of organizing industrial production that struck many people in Ontario as either impressively or disturbingly new. The discussion of workers and factories that follows here leans heavily on this great volume of writing that appeared in the 1880s, but also moves back through the more opaque preceding half century, much of it explored by other scholars, to try to appreciate how much had changed since the 1840s and why.

Within the limitations of the research and the constraints of space, it is possible only to sketch a general outline of regional industrial change that may help to guide future research. Each of the main sections in this essay presents one piece of an argument about this period of Ontario working-class history. The first section suggests the limited scope of Ontario's industrial revolution and the diversity of experience within it, especially the striking regional differences throughout the province. The second points to the equally limited and uneven transformation of the work processes in the province's factories, which left in place a considerable amount of manual labour, both skilled and unskilled. The third outlines the complicated recruitment methods of industrial employers. The fourth section explores the emerging systems of factory management and the continuing importance of paternalism in the social relations of the Ontario factory regime. And the final section considers the rise of substantial organized resistance from Ontario factory workers in the 1880s, when the practice and promise of paternalism began to crumble.

Ontario's Industrial Revolution

Debating the Concept

In 1871 a Hamilton journalist announced that the country had been passing through an "industrial revolution."[2] It was to be a full century before many scholars began to take notice of this great change in Canadian social and economic life. What exactly were these writers separated across time talking about? The phrase has always been more of an evocative metaphor than a term of precise analysis. In the broadest sense, it has been used to denote the emergence of a new phase of capitalist accumulation through more effective use of labour power. Within the work world itself, it appeared as a shift from independent commodity production to wage-earning in some kind of large-scale workplace. The form could vary between industrial sectors, but in manufacturing the long-term transition was from household or artisanal workshop to factory. Implicit in the term are new technology, power sources, and management practices, larger units of production, and in many cases a concentration in urban areas, all of which profoundly disrupted not only older forms of work, but also the whole societies in which they existed. In particular, the industrial revolution is credited with accelerating the formation of new social classes, especially the working class, and creating the conditions for serious social conflict. The distance between "pre-industrial" and "industrial" could be long, circuitous, and tortuous and was sometimes never finally bridged, but with time this transformation brought into being new ways of working and living in the shadow of urban factories.

Ironically, at roughly the same time that writers and researchers were first discovering an industrial revolution in Canada, the term was falling into disfavour among many scholars of British and European history. They were reacting against the limitations of both the critical anticapitalist and the more celebratory neoclassical traditions in the writing about industrialization in the eighteenth and nineteenth centuries. In their divergent ways, both had emphasized a dramatic, cataclysmic breakthrough (or "take-off") from a pre-industrial to an industrial society in a brief, concentrated period, during which large, centralized, highly mechanized, steam-powered factories came to dominate production and introduce shockingly new forms of work.[3] In the late 1970s, an alternative perspective began to take shape in much of the new social history of the working class and in the renewed theorizing about labour processes and labour markets. This new view involved three new analytical departures. First, the various "big-bang" theories of industrialization fell apart under closer scrutiny. It became clear that even in Britain there had been a widespread expansion of industrial production, wage-earning, and capitalist social relations in the rural countryside before the putative great turning point at the end of the eighteenth century – a phase eventually known as "proto-industrialization."[4] Even by the mid-nineteenth century, moreover, the industrial transformation remained incomplete and uneven across the industrial landscape; as the new terminology would have it, it was a process of "combined and uneven" development. This new appreciation of the industrialization process did not assume that "traditional" sectors simply lagged behind the "modern" sectors, but that apparently pre-industrial, labour-intensive forms of production would continue to coexist with newer production, albeit in a somewhat altered state. Such a new perspective drew into the analysis the often neglected (and poorly quantified) household production, frequently carried on by women and children outside the framework of formal wage-earning.[5] These new writers have emphasized the complexity and contingency of the industrializing process.[6]

As several of them now argue, however, it would not be helpful to jettison completely the idea that one period of industrial development was distinct in important ways from another. Certainly there was a constantly evolving process of industrial recomposition, rather than a single leap or "take-off," but closer examination has revealed a pattern of sharply demarcated phases in that evolution. These are much clearer when we move further away from the aggregate economic data that dominate the neoclassical economic histories and towards a wider appreciation of what have been called "social structures of accumulation" – that is, when we think of a process that integrates the dominant forms of capitalist activity, systems of production, state intervention, and social relations among classes, sexes, and ethnic groups. Over the past two centuries we can see three major phases, each with both old and new elements – probably best understood as three successive and distinct "industrial revolutions."[7] In each we find plenty of continuity from the past, but also enough abruptly new developments to suggest that the social structure of accumulation has lurched decisively in a new direction and that a "revolution" is once again under way in production. From this perspective, we would not expect to find a single moment of accelerated growth that created a new industrial capitalist economy in Canada at the end of the nineteenth century, but rather an initial phase stretching from the 1840s to the 1890s, to be followed by a fundamental restructuring of industrial production and of the working class in a "Second Industrial Revolution" after the turn of the century and a third reconstitution after 1940. (It can be argued that we have been living through a fourth since about 1975.) This essay is concerned with the working-class experience in the first phase only.[8]

A second intellectual and political influence has altered our view of an industrial revolution. Feminist writers have reminded us that industrial capitalism was also patriarchal, that is, that male power was reconstituted on a new basis within the working-class family and the capitalist workplace. Working-class men found wage-earning jobs and became the chief breadwinners for their families, while the primarily domestic responsibilities of the females in these families limited their occupational and income-earning opportunities in the capitalist labour market and heightened their dependence on men's wages. Specifically, working-class women were much more likely than men to be working at home for no wages or to have only a brief, premarital spell as a wage-earner in a cheaply paid job ghetto designated as "women's work." Male factory owners built the patriarchal social relations of the family into their management systems, while skilled craft workers wove their gendered privileges into their sense of their own skill and "manhood." For workers, then, an Industrial Revolution was also an experience of gender as well as class.[9]

The third important new insight emerging from the new social history of industrialization was the variation in the process among nation states and among regions within them. An industrial revolution did not involve simply carrying the pioneering British model far and wide (in a process loosely dubbed "modernization"). Factories and workshops appeared and evolved in different countries in response to particular resource endowments, state policies, and markets for products and labour.[10] In the same vein, the new research has stressed the regional diversity within countries.[11] In Canada there are now various local studies suggesting that, despite some striking parallels, the major regions of the country all followed different paths of industrialization.[12]

Gradually these insights have been incorporated into the writing on Ontario's First Industrial Revolution. Factories did not loom large in the economic landscape of the province charted by the two dominant schools of economic history in Canada before the 1970s. The "staples" school of political economists concentrated exclusively on the export of primary resources and the economic relationships that resulted. In all his voluminous writings, the commanding figure among these political economists, Harold Innis, wrote nothing substantial about manufacturing in the Canadian economy. His brief 1934 essay on Ontario scarcely acknowledged the secondary manufacturing that sustained the southern part of the province.[13] The new generation of scholars who undertook to revive and build on the older school of Canadian political economy was often at pains to minimize the importance of manufacturing in Canadian economic development and indeed to suggest that it was deliberately stifled by commercial and financial interests in the Canadian bourgeoisie.[14] The second group of economic historians, those of the neoclassical persuasion, showed somewhat more interest in manufacturing, but usually only in the statistical evidence of its output and in the folly of Canadian tariff policies for protecting it.[15] Neither the factory itself nor the social relations that it embodied were ever in the foreground. So, as late as the early 1970s, the story of industrialization in Canada, particularly in Ontario, had to be pieced together from a variety of other sources – company histories, local community studies (both antiquarian and scholarly), the scattered observations of historical geographers, and the writings of two mavericks influenced by Marxism – Stanley Ryerson and H. Clare Pentland (whose unpublished doctoral thesis was soon to become an underground classic).[16]

It was labour historians digging into the nineteenth-century experience of Canada's first working class who began to tackle the questions of industrialization more systematically. They were eventually joined by a few practitioners in economic, urban, and women's history, and a new general framework of Canada's industrial development began to take shape. The most influential voice at the outset of this new scholarship was Clare Pentland. He brought to light many pockets of pre-industrial wage-earning and the paternalistic social relations within them and also investigated the conditions that permitted the creation of a capitalist labour market in central Canada. Eventually he was criticized for seriously misunderstanding and distorting that transition from pre-industrial to industrial.[17] Steven Langdon undertook a more detailed exploration of the process of capitalist industrialization and workers' active role within it.[18] The historians who contributed most to this new history of the Ontario working class, however, were Gregory Kealey and Bryan Palmer, who used their separate, penetrating studies of Toronto and Hamilton and their jointly written work on the labour movement of the 1880s to open up the industrial transformation in late nineteenth-century Ontario, especially the fascinating contours of working-class resistance, to more sensitive, sophisticated analysis.[19] The extensive groundwork they laid was immeasurably useful for an understanding of working-class experience in this province.

All this preliminary scholarship had three related weaknesses, however. First, it presented the Ontario evidence within a universal paradigm of industrial capitalist development; in other words, the formation and struggles of the working class seemed to unfold in a pattern roughly similar to those in most other industrializing areas of the world in the period, especially Britain and the United States. By extension, readers might also easily assume that the wider experience in Ontario was simply Toronto and Hamilton writ large. Second, this work placed the male craft worker, his union, and his public life at the centre of the story, to the virtual exclusion of all others, most particularly female wage-earners. And third, these writers said little about the effects of gender within the process of class formation. Marjorie Griffin Cohen underlined this neglected element in her important study of the transition from rural independent commodity production to urban wage-earning in nineteenth-century Ontario. She emphasized the crucial ways in which women's unpaid domestic labour in patriarchal households shaped their experience in the capitalist labour market.[20]

In the end, all these debates have taught us that to assess the experience of workers in Ontario's First Industrial Revolution requires a sensitivity to structure as well as agency, to continuity as well as change, to diversity as well as shared experiences, to the differences, in particular, of occupation, region, and sex.

Ontario Industrializes

Before 1840, manufacturing in Upper Canada felt virtually none of the shock waves hitting industrial life in the imperial heartland. By the 1820s and 1830s Canadian merchants were finding markets in Britain for the small surpluses of grain and square timber produced in the colony, and shipbuilding in several small Great Lakes ports became a significant industrial spin-off of such trade. But the fluctuations in imperial demand made this an unstable basis for economic expansion. Local markets were active but small. The great majority of the population lived and worked in semi-isolated farms. Like European peasants, the farm families produced a great many of the goods they needed in and around their households. From the beginning they also relied on artisans sprinkled through the countryside. Local millers processed their wheat, wood, wool, and leather for family use, often on a barter basis or in return for up to half the product. Eventually skilled artisans such as blacksmiths, millwrights, weavers, shoemakers, and other well-rounded craft workers also supplied from their workshops a considerable range of articles not made at home or imported from Britain or the United States; these goods were sold by pedlars and shopkeepers.

Local merchants often combined several of these industrial and marketing activities for the pioneering communities. In the handful of larger towns in the colony, some artisans produced bread and a few other essentials for urban and military populations that could not produce for themselves; others turned out such luxury goods as wigs, watches, or carriages for an upper-class clientele. All of this localized production benefited from the "tariff of bad roads" – the poorly developed transportation system that limited the circulation of cheaper mass-produced goods from outside the colony – but it also suffered from the insecurities of consumer demand. This was not a ripe terrain for industrial capitalist investment, as the frustrating efforts to get a number of ironworks well established in the province made clear. Many artisans survived only by trying out or combining a variety of occupations, including farming.[21]

During the 1840s and 1850s, the shifting structures of the Upper Canadian economy and society opened up the first opportunities for significant industrial innovation. When the British mercantilist system that had partially protected Upper Canadian trade in natural resources was dismantled in the mid-1840s in favour of freer international trade, some wild fluctuations threw the export industries into temporary tailspins. Yet the demand for the principal Upper Canadian products grew steadily in Britain and increasingly in the United States, especially after the signing of the Reciprocity Treaty of 1854. Within the colony, a new class of merchant-capitalists and liberal politicians steadily assumed control of the state from the old aristocratic oligarchy and began to overhaul state apparatuses and policies to facilitate the development of a bourgeois capitalist society. In civil society various voluntary societies, from evangelical churches to mechanics' institutes, promoted the ideas, values, and morality of the new bourgeois culture. The colony's population began to grow more and more quickly as immigrants arrived in huge numbers after 1840, principally from the British Isles; at the same time cheap, easily accessible farm land was getting scarcer. A new social structure of accumulation was emerging based on larger, more secure markets, a new economic elite, a new bourgeois culture, state support, and, above all, wage labour.[22]

The main stimulus to industrialization in this period was the growth of trade in natural resources from Upper Canadian forests and farms, whether for export, for down-river sales in Lower Canada, or for the growing urban markets in the province. The first steps came in three sectors. One was the processing of agricultural and forest products.

Early in the nineteenth century merchant-millers in the settled parts of the province had begun to expand beyond "custom work" for the local population to wider trade, but after 1840 they sold much more. Operators of flour and woollen mills, tanneries, breweries, and distilleries still relied on farm families to supply them, and they benefited from the great expansion of commercial agriculture, mostly wheat production. The 1851 census takers found scores of flour and woollen mills across the province, a few of them among the largest employers in manufacturing. By 1871 Ontario had some 900 flour mills, and 210 woollen mills.[23] By the 1880s, however, these agriculturally based industries had peaked and were in many cases in decline. After 1860, other food-processing enterprises – first cheese, much later canning and meat packing factories – had begun to proliferate as urban populations expanded and farmers converted from wheat farming to commercial dairying and mixed farming.[24] In the forest-products industry, the growing shift by mid-century from squared timber to sawn lumber prompted numerous entrepreneurs to establish sawmills independent of farming populations and to process logs gathered by their own crews of wage-earners from the virgin forests well beyond the settlements, first along the lakefront and in the Ottawa Valley and then along the edge of the Canadian Shield through the centre of the province to Georgian Bay. Throughout the second half of the nineteenth century, sawmills provided more jobs than any other manufacturing industry in Ontario, with a total workforce rising from 6300 in 1861 to 17,000 in 1881 and 24,000 in 1891. The processing of minerals was much more limited and less important in Ontario's industrialization experience. The small primary iron industry collapsed completely after 1850, and most other mineral exploration projects were failures. There were two great exceptions: the oil boom in southwestern Ontario that began in 1861 and spawned forty-six oil refineries over the next decade, and the equally successful salt industry that grew up in the same period in the Goderich area.[25] In all, the processing of primary products employed roughly three factory workers out of ten in Ontario between 1871 and 1891.

The second stimulus to industrialization came from the transportation sector, as the colony's leading mercantile interests undertook to improve the flow of products from Upper Canada and the American Midwest to distant markets (and the profits into their pockets). This was done initially with steamboats on the lakes and rivers, then with new canals, and finally, by the end of the 1840s, with railways. Thus the artisans in the larger commercial towns found a growing demand for steam engines and other metal equipment, along with some orders for machinery for the many new mills.[26] The railways that started fanning out across southern Ontario after 1850 at first relied on these local workshops, but eventually they opened their own metalworking shops, which rapidly became the largest manufacturers of producer goods in the colony. By the early 1860s, railway companies were operating the province's only two rolling mills, in Toronto and Hamilton.[27] Late nineteenth-century census takers always found the various branches of metalworking to be the largest general category of manufacturing employment.

Third, after 1840, consumers on the more commercially successful farms and, eventually, in the growing towns and cities had somewhat more income to spend on household needs. And the railways made it much easier to reach many more of them. The major beneficiary of the new rural spending was undoubtedly the agricultural-implements industry, which began turning out mowers, reapers, and sundry farm machinery for the larger farm population interested in mechanizing. And with increasingly large, sophisticated factories, it was able to produce for international markets before the end of the century.[28] But farmers and city dwellers were also interested in buying boots and shoes, stoves, wagons, cloth, furniture, pianos, newspapers, and much more.[29] By the 1850s numerous artisans, often recent immigrants from the British Isles or the United States with capital and skill,[30] had responded to this demand by expanding their workshops, while many wealthy merchants who had been importing manufactured goods invested in new industrial enterprises.[31] In both cases, the goal was what has become known as "import substitution." The production of consumer goods, especially clothing, soon brought together some of the largest workforces in Ontario's industrial economy.

This industrialization process emerged in three spurts, each prompted by new market opportunities or difficulties. The first lasted to the economic collapse of 1857 and saw the rise of the first large saw, flour, and textile mills, railway shops, and expanded workshops in many industries. In the second phase – from 1860 to 1873 – in response to the expansion of railways and the stimulus of the American Civil War, "manufactories" proliferated across the province and the first more specialized factories emerged in industries producing such consumer goods as shoes, agricultural implements, stoves, sewing machines, newspapers, clothing, and furniture. In the final phase – from the late 1870s to the early 1890s – the resource industries geared to export, especially lumber, remained important, but proportionally much more new investment was driven by production for the domestic consumer market.

This was by no means a smooth path of growth and prosperity. The province's new industrial-capitalist economy was a chronically insecure and unstable edifice. Wage-earners had to cope with annual cycles that still brought seasonal shutdowns. In 1871 the census takers found that only three out of five industrial enterprises in Ontario ran the year round (though they employed 70 per cent of male workers and 75 per cent of female workers).[32] The climate dictated some of the seasonal shutdowns, especially in the many workplaces powered by water (62 per cent of those reporting any power),[33] which could be disrupted by winter freeze-ups, spring floods, or summer drops in water levels.[34] Hot summers could also curtail work in such places as tobacco factories, glass works, and even an Ottawa dressmaking and millinery shop.[35] Climate, however, was most important in shaping the annual cycle of natural resource production. The province's largest industrial sector, sawmilling, was organized entirely around the changing seasons, so that the mills were open only from about April to November. Oil too could be pumped only in the warmer months. Similarly, the processing of farm products covered only a short spell on the calendar, especially flour milling and the canning industry, which took off in the 1880s. Predictably the numerous agricultural-implement plants had to organize their production in reverse – from fall to spring, with a lengthy summer shutdown – in order to have equipment ready to sell to farmers during the summer.[36] Many of the new factories, however, had to follow a different pattern of seasonal swings based, not on the climate, but on cycles of consumer demand. The Labour Commission heard reports of two-to-four-month shutdowns every year in boot and shoe, confectionery, and tobacco factories and stove foundries; there were even longer closures in clothing workshops. Few industries escaped a shutdown of at least three to six weeks a year.[37]

The economic insecurity had more to do with larger structural problems in the new economy. Ontario manufacturers had to weather some dramatic swings in the international business cycle, notably the severe depression of 1857–60 and the prolonged slump that set in after 1873, which was relieved only for brief periods in the 1880s. Although it did not stop all industrial growth, as economists once argued, this so-called Great Depression certainly made survival and adaptation a challenge for the province's industrialists.[38] Equally troubling, though, was the small size of the domestic market available to industrialists, which limited their ability to expand and specialize their production facilities. Compared to the United States, Ontario's population was small, and after 1850 it grew much more slowly as immigrants increasingly tended to bypass the region. Moreover, its farmers had only limited cash for purchasing manufactured goods.[39] Here is undoubtedly a large part of the explanation for both the frequency of business failures (an international phenomenon)[40] and the slowness of some consumer-goods industries to emerge. The characteristic industry of the British and American industrial revolutions, cotton mills, arrived relatively late in Ontario – in 1871 there were only two good-sized mills, at Merritton and Dundas, and by the end of the decade only two more, at Cornwall.[41] Not surprisingly, then, Ontario's industrial establishments remained comparatively small. In 1871 the census takers discovered that the province's two largest employers were railway shops – the Great Western with 984 workers in Hamilton and the Northern with 561 in Toronto. But only three other firms – a Toronto boot and shoe factory, a Hamilton clothing enterprise, and a Toronto furniture works – had more than 400. In all, only 21 firms had more than 200 employees and only 19 more had over 150. Only 71 industrial establishments had more than 100 workers; they employed 14,091 workers (an average of 198.5 each), a mere 15 per cent of the province's industrial workforce. The mean size of Ontario's industrial establishments that year was only 4.4 employees. Roughly two out of every five firms had only one worker, and nearly 85 per cent had under six. In only a few industries – railway shops, rolling mills, cotton factories, engine works, and distilleries – did any firms come close to dominating production. In contrast, the handful of impressively large firms in sawmilling (such as those at Hawkesbury, Ottawa, Trenton, and Deseronto) and flour milling existed in a large sea of small-scale manufacturers and contributed only 12 and 18 per cent respectively of total value added in the province's production. By 1891 some sectors had relatively more large establishments – agricultural implements and cotton, in particular – but the average number of workers in all industrial establishments that year was still only five.[42]

To make matters worse, Ontario industrialists could not be certain of controlling their own markets against outside competition, either regional or international. Montreal had always loomed as the premier manufacturing centre of the St Lawrence waterway system, especially with its cheaply produced consumer goods. By the 1880s, Ontario boot and shoe manufacturers, some of the earliest contributors to the province's industrial revolution, had more or less given up the battle with Quebec producers, and textile and tobacco manufacturers were feeling the same pressure. Far more threatening, however, was the steady flow of cheap British and American goods into the province. The high American tariffs imposed in 1866 cut Ontario manufacturers out of the southern markets but did not prevent the dumping of cheaply produced American products in Ontario, especially in the deep depression of the 1870s. In that decade, the convergence of two sources of uncertainty for Ontario manufacturers – the business cycle and intense competition – created a crisis that threatened the survival of many of them. Some producers quietly colluded to control price competition among themselves, but the most widely discussed solution was tariff protection. From the beginning of Ontario's industrialization process, industrialists had campaigned for a state policy to limit competition in the domestic market by raising tariffs. They got some help in the provincial tariffs of 1858–9, watched that protection eroded in the new post-Confederation commercial policies, and then battled successfully for the elaborate package for stimulating manufacturing development in the National Policy inaugurated by the Macdonald Tory government in 1879. In the next four years there was a small flurry of new investment in manufacturing including a considerable expansion of the province's cotton textile production. Small-scale producers took a new lease on life, and overproduction was soon a serious problem in many sectors. "There is scarcely a little town or village in Canada but has a cabinet factory with power going," a Toronto cabinet manufacturer told the Labour Commission. "Those men are not making money … the market is not sufficient to keep all those factories in a healthy state of operation."[43]

For our purposes it is perhaps most important to note that, in the dark moments of the 1870s, many manufacturers had come to realize that tariffs were not a panacea and that, over the longer term, they needed to cut their costs of production to compete in the larger, more crowded Canadian and North American markets. The Chatham agricultural-implement manufacturer who argued in 1887 that he had to produce a thousand fanning mills to make the same profit he had made producing seven hundred five years earlier voiced a common concern.[44] It was the industrialists' drive to modify and intensify the labour process in various ways, as much as the proliferation of new factories, that gave so many Ontario workers a sense of living through a profoundly disturbing industrial transformation.

For the working-class experience within this process of industrialization, it is also important to note that the new industrial enterprises were widely scattered across the province, principally in regions not far removed from commercial agriculture and logging.[45] Much of the initial industrial development took place outside large cities, in communities of well less than five thousand people. This pattern was encouraged by the profusion of farm families with some disposable income and the many good sites for water power across the province; and by the proliferation of railway lines in the 1860s and 1870s throughout the settled agricultural regions. The industrial centres where the new enterprises clustered had many similarities, but between the 1840s and the 1890s they tended to be of three types. First and by far the most common was the small, multi-factory town serving a nearby (and, it hoped, growing) agricultural hinterland. Each one was unique, but one could expect to find in these places some combination of agricultural-implement works, woollen mill, stove foundry, furniture or woodworking factory, wagon shop, brewery, tannery, and eventually perhaps a knitting mill. Throughout the period, these businesses ranged in size from a cluster of artisanal workshops to quite a large factory. The large-scale enterprises that had emerged by the 1870s could be found even in towns and villages as small as Oshawa, Galt, and Dundas. Even before the 1890s some towns developed a degree of industrial specialization, notably in metalworking and machine building, or in woodworking, especially in southwestern Ontario, where much of the province's furniture and musical-instrument production was concentrated.[46]

The second type of manufacturing town was a commercial and transportation hub, generally with metropolitan ambitions to dominate the trade of a much wider hinterland. Toronto and Hamilton were the most successful contenders in the 1840s and 1850s, but towns like Sarnia, Windsor, London, Oakville, Port Hope, Whitby, Belleville, and Kingston shared some of the same characteristics.[47] In many ways, these towns had a mixture of industries similar to those of the agricultural service towns, but here one was less likely to find milling operations and more likely to encounter two additional economic sectors – metalworking shops turning out heavy transportation equipment (such as the Hamilton and Toronto rolling mills and the Kingston locomotive and steam-engine factories),[48] and the first large-scale producers of light consumer goods, such as boots and shoes, ready-made clothing, tobacco, daily newspapers, and some processed food and drink (such as biscuits and liquor), made possible by larger pools of labour (steadily restocked with new immigrants) and the extensive trading networks into the hinterland of each metropolis. Some of these were also administrative towns where manufacturers could sell to governmental institutions and a better-paid white-collar workforce. The Toronto and Ottawa printing industries, for example, grew up under those circumstances. In 1871 Toronto had only 12 per cent of Ontario's industrial production, in striking contrast to Montreal, which had 43 per cent of Quebec's production.[49] But by the 1880s Toronto had won its commanding position over all other towns of the region – symbolized by the relocation of the Massey agricultural-implement works from Newcastle to Toronto in 1879.

The third sort of industrial centre – the more specialized mill town – was considerably different. Ottawa, Belleville, Peterborough, Bracebridge, and Collingwood, and many more, were the sites of extensive sawmilling. Others were specialized textile centres, first the larger woollen-mill towns that began in the 1860s (especially such eastern Ontario centres as Almonte and other mill villages on the Mississippi in Lanark County and towns on the Grand River in Waterloo County) and then cotton-mill towns in the 1870s (notably Merritton, Dundas, and Cornwall, which by 1878 reputedly had the largest cotton factories in the Dominion). The sawmilling communities were often short-lived, as the nearest forests fell to the logger's axe, and they tended to have many fewer spin-off industries, beyond the production of such simple wood products as staves, shingles, and other construction materials. Western Ontario also had its own distinct resource towns – the oil-refining centres of Oil Springs, Petrolia, and Sarnia, which were also in decline by the end of the century when the resource was exhausted.

These three urban forms were not neatly divided into distinct regions, but by the 1880s a slight regional specialization had begun to emerge. The leading metropolitan centres were clustered on the west end of Lake Ontario. The most successful mixed-factory towns were spread through the south-central and southwestern part of the province, while such eastern Ontario towns as Belleville, Kingston, and Brockville were clearly stagnating – only 30 per cent of Ontario's manufacturing employment was found in this region in 1881. The mill towns tended to be dispersed along the extremities of eastern, central, and western Ontario, though clearly the Grand River textile centres were exceptions. There was also a discernible west-central region of faster growth and partial concentration, especially of larger metalworking firms; this region started in Toronto and extended around the west end of Lake Ontario and westward up the Grand River Valley through Wentworth, Brant, and Waterloo counties, with a leap over to London in Middlesex County.[50]

So, to a considerable extent, the first phase of industrialization in Ontario was a decentralized process based on the proliferating opportunities in an expanding economy of farm, forest, and transportation. Compared with the British and European experience, or even that of Quebec and the Maritimes, Ontario's First Industrial Revolution was at first based much more heavily on the processing of natural resources produced in the countryside and on serving the needs of those rural producers. (In Britain much more of the countryside was filled with rural outworkers engaged in manufacturing.) The small factory town with its close hinterland figured much more prominently in Ontario than in the other Canadian provinces, where industrialization was much more concentrated in large cities. The output of Ontario factories also had its own special industrial mix. Forest products loomed extremely large. The textile industry concentrated predominantly on coarser woollen goods, and, in contrast to Britain and the United States, did not include cotton mills until relatively late. There was no munitions industry to compare with the extensive armament factories that were so important to the development of precision metalworking elsewhere.[51] Metalworking was concentrated, to a limited extent, in machinery production for the transportation industries, but far more in consumer goods, so that the iron moulder was more common than the machinist or boilermaker. Perhaps most important, in the absence of coal resources or high-quality iron deposits, there was no primary iron and steel industry. Even the rolling mills that had opened in the 1850s were closed in 1872, when foreign steel rails began to replace the iron rails previously rolled in Ontario's mills. (Hamilton's rolling mills reopened in 1879, but they simply rolled scrap for nails and other metal goods produced locally).[52] The province's extensive metalworking industries had to rely on imported iron. Finally it is worth remembering that, despite all the remarkable growth of industrial enterprises, manufacturing in this predominantly agrarian province still drew in the same proportion of the gainfully employed in 1891 that it had in 1851 – roughly one-fifth. To point to all these limitations is not in any way to diminish the sense of a "revolution" that people thought, quite correctly, they were living through. At the end of the period, Ontario may still have lacked the concentrations of large factories that had grown up in Manchester and Chicago, but workers in the province's factories found themselves confronting a system of production that had profoundly new elements.

Reorganizing the Work

In pre-industrial Upper Canada manufacturing generally meant the exercise of manual skill and strength with simple tools and occasionally animal or water power to make a product from start to finish. The work was done by an individual or a small work team either in and around the family household or in a relatively primitive mill or artisanal workshop. Wage labour was not the predominant way to get this work done, but it was certainly not unknown. In the small workshops, especially in the towns, craft workers might take on a journeyman or, more likely (to avoid high journeymen's wages), an apprentice or two to work with them on the skilled work, and occasionally a day labourer to help with the heavy unskilled tasks. Mill owners often hired millers and sawyers. In the few large manufacturing enterprises that existed, such as the iron works and the shipyards, owners relied on a more regular wage-earning force. To curb footloose habits at a time when labour was scarce, these workers were sometimes legally bound to their "masters" with contracts of indenture that stipulated the mutual obligations between the parties, but by the early nineteenth century that understanding was most often informal and unwritten. In a relationship of "paternalism," workers would be expected to serve faithfully and obediently, while the employers promised to pay both a wage and some part of their employees' room and board, often taking them into their own houses, where their wives would be expected to provide for the workers' daily needs. Many more workers in all occupational groups probably had briefer, more casual relations with employers that took them away from farming or other independent production for only short spells. By the 1830s, in the larger lakefront towns, especially Toronto, the odd woodworker or metalworker was using a simple machine, such as a lathe powered by water or, in a few cases, by a small steam engine. Yet with only these few isolated exceptions, employers put these men and women to work on well-recognized skilled and unskilled manual tasks and, aside from trying to exercise strict discipline and to keep wages reasonably low, undertook no fundamental restructuring of work routines and practices.[53]

By the 1840s and 1850s, however, competition in the new industrial-capitalist economy stimulated would-be industrialists to organize production in new ways in the hopes of substantially increasing their profits. They had no set formula for how their new operations might run.[54] Some production problems had already been addressed elsewhere, notably in the textile industry, and the managerial and technological solutions could simply be imported. In others, such as metalworking, it made no sense to introduce technology and work routines that would not pay in the colonial economy. (Puddling furnaces and rolling mills were much slower to appear in British North America than in Britain, for example.)[55] In many industries, it was an age of considerable local experimentation. Over the second half of the nineteenth century, more and more Ontario employers had to find ways to extract the maximum effort and highest output from the wage labour they paid for. This eventually forced them to reorganize the labour process, recruit from new pools of labour, and develop new systems to instil the necessary discipline and morale. There were some clear continuities from the past, but some dramatically new departures.

Throughout the period, however, in many Ontario enterprises, the lack of a large, secure market for identical products put sharp limits on capitalists' ability to alter the labour process. From the early days of industrialization, most Ontario manufacturers trying to make more money had found that to reach more customers they had to expand their product lines rather than increase the number of identical products. Lumbermen and flour millers were almost unique in their ability to produce huge quantities of identical or similar products.[56] In 1871 census takers concluded that "the division of labour is not carried on to the same extent as in the older societies of Europe, and in the same establishments there are often to be found grouped together several branches of industry." Many manufacturers complained to parliamentary committees in the 1870s that their markets were too small to permit product specialization. "They have factories on the other side where they can complete one hundred machines where we can complete ten," a London machinery manufacturer told the Labour Commission a decade later. "The only thing running against us is that we have not quite enough people in Canada to let us run into specialties." These structural limitations were to have important consequences for what many Ontario employers expected from their workers.[57]

Towards Factory Production

At first, in most industries, the new capitalists probably tried to turn out more goods for the expanding markets simply by hiring more workers, especially skilled workers to carry on their customary craft production under the entrepreneur's roof but with their own tools.[58] For the many firms producing a wide range of goods for a small market, the flexibility and ingenuity of these workers were crucial. Their bosses relied heavily on their expertise and inventiveness and often gave them considerable independence and supervisory responsibility in their work.[59] The smaller number of industrialists able to increase specialized production of a narrow range of goods in larger workplaces, however, soon discovered that craft workers were not an easy workforce to push harder. As we will see, they had a strong spirit of independence and carefully guarded the "arts and mysteries" of their craft, which included the technical details and rhythm and pace of their daily work. And employers believed that there were seldom enough of them in the provincial labour market. So employers began altering workplace practices to use this labour more effectively, or even to do without it altogether. Many scholars have adopted the term "manufactory" used by Marx and many Canadian contemporaries for this kind of expanded workshop that still functioned primarily on manual skill but was moving sharply away from artisanal practices.[60] Across the industrial landscape, the ways in which the capitalists reshaped the labour process in manufactories fall into five categories, each of which eroded the artisanal practices still further.

The first was an attempt to limit the range of products the craft worker was expected to turn out, on the largely correct assumption that repetitive work on similar goods could encourage a speed-up. As a machinist told the Labour Commission in 1888, "a journeyman going into such a shop will be at the same job all the time for he gets perfect at that kind of work and it pays the employer better to have him kept at it."[61] The skilled wage-earner thus lost the artisan's contact with his customers and control over the choice of products to manufacture, and some of the crafts began to fragment internally between those workers making goods to order and those producing for mass markets. By 1870 Ontario's moulders were becoming segmented into specialists working on either brass or iron and, within the latter group, on stoves, agricultural implements, or machinery. Printers had separated into newspaper, book-publishing, and jobbing labour markets. Some furniture makers made only chairs. Movement between the branches of these industries became less and less common, and union solidarity between them was not even assured.[62]

Closely tied to this kind of narrowing of craft practice was a second innovation – a narrowing of the range of tasks that the craft worker would be expected to perform by using cheaper, less-skilled labour for work that did not require his knowing hand. Craft skill remained at the centre of production, but it was to be applied more intensively, with fewer interruptions for lifting, hauling, and fetching. The cigarmaker could stay at his bench while others prepared the tobacco and brought it to him. The cabinet-maker would have his wood cut and planed by other workers. The stove moulder did not assemble the parts of the stove he had cast; that became the job of the new occupational group known as "stovemounters" (one of whom, Alan Studholme, served as the only independent labour member in the Ontario legislature from 1906 to 1919).[63] Inside the larger foundries, patternmakers and coremakers became new occupations distinct from moulding, and "bench" moulders (who worked on smaller parts) became distinct from those making the larger castings on the sandy floor. Likewise in large machine shops, such as at the Massey works, "fitters" became a separate occupational category from machinists.[64]

In many industries, especially metalworking, this narrowing and specialization of skill was about as far as managerial innovation could go. The pressure then built up for the third step – simplifying or reducing as much as possible the training period for skilled work and recruiting workers who had not served full apprenticeships. These efforts produced some of the fiercest battles with printers, moulders, cigarmakers, and any other trades where craft skills remained important throughout the period.[65] In the midst of a major confrontation with the shoemakers' new union, for example, a frustrated boot and shoe manufacturer denounced the hundred men in his factory for refusing to allow a single boy to work with them: "The consequence was that men had to do the boys' work; and what could be done by a boy for two dollars a week the firm had to pay a man ten dollars to do."[66]

In many other industries, where the market was large enough to allow for high-volume output, industrialists moved towards a fourth form of industrial transformation – a much more extensive subdivision of skilled labour into simpler tasks that could each be carried out by narrowly specialized, minimally trained, and cheaply paid workers. In the 1840s and 1850s subdivided labour was most evident in the textile, sawmilling, and boot and shoe industries. Others soon followed. A visitor to an Oshawa agricultural-tool plant in 1862 was quite struck by this process: "While in ordinary cases – such as axe making – the one person can do the various parts necessary, in this establishment they pass through the hands of eight persons before they are finished." He also stopped at the province's largest factory, E.B. Eddy's woodworking operation near Ottawa, and found that making a pail involved "a good many operations, and at each time by a separate individual." Likewise, in the chair department of a Bowmanville furniture factory, "each man has his part to do, a chair having to pass through six different hands before being completed." A tour of the Joseph Hall agricultural-implement works a few years later prompted a similar observation: "Each man has his own specified work to perform, and by this system an agricultural machine was able to be finished, not only in much shorter time, but in a much better manner, than could be done by other means." At the end of the decade a journalist found the division of labour in Wantzer's large sewing-machine factory in Hamilton "carried to the last point of perfection."[67] Between the 1860s and 1880s many other large factories incorporated this kind of advanced subdivision of labour. By 1888 the manager of Toronto's largest boot and shoe firm, J.D. King, could claim that a boot passed through the hands of fifty workers before it was completed.[68]

Some industrialists organized a division of labour between their central factory building and the households of workers or small workshops of subcontractors. This kind of "putting out," or outwork, was primarily an attempt to build on female domestic skills and to avoid the risks of full-time recruitment and management. From the 1860s onward, it was widespread in the emerging ready-made clothing industry, especially in Toronto and Hamilton, where women took home bundles of pre-cut cloth to stitch into garments, or worked in small subcontractors' workshops (known as "sweat shops" by the end of the century).[69] Occasional references to putting-out have surfaced in other industries, such as paper-box-making for the E.B. Eddy works and weaving cane seats for chairs at the Bowmanville furniture factory in the 1860s,[70] but, overall, outwork played no significant part in Ontario's First Industrial Revolution, except in the garment industry.

The fifth possible workplace innovation was closely connected to the subdivision of labour, namely, mechanization, a process that seemed to accelerate in the 1870s and 1880s. By 1871 half the province's industrial employees (nine out of ten of those in the sixty largest firms) worked in establishments with the most powerful new machinery – improved water-powered engines and steam engines.[71] These could simply make available unprecedented strength – to grind wheat or to shape iron in huge forges and rolling mills or tobacco in plug moulds, for example.[72] But more often these power sources were linked to specialized machinery that was · intended to replace some part of craft skill and thus cut labour costs. Looking back at a family business built up to a workforce of 150 by 1875, a Smiths Falls agricultural-implement manufacturer bragged to a parliamentary committee that productivity had increased with mechanization: "There was a time several years ago when we could not produce over $1000 per man; but with improved machinery we can now turn out from 30 to 40 per cent more."[73] Many industrialists must have expected the same results.

From the 1840s Ontario's textile mills offered some of the most prominent examples of relatively complex machinery for carding, spinning, weaving, and so on, all of it developed in Britain or the United States.[74] Equally striking were the lumber mills, where by the 1850s multiple-blade gang and circular saws powered by water or steam were rapidly replacing the manual routines of the hewer of squared timber and the hand sawyer with the simple, single-blade saws. The fact that these mills ran smoothly with considerable labour turnover suggests their considerable success in reducing skill requirements for the province's leading mass-production industry.[75] In the 1850s skilled tailors and shoemakers also first faced the disruptive effects of the sewing machine.[76] After 1850, in fact, dewy-eyed visitors to the province's new industrial workplaces began reporting regularly on the machinery used by metalworkers, woodworkers, and many others.[77] Invariably such commentators praised the speed of the new machinery. In a typical account, a tourist in 1850 reported his amazement at the woodworking machinery in the already large Jacques and Hays furniture works in Toronto: "From the rough timber a neat bedstead can be made and put together in the short space of two minutes." Fourteen years later, another visitor to the same factory marvelled at "an admirable contrivance for doing perfectly in less than a minute that would require an hour to do imperfectly by hand labor." The Labour Commission heard similar comments. "Spokes were formerly made by hand, but it was an everlasting job," a St Thomas manufacturer of carriage woodwork explained in a characteristic defence of technological change. "The only successful way of conducting the trade is with the aid of machinery." An Ottawa furniture manufacturer boasted that his output had increased by 50 per cent in ten years "in consequence of improved machinery and the men being able to turn it out faster."[78] Of course, a parallel series of newspaper stories made it clear that this fastpaced new technology often made the factories much more dangerous workplaces and the scenes of innumerable grisly accidents.[79]

The "labour-saving" (i.e., labour-displacing) qualities of the new machines also got plenty of attention. Towards the end of the period, a

Globe reporter found the Massey factory in Toronto "a marvellous study in labor-saving machinery; it really looks as if it was the machines that are human and the men that were machines. The steam-driven tools pick up bars and rods of iron, bend them, and shape them as if they were bits of tin."[80] The Labour Commissioners heard much about labour displacement. "I know they have one machine in the waggon shop here that takes the place of about twenty men," a Chatham man reported. A Toronto carpenter was convinced that a particular woodworking machine would "mortise as much as fifty men in a day, or probably a hundred men." Some employers agreed. "One machine may do the work of seven or eight hands, sometimes, and thereby might throw six hands out," the manager of a Kingston hosiery company admitted. "I think the tendency of machinery is to displace men," a Toronto cabinet manufacturer declared. "You turn out more work with the same number of men." Most industrialists tried to dodge the issue of technological unemployment by arguing that the new technology had allowed them to expand their businesses and increase employment overall or that the job opportunities in the wider economy had grown. Few workers bought this argument.[81]

Perhaps most disturbing for Ontario's craft workers was the potential for deskilling through mechanization. Of all the many voices the Labour Commission heard on this question, two will suffice to convey employers' satisfaction and workers' grief. A Chatham flour-mill owner explained:

> With the introduction of roller mills and improved machinery, we do not need so many skilled men. An ordinary intelligent mechanic, or an intelligent man, is able to run a roller mill as well as a skilled miller could do. When there were stones to be dressed, under the old system of grinding, a man required to serve an apprenticeship to the business, and have a great deal of practice, but now machinery has changed all that.

With much more regret, an aged millwright described how new machinery had changed his craft:

> When I first went to the trade we had a casting from the foundry. An ordinary mechanic like myself would take and lay the work out. Then he would chip it with the hammer and chisel, and after that chiselling process he would file it to make it true, square, and clear of twist. Since the introduction of the planer has become universal, an unskilled man starts a

planing-machine, which moves back and forth, and does the work silently and cheaply, and to a certain extent only does it better, but it may be at one-fourth the cost, and in one third the time.[82]

At the same time, the popular fascination with the new technology in the Ontario factory system should not blind us to the relatively small extent of mechanization in Ontario's First Industrial Revolution (as in Britain's).[83] In most industries the organizational changes in the workplace were at least as important as the technological. In some, the subdividing of labour was adequate. In many cases, machinery did not yet exist to replace craft skill or, quite commonly, could only be introduced in part of the operation. A visitor to a large Cobourg woollen mill in 1864 extolled the virtues of the machinery used to process the wool into cloth, but also paused to describe the skilled manual tasks of the "burler," who spread out the woven wool and corrected the imperfections left by the machines – undoing knots, "picking out gouty threads and mending the gaps thus made by running in even ones, and rendering it as perfect as possible."[84] The large Jacques and Hay woodworking factory in New Lowell still relied heavily on hand lathes as late as the 1870s.[85] Hart Massey's agricultural-implement works included some impressive technology in the woodworking and machine shops, but nothing to speak of in the firm's large iron foundry, where, as in most of the province's foundries, moulders still made their castings by hand.[86] George Brown and many of his fellow newspaper publishers had installed steam presses run by specialized machine operators, but until the arrival of the linotype machine in the 1890s, they had to rely on skilled compositors to set the type by hand.[87] On one floor of Jacques and Hay's much admired furniture factory in Toronto, narrowly specialized workers mass-produced simple chairs on whirring machinery, while upstairs skilled cabinetmakers assembled fine furniture by hand. In a Kingston bakery, the bread was prepared by hand while the biscuits were machine-made.[88] In the province's few glass works, glass-blowers still used their own strength and dexterity.[89] There were also contrasts between sectors of particular crafts; for example, coopers worked by hand for breweries and flour mills but with new machinery for the distilleries and the burgeoning oil industry.[90] In general, the smallness of the product markets open to most Ontario manufacturers meant that the production runs in their factories were too small and varied to allow for the specialization of tasks either by hand or with machines that would make much of the new machinery pay. They needed workers and machines with the flexibility to shift to the constantly changing specifications of new orders.

Skill

There was clearly a trend here towards skill dilution as a solution to the high cost and inflexibility of labour in Ontario's first industrialization process. Yet even where machines were in place, we should not assume that they wiped out manual skill. The ability of textile machinery to completely replace hand spinning and weaving, and of the rolling-mill technology to displace traditional blacksmithing were exceptions. Just as often the new machinery was simply incorporated into the craft. The tailor's adaptation to the sewing machine without losing his craft status was perhaps the best example. Even more important, many new machines demanded new skills (though employers were seldom eager to admit this). Operating a machine in this period was generally far from mindless. The stationary engineers eventually convinced the public that their work tending the new steam engines demanded careful training.[91] The millers in the highly mechanized flour mills continued to be highly valued for the considerable skill in their jobs, and even after the introduction of new rolling technology in the 1870s and 1880s, the Chatham mill owner who praised its deskilling qualities was frustrated with the improperly trained "unskilled men ... not fitted for their duties" who presented themselves as millers. "You have got to trust certain things to them," he complained, "and they learn at your expense." Likewise the sawyer in even the most mechanized sawmills had to be "a man of outstanding ability, intelligent, agile and well-trained."[92] The new occupational category of machinist similarly denoted men who used more sophisticated machinery to add more precision to their skills. In the rolling mills the puddlers who purified the iron and the rollers who passed it back and forth through the mills also became extremely valuable skilled workmen.[93] Amidst the whir of the deskilling machinery in the province's largest furniture factory, an observer was still impressed that in much of the wood turning "the hand still guides the tool, and guides it to admiration," and that fine furniture production still required "skill and dexterity."[94] The cutters inside the province's clothing factories quickly won their employers' respect for their abilities. Even in the highly subdivided textile industry, mule spinners and weavers emerged as powerful groups of skilled men (and, occasionally, women).[95] The most skilled element in the new boot and shoe factories, the male lasters who put together the uppers and soles, had a similar status. A Hamilton shoemaker who worked at trimming described how men who were able to run one of the new machines could earn the high wage of $15 a week: "It is a new machine, and there are not many who understand its working."[96]

Unlike old-time artisans, most of these workers had more narrowly focused skills that had to be exercised in quite specific industrial situations, but they had to use considerable judgment and discretion to do their job properly and were generally allowed considerable independence on the shop floor. Employers often made every effort to hold onto such a workforce, especially by moving to "short time" (a shorter work week) rather than shutting down completely during economic crises.[97] As we will see, several of these new skilled groups struggled hard to get some recognition of their new skills and emulated the older trades in creating craft unions.

In a few of the highly mechanized operations, we also hear the first assertions of pride from those whom social scientists would eventually call "semi-skilled" – machine operators engaged in repetitive work. A nail maker who had just described to the Labour Commission the routine of his job as "sitting down and turning a rod in the machine" bristled when a commissioner suggested, "There is not much skilled labor about it, is there?" The indignant worker insisted, "It is skilled labor making these nails … and I have been twenty-eight years in the business, and should know something about it." A machinist with a seven-year apprenticeship and thirty-two years' experience behind him who was working on a planer in a Hamilton factory reported, "Before I came here they had a man four years at it, but they could not run it satisfactorily till I came. He spoiled work which had to be done over again. There is no man who can run a machine properly after [only] three years' apprenticeship." A Toronto machinery manufacturer similarly explained, "We have laborers who we considered skilled, because they have worked so long at the trade." These workers were not interchangeable parts in some huge industrial machine. Their pride in their competence would help to fuel working-class resistance to the new industrial practices by the 1880s.[98]

We must also recognize the gendered dimensions of skill. In this industrializing period (as later), technical skill was formally recognized and rewarded only if it was found in male hands. Craftsmen tied their manual competence closely to their masculine identity – their much vaunted "manhood" – as breadwinners, and, as we will see, employers incorporated these assumptions into their wage structures, despite clear evidence that not all women wage-earners were simply untrained and unskilled. A woman working in an Ottawa printing office claimed that it would take "pretty near a year" for women like her to become competent folders. A foreman in the city bindery agreed. Similarly, as their employers readily admitted, female stitchers in Toronto and Chatham corset factories needed at least six to eight months to learn their skilled tasks properly.[99] A Paris knitting-mill owner might similarly contend that female labour naturally had "a quickness and deftness not obtainable otherwise," but like other employers, he never elevated these valued attributes to the level of well-rewarded skill. The chief employer in that town, John Penman, regularly had to reach outside the country to find female weavers and knitters for his knitting mill, but he still paid women less than men. So too did the Cornwall cotton manufacturers.[100] Skill, then, was socially constructed, and to be a woman was to be denied full recognition for technical competence.

Not all manual labour was skilled, of course. The new factory system was no less reliant on the brute muscle power of unskilled labourers. Occasionally steam or water power could be used to replace their work. By far the most impressive examples were in the flour mills, where closely linked mechanical devices driven by water power carried the wheat through its several stages of transformation into flour without contact with human hands, and in the saw mills, where a handful of workers used primitive conveyor belts to move the logs from the millpond, through the saws, and out to the lumber yard in a matter of minutes.[101] But outside these industries, the mechanization of the lifting, hauling, loading, and unloading of raw materials and finished products was generally a feature of the Second Industrial Revolution, not the First. Indeed, a visitor to state-of-the-art rolling mills in Toronto in 1864 described men carrying iron rails by hand, and commented on how he was nearly knocked down by the many labourers scurrying to and fro with wheel barrels full of material. A former executive of the Ontario Rolling Mills Company in Hamilton later recalled similar work in the 1880s: "All the lifting was done directly by hand labor and so cheap was this labor that it was really more economical to employ direct human effort than machinery. Even cranes, derricks, tackle and all the various simple labor-saving devices were rarely used in any factories at that time." Reports and statistics from other establishments in the same decade suggest the same continuing reliance on the brute strength of many unskilled labourers, rather than the twentieth-century world of conveyor belts, travelling cranes, and fork-lift trucks.[102]

Human mental and manual capacities were thus by no means eliminated in Ontario's First Industrial Revolution. Certainly, few of the province's craft workers could claim to work in conditions identical to the self-employed artisan – the shift to wage-earning had deprived them of too many crucial elements of control over investment and marketing. But in many industries across the province, considerable numbers of skilled workers in both old and new occupations and in large and small factories were essential to the production process and thus retained varying degrees of job control. Indeed, the importance of the "manufactory" brought a large increase in craft workers rather than a decline. The persistence of skilled work inside the Ontario factory system down to the 1880s helps to explain how some wage-earners continued to be able to shift into self-employment or small-scale entrepreneurship,[103] but also how craft unions could remain such a potent force in several cities until the end of the century.

In the broadest sense, then, Ontario manufacturers put together what we can call a "factory system." As the workplaces got larger (fifty workers might be some kind of turning point), as specialization and the subdivision of labour expanded, and as more machinery was installed, a transition from "manufactory" to full-fledged "factory" eventually took place. By the 1880s this kind of new capitalist workplace included the larger saw and flour mills, agricultural-implement works, woollen, cotton, and paper mills, distilleries, tobacco factories, boot and shoe factories, sewing-machine factories, and some furniture factories. But many workplaces had not evolved far in this direction. The outcome of the capitalist reorganization was extremely uneven within and between industrial sectors. The small size of markets and units of production and the workers' own insistence on defining and shaping their own work practices guaranteed that. Ontario's late nineteenth-century factory system remained a patchwork of varied approaches to organizing work and cheapening the costs of production in an increasingly competitive economy. As I continue to use the term "factory" in this chapter, it will be intended to encompass all this diversity, rather than to mean a narrowly specific form of industrial-capitalist workplace.

Finding the Labour Power

Where could Ontario manufacturers hope to find the workers for their new factories? In time, they might expect that a well-stocked, self-regulating capitalist labour market would supply their needs, but for much of the last half of the nineteenth century no such equilibrium of supply and demand was possible.[104] To mobilize and hold on to a suitable, reliable factory workforce was no easy task. There was no large reservoir of craft workers in the countryside comparable to that available to British industry. After 1850 the number of immigrants declined and many still found their way into farming or moved on to the United States. Indeed, the little research done so far suggests that many workers were highly mobile in this period, moving often between jobs and communities. Frequently they followed the custom of their trade in travelling extensively to broaden their experience or, more often, simply looked for steady, more satisfying employment. Indeed, all these perambulations eventually created a continental labour market in particular skills, a growing craft identity, and the basis for a continental labour movement.[105] Moreover, potential wage-earners had their own inclinations about how a capitalist labour market should work. Many craft workers tried to control the market for their skills by using their unions to restrict the number of practitioners. Employers also had to recognize (as modern economists seldom do) that workers were not isolated individuals in an impersonal labour market, but rather members of families rooted in a variety of household economies. Both rural and urban families determined who among them should be sent out to earn wages and under what conditions. The male head of household was the most likely to be the chief breadwinner, but children and young adults, especially the males, might also be sent out to increase the family income. The young females might also be withdrawn from the paid workforce from time to time to help out with the family's domestic labour. These family decisions could mesh with industrialists' needs, but they could also frustrate them if urban wage-earning became a less attractive option, or if prospects looked brighter elsewhere. A Cornwall cotton manufacturer highlighted this problem in his 1876 testimony to a parliamentary committee: "If we had more working people among us their families would be a great help; we have to draw largely from well-to-do farmers. This kind of help has to go home during the harvest and Christmas holidays. All these things work against us."[106] Under these complex and shifting circumstances, Ontario's first industrialists tried to find the labour power to run their factories, primarily through labour migration and on-the-job training.

Men

Skilled male workers inevitably posed the biggest headache for employers – a North-America-wide malady, in fact. Not only were there frequently not enough of them,[107] but they were highly mobile and liable to leave one employer or one community after only a short stay, especially if they were young or were recent immigrants.[108] A few manufacturers experimented with the labour of Ontario prisoners, but those projects generally proved too unpopular and unproductive for widespread adoption.[109] Most employers expected the pool of new immigrants to wash up willing workers on their doorsteps. By the time of the Labour Commission hearings in 1888, there seemed to have evolved two distinct sources for skilled migrant labour. One group came from outside the country, the most well-rounded generally from Britain, the most specialized from the United States.[110] In general, those skilled men who arrived from abroad to work in Ontario factories were more likely to have served a formal apprenticeship elsewhere and to have accumulated experience in several larger industrial cities. Often they were specifically recruited and imported during a strike,[111] or at the start-up of a new industry, especially those with technologically sophisticated workplaces such as railway shops or textile and lumber mills.[112] But gradually, cheap transatlantic steamship fares and railway tickets encouraged the migration of new recruits more or less regularly. Throughout the second half of the nineteenth century, the transportation companies and the Dominion and provincial governments spewed out glowing advertisements to entice British, western-European, and American immigrants. Emigration societies in Britain also sponsored the emigration of unemployed workers. To stimulate the recruitment of newcomers, the Canadian state paid bonuses to emigration agents and gave discounts on travel fares to bona fide immigrants, in the face of growing criticism from the labour movement that the local labour markets were being flooded. State and business nonetheless had difficulty holding new immigrants in the labour pool of such an uncertain regional economy.[113]

The second group of potential recruits into skilled jobs were workers migrating from the villages of the Ontario countryside. They had probably grown up in rural, even agrarian surroundings and had picked up what skills they had more informally among family, relatives, and neighbours on farms or in small country workshops, where strict apprenticeships might be rare. In his autobiography, John Woodside, a moulder, recalled how he left his family's farm to learn his trade in an Owen Sound foundry in the 1860s and ten years later got a job in the Joseph Hall agricultural-implement works in Oshawa with the help of a boyhood friend. The best-studied examples of this pattern of labour migration are blacksmiths, moulders, and the woodworkers of Waterloo, Grey, and Bruce counties, who were steeped in German rural craftsmanship. Employers and workers in several trades – printers, moulders, harness makers, carriage builders, and bakers – told the Labour Commissioners about the "country boys" who arrived in their midst. Manufacturers in the smaller towns probably drew regularly on such a labour pool, but these workers also migrated to the larger cities. A Toronto moulder with thirty years of work experience told the Labour Commission, "There are a great many moulders, or boys, who learn the trade outside in the country towns who come into the city and they do not even have to serve their time at all." This resentment prompted urban craft workers to intensify their efforts to block the flow of these competitors with demands for strict apprenticeship training.[114]

Many industrialists hoped that the overall growth of their industry in a particular district would build up a sufficient pool of experienced labour. "The Gartshore Works many years ago caused Dundas to abound in thoroughly trained and skilled workers in iron," a newspaper reported in 1872, "and the 'graduates' of the old Establishment – if we may use the expression – have made Dundas an iron working town." Hamilton had a similar opportunity thanks to its many foundries. By the 1880s the Toronto garment industry had benefited from the increasing concentration of skilled Jewish tailors. At that point, too, Toronto's largest boot and shoe manufacturer, J.D. King, explained that "shoe factories have been going on so long in Toronto that we never take on inexperienced hands at all." This was likewise a crucial factor in the success of the Lanark County woollen industry. Yet it could take time to reach that critical mass, and an Oshawa agricultural-implement maker and the Cornwall cotton manufacturers lamented in the mid-1870s that they still lacked such a pool of skilled workers.[115] Until the end of the century, neither the Ontario government nor the municipalities put any money into technical schools that might have helped to increase their labour pools.[116]

In the face of an uncertain labour market, industrialists could train their own labour, and many did, at least to some extent. Boys from their own employees' families or from the town beyond the factory walls were regularly presented to them to be trained.[117] There is also evidence that apprenticeship did not disappear quickly from all trades. In 1865 a London printing office was still announcing the availability of apprentice indenture forms,[118] and the newspapers sometimes published both advertisements for apprentices in printing, blacksmithing, moulding, baking, and other trades[119] (including only two for young women – dressmaking and millinery)[120] and reports of court cases about apprentices' conflicts with their masters.[121] The 1888 Labour Commission heard a great deal about the decay of apprenticeship in many industries, though probably some witnesses' points of comparison were outside the country rather than in Upper Canada,[122] but in several branches of metalworking and woodworking, it still survived on a small scale, generally for only three to five years rather than the seven that British craftsmen served.[123] By that time, few Ontario employers bound their apprentices with indentures because in their experience too many would leave before completing their term.[124] "Boys, after they had served a year or two, thought they were full-fledged machinists," a Hamilton machinery manufacturer said, "and they could do better elsewhere, and they wanted to go away." A Chatham flour-mill owner had a similar experience: "Boys will come into the shop, and in a year or so they will pick up a sort of trade, and start out thinking they are skilled mechanics." A foreman in a St Thomas woodworking factory (who twenty years earlier had been the last in his workplace to be indentured) voiced a common complaint about boys' cheekiness when he told the Labour Commission, "If you take a young man in now, you do not know the minute he is going to get saucy and leave you, after you have shoved him along a bit"; in eight years only two or three workers had stayed long enough in this factory to accumulate much proficiency as woodworkers.[125] To encourage their long-term commitment, some employers introduced graduated annual wage increases instead.[126] In any case, unionized craft workers, especially printers, fought a steady battle to prevent the shops from being flooded with apprentices and to ensure proper training.[127] "A boy comes into an office scarcely able to read or write, and is taken on to sweep the room and go on messages," an Ottawa printer complained, "and when he takes up with business he is not taught it, but picks it up the best way he can, and to a right-thinking man that is totally wrong."[128] Many craft workers told the commissioners that they would prefer to have indentures restored to apprenticeship.

In less clearly defined crafts, a more informal on-the-job training often took place.[129] In industries with any degree of subdivision of labour, some employers began to develop internal labour markets, to recruit and promote the less skilled into the more skilled machine operating jobs, thus benefiting from their informal on-the-job training. W.E. Sanford of Hamilton described a "school of labour" connected with his clothing enterprise, "where we help young girls by teaching them the business, and in that we have been able to keep up the supply of labour which we require." The railway shopcraft workers had always risen through the ranks in this informal way. George Tuckett also described this as his preferred method of filling positions in his Hamilton tobacco factory in the 1880s, and Samuel Lennard said that, to get skilled workmen for his knitting mill in the same city, "we have educated them since we commenced ... in the art of knitting." Other testimony described the same on-the-job training for Windsor wire workers, St Thomas woodworkers, and Ottawa flour-mill workers, box makers, and biscuit makers.[130] This could be reliable but also cheaper labour, as an Oshawa agricultural-implements manufacturer explained: "When we teach a man to make forks in our neighbourhood we can get him at a cheaper rate than by employing a man from the States."[131] This was a slow, uncertain process of recruitment, however, and few firms had the stability to guarantee the long-term employment that these internal job ladders assumed. In any case, many workers moved on too frequently.

On the whole, apprenticeship, formal or informal, was not the way most employers of skilled labour expected to find their skilled help. More often they looked outside their own enterprises. Whatever the source, Ontario's first industrialists learned that the capitalist labour markets for various kinds of skilled labour functioned unpredictably, and to whatever extent possible it was important to hold onto the experienced skilled men they had attracted into their factories.[132]

In their fluctuating and uncertain needs for less skilled labour, Ontario's industrialists had more choice and flexibility. Manufacturers admitted to parliamentary investigators in the 1870s that they had little trouble finding their unskilled help and that it was consequently cheaper on the whole than for their competitors to the south.[133] Usually, it seems, they could find strong young men recently off the immigrant ships[134] or just in from the farm willing to do heavy labouring work for low wages and for the short spells that they were needed. A Brantford unionist complained in 1884 that, owing to mechanization, "the shops are filled with young men from the country, leaving their regular avocations and working cheap." A Woodstock unionist reported a similar development two years later: "Some firms are in the habit of putting green hands from the country on machines they know nothing about." Sawmills certainly drew on this kind of labour for their seasonal work.[135] They also encouraged another form of occupational pluralism by using some mill hands as lumberjacks in the woods in the winter.[136] Few manufacturers recruited from the new pools of immigrants from southern and eastern Europe that had found their way into American factories by the 1870s and 1880s.[137] But tobacco firms brought in American blacks, and Jacques and Hay imported some for the unpleasant work in their chair factory at New Lowell. The sawmills often used the muscle power of male French-Canadian migrants,[138] and the textile industry in eastern Ontario, and even in Dundas, reached out to the growing number of French-Canadian cotton workers with experience in the New England mills.[139]

Women

Employers could also hire female workers, especially those under thirty, who were available in Ontario cities in even larger numbers than men in this industrializing period.[140] And the census reports on manufacturing show that many more women found manufacturing jobs after 1870; the number rose rapidly from just under 10,000 in 1871 to nearly 25,000 in 1891, while their proportion of the manufacturing workforce climbed from 11.6 to 16.1 per cent. Yet their participation in the labour force was strictly limited by their families and by the industrialists themselves. In Ontario, in contrast to Britain, several European countries, and the New England textile communities,[141] married women seldom worked outside the household for wages, even in textile towns. With only rare exceptions, wage-earning females were young, single, and solidly attached to the patriarchal household economies of their working-class families. They found wage-earning jobs intermittently between the end of school and the beginning of their marriages, in response to their families' varying need for their wages or their domestic labour. That period usually lasted into their mid-twenties, as the age of marriage rose in Ontario in the last half of the nineteenth century.[142] The gender of the "working girls," as they were popularly known, was crucial in determining their factory experience both in their families' expectations and their employers' employment policies. Industrialists knew that women could not demand a breadwinner's "family wage," and therefore they could get away with paying them much less than men, as we will see below.

In the blunt words of a London cigar manufacturer, "It is more profitable to us or we would not employ them." He also claimed that "women do not go on strike and do not get drunk."[143] A London printer voiced the suspicions of many male workers in 1888: "The proprietor says he likes to have girls because they never ask for a raise of wages, and he can get rid of them some day when he does not need them. They get married."[144] But industrialists also knew that bourgeois Victorian notions of fragile femininity and inevitable motherhood – the so-called cult of true womanhood – limited the kinds of jobs that they could ask women to do. The industrial workplaces into which wage-earning women were drawn were therefore predominantly extensions of their long-established spheres of labour in the family household – clothing, textiles, food processing, and the like – or involved light tasks that could be construed as needing special female attributes, notably "nimble fingers." It was the latter ideological rationale that allowed manufacturers to introduce women workers into several different industries where they had seldom been before in the days of pristine craftsmanship.

How, then, could a factory owner use female labour? Only in dressmaking and millinery shops did women apprentice to be the main craft workers of the trade, and they dominated this popular, more respectable work as they did no other industry.[145] In a few other crafts involving relatively little manual strength, especially tailoring, and, to a lesser extent, cigarmaking and typesetting, employers introduced women as cheap substitutes for male craft workers, sometimes in the midst of a strike,[146] and usually in a restricted role in production. Generally, though, they did "women's work" in female job ghettoes and did not compete directly with men. In 1871 and 1881 more than four out of five adult female wage-earners could be found in clothing and textile production, and by 1891 the proportion was nearly nine out of ten. Other than in some food processing,[147] women formed an insignificant proportion of the workforce in primary industries, metalworking, and woodworking.

Wherever they worked, women factory operatives most often became a part of the overall process of the subdivision of labour and dilution of skill, usually filling the least skilled jobs in the new occupational hierarchies. The province's woollen and cotton industries had used them from the beginning as carders, weavers, and ring spinners (though never as mule spinners, loom fixers, or dyers).[148] Both custom tailors and the ready-made clothing industry relied heavily on their labour power, principally for the simpler work on pants and vests (though sometimes on more complicated garments too).[149] In shoemaking they did basting and tacking and plain stitching on sewing machines.[150] In cigarmaking they packed tobacco or rolled cheaper cigars.[151] In baking they worked with the machines to make biscuits, crackers, and candies, while men made the bread.[152] In the less conventional occupations that became "women's work" in the new factory system, small handfuls of women were put to work on simple, repetitive tasks, often with light machinery. Visitors to Eddy's huge woodworking factory at Ottawa found young women in the "rather *ominous*" sulphuric haze of the match department, not by the saws.[153] Elsewhere, in printing they fed the presses, and folded, stitched, and collated books in the bindery, but only occasionally set type.[154] Hardly any women showed up in the province's heavy metalworking factories, but small clusters appeared in shops producing screws or sheet-metal products and occasionally in a foundry fashioning small sand cores for the male moulders, or perhaps doing a little soldering.[155] They also found work in paper factories and worked on paper products, such as boxes and stationery.[156] In a few cases, as we have seen, industrialists got around the controversial issue of bringing women into factories by organizing the subdivision of labour so that women worked in their own households; many of these women were widows or married women who were the chief breadwinners. This may have been the largest single category of factory-related employment for women, though the statistical reporting of homework is unreliable.

The use of female labour in these ways to degrade established craft practices raised the hackles of adult male workers, especially the skilled workmen. Caught on the horns of a patriarchal dilemma, these men could readily recognize how important a woman's wages could be for her family, but they also worried about threats to their role as chief breadwinners if they had to compete with poorly paid women. Their masculinity was bound up in their pride as competent producers deserving of good wages and thus as good providers for their families.[157] Several groups of craftsmen in late nineteenth-century Ontario criticized the employment of women as degrading to their craft – notably tailors, printers, and cigarmakers. In 1856 the London tailors' society linked the arrival of women with all the degrading tendencies within their trade by demanding that "all custom work … be done on the premises at which it's offered for sale, a discharge of female tailors and an end to the use of sewing machines." A decade later these men were still bemoaning the fact that "so much is given out to women that the tailoring business is fast degenerating." Not surprisingly, craft unions showed a general indifference to organizing the female practitioners of their trade.[158]

To some extent, the perspectives of male bosses and their male workers converged. In the 1888 Labour Commission hearings, they both often shared a discourse of disparagement and exclusion. Repeatedly men argued that women wage-earners were incompetent or unreliable, either because of biological or physiological limitations or because of their brief stint in the paid workforce. "Almost invariably they do their work in a very inferior manner," a Toronto printer insisted. "They do not take the trouble." Printing was "a life occupation for the men" but "only a temporary occupation" for the women. A Windsor publisher was similarly dismissive: "They are not as good as men, and cannot make themselves as useful. If they had nothing to do but set type they would be all right, but they have not the endurance of men, and that is another drawback." A London cigar manufacturer who had filled his factory with female labour was nonetheless similarly contemptuous of their abilities: "As between a man and a woman, a woman can never make as good a cigar as a man, that is taking ten men and ten women … A man will take a pride in getting up an article nicely where a woman will not." Unfortunately, he explained, since cigars produced by men and women sold at the same price, his profits would be larger with cheaper female labour. One of this man's competitors in Kingston shared these sentiments: "They don't work as hard as the men do: they are not so ambitious." When asked if a tailoress could make as good a vest as a man, a London tailor replied, "She might manage to make one that would pass as well, and a man not as experienced as a tailor would not know the difference … [But] a practical tailor could tell the difference." Again, she found work in some of the city's clothing shops only because her labour was cheaper.[159] There were nonetheless class differences in this wall of masculine scorn that relegated women to narrowly circumscribed occupational niches. Employers were more frustrated that the demands of the household economy made these women less reliable sojourners in the wage labour market, but the male workers more often feared the degradation of their crafts and the threats to their status as breadwinners. They also showed more sympathy with their bargaining power as wage-earners and thus became a leading voice in pushing for the Ontario Factory Act (enacted in 1886), which put special protections on the working hours of female labour.[160]

Women thus found themselves in a paradoxical position as wage-earners. More and more jobs were opening up for them in the new industrial workforce, but their family responsibilities, even before marriage, and the attitudes of male manufacturers and male wage-earners, and the larger patriarchal ideologies restricted their employment possibilities to only a few industries and only a few job ghettoes – the less skilled, more repetitive, less well-paid, dead-end work, often attached to specialized machinery.

Children

In similar ways, child labour in factories was rooted both in the new needs of industrialists for cheap, unskilled labour and in the customary place of children in the family economies of both rural producers and urban workers. Boys and girls had long been expected to contribute their paid or unpaid labour to the well-being of their families from an early age, and, as opportunities for young workers began to open up in the rapidly expanding industrial workplaces of the 1860s and 1870s, many youngsters from working-class families began to march through the factory doors to earn wages for their family coffers. Throughout the period many commentators saw parental greed behind child labour in Ontario.[161] In the same vein, the Labour Commission heard numerous employers of juvenile labour justify their profit-making employment practices virtually as charity. "It would be a great grievance to some parents if we refused to employ their children," a Dundas cotton manufacturer insisted. "Their work is a great assistance to them." According to Hamilton's leading tobacco manufacturer, George Tuckett, some parents saw a factory as a reform school: "The mothers come to me and say that their children will not go to school, and in order to keep them off the streets, they send them to me." (Ironically, when pressed, employers seldom knew anything about local working-class household economies.) The Cornwall correspondent of the Ontario Bureau of Industry was closer to the mark when he said in 1887, in tune with his fellow reporters across the province, "The reason of their employment is mainly because the wages paid to heads of families are insufficient to maintain all without the aid of the children."[162] School officials wanted these youngsters to spend more of their time in the classroom, but such schooling as they got had to be sandwiched between their work at home and in the factory. "Sure she needs meat first," the guardian of a thirteen-year-old mill girl told a factory inspector, James Brown, when he suggested schooling for the girl. Of course, many children themselves would often "rather work than go to school," as one told a government commissioner in 1882.[163]

Until the late 1880s, there was no popular consensus on a suitable age for starting full-time wage labour. In Hamilton in 1871, working-class boys tended to begin work at age twelve and girls a couple of years later; scattered evidence over the next twenty years suggests that this may have been the threshold for much juvenile wage-earning.[164] Certainly some children, especially boys, started as young as nine or ten, but they were probably a small proportion. A letter to the *Almonte Gazette* in 1862 complained that there was a "considerable number in Almonte working in the woollen mills who are under 12 years."[165] Two decades later, a special federal Royal Commission on factory labour counted 173 children under age ten (and over 2,000 between ten and fourteen) in the 465 factories and mills in the five eastern provinces it visited.[166] The 1888 Labour Commission heard several reports of Ontario boys starting work at nine, ten, or eleven – in Ottawa sawmills, in a Toronto box factory, in cotton mills (where a boy of eight managed to earn ninety-two dollars in one year), and in southwestern-Ontario canning factories.[167] The first factory inspections in the late 1880s and early 1890s also turned up quite young workers, who were usually sent home immediately. But these were probably instances of dire family need and not typical cases.

Most employers claimed, probably truthfully, not to know the real ages of their young workers. Before the 1886 Factory Act required employers to get age certificates from the parents of young employees, they probably cared much more whether the child was physically fit for the job, and perhaps whether he or she was related to a highly valued adult worker. The 1882 commission on factory labour found employers had had no record of their employees' ages.[168] Inevitably that looseness brought many children aged twelve to fourteen, especially boys, inside the Ontario factory system, as the nervous defensiveness of employers in the late 1880s suggests: "I don't think there are more than six under fourteen years, and they have worked at the mill a long time," the manager of a Kingston cotton company proclaimed. The first Ontario factory inspectors had an extremely difficult time determining precise ages. Under the Factory Act, the legal age for wage-earning – and thus the effective end of "childhood" – was set at fourteen for girls and twelve for boys (the difference was eliminated in 1895; Ontario's compulsory school-attendance legislation of 1891 similarly set fourteen as the common cut-off point). Both before and after the new legislation, "child labour" in this strictly defined sense seems to have had a relatively small place in Ontario's industrial economy – manufacturers did use such young workers but were simply not dependent on recruiting a huge proportion of their juvenile workforce from this age group. But if we extend the definition into early adolescence, as school reforms did in the 1920s, we find a large number of young workers under sixteen. Overall, between 1871 and 1891, they never made up much more than 8 per cent of the total manufacturing workforce, but in some industries their proportion ranged between a quarter and a half. In fact, by the early 1880s the Dominion government thought that child labour had become a serious enough problem to merit particular investigation.[169]

It would be misleading to lump boys and girls into one category of juvenile labour, since the patterns of their employment were, on the whole, quite different. Far more adolescent boys than girls worked for wages and in far more industries, and they seldom did the same jobs.[170] Industrial capitalists put boys to work in three different ways. A few might be recognized apprentices, as we have seen. Many more did light labouring – carrying, fetching, sweeping, and generally helping (some were specifically named "helpers"). In fact, few industrial operations were without at least a handful of young male teenagers on the premises. Saw operators used many such boys to cart away scrap and small pieces of wood – an extremely dangerous job.[171] But both boys and most wage-earning girls also got low-skilled jobs directly in production processes that had been extensively subdivided and, in many cases, mechanized. Their labour thus played a vital part in the transformation of the labour process in this period; as a Toronto shoemaker lamented in 1871, "Boys and girls were placed at work which the skilled mechanics ought to have done."[172] They could not be used in all industries – the heavier metalworking factories, in particular, seldom took on young workers below age sixteen.[173] This young labour was most heavily concentrated in the textile, clothing, woodworking, food processing, and tobacco industries.[174] Nor was juvenile labour evenly distributed across the province. Young workers appeared in some of the consumer-goods industries in the metropolitan centres and were certainly crucial to the mill towns that produced textiles and wood products. But, as the

Bureau of Industry correspondents confirmed in the 1880s, they were far less common in the small, mixed factory towns, where the subdivision of labour and skill dilution might not have advanced as far, and where, presumably, there were enough adult workers willing to take on the lower-paid unskilled jobs.[175]

Generally the youngest workers could be found feeding or tending light machinery, in the spinning departments of cotton mills, on picking and carding machines in woollen mills, on knitting machines, cork-making machines, tin-can stamping machines, nail-making machines, wiremaking machines, biscuit-making machines, folding machines in bookbinding operations and printing presses, and on planers, rip-saws, cross-cut saws, sandpapering machines, and jointers in woodworking factories. In 1852 an Ottawa reporter found a thirteen-year-old boy running a steam engine, and thirty years later the 1881 commission on factory labour claimed to have discovered several boys of that age in charge of boilers and engines.[176] In some cases they became part of a largely nonmechanized labour process. Most young male and female tobacco workers were hired to stem the leaves. "The older hands would not be so nimble," George Tuckett of Hamilton argued in defence of employing 120 to 150 boys and girls, many as young as fourteen. Some worked directly on the cigars: "We take a girl and teach her to make the inside of a cigar, what is called the bunch," John Rose, the London cigar manufacturer, explained, "and we teach another girl to roll them up." Girls might be used for other simple manual tasks – cleaning fruit in a canning factory, pasting and tacking in a shoe factory, japanning tin cans, finishing blinds in window-shade factories, rolling chocolates in candy factories, or wrapping and packing the end product in biscuit, confectionery, soap, seed, or other factories.[177] Some employers continued to use the term "apprentice" for this kind of wage-earner, and in a few cases, especially textile and clothing production, they paid the newcomers to the job nothing while they learned (for up to six months).[178] Yet generally the range of tasks they learned was far too narrow to be considered an apprenticeship for skilled adult work. "They go around taking up what they can, but do not become thorough mechanics," a Toronto journeyman gilder told the Labour Commission. A St Thomas manufacturer of carriage woodwork admitted that the work of his young male machine operators was "no trade to them," though they might graduate to heavier, better-paid men's work. A woodworker in a London agricultural-implement works explained that becoming a well-rounded workman was impossible as long as the boys were "always kept on that saw or machine." A tobacco manufacturer in the same city was even blunter: "As soon as they are out of their time, they demand journeymen's wages, and I have no more use for them."[179]

Throughout most of this period, boys and girls responded to the same factory bell and worked the same hours as their adult workmates, sat on oversized, uncomfortable benches and stools designed for adults,[180] and were otherwise treated like adults except for their much lower wages. So, to take a stark example, twelve-year-old boys worked in Ottawa lumber mills six days a week from 6 a.m. to 6:30 p.m., with fifty minutes at noon for lunch and frequent overtime, for forty cents or less a day. Small wonder, in the words of a factory inspector, that "the employer seemed to consider that class of labor as very saving and economical."[181]

Juvenile labour evidently posed problems for Ontario industrialists, however, and by 1891 some seem to have stopped relying so heavily on children under sixteen.[182] The decline was not precipitous but steady. Overall, the proportion of wage-earners under sixteen declined from 8.3 per cent of the manufacturing workforce in 1871 to 6.5 in 1891, but mostly it was boy labour that was slowly contracting: the percentage of girls (most of them in clothing and textiles) remained roughly the same. Perhaps the lower number was merely due to the economic slump in that year. Or perhaps employers had learned that boys caused so many accidents and disciplinary problems – by joyriding on overhead pulleys, for example[183] – that they were too severe a drain on productivity. A foreman in a large western-Ontario furniture factory told an inspector that as boys became familiar with the machinery they became "correspondingly reckless."[184] The central-district inspector similarly noted the "tendency of young people to talk and 'lark' with each other while operating dangerous machines or working near them." His eastern-Ontario colleague noted "in every instance where children are employed their extravagance and carelessness in the performing of their work."[185] Girls were not exempt from this criticism: a Kingston cigar manufacturer complained to the Labour Commission that the young girls in his factory "could make so much more than they do, but there is too much nonsense about them.[186] Occasionally these workers might even strike, as they did at the Wanzer sewing machine works in 1886.[187] A few years later, a factory inspector suggested that canning companies were replacing their young workers with machines.[188] Certainly, as the Second Industrial Revolution unfolded after 1900, the mechanization of the work once done by young hands was to become common. But there is no evidence that this was a widespread trend across the industrial landscape in the 1890s. More likely young women were the immediate replacements; in the industries where boy labour was falling off, adult female employment was rising by 1891, notably in the production of food, chemical, printed and published, textile, and wooden products. Perhaps, too, by the 1890s, the public disapproval embodied in the new Factory Act had given some employers second thoughts about using particularly young workers. The much publicized debates about child labour that had preceded the legislation must have sensitized many industrialists to the issue and encouraged them to avoid the prodding of even the most polite inspectors.[189]

Of course, in the face of a weak system of inspection and enforcement, some child labour simply went underground. A factory inspector told the Labour Commission how one firm "had two boys under packing cases while we were going up the stairs and they sent them down by the hoist."[190] And both parents and bosses undoubtedly continued to misrepresent children's ages easily enough, as the inspectors regularly lamented. The same inspector reported:

> Parents having in the majority of cases, neglected to register the births of their children, it is difficult to verify the certificates of age given by them. Out of nearly one hundred, considered doubtful and sent in to the Registrar-General's Department for verification, only twenty-five per cent were found to have been registered. I have reason to believe that children have, in many cases, been instructed to state their age as greater than it really was.

A Cornwall doctor, hired to assist the eastern-Ontario inspector, was likewise convinced that the children he interviewed at the large cotton factories "had been coached as to their ages, as they seemed to know how old they were required to be in order to obtain employment in the mill." At the turn of the century, an inspector discovered that only eight of fifty-three age certificates provided by parents matched the government birth records.[191] Ultimately, it is impossible to know precisely how much young labour continued in Ontario manufacturing at the end of the century. Certainly few late nineteenth-century photographs taken on the back steps of the province's factories lack a fresh young face or two, testifying to the importance of juvenile labour markets in Ontario's First Industrial Revolution. And the objections to their employment continued into the early twentieth century.[192]

Wages

Finding the necessary labour power for Ontario factories in the late nineteenth-century, then, involved the creation of a number of distinct labour markets, each with its own difficulties and possibilities for employers and each offering quite different rewards for wage-earners. A complex structure of wage payment that corresponded to the new divisions of labour, dilution or continuities of skill, and gender differences had emerged by the 1880s. To some extent, the overall patterns are elusive, since the forms of wage payment still varied widely. Some employers, as we will see, continued to provide amenities beyond simple wages. Others paid their workers enough to hire their own helpers. Still others paid "learners" nothing at all. Throughout the period, wages could still be earned by the month, by the day, by the hour, or, in a growing number of industries, by the piece. Moreover, the surviving data on wages are scattered and limited. No consistent statistics were collected before the 1880s. Nonetheless, from the surviving data we can glean some idea of how the dramatic changes in industrial life affected the relationships among the various wages of Ontario workers. An examination of the information on workers' weekly wages gathered by the Ontario Bureau of Industries for the week ending 25 April 1885, a relatively good year in the Ontario industrial economy, is revealing. The wage-earners in manufacturing have been clustered into a ranking by income to suggest something about their value on the Ontario labour market. Unfortunately, there is no way to control for experience within a single craft or industry, which could obviously affect some rates of pay, but as a snapshot of industrial wages in the late nineteenth-century Ontario economy, the data are suggestive.

Several important patterns emerge. The most striking are clearly based on age and sex. Across all industries, workers under sixteen, whether male or female, earned less than $4 a week, and females less than $3 (with only one exception, an unspecified cotton worker).[193] Similarly, no women earned more than $6, and only two highly skilled groups – cotton weavers and milliners – took home more than $5. Those earning between $4 and $5 were found in only boot and shoe, carpet, corset, and cotton factories. All other women wage-earners were paid roughly the same as adolescent boys, and occasionally less. At the same time, no males over sixteen earned less than $4 a week, and most of those under $6 were probably teenagers. Equally significant, in the seventeen jobs where the bureau listed both men and women with the same job titles (admittedly with no indication of different responsibilities), females earned on average only half as much as their male counterparts, and ten of these female groups earned even less.[194]

Other patterns in these wage data are more subtle. The tiny elite that earned more than $11 a week were clearly the most highly skilled men, either in a few old, still vibrant crafts (such as glass-blowing or iron moulding) or, more commonly, at the pinnacle of a new occupational ladder, where they applied their craftsmanship as low-level supervisors (such as brewers, distillers, or wheelmakers) or as highly valued contributors to a subdivided labour process (notably in metalworking and the production of carriages, furniture, and musical instruments). The ranks of those earning from $9 to $11 a week contain some of the same groups but also many craft workers (such as bakers, brushmakers, and coopers) who were holding on with somewhat more difficulty and larger numbers of men with narrowly specialized jobs, rather than crafts, in a new industry (agricultural implements, textiles, tobacco, and so on), each demanding considerable manual competence. Virtually no full-fledged craft workers appear below that line, but in several industries with a more advanced subdivision of labour in their workforce, the occupational hierarchy slopes gently downward through various semi-skilled workers in the $7- to $9-a-week range. Mixed in here too are the adult male labourers. In cotton and woollen mills the jobs have extremely narrow labels and are separated by only slight gradations in pay.

So the creation of a well-stocked, impersonal, self-regulating capitalist labour market was no less complicated than the reorganization of labour processes in the new factories. Industrialists had to work with the unpredictable flow of regional and international migration, deeply rooted conventions about men's and women's "spheres," and workers' own sensitivity about status and remuneration. In the face of these difficulties, Ontario's first industrial capitalists undoubtedly found the labour power to make their factories work, though sometimes not as profitably as they would have liked. The scarcity of labour nonetheless haunted them at many points and shaped a crucial element in their management practice – industrial paternalism.

The Art of Handling Labour

"There is a great art in handling labour so as to make the most of it," Canada's leading business publication explained in an 1871 editorial entitled "The Effectiveness of Labour." "Let it be taken for granted that the object of the employer is to get as much for his money as possible."[195] Given the limited substitution of machines for humans in Ontario's new industrial workplaces, the knowledge and discretion still required of many workers, including machine operators, and the all-too-common scarcity of labour in the industrializing economy, industrialists had to work out appropriate management policies. In part this was a question of morale and of loyalty to the industrial enterprise and its owner, in part one of discipline to increase what in the twentieth century would be called productivity, that is, getting more work out of the worker. The solutions developed fell within a general framework of paternalism, which required deference to the authority of the capitalist owner, and of patriarchy, which meant that authority was male and modelled after the hierarchical power relations of the patriarchal family.

The Personal Touch

In the evolving system of capitalist ownership and control, the years between 1840 and 1890 were the age of the capitalist patriarch. Most new industrial enterprises were owned and operated by one capitalist and his male kin, occasionally in partnership with another male partner or two. A single capitalist could, of course, preside over a huge enterprise, as many of the lumber magnates did, for example, but the firm retained their personal stamp. Even when there was important investment from outside, as in the case of Montreal capitalists' interest in eastern-Ontario textile mills, the operating control generally stayed in the hands of the local entrepreneur – in contrast to the great railway corporations of the period.[196]

Not surprisingly, then, the workplace relations of the new factory age were in many ways a continuation of what has been called the "personal" labour relations of the pre-industrial era in British North America, in which the male head of the household had directed artisanal or domestic production for the market. The "master's" hold over his "servant" had been a blend of material provision (room, board, and other necessities), stern punishment, and legal prerogative occasionally codified in a formal indenture and always backed by the common law notion of a contract of employment enforceable in the courts. In return he had expected loyal service and obedience.[197] The industrial-capitalist employer of the second half of the nineteenth century used many of the same paternalist tools of workplace control. Payment by "truck" (i.e., scrip redeemable for merchandise, usually at a company store) survived into the 1870s in several mill towns, though workers elsewhere seem to have succeeded in driving out this constraint on their independence.[198] More important, an industrialist's legal powers were enhanced by the new master and servant legislation of 1847, and newspapers carried regular reports of workers and apprentices being dragged before a magistrate to be punished for disobedience or for abandoning their employers without permission. "From the frequent lessons taught at the Police Court," the *Ottawa Citizen* warned in 1866, "servants should have a care lest they, in foolishly leaving their situations, lose their hard earned wages in law costs." Not until 1877 did a disobedient worker cease to be a criminal in Ontario.[199]

Paternalism worked not simply because of coercion, however, but also because of industrialists' efforts to cultivate respect and loyalty among their workers. Inside Ontario's many diminutive workshops, especially in the smaller towns, the bond between owner and skilled men doubtless remained close and reciprocal in day-to-day work routines, including some elements of masculine solidarity among skilled men, since the owner was so often an accomplished craft worker himself and it was often possible for his employees to become self-employed.[200] Yet among these and other less skilled, female, or juvenile workers, the success of this relationship in the individual enterprise probably hinged most often on guarantees of employment at a time when workers were almost completely reliant on wages for their survival. Their boss would look after them, it often seemed, especially if they were valuable to the firm. In a few cases, they continued to get some kind of board from small-scale or isolated employers as late as the early 1870s. In many more, they were no doubt grateful for the minimal job security they received, as their bosses attempted to maintain a seasoned workforce through difficult times without complete shut-downs. One of the "old hands" at the Waterous engine works in Brantford recalled in 1887 that C.H. Waterous had been "more like a father than an employer," especially in the depression of the late 1850s, when "he said he could not bear to see the old hands in want and so kept open, when we knew it was a great loss to him"; in fact, "short time," rather than a full lay-off, was a common and sensible practice among capitalists anxious to hold on to valuable workers in an uncertain labour market. One employee at the Massey agricultural-implement plant later claimed that Hart Massey went one step further and guaranteed life employment to anyone injured on the job. Workers may have been similarly appreciative of the efforts to hire members of their families, which helped stabilize the household economy and allowed working-class parents to give their sons a start in life.[201] Some workers (we will never know how many) waited patiently and deferentially to be promoted within the factory to more skilled work or even to a foremanship. Eighteen-year-old William Holden, a three-and-a-half-year veteran of a Hamilton tobacco factory, confessed to the Labour Commission his aspirations in the internal labour market: "I consider they will put me in another year at making lumps for plugs ... They never take them on unless they have worked there a long time."[202]

The power of the paternalistic capitalist, however, often extended well beyond his factory walls. Outside the large cities, workers would have encountered visible reminders of the class structure of their society, most particularly the baronial mansions that the capitalists and their families were moving into by the 1870s and 1880s. Within the town's community life, they might take a leading role in town councils, churches, and voluntary societies. They might subsidize schools, churches, and various leisure activities. They probably tried to infuse their working-class fellow citizens with the small-town boosterism spearheaded by local capitalists to promote profit making in their municipalities, in competition with other Ontario communities. Their political opponents complained, probably with good reason, that they also led their workers to the polls in elections, and although many workers would have been unable to vote before 1885 (and even after), we now know that the manufacturers who were rallying to the Tory party in the 1870s made particular efforts to build an alliance of "producers" in support of the National Policy.[203]

In towns where a single employer was dominant, especially the small, single-industry mill towns, paternalism was less personal and more all-encompassing. Many workers lived in company housing, shopped in a company store, and benefited from services arranged or supported by the company, such as a school, church, doctor, or even accident insurance. Textile towns like Hespeler, Paris, Almonte, and, to some extent, Cornwall ran this way, as did Walkerville, the company town of distiller Hiram Walker in southwestern Ontario.[204] In the dozens of isolated sawmill towns, employers had little choice but to provide basic shelter, provisioning, and community services if they wanted to hold onto a workforce. Of course, once established, these facilities allowed the companies to cast a blanket of paternalistic discipline over the workforce. The major sawmilling company on Georgian

Bay, for example, imposed a ban on alcohol in its mill towns. Since the company owned virtually all the property in Waubaushene, the site of its headquarters, there was no municipal government, and the magistrate was a company official.[205]

This kind of paternalism was reconsecrated in regular ceremonies. Each year industrialists across the province hosted picnics, Christmas dinners, or summer afternoon excursions for their workers and their families to symbolize the "harmony of interests" that newspaper editors liked to extol.[206] Some firms equipped baseball teams, marching bands, or floats for the ever popular industrial parades through the city streets.[207] Occasionally workers responded with collective tributes to their employer. During a New Year's oyster supper hosted by an Ottawa employer, an older worker rose to speak: "Sometimes you appear rather rough, when matters don't go right," he declared, "but then it's over in a minute, and after all we rather like to hear you scold a bit, for then we know that work is on hand and must be put through." In 1868 a workman from E.B. Eddy's factory dropped by his house on Christmas Day to give him a dollar to help replace the part of his operation destroyed in a fire. A few days later the workers at Eddy's match factory (arguably one of the least pleasant workplaces in the province) presented his daughter with a piano. In 1872 L.C. Northrup's woollen workers in Almonte presented him with a Family Bible, a Masonic ring, and a silver pencil on his retirement. In the same period, workers in that town and in Lanark Village organized Christmas or New Year's dinners for the woollen manufacturers who employed them. When all of Almonte's woollen mill owners announced a reduction to ten hours a day in June 1872 (for which the employees had petitioned the previous fall), their workers were "so much pleased … that a band serenaded the residences of the employers."[208] Similarly, cotton-mill workers paraded the streets of Paris and Cornwall to defend their employers and themselves against attacks published in the Toronto *Globe* in 1882 by labour reformer Phillips Thompson.[209] A Brantford foundry worker addressing the first employees' picnic of the William Buck Company in 1886 praised his boss: "The ministers of the city have been trying to settle what is termed the vexed question of capital and labor by words. But our employer took the best way, the practical way, by giving his means to enhance the enjoyment of all." A weaver in the same town explained his workmates' sense of bereavement when the owner of the town's small cotton mill died in 1890: "Most of the help of the cotton mill was brought to this country by Mr. Slater, and they realize that they have lost a friend, and they naturally desired to see their beloved master for the last time and attend his funeral."[210]

However much these forms of paternalism may have infused small-scale or small-town industry during Ontario's First Industrial Revolution, it was much more difficult to find equally strong social cement in the larger industries in the bigger metropolitan centres, where a single employer had less influence on the local labour market and was less likely to cut as big a swathe in social life off the job, and where, as we will see, the alternative loyalties of the urban crafts had taken root. More elaborate means were needed to attempt to continue the ideal of paternalistic control. The railways were the pioneers, in the 1850s, in establishing recreation programs for their shop-craft workers in order to co-opt and shape working-class leisure activities.[211] Elsewhere employers funded reading rooms or local mechanics' institutes to promote "rational" leisure.[212] Few other factory owners did much more before the 1880s. The McCormick biscuit and confectionery company in London provided dining rooms for men and women. Hamilton's tobacco magnate, George Tuckett, doled out small Christmas bonuses to loyal workers in proportion to their apparent merit; "They notice that we are watching their interests and rewarding merit, and therefore they watch our interests," the firm's owner explained. The large Rathbun lumber company based in Belleville published a company newspaper known as the *Tribune* in the 1880s.[213]

Undoubtedly the most elaborate program to appear in that decade was introduced in the Massey agricultural-implement works in Toronto. The firm sponsored a benefit society, medical care, a brass band, a string orchestra, a glee club, a library association (which ran a reading room and lectures and debates), outing clubs, sports teams, a seven-hundred-seat meeting room known as Memorial Hall, and a company magazine, the *Trip Hammer*.[214] As the railways had already discovered by that point, however, this form of paternalism did not cement enough loyalty to prevent workers from forming unions. Massey had already had weak support and attendance for most of its program, but the walk-out of Massey's workers in early 1886 was the most overt, massive rejection of the family's paternalism, symbolized by the immediate collapse of the *Trip Hammer*.[215] Tuckett's workers were similarly contemptuous of their employer's paternalism that year and struck for two weeks before winning a settlement.[216] Most Ontario employers showed no interest in this scale of company welfarism in any case. Their workers considered themselves lucky to have clean drinking water, and they ate their lunch outside or at their bench or in improvised eating areas, not in company lunchrooms. They washed up on the shop floor or in nearby streams or waited until they got home.[217] They tended to their own injuries without a plant nurse. And they organized their own recreation with workmates, family, and neighbours. Only by the 1920s did "welfare capitalism" become a significant force in the province's factory management.[218]

Supervision

Ultimately strict application of the workers' labour power was more important to companies' profit margins than welfarism. Who, then, supervised the wage-earners of Ontario's First Industrial Revolution? Because so many manufacturing enterprises in Ontario in the second half of the nineteenth century were very small, most employers could oversee their workers directly. Indeed, with only rare exceptions (notably the railways)[219] we find no large new class of professional factory managers in the province's industries before the end of the nineteenth century. Many of the managers who appear in the historical record were either the partner in charge of operations or a member of the owning family. The Labour Commission was presented with a striking example of limited management when a clerical worker at Ottawa's large lumber firm, Gilmour and Company, explained, "They have no manager; my position is that of book-keeper. I am sort of manager."[220] At the same time, however, old-fashioned paternalism and patriarchy required innovation and adaptation in the new factory system, especially as workplaces got larger.

Some industrialists tried to maintain a system of direct supervision by delegating authority to some kind of subcontractor who undertook to produce goods for a stated fixed price. He would be provided with raw materials, whatever machinery was needed, and, in most cases, space inside the factory, and would hire, pay, and supervise his own labour without any interference from the factory owner. Existing research has so far told us little about the importance of this figure in Ontario's nineteenth-century industrial life. Elsewhere, we have learned, subcontracting took varied forms and did not appear in all industries or all departments of a company's operations.[221] By the end of the 1880s, the system was common in Ontario in some parts of large sawmills, tobacco factories, and rolling mills, and occasionally it cropped up in woodworking, as in London and Chatham furniture factories.[222] In most of these settings, the man in question was a skilled worker who worked by the piece and hired one or more boys as helpers at the lowest possible wages. In some cases, however, subcontractors organized production teams of predominantly adult workers. Since the early 1860s, clothing manufacturers in the bigger cities had used this system most extensively, turning over batches of garments to be sewn either in households by women and members of their families or in small contract shops outside their premises with anywhere from three to twenty workers. The number of women and men employed this way by one clothing firm could vary from a few dozen to some two thousand in the industry's giant, W.E. Sanford and Company in Hamilton.[223] In the testimony to the Labour Commission, it is clear why, wherever it appeared, this system soon became known as "sweating." A Toronto harness maker described the system in one American-owned leather-working factory:

> The firm employs a contractor who contracts to make so many dozen sets for a certain wage; then he hires a fitter and finisher who fits and finishes the work with the contractor and then they employ either a lot of boys or young fellows who can just stop the men who are out of work. They are obliged to do that or starve. They pay next to nothing and if they work very hard and manage to knock out a dollar a day they do very wel1.[224]

In Chatham, which seemed to be either an unusual hotbed of subcontracting or else an example of its popularity in small towns, the Labour Commission discovered in 1888 that the owners of a small agricultural-implement factory had recently reverted to subcontracting. A woodworker explained what had happened:

> One of the contractors was the foreman last year, and he has two other men with him, and the foreman who worked here for a number of years is one of the subcontractors. I say that same foreman has worked the men harder, less wages have been paid, a cheaper class of men have been employed, and he has made a large profit, the proprietor paying him the same rate per fanning mill as the mills cost him last year, when he did the work by day work. The foreman, who, I say, is one of the sub-contractors, has made better wages for himself, and a large profit besides, out of the men under him.[225]

In this case, the employer's version of the story was not much different: "The profit that the sub-contractor made was by looking after matters, and working the men a little harder, and looking after his own interest sharper than he would look after mine."[226] This arrangement of work was not some kind of residue of the past, but rather a revival of an older form of supervision in new circumstances that allowed the industrial capitalist to stabilize labour costs and intensify work without any direct involvement himself.[227]

However widespread it may once have been, subcontracting was not typical in industrial Ontario by the 1880s. Generally, it was more common in larger factories to hire salaried foremen empowered to hire, fire, and discipline the workers in specific branches of the company's operations within a loose general framework of company policy.[228] "We expect and exact a fair day's work," a Chatham agricultural-implement manufacturer explained. "It is mostly left to the foreman." According to the manager of a Kingston knitting mill, "that part of the business is in his charge. If he gets the work out it suits us, and he can do as he likes." A labourer in the same city's locomotive works discovered that "the foreman was the man to judge what a man was worth." The manager of a Cornwall cotton mill agreed that these front-line officials had "full control over their department ... and I would not interfere with their work."[229] Some of the industrialist's paternalism inevitably passed over to the foreman, whose rule was based to a great extent on his personal rapport with his subordinates. Scattered through the daily press are accounts of testimonials and gifts for these front-line supervisors from allegedly grateful employees.[230] The relationship could also involve sponsorship and patronage, as a London moulder made clear when he complained that an American foreman at the local car works was firing local workers in favour of his compatriots.[231]

Discipline

If the personal touch of direct supervision remained in the transition to factory production, there were also many new managerial policies that deliberately sought to disrupt older patterns of industrial work. These began to appear in the larger, more aggressively managed workplaces as early as the 1860s, but they seemed to have spread much further once the post-1873 depression had convinced industrialists of the need for more intense use of the labour power they were purchasing. Central to the new industrial discipline was imposing a new sense of industrial work time. New disciplinary controls were imposed on all workers to instil more punctuality and commitment to regular wage-earning than had often existed in pre-industrial British North America. Workplaces ran to the rhythms of clocks, not tasks to be completed each week or each season. Such dissolute habits as the extended weekend known as "Saint Monday" had to stop. The working day was sharply demarcated by bells and whistles. "They are supposed to be in their places and prepared to commence work when the whistle blows," the managing director of Kingston's locomotive works insisted.[232] Many workers found their wages reduced for arriving a few minutes late. "If they cannot cure themselves of that habit," the manager of a Kingston cotton mill said, "we discharge them." Several other employers agreed. Some factory owners had all the doors to their premises locked except the main entrance where tardy workers had to present themselves to timekeepers. At the other end of the working day, a Cornwall cotton factory restricted access to the washroom just before closing time.[233]

Once the workers were under a capitalist's factory roof, he most often demanded that they stay at their jobs for a good long stretch, since the labour-intensive production systems of the period allowed for only limited increases in productivity. Factory buildings were designed with large windows to make maximum use of daylight, and gas lighting was often installed to keep workers on the job after dark. Ten hours was the typical working day across the province. Highly mechanized processes did not bring any reduction – indeed some of the most technologically sophisticated factories with the most advanced division of labour, notably the lumber, textile, and flour mills, frequently ran for eleven or twelve hours a day. Few industries besides the lumber and flour mills, and distilleries incorporated a night shift,[234] but overtime was common in busy spells. Most Ontario factory workers also worked a six-day week. By the 1880s there was pressure from workers for a half-day on Saturday, but outside Toronto the few establishments that cut back on Saturday working hours usually expected the workers to make them up during the week. In the sawmills, which generally ran no more than five or six months a year, seven-day weeks were not uncommon.[235] Relief from the gruelling routine of the typical fifty- to sixty-hour week came during the seasonal shutdowns that hit so many industries, or during economic slumps, when "short time" or full-scale lay-offs were invoked.

Employers most often justified the long working days as a means of curbing working-class dissipation after work. "The more spare time men have the more they are likely to form intemperate habits," a Belleville manufacturer insisted. "Shortened hours of labor, we believe, in 75 per cent. of cases would only tend to mischief," an Owen Sound foundryman claimed. According to a Toronto watch-case manufacturer, shorter hours "would simply mean in most cases more time to loaf and spend money in dissipation, and in very few cases would it be employed for mental improvement." A Huntsville lumberman waxed philosophical on the subject: "Long hours and low wages love the working classes, short hours and high wages are their curse." Workers predictably denied such charges and, as we will see, organized to get more time away from the job.[236]

During these long working days, factory owners expected industriousness but also self-discipline. Stern rules were posted on many factory walls and on pay envelopes to remind employees that their time on the job was not to be disrupted by socializing, joking, swearing, or even smoking.[237] The pre-industrial work routines that could involve conviviality with visitors, drinking at work, and other forms of integrating work and leisure were banished. A Toronto moulder may have believed that in the foundry where he worked every man, except himself and one other, was "drunk every chance he could get," but the Georgian Bay Lumber Company fired any worker found drinking alcohol on the company's extensive premises.[238] A Kingston cotton-mill worker found herself sent home for two days "as a correction" when she and her workmates were discovered "getting in the hallway and making a noise at noon-hour." Similarly a group of Cornwall's female cotton workers were disciplined for "talking and laughing and clapping hands" in the presence of their foreman in the lunchroom. "They are supposed to conduct themselves quietly during working hours," their overseer said.[239]

At the same time, to tie workers down to their jobs and discourage sudden departures, the first industrialists appear to have made good use of the master and servant legislation that allowed them to take employees to court for running off. Even before the decriminalization of this workplace discipline through legislation in 1877,[240] they tried other methods too. In the 1860s the newly formed province-wide employers' association among foundrymen kept a blacklist of moulders who left their employment without their boss's permission – a "slave law," in the workers' eyes. So too did London's cigar manufacturers twenty years later. In the aftermath of the agitation for shorter hours in 1872, some Ontario manufacturers compelled their workers to sign "iron clad" documents that, among other provisions, attempted to tie the workers to their jobs for as long as a year. In addition, the owners of large factories regularly held back up to two weeks' wages to inhibit footloose behaviour. "That has been the custom in mills ever since I knew anything about it," the manager of Cornwall's Stormont Cotton Mills told the Labour Commission.[241]

Of course, the coercion could be indirect. One of the best ways to instil industrious habits, many employers concluded, was to tie the workers' wages to their output. In the 1860s there were reports of daily quotas in the larger factories. At E.B. Eddy's huge woodworking complex near Ottawa, "like most of the establishments where Americans are proprietors," a respectful visitor reported in 1862, "the articles are made by the dozen or the gross; each person is bound to turn out so much each day; if they fail in this they are discharged." Workers in Wanzer's sewing machine works had to produce five hundred a week in 1870 or "return to work at night," according to a posted sign. But far more important and eventually more widespread was the introduction of piecework. In pre-industrial Ontario, workers were accustomed to being paid by the day or the month. As late as the 1880s, wage rates in some industries might still be quoted by the month, but after 1870 wages per day and, in a few cases, per hour became more typical across the industrial landscape. Wherever the product market could absorb enough of a firm's output, however, workers were put onto piecework to encourage them to speed up. This incentive system had appeared in some larger Ontario enterprises by the early 1860s. In a Hamilton garment factory, employees were seen in 1862 "working in gangs and by the piece." An Oshawa agricultural-implement manufacturer required his fifty employees to accept piecework and "to make so many dozen per day," thus being able to "tell exactly how much each piece will cost, and what the value of each man is to him." Twenty years later, at the end of their hurried visit to factories across central and eastern Canada, two royal commissioners tallied up roughly equal numbers of workers paid by the day or week and by the piece. But the much fuller labour commission testimony revealed that this kind of incentive wage had taken root most commonly in specific industries with large outputs for large markets, and not where short product runs or careful craftmanship predominated. Piecework thus became another part of the process of splitting a craft between those doing made-to-order work and those in mass production, such as machinery and stove moulders, and printers in jobbing and newspaper shops.[242]

In many industries piecework took hold without much opposition from the workers. The divisiveness of the issue was evident when the

1882 commissioners could get "no definite answer" from the Toronto Trades and Labor Council on whether "your trades prefer time or piece work.'[243] A few years later the Labour Commissioners heard that printers and iron workers seemed satisfied to work on piece rates.[244] But moulders were less certain. Some readily accepted it as a way to increase their earnings. A Toronto moulder lamented the "selfishness of men" that made piecework so successful: "So long as they can get dollars and cents they do not care as the amount of work they do." Another in Hamilton saw the same problem: "A man will be covetous and work himself tight out to try to earn a few cents more than his day pay." But others grew to hate the system. Craftsmanship could suffer: "In doing piece-work a man never tries to remedy his mistakes," a London moulder insisted; "he just goes right along, and if the work will pass he thinks it is all right. He will not take time to use his judgment in trying different ways of making work properly and in adopting a proper way of making a piece. He gets a job and runs it for all he is worth." Speed-up was the inevitable result. "It is better of course for the bosses," a Toronto stove moulder argued; "they can get more work for less money" by creating "a rushing tendency on the part of the men and consequently a cutting down of prices." Small wonder that a factory inspector would warn that pieceworkers, "in order to earn a fair wage, must take great risks." Some workers also believed that both seasonal and structural unemployment increased. As the moulder's journal had noted in 1873, a stove moulder was "doing the work of eleven months in eight, for eight months pay; and then has the satisfaction of starving the balance of the year." In a similar vein, a Toronto moulder argued that piecework was directly responsible for the high unemployment in the trade for the previous fifteen years: "Where there are two men at present employed on piece work three men would be required if they were working day work."[245]

But piecework did not guarantee limitless increases in productivity. Some unions began to impose limits on their members' daily production and led strikes against payment by results, though the outcomes were mixed. Whether or not they were unionized, many workers eventually learned to restrain their own effort and to impose limits on each other, rather than risk lower piece rates that would make them work harder for the same money. "I have heard it said that the girls [in a paper-box factory] did not want to make more, for the employers might cut them down on their piece work," a Toronto worker reported. By the turn of the century, a new school of North American management experts would be looking for new ways around this widespread restriction of output that they dubbed "soldiering."[246]

Patriarchy

The patriarchal quality of the disciplinary codes and sanctions in the new factory system shone through in the different treatment of women and children from that of men. In some industries, as we have seen, employers allowed their male workers to hire the children and youths they needed as helpers and to exercise a father's authority over them. More generally, women and children, unlike most men, were fined for tardiness, unacceptable work, insubordination, and sundry other minor misdemeanors (including spitting on the floor or fixing their hair). "Men will not put up with deductions from wages which they have toiled to obtain," the pro-labour group of Labour Commissioners reported in 1889, "and therefore the system is not applied to them."[247] Sometimes the fines were clearly stated in posted notices, but more often foremen seem to have had the discretion to deal with the "childlike" behaviour of women and children as they pleased. "I happened to be out about an hour," an Ottawa print-shop foreman related. "When I returned I found them pulling each other's hair, and running about the floor; and as I came in I saw all this, I said: 'You will lose an hour' ... [;] something has to be done to keep order in establishments of this kind."[248] In Ontario the Labour Commission did not hear any evidence of physical abuse to compare with the harsh disciplinary regime in Montreal's infamous tobacco factories. But there were strong hints that male foremen (there appear to have been relatively few women overseers)[249] were not above browbeating their female and juvenile labour with gruff or abusive language. "I am no angel," a foreman in an Ottawa printing office admitted; "occasionally I might swear."[250] There were also occasional hints of sexual harassment, such as the charges laid by some women in Elora's carpet factory in 1882, resulting in a criminal prosecution.[251] Almost all female wage-earners also felt the indirect prod of piecework to make them work faster.[252]

As the Labour Commission often discovered, most male wage-earners were not subjected to quite the same rigid authoritarianism. They tended to fill more skilled, more responsible jobs, and, far more often, it seems, they demanded and got respect for their "manhood" – in this case, independent control over the labour process exercised individually and together with their male workmates. They knew their work and, in many manufactories and factories, were left to do it. Yet deference to the overall paternalistic authority was expected, and when the independence and solidarity of the shop floor stood in the way of profit making, industrialists were not shy about attempting to bring the men to heel. The various tactics of diluting craftsmanship with poorly trained workers or dissolving it with the subdivision of labour, the use of children and women, and mechanization showed that the capitalist was willing to abandon his respect for his workmen and often to precipitate a confrontation with the men. Even more important, the disloyalty of joining a union of other craft workers outside the factory could not be tolerated. Union requests for negotiation were regularly brushed aside, strikes were fought and broken, ringleaders were dismissed and blacklisted, and occasionally ironclad contracts against union membership were forced on workers. In the colourful metaphor of a Hamilton rolling-mill official, when the owners could not tolerate the union among their workers, "they just sat upon it and squelched it."[253] In a few industries or towns, employers formed their own organizations to defeat the unions, though these "bosses' unions" were never typical of industrial relations in the period.[254] Nowhere in Ontario did industrialists show any serious interest in stabilizing industrial relations with the kind of formal collective bargaining that was emerging in several British industries in this period.[255]

We can see then that managerial authority in the new factory regime of late nineteenth-century Ontario rested on the continuing power of paternalism and patriarchy but with a few new variations. A single male figure still tended to preside over each unit of production, and he still exercised his authority by the double-sided process of paternalism – the promise to care for his industrial flock and the coercion to keep them in line. But a primary goal of the emerging system was to concentrate and intensify their labour through long hours and strict discipline in the workplace. There was no fixed managerial formula, however, and the new factory regime across the province varied considerably according to the skill and strength demanded of the workers, the volume of identical products turned out, the age and sex of the workforce, and occasionally the whim of the capitalist himself. The contrast between Tuckett's Christmas gifts to his tobacco workers in Hamilton and Rose's draconian authoritarianism in his London tobacco factory points to different possibilities. More often, however, each industry developed its own practices. The most rigid management appeared in the mill towns and in the "mass production" industries in the larger cities, while somewhat more flexible paternalism tended to continue in the hundreds of smaller-scale workplaces sprinkled through the mixed factory towns of the region. Yet, as industrialists across the province struggled to find their feet in the harsh economic climate that settled in after 1873, the efforts to intensify labour spread through much more of industry. The Labour Commission heard numerous voices of working-class outrage at many quite recent changes in industrial management – the new subcontracting schemes in a Chatham wagon works or a London furniture factory were striking examples. Perhaps the most bitterly resented practice, which revealed the shallowness of paternalism, was the bluntest method of reducing labour costs – slashing wages in times of economic depression, as many industrial enterprises did in the mid- 1870s and again a decade later. The breakdown of paternalistic authority in so many Ontario industrial workplaces in the 1880s suggests how fragile and unstable this form of factory management could be once the workers discovered a common sense of injustice at the ways the factory system was working against their interests. "Under the factory system, many employers fail to recognize an essential difference between machines and the human labor by which they are operated," an editorial writer observed in 1896; "kindly interest and consistent devotion have been replaced by indifference and distrust." Ironically, this was not the voice of outraged labour, but of perceptive business opinion, the venerable *Monetary Times*.[256]

Resistance and Struggle

Paternalism is a system of unequal social relations, but also one of reciprocity. It works to the extent that both sides are able to find some balance of separate and distinct interests through a complex process of negotiation and accommodation. We have already seen that within industry the dominant figure in the relationship might feel called upon to wield an authoritarian whip over the subordinate element to bring them into line. Yet the reverse could also be true. Occasionally the normally deferential workers might strike a defiant posture to remind the paternalist of their needs and interests. The outcome of that confrontation would probably be a new equilibrium within industrial paternalism. Many workers probably moved around between jobs and communities too often to settle comfortably into such a relationship, but before 1880 in Ontario, outside a handful of industries and trades in the larger cities, it was the struggles to ensure the mutuality between workers and bosses that seemed to form the main pattern of what would later be called "industrial relations." As we have seen, however, many Ontario industrialists began to shuck off the yoke of real, reciprocally based paternalism during the later 1870s and the 1880s, and to treat the labour power they purchased much more as an expendable commodity that could be intensified or dispensed with without the older sense of obligation. Bitter confrontations with their workers then erupted over the threat to their living standards from irregular employment and wage cuts or to their pride and self-esteem as producers, and many more workers put their faith in labour organizations to promote and defend their particular interests as wage-earners. The 1880s thus became a decade of widespread working-class organization and intense industrial conflict never before seen in the province.

The Revolt of the Urban Craft Workers

As the First Industrial Revolution unfolded in Ontario, working-class defiance percolated through many workshops, manufactories, and factories. Occasionally we can catch a glimpse of the work-group solidarity that must have flourished (as it certainly did later) as a source of resistance to unbridled managerial control. In Berlin (now Kitchener) unknown pranksters hid the factory bell down a well. In New Hamburg, carpet-mill workers let tardy workers in a window to avoid the foreman's wrath. A group of high-spirited women in a Kingston cotton mill derided and ridiculed their foreman when he tried to supervise their behaviour during their lunch break (we have already met him and his methods above). Rolling-mill men in Hamilton smuggled beer onto the shop floor. Boys and girls regularly turned some parts of their factory workplace into illicit playgrounds.[257] This kind of informal trench warfare against the elements of the new factory regime they disliked relied on conspiracies of silence and cooperation within a workforce. There were also more open collective efforts to change the terms of employment. In 1872, for example, sawmill workers in Ottawa and woolen-mill workers in Almonte petitioned their respective employers for shorter hours, apparently with some success.[258] Workers sometimes also refused to work until the terms of their employment had been modified, though often their bosses refused to deal with them and broke the strike as quickly as possible.[259] The ironies were evident in 1872, when the workers of Wanzer's sewing-machine factory in Hamilton presented the firm's manager with a glowing tribute on the occasion of his retirement only a few short months after their bitter dispute with him over the nine-hour day.[260]

A turning point was first seen in the late 1860s and early 1870s, when both strikes and union organizing increased in the province. Yet before 1880 this working-class resistance never extended much beyond a handful of crafts and the largest cities. Many efforts have doubtless been lost to the historical record (Ontario had no official labour statistics before the 1880s), but it is hard to escape the conclusion that strikes and unions were the exception rather than the rule in this early period. In the 1860s and 1870s more than three-quarters of the strikes uncovered in the most thorough study to date involved craft workers in only six trades, and three-quarters took place in Toronto, Hamilton, Ottawa, and London. The rest were spread thinly through small-town Ontario. Similarly, the most encyclopaedic research on unions turned up only 17 local organizations in Ontario manufacturing in the 1850s, 36 in the 1860s, and 77 in the 1870s. In each decade more than half of these were in Hamilton, Toronto, and London; most other towns had only one or two. The explanation for this limited level of organization lies in the constraints of the general economic situation and in the unevenness and diversity of workers' experience across the province.

Before the 1880s, the structures of the employment relationship in most late nineteenth-century Ontario manufactories and factories did not promote a militant class consciousness among the wage-earners within them. A stable working-class community was certainly less likely to emerge amid the insecurities and irregularities of Ontario's industrial economy. So many industries had prolonged seasonal shutdowns that many workers would doubtless have returned to farming or other occupations. During the deep economic slumps, especially after 1873, as businesses closed or went into bankruptcy, many wage-earners and their families must have moved on.

At the same time, we have seen that Ontario's First Industrial Revolution was an extremely uneven process, moving through particular industries and towns in very different ways. Three different kinds of manufacturing centres appeared – mill town, mixed factory town, and metropolitan centre. In each of these, industrialists brought together the raw materials for distinctive working-class communities with their decisions to invest in certain kinds of production to compete in particular markets, to organize specific work processes, and to recruit the necessary kinds of labour. The workers who gathered in each of these industrial centres proceeded to shape their own patterns of association, organization, and resistance or accommodation according to the structural constraints and opportunities they found. We still know little about how these local working-class communities took shape in Ontario, but it is clear that the result was three different patterns of working-class experience in the province's factory towns. In only a few of the larger cities did workers produce a self-conscious, independent, and aggressive form of resistance to the new industrial capitalism before 1880. After that date, a more generalized spirit of class-conscious protest began to percolate throughout industrialized Ontario, though the differences persisted.[261]

Two of the three kinds of working-class community were weak recruiting ground for independent working-class organization and action. Compared to workers in the average Ontario factory, mill-town workers – especially sawmill and textile hands – tended to work for large, impersonal firms with more advanced subdivision of labour, mechanization, and, in the case of textiles, female labour. Because their jobs were tied closely to one industry and had little independent status as crafts, these workers would have fallen more easily into the deference expected by the industrial patriarchs who effectively controlled the local labour market and most social institutions. In contrast, workers in the many small, multi-industry towns were more likely to find themselves in much smaller establishments, often with only a handful of employees, many of whom were probably versatile, skilled men. There it would not be easy for an occupational identity to develop among the sprinkling of workers in any trade, and there was not likely a yawning social gulf between them and the owner, who was often a skilled manual worker himself. Even in the growing numbers of somewhat larger factories in these towns, this respect for, and masculine solidarity with, a former-artisan-turned-capitalist could be potent cement between master and men. Craft workers were a prominent part of this small-town world, but in many cases their occupational trajectory and general craft experience were considerably different from those of their counterparts in the larger cities. As we have seen, Ontario had two different sets of craft traditions – one rural, the other urban. The rural craft worker was rooted in the agrarian experience, where skills were learned more informally and sometimes practised together with agriculture. These men had none of the corporate organizations of their urban counterparts.[262]

It is the workers in the few big cities, especially Toronto and Hamilton, who have become best known for determined self-organization in the late nineteenth century. These cities contained a remarkable range of factory wage-earning experience, including substantial clusters of women, children, and other unskilled recruits to the large consumer-goods factories that served the cities' extensive hinterlands with boots and shoes, clothing, tobacco, and so on. Yet, far better studied are the large numbers of urban craft workers, both specialized men in manufactories that produced such mass-market goods as stoves and ironware, newspapers, and the like; and the more all-round men in generally smaller workshops that turned out machinery, fine furniture, and a host of other consumer and producer goods. It was among these urban craft workers that the first elements of a labour movement emerged. Their experience with managerial innovation in the rapidly expanding manufactories sharply challenged the long-standing craft traditions with which so many craft workers in the larger towns and cities identified and the newer craft practices that these skilled wage-earners were evolving. By mid-century, they had a tradition of mutual support in times of economic distress. They also gathered in growing numbers in taverns and banquet halls to toast their patron saints. They marched proudly in parades beneath banners celebrating the glories of their trade and the virtues of manly independence and popular democracy. They reinforced their occupational solidarity in baseball games, balls, and family picnics.[263] And they dug in their heels against any effort to erode their crafts in the new manufactories where they were employed in growing numbers. Indeed these journeymen came to assume that only they could defend the integrity of their craft, as master artisans became more interested in profit than craftsmanship. Starting in the 1850s, they formed craft unions to control the daily labour process and to maintain their relatively high wages and occupational status. They tried to regulate the labour supply with formal apprenticeship training and unemployment programs that helped the jobless in their trade to set off "tramping" in search of work. In fact, these craft workers were highly mobile, carrying their principles of organization, fellowship, and independence around the continent. The links between Ontario unions and American national craft organizations that began in the 1850s and 1860s – the origins of so-called international unionism – were due to this mobility and the desire to control the continental labour market in their skills. The biggest industrial conflicts in southern Ontario took place whenever this kind of craft unionism collided with the new capitalist authoritarianism. These battles were often framed dramatically as a struggle for control of the workplace.[264]

Before 1880, then, unions in manufacturing industries were primarily a metropolitan phenomenon. Perhaps even more striking was the small number of occupations covered. Four-fifths were found in seven crafts – shoemakers, moulders, machinists, printers, cigarmakers, coopers, and tailors. More detailed studies have revealed why these were the wage-earners who unionized. In each case these industries were reaching out to a mass market, and the capitalist employers were consequently pushing hard to intensify the labour process and where possible to transform it. In each case, they had to confront large numbers of well-entrenched male craft workers whose skill was still vital to production. In the 1860s shoemakers were the first to encounter skill dilution, subdivision of labour, and mechanization on a large scale, and they launched a substantial resistance movement in the early 1870s. They set up branches of their new organization, the Knights of St Crispin, in twenty-one towns across the province.[265] Coopers made a similar stand against employers who adopted new methods for barrel production in response to the demands of the distillers, oil refiners, and salt producers. [266] Tailors met the challenge of the sewing machine in the 1850s by incorporating it into their craft, but they felt the new pressures of subdivision of craft skill as the ready-made clothing industry emerged in the larger cities.[267] Cigarmakers too had to confront such changes inside the big new tobacco factories.[268] Two large groups of craft workers – the iron moulders in the province's many foundries (especially the stove foundries)[269] and the compositors who set type in the offices of the new daily newspapers[270] – retained crucial manual skills and maintained persistent, determined organizations in the face of their employers' attempts to flood the respective labour markets with poorly trained, cheaply paid workers and to break their unions. At the same time, one group of craft workers who had emerged within the First Industrial Revolution rather than out of pre-industrial experience, the machinists, stood their ground in the railway shops, the province's largest industrial employers in the 1870s. They organized mostly within branches of the British-based Amalgamated Society of Engineers.[271] The common experience of all these unionists was the confrontation between capitalist market principles and their craft identity and practices.

Occupational solidarity was strong among these workers, but the exclusiveness evident in their desire to restrict access to craft training did not encourage much organizational initiative among the unskilled. (The moulders, for example, never tried to rally their less skilled workmates in stove factories or agricultural-implement works.)

It even created divisions within crafts, between compositors and pressmen, and between stove and machinery moulders, for example.[272] But workers who regularly extolled the value of craftsmanship had little difficulty striking up bonds of solidarity with craft workers in other manufacturing trades and those in construction and transportation. By the early 1870s craft unionists had created the first "trades assemblies" of craft union locals in Hamilton, Toronto, Ottawa, and St Catharines. The growing consciousness of a generalized craft worker identity was evident in the appearance of several additional unions of manufacturing craft workers in the larger cities in the late 1860s and early 1870s. Among them were bakers, butchers, carriage makers, broommakers, hatters, boilermakers, varnishers, and polishers. It was this expanding craft-union movement that fuelled the spectacular Nine-Hours movement in the spring of 1872 and launched the Canadian Labor Union (which was never more than an annual meeting of southern-Ontario craft-union locals) the next year. Most of this labour movement died in the depression of the mid-1870s.[273]

We should never forget, however, that this well-studied movement made few inroads into the Ontario manufacturing workforce. Before the 1880s, unions touched only a small minority of Ontario factory workers, namely, the adult male craft workers in the manufactories of the rapidly expanding industries, principally in five of the largest industrial towns – Hamilton, Toronto, London, St Catharines, and Brantford. Aside from the odd local of moulders or shoemakers, small-town Ontario never saw unions in their manufactories and factories in these early years, and there is no record of organization in such major resource-processing industries as sawmilling, flour milling, or textiles. At least for factory workers, then, it is not helpful to imagine that before 1880 Ontario wage-earners had "a long history of resistance, challenge, and organization."[274]

The Great Upheaval

After 1880, however, workers across the province organized in unprecedented numbers. Part of this expansion was the resurgence and reinvigoration of craft unionism.[275] But much more remarkable was the broadening of working-class organization, principally through a new movement known as the Noble and Holy Order of the Knights of Labor, which drew in thousands of workers who had never before belonged to unions and which touched towns that had never seen a union. The Knights' story has been well told elsewhere and need not be repeated here in detail.[276] In all, the order's "missionaries" to the working class, as one of their Toronto leaders dubbed them,[277] probably recruited some 22,000 wage-earners in Ontario. The predominance of Toronto, Hamilton, Ottawa, London, and Kingston, which together had four-fifths of the Knights' "local assemblies," is not surprising. Yet the Knights' organizational flexibility, which permitted both occupationally based assemblies and "mixed" assemblies of diverse crafts and occupations, made possible the appearance of labour organizations in some eighty-three municipalities, including all those with a population over 5,000 and four-fifths of those over 3,000. Craft workers took the lead and probably predominated numerically. But the less skilled and more narrowly specialized factory workers also joined in substantial numbers. Local assemblies of workers in boot and shoe, textile, lumber, agricultural-implement, and other large establishments dotted urban Ontario in the second half of the 1880s. For the first time in the province's history, women were included, either as members of mixed assemblies or in their own female locals.[278] Debates over the statistics on membership [279] cannot undermine the remarkable change that was evident among factory workers (and other wage-earners) after 1880. Far more of them were expressing a sense of collective working-class identity than ever before in the province's history.

Any explanation for such a change must begin with the larger industrial context. As we have seen, industrialists had done some serious soul searching in the severe depression of the 1870s and saw the need for some major new departures. The most celebrated, the National Policy tariff, restricted foreign competition but stimulated a lot of new internal competition, as new factories opened, older firms expanded, and most industrialists simply jostled desperately for space in the limited domestic markets. By the mid-1880s overproduction was a serious problem. Survival required a cutting of production costs wherever possible. Some factory owners resorted to the familiar nineteenth-century solution by slashing wages. Still others looked for changes in the labour process that could help them. The increase in immigration also provided some relief.[280]

For most workers, then, the 1880s became a decade not of prosperity,[281] but of economic and occupational insecurity and uncertainty. Percolating through the language of the Knights' activity in Ontario were a sense of outrage and injustice and a palpable loss of faith in the industrial-capitalist economy in which they worked. Often it was the over stocked labour market and the consequent unemployment and economic insecurity that they attacked.[282] Pressures on the job were troubling as well, and, not surprisingly, strikes proliferated. Craft workers in the most dynamic industries once again rose in vigorous opposition to the continuing degradation of their crafts and struggled to establish the formal job-control mechanisms devised by their unions. Workers in a wide variety of occupations – including some tough minded, determined women[283] – also struck to protest wage cuts[284] and other threatening managerial innovations aimed at intensifying their labour, frequently through some complicated adjustment of piecework.[285] These defensive struggles suggested that many of these workers without strong craft identities had developed a clear sense of what was customary and fair in their workplace routines and their living standards and what should not be tolerated. They expressed the evidently widespread commitment among many factory workers to maintaining the dignity of labour – the Knights' central message – and often fuelled the growth of the Order's local assemblies. In many factory towns and villages, the demand that seemed to encapsulate their resistance to the new capitalist labour market and employment conditions was a shorter working day. With only eight or nine hours on the job, male workers could both spread employment to the unemployed and limit the encroachment of the waged workplace on their domestic, social, and civic lives. In town after town, Knights' assemblies discussed the shorter working day and in some cases tried to get their employers to adopt it, generally without success. The town of Chatham saw one of the most concerted campaigns, as the local Knights of Labor asked all the town's manufacturers for an extra hour off on Saturday afternoon, only to be confronted with a lockout by a new employers' association.[286]

The "Great Upheaval," then, encapsulated the anger and concern of a great many Ontario factory workers about the transformation that had taken place in the province's First Industrial Revolution. It showed that the earlier willingness among both employers and workers to allow some version of paternalism to govern their relations had broken down, and that workers were now more likely than ever before to look to their own collective power to pursue their interests. Ultimately, though, what can we conclude about the effects of this wave of working-class resistance, spearheaded by the Knights of Labor, on Ontario's industrial life? The pinnacle of labour strength in the 1880s was undoubtedly Toronto, where by 1886 organized workers totalled five thousand and concessions on wages and hours were apparently extracted from some reluctant employers – probably most dramatically from the city's largest employer, the Masseys, in 1886. "As labour organizations exist in greater numbers in Toronto than any other city in Ontario, or in the Dominion in fact, the consequence is seen in its generally higher average wages in all callings," the Bureau of Industry's labour statistician reported in 1884.[287] Hamilton was close behind with some three thousand organized wage-earners. These metropolitan centres nourished the provincial leadership of the Knights, the most articulate intellectuals of the movement (like Phillips Thompson), and the most vibrant labour press.[288] In these cities the daily press also expressed fascination with and support for the cause,[289] and federal and provincial politicians scrambled to make legislative concessions. (The most notable were the collecting of labour statistics by the Bureau of Industries and the Factory and Workmen's Compensation acts in Ontario and the federal government's appointment of the Labour Commission.)[290]

But in the smaller factory towns and mill towns, a different story unfolded. Certainly several employers across the province felt pressured enough by the apparent strength of this labour organizing to try to shore up their workers' loyalty. Some took their first steps into paternalistic welfarism with new company picnics and the like, which may have reassured some workers.[291] Some reduced working hours slightly in 1886–7,[292] and there was a flurry of debate in at least three towns about ringing the towns' bells at seven o'clock to signal the end of all work.[293] Few of these changes seem to have lasted, however, and far more often the industrialists refused to make any concessions. Although there have been no careful statistical studies, impressionistic evidence suggests that far more strikes in small-town Ontario resulted in defeat in the face of the relentless hostility of the employers, and that workers' resistance in general made few dents in local employment practices. Outside the metropolitan centres, the influence of the Knights seems to have been fleeting: two-thirds of the local assemblies across the province appeared in the five years between 1885 and 1889, and outside Toronto they were in decline in most places, including Hamilton, by 1888. In the seven district assemblies organized after 1885, 87 of the 137 local assemblies whose dates are known – that is, nearly two-thirds – lasted only three years or less. A significant minority died after only one or two years.[294] It is hard to see how this brief "upheaval" could have blunted the effect of industrial capitalism on the Ontario working class to any significant extent.[295] The reasons for this lack of success are not hard to find. Ontario's factory workers had to take their stand on the shaky ground of renewed large-scale unemployment[296] and in the face of dogged capitalist hostility. In these circumstances, they seemed to be quickly disillusioned with the Knights over their half-hearted strike leadership, partisan political squabbles, and insensitivity to craft-union prerogatives. The aggressive working-class consciousness and militancy soon ebbed away.

Weighing the Evidence

More than a century after the Labour Commission undertook its work, the efforts of the commissioners and so many of their contemporaries have helped us see the broad contours of labouring lives inside the new factory regime that had emerged in late nineteenth-century Ontario. A great deal more research in company records, local newspapers, unpublished census data, and so on will be necessary before the picture comes into sharper focus. But in the commissioners' work we can find some guideposts for understanding the process.

The transformation involved in this First Industrial Revolution disrupted much of the province's early nineteenth-century manufacturing practices. A large proportion of production was moved out of the household and artisanal workshop into new workplaces staffed by wage-earners. Wherever possible, aggressive industrial capitalists expanded their workforces and attempted to apply their workers' labour power more intensively. Their efforts included some combination of dilution of skill, subdivision of labour, mechanization, recruitment of poorly paid, unskilled workers, including women and children, and new supervisory techniques, from fines to piecework. The large new factories where these innovations were pushed furthest gave contemporaries the unmistakable sense of living through an industrial revolution (and historians the grounds for agreeing with them). Yet the transition to this new phase of industrial capitalism was more uneven among manufacturing industries and towns and less thoroughgoing than popular and academic notions of such a revolution might suggest. In fact, despite the many technological and managerial changes, the new factory regime continued to rely to a considerable extent on manual labour, both skilled and unskilled, especially in the many 'manufactories' that proliferated across the province. In only a small number of industrial situations could Ontario industrialists escape their need for manual skill by dissolving crafts into narrowly subdivided, mechanized jobs for unskilled operatives. They were hampered not only by the smallness of the markets, which made 'mass-production' difficult in so many sectors in Ontario, but also by the deepening ideological (and legal) constraints on their use of female and juvenile labour. They most often also had trouble finding the skilled labour they needed. Consequently Ontario industrialists tended to retain and adapt some form of industrial paternalism to hold onto and motivate their valuable workers.

Of course, the same conditions laid the groundwork for industrial conflict, first, between the most capitalistic owners of manufactories in the larger towns and the growing numbers of their increasingly well organized craft workers, and, then, as the promise of paternalism began to falter by the 1880s, between many more industrialists and all kinds of factory workers in towns and cities across the province, who were dismayed by the accelerated pace of change in their workplaces and in the capitalist labour market generally. By the 1880s workers were organizing in unprecedented numbers to try to impose some of the ethical constraints on the new industrial system that had begun to disappear with the decline of paternalism. Their resistance brought some concessions – higher wages and shorter hours in some cases, the first, quite limited labour-standards legislation – but it was floundering by the early 1890s. The industrial system was stabilized with a reinvigoration of paternalism where possible, but more often now with the more coercive power of an overstocked labour market to ensure compliance.

The Labour Commissioners developed a strong sense of this transformation from their trips through Ontario and the industrial towns of Quebec and the Maritimes. When they sat down to deliberate on the evidence they had gathered, they split roughly along class lines and issued separate majority and minority reports. The tone of these documents varied, but both saw the need for several government measures to make wage-earning in this new industrial economy slightly safer and more just. Unfortunately for the Ottawa millmen, bookbinders, and young labourers who took time off their jobs on 4 and 5 May 1888 to tell their stories to the commission, the Dominion government did not share this belief in state action to protect working people. It is perhaps fitting that this essay should be appearing exactly one century after the government's only legislative response to the commissioners' recommendations – the adoption of Labour Day.[297]

[The extensive tables attached to this article when originally published can be found in Paul Craven, *Labouring Lives: Work and Workers in Nineteenth-Century Ontario* (Toronto: University of Toronto Press 1995)].

Notes

1 *Ottawa Citizen* 3, 5 May 1888. On the Labour Commission see Greg Kealey, "Introduction," *Canada Investigates Industrialism: The Royal Commission on the Relations of Labor and Capital, 1889 (Abridged)* (Toronto: University of Toronto Press 1973), ix–xxvii.
2 Quoted in Steven Langdon, "The Political Economy of Capitalist Transformation: Central Canada from the 1840s to the 1870s" (MA thesis, Carleton University 1972), 107.
3 For a review of the evolving conceptualization, see David Cannadine, "The Present and the Past in the English Industrial Revolution, 1880–1980," *Past and Present* 103 (May 1984), 131–72.
4 Maxine Berg et al., eds., *Manufacture in Town and Country before the Factory* (Cambridge: Cambridge University Press 1983); L.A. Clarkson, *Proto-Industrialization: The First Phase of Industrialization* (London: Macmillan 1985).
5 See, in particular, Raphael Samuel, "The Workshop of the World: Steam Power and Hand Technology in Mid-Victorian Britain," *HW* 3 (Spring 1977), 6–72; Pat Hudson, "The Regional Perspective,' in Hudson, ed., *Regions and Industries: A Perspective on the Industrial Revolution in Britain* (Cambridge: Cambridge University Press 1989), 5–38.
6 For strong statements on the validity of the concept of an Industrial Revolution, see Pat Hudson, *The Industrial Revolution* (London: Edward Arnold 1992); and Peter Stearns, *The Industrial Revolution in World History* (Boulder: Westview Press 1993).
7 David M. Gordon, Richard Edwards, and Michael Reich, *Segmented Work, Divided Workers: The Historical Transformation of Labor in the United States* (New York: Cambridge University Press 1982); Gregory S. Kealey, "The Structure of Canadian Working Class History," in W.J.C. Cherwinski and Gregory S. Kealey, eds., *Lectures in Canadian Labour and Working Class History* (St John's: Committee on Canadian Labour History 1985), 23–36; Craig Heron and Robert Storey, "On the Job in Canada," in Heron and Storey, eds., *On the Job: Confronting the Labour Process in Canada* (Kingston and Montreal: McGill-Queen's University Press 1986), 3–46.
8 I have written about the Second Industrial Revolution elsewhere; see "The Second Industrial Revolution in Canada, 1890–1930,' in Deian Hopkin and Gregory S. Kealey, eds., *Class, Community, and the Labour Movement: Wales and Canada, 1850–1930* (Aberystwyth: Llafur and Committee on Canadian Labour History 1989), 48–66; "The Crisis of the Craftsman: Hamilton's Metal Workers in the Early Twentieth Century," *L/LT* 6 (Autumn 1980), 7–48; and *Working in Steel: The Early Years in Canada, 1883–1935* (Toronto: McClelland and Stewart 1988).

9 See, in particular, Judy Lown, *Women and Industrialization: Gender at Work in Nineteenth-Century England* (Cambridge: Polity Press 1990); Harold Benenson, "Victorian Sexual Ideology and Marx's Theory of the Working Class," *International Labor and Working-Class History* 25 (Spring 1984), 1–23; Sally Alexander, "Women, Class, and Sexual Differences in the 1830s and 1840s: Some Reflections on the Writing of a Feminist History," *HW*, no. 17 (Spring 1984), 125–49; Sonya O. Rose, "'Gender at Work': Sex, Class, and Industrial Capitalism," ibid., no. 2 1 (Spring l 986), 113–31.

10 See E.J. Hobsbawm, *Industry and Empire* (Harmondsworth: Penguin 1968); Ronald Aminzade, "Reinterpreting Capitalist Industrialization: A Study of Nineteenth-Century France," *SH* 9 (October 1984), 329–50; William Sewell, "Artisans, Factory Workers, and the Formation of the French Working Class, 1789–1848," in Ira Katznelson and Aristide R. Zolbereg, eds., *Working-Class Formation: Nineteenth-Century Patterns in Western Europe and the United States* (Princeton: Princeton University Press 1986), 45–70. For stimulating efforts to place Canada within a comparative framework, see Philip Ehrensaft and Warwick Armstrong, "The Formation of Dominion Capitalism: Economic Truncation and Class Structure," in Allen Moscovitch, ed., *Inequality: Essays on the Political Economy of Social Welfare* (Toronto: University of Toronto Press 1981); and Gordon Laxer, *Open for Business: The Roots of Foreign Ownership in Canada* (Toronto: Oxford University Press 1989).

11 Sidney Pollard, *Peaceful Conquest: The Industrialization of Europe, 1760–1970* (Oxford: Oxford University Press 1981); Hudson, "Regional Perspective"; Hudson, *Industrial Revolution.*

12 See John McCallum, *Unequal Beginnings: Agriculture and Economic Development in Quebec and Ontario until 1870* (Toronto: University of Toronto Press 1980); Gerald J.J. Tulchinsky, *The River Barons: Montreal Businessmen and the Growth of Industry and Transportation, 1837–53* (Toronto: University of Toronto Press 1977); Brian Young and John Dickinson, *A Short History of Quebec: A Socio-Economic Perspective* (Toronto: Copp Clark Pitman 1988); T.W. Acheson, "The National Policy and the Industrialization of the Maritimes, 1880–1910," in P.A. Buckner and David Frank, eds., *Atlantic Canada after Confederation: The Acadiensis Reader, Volume Two* (Fredericton: Acadiensis Press 1985), 176–201; Ian McKay, "Capital and Labour in the Halifax Baking and Confectionery Industry during the Last Half of the Nineteenth Century," *L/LT* 3 (1978), 63–108; L.D. McCann, "Staples and the New Industrialism in the Growth of Post-Confederation Halifax," *Acadiensis 8* (Spring 1979), 47–79; L.D. McCann, "The Mercantile Industrial Transition in the Metal Towns of Pictou County, 1857–1931," ibid., 10 (Spring 1981), 24; Robert Babcock,

"Economic Development in Portland (Me.) and Saint John (N.B.) during the Age of Iron and Steam, 1860–1914," *ARCS* 9 (Spring 1979), 1–37; Kris E. Inwood, "Maritime Industrialization from 1870 to 1910: A Review of the Evidence and Its Interpretation," *Acadiensis* 21 (Autumn 1991), 132–55; Phillip Wood, "Barriers to Capitalist Development in Maritime Canada, 1870–1930: A Comparative Perspective," in Peter Baskerville, ed., *Canadian Papers in Business History* (Victoria: Public History Group 1989), 33–58; Phillip Wood, "Marxism and the Maritimes: On the Determinants of Regional Capitalist Development," *SPE* 29 (Summer 1989), 123–53; John Lutz, "Losing Steam: The Boiler and Engine Industry as an Index of British Columbia's Deindustrialization, 1880–1915," *HP* 1988, 168–208.

13 Harold A. Innis, "An Introduction to the Economic History of Ontario from Outpost to Empire," in Mary Q. Innis, ed., *Essays in Canadian Economic History* (Toronto: University of Toronto Press 1956), 108–22. Similarly a textbook of primary documents in Canadian economic history prepared by Innis and A.R.M. Lower contains only the flimsiest scraps of evidence of industrialization, most of which involved resource processing; see *Select Documents in Canadian Economic History, 1783–1885* (Toronto: University of Toronto Press 1933).

14 The leading voice of this new school of economic historians was Tom Naylor, whose first essay on the subject ("The Third Commercial Empire of the St. Lawrence," in Gary Teeple, ed., *Capitalism and the National Question in Canada* [Toronto: University of Toronto Press 1972], 1–42) became extremely influential in the Canadian social sciences and grew into a factually unreliable two-volume study, *The History of Canadian Business* (Toronto: James Lorimer 1975). A much more respectable study of Ontario's resource industries by H.V. Nelles, *The Politics of Development: Forests, Mines, and Hydro-Electric Power in Ontario, 1849–1941* (Toronto: Macmillan 1974), inadvertently reinforced this overemphasis on "staples" at the expense of a fuller understanding of Ontario's industrialization. For critiques of this perspective, see L.R. Macdonald, "Merchants against Industry: An Idea and Its Origins," *CHR* 66 (September 1975), 263–81; Robin Neill, "The Politics and Economics of Development in Ontario," *OH* 70 (December 1978), 281–90.

15 Several Canadian neoclassical economists produced a flood of statistics in the 1960s on the timing of industrialization in Canada. The most important contributions were O.J. Firestone, *Canada's Economic Development* (London: Bowes and Bowes 1958), and "Development of Canada's Economy, 1850–1900," in *Trends in the American Economy in the Nineteenth Century* (Princeton: Princeton University Press 1960); G.W.

Bertram, "Economic Growth in Canadian Industry, 1870–1915: The Staple Model and the Take-Off Hypothesis," *CJEPS* 29 (May 1963), 159–84; G.W. Bertram, "Historical Statistics on Growth and Structure of Manufacturing in Canada, 1870–1957," in J. Henripin and A. Asimakopolas, eds., *Canadian Political Science Association Conference on Statistics, 1962 and 1963: Papers* (Toronto 1964), 93–146; J.H. Dales, "Estimates of Canadian Manufacturing Output by Markets, 1870–1915," ibid., 61–91; Edward J. Chambers and Gordon W. Bertram, "Urbanization and Manufacturing in Canada, 1870–1957," in Sylvia Ostry and T.K. Rhymes, eds., *Canadian Political Science Association, Conference on Statistics, 1964* (Toronto 1966), 225–57; and Robert E. Ankli, "Reciprocity Treaty of 1854," *Canadian Journal of Economics* 4 (February 1971), 21–33. The outcome of that debate was a recognition that decennial census statistics revealed steady, if erratic growth in Canadian manufacturing in the late nineteenth century. This consensus frames the more detailed work of Ian Drummond on the Ontario economy in *Progress without Planning: The Economic History of Ontario from Confederation to the Second World War* (Toronto: University of Toronto Press 1987). For a slightly less blinkered neoclassical perspective, see Douglas McCalla and Peter George, "Measurement, Myth, and Reality: Reflections on the Economic History of Nineteenth-Century Ontario," *JCS* 21 (Fall 1986), 71–86.

16 Stanley B. Ryerson, *Unequal Union: Confederation and the Roots of Conflict in the Canadas, 1815–1873* (Toronto: Progress Books 1968); H. Clare Pentland, "Labour and the Development of Industrial Capitalism in Canada" (PhD dissertation, University of Toronto 1961), later published in revised form as *Labour and Capital in Canada, 1650–1860* (Toronto: James Lorimer 1981).

17 Allan Greer, "Wage Labour and the Transition to Capitalism: A Critique of Pentland," *L/LT* 15 (Spring 1985), 7–24.

18 Stephen Langdon, "The Emergence of the Canadian Working Class Movement, 1845–75," *JCS* 8 (May 1973), 3–13, and 8 (August 1973), 8–24; see also Robert H. Storey, 'Industrialization in Canada: The Emergence of the Hamilton Working Class, 1850-1870s' (MA thesis, Dalhousie University 1975).

19 Bryan D. Palmer, *A Culture in Conflict: Skilled Workers and Industrial Capitalism in Hamilton, Ontario, 1860–1914* (Montreal: McGill-Queen's University Press 1979); Gregory S. Kealey, *Toronto Workers Respond to Industrial Capitalism, 1867–1892* (Toronto: University of Toronto Press 1980); Gregory S. Kealey and Bryan D. Palmer, *Dreaming of What Might Be: The Knights of Labor in Ontario, 1880–1900* (New York: Cambridge University Press 1982).

20 Marjorie Griffin Cohen, *Women's Work, Markets, and Economic Development in Nineteenth-Century Ontario* (Toronto: University of Toronto Press 1988); see also Janice Acton et al., eds., *Women at Work: Ontario, 1850–1930* (Toronto: Canadian Women's Educational Press 1974).

21 Robert Gourlay, *Statistical Account of Upper Canada* (London 1822; abridged edition Toronto: McClelland and Stewart 1974); Edwin C. Guillet, *Pioneer Arts and Crafts* (Toronto: University of Toronto Press 1968); Felicity L. Leung, *Grist and Flour Mills in Ontario: From Millstones to Rollers, 1780s–1880s* (Ottawa: Parks Canada 1981); Elizabeth Price, "The Changing Geography of the Woollen Industry in Lanark, Renfrew and Carleton Counties, 1830–1911" (Master's research paper, University of Toronto 1979); Mary Quayle Innis, "The Industrial Development of Ontario, 1783–1820,' in J.K. Johnson, ed., *Historical Essays on Upper Canada* (Toronto: McClelland and Stewart 1975), 140–52; Douglas McCalla, *Planting the Province: The Economic History of Upper Canada, 1784–1870* (Toronto: University of Toronto Press 1993); Sidney Thomson Fisher, *The Merchant Millers of the Humber Valley: A Study in the Early Economy of Canada* (Toronto 1985); Leo Johnson, *History of the County of Ontario, 1615–1875* (Whitby: The Corporation of the County of Ontario 1973), 38–81; W. John McIntyre, "From Workshop to Factory: The Furnituremaker,' *MHB 19* (Spring 1984), 25–8; Thomas McIlwraith, "The Adequacy of Rural Roads in the Era before Railways: An Illustration from Upper Canada," *Canadian Geographer* 14 (1970), 344–60; Thomas McIlwraith, "Transportation in the Landscape of Early Upper Canada," in J. David Wood, ed., *Perspectives on Landscape and Settlement in Nineteenth-Century Ontario* (Toronto: McClelland and Stewart 1975), 51–63; James Herbert Bartlett, *The Manufacture, Consumption and Production of Iron, Steel and Coal in the Dominion of Canada, with Some Notes on the Manufacture of Iron and on the Iron Trade, in Other Countries* (Montreal: Dawson 1885); T. Ritchie, "Joseph Van Norman, Ironmaster of Upper Canada," *CGJ* 78 (August 1968), 46–51.

22 Pentland, *Labour and Capital*; McCalla, *Planting the Province*; Johnson, *Ontario County*, 128–71; Allan Greer and Ian Radforth, eds., *Colonial Leviathan: State Formation in Nineteenth-Century Canada* (Toronto: University of Toronto Press 1991); Bruce Curtis, *True Government by Choice Men? Inspection, Education, and State Formation in Canada West* (Toronto: University of Toronto Press 1992); Leo Johnson, "Land Policy, Population Growth, and Social Structure in the Home District, 1793–1851," in J.K. Johnson, ed., *Historical Essays*, 32–57; Gary Teeple, "Land, Labour, and Capital in Pre-Confederation Canada," in Teeple, *Capitalism*

and the National Question, 43–6; Graeme Wynn, "Notes on Society and Environment in Old Ontario," *JSH* 13 (Fall 1979), 49–65.

23 Leung, *Flour and Grist Mills*; W.P.J. Millar, "George P.M. Ball: A Rural Businessman in Upper Canada," *OH* 66 (June 1974), 65–78; Fisher, *Merchant Millers*; Price, "Changing Geography"; North Lanark Historical Society, *The Development of the Woollen Industry in Lanark, Renfrew and Carleton Counties* (Erin: Porcupine's Quill 1978); McCalla, *Planting the Province*, 94–104.

24 McCalla, *Planting the Province*; Robert Leslie Jones, *History of Agriculture in Ontario, 1613–1880* (Toronto: University of Toronto Press 1946); J.A. Ruddick, "The Development of the Dairy Industry in Canada," in H.A. Innis, ed., *The Dairy Industry in Canada* (Toronto: Ryerson Press 1937), 15–123; D.A. Lawr, "The Development of Ontario Farming, 1870–1919," *OH* 64 (December 1972), 239–51; Robert Ankli and Wendy Millar, "Ontario Agriculture in Transition: The Switch from Wheat to Cheese," *JEH* 42 (1982), 207–15; Marvin McInnis, "The Changing Structure of Canadian Agriculture, 1867–1897," ibid., 191–8; Michael Bliss, *A Canadian Millionaire: The Life and Business Times of Sir Joseph Flavelle, Bart., 1858–1939* (Toronto: Macmillan 1978), 27–52. Kris Inwood and Tim Sullivan raise questions about the link between agricultural "improvement" and industrialization; see "Comparative Perspectives on Nineteenth-Century Growth: Ontario in the Great Lakes Region," in Peter Baskerville, ed., *Canadian Papers in Business History*, vol. 2 (Victoria: Public History Group, University of Victoria 1993), 71–101.

25 W.H. Smith, *Canada: Past, Present and Future, Being a Historical, Geographical, Geological and Statistical Account of Canada West* (Toronto: Thomas MacLear 1851); Jacob Spelt, *Urban Development in South-Central Ontario* (Toronto: McClelland and Stewart 1972), 55–100; A.R.M. Lower, *Settlement and the Forest Frontier in Eastern Canada* (Toronto: Ryerson 1936); A.R.M. Lower, *The North American Assault on the Canadian Forest: A History of the Lumber Trade between Canada and the United States* (Toronto: Ryerson 1938), 27–52; Michael S. Cross, "The Lumber Community of Upper Canada, 1815–1867," *OH* 52 (November 1960), 213–32; Richard M. Reid, "Introduction," *The Upper Ottawa Valley to 1855* (Ottawa: Carleton University Press 1990), xlvii–lxxiii; James T. Angus, *A Deo Victoria: The Story of the Georgian Bay Lumber Company, 1871–1942* (Thunder Bay: Severn Publications 1990); McCallum, *Unequal Beginnings*, 9–74; Leung, *Grist and Flour Mills*; Fisher, *Merchant-Millers*; Drummond, *Progress without Planning*, 93–7; Elizabeth Bloomfield and Gerald Bloomfield, *Industrial Leaders: The Largest Manufacturing Firms of Ontario in 1871* (Guelph: University of Guelph, Department of

Geography, Canadian Industry in 1871 Project 1989), 45; Dianne Newell, *Technology on the Frontier: Mining in Old Ontario* (Vancouver: UBC Press 1986); Edward Phelps, "Foundations of the Canadian Oil Industry, 1850–1866," in Edith Firth, ed., *Profiles of a Province: Studies in the History of Ontario* (Toronto: Ontario Historical Society 1967), 156–65; W.E. Brett Code, "The Salt Men of Goderich in Ontario's Court of Chancery: *Ontario Salt Co. v. Merchants Salt Co.* and the Judicial Enforcement of Combinations,' *McGill Law Journal* 38 (1993).

26 See, for example, *Citizen* (Otawa), 12 March 1852.

27 Peter Baskerville, "Donald Bethune's Steamboat Business: A Study of Upper Canadian Commercial and Financial Practice," *OH* 67 (1975), 135–49; George Richardson, "The Canadian Locomotive Company," in Gerald Tulchinsky, ed., *To Preserve and Defend: Essays on Kingston in the Nineteenth Century* (Montreal: McGill-Queen's University Press 1976), 157–67; William Kilbourn, *The Elements Combined: A History of the Steel Company of Canada* (Toronto: Clarke Irwin 1960), 33–62; Paul Craven and Tom Traves, "Canadian Railways as Manufacturers, 1850–1880," *HP* 1983, 254–81.

28 W.G. Phillips, *The Agricultural Implement Industry in Canada: A Study of Competition* (Toronto: University of Toronto Press 1956); Merrill Denison, *Harvest Triumphant: The Story of Massey-Harris* (Toronto: Collins 1949).

29 Gerald Tulchinsky, "Aspects of the Clothing Industry in Canada, 1850s to 1914" (paper presented to the Business History Conference, Trent University, 1984); Gerald Tulchinsky, "Hidden among the Smokestacks: Toronto's Clothing Industry, 1871–1901," in David Keane and Colin Read, eds., *Old Ontario: Essays in Honour of J.M..S. Careless* (Toronto: Dundurn 1990), 257–84; Peter Bischoff, "Tensions et solidarité: La formation des traditions syndicales chez les mouleurs de Montréal, Hamilton et Toronto, 1851 à 1893" (PhD dissertation, Université de Montréal 1992), 35–77; McIntyre, "From Workshop to Factory"; Joan MacKinnon, *A Checklist of Toronto Cabinet and Chair Makers, 1800–1865* (Ottawa: Parks Canada 1975); John Hall, "One Hundred Years of Piano Making in Kingston," *Historic Kingston* 39 (1991), 36–51; Wayne Kelly, *Downright Upright: A History of the Canadian Piano Industry* (Toronto: Natural Heritage/Natural History 1991); Martha Eckmann Brent, "A Stitch in Time: The Sewing Machine Industry of Ontario, 1860–1897," *MHB* 10 (Spring 1980), 1–30; Thomas L. Walkom, "The Daily Newspaper in Ontario's Developing Capitalist Economy: Toronto and Ottawa, 1871-1911" (PhD dissertation, University of Toronto 1983).

30 T.W. Acheson, "The Social Origins of the Canadian Industrial Elite, 1880–1885," in David S. Macmillan, ed., *Canadian Business History: Selected Studies, 1497–1971* (Toronto: McClelland and Stewart 1972), 143–74.

31 There is no space here for an extensive digression on the question of the alleged conflict between industrial and commercial capital in this period, first argued by Tom Naylor and subsequently repeated by many other social scientists. There is now plenty of evidence to establish that no such split took place, that indeed merchants in many communities invested heavily in the new factories, and that the alleged American domination of manufacturing was still many decades in the future. For examples in specific industries and industrial centres, see Macdonald, "Merchants against Industry"; Kealey, *Toronto Workers;* Kris Inwood, "Inter Sectoral Linkages: The Case of Secondary Iron and Steel" (paper presented to the Canadian Business History Conference, May 1984); David G. Burley, "The Businessmen of Brantford, Ontario: Self-Employment in a Mid-Nineteenth Century Town" (PhD dissertation, McMaster University 1983).
32 Elizabeth Bloomfield and G.T. Bloomfield, *Patterns of Canadian Industry in 1871: An Overview Based on the First Census of Canada* (Guelph: University of Guelph, Department of Geography, Canadian Industry in 1871 Project, Research Report 12 1990), 28–30.
33 Elizabeth Bloomfield, *Water Wheels and Steam Engines*, 8.
34 Canada, Royal Commission on the Relations of Labour and Capital, *Report – Evidence, Ontario* (hereafter RCRLC), 1062; Ontario, Bureau of Industries, *Report* (hereafter OBIR), 1887, 39; 1889, 16; Knowles, "Beyond Domesticity," 104.
35 RCRLC, 743, 1 185; *Canadian Manufacturer*, 30 June 1882, 258.
36 *Canadian Manufacturer*, 21 July 1882, 355; September 1882, 546; Angus, *A Deo Victoria*; RCRLC, 261, 707, 882, 891, 1137, 1176; Ontario, Inspectors of Factories, *Report* (hereafter OIFR), 1888, 10, 1891, 7; Canada, House of Commons, *Journals* (Ottawa), vol. 10 (1876), App. 3 ("Select Committee on the Causes of the Present Depression of the Manufacturing, Mining, Commercial, Shipping, Lumber and Fishing Interests, Report") (hereafter Select Committee on the Causes of the Present Depression), 115.
37 RCRLC, 666, 685, 743, 784, 794, 842, 885, 936, 953, 1130, 1185; see also OBIR, 1889, 16; OIFR, 1889, 7, 40.
38 The pessimistic view of the period and the optimistic revisionism are set out in, respectively, O.D. Skelton, *General Economic History of the Dominion, 1867–1912* (Toronto: Publishers' Associates 1913); and Drummond, *Progress without Planning*, 103–33. For a statistical outline of business cycles based on the extremely limited data available from the late nineteenth century, see Edward J. Chambers, "Late Nineteenth Century Business Cycles in Canada," *CJEPS* 30 (August 1964), 391–412; for more qualitative discussions of unemployment in the period, see OBIR, 1884–90; OIFR,

1888–90; Debi Wells, "'The Hardest Lines of the Sternest School': Working Class Ottawa in the Depression of the 1870s" (MA thesis, Carleton University 1982); James M. Pitsula, "The Treatment of Tramps in Late Nineteenth Century Toronto," *HP* 1980, 111–32; Richard Anderson, "'The Irrepressible Stampede': Tramps in Ontario, 1870–1880,' *OH* 84 (March 1992), 33–56.

39 McInnis, "Marketable Surpluses in Ontario Farming, 1860," in Douglas McCalla, ed., *Perspectives on Canadian Economic History* (Toronto: Copp Clark Pitman 1987), 37–57.

40 Of the province's sixty leading industrial firms in 1871, thirty-seven had ceased operation by the end of the century. Bloomfield and Bloomfield, *Industrial Leaders*, 53.

41 Ibid., 46; Elinor Kyte Senior, *From Royal Township to Industrial City: Cornwall, 1784–1984* (Belleville: Mika Publishing 1983).

42 Bloomfield and Bloomfield, *Industrial Leaders*, 13, 62–3; *Census of Canada*, 1891, vol. 3. Some calculations are mine.

43 A.H. Blackeby, *Report on the State of the Manufacturing Interests of Ontario and Quebec* (Ottawa: Queen's Printer 1885); RCRLC, 354; Kealey, *Toronto Workers*; Ben Forster, *A Conjunction of Interests: Business, Politics, and Tariffs, 1825–1879* (Toronto: University of Toronto Press 1986); Ben Forster, "Finding the Right Size: Markets and Competition in Mid- and Late-Nineteenth-Century Ontario," in Roger Hall, William Westfall, and Laurel Sefton MacDowell, eds., *Patterns of the Past: Interpreting Ontario's History* (Toronto: Dundurn Press 1988), 150–73.

44 RCRLC, 494.

45 James M. Gilmour, *Spatial Evolution of Manufacturing: Southern Ontario, 1851–1891* (Toronto: University of Toronto Press 1972).

46 Elizabeth and Gerald Bloomfield, *The Ontario Urban System at the Onset of the Industrial Era* (Guelph: Canadian Industry in 1871 Project, Research Report 3, Department of Geography, University of Guelph, 1989), 26; Elizabeth and Gerald Bloomfield, *The Hum of Industry: Millers, Manufacturers and Artisans of Wellington County* (Guelph: Canadian Industry in 1871 Project, Research Report 9, Department of Geography, University of Guelph 1989); Joy Parr, *Gender of Breadwinners: Women, Men, and Change in Two Industrial Towns, 1880–1950* (Toronto: University of Toronto Press 1990); Kelly, *Downright Upright*; Spelt, *Urban Development*; Johnson, *County of Ontario*; Johnson, *The History of Guelph, 1827–1927* (Guelph: Guelph Historical Society 1977); John English and Kenneth McLaughlin, *Kitchener: An Illustrated History* (Waterloo: Wilfrid Laurier University Press 1983). By 1871 the province's leading producers of

agricultural implements were spread through such towns as Oshawa, Mitchell, Smith's Falls, Ingersoll, Brampton, Newcastle, Aurora, Gananoque, Bradford, Dundas, St Mary's, Belleville, Napanee, Strathroy, New Hamburg, Waterloo, Brockville, Seaforth, Milton, Galt, Clinton, Caledonia, Chatham, Lindsay, London, and St Catharines. Elizabeth and Gerald Bloomfield, "Mills, Factories, and Craftshops of Ontario, 1870: A Machine-Readable Source for Material Historians," *MHB* 25 (1987), 44. By no means all small towns made this leap into the industrial age; Bloomfield and Bloomfield found that in 1871 only 67 of 148 urban and "proto-urban" places in Ontario had at least one factory and only 23 had at least one manufactory; see *Ontario Urban System*, 34; also Stephen Edward Thorning, "T.E. Bissell of Elora, Ontario: A Small Town Manufacturer and His Milieu' (MA thesis, McMaster University 1986), 15; OBIR, 1884, lxix. On the continuity of small-scale producers, see Gordon Darroch, "Class in Nineteenth Century Ontario: A Reassessment of the Crisis and Demise of Small Producers during Early Industrialization, 1861–1871,' in Gregory S. Kealey, ed., *Class, Gender and Region: Essays in Canadian Historical Sociology* (St John's: Committee on Canadian Labour History 1988), 49–72.

47 J.M.S. Careless, "Some Aspects of Urbanization in Nineteenth-Century Ontario," in P.H. Armstrong et al., eds., *Aspects of Nineteenth-Century Ontario: Essays Presented to James J. Talman* (Toronto: University of Toronto Press 1974), 65–79; Frederick H. Armstrong and Daniel J. Brock, "The Rise of London: A Study of Urban Evolution in Nineteenth-Century Southwestern Ontario," ibid., 80–100; Langdon, "Political Economy," 88–94; Kealey, *Toronto Workers*, 18–34; Douglas McCalla, *The Upper Canada Trade, 1834–1872: A Study of the Buchanans' Business* (Toronto: University of Toronto Press 1979); Douglas McCalla, "The Decline of Hamilton as a Wholesale Centre," *OH* 65 (1973); John C. Weaver, *Hamilton: An Illustrated History* (Toronto: James Lorimer 1982), 41–77.

48 Craven and Traves, "Canadian Railways as Manufacturers"; Richardson, "Canadian Locomotive Company."

49 Bloomfield and Bloomfield, *Industrial Leaders*, 30–3.

50 Ibid., 26; Gilmour, *Spatial Evolution*, 121–52; Warren R. Bland, "The Location of Manufacturing in Southern Ontario in 1881," *Ontario Geography* 8 (1974), 8–39; Edward J. Chambers and Gordon W. Bertram, "Urbanization and Manufacturing in Central Canada, 1870– 1890," in Sylvia Ostry and T.K. Rymes, eds., *Canadian Political Science Association, Conference on Statistics, 1964* (Toronto 1966), 225–57; John C. Weaver, "The Location of Manufacturing Enterprises: The Case of Hamilton's Attraction of Foundries, 1830–1890," in Richard A. Jarrell and Arnold E. Ross, eds.,

Critical Issues in the History of Canadian Science, Technology, and Medicine (Thornhill: HSTC 1983); Bischoff, "Tensions et solidarité," 44–60; Randy William Widdis, "Belleville and Environs: Continuity, Change, and the Integration of Town and Country during the 19th Century," *UHR* 19 (February 1991), 181–208.

51 Gordon Laxer pursues the implications of this gap in the industrial structure in *Open for Business.*

52 Kilbourn, *Elements Combined*, 41.

53 There has not been much careful research of pre-industrial wage-earning in Upper Canada before 1840. This sketch is based on Pentland, *Labour and Capital*; Peter A. Russell, "Wage Labour Rates in Upper Canada, 1818–1840," *HS/SH* 16 (May 1983), 61–80; McCalla, *Planting the Province*, 92–115; William N.T. Wylie, "The Blacksmith in Upper Canada, 1784–1850: A Study of Technology, Culture, and Power," *Canadian Papers in Rural History* 7 (1990), 50–3; Elijah Leonard, *A Memoir* (London: Advertiser Printing n.d.); Innis and Lower, *Select Documents*, 296–7; Sally Zerker, *The Rise and Fall of the Toronto Typographical Union, 1832–1972: A Case Study of Foreign Domination* (Toronto: University of Toronto Press 1982), 3–49; McIntyre, "From Workshop to Factory"; Upper Canada, House of Assembly, *Journal*, 1836, vol. 3, App.102 (thanks to Paul Craven for this reference); Bryan Palmer, "Kingston Mechanics and the Rise of the Penitentiary, 1833–1836," *HS/SH* 13 (May 1980), 7–82; Jeremy Webber, "Labour and the Law," in Paul Craven, ed., *Labouring Lives: Work and Workers in Nineteenth-Century Ontario* (Toronto: University of Toronto Press 1995), 105–201. Rusty Bitterman's stimulating new work on pre-industrial wage-earning in Nova Scotia is suggestive of new directions that research on Ontario could fruitfully take; see Bitterman, "Farm Households and Wage Labour in the Northeastern Maritimes in the Early 19th Century," *L/LT* 31 (Spring 1993), 13–45. The Lower Canadian artisanal experience has been covered more fully in Pierre H. Audet, "Apprentices in Early Nineteenth Century Montreal, 1790–1812" (MA thesis, Concordia University 1976); Jean-Pierre Hardy and David-Thiery Ruddell, *Les apprentis artisans à Québec: 1660–1815* (Montreal: Les Presses de l'Université du Québec 1977); Joanne Burgess, "Work, Family, and Community: Montreal Leather Craftsmen, 1790–1831" (PhD dissertation, Université du Québec à Montréal 1986); Grace Laing Hogg, "The Legal Rights of Masters, Mistresses, and Domestic Servants in Montreal, 1816–1829" (MA thesis, McGill University 1989).

54 A considerable variety of "factories" appeared in Ontario, as elsewhere. The term itself was certainly not used precisely. In the 1860s "manufactory" was more common to describe the new larger units

of manufacturing, while "factory" seemed to have a more specialized meaning alongside "mill" – cheese factories and so on, none of which were necessarily large or highly mechanized. By the 1880s, factory seems to have become the standard term for the industrial capitalist workplace, while "workshop" had come to mean something much smaller and run on distinctly different lines. For the contrast, see, for example, the *Journal* of the Board of Arts and Manufactures in the 1860s and the reports of the Ontario factory inspectors in the 1880s.

55 Bartlett, *Manufacture.*

56 In the 1850s and 1860s, for example, Toronto's largest foundries each manufactured a considerable variety of iron goods – stoves, hollowware, engines, and sundry milling machinery. Only in the 1860s, at the time of railway expansion and the boost given to the economy by the American Civil War, was there a marked increase in specialization of production, and then only in some sectors – notably boots and shoes, woollen textiles, agricultural implements, and sewing machines. Nonetheless, even the province's largest agricultural-implement plant, the Joseph Hall works in Oshawa, which employed over three hundred men in 1872, was also producing an extensive line of other industrial machinery, including printing presses. *Globe*, 13 December 1856; *Mail* (Toronto), 8 April 1872; Bischoff, "Tensions et solidarité," 46.

57 *Census of Canada* (Ottawa), 1871, vol. 3, x; Canada, House of Commons, *Journals* (Ottawa), vol. 8 (1874), App.3 ("Select Committee Appointed to Enquire into and Report to the House on the Extent and Condition of the Manufacturing Interests of the Dominion") (hereafter Select Committee on Manufacturing Interests); and Select Committee on the Causes of the Present Depression; RCRLC, 674. It was not usual for companies to specialize in only one part of their operation; for example, the huge Jacques and Hay factory in Toronto in the 1860s mass-produced chairs but made much smaller runs of other furniture; Board of Art and Manufactures of Upper Canada, *Journal* (Toronto) (hereafter BAMUCJ), July 1864, 194–5.

58 *Free Press* (London), 17 January 1864, 12 September 1870; Kealey, *Toronto Workers*, 46–7.

59 Pollin, "Jacques and Hay," 9–10, 24–5, 29–30; Kealey, *Toronto Workers*; Parr, *Gender of Breadwinnners.*

60 Elizabeth and Gerald Bloomfield have attempted to refine the concept of manufactory by separating out those that, according to the 1871 census, had water or steam power and those with more than twenty-five workers (see *Hum of Industry*, 39–40). Their elegant schema of factories, manufactories,

mills, powered craftshops, and so on, however, does not seem helpful for understanding the evolving factory system in the period. In the first place, the presence of inanimate power tells us nothing about how it was being used in the labour process – often much of the production process remained manual, or the machinery simply allowed for more precision in skilled work (especially among machinists). And equally important, in 1871 few enterprises were so specialized that their whole operations could be easily slotted into one category – as we will see, powered machinery in one department might have no counterpart in another. For these reasons, I will continue to use the term "manufactory" as a broad, relatively loose term to indicate workplaces where skilled workers still exercised significant amounts of manual control over the labour process.

61 RCRLC, 67.

62 Bischoff, "Tensions et solidarité"; Gregory S. Kealey, "Work Control, the Labour Process, and Nineteenth-Century Canadian Printers," in Heron and Storey, eds., *On the Job*, 75–101; RCRLC, 608–9, 1118.

63 W. Craig Heron, "Working-Class Hamilton, 1895–1930" (PhD dissertation, Dalhousie University 1981).

64 Bischoff, "Tensions et solidarité," 51; RCRLC, 608. For drawings of a fitter in the Massey plant, see *Massey's Illustrated* 1 (May 1889), inside front cover, and Massey-Harris Co., *Visitors' Souvenir* ([Toronto] n.d.), in Ontario Agricultural Museum (hereafter OAM), Massey-Ferguson Collection, MH 154.

65 Kealey, "Work Control"; Bischoff, "Tensions et solidarité"; Palmer, *Culture in Conflict*.

66 *Globe*, 10 April 1871, quoted in Langdon, "Emergence," 16.

67 BAMUCJ, May 1862, 137; December 1865, 310; *Canadian Illustrated News*, 17 January 1863, 112; *Spectator* (Hamilton), 22 December 1870 (quoted in Palmer, *Culture in Conflict*, 16).

68 RCRLC, 336.

69 *Globe*, 28 October 1868; Select Committee on Manufacturing Interests, 17; RCRLC, 629, 829; A.W. Wright, *Report upon the Sweating System in Canada* (Ottawa: Queen's Printer 1896); W.L. Mackenzie King, *Report to the Honourable Postmaster General on the Methods Adopted in Canada in the Carrying Out of Government Clothing Contracts* (Ottawa: Queen's Printer 1898); Tulchinsky, "Hidden among the Smokestacks," 272–6; Robert Mcintosh, "Sweated Labour: Female Needleworkers in Industrializing Canada," *L/LT* 32 (Fall 1993), 105–38.

70 BAMUCJ, May 1862, 137; *Canadian Illustrated News*, 17 January 1863, 112. Penman's knitting mill in Paris may also have had "inside" and "outside" employees; see Knowles, "Beyond Domesticity," 170–1.

71 Bloomfield and Bloomfield, *Industrial Leaders*, 33–4. Water power was by no means a declining technology across Ontario. The abundance of streams cascading down to the lakefront made it an abundant source, and several communities developed water power canals in order to attract factories. Moreover, all but eight of the forty-three largest consumers of power in the province in 1871, the overwhelming majority of them saw and flour mills, used water power (one used both water and steam). Steam engines tended to have smaller capacity (typically 20 h.p.) but to be more flexible. More industrial workers would have encountered them in 1871: of the 48 per cent of the Ontario industrial workforce that worked in establishments with either form of power, twice as many (32 per cent) found steam rather than water power on the premises. The larger the town, the more likely was steam to be the motive power, reaching 95 per cent in Toronto and 98 per cent in Hamilton.

72 BAMUCJ, March 1863, 84; January 1864, 1.

73 Select Committee on the Causes of the Present Depression, 115–16.

74 For descriptions of the technology and division of labour in Ontario's textile mills, see BAMUCJ, September 1864, 255–7; July 1866, 198–9; RCRLC, 892–3; A.B. McCullough, *The Primary Textile Industry in Canada: History and Heritage* (Ottawa: Environment Canada, Parks Service, National Historic Sites 1992), 13–23.

75 John W. Hughson and Courtney C.J. Bond, *Hurling Down the Pine: The Story of the Wright, Gilmour and Hughson Families, Timber and Lumber Manufacturers in the Hull and Ottawa Region and on the Gatineau River, 1800–1920* (Old Chelsea, Quebec: Historical Society of the Gatineau 1965), 68–78; McIntyre, "From Workshop to Factory," 32; Angus, *A Deo Victoria*, 87–8; Charlotte Whitton, *A Hundred Years A-Fellin': Some Passages from the Timber Saga of the Ottawa in the Century in Which the Gillies Have Been Cutting in the Valley, 1842–1942* (Ottawa: Runge Press [1943]), 141–2; Jack Brown, *The Sawmills of Lanark and Renfrew* (Mallorytown: Author 1976); Donald M. Wilson, *Lost Horizons: The Story of the Rathbun Company and the Bay of Quinte Railway* (Belleville: Mika Publishing 1983), 18; Barbara R. Robertson, *Sawpower: Making Lumber in the Sawmills of Nova Scotia* (Halifax: Nimbus Publishing and the Nova Scotia Museum 1986).

76 Kealey, *Toronto Workers*, 39–40; Storey, "Industrialization"; Palmer, *Culture in Conflict*, 12. Technological change in the clothing industry would continue in the late nineteenth-century with special adaptations for pocket stitching and buttonholing, steam-powered cutting, gas-heated pressing, and other minor modifications. Tulchinsky, "Aspects of Clothing Manufacturing," 13–14.

77 See, for example, *Citizen* (Ottawa), 27 November 1852 (Ottawa woodworking factory); *Canadian Illustrated News*, 3 January 1863, 95 (Taylor safe works, Toronto); *Spectator* (Hamilton), 1 May 1871 (Wanzer's sewing machine factory, Hamilton); *Mail* (Toronto), 15 April 1872 (Canada Tool Works, Dundas); *Globe*, 3 September 1888 (Massey works, Toronto).

78 William Chambers, *Things as They Are in America* (London and Edinburgh 1854), 115 (quoted in McIntyre, "From Workshop to Factory"); BAMUCJ, July 1864, 194–5; RCRLC, 508, 1117. Similar woodworking machinery was reported frequently in testimony to the Labour Commission; see pp. 403, 422–3, 442, 462, 467, 509, 530–1, 607–10, 623–6, 647, 939, 947.

79 See, for example, *Almonte Gazette*, 16 July 1870, 26 July 1872, 27 June, 4 July 1873, 20 March 1874 (courtesy of Elizabeth Price); Eric Tucker, *Administering Danger in the Workplace: The Law and Politics of Occupational Health and Safety Regulation in Ontario, 1850–1914* (Toronto: University of Toronto Press 1990), 15–37.

80 *Globe*, 3 September 1888.

81 Amidst the voluminous commission testimony on technological change, see in particular RCRLC, 9–10, 38, 55, 61, 114–15, 124, 130, 141, 354–5, 443, 461–3, 472, 490, 509, 566, 596, 663, 669, 671, 677, 826, 884, 925, 929, 930, 980–2, 1034, 1117.

82 RCRLC, 490, 826.

83 Samuel, "Workshop of the World." Stephen Langdon's preliminary discussion of the First Industrial Revolution put too much emphasis on mechanization; see "Political Economy," 102–6, and "Emergence."

84 BAMUCJ, September 1864, 257.

85 Pollin, "Jacques and Hay," 28.

86 The main exception was the sewing-machine industry, where the tiny parts required encouraged the introduction of some mechanization in the 1870s and 1880s. The giant Massey agricultural-implement works did not have any moulding machines until 1889. Bischoff, "Tensions et solidarité," 95–8; Kealey, *Toronto Workers*, 75.

87 Kealey, "Work Control."

88 Massey-Ferguson Collection; Bischoff, "Tensions et solidarité"; Kealey, "Work Control"; *Northern Advance*, 8 December 1863, 19 September 1866; BAMUCJ, July 1864, 194; RCRLC, 997.

89 Palmer, *Culture in Conflict*, 75–6.

90 RCRLC, 261, 400, 489; Kealey, *Toronto Workers*, 53–63.

91 They presented plenty of evidence to the Labour Commission that too many incompetent men ran steam engines and boilers and that public safety was consequently in danger. RCRLC, 207, 257–8.

92 Leung, *Grist and Flour Mills*; Hughson and Bond, *Hurling Down the Pine*, 75–6; *Northern Advance*, 27 August 1857, 15 August 1860; *Free Press* (London), 8 July 1865, 15 October, 4 November, 2 December 1868. RCRLC, 377, 490.

93 RCRLC, 786.

94 BAMUCJ, July 1864, 195. On the continuing skill requirements in furniture manufacture, see Parr, *Gender of Breadwinners*; Forster, "Finding the Right Size"; Ruth Cathcart, *Jacques and Hay: 19th Century Toronto Furniture Makers* (Erin: Boston Mills Press 1986), 31.

95 RCRLC, 893.

96 Ibid., 884.

97 OBIR, 1886, 205. Similarly, the Dominion Starch Works took its experienced workforce with it when it moved from Edwardsburg to Walkerville. RCRLC, 379.

98 RCRLC, 327, 762, 880–1.

99 Ibid., 287, 536, 1171, 1173.

100 Knowles, "Beyond Domesticity," 39, 96–8; Parr, *Gender of Breadwinners*, 15–17; Committee on the Causes of the Present Depression, 146.

101 The flour mills were mechanized quite early in the nineteenth century, the sawmills from the 1850s onward. Leung, *Grist and Flour Mills*; Angus, *A Deo Victoria*, 88–9; Whitton, *A Hundred Years A-Fellin'*, 141–2; Wilson, *Lost Horizons*, 18; Clyde C. Kennedy, *The Upper Ottawa Valley: A Glimpse of History* (Pembroke: Renfrew County Council 1970), 125–9.

102 BAMUCJ, January 1864, 1; W.A. Child, "Iron Trade Built by Determined Men," *Spectator* (Hamilton), 15 July 1926. The Joseph Hall works reported only one six-ton steam hoist in its large agricultural-implement factory in Oshawa in 1872 in the midst of over three hundred workers (*Mail*, 8 April 1872). A detailed drawing of the huge Massey machine shop in Toronto in the 1880s showed manual lifting and carrying (OAM, Massey-Ferguson Collection, MM 127).

103 Bischoff, "Tensions et solidarité," 19–20; Price, "Changing Geography," 62 and App.A; North Lanark Historical Society, *Development of the Woollen Industry*, 13; Burley, "Businessmen of Brantford." In 1870 a British stonemason, Thomas Connolly, wrote to the Ontario minister of agriculture and public works to express his favourable impressions of industrial prospects in Ontario after a tour through the province earlier that year; among his observations, he noted that a mechanic's "chance to become an employer or the owner of property is much greater" than in Britain; Ontario, Commissioner of Agriculture and Public Works, *Annual Report on Immigration* (Toronto), 1870, 28. Bryan Palmer has shown how

these artisanal businesses could be perilous, however, and David Burley has revealed that they were much harder to start up by the 1870s; Palmer, *Culture in Conflict*, 13–14; Burley, "Businessmen of Brantford," 133–71.

104 H.C. Pentland has probably overstated the ease with which a capitalist labour market came into being in this period; see *Labour and Capital.*

105 RCRLC, 478, 535, 623; Zerker, *Rise and Fall*; Bischoff, "Tensions et solidarité," 134–43, 171–207; Michael B. Katz, *The People of Hamilton, Canada West: Family and Class in a Mid-Nineteenth-Century City* (Cambridge: Harvard University Press 1975); Michael B. Katz et al., *The Social Organization of Early Industrial Capitalism;* A. Gordon Darroch, "Migrants in the Nineteenth Century: Fugitives or Families in Motion?" *Journal of Family History* 6 (Fall 1981), 257–77; Palmer, *Culture in Conflict*, 3–4; Alan Wilson, *John Northway: A Blue Serge Canadian* (Toronto: Burns and MacEachern 1965), 14.

106 Committee on the Causes of the Present Depression, 146. See also Bettina Bradbury, "The Home as Workplace," in Craven, ed., *Labouring Lives*, 412–76; John Bullen, "Hidden Workers: Child Labour and the Family Economy in Late Nineteenth-Century Urban Ontario," *L/LT* 18 (Fall 1986), 163–87; John Bullen, "Children of the Industrial Age: Children, Work, and Welfare in Late Nineteenth-Century Ontario" (PhD dissertation, University of Ottawa 1989); Chad Gaffield, "Children, Schooling, and Family Reproduction in Nineteenth-Century Ontario," *CHR* 72 (June 1991), 157–91; Gordon Darroch and Michael Ornstein, "Family Coresidence in Canada in 1871: Family Life-Cycles, Occupations and Networks of Mutual Aid," *HP* 1983, 30–55.

107 In 1870, after surveying the province, a British workman concluded that "a mechanic when in employment here is better paid than in England or Ireland, and has less competition in the labour market." A few years later, parliamentary committees heard regular complaints from manufacturers of clothing, agricultural implements, and cotton about the difficulty of finding enough skilled labour and its consequent high cost; see Ontario, Commissioner of Agriculture and Public Works, *Annual Report on Immigration*, 1870, 28; Select Committee on the Manufacturing Interests, 8, 41–4, 142–8; see also Pollin, "Jacques and Hay," 15; BAMUCJ, 1865, 305; *Monetary Times*, 17 November 1871, 387; *Canadian Manufacturer*, 1 September 1882, 543; RCRLC, 710.

108 RCRLC, 37, 65, 66, 110, 146, 248–9, 251, 260, 372, 389, 398–9, 483, 630, 707, 749, 856, 1069, 1097.

109 *Monetary Times*, 11 December 1874, 656; 1 June 1877, 1383; *Ontario Workman*, 3, 24 October, 21, 28 November 1872; Osborne and Swainson, *Kingston*, 192; Kealey, *Toronto Workers*, 140.

110 A London moulder explained to the Labour Commission, for example, that among his workmates those from Britain were the well-rounded moulders who worked on machinery, while those from the United States were narrower specialists in stove and hollowware work. RCRLC, 601–2. Years earlier a lumberman had warned the furniture manufacturer Robert Hay that British and American skills were not interchangeable: "Canadian and old country people don't know how to saw or pile lumber properly for the American market." Pollin, "Jacques and Hay," 30. On the general importance of immigrant labour for Ontario factories, see RCRLC, 65, 66, 117, 152, 372, 389, 391, 601–2, 625, 628, 630, 635, 797, 813, 958, 1007, 1027.

111 RCRLC, 842.

112 The new railways of the 1850s generally brought their skilled labour with them from Britain, Cobourg's Ontario Woollen Mill imported a skilled dyer first from France and then from Scotland, and the huge Georgian Bay Lumber Company brought the skilled labour for its many sawmills from the United States, especially Pennsylvania. A correspondent for the *Journal* of the Upper Canada Board of Arts and Manufactures reported numerous examples of this kind on his tour through the emerging industrial centres in 1862. A new carpet factory in Elora similarly imported skilled workers, mostly from Philadelphia. Paul Craven and Tom Traves, "Dimensions of Paternalism: Discipline and Culture on the Canadian Railways of the 1850s,' in Heron and Storey, *On the Job*, 47–74; BAMUCJ, September 1864, 255; Angus, *A Deo Victoria*, 64; BAMUCJ, January 1862, 9–10; February 1862, 47; Thorning, "T.E. Bissell," 10; see also *Canadian Manufacturer*, 22 March 1883, 219. Direct importation continued when the local supply was insufficient, notably in the textile industries; see Ontario, Department of Immigration, *Report*, 1878, 21; 1881, 34; 1882, 37; 1885, 18; 1886, 18–19; *Canadian Manufacturer*, 20 January 1882, 25; 17 March 1882, 99; 6 October 1882, 722; RCRLC, 265, 1069. Federal and provincial immigration agents seem to have done little to supply specific needs for industrial labour. For a few years in the late 1860s and early 1870s, the provincial immigration department sent a circular to local mayors, wardens, and reeves, soliciting specific information on local labour needs, but the replies were spotty and the practice was discontinued. Ontario, Commissioner of Agriculture and Public Works, *Annual Report on Immigration* (Toronto), 1869–72.

113 Ontario, Department of Immigration, *Report* (Toronto), 1869–90; Macdonald, *Canada: Immigration and Colonization*. The peaks of immigration into the province in this period were in 1873 and 1883 at

around 40,000 per year; except in the deep depression of the late 1870s, annual figures were usually well above 20,000. OBIR, 1886, 236.

114 Woodside's autobiography appeared in instalments in the *Canadian Foundryman* 8 (November 1917), 195–6; 10 (August 1919), 221; (September 1919), 270–1; (December 1919), 360; 11 (January 1920), 15; (February 1920), 48; (April 1920), 17; 13 (May 1922), 47; (July 1922), 36–7. Wylie, "Blacksmith"; Bischoff, "Tensions et solidarité"; Parr, *Gender of Breadwinners*; RCRLC, 37, 105, 146, 152, 213, 214, 362, 1155. Similarly, a Toronto horseshoer told the Labour Commission that apprenticeship was almost unknown: "They generally come from the country shops"; RCRLC, 105.

115 *Mail*, 15 April 1872; Weaver, "Foundries"; Tulchinsky, "Hidden among the Smokestacks," 261; RCRLC, 336; Price, "Changing Geography," 51; Select Committee on Manufacturing Interests, 40–4, 142–7.

116 Robert M. Stamp, *The Schools of Ontario, 1876–1976* (Toronto: University of Toronto Press 1982), 43–4. Toronto took the first step in 1891.

117 Peter Bischoff has painstakingly traced the transmission of the craft from father to son among moulders in central Canada in "Tensions et solidarité," 150–3.

118 *Free Press* (London), 13 November 1865.

119 Ibid., 7 April 1857, 14 March 1866, 5 November 1869, 14 February, 12 March 1870; *Citizen* (Ottawa), 31 July 1847, 5, 19 May 1849, 29 November 1851, 10 July 1852, 24 June, 19 August, 7 October 1854, 5 January, 9 March 1855, 5 December1856, 11 May 1859, 20 November 1865, 29 November 1872.

120 *Free Press* (London), 9 April 1856, 4 August 1862, 17 April 1864, 29 September, 6 October 1865, 24, 26 August 1869, 13, 19 November 1880; RCRLC, 347, 358; Burley, "Businessmen of Brantford," 109–10; Madeleine Muntz, "An Early Parry Sound Millinery and Fancy Goods Shop," *East Georgian Bay Historical Journal* 5 (1989), 80–95.

121 *Free Press* (London), 8, 14 January, 4 March 1856, 10 April 1861, 9 May, 31 October 1864, 27 July 1865, 10 March, 11 July 1866, 17, 19 November 1868, 21 July, 28 August 1869, 19 April 1870, 9 February 1871, 17 April 1872, 20 April 1875, 24 January 1876, 13 September 1877, 16 March, 8 August, 28 December 1878, 10 March 1879; *Ottawa Citizen*, 19 March, 23 July 1853, 24 March, 11 July, 22 August, 29 September, 8 November, 21 December 1866, 11 February, 18 November 1868, 16 May 1870, 1 February 1872.

122 RCRLC, 177, 623, 1181; Webber, "Labour and the Law." The commission heard that apprenticeship no longer prevailed in brass finishing (RCRLC, 427), for example.

123 See, for example, RCRLC, 1116. The 1891 occupational census listed only 157 apprentices across the whole province. *Census of Canada, 1891*, vol. 2, 164. For a comparative perspective, see W.J. Rorabaugh, *The Craft Apprentice* (New York: Oxford University Press 1985).
124 A major exception was the Bertram tool and machine works in Dundas, where apprentice machinists were still indentured in 1888 under a $200 bond posted by the boy's parents (RCRLC, 956). This system was still in effect in the plant in the mid-1920s. A similarly large London machine shop also used indentures (ibid., 672).
125 Ibid., 490, 532, 902; see also 1097.
126 Ibid., 565, 1116.
127 Ibid., 38, 40, 41–2, 44 (Toronto), 1157 (Ottawa), on printers; 65, 67 (Toronto), on machinists.
128 Ibid., 1181.
129 Ibid., 509 (St Thomas carriage works); 431 (St Thomas woodworking factory); 565 (St Thomas car shop); 1117 (Ottawa furniture factory).
130 Select Committee on Manufacturing Interests, 28; Craven and Traves, "Dimensions of Paternalism"; Paul Craven, "Labour and Management on the Great Western Railway," in Craven, ed., *Labouring Lives*, 335–410; RCRLC, 427, 431, 743–4, 808, 859, 1095, 1102.
131 Select Committee on the Causes of the Present Depression, 75.
132 The managing director of Kingston's locomotive works told the Labour Commission that this concentration of skilled labour accounted for the new owners' decision to keep the operation in that city. RCRLC, 1027, 1029.
133 Select Committee on Manufacturing Interests, 40; Select Committee on the Causes of the Present Depression, 143.
134 The supply of immigrants was not always steady, however, especially in the smaller inland towns. In 1869, for example, Jacques and Hay made a visit to the "Emigration Office" to try to get more hands for their lumber mill at New Lowell. McIntyre, "From Workshop to Factory," 32.
135 OBIR, 1884, lxviii; 1886. We need far more research to determine the flow of men and women between the factory labour markets and their own families' household economies, especially those on Ontario farms. For some important insights, see Chad Gaffield, *Language, Schooling, and Cultural Conflict: The Origins of the French-Language Controversy in Ontario* (Kingston and Montreal: McGill-Queen 's University Press 1987), 78–9.
136 Workers in the mills of the Georgian Bay Lumber Company got free housing if they agreed to work in the lumber camps in the winter. In 1883

the company's new president announced a preference for married men and built many more houses to accommodate a more settled workforce. Angus, *A Deo Victoria*, 89–90, 188–9; see also RCRLC, 1175.

137 A few workers gave the Labour Commission information on the highly atypical use of such workers – Italians in Toronto clothing shops and a London cabinet works and German strikebreakers in a London cigar factory. RCRLC, 628, 653, 690.

138 Angus, *A Deo Victoria*, 67, 205; C. Grant Head, "An Introduction to Forest Exploitation in Nineteenth Century Ontario," in Wood, *Perspectives*, 104–5; Pollin, "Jacques and Hay," 12.

139 OBIR, 1884, lxix; 1886, 210.

140 Cohen, *Women's Work*, 120–1.

141 Louise A. Tilly and Joan W. Scott, *Women, Work and the Family* (New York: Holt, Rinehart and Winston 1978), 123–36; Tamara K. Hareven, *Family Time and Industrial Time: The Relationship between the Family and Work in a New England Industrial Community* (New York: Cambridge University Press 1982), 190–217.

142 Cohen, *Women's Work*, 118–51; Jean Thompson Scott, *The Conditions of Female Labour in Ontario* (Toronto: University of Toronto 1892); Karen Dubinsky, "'The Modern Chivalry': Women and the Knights of Labor in Ontario, 1880–1891' (MA thesis, Carleton University 1985), 14–29; Knowles, 'Beyond Domesticity.'

143 RCRLC, 617, 620.

144 Ibid., 598; see also Langdon, "Emergence," 8.

145 *Globe*, 28 October 1868; Beth Light and Joy Parr, eds., *Canadian Women on the Move, 1867–1920* (Toronto: OISE Press and New Hogtown Press 1983), 90–1.

146 *London Free Press*, 12 February 1856; Kealey, "Work Control," 84.

147 Marjorie Cohen has clarified how women could be excluded from some important food-processing industries that had been previously part of their work in rural households, especially in dairy production. The same constraints did not hold for the canning industry, however, where females made up more than three-quarters of the workforce by 1891. Cohen, *Women' s Work*, 93–117.

148 *Citizen* (Ottawa), 26 July 1851; *Almonte Express*, 30 May 1862 (courtesy of Elizabeth Price); BAMUCJ, May 1862, 137; RCRLC, 859–61, 875, 877, 892, 893, 894, 1058, 1061, 1063, 1068, 1074–5, 1086, 1087, 1144; *Illustrated Historical Atlas of the County of Carleton, Ontario* (Toronto: H. Beldon and Company 1879), xxix. Females typically made up a larger proportion of the workforce in a cotton mill than in a woollen mill.

149 BAMUCJ, January 1862, 9; *Globe*, 28 October 1868; RCRLC, 406–7, 627, 629, 829–33, 1164; Wright, *Sweating System*; King, *Clothing Contracts*; Tulchinsky, "Hidden among the Smokestacks."

150 RCRLC, 307, 309, 336–7, 885.

151 BAMUCJ, March 1863, 84; *Globe*, 28 October 1868; RCRLC, 617–21, 810, 962–3.

152 RCRLC, 1001, 1102; McKay, "Baking and Confectionery Industry"; Margaret E. McCallum, "Separate Spheres: The Organization of Work in a Confectionery Factory: Ganong Bros., St. Stephen, New Brunswick," *L/LT* 24 (Fall 1989), 69–90.

153 BAMUCJ, May 1862, 137; *Illustrated Historical Atlas of the County of Carleton*, xxvii.

154 RCRLC, 40–1, 44, 47, 108, 110, 113, 596, 1141–3, 1146, 1161–3, 1171–3. By the end of the 1880s virtually all the 35 women working as compositors in Toronto (alongside 595 men) were unapprenticed "learners" who worked in non-union printing shops. In London there were apparently 10 female compositors, but none in St Catharines or Hamilton. Christina Burr, "'That Coming Curse – The Incompetent Compositress': Class and Gender Relations in the Toronto Typographical Union during the Nineteenth Century," *CHR* 74, no. 3 (September 1993); RCRLC, 635, 748, 925.

155 RCRLC, 326, 613.

156 Ibid., 110.

157 On the general question of working-class masculinity in this period, see Christina Burr, "Class and Gender in the Toronto Printing Trades, 1870–1914" (PhD dissertation, Memorial University of Newfoundland 1992); Burr, "That Coming Curse"; Burr, "Defending 'The Art Preservative': Class and Gender Relations in the Printing Trades Unions, 1850–1914," *L/LT* 31 (Spring 1993), 47–74; Ava Baron, "Questions of Gender: Deskilling and Demasculinization in the U.S. Printing Industry, 1830–1915," *Gender and History* 1 (Summer 1989), 178–99; Keith McClelland, "Some Thoughts on Masculinity and the 'Representative Artisan' in Britain, 1850–1880," *Gender and History* 1 (Summer 1989), 164–77.

158 *London Free Press*, 29 May 1855, 25 September 1865; RCRLC, 40–7, 108, 113; Burr, "That Coming Curse."

159 RCRLC, 41, 47–8, 392, 618, 627, 962. The Labour Commission did hear occasional admissions that women were just as competent as men; see the testimony of a Hamilton cotton weaver (893) and a St Catharines cigarmaker (919). But these voices were generally drowned in the flood of disparagement.

160 Tucker, *Administering Danger*, 76–136.
161 See, for example, *Globe*, 28 October 1868; CMFR, 2. The first factory inspectors tended to share this view of parental responsibility for child labour; "in nine-tenths of the cases," eastern-district inspector O.A. Rocque argued in 1891, "they are forced upon the employer through the influence of leading workmen or their parents employed themselves in the factory, under the pretence that they refuse to go to school and if not employed would remain on the streets and be out of their surveillance; whilst the true reason is a selfish desire to increase the revenue of the parents to enable them to live more in luxury and extravagance. In other cases children are sent to work to allow parents to remain idle and live in laziness and in all the evils which follow." OIFR, 1891, 18.
162 RCRLC, 743, 879, 893, 895, 973; OBIR, 1887, 38–9. See also OBIR, 1890, 17; 1891, 8, 15, 18.
163 OIFR, 1890, 17; CMFR, 2.
164 Ian E. Davey, "Educational Reform and the Working Class: School Attendance in Hamilton, Ontario, 1851–1891" (PhD dissertation, University of Toronto 1975); Knowles, "Beyond Domesticity," 88–94.
165 *Almonte Gazette*, 15 March 1872. The woollen industry apparently used less child labour than the cotton industry: in 1871 census takers counted only 48 children under age 16 in Almonte's woollen mills, who made up only 13.6 per cent of the workforce; Canada, Manuscript Industrial Census, 1871 (calculations are mine). Both references courtesy of Elizabeth Price.
166 CMFR, 10–13.
167 RCRLC, 73, 141, 316, 651, 1136, 1152.
168 CMFR, 2.
169 Ibid., 2, 8, 10–13; RCRLC, 73, 141, 316, 651, 896, 972, 1136, 1152; OIFR, 1888, 10, 18, 30; 1889, 26, 28; 1890, 5, 20–1, 23; 1891, 14; Department of Labour, *The Employment of Children and Young Persons in Canada* (Ottawa: King's Printer 1930), 111–12.
170 In only a few industries were boys and girls at this young age used interchangeably for light, unskilled jobs, in contrast to their treatment at a slightly older age. In cotton mills, for example, children of both sexes under sixteen could be doffers and spinners, though only boys were packers, card tenders, and roving hands, and only girls were spoolers, weavers, and winders. OBIR, 1884, 35.
171 Pollin, "Jacques and Hay," 14–15; RCRLC, 141, 311 (Toronto), 649 (London), 689 (London), 1100, 1135–9, 1149–52 (Ottawa); OIFR, 1888, 30. For use of this kind of young labourer by other industries, see RCRLC,

613 (tin department of McClary's London foundry), 1075 (Canada Cotton Mill in Cornwall), 1117(Ottawa furniture factory).

172 Quoted in Langdon, "Emergence," 16.

173 RCRLC, 427 (Windsor wire works); 565 (St Thomas car shops); 784 (Hamilton emery-wheel factory), 787 (Hamilton rolling mills); 820 (Hamilton forge works); 856 (Dundas machinery works); according to the Oshawa correspondent of the Ontario Bureau of Industry, the moulders did not allow apprentices to start at the trade before age sixteen. OBIR, 1887, 38. It is significant that when the Ontario Manufacturers' Association first formally considered proposed new factory legislation, they passed no comment on the child-labour sections "as so few members present were interested in child labor." CMFR, 15.

174 RCRLC, 305, 890–1; OBIR, 1887, 38–9; 1889, 10; Scott, *Conditions of Female Labour*, 20; Hughson and Bond, *Hurling Down the Pine*, 76. They accounted, for example, for 120–50 out of 425 workers in a Hamilton tobacco plant, 82 of the 208 in a Kingston cotton mill, 98 of 670 in a Cornwall cotton mill, and about a third of 80 in an Ottawa box factory. RCRLC, 743, 971, 1063.

175 RCRLC, 931, 933; OBIR, 1887, 38–9; 1888, 10–12; 1889, 10–14. The Perth correspondent noted that children under fourteen were unnecessary since "there is an abundance of adult help at low wages."

176 RCRLC, 308, 311, 424, 475, 623, 663, 840, 895–6, 933, 1102, 1144; CMFR, 6, 16; OIFR, 1889, 5; 1891, 23, 25; *London Free Press*, 3 January 1877, 15 November 1880; *Citizen* (Ottawa), 13 March 1852, 16 February, 25 July 1870, 16 January 1872, 12, 20 August 1873.

177 *Globe*, 28 October 1868; RCRLC, 305, 309, 435, 473, 617, 666–7, 807–8, 962, 1104; Scott, *Conditions of Female Labour*, 20, 22–3.

178 *Globe*, 28 October 1868; RCRLC, 347, 893, 1074; Scott, *Conditions of Female Labour*, 20.

179 RCRLC, 178, 509, 618, 623.

180 Factory inspectors claimed this inadequate seating contributed to "crooked spines, round shoulders and contracted chests." OIFR, 1888, 5.

181 Ibid., 1891, 18.

182 The Bureau of Industry correspondents and factory inspectors had already noted a decline in the employment of children under fourteen after the introduction of the Factory Act. OBIR, 1887, 38; OIFR, 1889, 7, 8, 14, 19; 1891, 7.

183 Their exploits usually surfaced when one of them had a serious accident; see OIFR, 1888, 23; 1889, 26; 1891, 22, 23.

184 OIFR, 1888, 8.

185 Ibid., 1890, 20; 1891, 16.

186 RCRLC, 962.

187 Palmer, *Culture in Conflict*, 25.

188 "The corn is hulled, the peas podded, the cherries pitted and the apples prepared by machinery nowadays, dispensing almost entirely with child labor," the inspector wrote; "Even where light manual labor is required the canners prefer older hands to do it." OIFR, 1891, 7. See also Lorna Hurl, "Overcoming the Inevitable: Restricting Child Factory Labour in Late Nineteenth Century Ontario," *L/LT* 21 (Spring 1988), 87–122.

189 The inspectors were mostly confident that the new legislation had a deterrent effect. OIFR, 1888, 6; Tucker, *Administering Danger.*

190 RCRLC, 316. He also later reported that one female employer "of a masculine turn" had threatened to tar and feather him if he returned, after he had launched a prosecution against her for employing three girls aged nine, ten, and twelve. OIFR, 1890, 14.

191 OIFR, 1889, 28; 1900, 12.

192 Craig Heron, "The High School and the Household Economy in Working-Class Hamilton, 1890–1940," *HSE* 7, no. 2 (Fall 1995), 217–59.

193 Evidence presented to the Labour Commission also indicated juvenile wages ranging from $1.50 to $4.00 a week (with girls on the lower end), or roughly a fifth to a third of that of a skilled man. RCRLC, 305, 308, 309, 424, 427, 475, 617, 665, 666, 667, 807, 837, 840, 879, 883, 962, 972, 973, 1100. In one Cornwall cotton mill boys got 15 cents a day, according to a carder working there, and a boy in an Ottawa box factory said he got 25 cents a day. Ibid., 1075, 1151. See also Scott, *Condition of Female Labour*, 22.

194 This ratio was determined by a separate calculation with the same statistics. Other sources confirm this ratio. In 1862 a reporter for the *Journal* of the Board of Arts and Manufactures of Upper Canada found women in textile and clothing enterprises paid approximately half what the men got (45 and 75 cents a day respectively, in contrast with $1 and $1.50) (BAMUCJ, January 1862, 9; May 1862, 137). Roughly the same proportions held through the 1880s; the Labour Commission learned that most women were paid in the range of $3 to $6 per week, again up to half the average male wages (RCRLC, 110, 287, 307, 336, 347, 365, 478, 596, 635, 810, 877, 885, 894, 1009, 1068, 1141, 1162, 1171, 1173).

195 *Monetary Times*, 8 December 1871, 446. A writer in the *Ontario Workman* on 13 June 1872 agreed: "Employers generally strive to get as much labor and as many hours as possible from the workingmen for the lowest possible remuneration."

196 R.C.B. Risk, "The Nineteenth-Century Foundations of the Business Corporation in Ontario," *University of Toronto Law Journal* 33 (1973), 270–306; Douglas McCalla, "An Introduction to the Nineteenth-Century Business World," in Tom Traves, ed., *Essays in Canadian Business History* (Toronto 1984), 13–23; T.W. Acheson, "The Changing Social Origins of the Canadian Industrial Elite, 1880–1910,' in Glenn Porter and Robert Cuff, eds., *Enterprise and National Development: Essays in Canadian Business and Economic History* (Toronto: Hakkert 1973), 51–79. In 1871 there were only six incorporated firms among the sixty industrial leaders – three railway companies, two textile firms, and one locomotive manufacturer. Only eleven more of this group had incorporated by 1891. Bloomfield and Bloomfield, *Industrial Leaders*, 36–9.

197 Pentland, *Labour and Capital*, 24–60; Cohen, *Women' s Work*, 29–117. See also Webber, "Labour and the Law."

198 Akenson, *Irish*, 310; Wylie, "Blacksmith," 50; Johnson, *Ontario County*, 214; Gaffield, *Language*, 84; Wilson, *Lost Horizons*, 45. In 1852–3 workers in Brantford, Hamilton, and London unsuccessfully petitioned the provincial government to "prohibit the payment to mechanics ... of wages in goods or way of truck" (quoted in Langdon, "Emergence," 8; see also Palmer, *Culture in Conflict*, 11–12), and the *Ontario Workman* railed against it twenty years later (9 May 1872). The Labour Commissioners asked many witnesses about the system, but found almost no trace of it.

199 *Citizen* (Ottawa), 29 September 1866; Craven, "Law of Master and Servant," 200–4; Kealey, *Toronto Workers*, 148–52; Palmer, *Culture in Conflict*, 25.

200 Bischoff, "Tensions et solidarité," 60; Parr, *Gender of Breadwinners*; Margaret Watson, "The Transformation of Paternalism: Workers and Capitalists in Brantford, 1880 to 1900' (MA research paper, York University 1985), 13–14. David Burley has established that the opportunities for self-employment were definitely narrowing by the 1870s in the important manufacturing town of Brantford; see Burley, "Businessmen of Brantford," 133–71.

201 *Expositor* (Brantford), 28 October 1887, quoted in Watson, "Transformation of Paternalism," 14; Pollin, "Jacques and Hay," 15–18; Select Committee on Manufacturing Interests, 57; RCRLC, 880, 1099, 1173; OBIR, 1887, 40; Mollie Gillen, *The Masseys: Founding Family* (Toronto: Ryerson Press 1965), 61–2. Little systematic research has yet been done on family and kinship links inside nineteenth-century Ontario factories. In Almonte, family groupings are evident in the woollen mill workforce found in the 1861 manuscript census (courtesy of Elizabeth Price).

202 The Masseys, like other employers, liked to brag about long-service employees who had risen through the ranks; see the story on W.F. Clarke, moulding-shop foreman in the 1880s, who had started work for Daniel Massey forty years earlier. *Trip Hammer*, June 1885, 55. See also Wilson, *Lost Horizons*, 44–5; Craven and Traves, "Dimensions of Paternalism"; RCRLC, 427, 431, 533, 743–4, 808, 859, 898, 1095, 1102.

203 Thorning, "Bissell," 10; Palmer, *Culture in Conflict*, 97–122; Kealey, *Toronto Workers*, 154–71; Peter Warrian, "'Sons of Toil': The Impact of Industrialization on Craft Workers in Late 19th Century Ontario," in David F. Walker and James H. Bater, eds., *Industrial Development in Southern Ontario: Selected Essays* (Waterloo: Dept. of Geography Publication Series no. 3, University of Waterloo 1974), 69–99. On boosterism in late nineteenth-century Ontario, see Robert J. Morris, "The Reproduction of Labour and Capital: British and Canadian Cities during Industrialization," *UHR* 18 (June 1989), 55; Thomas William Acheson, "The Social Origins of Canadian Industrialism: A Study in the Structure of Entrepreneurship," (PhD dissertation, University of Toronto 1971), 188–260; Johnson, *Ontario County*, 247–52, 282–316; Leo Johnson, "Ideology and Political Economy in Urban Growth: Guelph, 1827N1927," in G.A. Stelter and A.F.J. Artibise, eds., *Shaping the Urban Landscape: Aspects of the Canadian City-Building Process* (Ottawa: Carleton University Press 1982), 30–64; Elizabeth Bloomfield, "Building the City on a Foundation of Factories: The 'Industrial Policy' in Berlin, Ontario, 1870–1914," *OH* 75 (September 1983), 207–43; Elizabeth Bloomfield, "Municipal Bonusing of Industry: The Legislative Framework in Ontario to 1930," *UHR* 9 (February 1981), 59–76; Elizabeth Bloomfield, "Community Leadership and Decision-Making: Entrepreneurial Elites in Two Ontario Towns, 1870–1930," in G.A. Stelter and A.F.J. Artibise, eds., *Power and Place: Canadian Urban Development in the North American Context* (Vancouver: UBC Press 1986), 82–104; E.J. Noble, "Men and Circumstances: Entrepreneurs and Community Growth: A Case Study of Orillia, Ontario, 1867–1898" (PhD dissertation, University of Guelph 1980); *Northern Advance*, 4 January, 1, 8 February 1860.

204 Reid, "Rosamond Woolen Company," 279–80; Knowles, "Beyond Domesticity," 44–5; *Ontario Workman*, 27 June 1872; *Canadian Illustrated News*, 26 January 1878, 55; *Globe*, 27 May 1882; R.G. Hoskins, "Hiram Walker and the Origins and Development of Walkerville, Ontario," *OH* 65 (1973), 122–31.

205 Angus, *A Deo Victoria*, 27–46, 55–71, 151–4, 175–9, 185–8; see also Radforth, "Confronting Distance," 82–4; Pollin, "Jacques and Hay," 8, 11; Wilson, *Lost Horizons*, 22, 45, 47, 53; OA, F209, MU 1957, vol. 2, ii.

206 *Almonte Gazette*, 3 January, 24 July 1868, 11 August 1871 (courtesy of Elizabeth Price); *Citizen* (Ottawa), 4 January 1866, 11, 15 January 1867, 26 August 1869, 24 November 1869, 7 April 1879; *London Free Press*, 25 July 1865, 7, 19 July, 26 November 1869, 13 July 1870, 24 January, 16 February 1871, 7 February 1874; *Advance* (Barrie), 13 July, 10 August 1864, 29 August 1866; Bischoff, "Tensions et solidarité," 21–2; Burley, "Businessmen of Brantford," 110–11 ; Watson, "Transformation of Paternalism," 18–19, 34–7; Knowles, "Beyond Domesticity," 43, 46.
207 Lisa Bowes, "George Sleeman and the Brewing of Baseball in Guelph, 1872–1886," *Historic Guelph* 27 (1987–8), 45–57; Kelly, *Downright Upright*, 55.
208 *Citizen* (Ottawa), 11 January 1867, 28 December 1868, 4 January1869; *Almonte Gazette*, 13 October 1871, 9 February, 21 June 1872, 2, 17 January 1873, 2 January 1874 (courtesy of Elizabeth Price). See also *Ontario Workman*, 30 May 1872, for a similar expression of gratitude in Toronto.
209 Kealey, *Toronto Workers*, 221–2.
210 *Expositor* (Brantford), 11 June 1886, 5 December 1890, quoted in Watson, "Transformation of Paternalism," 33–4, 36.
211 Craven and Traves, "Dimensions of Paternalism," 63–70.
212 Archives of Ontario (hereafter AO), F209, MU 1957 (McLauchlin Brothers' Lumber Company), vol. 9, ii (Arnprior 1858); Burley, "Businessmen of Brantford," 111; *Free Press* (London), 19–20 November 1872; *Ontario Workman*, 28 November 1872 (East London oil refiners).
213 RCRLC, 666, 745, 808, 810, 816; Wilson, *Lost Horizons*, 32.
214 *Trip Hammer*, February 1885–February 1886; Denison, *Harvest Triumphant*. None of these employers tried profit-sharing, however. Michael Bliss, *A Living Profit: Studies in the Social History of Canadian Business, 1883–1911* (Toronto: McClelland and Stewart 1974), 89–91.
215 *Trip Hammer*, February 1885, 4–5; April 1885, 26; November 1885, 137; January 1886, 180; February 1886, 183–4, 193; Kealey, *Toronto Workers*.
216 OBIR, 1886, 206–7.
217 When the Gurneys installed washing facilities in their Toronto foundry, the moulders spurned the paternalism and refused to use the new sinks. Another Hamilton foundryman was convinced that moulders would never use company washrooms.
218 James Naylor, *The New Democracy: Challenging the Social Order in Industrial Ontario, 1914–25* (Toronto: University of Toronto Press 1991), 159–88; Heron, *Working in Steel*, 98–111.
219 Paul Craven and Tom Traves, "Labour and Management in Canadian Railway Operations: The First Decade" (paper presented to the Commonwealth Labour History Conference, Coventry, England 1981);

Craven and Traves, "Dimensions of Paternalism"; Craven, "Labour and Management."

220 RCRLC, 1176.

221 Sidney Pollard, *The Genesis of Modern Management: A Study of the Industrial Revolution in Great Britain* (London: Penguin 1965), 51–63; John Buttrick, "The Inside Contract System," *JEH* 12 (Summer 1952), 205–21; Dan Clawson, *Bureaucracy and the Labor Process: The Transformation of U.S. Industry, 1860–1920* (New York: Monthly Review Press 1980), 71–125; David Montgomery, *Workers' Control in America*, 11–12; David A. McCabe, *The Standard Rate in American Trade Unions* (Baltimore: Johns Hopkins University Press 1912), 62–5. In the United States, the system was most elaborately developed in the munitions industry, for which Ontario had no counterpart in this period.

222 Jacques and Hay ran the woodturning and chair-making branches of their operations in New Lowell on a contract basis; Radforth, "Confronting Distance," 94. See also RCRLC, 442, 602, 691, 743, 760, 810–1, 1105, 1134–5, 1137; OBIR, 1888, 11; OIFR, 1889, 5, 26; CMFR, 4; Palmer, *Culture in Conflict*, 255. Moulders had long been accustomed to hiring their own helpers, often known as "berkshires," though their union fought the system vigorously (Kealey, *Toronto Workers*, 67–8). The large Georgian Bay Lumber Company used subcontractors for piling lumber and for running lath mills at Waubaushene and Port Severn (Angus, *A Deo Victoria*, 88–9), and in 1886 Hamilton Brothers similarly contracted for saw filing in their mills for the following season (AO, F 131, MU 1221, Box 9, Contract, 8 September 1886); the Gillies Brothers received an enquiry about similar work (AO, F 150–4, 2–7, 18 March 1872). In an interesting variant, William Doherty, a merchant-turned-organ manufacturer in Clinton in 1876, was given access to equipment inside a local planing mill to build the cabinets. Kelly, *Downright Upright*, 46.

223 BAMUCJ 1862; E.P. Morgan and F.L. Harvey, *Hamilton and Its Industries: Being a Historical and Descriptive Sketch of the City of Hamilton and Its Public and Private Institutions, Manufacturing and Industrial Interests, Public Citizens, etc.* (Hamilton 1884), 21–4; RCRLC, 359, 628–9, 829–30, 931; OIFR, 1889, 7; 1891, 13; McIntosh, "Sweated Labour."

224 RCRLC, 213.

225 Ibid., 474; see also 469–71. In addition to the furniture finishing already mentioned, a local flour mill also subcontracted its coopering; ibid., 489.

226 Ibid., 494.

227 In 1892 a Hamilton foundryman introduced the system in the midst of a strike. Palmer, *Culture in Conflict*, 90.

228 It is interesting that the Masseys' first proposal for a kind of centralized cost accounting in their Toronto operations, distributed to foremen in October 1888, used the subcontracting model. "Each department shall be considered and treated as a separate business establishment independent of the Massey M'f'g. Co.; its foreman considered as the proprietor, who shall jealously look after its interests, curtail expenses as far as possible, and do all in his power to make a creditable showing," the memorandum read, but there was no indication that the salaried foreman would get to keep any profits made this way, as the inside contractor would have. OAM, Massey-Ferguson Collection, MM 69 ("Prospectus of a System of Records to Show the Relative Standing of Individual Departments," October 1888). In this large factory, moreover, foremen were not supposed to make a final decision about hiring or setting wages without consulting the superintendent; ibid., MM 32 ("General Rules and Regulations Regarding Foremen," 1890).

229 RCRLC, 441, 982, 999, 1067; see also ibid., 1018, 1023–4, 1037, 1088.

230 *Almonte Gazette*, 10 April 1868, 24 December 1870, 4 April 1873 (courtesy of Elizabeth Price); *Citizen* (Ottawa), 18 May 1867, 4 January 1868, 3 November 1869; *Ontario Workman*, 21 May, 27 June 1872. One of E.B. Eddy's foremen revealed how this relationship could involve collusion to defraud the owner, when he was caught in a scam of regularly "giving in more time than was due and sharing with the men the proceeds of this nefarious practice." *Citizen* (Ottawa), 17 February 1867.

231 *Free Press* (London), 11 January 1877. There was also some ambiguity about the ultimate loyalty of foremen, who had almost invariably emerged off the shop floor as skilled workers. In the 1872 shorter-hours strike in Hamilton, three foremen joined striking machinists at a sewing-machine works and publicly denounced their boss (Palmer, *Culture in Conflict*, 135). The printers were the only craft to succeed in keeping their foremen inside their union. Kealey, "Work Control."

232 RCRLC, 1024.

233 Palmer, *Culture in Conflict*, 21; Kealey, *Toronto Workers*, 54, 68; RCRLC, 376, 886, 978, 1024, 1067, 1174; OAM, Massey-Ferguson Collection, MM 33 (Massey Manufacturing Company, *Agreement between Employers and Employed: Rules and Regulations. General Instructions* (Toronto [c. 1888–90]), 4. The practice of locking doors was frequently mentioned but was evidently far from universal since several of the Ontario Bureau of Industries correspondents reported in 1888 that it was actually not common in their towns. OBIR, 1886, 204; 1888, 10–12.

234 The Gooderham and Worts distillery in Toronto ran day and night, as did flour mills in busy periods. Many lumber mills also ran two shifts,

one from 6 a.m. to 6 p.m. and another from 7 p.m. to 5 a.m. BAMUCJ, May 1862, 135; *Northern Advance*, 29 August 1866; *Mail*, 23 April 1872; *Canadian Manufacturer*, 21 July 1882, 355; 20 April 1883, 296; RCRLC, 489, 882, 1125–6, 1152. One of the first items of business of the newly organized Lumberman's Association of Ontario in 1888 was to urge the Georgian Bay Lumber Company to lengthen its work day from ten and a half hours to eleven to conform with other mills on the bay (AO, F 248, MU 1745, vol. 1, 8 February 1888, 132). The Waterous Engine Works began round-the-clock operations to cope with increased business in 1880 (Burley, "Businessmen of Brantford," 121). Bakeries, of course, and publishers of morning newspapers also expected night work from their operatives (Palmer, *Culture in Conflict*, 129; Kealey, "Work Control," 84; RCRLC, 1118).

235 Angus, *A Deo Victoria*, 89.

236 OBIR, 1886, 204–6; see also Palmer, *Culture in Conflict*, 26.

237 Massey Manufacturing Company, *Agreement between Employers and Employed*; RCRLC, 1102, 1058, 1116; Palmer, *Culture in Conflict*, 20–1.

238 RCRLC, 171; Angus, *A Deo Victoria*, 73; Peter Bischoff found a high incidence of drunkenness among moulders in the Hamilton police records; see "Tensions et solidarité," 110.

239 RCRLC, 976, 1074–5.

240 Some employers might still have recourse to the courts when an apprentice broke his indenture; RCRLC, 750.

241 Ibid., 654, 1061, 1068; Palmer, *Culture in Conflict*, 78–9, 81, 85; see also *Ontario Workman*, 23 May 1872; OBIR, 1885, cxxx; 1886, 202–3; 1888, 7–9; 1889, 2–4.

242 Russell, "Wage Rates"; AO, F 150 (Gillies Brothers Lumber Company), 13-6-1, No. 29 (March 1872); 3-0-2, 19 April 1875; 3-0-3, 10 March 1876; 3-0-7, 5 March, 28 June, 2 July 1879; 3-0-8, 27 January, 29 March, 19, 25, 28 April, 1 September, 11 October 1880 (on the emergence of hourly wages, see Craven, "Labour and Management"); BAMUCJ, January 1862, 9; April 1862, 112–13, 137; Palmer, *Culture in Conflict*, 26. See also Pollin, "Jacques and Hay," 14; Select Committee on Manufacturing Interests, 44, 47, 58; Select Committee on the Causes of the Present Depression, 180; CMFR, 15; Karl Marx, *Capital*, vol. 1 (Harmondsworth: Penguin 1976), 692–700. The Labour Commission heard evidence on piecework in barrels (RCRLC, 261, 398–9, 489); cigars (305, 962), clothing (287–8, 359–60, 406, 627, 829, 1187); confectionery (666–7); cotton (879, 893, 973, 1058, 1068, 1082, 1086, 1087, 1094); furniture (441, 443, 609, 691); harness (213); knit goods (859, 980–2); paper boxes (110, 364–5); pianos (947); rolling-mill products (760, 763, 786, 790); shoes (431, 884–5, 1049); stoves (144, 158,

173, 295, 373, 601, 612, 658, 784, 802, 821, 903, 949); tobacco (809); wool (665). See also Bischoff, "Tensions et solidarité," 104–7.

243 CMFR, 17.

244 RCRLC, 45, 763.

245 Ibid., 152, 158, 178, 822; see also 144, 431, 763, 802, 884; Bischoff, "Tensions et solidarité," 105. A gilder in the same city recalled that in 1885, when put on piecework, his fellow workers had "worked so hard as to work themselves out of work." OIFR, 1888, 20.

246 RCRLC, 110; Kealey, *Toronto Workers*, 66–7; Kealey and Palmer, *Dreaming*, 113; Craig Heron and Bryan D. Palmer, "Through the Prism of the Strike: Industrial Conflict in Southern Ontario, 1901–14," *CHR* 58 (December 1977), 423–58.

247 Their report also indicated that fining was a recent innovation, "only in its infancy." Kealey, *Canada Investigates Industrialism*, 46–7.

248 RCRLC, 1175; see also 287, 337, 861, 879, 892, 1058, 1069–70, 1074, 1076, 1079, 1144, 1162–3. A moulder remembered that once it had been common to fine workers for breaking a mould, but that system had been abandoned long ago; ibid., 798. The Masseys' detailed system of fines for infractions of company rules seems to have been an exception; see Massey Manufacturing Company, *Agreement between Employers and Employed*, 11–12.

249 The Labour Commission heard of them in a St Thomas "featherbone" factory and an Ottawa print shop (RCRLC, 536, 1171).

250 Ibid., 1074–5, 1085, 1163, 1174–5.

251 Thorning, "Bissell," 17. It must be said that the Labour Commissioners pursued this issue relentlessly, but accumulated little evidence, probably because of the little testimony they heard directly from women; see Susan Mann Trofimenkoff, "One Hundred and Two Muffled Voices: Canada's Industrial Women in the 1880s," in Michael S. Cross and Gregory S. Kealey, eds., *Readings in Canadian Social History, Vol. 3, Canada's Age of Industry, 1849–1896* (Toronto: McClelland and Stewart 1982), 210–29.

252 RCRLC, 47, 110, 287, 359, 364–5, 406–7, 627, 665, 667, 829, 885, 893.

253 Ibid., 601, 614–15, 625, 650–1, 790, 1083, 1085, 1088; OBIR, 1884, lxix; 1885, cxxxiv.

254 Examples included the province's largest stove foundrymen from 1866 on, known as the Canadian Iron Founders' Association (*Free Press* [London], 2 May 1866; *Ontario Workman*, 30 May 1872; Select Committee on the Causes of the Present Depression, 180; Canada, House of Commons, *Journals* [Ottawa], vol. 22 [1888], App. 3 ["Report of the Select Committee Appointed to Examine into Combinations Said to Exist with

Reference to the Purchase and Sale or Manufacture and Sale in Canada of Any Foreign or Canadian Products"], 8–9, 391–407, 699, 791–5, Bischoff, "Tensions et solidarité"); newspaper publishers in Toronto in 1872 and in Ottawa in 1873 (Zerker, *Rise and Fall*, 78–91; *Citizen* [Ottawa], 4 August 1873); London's cigar manufacturers in 1883 and Hamilton's in 1885 (RCRLC, 620–1, 650; Kealey and Palmer, *Dreaming*, 159); all manufacturers in Chatham in the mid-1880s (RCRLC, 438–9), 443; Kealey and Palmer, *Dreaming*, 355–6); and the Lumberman's Association of Ontario, founded 1887 (AO, F 248, MU 1745).

255 See C.J. Wrigley, ed., *A History of British Industrial Relations, 1875–1914* (London: Harvester Press 1982).

256 Quoted in Bliss, *Living Profit*, 75.

257 Hamilton Group Archives (Burlington), New Hamburg Curtain and Rug Company, Letterbook, 1898; RCRLC, 790, 1074–5; OFIR, 1888, 23; 1889, 26; 1891, 23.

258 *Almonte Gazette*, 13 October 1871, 21 June 1872; *Citizen* (Ottawa), 26 September, l June 1872; North Lanark Historical Society, *Development of the Woollen Industry*, 22. Jonathan Prude's discussion of this kind of informal protest in small New England textile towns offers some fascinating insights that could be pursued in Ontario mill towns; see *The Coming of Industrial Order: Town and Factory Life in Rural Massachusetts, 1810–1860* (New York: Cambridge University Press 1983).

259 For example, strikes at Ottawa sawmills in 1874, 1875, and 1877, all of them over wage cuts; see *Ottawa Citizen*, 29 May 1874, 13 July 1877, 10 July 1877.

260 Palmer, *Culture in Conflict*, 150.

261 The recent emphasis on community studies of the nineteenth-century working-class history in North America thus has considerable validity, though the less organized working-class communities have had far less attention than the centres of active working-class resistance.

262 Wylie, "Blacksmith"; Bischoff, "Tensions et solidarité"; Parr, *Gender of Breadwinners.*

263 Palmer, *Culture in Conflict*; Kealey, *Toronto Workers*; Forsey, *Trade Unions*; *London Free Press*, 13 September 1869, 18 January 1870, 21 January 1871, 11 August 1873, 7 April 1874; *Citizen* (Ottawa), 15 April 1867.

264 Langdon, "Emergence"; Forsey, *Trade Unions*; Zerker, *Rise and Fall*, 53–156; Kealey, *Toronto Workers*, 37–97; Kealey, "Work Control"; Palmer, *Culture in Conflict*, 71–95; Bischoff, "Tensions et solidarité"; Bliss, *Living Profit*, 86–9.

265 Langdon, 'Emergence,' 7; Kealey, *Toronto Workers;* Storey, 'Industrialization'; *Free Press* (London) 2 December 1852, 15 May 1873.

266 Kealey, *Toronto Workers*; Code, "Salt Men of Goderich"; *Free Press* (London), 2, 3, 8, 9 November 1869, 27 April, 20 May, 6 June, 10 September 1870, 12 June 1873, 29 August 1876, 5 February 1877, 5, 7, 21 October 1880. Even in the village of Elora, a newspaper editor could complain that the coopers, the only unionized workers in town, were "striking too much lately for their own good"; quoted in Thorning, "Bissell," 10.
267 *Free Press* (London), 2 December 1852, 10 January, 29 May 1856, 25 September 1865.
268 Ibid., 30 October 1878, 12, 13 November 1880.
269 *Free Press* (London), 2 May 1866, 17 March 1873, 11 August 1873, 13 January, 7 April 1874, 14 January 1879; Bischoff, "Tensions et solidarité"; Kealey, *Toronto Workers*; Palmer, *Culture in Conflict.*
270 *Free Press* (London), 14 January, 12, 25 February 1856, 13 September, 20 November 1869, 8 November, 6 December 1870, 6 June 1871, 25 January, 5 June 1872, 6 March 1873; Kealey, "Work Control"; Zerker, *Rise and Fall.*
271 Kealey, *Toronto Workers*; Craven, "Labour and Management on the Great Western Railway."
272 Kealey, "Work Control"; Bischoff, "Tensions et solidarité."
273 Langdon, "Emergence," 12–23; Forsey, *Trade Unions*, 3–127; John Battye, "The Nine Hour Pioneers: The Genesis of the Canadian Labour Movement," *L/LT* 4 (1979), 25–56; Kealey, *Toronto Workers*, 124–53; Palmer, *Culture in Conflict*, 125–52.
274 Kealey and Palmer, *Dreaming*, 45.
275 See Forsey, *Trade Unions*, 201–87, 320–38.
276 Kealey and Palmer, *Dreaming*. For local studies of the Knights, see George De Zwaan, "The Little Birmingham on the St. Lawrence: An Industrial and Labour History of Gananoque, Ontario, 1871–1921" (PhD dissertation, Queen's University 1987); Edward McKenna, "Unorganized Labour versus Management: The Strike at the Chaudiere Lumber Mills, 1891," *HS/SH* 5 (November 1972), 186–211; Senior, *Royal Township to Industrial City*, 236–45; Dale Chisamore et al., *Brockville: A Social History, 1890–1930* (Brockville: Waterway Press 1975), 85–91.
277 Kealey and Palmer, *Dreaming*, 7 1.
278 Dubinsky, "Modern Chivalry."
279 Michael Piva, "The Bonds of Unity: A Comment," *HS/SH* 16 (May 1983), 169–74; Gregory Kealey and Bryan Palmer, "The Bonds of Unity: Some Further Reflections," ibid., 175–89.
280 Acheson, "Social Origins," 194–226.
281 Drummond, *Progress without Planning.*

282 See, for example, the reports of the Ontario Bureau of Industry correspondents in 1883–4; OBIR, 1883, 37; 1884, lxix.
283 See, for example, RCRLC, 288, 338, 1074–5; OBIR, 1884, lxx.
284 The great majority of the strikes reported to the Bureau of Industries after its labour statistics began appearing in 1883 were against wage cuts of some sort; OBIR, 1883, 39; 1884, lxix, lxx, lxxii, lxxiii; 1885, cxxxi; 1888, 5, 16; 1889, 22, 23.
285 See, for example, the confrontation with Hamilton cotton weavers over "an increased length in cuts or pieces woven," and the extended conflicts in the Cornwall cotton mills in 1888 and 1889 over piece-rates; OBIR, 1884, lxix; RCRLC, 1059, 1062, 1066, 1068, 1070; Senior, *Royal Township to Industrial City*, 240–2; Kealey and Palmer, *Dreaming*, 358–9.
286 The outcome of this confrontation was fragmentation and at best partial success for some workers. RCRLC, 437–9, 441–3, 462, 468, 476; OBIR, 1886, 207; Kealey and Palmer, *Dreaming*, 355–6.
287 OBIR, 1884, lxxiii. Two years later the bureau reported that only in Toronto had "the nine hour movement made great strides" (ibid., 1886, 205); in fact, from 1884 to the end of the decade, provincial averages for hours of work per week hovered around 58–9, while in Toronto the average dropped to 53–4 (ibid., 1887, 4; 1888, 24; 1889, 32, 34–5).
288 Kealey and Palmer, *Dreaming*.
289 Russell Hann, "Brainworkers and the Knights of Labor: E.E. Sheppard, Phillips Thompson, and the *Toronto News*, 1883–1887," in Gregory S. Kealey and Peter Warrian, eds., *Essays in Canadian Working Class History* (Toronto: McClelland and Stewart 1976), 35–57; Desmond Morton, "The *Globe* and the Labour Question: Ontario Liberalism in the 'Great Upheaval,' May, 1886," *OH* 73, no. 1 (March 1981), 19–39.
290 Margaret Evans, *Sir Oliver Mowat* (Toronto: University of Toronto Press 1992), 191–7; Tucker, *Administering Danger*; Kealey, "Introduction," *Canada Investigates Industrialism.*
291 Belleville's Rathbun Company began publishing a company magazine for its millmen. Brantford foundryman William Buck held his first company picnic in 1886. Wilson, *Lost Horizons*, 32; Watson, "Transformation of Paternalism," 33.
292 John Penman of Paris took this step in April 1886, as did the Gravenhurst lumbermen a year later. George Tuckett of Hamilton also proudly explained the new nine-hour regime in his tobacco factory to the Labour Commission. Knowles, "Beyond Domesticity," 41; Kealey and Palmer, *Dreaming*, 359; RCRLC, 745.

293 The towns were London, Galt, and Paris. Kealey and Palmer, *Dreaming*, 354–5; Knowles, "Beyond Domesticity," 173.

294 Calculated from the lists provided in Kealey and Palmer, *Dreaming*.

295 Gregory Kealey and Bryan Palmer made this questionable claim in their otherwise superb study; see ibid., 32–3.

296 OBIR, 1884–90.

297 Kealey, "Introduction," *Canada Investigates Industrialism*.

Chapter Three

Work and Struggle in the Canadian Steel Industry, 1900–1950

Until quite recently, a steel plant was a vast, terrifying inferno. The heat was scorching, the air thick and choking, and the noise overpowering. Blinding flashes and showers of sparks would explode in the gloom of smoke and dust beneath towering hulks of machinery. Deafening roars, wailing sirens, and clattering bells heightened the atmosphere of tension and danger. Out of this eerie world of fire-breathing machines and toiling men flowed a vital commodity for modern industrial society – primary steel.

Canadian steelworkers participate in a labour process that we have come to know as mass production – a large-scale, high-speed, continuous, and technologically sophisticated system of production. In Canada, researchers and writers have seldom asked how industries like steel (or auto or any of a number of others) evolved to this stage of development. This paper attempts to begin to fill that gap in our understanding of Canadian industrial life. It will carry the reader from the formative years of the modern, mass-production steel industry at the turn of the century to the early 1950s, when steel-plant work relations reached a new stability. We begin by outlining the economic structure of the industry and then consider the nature and impact of technological change and managerial labour policies; we discuss the responses of the steelworkers themselves to this new work world, and finally, the consolidation of industrial unionism in the 1940s.

Open-hearth department at Stelco in Hamilton.
Library and Archives Canada, PA 17740

The story that unfolds suggests some of the main dynamics of the mass-production labour process in Canada. New machines and new managerial policies provided a substantial increase in the power of owners and managers to control the workplace and thus to boost productivity. Resistance to that unbridled control arose from the workers, whose role in the steel-making process gave them some independence on the shop floor. These men led an ultimately successful effort to give steelworkers some power to negotiate the terms of their employment and to impose new standards of fairness on steel-plant administration. Yet they neither demanded nor won any fundamental change in the essential shape of the labour process that had been created in the early years of the twentieth century: the technology, the work routines, and the power to control the process.

The Anatomy of an Industry

In 1896 the manager of Nova Scotia's Londonderry Iron Company raised few eyebrows among his fellow industrialists when he lamented that "there is only one country under the sun with 15,000 miles of railway that does not manufacture a single steel rail, and that country is Canada."[1] Canadian businessmen could only nod soberly in agreement that the history of iron and steel production in the country up to that point had been a tale of failures and disappointments. Why?

Three problems had plagued would-be ironmasters in Canada – problems that would persist well into the twentieth century.[2] First, Canada lacked large, known supplies of good-quality iron ore, and only in Nova Scotia was coal easily accessible. Second, foreign competition was crippling. The small Canadian market had not permitted the economies of scale and technological innovations of the British and American producers. And third, tariff protection was inadequate to meet this competition. The numerous consumers of primary iron and steel – particularly railways, agricultural-implement firms, foundries, and independent rolling mills – did not believe that the small, inefficient primary industry in Canada could provide cheap-enough metal and convinced the Canadian state that the tariff system should have major loopholes to allow in various primary and semi-finished steel products. Canadian steel producers, especially in Sydney and Sault Ste Marie, were still agitating for more effective tariff protection as late as the 1920s, when Canada's primary producers supplied only half of all primary iron and steel products consumed in the country.[3]

Clearly the economic and political climate was far from favourable for a large, successful steel industry in Canada. There were some major structural constraints that would inhibit development and provide chronic instability for any steel-makers who undertook production in this context. Under these circumstances, the Canadian steel industry developed along two separate paths in the late nineteenth and early twentieth centuries. The first, pioneered by the Nova Scotia Steel Company at Trenton, NS, in the 1880s, involved slow, cautious growth with diversified markets and close integration with the finishing industries. The most successful example of this development path began as the Hamilton Blast Furnace Company in 1895, and after a series of mergers with a string of finishing plants, became the Steel Company of Canada (Stelco) in 1910.[4]

The second path was more dramatic and posed more risks. At the turn of the century, two free-wheeling American entrepreneurs launched widely hailed steel-production projects at Sydney in Nova Scotia and Sault Ste Marie in northern Ontario. H.M. Whitney organized the Dominion Iron and Steel Company (Dosco) in 1899, and Francis Clergue created the Algoma Steel Company in 1901. Both firms opened highly specialized facilities capable of turning out a large-enough volume to keep costs competitive with the Americans, and both looked to the new Canadian railways for their principal market, especially for steel rails. Both were also in serious trouble by the 1920s when their over-specialization and distance from markets in the industrial heartland of southern Ontario forced them to curtail production drastically. Nova Scotia Steel was dragged down at the same time, when it merged with Dosco into Cape Breton's new corporate monster, the British Empire Steel Corporation (Besco), after the First World War.[5] Of the three major steel producers, only Stelco consistently turned a profit, not only in the 1920s but in each year of the 1930s depression.

The Second World War saved most of the teetering Canadian steel industry. The renewed demand for steel products in munition plants helped, but equally important was the active intervention of the Canadian state. A steel controller in C.D. Howe's Department of Munitions and Supply presided over a revitalization of steel-making facilities. An essential component of this resurgence was the provision, for the first time, of generous depreciation allowances that encouraged rapid expansion and modernization of their facilities. The major Ontario producers emerged into the postwar world as efficient, diversified, integrated industrial complexes capable of surviving in a continental market. The Sydney operations, however, continued their steady decline into marginality in Canadian steel production.[6]

The structure of the Canadian steel industry, then, would have major implications for the country's steelworkers. They had to confront three large, powerful corporations that controlled all primary steel production.[7] The workers were grouped in three major centres, each hundreds of miles from the others. Small and unsteady orders for steel, along with over-specialization, created an uneven demand for labour and fear among workers for the existence of their jobs. But, probably most important, these workers would find that their employers all recognized the need for cutting costs to match American standards of productivity if their products were going to find a market. The results for the labour process in Canada's steel plants were profound.

Machines and Men

In 1924 a business journalist emerged from a Canadian steel plant marvelling at what "a gigantic automaton" it was. On his tour he had found huge mechanical devices for handling and treating the iron on its progress through to rolled steel, and the workers he encountered seemed to be overwhelmingly machine-operators: "The labor in every branch of the industry consists mainly in the supervision and maintenance of machinery," he wrote.[8] The labour process this writer observed was, in fact, the recognizably modem mass-production system of steel making, which would see few significant changes in the next quarter century.

The mechanization of the Canadian steel industry had been a fairly abrupt process beginning at the turn of the century, and leaving behind the slow, labour-intensive methods of the scattered nineteenth-century producers. In part, Canadian steelmasters simply installed the most advanced technology available, virtually all of it American.[9] They were thus able to incorporate into their production processes many years of experimentation by American manufacturers aimed at reducing costs through eliminating as much self-directed manual labour as possible and using their control over the new machinery to intensify the work in the mills.[10] At the same time, in response to local experience turning out steel and managing steelworkers, Canadian companies continued to innovate with production techniques of their own. As a result, each of the three main stages of steel production – the blast-furnace, steelmaking, and rolling-mill departments – was transformed in the late nineteenth and early twentieth centuries.

The blast-furnace had been at the core of the typical early Canadian ironworks. A small, perhaps thirty-foot stone stack would be built beside a hill, and wheelbarrows full of raw materials for the furnace would be trundled from the hilltop, across a ramp, and into the top of the furnace. Along with iron ore and limestone, quantities of charcoal, prepared by simply burning a large pile of local trees, would be dumped in. The "blast" of air blown into the bottom of the furnace would normally be powered by a simple waterwheel. The molten iron that flowed out at the bottom of these primitive furnaces would most often be directed along channels in the sandy floor of the casting house to form blocks of iron known as "pigs." Once cooled, these pigs were separated by brawny men with sledge-hammers and piled up by hand. These methods could produce no more than 5–10 tons of iron per day, and numerous labourers were required to run to and fro around the furnace with their barrows, shovels, and hammers.[11]

The typical blast-furnace of the 1890s had changed remarkably little. It had a larger capacity, steam had replaced waterpower, and in the newer operations, elevators carried the wheelbarrows of raw material up the side of the furnace. But the brigades of shovellers and "barrowmen" still hauled the material from piles by the railway tracks into and out of the elevators. At the base of the furnace, labourers still scampered about in the smokey heat and deafening noise to direct the molten iron into the beds of pigs. By this point, many firms were abandoning charcoal in favour of coke, and several companies had developed coke ovens for preparing coal for use in the furnace. These so-called bee-hive ovens required men to shovel coal into a small car, shove it in and out of ovens, hose it down, and fork the still-warm coke into wheelbarrows.[12]

The opening of the Dosco plant in 1901 unveiled much more sophisticated techniques of blast-furnace work that eliminated a large amount of brute labour, and that most other Canadian steel plants promptly adopted.[13] Workers now ran new electrically powered machines for hoisting coal and ore out of ships, for scooping them up from the stockyard and transporting them to the furnace, and for carrying them up and dropping them into the top of the furnace without any manual assistance. Crane operators now caught the molten pig iron in huge ladles and swept it away for use immediately in the steel-making departments, or else emptied the hot metal into new "pig-casting machines" – conveyor belts of metal moulds, which eliminated the old work in sand on the casting-house floor. The new coke ovens built at Canadian steel plants after 1900 were similarly mechanized, so that conveying vehicles and belts moved the coal speedily through its stages of preparation into coke.[14] Gone from all this work were most of the shovels, wheelbarrows, and small armies of brawny labourers, and in their place were a few handfuls of men who manipulated gears.[15]

In the nineteenth century, most Canadian ironmasters had sold the pig iron produced in their furnaces either to foundries, which would turn it into "cast iron" goods, or to forges and rolling mills, where the iron would be reheated and shaped into usable "wrought iron" products. The earliest method of producing wrought-iron goods had involved heating the iron in forges and hammering out the impurities – the work of the all-round blacksmith. In the last quarter of the nineteenth century, however, the more common procedure was "puddling" the pig iron – that is, while heating it in a special furnace, to stir the iron to separate out the dross, to form it into pasty balls of iron, and to put the balls through a "squeezer" to extract the last impurities. The iron could then be sent through the rolling mills to produce bars and other shapes. The slow, painstaking labour of the iron puddler, a highly skilled craftsman, made this a costly process, and, while iron enterprises at Londonderry and Hamilton employed these men from time to time, most rolling mills in the country preferred working with scrap iron, which was cheaper and did not require this purification process. The iron puddler who was so important in the American and British industries was, therefore, comparatively less so in Canada.[16]

In any case, by the 1890s, wrought iron was no longer the wave of the future. Puddling would not be challenged and transformed; it would simply be bypassed. Experiments in Britain and Germany in the 1870s had brought about a new, tougher, more-resilient type of iron, with a lower carbon content that was soon known as steel. The processes developed in Britain and the United States for producing steel from pig iron avoided the labour-intensive routines of puddling. The first and initially most popular was the Bessemer process: in a huge pear-shaped converter, air was blown through the molten iron to oxidize or burn out the impurities; the vessel would then be tilted to drain out the steel thus formed. The Bessemer method, however, required a high quality of ore, which was becoming scarce in North America by the turn of the century. Francis Clergue installed Bessemer converters at Algoma Steel in 1902, to use the ores of the corporation's nearby Helen Mine, but unending problems with the process forced the firm to abandon these converters completely in 1916.[17]

By 1900, in fact, the increasingly more common method of steel making in North America was "open-hearth" production.[18] Molten pig iron and a quantity of scrap metal would be exposed to the intense heat of a gas flame in special furnaces to draw out the last impurities in the iron, and, once small quantities of ferro-alloys had been shovelled in to adjust the chemical composition for hardness, the molten steel could be tapped from the back of the furnace in a thunderous explosion of liquid fire – perhaps the most dramatic spectacle in a steel plant. The first open-hearth installation in Canada was a small operation at the Trenton works of Nova Scotia Steel in 1883. The chemical process within these large new furnaces had replaced the puddler's craft, but human muscle was still straining to produce the steel. The furnaces were charged by hand, according to old-timers:

> The crew of four helpers charged their furnace, then pushed buggies to outdoor scrap and ore piles, loaded up the buggies by hand, then pushed them back to the furnace, to be ready for the next charging. They helped the Ladleman push the molten ladle of steel suspended from a swinging arm over the ingot mould. Rain or shine, snow or frost, the buggies were loaded outdoors. Indoors, the temperature near the furnaces was between one hundred and one hundred and thirty degrees F., depending upon the season.[19]

The open-hearth departments, which opened in the main steelmaking centres between 1900 and 1907, incorporated numerous "labour-saving devices," which eliminated much of this manual labour.[20] Skilled furnace-tenders, known as "melters," still had to use considerable discretion in determining the quality and timing of the brew, and at regular intervals melters' helpers had to face the gates of hell with shovels full of chemicals;[21] but machinery had replaced most other manual labour. Men now drove small vehicles mounted on railway tracks for thrusting iron and scrap into the furnaces. Others used powerful electric cranes to pick up ladles of molten steel and to fill ingot moulds sitting upright on railway cars. Other operators handled specially designed "stripping cranes" to slip off the moulds, while another crane carried them off to the "soaking pits," where they were heated to a uniform temperature for their trip through the mills. A few key workers were still responsible for quality control, but, in contrast to the arduous, manual work of the old puddlers, many more men in the open-hearth department were operating or helping to maintain machinery, which handled the tasks of large-scale steel production quickly and smoothly.

The final phase of steel production took place in the rolling-mill plants, where the ingots passed back and forth between sets of massive rolls (like an old-fashioned wringer washing machine) to produce smaller shapes, from rails to structural steel to wire rods. The first rolling mills had appeared in Canada between the 1850s and 1880s to meet the needs of, first, the railway industry and eventually a wide range of metal-working enterprises. By the turn of the century, there were numerous independent firms still running on the older technology of that era.[22] Most continued to produce relatively small quantities of varied products for the small Canadian market and consequently could not afford the expensive investment in highly specialized, highly mechanized rolling-mill equipment. In 1910 a supervisor at Stelco, a company that had brought a number of these older operations into its merger that year, told a parliamentary committee: "We consider we would have a very good order if we ran a day on it."[23] As a result, many Canadian rolling-mill operations still needed the muscle and the savvy of the "heaters" and "rollers" – the men who used simple tongs to snatch the hot bars from reheating furnaces and thrust them into the successive sets of rolls, working at their own pace and judging the quality of the product themselves. "We knew when we were handling that steel what its potentials were, what we could and couldn't do with it," one rolling-mill worker explained many years later. "We had to do it all with our eyes and judgment, mainly judgment. There were no gauges like today."[24]

Besides these older, hand-operated mills, however, each of the big three firms opened specialized rolling-mill facilities before the First World War that transformed the traditional labour process. In these operations, a crane operator would fetch a reheated ingot from the soaking pit and place it on a bed of rollers. From here men perched high up in "pulpits" controlled the complex machinery by pulling levers and pressing buttons, sending the hot steel block back and forth through the rolls. Each time through, the flip of one lever would raise or lower the large table on which the ingot rested, while another would activate mechanical arms called "manipulators" for turning it over. The "bloom" that emerged from this process would then be sent along more automatic conveyors to giant shears, where men cut it into appropriate lengths, and then on to smaller sets of rolls. As the *Canadian Foundryman* noted after surveying Stelco's new continuous, electrically driven operation in 1913: "Modern rolling mills are really automatic machines on a large scale, one machine sometimes covering an acre or more of ground, and operated by a few men almost entirely without hard muscular labour." The efforts to modernize the older, smaller rolling-mill plants, which in some cases would last until the 1930s, aimed at achieving the same level of mechanization.[25]

The techniques of steel making in Canada thus changed quickly and dramatically after 1900. Much of the old craft knowledge of preparing and shaping metal had been embodied in large, complex, new machinery. Perhaps even more important, powerful, fast-paced lifting and conveying devices were performing feats of superhuman strength in moving raw materials and finished steel through the plants. The unprecedented speed and reliability of these machines was pushing up the pace of production and closely integrating all the stages in the process. Wherever possible, machines had replaced men. The object of all this mechanization was not to save sweat, but to cut production costs. As the directors of Algoma Steel boasted in 1902: "The arrangement of the plant is such that the material can be handled at a minimum labor cost, and an unusually large output per man is thus obtainable." Twenty years later, a business journalist found this claim true for the whole industry: "The products could not be turned out at anything even approaching their present low price if human labour had to be utilized to do what is now done by mechanism." Federal government statistics also sustain these claims of higher productivity: in 1901 some 4,110 workers were needed to produce the country's 245,000 long tons of pig iron and 26,000 tons of steel; by 1929, the number of workers had risen to 10,500, but they were turning out 1.1 million tons of pig iron and 1.3 million tons of steel.[26] Machines could work faster, more reliably, and with fewer interruptions from human frailty or wilfulness. Human foibles had confronted the steelmasters in the form of occasional labour shortages and frequent unruliness – both strikes (as we will see) and labour turnover. "Workmen find it bad enough to be forced to handle frozen pig and scrap iron in the winter," the *Canadian Foundryman* noted, "but when the sun comes beating down the men become inefficient and discontented. Many of them leave."[27] Machines in a steel plant that eliminated such men, therefore, embodied more effective managerial control over production.

Journalistic enthusiasm for the new technology could also mask the hazards of the new work environment. The vast new steel plants became fiercely hot, smoky, deafeningly noisy caverns filled with massive, towering machinery that dwarfed the workmen toiling below. Brilliant, fiery flashes from the mouths of furnaces or showers of sparks from cauldrons of molten metal penetrated the gloom and seared the flesh of any nearby workers. If the men were not scampering out of the way of ladles, moulds, and great hunks of glowing steel that soared through the air at the end of giant cranes, they were dodging locomotives or charging machines whose tracks criss-crossed the plants. Dirt and danger remained hallmarks of the work experience in the steel industry.

The labour requirements of Canadian steel plants changed as rapidly as the technology. The observation of a Nova Scotia royal commission in 1910 that Dosco's workforce had been "enormously reduced" in order to "eliminate needless cost wherever possible" reflected the trend in the industry.[28] Yet "labour-saving devices" by no means displaced all manual labour. Mishaps, delays, and clean-up and maintenance functions still demanded both skill and brute labour; so, too, did the crucial judgments of the men at the furnace doors and on some of the old rolling mills. As Stelco's open-hearth superintendent explained in 1910: "You cannot go and round up the skilled men and pick them up on the street corner. Take our melters, rollers and first helpers, they are skilled men and the next man to one of these cannot take his place. The second helper or third helper cannot take the place of the first helper and the same with the men at the ladles."[29] Over the long term, however, the jobs eliminated were the most skilled (notably the work of the puddlers) and the least skilled. In 1923, for example, a royal commission on industrial unrest in the Sydney steel industry learned that only about 20 per cent of Dosco's total staff was "common labour."[30] On the whole, the new technology had replaced the old nineteenth-century dichotomy between craftsman and labourer with more homogeneity among the steelworking occupations, a large percentage of which now involved machine operation.

The term for this new body of workers, which became current in the early twentieth century, was "semi-skilled," but the phrase disguised how little skill was required in most jobs and how easily these workers could be replaced. In an address to the American Iron and Steel Institute in 1919, Stelco's president proudly announced that in four-and-a-half years of operating the company's new electrically driven blooming mill, less than an hour and a half had been necessary for "breaking in new men to operate the motor for the mill."[31] For a former labourer, the most significant changes in the shift to semi-skilled work in a steel plant were the move from the periphery to the centre of the production processes and an increased responsibility for the machinery and for output. He was not as indispensable as the old craftsman, but his employer would soon grow reliant on the regularity, stability, and experience of these new mass-production workers.

Labour economist Richard Edwards has applied the term "technical control" to managerial systems in which "the entire production process of the plant or large segments of it are based on a technology that paces and directs the labor process."[32] The term is only partially applicable to the Canadian steel industry. While machines in a steel plant could replace slow-moving, obstreperous, unreliable labourers and independent-minded craftsmen, they did not necessarily discipline the workers who remained. The chemical processes in the furnace played an autonomous role in setting work rhythms, as did the close integration of processes that demanded speedy movement of molten metal about the plant. Yet few steelworkers fit Charlie Chaplin's stereotype of the assembly-line worker feverishly struggling to keep up with the relentless pace of self-propelled machinery. Most of the individual machines, whether hoists, cranes, conveying vehicles, charging devices, or even furnaces, had to be activated by workers making their own judgments about timing and pacing. Under these circumstances, new technology was not enough: owners and managers of Canada's steel plants recognized the need for new policies for managing their workers – policies designed to extract from them the maximum effort in their hours on the job, with a minimum of resistance.

Managers and Men

In the nineteenth century, ironmasters had most often left direct supervision of the work process to their most skilled workers. Subcontracting the work to these men had been common in the British and American industries[33] and in the early years at Londonderry, but such practices seem to have largely disappeared in Canada by the late 1880s.[34] Skilled workers nonetheless still had responsibility for directing the work of their less-skilled workmates. Ironmasters indirectly disciplined these skilled work leaders by tying their earnings to the company's economic fortunes: they were paid on a tonnage basis and on a sliding scale that reflected the selling price of iron products. A unionist in a small rolling-mill department at the Hamilton steel plant described this system still in use in 1910: "Our scale is what is called the sliding scale, and our officials examine the books of the Iron and Steel Company every six months – every sixty days I should say – and if the selling price of iron and steel has gone up we will say one point, why we get a two per cent advance. If it goes down one point, we get a two per cent reduction."[35] The historic defeat of the skilled workers' union in the brutal Homestead strike of 1892 sounded the death knell for these practices and, combined with ongoing technological innovations, allowed the major American steel companies to break the connection between corporate earnings and skilled workers' pay. Henceforth the pattern – soon copied in Canada – was to establish wage scales from the base rate for unskilled labour.[36]

After 1900, new Canadian steel-making corporations were too obsessed with cutting costs to tolerate an indirect form of management. Productivity, they believed, would rise only if managers exercised a centralized control over the labour process. Although there is no evidence of simon-pure scientific managers in Canadian steel plants,[37] the companies' owners and managers showed the characteristic mania for "efficiency" that swept through industrial Canada in the early twentieth century: meticulous calculation and minimizing of costs, careful planning and scheduling in the front office, centralized job redesign, and so on.[38] It would be a mistake, however, to expect to find many white-collared men with stop watches roaming about amidst the smoke and din. The steel companies' management of their workforce was less genteel than all that. Their labour policies in the early twentieth century were reminiscent of the techniques of the pioneers in Britain's Industrial Revolution a century earlier: new machines, a new workforce, long hours, and a rigid discipline based on the carrot and the stick. In this case, the new industrial recruits were migrant labourers from the villages of southern and eastern Europe and the outports of Atlantic Canada. The workplace discipline came from both rigid, authoritarian direction of the workers and the incentives of piecework and welfare capitalism.

Canadian iron and steel producers who pondered the weakness of their industry in the 1890s recognized that their chief competitors south of the border had reduced their labour costs by hiring European immigrants and American blacks. As John F. Stairs of Nova Scotia Steel told a gathering of iron men in 1897: "If we in Nova Scotia were able to compete in wages with those in Alabama we could make iron as cheap as they do."[39] By the early 1900s each of the major corporations in the industry was trying to "compete in wages" with the Americans by recruiting from new pools of cheaper labour. Both Dosco and Algoma found the large number of Italians hired to build their new plants or nearby railways could be profitably shifted into manufacturing jobs. Each of these firms also actively recruited European migrants in Europe and the United States through special employment agencies.[40] Similarly, the Hamilton Steel and Iron Company, Stelco's predecessor, imported a trainload of Italians to help break a turn-of-the-century strike and encouraged these newcomers to set up shacks on the company's lakefront property.[41] Nova Scotia Steel was the only large steel firm that shunned this "foreign" labour force, but, like Dosco, it employed migrant labour from the outports of Newfoundland.[42] Eventually, once a decided preference for certain ethnic groups was known, intermediaries in the immigrant communities, usually labour agents of some kind, would keep up the flow of new workers into the plants.[43] In the pre-war decade, therefore, the steelworking labour force became a multicultural patchwork, including Italians, Poles, Hungarians, Ukrainians, southern blacks, and Anglo-Celtic Newfoundlanders, Canadians, and Americans.

This new workforce had several advantages for the steelmasters. In the first place, large numbers of these workers were transients, migrating from distant villages or outports in search of cash to help their peasant families back home cope with worsening underemployment, overpopulation, and agricultural depression. They tended to come alone and to board in tightly packed little ethnic ghettoes near the steel plants.[44] Their economical lifestyle allowed them to save much of their earnings, but also to work for unusually low wages. "The Italian will board himself and thrive upon a dollar a week, on which men of any other nationality would starve," the Sault *Star* complained in 1903.[45] These migrant labourers who were only expecting to work for short spells in a steel plant were, therefore, cheap labour for the companies. "It would be a very serious matter to do away with foreign labour," a Stelco official warned in 1919 during heated debates about deporting the "aliens." "If we expect returned soldiers to do the rough, rugged work, many of us would be out of business because we could not produce at anything like low enough cost."[46]

The transiency and inexperience of this new workforce had a second advantage for the steel companies. Since they had no long-term commitment to their jobs in the steel plants and seldom stayed more than a few years at the most,[47] their bosses could intensify the labour process to extract the maximum from their labour power in a working day. One technique was the twelve-hour day (eleven on the day shift, thirteen at night) in the continuous production departments:

blast-furnace, open hearth, and, quite often, the larger rolling mills. The companies repeatedly resisted efforts to introduce the eight-hour day, and they won support from a Nova Scotia Commission on Hours of Labour in 1910. "No one can deny," the commissioners reported, "that a day of twelve hours' manual labor, or of twelve or ten hours of attendance on ovens, furnaces, and machines, amid the conditions of such an industry, is long, and leaves the man little time, inclination or energy for other interests"; but "as the business stands at present, the men cannot live on 8 hours pay, and the Company cannot afford 12 hours pay for 8 hours work." Not surprisingly, the commission found the heaviest concentration of Europeans and Newfoundlanders in departments on twelve-hour shifts, especially around the coke ovens and blast- and open-hearth furnaces.[48] Probably only these "sojourners" could tolerate such exhausting work.

The twelve-hour day and seven-day work week also had a disciplinary power, which Stelco's steel-plant superintendent explained to a parliamentary committee on the eight-hour day in 1910. In describing the long night shift, he noted that the men did nothing but work and sleep: "They prefer to work at night and then go home, go to bed right away and sleep all day. They get up at five or half-past five and go to the plant." This endless cycle of work made the men easier to manage. "We get better results from our men where we have them work 11 and 13 hours," the official stressed repeatedly in his testimony; moreover, "the best men we have and from whom we get the best results are the men who stay at work at least 325, 330, or 340 days a year." Shortening the work week, especially by shutting down on Sundays or holidays, created "constant trouble" and "dissipation": "It seems to give them too much time off; too much chance of spending money or to get around." Evidently the long hours in the steel industry gave the companies control over the whole lives of their workers. These hours would last until 1930 in Hamilton, and 1935 in Sydney and Sault Ste Marie.[49]

Steel company managers also wanted to provide incentives to drive the workers harder during their long hours on the job. In the decade before the war, superintendents and foremen were under steady pressure to increase the daily output beyond the rated capacity of the steel-making facilities. In April 1906, for example, Algoma proudly announced that its rail mill had set a new record: 859 tons of rails had been turned out in 24 hours, on equipment built to produce 500 tons per day, and Dosco' s previous record had been smashed by 50 tons.

By September, the daily output had passed 1,000 tons, and seven years later reached 1,400. Both these plants continued to report "record months" in all departments.[50]

In part, this increased output came from close supervision by foremen whose tyrannical rule was notorious. A Stelco executive admitted in 1919 that "we have more trouble through workmen and foremen than anywhere else," and until the 1940s workers had to learn to curry the favour of foremen with money, food, liquor, and occasionally even the sexual services of their wives.[51] An important figure in this system of control was the ethnic "straw boss" who imposed managerial discipline on small groups of workers of the same nationality. At the same time, however, managers were making full use of piecework to stimulate the individual worker's effort. Payment by tonnage rates had begun in the late nineteenth century and was well established throughout the industry by the First World War. In 1923, Stelco's blast-furnace superintendent described "good incentive wages" as one of the keystones of the firm's industrial relations policies.[52] The federal government's statistics on average annual wages suggest that the long hours on piecework did pay off for those who held onto their jobs: as table 1 (p. 170) indicates, steelworkers' annual earnings were always well above the average manufacturing wage, and even above the earnings of the largely skilled workers in printing; among mass-production workers, only workers in the auto and pulp and paper industries did better (like steel, both these industries had virtually no women workers whose low wages would drag down the average figure).

In this context, the new immigrants' desire for quick money was a boon to employers who were undertaking to intensify production in their plants. Two American scholars, for example, noted in 1918 how migrant Polish peasants in Europe had already adjusted their work rhythms in order to earn as much and as fast as possible:

> The peasant begins to search, not only for the best possible remuneration for a given amount of work, but for the opportunity to do as much work as possible. No efforts are spared, no sacrifice is too great, when the absolute amount of income can be increased. The peasant at this stage is therefore so eager to get piece-work … They take the hardship and bad treatment into account, but accept them as an inevitable condition of higher income. When they come back [home], they take an absolute rest for two or three months and are not to be moved to do the slightest work.[53]

Table 1 Average annual wages in selected Canadian manufacturing industries, 1917–50

Year	All manufacturing	Agricultural implements	Automobiles	Electrical parts	Printing & publishing	Pulp & paper	Steel
1917	$759	$838	$970	$736	$776	$865	$1,217
1918	878	934	1,191	856	775	1,020	1,371
1919	938	1,047	1,397	854	989	1,230	1,246
1920	1,109	–	–	–	–	–	–
1921	1,002	1,193	1,458	1,091	1,238	1,251	1,441
1922	939	1,004	1,400	948	1,135	1,145	1,259
1923	959	1,043	1,500	957	1,233	1,186	1,746
1924	972	1,086	1,387	1,012	1,343	1,247	1,262
1925	971	1,101	1,577	992	1,305	1,267	1,325
1926	1,003	1,178	1,535	1,061	1,365	1,302	1,382
1927	997	1,147	1,581	1,070	1,333	1,265	1,529
1928	1,024	1,158	1,697	1,080	1,397	1,282	1,650
1929	1,045	1,188	1,530	1,121	1,465	1,340	1,598
1930	1,001	1,145	1,422	999	1,459	1,221	1,449
1931	957	–	1,133	970	1,457	1,146	1,252
1932	852	859	1,063	846	1,364	984	1,117
1933	785	806	809	746	1,243	956	1,049
1934	837	859	1,191	750	1,254	1,098	1,135
1935	874	962	1,321	906	1,275	1,143	1,247
1936	896	996	1,286	924	1,316	1,201	1,144
1937	965	1,051	1,371	996	1,338	1,344	1,333
1938	956	1,088	1,263	976	1,334	1,192	1,284
1939	975	1,028	1,263	982	1,324	1,271	1,373
1940	1,084	1,199	1,781	1,123	1,397	1,475	1,566
1941	1,220	1,331	1,963	1,280	1,444	1,855	1,855
1942	1,383	1,516	2,135	1,443	1,505	1,701	1,797
1943	1,525	1,718	2,351	1,518	1,575	1,787	1,883
1944	1,564	1,762	2,347	1,548	1,657	1,858	1,930
1945	1,538	1,739	2,365	1,576	1,705	1,873	1,907
1946	1,516	1,735	1,887	1,523	1,775	2,113	1,998
1947	1,713	1,898	2,337	1,817	1,975	2,443	2,149
1948	1,960	2,306	2,639	2,125	2,440	2,764	2,651
1949	2,067	2,506	2,660	2,212	2,255	2,851	2,757
1950	2,183	2,574	3,045	2,336	2,621	3,051	2,841

Source: *Canada Year Book* (Ottawa), 1917–50.

One unfortunate by-product of the speed-up that was possible in this situation was a deplorably high accident rate. Industrial accidents were not reported with any consistency before 1910, but in Ontario, in 1912, at least 388 Algoma employees and 113 at Stelco suffered occupational injuries requiring at least a week off work. Four years later, the last detailed statistics available included 473 and 488 victims respectively, amounting to almost one worker in six at Stelco and involving four deaths at the two plants. The same year, Nova Scotia's factories' inspector reported 345 injuries at Dosco, nine of them fatal. In 1917 he commented on the connection between transiency and accidents:

> Most of the accidents are due to inexperience, and happen mostly to unskilled labourers about the large plants. Large numbers are injured by material of all kinds falling on their heads or feet, by being jammed between objects, by falling or tripping, and in many other ways, which can only be avoided by experience or when workmen get to know the dangers and mishaps liable to occur while they are at their work.[54]

There was one final bonus for the steel companies who hired these "birds of passage" – the cultural gulf that set them apart from the rest of the city's working class and inhibited class-conscious activity. These were men from peasant or outport backgrounds whose ties were usually stronger with family and village across the water than with fellow workers a few blocks away. The presence of so many Europeans, moreover, deeply troubled the native-born and American workers, who charged that these "foreigners" had been "brought over to lower the standard of living."[55] There were a few incidents (surprisingly few, actually) of open conflict between these two distinct groups of workers before the First World War, such as a 1912 strike precipitated by the introduction of two Poles into Stelco's wire-drawing department.[56] The war, however, ignited some vigorous nativist sentiments, often based on resentment of the better jobs the "foreigners" had acquired in the wartime prosperity and the higher earnings they were stashing away. By 1919, Anglo-Canadian workers in the three major steel centres were agitating for exclusion of "aliens" from "white" jobs. "The Government should be told now and told plainly," a Nova Scotia labour paper argued early that year, "that restrictions should be placed on all cheap European labor, especially should this apply to Germans, Austrians, Hungarians, and Russians"; and another voice of labour in the same steel towns insisted a few months later: "Cheap alien labour must not be allowed to encroach on the hours and wages of good Anglo-Saxon wage-earners." In Hamilton in February 1919, a boisterous crowd of 10,000, in which "returned soldiers and working men seemed to predominate," demanded the deportation of "enemy aliens and other undesirables."[57]

As important as these thundering denunciations were, it should be borne in mind that there were no race riots comparable to those in

British Columbia or the United States at the time. Ultimately, it was not so much the open conflict between ethnic groups under one factory roof as their completely separate social worlds. An Italian blast-furnace worker would return to his boarding house, or perhaps later to his own home, in a continental European enclave where he enjoyed the support of his own community institutions distinct from those of the English-speaking workers. A common working-class community developed only with great difficulty in these circumstances.

A Hamilton newspaper had early on observed how advantageous this ethnic segmentation of the steel-making workforce could be. In the wake of a large strike at the Hamilton Steel and Iron Company in 1910, it noted how the transiency and the strangeness of so many of the city's steelworkers left the public "comparatively indifferent to their claims." The "great manufacturing corporations" thus reaped a twofold benefit: "They get work done at a cost less than the cost of getting it done by English-speaking workmen, and they prevent the enlistment of public opinion on the side of the workers when troubles arise with their foreign employees."[58] For these companies the interests of the migrant labourers in quick cash earnings meshed well with corporate strategies aimed at intensifying production and increasing productivity.

Modern theorists of "segmentation" in the working class have focused on the narrowing of the job hierarchy and concluded that homogenization was the main theme in the development of the labour force between 1870 and the Second World War, at which point segmentation began to emerge between core and peripheral sectors of the labour market.[59] This perspective misses the crucial divisions within mass-production industries along ethnic lines, which in Canada date from the turn of the century. Until the 1940s, ethnic fragmentation was a persistent counterpoint to occupational homogeneity.[60] Intensive use of migrant workers unfamiliar with the industry's traditional work routines would bring results only with that part of the workforce that could be easily replaced. But, as we have seen, technological and managerial innovations in the steel industry had not completely eliminated the need for skill and experience; in fact, they may have heightened the importance of permanently employed, experienced, responsible steelworkers. In the nineteenth century, Canadian ironmasters had generally imported their skilled labour, often from Britain, and all the new steel corporations in the early twentieth century had similarly turned to the United States and, to a lesser extent, to Europe for their first skilled workers.[61] The services of these men could not be treated as cavalierly as those of the thousands of unskilled labourers who flocked to the factory gates looking for work. Policies had to be developed that tied these workers to their employers without at the same time granting them too much autonomous shop-floor control (to prevent the re-emergence of the kinds of independent craftsmanship that had characterized nineteenth-century iron work). The key seemed to be ensuring worker dependence on the company.

One set of employment policies that helped immensely to heighten the dependency of the more skilled workers on their employers was internal recruitment. After the initial importation of skilled men, Canada's steel companies apparently made every effort to hire replacements from within their own workforces. Like its American counterparts, Nova Scotia Steel had first used a policy of training local residents for as many jobs as possible and drawing them up "job ladders" into more-skilled, higher-paying jobs. Presiding over this process of job placement were the foremen, who were able to develop powerful systems of patronage in the plants. Not only did this kind of promotion system encourage men to stay in their jobs (and to curry favour in the hopes of advancement), it also left them with skills that were seldom easily transported to other industries, or even to other Canadian steel plants, which were hundreds of miles away. This dependent status contrasted with that of the older-style craftsman, like a moulder or pattern-maker, whose skills were learned within independent craft traditions and controlled by craft unions.[62]

At the same time, the Canadian steel companies all sponsored welfare programs, which would encourage their more valuable employees to identify their long-term economic security with the company. Employees' benefit societies in each of the films provided insurance against sickness and death, and pension, stock-subscription, and group-insurance plans were gradually added. So, too, were some limited, long-overdue safety programs. The range of welfare programs increased whenever industrial conflict intensified in the steel plants and the spectre of trade unionism appeared, notably after the First World War and in the later 1930s.[63] The most elaborate, and ultimately the most successful plan, introduced at the Dominion Foundries and Steel (Dofasco) plant in Hamilton in 1937, showered steelworkers and their families with recreational activities and, more important, incorporated them into a much publicized profit-sharing scheme.[64] Dosco and Stelco also cast the illusion of industrial democracy over their plants in 1923 and 1935 respectively, by organizing "industrial councils" of equal numbers of workers and management staff, with limited powers to recommend changes in working conditions (though seldom in hours or wages).[65] In 1943 Stelco took the further step of sponsoring a company union – a move Algoma was originally contemplating before it recognized an independent union in 1935.[66] The steel companies were invariably pushed into these welfare-capitalist measures by restlessness among their more stable employees. In 1919, Stelco's vice-president explained to a royal commission that they were not acts of philanthropy towards the firm's employees, but were intended "to give them a direct interest in the business and promote continuity of employment," since "continuous and contented service is an asset to any company."[67]

Maintaining an internal labour market and spinning a web of welfare capitalism over the workers were techniques for ensuring a stable, dependent workforce that the American steelmasters had also developed. But there was a third force in Canada that tightened the bonds between these steelworkers and their employers: the chronic instability of much of the Canadian industry. The stable core of steelworkers who clung desperately to their jobs in the 1920s and 1930s occasionally joined company delegations to Ottawa to beg for better tariff protection or for government spending to stimulate the industry. The federal Advisory Board on Tariffs and Taxation heard particularly earnest pleas from Algoma's steelworkers requesting some state intervention to overcome the pattern of sporadic employment. Appealing to the same spirit, Algoma circulated a handbill in its plant in 1937: "Don't fight this Company but with it, come to Ottawa with us and get a 100,000 ton rail order."[68] Clearly the dependence of these steelworkers on their employer went beyond social mobility and a modicum of social security, to the very existence of their jobs.

The Canadian steel companies did not fashion this whole set of labour policies according to any industrial engineer's master plan. Most of the key practices were borrowed from the United States and implemented by managers with American experience, but there was plenty of experimentation in local contexts, particularly in the first twenty years. The pool of cheap, inexperienced, migrant labour provided the flexibility necessary for extracting unprecedented levels of productivity from the steelworkers. Out of the somewhat chaotic early years came distinctive patterns of managing men in the steel plants. Management emerged securely in the saddle of production, with the tyranny of the foreman as the spur and the cultivated self-interest of wage-incentive plans and internal promotion as the bit. Centrally important was a relentless effort to eliminate as far as possible the autonomy of workers on the job and to heighten their dependence on their employer. Despite the modest gestures of welfarism, the managerial style was ruthlessly authoritarian, and supervisors ruled their industrial domains with iron fists, supplementing their gruff commands and arbitrary patronage systems with spies, blacklisting, and company police.[69] Mechanization had facilitated predictability and speed-ups, but these shop-floor despots guaranteed to Canada's steelmasters that their workers' labour-power would be used to the fullest. Not surprisingly, most steelworkers eventually toiled in an atmosphere of fear – fear of injury in the heat, dust, and noise of fire-breathing machines and fear of losing their jobs for insubordination. Ultimately that fear was mixed with a deep resentment.

Resistance

The response of Canada's steelworkers to their work environment followed two paths in the twentieth century. Before the Second World War, the predominant response was individualized and took two forms: initially, casual, short-term attachment to jobs; and, then, by the 1920s, integration into the web of longer-term dependency on employers. Yet groups of workers in the industry regularly challenged that pattern with forms of collective resistance. In the early years, before the First World War, that resistance surged up in the apparently spontaneous strikes of migrant labourers. By the end of the war, more-formal trade unionism had become the vehicle of worker protest. Only in the course of the next world war, however, did that challenge to the relationship of dependency finally succeed.

The first generation of twentieth-century steelworkers in Canada had come of age by the 1920s. It had taken roughly twenty years for that workforce to develop any cohesion and self-consciousness. In the two preceding decades, a large proportion of the new steelworkers seemed to be just passing through. These workers had no steady attachment to the industry and seemed to see their jobs as a short, if unpleasant, episode in a personal or family-oriented strategy for survival. As in so many other mass-production industries, they changed jobs frequently, partly as a result of the economic instability of the manufacturers and partly as means of dealing with intolerable working conditions.

"Floating" between jobs was a much discussed phenomenon in Canadian industrial life of the early twentieth century, one that had attracted the label of "labour turnover" by 1920.[70] This behaviour became a serious problem for managers only when the reserve army of labour dried up, especially during the First World War. At that juncture, the companies faced wartime labour shortages and declining productivity. Without the whip of poverty to discipline them, workers quit or took days off, confident of their ability to find work again soon. Dosco's general manager reported in 1916: "The foreigners in our employ, particularly the Austrians, realizing the scarcity of labour, are not doing a fair day's work. It is extremely difficult to keep them in hand." The next winter, Algoma's president reckoned the "efficiency" of the company's workforce at about 60 per cent. In 1918, a federal board of conciliation was appalled to discover this attitude in Algoma's coke-oven and open-hearth departments:

> In these basic departments there are nearly twelve hundred (1200) Austrians employed (alien enemies); they almost entirely run the coking ovens; they have been hard to control; they receive such good pay that they do not require to work all the time, so they knock off whenever they like, and do not come back until their money is spent, or they are good and ready. On occasion the company has been obliged to round these men up with the police in order to get men enough to operate this department, so as the mills could be kept going.

An official at Dosco told a royal commission in 1919 that labour turnover during the war was well above 20 per cent – "forty and fifty and maybe a hundred."[71]

Drifting between jobs, however, had become less common by 1930. In the first place, it proved to be a less successful strategy for survival in a period of depression, since there might be no job to move on to. Second, the flow of transatlantic migration was curtailed by the Canadian government between 1920 and 1925 and again for more than a decade in the 1930s. The footloose proletariat of the pre-war years that planned only brief work tours of North America was gradually disappearing. The European migrant community shrank most noticeably in Sydney, from 8 per cent in 1911 to 5.2 per cent in 1931. Those who remained were more settled: in 1927 a delegation of Algoma steelworkers informed the federal tariff board that only one-third of their ranks were "of foreign extraction," and two-thirds of those were naturalized citizens. It should not be surprising, therefore, that Stelco was able to report in 1935 that 88 per cent of its employees had been with the company at least five years.[72] Third, many of these former migrants were beginning to work their way into the semi-skilled jobs in steel making. The labour shortages of the First World War seem to have opened up new opportunities that continued in the postwar world. These three new patterns of employment experience were producing a more stable workforce, much more fully integrated into the structures of control that the companies had developed. Any working-class challenge to that control would have to reckon with deeply ingrained habits of fearful deference.

Steelworkers had, nonetheless, challenged their employers almost from the beginning. Surprisingly, the most consistent source of opposition arose from the supposedly docile continental European labourers. Each of the three companies discovered that these workers were capable of launching surprise strikes, using the ethnic solidarities cultivated in their close-knit little ghettos and on the job. These actions were often well timed to catch the companies in temporary labour shortages. One of the most dramatic of these incidents occurred in Hamilton in 1910, when the entire steel-making operations were shut down for two days by some 1,000 European workers. The strike spread alarm through much of the city's Anglo-Celtic population and made Stelco aware of the potential power of these groups of workers.[73] Despite their lack of permanent organization, these strikers always framed clear demands directed against unacceptable employment policies, especially low wages. For if the object of "sojourning" in North America was to accumulate as much cash as quickly as possible, it made sense to press for higher wages, just as it did on the many other work sites in Canada where immigrant workers seemed so rebellious.[74] In fact, it was the impermanence of their employment in the steel plants and the strength of their ethnic bonds that gave them a minimal autonomy from the steelmasters not shared by their Anglo-Celtic workmates. That form of resistance declined, however, as the steel companies used machines to reduce their reliance on unskilled labourers and as the workforce began to stabilize after the First World War. Henceforth, steelworkers who wanted to stand up to their employers were more likely to be the more skilled workers turning to some brand of trade unionism, although workers were not successful in forcing recognition of their unions in the industry until 1946. The half-century of struggle that culminated in that victory followed an uneven pattern, in which unionizing efforts were restricted to three distinct periods, each more intense than the last: 1901–4, 1917–23, and 1935–46.

The first union organization in the twentieth-century industry appeared in the new Dosco plant in 1901–2, in the form of two lodges of the Provincial Workmen's Association (PWA). The PWA had represented Nova Scotia miners for nearly twenty-five years, and at the turn of the century had widened its membership base to include many other occupations. In 1904 the PWA lodges in Sydney launched a long, bitter strike against the company that shattered the steelworkers' organization and led to extensive blacklisting.[75] No further unionization was seen in the Canadian steel industry until the war. This time, the workers used the vehicle of the Amalgamated Association of Iron, Steel, and Tin Workers. An erstwhile craft union, this association had formally opened its ranks to the unskilled but still drew the bulk of its membership from the technologically backward nooks and crannies of the American steel industry, particularly the older rolling mills. Its first Canadian lodge was organized in Gananoque in 1914, but the great burst of organization in Canada began in 1917, leading to thirteen lodges from Sydney to Red Deer, Alberta, with perhaps 8,000 members.[76]

Overwhelmingly, this was a union of rolling-mill men in the older, hand-operated mills, who, as we have seen, often still exercised considerable skill in handling iron and steel between the rolls. Steelworkers in Sydney, Sault Ste Marie, and Gananoque made significant efforts to create all-inclusive industrial unions, but the international's official policy by 1919 was to subdivide the membership into smaller lodges based on occupational and skill groups. At Algoma and Stelco this quasi craft-unionist policy seriously weakened the local lodges. The Amalgamated Association's move away from craft unionism was ultimately only half-hearted, and a prominent Canadian member later reflected that "the division of the mills by crafts was its outstanding weakness."[77] A few of the association's lodges won temporary informal bargaining rights at the end of the First World War, but virtually all of them collapsed in the depression of the early 1920s, in the face of aggressive employer hostility. The Sydney steelworkers fought the longest, most brutal battle in 1923, with the help of Cape Breton's militant coal miners, who struck in sympathy when federal troops violently attacked the striking steelworkers. The strike was broken, and, as in important sectors of the American steel industry after the historic 1919 strike, Besco established an industrial council as its pale alternative to trade unionism.[78]

The next attempts at organization began in the mid-1930s when independent steelworkers' unions appeared in Hamilton, Sault Ste Marie, Sydney, and Trenton. In 1936, the Steel Workers' Organizing Committee (SWOC) emerged in the United States, and the locals in Sydney, Trenton, and Hamilton resolved quickly in favour of affiliation. Algoma's workers waited until 1940, when a new leadership had emerged in the local, and when SWOC's Canadian national office had been purged of its Communists. In their rush to affiliate, these Canadian steelworkers were responding to the almost magic appeal of the Congress of Industrial Organizations (CIO), of which SWOC was one of the first and most significant members. Yet the early successes of the American steelworkers were not matched in Canada: after the first wave of enthusiasm and rising membership levels, the Canadian steel companies fought back, and the struggle for collective representation became bitter and protracted. Indeed, despite the strength of the union in Sydney and the imminent affiliation of the Algoma local, SWOC, and Canadian steelworkers, were on the defensive by the end of the 1930s.[79]

The union's basic weakness in Canada lay in Stelco's Hamilton plant – the industry's trend-setter. There the local union members, the core of whom were the more skilled workers of the sheet mill, had been unable to build a successful union in the face of workers' fear, loyalism, and apathy, and in competition with a works council, started in 1935. In the context of new wartime labour shortages, however, the balance of forces at Stelco gradually shifted to the workers. The victory of eight of the eleven union candidates for the works council in 1942 emboldened Local 1005 to demand company recognition of the union – a demand raised in the midst of strikes by Algoma, Sydney, and Trenton steelworkers against company refusals to meet wage demands that government regulations forbade. Industrial relations within the industry had reached crisis proportions. In response to this and similar situations in other industries, the Mackenzie King cabinet enacted an order-in-council, PC 1003, which established state-supervised union certification and collective bargaining.[80]

Events now moved quickly at Stelco. Local 1005 was certified in 1944, and the first contract was signed in February 1945. As both sides were aware, however, this was a paper agreement: the real confrontation would take place once the government's intervention into the field of industrial relations ended after the war. The Canadian steel companies were eager to return to the pre-war days of unfettered managerial control. Stelco became the main battleground for the industry. As the strike deadline approached, and the Algoma and Sydney plants seemed certain to be completely shut down by the overwhelming strength of the unions there, Stelco answered demands for union security (the "checkoff"), wage increases, seniority, and grievance procedures with a proclaimed determination to keep its Hamilton plant open during any strike. The workers themselves squared off along pro-union and pro-company lines. At the forefront of the strikers' ranks were the eastern and southern European workers, who were the most vulnerable to the capricious powers of supervisors and who were keenly interested in establishing the forms of security that union recognition promised. The steelworkers drew support from Hamilton rubber and electrical workers, themselves on strike and highly aware that the outcome of their conflicts depended on the fate of the Stelco strikers. Indeed, it was the support of these workers – and of the Hamilton working class generally – that sustained the picket lines at Stelco, perhaps the critical determinant in the ultimate victory of the strikers. After 81 days, Stelco and Local 1005 reached an agreement, and settlements at Sydney and Sault Ste Marie followed quickly. Stelco workers had established their union and had helped to set industrial relations in Canada on a completely new footing.[81]

Three features of this record of unionizing in the Canadian steel industry should be emphasized. The first is the social complexion of union enthusiasts. The initiative in each wave of organizing unquestionably came from some of the most skilled steelworkers, notably the rolling-mill hands, whose small edge of functional autonomy on the job gave them the pride, confidence, and leverage to challenge the companies' authoritarian rule.[82] In some cases in the SWOC era, these union militants had the additional leaven of radical politics sprinkled through their leadership, both Communist and social-democratic.[83] It was evident, moreover, that union success would be greater where steelworkers could draw on a vibrant, independent working-class community outside the steel plants. In Cape Breton the coal miners' advice and solidarity helped Sydney steelworkers in each wave of organizing. Hamilton, however, provided the striking contrast of a city of huge factories where traditions of workplace solidarity had largely been shattered by the 1920s.[84] In both wartime upsurges of union organizing, Hamilton lagged far behind the other major centres.

In fact, the importance of the tough-minded militants operating from a sphere of relative shop-floor independence and radical commitment should not blind us to the limited support they could count on. Thousands of workers were reluctant or unwilling to step outside the structures of dependence, deference, and loyalism to the firm. Nowhere was this more evident than in Hamilton, where more than 1,000 steelworkers stayed inside the plant during the 81-day strike of 1946 and organized themselves into the "Loyal Order of Scabs." These were predominantly men with long service to the company who saw their lifetime security tied to their employer. The more permanent monument to this working-class loyalism was next door at Dofasco, where prompt moves by the company in 1937 to break up an incipient union local and to launch an imaginative program of welfare capitalism solidified this alternative to the unionized workplace – the so-called Dofasco Way.[85]

Second, the context of these unionizing efforts was crucial. Some crisis was necessary to overturn the stability and legitimacy of the steel companies' control over their work processes. In Cape Breton, the arrogance of outside corporate manipulations, especially in the 1920s, created a rupture. But more than any other factor, the two world wars disrupted established notions about the distribution of power and wealth and provided the catalyst for union growth. The labour shortages during both wars gave workers greater independence from the discipline of poverty, and the pressure to turn out munitions strengthened their hand with employers. During the Second World War, moreover, federal regulations froze essential workers in their jobs and effectively prevented employers from firing them in the traditional arbitrary fashion.[86]

Third, and even more important, was the wartime political climate. During both wars, Canadian workers were urged to sacrifice personal goals in the struggle for democracy. Unionists quickly transformed this rhetoric into demands for *industrial* democracy. In 1918 the Sydney steelworkers' newspaper attacked Dosco for its "attitude of stubbornness, of tyranny, of Steel-gloved Kaiserism"; it insisted that "the people of Cape Breton have suffered too dearly on the fields of Flanders and at home to be ruled by an autocracy."[87] A quarter of a century later, a Hamilton union bulletin declared that "every individual must decide whether he is for democracy or dictatorship – whether he supports 'der fuehrer' policy of having the bosses say how workers may present their case."[88] The strength of that sentiment ultimately pushed the Canadian state into a new activist role in industrial relations. The wartime political environment also generated the demand for social security, raised by workers during both wars. It was not until 1943–4 that the federal government began to act on questions of family allowances, contributory health insurance, and a contributory old-age pension scheme, promising as well to create a new Department of National Health and Welfare.[89] Organizers for the new industrial unions who took up Canadian workers' demands for these measures made the connections between industrial democracy and social security, and, by inaugurating the welfare state in Canada, Mackenzie King hoped to sap the new-found strength of the Cooperative Commonwealth Federation (CCF), as well as short-circuiting the alarming growth in industrial conflict. In general, this wartime experience not only demonstrates the impact of workplace relations on the political climate; it points as well to the ways in which workplace relations can themselves be profoundly influenced by the changing nature of politics and political behaviour.[90]

Finally, it is important to note the goals of industrial unionism in the Canadian steel industry. Neither the Amalgamated Association nor the United Steelworkers ever questioned the employers' right to control work routines in their plant. In part, these unions sought instead to reduce workers' contact with the job – through demands for an eight-hour day in the early years and for a forty-hour week and regular vacations in the 1940s. But even more important for these steelworkers was an industrial administration that was inherently *fair* and which assured a level of economic *security* for steelworkers. The means to those ends was a further bureaucratization of workplace relations – in effect, the creation of a "rule of law" within the steel plants.[91] The rules and regulations for hiring, promotion, wage payment, and settlement of grievances were to be clearly specified in a binding contract. Not surprisingly, one of the key provisions in the Algoma steelworkers' first contract in 1936 was a system of promotion based on seniority, which promised an end to nepotism, favouritism, and other forms of arbitrary supervision.[92] Seniority, grievance procedures, and union security were likewise at the heart of the great 1946 upheaval. A similar desire to inject new standards of equity was reflected in the union's drive, begun during the war, to standardize wage rates across the industry. In the early 1950s, successful efforts to rationalize the myriad unequal distinctions along the "job ladders" involved an extensive program of job evaluation and classification jointly by unions and management, known as the "Co-operative Wage Study." The union went so far as to develop its own industrial-engineering department! As a result, according to the most thorough study of the program, "the rate for a particular job no longer depends upon such intangible factors as the personality of the worker or the whim of the foreman, but upon the job itself."[93]

For these steelworkers, the central concern lay in minimizing competition between themselves in the workplace, to avoid a return to the often degrading practices of the preceding decades. Their success altered one important element in the traditional administration of the steel-making work process – the unchecked authoritarianism of front-line supervisors, those ruthless, much despised "drivers" on the shop floor. Yet the "rule of law" within the industry did not mean any serious erosion of managerial power in the workplace; it affected only the *way* in which that power was wielded. In the words of Stelco's historian, William Kilbourn, the company avoided an "abdication of a certain basic responsibility of management for determining work rules ... Sound seniority provisions ... were thus prevented from becoming mere rigid ritual codes for the consecration of inefficiency."[94] In the late nineteenth century, those "rigid ritual codes" had been the workplace customs and regulations of the skilled craftsmen and their union. The consolidation of industrial unionism in the steel industry in the 1940s had clearly not brought back those mechanisms of workplace control. Moreover, steel companies, which had vigorously resisted collective bargaining and even, in some cases, the Cooperative Wage Study, learned the value of the new bureaucratized work relations. State legislation had not only bound the employers to recognize their employees' union, but also confined workers to the rigid channels of legally enforceable contracts and grievance procedures. Disruptions to the flow of production could be minimized when the union officials became the policemen of work relations. The steelmasters' long-standing concerns with predictability thus had a new solution.

For Canada's steelworkers, then, the victories of the 1940s had ensured formal negotiations over the price of their labour power, more consistency and equity in management labour policies, and a minimum level of job security. But their new power to influence the administration of the steel plants did not confront the deepest source of tension in their workplace – the relentless efforts of owners and managers to cheapen the cost of production by intensifying the use of the workers' labour-power. Those initiatives were outside the realm of collective bargaining, and the new bureaucratized structures of the Canadian industrial-relations system made resistance to them more difficult and more likely to find expression in absenteeism, sabotage, or wildcat strikes.[95] Industrial unionism brought undeniable benefits to workers like these, but it fell short of its potential.

The primary steel industry that emerged in Canada at the turn of the twentieth century made a radical break with the past. In contrast to the small, widely scattered ironworks of the nineteenth century, a handful of large corporations integrated all stages of primary steel making within large new production facilities at Sydney, Hamilton, and Sault Ste Marie. Inside these mammoth mills, the companies also introduced major changes in the way that steel and iron had previously been produced in Canada. A visitor to the plants would have been struck by the elaborate new machinery, which reduced or eliminated the firms' reliance on both highly skilled craftsmen and unskilled labourers. The same visitor might also have noticed the babble of strange tongues among the workers in the plants, since the companies had learned to make full use of inexperienced, tractable, transient labour from continental Europe, in order to extract the maximum from the new equipment and to push up productivity. Twelve-hour days, harsh, autocratic supervision, and high accident rates were the results. Mass production in the steel industry was born.

As the new work routines became firmly established, a new workforce emerged – for the first time known as "steelworkers." Their "semi-skilled" jobs generally had low skill requirements, and only the long hours and incentive wages assured them a steady income. These men found themselves enmeshed in a relationship of almost inescapable dependency on their employers: few of them had portable skills, and most relied on promotion within the firm for any modest improvement in status and earnings; they were at the mercy of departmental despots for any promotion or even for keeping their jobs; and many had their long-term economic security tied to company welfare programs. The strands of this web of dependency were primarily deference and fear.

The first challenges to these work relations arose from those with a modicum of independence – the European labourers – who had no permanent commitment to the industry and whose ethnic enclaves in the steel towns provided the collective resources for successful resistance, and also from small groups of workers, especially in the rolling mills, whose jobs still demanded some skill and allowed some workplace autonomy. The footloose Europeans declined in importance as the steel workforce stabilized, but the more skilled workers led the efforts to establish industrial unionism for all steelworkers. The companies' policies to promote a stable workforce ultimately backfired when these more settled workers began to assert their own rights within the industry. The victory of the United Steelworkers of America by 1946 brought a significant shift in the administration of the steel-making labour process – from autocracy to bureaucracy. Henceforth, work relations were governed by a negotiated "rule of law," which would guarantee equitable treatment on the shop floor, job security, and, if possible, a decent wage. The labour movement's old adage of "a fair day's work for a fair day's wage" had finally won some acceptance in the industry. What did not change fundamentally, however, was the actual organization and execution of work. The early twentieth-century transformation of the labour process survived intact, and the steel companies could continue to use their highly mechanized, speeded-up system of production to maintain and increase productivity.

Notes

1 *Canadian Mining Review* (hereafter *CMR*) 16, no. 2 (February 1897), 51. The contrast was quite clearly with the United States, where more than half the steel production was in the form of rails; Bernard Elbaum and Frank Wilkinson, "Industrial Relations and Uneven Development: A Comparative Study of the American and British Steel Industries," *CJE* no. 3 (1979), 279.

2 The history of the Canadian iron and steel industry can be traced in the following: James M. Cameron, *Industrial History of the New Glasgow District* (New Glasgow: n.p. n.d.); W.J.A. Donald, *The Canadian Iron and Steel Industry: A Study in the Economic History of a Protected Industry* (Boston: Houghton Mifflin 1915); Donald Eldon, "American Influence in the Canadian Iron and Steel Industry" (PhD dissertation, Harvard University 1952); William Kilbourn, *The Elements Combined: A History of the Steel Company of Canada* (Toronto: Clark Irwin 1960); L.D. McCann, "The Mercantile Industrial Transition in the Metal Towns of Pictou County, 1857–1931," *Acadiensis* 10, no. 2 (Spring 1981), 29–64; Edward J. McCracken, "The Steel Industry of Nova Scotia" (MA thesis, McGill University 1932); Duncan L. McDowall, "Steel at the Sault: Sir James Dunn and the Algoma Steel Corporation, 1906–1956" (PhD dissertation, Carleton University 1978); Tom Traves, *The State and Enterprise: Canadian Manufacturers and the Federal Government, 1917–1931* (Toronto: University of Toronto Press 1979), 121–54.

3 This situation helps to explain why there were no significant American branch plants in the Canadian primary steel industry – there was no substantial tariff wall behind which to set up production facilities. The United States Steel Corporation secured lands at Ojibway in southwestern Ontario and announced elaborate plans for a branch plant in 1912 and then again in 1920. But much more modest facilities opened in 1927, only to close five years later. In 1938, Dosco bought out US Steel's handful of Canadian subsidiaries, which were mostly in the finishing branches of steel production (Eldon, "American Influence," 163–4).

4 McCann, "Mercantile-Industrial Transition," 29–64; Kilbourn, *Elements Combined*, 51–96.

5 Don Macgillivray, "Henry Melville Whitney Comes to Cape Breton: The Saga of the Gilded Age Entrepreneur," *Acadiensis* 9, no. 1 (Autumn 1979), 44–70; David Frank, "The Cape Breton Coal Industry and the Rise and Fall of the British Empire Steel Corporation," ibid., 7, no. 2 (Autumn 1977), 3–34; McCracken, "Steel Industry," 96–127, 180–232; McDowall, "Steel at the Sault," 26–150; Margaret Van Emery, "Francis Hector Clergue and the Rise of Sault Ste Marie as an Industrial Centre," *OH* 56, no . 3 (September 1964), 191–202. Several similar, though more limited, entrepreneurial ventures were undertaken in Ontario at the turn of the century, principally by American capitalists – at Midland, Collingwood, Deseronto, and Port Arthur – but most had given up the ghost by the First World War.

6 McDowall, "Steel at the Sault," 306–67; Kilbourn, *Elements Combined*, 159–81; Robert H. Storey, "Workers, Unions, and Steel: The Shaping of the Hamilton Working Class, 1935–1948" (PhD dissertation, University of Toronto 1981), 302–8; Steel Research Group, "Report on Sydney Steel," *CD* 14, nos. 4–5 (February–March 1980), 33–52.

7 Alongside the big three stood a few smaller, more specialized companies – older rolling mills like the Manitoba Rolling Mills, and steel foundries like Dominion Foundries and Steel (Dofasco) and Canadian Steel Foundries in Montreal. Some of these firms had modest facilities for producing steel from pig iron, but none had blast furnaces before 1950.

8 A.R.R. Jones, "A Gigantic Automaton," *Iron and Steel of Canada* (hereafter *ISC*), April 1924, 61.

9 Eldon, "American Influence," 294–328.

10 David Brody, *Steelworkers in America: The Nonunion Era* (New York: Harper and Row 1960), 1–26.

11 B.J. Harrington, "Notes on the Iron Ores of Canada and Their Development," in Canada, Geological Survey, *Report of Progress* (Montreal 1873–4), 242–59; Henry How, *The Mineralogy of Nova Scotia: A Report to the Provincial Government* (Halifax: C. Annand 1869), 84–95; Nova Scotia, Department of Mines, *Report* (Halifax 1877), 45–6; Michel Gaumond, *Les forges de Saint-Maurice* (Quebec: Société historique de Québec 1969), 11–13; Dollard Dubé, *Les vieilles forges il y a 60 ans* (Trois-Rivières: Éditions du Bien public 1933), 21–51; J.A. Bannister, "The Houghton Iron Works," in Ontario Historical Society, *Papers and Records* 26 (1944), 80–1; W.J. Patterson, "The Long Point Furnace," ibid., 73–6; E.A. Owen, *Pioneer Sketches of Long Point Settlement* (Toronto: William Briggs 1898), 452–7; Elijah Leonard, *A Memoir* (London: Advertiser Printing Company, n.d.); T.J. Drummond, "Charcoal and Its Bearing on the Utilization of Our Forests," *Canadian Engineer* (hereafter *CE*) 2, no. 10 (February 1895): 288–9;

and no. 11 (March 1895), 310–12; John Birkinbine, "The Old and New Industry Compared," *CMR* 21, no. 4 (April 1902), 90–2.

12 *Canadian Mining Manual* (hereafter *CMM*), 1897, 58–111; and 1900, 65–7; Nova Scotia, Department of Mines, *Annual Report*, 1893, 38–42; Ontario, Bureau of Mines, *Annual Report* (hereafter OBMAR) (Toronto), 1902, 27–30; 1908, 314; *CMR* 15, no. 2 (February 1896), 39; *CE* 3, no. 7 (January 1896), 248–9; *Spectator* (Hamilton), 10 February 1896; *Stelco Flashes* 14, no. 6 (June 1950), 6; Jones, "Gigantic Automaton," 63–4; Charles Reitell, *Machinery and Its Benefits to Labor in the Crude Iron and Steel Industries* (Menasha, WI: Banta 1917), 8–21.

13 The Dosco blast-furnace operations are described in *CMR* 20, no. 10 (October 1901), 240; *CMM*, 1901, 129–30; Canada, Department of Mines, Mines Branch, *Report on the Mining and Metallurgical Industries of Canada, 1907–8* (hereafter RMMIC) (Ottawa 1908), 528–300. For descriptions of the new blast-furnace equipment introduced at Collingwood in 1902, Sydney Mines in 1904, Sault Ste Marie in 1905, and Hamilton in 1907, see ibid., 325–6, 546; OBMAR, 1902, 2, and 1908, 291–7, 301–4; E.G. Brock, "Making Pig Iron at Hamilton," *Canadian Foundryman* (hereafter *CF*) 19, no. 2 (February 1928), 7–10.

14 *CMR* 21, no. 7 (July 1902), 195; F.E. Lucas, "By-Product Coke Manufacture at Sydney," *Canadian Mining Journal* (hereafter *CMJ*) 32, no. 18 (15 September 1912), 641–3; C.E. Wallin, "The Dominion Iron and Steel Coke Plant at Sydney, N.S.," *ISC*, December 1919, 291–7; W.S. Wilson and A.P. Theurkauf, "What the Eyes Behold at Sydney Steel Plant," ibid., November 1927, 333–4; W.J. Dick, "By-Product Coke Ovens at the Algoma Steel Company, Sault Ste Marie, Ont.," *CMJ* 35, no. 13 (15 July 1914), 487; William Seymour, "By-Product Coke Plant of the Algoma Steel Corporation at Sault Ste Marie, Ont.," *ISC*, November 1919, 262–8; J.F. Slee, "The By-Product Coke Plant of the Steel Company of Canada at Hamilton, Ontario," ibid., February 1929, 40.

15 Harry Jerome calculated that the greatest "labour-saving" innovations in the American steel industry were in blast-furnace work. See *Mechanization in Industry* (New York: National Bureau of Economic Research 1934), 58–66.

16 Peter Temin, *Iron and Steel in Nineteenth-Century America: An Economic Inquiry* (Cambridge: MIT Press 1964), 14–18; James J. Davis, *The Iron Puddler: My Life in the Rolling Mills and What Came of It* (Indianapolis: Bobbs Merrill 1922), 85–113; Donald, *Canadian Iron and Steel*, 99–101; Elbaum and Wilkinson, "Industrial Relations."

17 Temin, *Iron and Steel*, 125–38; *Star* (Sault Ste Marie), 20 February 1902; Library and Archives Canada (hereafter LAC), RG 36/17 (Fielding Tariff Inquiry Commission, 1898–1906), vol. 5, 858–60; MG 31, B 3 (C.H. Speer,

"Algoma Steel Corporation"), 86; McDowall, "Steel at the Sault," 74, 88; Eldon, "American Influence," 127.

18 Temin, *Iron and Steel*, 138–45.

19 Cameron, *New Glasgow*, V2.

20 RMMIC, 327, 337–8, 530–1, 548–9; OBMAR, 1902, 24; 1908, 304–7.

21 Jones, "Gigantic Automaton," 100–3; Charles Rumford Walker, *Steel: The Diary of a Furnace Worker* (Boston: Atlantic Monthly Press 1922), 21–6, 46–7, 52–3. The companies eventually developed laboratory staff who took full responsibility for testing the steel.

22 Kilbourn, *Elements Combined*, 3–50; Donald, *Canadian Iron and Steel*, 60–3; LAC, RG 87 (Mineral Resources Branch), vol. 18, F. 81.

23 Canada, House of Commons, *Journals*, vol. 45 (1909–10), Appendix, Part III ("Proceedings of the Special Committee on the Bill No. 21, "An Act Respecting Hours of Labour on Public Works" ... December 9, 1909–May 3, 1910") (hereafter "Eight-Hour Committee"), 183. See also the testimony of Stelco president Robert Hobson in 1919: LAC, RG 36/8 (Tariff Commission, 1920), vol. 8, F. 21 (Hamilton), 3777.

24 Quoted in Wayne Roberts, ed., *Baptism of a Union: Stelco Strike of 1946* (Hamilton: Labour Studies Program, McMaster University 1981), 16. See also John Fitch, *The Steel Workers* (New York: Charities Publication Committee 1910), 51.

25 *Star* (Sault Ste Marie), 10 April 1902; OBMAR, 1908, 299; C.H. Speer, "The New Merchant Mills of Algoma Steel," *ISC*, March 1930, 53–7; *CF* 4, no. 9 (September 1913), 142–4; *CMJ* 24, no. 5 (1 August 1913), 489; *Stelco Flashes* 14, no. 6 (June 1950); C. Ochiltree Macdonald, *The Coal and Iron Industries of Nova Scotia* (Halifax: Chronicle 1909), 84–9; *CE* 13, no. 2 (February 1906), 38–43; 25 (31 July 1913), 251–2; (4 September 1913), 416–18; *ISC*, May 1920, 113–19; Wilson and Theurkauf, "Sydney Steel Plant," 337–40; Cameron, *New Glasgow*, V1–V40.

26 *Star* (Sault Ste Marie), 6 October 1902; Jones, "Gigantic Automaton," 118; *Canada Year Book* (Ottawa: King's Printer 1908), 138; Canada, Dominion Bureau of Statistics, *Iron and Steel and Their Products* (Ottawa: King's Printer), 1929, 18; 1930, 68, 73.

27 F.H. Bell, "Lifting and Conveying Material in the Foundry," *CF* 12, no. 3 (March 1921), 19.

28 Nova Scotia, Commission on Hours of Labor, *Report* (Halifax 1910) (hereafter CHLR), 66.

29 "Eight-Hour Committee," 166.

30 University of British Columbia Library, Special Collections, James Robertson Papers, Box 5, F.1, handwritten memorandum, 3.

31 American Iron and Steel Institute, *Yearbook* (New York), 1919, 414. A special report on the American steel industry also noted this change in the labour force: "The semi-skilled among the production force consist for the most part of workmen who have been taught to perform relatively complex functions, such as the operation of cranes and other mechanical appliances, but who possess little or no general mechanical or metallurgical knowledge." (United States, Bureau of Labor, *Report of Employment in the Iron and Steel Industry*, 4 vols. [Washington 1911–13], Vol. 3, 81).

32 Richard Edwards, *Contested Terrain: The Transformation of the Workplace in the Twentieth Century* (New York: Basic Books 1979).

33 Elbaum and Wilkinson, "Industrial Relations," 283–93; David Montgomery, *Workers Control in America: Studies in the History of Work, Technology, and Labor Struggles* (New York: Cambridge University Press 1979), 11–12; David A. McCabe, *The Standard Rate in American Trade Unions* (Baltimore: Johns Hopkins University Press 1912), 62–5; Katherine Stone, "The Origin of Job Structures in the Steel Industry," *Radical America* 7, no. 6 (November December 1973), 20–5.

34 Canada, Royal Commission on the Relations of Capital and Labor, *Report* (hereafter RCRCLR), Vol. 2: *Evidence – New Brunswick* (Ottawa: Queen's Printer 1889), 17–18, 107; Vol. 3: *Evidence – Nova Scotia*, 237–68, 388–407; Vol. 4, *Evidence – Ontario*, 760–4, 786–94; Cameron, *New Glasgow*, VI–VI 6. This was evidently a transitional point: when asked if he paid his own helpers, a Londonderry puddler explained, "It comes out of the puddlers' wages but the company pay them" (RCRCLR, Vol. 3, 247).

35 "Eight-Hour Committee," 188. See also RCRCLR, Vol. 3, 237, 240, 242, 249, 257–9, 266, 268, 390, 394–5, 398; Vol. 4, 760, 763, 786–7.

36 Brody, *Steelworkers*, 27–9; Robertson Papers, "Notes from Conversations with Officers of the Steel Company of Canada, Hamilton, Ont., Dec. 21 / 23," 1.

37 F.W. Taylor, the "father" of scientific management, conducted some of his most important experiments at the Midvale Steel Company and later at the Bethlehem Steel Company. See Daniel Nelson, *Frederick W. Taylor and the Rise of Scientific Management* (Madison, WI: University of Wisconsin Press 1980).

38 Kilbourn, *Elements Combined*, 84–5; Craig Heron and Bryan D. Palmer, "Through the Prism of the Strike: Industrial Conflict in Southern Ontario, 1901–14," *CHR* 58, no. 4 (December 1977), 430–4; Graham S. Lowe, "The Rise of Modern Management in Canada," *CD* 14, no. 3 (December 1979), 32–8; Paul Craven, *"An Impartial Umpire": Industrial Relations and the Canadian State, 1900–1911* (Toronto: University of Toronto Press 1980), 90–110.

39 *CMR* 16, no. 2 (February 1897), 52; see also C.A. Meisner, "Notes on Some Comparisons between Southern and Nova Scotia Iron Methods," ibid., 16, no. 1 (January 1897), 12–15.
40 *Labour Gazette* (hereafter *LG*), 1, no. 8 (April 1901), 389; Labour Canada Library (Hull), Provincial Workmen's Association, Grand Council, Minutes, III, September 1904, 442; Ronald F. Crawley, "Class Conflict and the Establishment of the Sydney Steel Industry, 1899–1904" (MA thesis, Dalhousie University 1980), 52–61; CHLR, 65–72; Emilia Kolcon-Lach, "Early Italian Settlement at Sault Ste Marie, Ontario, 1898–1921" (MA thesis, University of Western Ontario 1979), 1–21; Livo Ducin, "Labour's Emergent Years and the 1903 Riots," in *50 Years of Labour in Algoma: Essays on Aspects of Algoma's Working-Class History* (Sault Ste Marie: Algoma University College 1978), 5–6; Francis M. Heath, "Labour, the Community, and Pre-World War I Immigration Issue," ibid., 41–2.
41 Craig Heron, "Hamilton Steelworkers and the Rise of Mass Production," *HP* 1982, 114.
42 CHLR, 65–72.
43 Public Archives of Nova Scotia, MG 1, no. 1191C (Thomas Cozzolino Autobiography); R.W. Ripley, "Industrialization and the Attraction of Immigrants to Cape Breton County, 1893–1914" (MA thesis, Queen's University 1980); *Labor News* (Hamilton), 30 October 1914; Robert F. Harney, "The Commerce of Migration," *CES* 9, no. 1 (1977), 42–53; Robert F. Harney, "Montreal's King of Italian Labour: A Case Study of Padronism," *L/LT* 4 (1979), 57–84.
44 W. Craig Heron, "Working-Class Hamilton, 1895–1930" (PhD dissertation, Dalhousie University 1981), 330–41; Kolcon-Lach, "Italians"; Ripley, *Industrialization.*
45 *Star* (Sault Ste Marie), 5 March 1903.
46 *Spectator*, 15 February 1919.
47 Kolcon-Lach calculated that of 252 Italians listed on Algoma's employment rolls in 1905, only 25 were still there in 1910.
48 CHLR, 64–75.
49 Ibid., 168–9, 171, 174; *LG* 30, no. 1 (January 1930), 2; McCracken, "Steel Industry," 269–70; McDowall, "Steel at the Sault"; University College of Cape Breton, Beaton Institute, William G. Snow, "Sydney Steelworkers: Their Troubled Past and the Birth of Lodge 1064" (typescript 1979), 20.
50 *LG* 5, no. 11 (May 1905), 1174; 6, no. 17 (January 1906), 703; no. 11 (May 1906), 1225; no. 12 (June 1906), 1336; 7, no. 3 (September 1906), 258; no. 4 (October 1906), 367; no. 6 (December 1906), 945; no. 9 (March 1907), 939; 8, no. 1 (July 1907), 13; 9, no. 4 (October 1908), 359; 10, no. 6 (December

1909), 634; 11, no. 5 (November 1910), 534; *Canadian Machinery* 10, no. 7 (14 August 1913), 170; John Ferris, *Algoma' s Industrial and Trade Union Development* (Sault Ste Marie: n.p. n.d.), 40–5, 61.

51 Storey, "Workers, Unions, and Steel," 208–11; Roberts, *Baptism*, 11–15; Harry J. Waisglass, "A Case Study in Union-Management Co-operation" (MA thesis, University of Toronto 1948), 89–94; George MacEachern, "Organizing Sydney's Steelworkers in the 1930s," in Gloria Montero, ed., *We Stood Together: First-Hand Accounts of Dramatic Events in Canada's Labour Past* (Toronto: James Lorimer 1979), 58.

52 CHLR, 70; Robertson Papers, "Conversations."

53 William I. Thomas and Florian Znaniecki, *The Polish Peasant in Europe and America*, 5 vols. (New York: R.G. Bager 1918–20), Vol. 1, 199. See also Montgomery, *Workers' Control*, 37.

54 Ontario, Inspectors of Factories, *Reports* (Toronto), 1912, 1916; Nova Scotia, Factories Inspector, *Reports* (Halifax), 1916, 32; 1917, 6.

55 LAC, RG 33/95 (Royal Commission on Industrial Relations, "Evidence"; hereafter RCIRE), 3744.

56 LAC, RG 27 (Department of Labour), vol. 299, F. 3475.

57 *Labour Leader*, 25 January 1919; *Eastern Federationist*, 22 March 1919; *Spectator*, 11 February 1919; see also *Amalgamated Journal*, 2 August 1917, 23; Kolcon-Lach, "Italians," 128–30.

58 *Herald* (Hamilton), 4 April 1910.

59 David M. Gordon, Richard Edwards, and Michael Reich, *Segmented Work, Divided Workers: The Historical Transformation of Work in the United States* (New York: Cambridge University Press 1982).

60 Probably the most pessimistic view of these ethnic divisions is presented in Gabriel Kolko, *Main Currents in Modern American History* (New York: Harper and Row 1976), 67–99.

61 Cameron, *New Glasgow*, V1–V40; RCRCLR, Vol. 3, 234–9, 241, 265, 268, 392, 407; "Eight-Hour Committee," 188; *Spectator*, 1 August 1901, 15 July 1926; Speer, "Algoma," 17–18, 23; Heath, "Immigration Issue," 39–56; Donald, *Canadian Iron and Steel*, 204; McCracken, "Steel Industry," 105; Crawley, "Class Conflict," 57; LAC, RG 36/8, vol. 6, F. 13.

62 Cameron, *New Glasgow*, V1–V40; RCRCLR, Vol. 3, 388, 391; Vol. 4, 761, 821; Fitch, *Steel Workers*, 141–2; Stone, "Job Structures," 40–3; Brody, *Steelworkers*, 85–7. On the general phenomenon of "internal labour markets," see Michael Burawoy, *Manufacturing Consent: Changes in the Labor Process under Monopoly Capitalism* (Chicago: University of Chicago Press 1979), 95–108; Edwards, *Contested Terrain*, 130–62. Elbaum and Wilkinson have correctly challenged Katherine Stone's suggestion that job

ladders were purely the creation of the steel companies; they were instead demanded by the less skilled well before the end of the nineteenth century to ensure fairness in promotion. See "Industrial Relations," 292.

63 Heron, "Hamilton Steelworkers," 118–19; *LG* 6, no. 12 (June 1906), 1301; 7, no. 7 (January 1907), 783–4; no. 12 (June 1907); 9, no. 1 (July 1908), 70–1; no. 12 (June 1909), 1344; 11, no. 12 (June 1911), 1334–5; 12, no. 8 (February 1912), 725; no. 12 (June 1912), 1135; 18, no. 9 (September 1918), 696; 21, no. 3 (March 1921), 521–2; 22, no. 10 (October 1922), 1041–2; 23, no. 1 (January 1923), 5; 26, no. 3 (March 1926), 237–9; no. 11 (November 1926), 1106; 28, no. 2 (February 1928), 172–3; no. 9 (September 1928), 942–3; 29, no. 1 (January 1929), 45–6; 30, no. 7 (July 1930), 783; *ISC*, August 1920, 208; August 1921, 198–200; August 1922, 147; September 1922, 168–9; July 1924, 129; January 1928, 24; March 1928, 68, 88; Speer, "Algoma," 122–35; LAC, RG 36/8, vol. 6, F. 13, 1764–9.

64 Robert Storey, "Unionization versus Corporate Welfare: The 'Dofasco Way,'" *L/LT* 12 (Autumn 1983), 7–42.

65 Storey, "Workers, Unions, and Steel," 190–3, 199–213; Canada, Commission to Inquire into the Industrial Unrest among the Steel Workers at Sydney, N.S. (hereafter CIIUR), *Report* (Ottawa 1924), 16–19; *LG* 26, no. 7 (July 1926), 665–6; McCracken, "Steel Industry," 261–4; MacEachern, "Organizing," 54–65.

66 Storey, "Workers, Unions, and Steel," 299, 336; "Early Union Reminiscing Reveals It Was Never Easy," *Algoma Steel News* 8, no. 3 (March 1977), 4.

67 RCIRE, Vol. 3, 2289, 2299.

68 LAC, RG 36/11 (Advisory Board on Tariff and Taxation), vol. 1, F. 2–1, exhibit 10; F. 3–6, exhibit 16; McDowall, "Steel at the Sault," 293.

69 LAC, MG 30, A16 (Sir Joseph Flavelle Papers), vol. 2, F. 11 (Department of Labour), R. Hobson to J.W. Flavelle, 8 July 1916; Provincial Archives of Nova Scotia (PANS), MG 2 (Armstrong Papers), vol. 670, F. 5; LAC, RG 27, vol. 69, F. 222(7).

70 William Davenport, "As a Britisher Sees It," *Western Clarion*, 30 June 1906; Ontario, Commission on Unemployment, *Report* (Toronto: Queen's Printer 1916), 9; G.W. Austen, "Excessive Labor Turnover and Its Remedies," *Industrial Canada* 21, no. 5 (May 1920), 74–5; "Cost of Labour Turnover," *LG* 20, no. 11 (November 1911), 1419; A.O. Dawson, "The Relations of Capital and Labour," *Social Welfare* 2, no. 7 (1 April 1920), 171–2; Paul F. Brissenden and Emil Frankel, *Labor Turnover in Industry: A Statistical Analysis* (New York: Macmillan 1922). On the transiency of workers in the period, see Edmund Bradwin, *The Bunkhouse Man* (Toronto: University of Toronto Press 1972); A. Ross McCormack, *Reformers, Rebels and Revolutionaries: The Western*

Canadian Radical Movement, 1899–1919 (Toronto: University of Toronto Press 1977), 98–117; John Herd Thompson, "Bringing in the Sheaves: The Harvest Excursionists, 1890–1919," *CHR* 59, no. 4 (December 1978), 467–89; Jack London, *The Road* (London: Arco 1967); G.H. Westerbury, *Misadventures of a Working Hobo in Canada* (Toronto: Routledge 1930).

71 LAC, MG 26, H 1(c) (Sir Robert Borden Papers), vol. 211, 118826 (D.H McDougall to Mark Workman, 2 September 1916); vol. 216, 121857 (W.C. Franz to J.W. Flavelle, 20 January 1917); *LG* 28, no. 3 (March 1918), 180; RCIRE, 3843. See also LAC, MG 30, A 16, vol. 2, F. 11, Thomas Findley to T. Crothers, 31 March 1916.

72 Canada, *Census* (Ottawa), 1911, 447; 1931, 756; LAC, RG 36/11, vol. 8, F. 3–6; Steel Company of Canada, *The Twenty Fifth Milestone, 1910–1935: A Brief History of Stelco* (Hamilton: Steel Company of Canada 1935), 54.

73 Heron, "Hamilton Steelworkers," 122–4; see also Crawley, "Class Conflict," 70, 72–4; *LG* 4, no. 11 (May 1904), 1074.

74 See McCormack, *Reformers, Rebels, and Revolutionaries*, 98–117; Harney, "King of Italian Labour"; Jean Morrison, "Ethnicity and Violence: The Lakehead Freight Handlers before World War I," in Gregory S. Kealey and Peter Warrian, eds., *Essays in Canadian Working Class History* (Toronto: McClelland and Stewart 1976), 143–60; Stanley Scott, "A Profusion of Issues: Immigrant Labour, the World War, and the Cominco Strike of 1917," *L/LT* 2 (1977), 54–78.

75 Provincial Workmen's Association (PWA), Grand Council, Minutes, II, September 1901, 368; III, September 1904, 429–30; September 1905, 521; Crawley, "Class Conflict," 70–146; Paul MacEwan, *Miners and Steelworkers: Labour in Cape Breton* (Toronto: Samuel Stevens Hakkert and Company 1976), 16–17; LAC, RG 27, vol. 69, F. 222(7).

76 *Amalgamated Journal*, 1914–23; Gordon Bishop, *Recollections of the Amalgamated* (n.p. n.d.), 4.

77 Bishop, *Recollections*, 5. See also Brody, *Steelworkers*, 255–8; Brody, *Labor in Crisis: The Steel Strike of 1919* (Philadelphia: J.B. Lippincott 1965), 166–8.

78 *Amalgamated Journal*, 1917–23; Donald Macgillivray, "Industrial Unrest in Cape Breton, 1919–25" (MA thesis, University of New Brunswick 1971).

79 Storey, "Workers, Unions, and Steel," 179–244; MacEachern, "Organizing," 60–1; Waisglass, "Case Study," 57; Irving Martin Abella, *Nationalism, Communism, and Canadian Labour: The CIO, the Communist Party, and the Canadian Congress of Labour* (Toronto: University of Toronto Press 1973), 55–60.

80 Storey, "Workers, Unions, and Steel," 297–370; MacEachern, "Organizing," 60–5; Ronald McDonald Adams, "The Development of the United

Steel Workers of America in Canada, 1936–1951" (MA thesis, Queen's University 1952); Laurel Sefton McDowell, "The Formation of the Canadian Industrial Relations System during World War Two," *L/LT* 3 (1978): 175–96; Laurel Sefton McDowell, "The 1943 Steel Strike against Wartime Wage Controls," ibid., 10 (Autumn 1982), 65–85. In 1942 SWOC changed its name to the United Steelworkers of America and two years later had 50,000 members in 113 Canadian locals.

81 Storey, "Workers, Unions, and Steel," 370–418; Roberts, *Baptism*; Adams, "Development," 129–56; C.D. Martin, "The 1946 Steel Strike," in *50 Years of Labour in Algoma*, 101–16.

82 *Amalgamated Journal*, 1917–23; Storey, "Workers, Unions, and Steel"; Waite interview; Snow, "Sydney Steelworkers," 20.

83 Storey, "Workers, Unions, and Steel," 184–5, 189, 358–61; MacEachern, "Organizing," 159–60; Adams, "Development," 78; Abella, *Nationalism, Communism, and Canadian Labour*, 55–60.

84 Heron, "Working-Class Hamilton."

85 Storey, "Workers, Unions, and Steel."

86 Desmond Morton, *Canada and War: A Military and Political History* ·(Toronto: Butterworths 1981), 115.

87 *Canadian Labor Leader*, 12 October 1918.

88 Quoted in Storey, "Workers, Unions, and Steel," 336.

89 Dennis Guest, *The Emergence of Social Security in Canada* (Vancouver: UBC Press 1980), 101–38.

90 This experience undermines Michael Burawoy's contention that the work process is "relatively autonomous." See *Manufacturing Consent*, 123–57.

91 See David Brody, *Workers in Industrial America: Essays on the Twentieth Century Struggle* (New York: Oxford University Press 1980), 173–214. Burawoy uses the term "internal state" to describe the same phenomenon, though he emphasizes the conservatizing effect of the bureaucratic work relations. See *Manufacturing Consent*, 109–20.

92 Waite interview.

93 Ronald B. Bean, "Joint Union-Management Job Evaluation in the Canadian Steel Industry," *RI/IR* 17, no. 1 (April 1962), 115–26; Ronald B. Bean, "The 'Cooperative Wage Study' and the Canadian Steelworkers," ibid., 19, no. 1 (January 1964), 55–70. See also C. Bryan Williams, "Collective Bargaining and Wage Equalization in Canada's Iron and Steel Industry, 1939–1964," ibid., 26, no. 2 (April 1971), 308–44.

94 Kilbourn, *Elements Combined*, 199–200.

95 See Maxwell Flood, *Wildcat Strike in Lake City* (Ottawa: Task Force on Industrial Relations 1968).

PART TWO

Workers' Cultures

GROCERIES

Chapter Four

Arguing about Idleness

Like others in the industrialized world, Canadians have a long history of arguing about work time. Many of those confrontations took place on the shop floor as workers attempted to resist their experience of time on the job – from speed-ups to layoffs. Many also resonated through the public arena as workers reached out for broader support. From the 1870s to the 1950s Canadian wage-earners and their allies repeatedly waged major campaigns to win more time away from paid work – shorter working days, longer weekends, more holidays and vacations, and retirement after age sixty-five. Each phase of their struggle had an international dimension, as their efforts fed on campaigns being waged simultaneously across the globe.[1] Through the same eight decades, the Canadian business community generally responded with intense opposition to any further reductions in working hours. As so many historians have reminded us, the clock stood at the centre of many confrontations between capital and labour. At stake was a division of the benefits of capitalist industrialization.[2]

This essay will look back a century and a half to examine more closely how people imagined the relationship between work time and time off the job and how they hoped to shift the balance between them to create more "free" time. It concentrates on the first phase of seven decades of campaigning for shorter hours, when concerns about "idleness" were prominent. A central point of what follows is that working hours did not shrink in any automatic way as productivity increased; rather it took persistent pressure from organized wage-earners to convince employers and politicians to shorten normal hours on the job.[3]

Nine-hour parade in Hamilton, May 1872. *Canadian Illustrated News*

To begin let's step back into the late nineteenth century and look inside the kitchen of a working-class household almost anywhere across the country in the early hours of a weekday morning. Wives and mothers would be scurrying about to fill the dinner pails of the family's wage-earners, so that they could be out the door in time to start work by 6:30 or 7 a.m. By the 1860s and 1870s most workers in manufacturing, mining, and construction worked a ten-hour day, six days a week – that is, a sixty-hour week. Each day that meant stopping for an unpaid hour for the noontime meal, and quitting work around 6 p.m. There is no record of other breaks in the workday. In busy seasons many might expect to work another hour or more of overtime. Workers in continuous-process industries often worked regular shifts of eleven, twelve, or even thirteen hours – notably iron and steel production, lumber and paper mills, distilleries, and sugar refineries – as did most stationary engineers and night watchmen. In some cases, there were night shifts in these plants to allow for non-stop production through the whole week, which could mean a twenty-hour swing shift every other weekend. Some other workers had extended work days broken up with enforced periods of idleness in the middle – railway workers, street car conductors, and telegraphers, for example. Within some industrial processes where wage-earners worked more independently and were paid by the piece, hours were more flexible. Foundry workers often worked a variable time to finish a specific number of "heats" in one day, and some Nova Scotia coal miners might quit work in the early afternoon if they were so inclined. In fact, in times of full employment, workers might not show up at all for a day or two, especially on Mondays, if they were confident of holding onto their jobs. Other than in day-labouring, which was certainly a significant category of employment, there was little of what we could now call part-time work. The regularity of all these jobs was nonetheless often disrupted by seasonality. Weather conditions curtailed construction and much labouring work (loading and unloading), and seasonal markets for products led to layoffs in many industries. Saw mills, for example, operated only from spring to fall, about six months a year. Fish-packing and canning were also seasonal, as were many other consumer-goods industries, such as clothing production. The working day of the late nineteenth century was long, but working time across a year was uneven and often unpredictable.[4]

For most workers, time off the job was thus limited to short evenings, Sundays, and a small number of one-day public holidays, which employers did not always honour. Longer periods of time away from paid work generally resulted from involuntary layoffs of uncertain length. Given their frequency, those spells of idleness probably filled some of the role that vacations would take up in annual work cycles after the Second World War.

In the early twentieth century, there were two notable changes to these patterns of work time. First, starting around the turn of the century, many working-class families could expect their breadwinners home at midday on Saturday, as most employers started granting the so-called Saturday half-holiday (sometimes this meant making up the time with slightly longer days Monday to Friday, but more often it was an overall reduction in weekly hours). The second change was a shortening of the working day for a few groups of workers with bargaining clout – miners, printers, and some building trades workers, who all won eight-hour days – and then a more general reduction of working hours to nine hours across many industries after the First World War. So by the 1920s a fifty-hour week had become more common, though a significant number of workers still had ten-hour days, and the twelve-hour day would last in some steel plants until 1935. The unpredictability of work had not changed, however, especially in the interwar period, when many workers faced persistent unemployment and underemployment through the first half of the 1920s and throughout the 1930s.[5]

These changes did not come without relentless efforts primarily by the Canadian labour movement. There were roughly five phases in the battles over time off the job, each part of widespread international debates and agitation for a reduction in working hours.[6] For more than thirty years after the nine-hours movement first raised these issues in 1872, workers' organizations tried to shorten their members' working hours through negotiations with their employers (although they also supported efforts to restrict the work time of women and children through legislation).[7] In the early 1900s, alongside the ongoing agitation on the economic front, they turned more decisively to the state for legislation to cut work time for everyone. Moving to the public realm encouraged them to reach out to wider audiences who might support their demands, such as clergymen and doctors. The workers' revolt at the end of the First World War provoked a new confrontation over the issue, and in the interwar years a patchwork of partial protection from long hours began to appear in the context of new international standards set by the International Labour Organization. The culmination of these long-standing efforts, however, peaked in the 1940s with the widespread adoption of a standardized eight-hour day and forty-hour week. Over the next decade the emphasis shifted to more "lumps of leisure" in the forms of paid holidays, long weekends, annual vacations, and fixed retirement dates. The debates in each stage of this long campaign had distinctive arguments. Here we focus on the early years, when the right to leisure was difficult to establish.

For Canadian capitalists, as for their counterparts elsewhere, the right to determine unilaterally the use of their employees' labour-power was non-debatable. The workplace should be a liberal space in which individual contracting prevailed. In the words of George Brown's Toronto *Globe* in 1872, it was a matter of "sound political economy."[8] Only five years earlier, Karl Marx had discussed capitalist employers' tenacious attachment to long hours in volume one of his magnum opus, *Capital*, and perceptively noted how they needed extensive working days to ensure the production of surplus value beyond the value of the labour expended on their products.[9]

Yet, from the beginning, the debates also had a wider resonance beyond the capitalist workplace for the evolving notion of "leisure." In mid-nineteenth-century British North America, the term had little of its present-day meaning, largely because *not working* was viewed with suspicion. Work was the central cultural reference point of the bourgeois epoch. The older aristocratic preference to avoid actual labour had been swept aside by a new insistence on the moral value of regular, purposeful, conscientious, diligent, and useful work for all social classes. A whole new way of thinking was expected, something that generations of scholars have usually labelled a new "work ethic." It was not merely to be imposed; individuals had to embrace and practise it. Children found these lessons in school primers. Preachers proclaimed them from their pulpits. Newspaper editors extolled the virtues of an economy built on such individual dedication to work, and extended such lessons to visions of national development through what they liked to call "progress." Social engineers turned poor houses, prisons, and lunatic asylums into laboratories for demonstrating the moral renewal that daily toil would bring. This embrace of work began before full-scale industrialization, but became central to the vision of a new society that the promoters of and apologists for the new work regimes of industrial capitalism were projecting. Industrialists also put new energy into intensifying the work experience for their employees to push up productivity and rates of profit.[10]

There was, of course, a working-class variant of this attachment to work. Working for wages was essential to the survival of a working-class family. A male breadwinner in such a household built much of his masculine identity on his ability and responsibility to bring home those wages. On the job and elsewhere, he also proclaimed his manhood through the social value of his manual labour, expressed in opposition to those who did not produce anything of worth. This was a working-class labour theory of value. "Now, sir, on whom has the progress of this country rested, and on whom will it depend in regard to her future wealth and glory?" asked F.C. Cole, a carpenter, in a letter to the Hamilton *Spectator* in 1872. "The mechanics are the palace-builders of the world; not a stick is hewn, not a stone is shaped in the great dwellings of our rich and princely merchants, that does not owe its fitness and beauty to the skilled hand of the sturdy mechanic. The towering spires that raise their giddy heads above all the clouds depend on the mechanic's art for their strength and symmetry. Not an edifice for devotion or business or comfort that does not bear the imprint of their hands."[11] In the 1880s that sense of self-worth blossomed into a large and influential workers' organization that chose a name to highlight the nobility of toil, the Knights of Labor, and in the early 1900s socialists would carry on that rhetorical thrust.[12]

But what about *not* working? The opposite of work in the mid-nineteenth century was not leisure but *idleness*, a term with two distinct meanings. On the one hand, idleness meant a lack of work (i.e., unemployment), a serious problem for families normally dependent on wages as their main source of income. On the other, the word was used to describe a wilful refusal to work and instead to engage in self-indulgent loafing and probably various kinds of dissipation, a characterization that was mostly aimed at working-class men and their recreational pursuits. "Idle hands are the devil's plaything," according to the old English proverb. The second meaning was often used to explain the first – the unemployed were simply lazy loafers. So too much leisure could be a social problem that required careful monitoring and regulation. In the words of an 1886 article in the *Canadian Manufacturer*, leisure required "the diligent and intelligent use of time." The prohibitionists undertook to tackle the potential dissipation by stopping alcohol consumption; the Sabbatarians worked on ensuring sober, restrained behaviour on the weekly day off work, Sunday. Not surprisingly, then, as the debates over shorter working hours took off in the last third of the nineteenth century, the chief protagonists frequently situated their arguments in relation to this central cultural nexus of work and idleness.[13]

As many scholars have told us, the first campaign to shorten the working day, the celebrated nine-hours movement that spread across central Canada in the first half of 1872, got its rhetorical energy from articulate white, male craftworkers, who were so central to that region's first wave of industrialization.[14] These men recognized that to ask for a reduction of one hour a day was to open themselves to charges that they couldn't handle more free time. In the first of several letters to the Hamilton *Spectator*, the secretary of the Hamilton Nine Hour League, James Ryan, lashed out at another city newspaper for going "out of its way to inflict a wanton and undeserved insult upon the whole body of workmen in Hamilton, by asserting that the nine hours movement was not required here, for if it was successful it would simply be an additional hour to spend in the saloon." He denied the charge that Hamilton workers were *"drunkards* or *loafers."*[15] Two weeks later, the first Toronto mass meeting called to build the nine-hour movement heard similar defensiveness. Robert Grant, a stonemason, got cheers for denying the claim "that the extra hour would be misspent by the workingmen"; looking around the meeting, he saw sober men who "knew how to spend their time usefully."[16]

So these craftworkers, and their successors in the shorter-hours campaigns over the next thirty years, constructed their arguments to avoid the charge of idleness by casting time off work as not wasteful but highly productive. Arguably, they were strengthening their case for the right to exercise more control over the labour processes within which they worked. Their resolutions and speeches were laced with references to "mental cultivation." In 1872 John Hewitt, a cooper and prominent leader of the nine-hour movement, "advocated the division of the day into eight hours for producing the necessaries of life, eight for improving the mental faculties, and eight for rest."[17] For these men, using time away from work in this way was not merely for personal enjoyment. Rather, they built on their claims about how valuable their skills were to industry to insist that their mental development would benefit society through enhanced work processes, especially new inventions. In James Ryan's oft-quoted language: "We want to better our physical constitutions, and increase our mental power, so that if we cannot equal our Yankee neighbours in the variety of our undertaking, we can at least compete with them in the artistic finish of our productions ... We want to become more skillful to use … machinery. We want time to study and learn."[18] F.C. Cole, the carpenter, insisted that "capital will accomplish nothing without the cooperation of the skilled hand and intellectual mind of the artisan."[19] John Collins, a furniture worker, provoked cheers at a Toronto mass meeting by arguing that workingmen were not "mere machinery; they had intellectual powers which needed cultivation. He contended that if the nine-hour system were introduced, they would "as a class very soon improve their mental, religious and intellectual qualities."[20] Many such comments linked workers' free time to adult education in some kind of evening school.[21] J.S. Williams's opening editorial in the new labour newspaper, the *Ontario Workman*, in April 1872 endorsed the nine-hour day as a means of the workingman gaining "improvement and elevation."[22]

These workers did not present work itself as a problem, except the fatigue when they finished for the day. The limited time after work and the exhaustion of the ten-hour working day prevented them from fulfilling their potential as "productive and mental labourers." James Dean, a Toronto shoemaker and leader of the Knights of St Crispin, declared:

> He, as a workingman, knew the time that was devoted to working ten hours a day left no time for mental cultivation. They had to rise at half-past five to get to work at seven in the morning. They got home in the evening about seven. At half-past nine, every workingman ought to be in his bed, so that he had only two hours to spare. After ten hours work they did not feel capable of entering on mental cultivation. They ought to have time to cultivate their intellectual faculties. (Applause)[23]

Education would also lead to the ability to participate in public life as informed citizens. At the first nine-hours mass meeting in Hamilton in January 1872, a resolution was passed calling for more time for education so that working men could "fulfil with credit to ourselves and advantage to the State, the various duties and responsibilities of Fathers and Citizens."[24] Toronto's John McCormick wrote that "they see that knowledge is power, that it is absolutely required in this age to enable them to be good citizens and fulfil the duties of true manhood."[25] Nine-hours advocates often spoke of the levelling up that would result from working men having the time to educate themselves more fully. As a writer in the *Ontario Workman* suggested, "The self-elevation of the working classes is one of the brightest hopes of our young and prosperous country. It is clear that the term 'working man' is rapidly acquiring a higher and more national significance than it ever bore before."[26]

The silences in these discourses are as interesting as what they said. The spokespersons of the earliest shorter-hours movement never talked about play or games, entertainment or amusement, shopping or consumerism, or even fun. They talked about rest and recreation, but tended to equate that with quiet time spent with families, and certainly not the rough pleasures of male-only bachelor cultures – drinking, gambling, fighting, or womanizing. Indeed, their masculinity had a strong domestic component. One of the resolutions passed at a Toronto mass meeting in February 1872 asserted that "the associations and endearments of an enlightened and intelligent home circle demand more time from him to whom they look, not only for support but for much of his presence to add pleasure and happiness to their mutual social intercourse."[27] Three months later the wife of a printer who had won the nine-hour day submitted a reassuring letter to the editor of the new *Ontario Workman*. "The extra hour is spent at home, 'tis true, but it is in the shape of gardening, fixing up things generally, or reading and writing, and – miserable fellow – playing with the children," she wrote; the extra free time would "not, as some have said, be spent in the tavern or in idleness."[28] Some advocates pushed this argument further by claiming that the extra time away from work would allow a man to shepherd his family to church on Sundays.[29] None of these claims suggested in any way that more free time would allow men to take on any of the domestic tasks normally expected of women.

In a general appeal to "The Workingmen of Ontario," James Ryan pulled together all these threads in a vision of what this "social revolution" would accomplish:

> Remember that whatever helps to raise us as a class tends to elevate the national character, tends to increase trade by refining the taste, tends to lower taxation by improving morality, tends to produce talent by promoting intelligence, tends to assist emigration by increasing the privileges we possess, tends to augment the power of Christianity by improving men.[30]

The "nine-hour pioneers" had therefore established a different framework for understanding leisure time, one that saw a positive relationship between free time and work time, and that dodged the moral quagmire of idleness. It came with a practice of sponsoring cultural programs and events in working-class communities that encourage "mental cultivation." The new Canadian Labor Protective and Mutual Association that the nine-hours activists from several cities set up in May 1872 envisioned "leagues in every ward, with a place of meeting containing a library and reading room, and having all the requirements suitable for the intellectual and social improvement of the working classes after their hours of labor," though it is not clear that any such neighbourhood institutions actually appeared until the Knights of Labor began to put such an agenda of "spreading the light" into practice in the 1880s.[31] When the Knights burst on the scene early in that decade, their "Declaration of Principles" argued for an eight-hour day "so that laborers may have more time for social enjoyment and intellectual improvement and be able to reap the advantages conferred by the labor-saving machinery which their brains have created."[32] A columnist in the Hamilton Knights' newspaper, the *Palladium of Labor*, argued that intellectual improvement could serve the collective good of working people: "Increased leisure will bring increased opportunities for reading and study, greater time for thought, mutual consultation and organization, a higher sense of the responsibilities of manhood and citizenship, and the energy and vigor necessary to assert the rights of Labor."[33]

When the first full-scale parliamentary investigation of shorter hours opened in Ottawa in 1910, letters poured in from unions with a similar message, and labour leaders showed up at the hearings to make the case. Paddy Draper, secretary-treasurer of the Trades and Labor Congress of Canada, hit all the familiar notes in his statement to the committee:

> Give us a chance to improve our minds, to build up our bodies, to cultivate our intellectual faculties and to call our souls our own once in a while. We want to get acquainted with our families, our pastors and our neighbours. Give us opportunity to read, learn and inwardly digest. Let us have time to straighten our backs from toil – to look around at what is transpiring in public life. If we are not to be led to the polls like sheep, then give us time to study the welfare of our country. Our response to the passage of this Bill will be early demonstrated in a readier interest in, and higher regard for, all those things that make for a better Christian civilization.[34]

Many of the hundreds of union letters sent in conveyed similar sentiments. A Montreal carpenter wrote: "A longer working day than an eight-hour day does not allow the workman time for cultivating his mind and for recreation as becomes an honest citizen of a free country."[35] Other labour voices sang a similar tune – carpenters from Sault Ste Marie and Sorel, a cotton worker from Valleyfield, machinist from Calgary and North Bay, railway workers from Fort William and Cranmore, moulders from Carleton Place and Port Hope, a printer from Chatham, telegraphers from Toronto, Winnipeg and Roland, Manitoba, and East Pubnico, Nova Scotia, and le Parti ouvrier from Montreal.[36] In debate in the House of Commons, the sponsor of the bill, Montreal's Alphonse Verville, a plumber and Congress president, insisted that workers would "be temperate – many are teetotallers – and [would] make conditions better, as regards themselves, their wives, families and homes … If they had more leisure they in this country would do the same as in other countries – the time would be well spent. We would see more people in libraries and reading rooms."[37]

That perspective on leisure allowed for some occasional alliances between labour and temperance advocates and Sabbatarians. In 1899, for example, a national leader of the temperance movement, F.S. Spence, wrote to Toronto city council in support of a resolution calling for a nine-hour-day clause in city contracts:

> Men that have more spare time will take more interest in public affairs. We will have more brain power at work on the great problems of life. We will have more religion and better religion, and more politics and better politics, and better laws, and better aldermen and better government, and everybody will be benefitted.[38]

The idea that shorter hours would bring moral renewal persisted within the Canadian labour movement in one form or another until at least 1920. It could certainly be heard in the eight-hour demands raised within the workers' revolt after the First World War.[39] It was also taken up by newer working-class ethnic groups that were building their own rich participatory cultures, notably the Jews who dominated the garment industry.[40]

For the whole half-century up to 1920, however, hostile voices, most often from employers, frequently expressed their scepticism about all this moral high-mindedness. George Brown's *Globe* had been blunt: "the man who thinks ten hours hurtful and oppressive is too lazy to earn his bread … [and] laziness is detestable." He dismissed the idea that very many working men wanted to educate themselves.[41] Fifteen years later, the commissioners sent out across the country by the federal government to investigate "the relations of labour and capital" repeatedly raised with witnesses the issue of workers' misuse of idle time with shorter hours of work, especially "increasing drinking habits." An executive officer of the Chatham Harvester Company took the opportunity to question the value of more free time: "I think extra time on their hands would not be used to advantage." When pressed to explain, he said: "The only reason I have is that if you take any holiday, if there is any drinking it goes on then. We have no men now who drink, but we used to have them, and they always came back used up the next day after a holiday." A St Thomas carriage manufacturer similarly claimed that "men with shorter hours invariably waste the balance of time." An iron master in the same city was also opposed to shorter hours: "I think it would be time wasted if it was lost," he argued; "there is so much trouble with men in the use of liquor …, and so many of them use that time for gratifying their own personal desires, that they don't take the time with their families that they might."[42] A few years later the *Canadian Lumberman*, a business paper, expressed doubt that many workers would use more free time for "self-improvement and education": "The men who spend their time now in ways that are neither healthful nor improving would in many cases only extend the dissipation of valuable time as a result of extra time on their hands."[43]

The same sentiments were alive and well at the 1910 hearings of the parliamentary committee on the eight-hour day. The Canadian Manufacturers' Association herded witnesses into the committee room, and at the front of their line-up were some employees of the Hamilton Steel and Iron Company (at that moment in the midst of a merger to create the Steel Company of Canada), a firm that ran much of its operations twelve hours a day. Frank McKune, a superintendent, was adamant that shorter hours meant dissipation and difficulties with work discipline. "From my experience the best men we have and from whom we get the best results are the men who stay at work at least 325, 330, or 340 days a year," he claimed. Whenever the firm shut down for a holiday, he noted, "we are always handicapped for two or three days afterwards to get the thing going again, to get it worked up and going smoothly … That is the trouble we find, and you would only multiply it by putting the work on an eight-hour basis." He predicted that too many men on an eight-hour day would misuse their time: "Men may work for eight hours and then spend the next six hours in dissipation."[44] A foreman in the rolling mill agreed; with shorter hours workers would be "apt to stay longer on the wayside, and would get more time to drink than they do at the present time."[45]

Among the hundreds of letters that the committee received from businessmen, a sprinkling were equally blunt. The eight-hour day would be "an encouragement to idleness," according to one harness manufacturer. An Ottawa foundryman said: "We find in our particular line of work that after every holiday a large percentage of the men are off duty for one or more days. It is a well recognized fact that when men are idle they are more libel to fall into temptation, and we believe the shorter day would certainly have an evil tendency." A leading manufacturer in Amherst, Nova Scotia, argued: "the unsteady men would have more time to spend in saloons and places of amusement than they now have, and the result would be they would have less money and poorer health." Another in Montreal wrote: "the working man who actually in his spare time finds occasion to spend the money he should keep for his family would ... be tempted to spend more money in the evening." A Toronto manufacturer similarly wrote: "We believe that too much idle time is a far greater injury than where the time is properly employed, and a man is happier and better at work if not excessive." The head of a tobacco firm in Granby, Quebec, believed: "On an eight-hour day the men are inclined to get into bad habits, too much leisure time on their hands, that they do not know how to dispose of." A Hamilton machinery manufacturer did a little sociologizing on excessive drinking:

> As the corner saloon in many cases is the working man's club, we believe the eight-hour day system is a direct temptation to him – not only does he get less money, but he is placed in the way of temptation to spend more. We know many good mechanics, whom, while they do not drink to excess, go into the corner saloon on the way home, and have one glass of beer, arriving home in time for tea. We have found that some of these men, when they have time on their hands, frequently take too much.[46]

Craft unionists repeatedly responded that these arguments had the issue backwards – it was actually long hours that encouraged heavy drinking. At the first nine-hours mass meeting in Toronto, a speaker insisted: "Nothing degraded a man so much as continuous toil, and he was apt to seek relief from his exhausted condition in intoxication and tobacco."[47] When asked "if a man works long hours he therefore becomes fatigued and is more liable to take a glass going home," a Toronto moulder told the royal commission in 1887: "I have often seen that occur, for it helps a man along on his way home." With shorter hours, he thought, "the men would feel more refreshed and there would be a chance to be better educated."[48] After listening to the Hamilton steel-mill superintendent at the 1910 eight-hour hearings, Paddy Draper exclaimed: "The great wonder to us is that the men did not keep themselves paralyzed with drink all of the time so as to forget the unhappy surroundings under which they were working."[49] A coal miner wrote to that committee that "the present work day is too long and keeps the great majority of workmen in a state of over-fatigue, which tends to drunkenness and other excesses."[50]

Yet, however often all these arguments about moral uplift were repeated, they gradually lost their power through the decades of unsuccessful struggles to shorten the working day in the late nineteenth and early twentieth centuries. They were increasingly eclipsed by other arguments. At the National Industrial Conference held in September 1919, only one speaker, a Cape Breton miner, raised the need for an "opportunity to study," and he suggested simply that it would enable bosses and workers "to get together in times of stress and to discuss problems."[51] Partly the fading away of the moral argument resulted from the fact that, by the late nineteenth century, critics of shorter hours from the upper and middle classes were speaking from a new cultural space, where they were more openly embracing the pleasures of leisure in huge, lavish urban households nestled in exclusive neighbourhoods, in expanding networks of extravagant socializing, in a blossoming public life of opera houses, symphony halls, and art galleries, in well-appointed clubhouses for yachting, tennis, golf, and much more, in commodious new summer residences (where businessmen could take a month-long vacation and their families stayed longer), and on lengthy, luxurious overseas junkets.[52] In a column entitled "Everyone Out of Town," Hamilton's *Palladium of Labor* observed in August 1883: "A hundred pleasure resorts easy of access by boat or rail offer to the wearied men of business an opportunity for rest and relaxation and to the do-nothings of society change of air and scene which may for a time dispel the ennui of a frivolous existence" – all of this in contrast to the workers who were still at their jobs and had no such holidays.[53] Conspicuous consumption replaced asceticism within bourgeois circles, and provided a new context for indulgence in structured play and genteel repose, both of which were carefully distinguished from idleness. Indeed, a new mental ailment resulting from overwork came into the English lexicon and medical practice – neurasthenia – the prescription for which was a rest cure. In the process of this cultural reconstruction, the old argument about the centrality of work and its demanding disciplines certainly lost some of its punch.[54] In the opening decades of the twentieth century employers began to offer their white-collar workers fixed vacations, and middle-class men turned their leisure-time energies towards "hobbies."[55] Not surprisingly, by the early 1900s, business leaders more commonly argued against shorter hours on economic grounds rather than the older morally based concerns.[56]

Parallel but different changes were underway in working-class life. Although there were working men and women who carried on the moral earnestness about avoiding dissipated idleness through their practice of evangelical Protestantism, pietistic Catholicism, or the orthodox Jewish faith, the craftworkers' view of the relationship between work and leisure was shared by a dwindling number of workers. Back in 1872, the nine-hours "pioneers" knew that many workers did not share their view of rational leisure, and that some might abuse their idleness. The editor of the *Ontario Workman* occasionally lectured men on their responsibilities to use their time wisely. In the fall of 1872 he warned that the approach of "long winter evenings" posed a challenge for working men, considering "the many enticements that are held out on every hand, to allure our unthinking young men to scenes of frivolity and even vice." There were "many habits to be improved." A few months later the writer disparaged the man who devoted his extra hour off work to "the shuffling of cards or the shaking of dice at the corner grocery store." He urged the worker to devote his free time "sensibly to better purposes than dissipation, or idleness, which leads to dissipation, if not to vagabondage and crime." Another editorial warning was blunt: "Don't carry these precious sixty minutes and slam them down upon a drinking bar, getting nothing in return for God's gift than poison and death and murder."[57] A decade later the Hamilton labour paper, the *Palladium of Labor*, complained that "the average workingman neglects mental culture. His leisure moments are not sedulously employed in training his mind, by means of books, to think on the great problems intimately connected with his welfare."[58]

Increasingly in the late nineteenth century, such earnest labour spokepeople were swimming against the current. It was becoming harder for most workers to define themselves through their work in the same old ways. Employers intensified time on the job by demanding stricter control of workers' bodies and minds, and in the process squeezed out of the working day as much pleasure and play as possible.[59] Workers' experience on the job was no longer as likely to be enhanced by educational enlightenment after work. A recognition of this change crept into the Knights of Labor's commentary on hours of work, alongside their calls for uplifting after-work pastimes. In the words of Toronto's Phillips Thompson:

> In many industries the employee is merely the slave of the machine – rendering his toil much more continuous, exhaustive and monotonous than in the case of the operative who regulates the rate of speed at which he works. His faculties are continually on the stretch without pause or rest. His movements are guided by the revolutions of the machinery and are purely automatic as though he were part and parcel of the elaborate mechanism of modern production. There is no scope for originality, no play for the creative faculty – nothing to interest or stimulate exertion … The need for rest and recreation is vastly increased when operatives are subjected to the continuous strain and tension amid the clang and clatter of machinery, incidental to modern industrial production.[60]

Another labour journalist sketched the difficult transition from work time to free time:

> After his day's work he is hungry and tired; sometimes he is discontented, especially Saturday night if he can't get any money. He has to work ten hours a day: sometimes he walks a mile or two before and after, and saws wood when he comes home. In that case he has not much energy left for culture and education, especially if the children have the whooping cough and his wife is worn out working.[61]

Another wrote: "After 10 hours steady work, keeping up with a machine, what is the average person good for? For nothing, except a frivolous pursuit that, by reason of change from the mental strain, gives some rest. Let nine out of ten wage-earners attempt to read a book requiring mental application and they will fall asleep."[62]

Under such circumstances, more workers were likely to want to distance themselves from the pressures and unpleasantness of paid labour in Canada's industrial capitalist economy. In fact, workers, like their bourgeois counterparts, were re-conceptualizing leisure in ways that imagined free time as fun time. In part, that involved the persistence of less respectable pre-industrial pastimes in boarding houses, saloons, pool halls, and brothels, especially among younger, unmarried, less skilled, and seasonally unemployed working men, some of them immigrants from peasant economies overseas. These workers resisted internalizing the new industrial discipline. As we saw, employers bewailed the persistent difficulty of bringing such men under the rule of the clock and of making sure they showed up sober on Monday morning. But, much more often, after the turn of the century, men of any age or skill, and increasingly young wage-earning women, were turning to the new commercialized amusements that were becoming available in urban centres in sports arenas, cheap theatres, amusement parks, skating rinks, and dance halls. Out of these after-work activities working people were constructing leisure as the opposite of work, as release from the authoritarian constraints of the working day and as the source of excitement that work too seldom made possible.[63]

The evolving bachelor cultures of the late nineteenth and early twentieth centuries in particular resonated with an ambivalence towards work bordering on contempt, and could include a celebration of idleness (which, of course, for them was most often involuntary unemployment). The stock character at the centre of this counterculture of loafing was the "tramp" or "hobo" or "bum," the single, itinerant male worker who hit the road with others like himself to search for work, or when necessary, to just get by. Their lives could be hard, but they appeared in hit songs, vaudeville acts, movies, cartoon strips, and eventually radio comedies as romantic symbols of the rejection of regular work routines and discipline – none more famous than Charlie Chaplin's "Little Tramp."[64] A more radical variant emerged after 1905 in the Industrial Workers of the World, which organized migratory "blanket stiffs" across western North America, and whose hugely popular song "Hallelujah, I'm a Bum" ended with the lines: "When springtime it comes, oh, won't we have fun;/ We'll throw off our jobs, and go on the bum."[65]

So, to be idle could also be to be engaged in a kind of subversive activity, refusing to comply with the increasing demands of industrial capitalist work discipline. This was an approach to shorter hours far removed from the moral earnestness of the spokepersons for craftworkers.[66] It was also one that brought many working men up against the law, in violation of the Vagrancy Laws against not working and, in 1918, against the so-called Anti-Loafing Law passed as an order-in-council to deal with growing evidence of workers' unwillingness to show up to work or to work as hard in the wartime economy.[67]

In this altered context, craft unionists pursuing shorter hours found their earnest discourses of improvement and uplift resonating far less convincingly.[68] So a different kind of argument began to take more prominence, one that took these labour leaders onto the favoured terrain of their employers – the economy. Since the days of George Brown and his fellow capitalists of the 1870s, opponents of shorter hours had insisted that they would be economically disastrous. Businessmen argued again and again that the young, fragile Canadian economy could not stand the shock of reduced working hours, which they believed would limit production, raise costs, and thus render Canadian enterprises uncompetitive. The Canadian Manufacturers' Association most often led the charge. In 1919 Stelco's senior executive F.H. Whitton read a stern lecture to the Royal Commission on Industrial Relations on the need for maintaining production and keeping down costs, and a few months later, as the chief spokesperson of the employers' group in the National Industrial Conference, Toronto industrialist M.P. White from Canadian General Electric used similar arguments in a lengthy, hard-hitting speech against eight-hour legislation.[69] White actually circled back to drop a hint of moralism, by suggesting that in the context of more intense international competition, "we have got to put forth much greater effort than ever before and we have got to make every citizen realize it." He decried the shorter-hour enthusiasts who "stand up and say, 'We must have shorter hours at once; we must not work so hard.'" This was an appeal to rallying around the private interests of Canadian business as a generalized national good. "We must learn to speak in terms of national interest, and not the interest of a particular class or a particular industry," White insisted. Like other businessmen in the period, he also questioned the principles of supporters of shorter hours by claiming that they really just wanted a basic eight-hour day and, rather than the time off, the right to work an hour or two of overtime at higher rates. In other words, the shorter-hours movement was merely a grab for more wages.[70]

By the early 1900s, as the language of "efficiency" spread through the Canadian business world, cutting working hours flew in the face of the emerging managerial consensus about extracting even more out of the labour-power that employers purchased from their workers.[71] Well before the First World War, labour leaders were responding to these challenges by arguing for the "efficiency" of the shorter working day.[72] The old claims that time away from work would allow for personal development were retooled; now rest and recreation would make more productive workers who could work harder and better in an eight-hour day. When Alphonse Verville finally got to present a rationale for his eight-hour bill to the House of Commons for the first time in May 1909, it was striking that he began not with arguments about moral improvement, but with the "question of the probable efficiency of the working people" under a shorter-hours regime: "As much is done in the short as was in the long day." After reviewing evidence from firms that had shortened their working day, he told his fellow parliamentarians:

> While it is proven that, under the short hours system, men work harder while they are at work than they do under the long hours system, it is then true that short hours and hard work impose less strain on the body than the long hours and dawdling, especially if the long hours are passed in a hot or dusty or poisoned atmosphere such as many trades are obliged to work in. Then the increased exertion during working hours has always been balanced and more than balanced by the restorative effects of a longer period of repose or recreation in good air. While the men do as good a day's work as they did before, they improve in health and vigour."

From the Liberal benches, the one-time Labour MP Ralph Smith chimed in: "The economic loss in reduced hours is overbalanced by the greater strength and efficiency of the workers."[73] Many witnesses and letter-writers to the parliamentary eight-hour committee made the same claim. In this line of thinking, labour leaders had allies among some middle-class professionals, intellectuals, and social critics concerned with "Progressive" reform in Canada and elsewhere.[74]

A decade later, when labour leaders were assembled with employers and "community" representatives in the great National Industrial Conference that the Borden government had called together, they made the issue of efficiency a central theme in their defence of the eight-hour day and forty-four-hour week. They picked through the burgeoning literature on industrial relations to find experts' studies that documented higher productivity with shorter hours, such as one by British Tory MP Lord Henry Bentinck (employers, of course, countered with different studies and different conclusions).They even overlooked Henry Ford's renowned anti-unionism and cited favourably his equally famous eight-hour-day experiment in his US auto plants (as a Ford official explained, Canadian autoworkers actually worked nearly nine hours a day).[75] As Sydney steelworker John A. Gilles stated, "The shortening of the hours of labour renders the men more efficient and consequently better able to give an honest day's work for an honest day's pay."[76] In essence, these men were suggesting that speeding-up production would be easier under an eight-hour day. While still soft-pedalling the notion that leisure should be about mental cultivation, they were now conceding it would help to make possible precisely what managers wanted – faster, more focused, more productive workers.

Labour also marshalled a related argument that brought workers' health into the question of efficiency. In the early twentieth century, shorter-hours advocates argued primarily against the bad effects of long hours and the advantages of less fatigue in eight hours for more work the next day, rather than in favour of the positive effects of leisure itself. They also emphasized the unhealthy impact of long hours on life beyond the job. They argued that such serious illnesses as tuberculosis would decline if workers were more rested. A Carleton Place moulder insisted in 1910 that "reducing the hours … adds longer and happier years to life, lessens disease and lowers the death toll of the white plague."[77] Supporters of laws limiting the working day of miners were particularly adamant about the dangers of overwork. When the machinists' union leader J.A. McClelland stood up before the National Industrial Conference in Ottawa in September 1919 to defend the eight-hour day on behalf of the labour group at the gathering, he focused on the workers' health.[78] "With the introduction of improved machinery the pace has been made so fast that it is absolutely impossible for the worker to maintain it for any length of time," he insisted. "The result is invariably that he falls ill, and his family or those dependent upon him suffer in consequence." He went on to cite physicians consulted by the US Bureau of Labor who supported an eight-hour day.[79] Vancouver's Helena Gutteridge stated that workers wanted "to recover from the fatigue of production, and sometimes the fearful speeding-up to which they are subject today." She was particularly concerned about women workers, noting that the British Ministry of Munitions had discovered that "because of the hours they were working they did not recover sufficiently from the fatigue day after day, until there was such an accumulation of fatigue at the end of the week that they did not properly recover at the week-end." She argued that "it pays to have healthy workers, because if workers are healthy and happy they will produce a great deal more than if they are in a constant state of irritation and ill-health."[80] Employers countered that only some industries were hard on their workers' health, and only those, not all, should have their hours reduced.[81]

By that point the debate was becoming a battle of the experts, and labour leaders felt they had to do their homework. Employers had economists to sustain their arguments about lower production under the eight-hour day, such as Adam Shortt from Queen's University and Robert Magill from Dalhousie University, and they presented studies of various kinds that, they contended, made shorter hours unacceptable, including the Health of Munitions Workers Committee of the British Ministry of Munitions and the US National Industrial Conference Board.[82] But there were middle-class voices in the public arena who had joined the chorus about the danger and unhealthiness of long hours and who could be relied upon to reinforce labour's case. Indeed, in contrast to the craftsmen of the late nineteenth century, labour leaders relied much more commonly on professional expertise to make their case. In 1925 a union brief to the federal government closed with reference to the "eminent medical authorities and prominent industrial engineers [who] have pronounced themselves in favor of the adoption of the eight hour day mainly on the grounds of physical and industrial efficiency."[83] This kind of argumentation had clearly moved away from the transformative possibilities of the early shorter-hours movements and to a more accommodationist framework. In 1927 a US journalist writing in the *Canadian Congress Journal* playfully traced how the fascination with productivity produced a "conservative" battle cry: "To suit the new discovery she [labour] turned economist, left behind, but not forgotten, her hope of a social revolution with labor supreme, and became intensely interested in industry, in production, in costs … [B]y shortening the hours you eliminate all waste caused by fatigue, your production is increased because your workers are rested, and able to do more in less time. Here was a battle cry … almost taken from the very lips of the employer!"[84]

Within a few years, however, a strand in the argumentation about shorter hours that had appeared earlier moved to the foreground and became almost the sole justification for less time on the job. That was the notion that reducing working hours for those employed would open up jobs for the unemployed (on the assumption that employers would have to hire more workers). Before the war, the Industrial Workers of the World had raised the six-hour day in their organizing campaigns with the unemployed. At its founding convention in 1919, the One Big Union resolved to conduct a referendum on holding a national general strike for a six-hour day and five-day week as a solution to the impending threat of postwar joblessness.[85] As underemployment of the 1920s turned into the mass unemployment of the early 1930s, the mainstream labour movement changed its demand to a six-hour day and a five-day week, that is, a thirty-hour week. This program of sharing the available work became labour's main panacea for solving the problem of unemployment. The craft union movement centred in the American Federation of Labor and the Trades and Labor Congress of Canada lobbied vigorously for this reform in working hours.[86] CCF MPs raised this demand repeatedly in the House of Commons, arguing against "technological unemployment," caused by rapid mechanization and managerial innovation that had reduced the need for human labour, and insisting that only a radical reduction in the working day (and week) would open up more jobs to the unemployed. In the words of Alberta's E.J. Garland, "continually and progressively we shall have to reduce the hours of labour as the scientific attainments of man develop and continue to displace labour."[87] In the first half of the 1930s this was a widely accepted premise that was influencing policy discussions across North America, including Roosevelt's New Deal and the debate around Prime Minister R.B. Bennett's eight-hour-day legislation in 1935.[88] It would continue as a rationale for shortening work hours well into the post-war period, even after unemployment had ceased to be such a burning issue. In that context, the older arguments about the moral worth of shorter hours and even the newer emphasis on enhanced productivity were totally eclipsed.

By the 1940s the argument that shorter hours would open up more jobs was more often twinned with the idea that leisure should be a positive experience. In 1949 the Canadian Congress of Labour's Research Department published a study of shorter hours, and emphasized: "A factor not to be overlooked is the recognition of adequate leisure time for recreation as an expression of a decent standard of living." It quoted an official in the US National Recreation Association:

> Recreation has come to be accepted as one of the fundamental needs for all people, and not just a birthright for children. The general acceptance of this broader meaning of recreation has given it its rightful place alongside religion, education, health, work, and the other essentials of life.[89]

Labour spokespeople also began to make a link between leisure and consumption. As early as 1932, a US labour leader wrote in the *Canadian Congress Journal* that "the wage-earner should have more leisure so that he would become a larger consumer by spending more money."[90] During and after the Second World War Canadian unions insisted on the right of workers to participate more fully in the consumer economy. This was of course sweet music to the ears of Canadian business.

So, in the rhetorical battle to get shorter working hours, the late-nineteenth-century debate about idleness was slowly pushed aside by an early-twentieth-century debate about efficiency, and then drowned in an interwar debate about unemployment. Only in the 1940s did the focus return to the issue of leisure time, but the difference between purposeful "mental cultivation" and playful consumption was vast. The modern view of leisure was as an end in itself, a compensation for alienating and enervating work, not something that could enhance work as the nineteenth-century craftworkers had argued. In essence, labour leaders had finally come around to a defence of shorter hours that resonated with where working-class popular culture had been for decades – in the words of the labour poet, "eight hours for work, eight hours for rest," but more ambiguously "eight hours for what we will."

Notes

1 Each of the first three Internationals, in particular, made shorter hours a priority, and the outcome of the peace conferences after the First World War brought the International Labour Organization on the world stage as a major player on the issue of work time.

2 For the larger picture, see E.P. Thompson, "Time, Work Discipline, and Industrial Capitalism," *Past and Present* 38 (December 1967), 56–97; Gary Cross, ed., *Worktime and Industrialization: An International History* (Philadelphia: Temple University Press 1988); David R. Roediger and Philp S. Foner, *Our Own Time: A History of American Labor and the Working Day* (London: Verso Press 1989).

3 Pietro Basso, *Modern Times, Ancient Hours: Working Lives in the Twenty-First Century* (London: Verso 2003).

4 See in particular the evidence presented in Canada, Royal Commission on the Relations of Labour and Capital, *Report: Evidence* (Ottawa: Queen's Printer 1888).

5 *Labour Gazette* (Ottawa), 1900–20; Craig Heron, *Working in Steel: The Early Years in Canada, 1883–1935* (Toronto: McClelland and Stewart 1988); James Struthers, *No Fault of Their Own: Unemployment and the Canadian Welfare State, 1914–1941* (Toronto: University of Toronto Press 1983).

6 Cross, ed., *Worktime and Industrialization*.

7 Lorna F. Hurl, "Overcoming the Inevitable: Restricting Factory Labour in Late-Nineteen-Century Ontario," *L/LT* 21 (Spring 1988), 87–123; Robert McIntosh, *Boys in the Pits: Child Labour in Coal Mines* (Montreal and Kingston: McGill-Queen's University Press 2000), 89–105.

8 *Globe* (Toronto), 20 May 1872, 2.
9 Karl Marx, *Capital, Volume 1* (New York: International Publishers 1967), chapter 10.
10 Daniel T. Rogers, *The Work Ethic in Industrial America, 1850–1920* (Chicago: University of Chicago Press 1978), 1–29; Craig Heron, "Factory Workers," in Paul Craven, ed., *Labouring Lives: Work and Workers in Nineteenth-Century Ontario* (Toronto: University of Toronto Press 1998), 479–590.
11 *Spectator* (Hamilton), 31 January 1872, 2; Gregory S. Kealey, *Toronto Workers Respond to Industrial Capitalism, 1867–1892* (Toronto: University of Toronto Press 1980), 130. See also John Hewitt's letter to *Ontario Workman*, 10 October 1872, 5.
12 Gregory S. Kealey and Bryan D. Palmer, *Dreaming of What Might Be: The Knights of Labor in Ontario, 1880–1900* (Toronto: New Hogtown Press 1987); Ian McKay, *Reasoning Otherwise: Leftists and the People's Enlightenment in Canada, 1890–1920* (Toronto: Between the Lines 2008).
13 *Canadian Manufacturer*, 3 December 1886, 707; Roediger and Foner, *Our Own Time*, 6, 13, 31, 37; Gary Cross, *A Quest for Time: The Reduction of Work in Britain and France, 1840–1940* (Berkeley: University of California Press 1989), 15–16.
14 Bryan D. Palmer, *A Culture in Conflict: Skilled Workers and Industrial Capitalism in Hamilton, Ontario, 1860–1914* (Montreal and Kingston: McGill-Queen's University Press 1979); Kealey, *Toronto Workers*; Robert Kristofferson, *Craft Capitalism: Craftworkers and Early Industrialization in Hamilton, Ontario, 1840–1872* (Toronto: University of Toronto Press 2007); John Battye, "The Nine Hour Pioneers: The Genesis of the Canadian Labour Movement," *L/LT* 4 (1979), 25–56; Paul Craven, "Workers' Conspiracies in Toronto, 1854–1872,' ibid. 14 (Fall 1984), 49–70; Paul Craven, "Labour and Management on the Great Western Railway," in Craven, ed., *Labouring Lives*, 381–4; Christina Burr, *Spreading the Light: Work and Labour Reform in Late-Nineteenth-Century Toronto* (Toronto: University of Toronto Press 1999).
15 *Spectator* 29 January 1872, 2 (emphasis in original).
16 *Globe*, 15 February 1872, 4. For a similar concern to deflect such assumptions, see *Ontario Workman*, 16 April 1872, 4. "The opponents of the short time movement were loud in their assertions that more leisure time meant more time for the billiard room and saloon," the *Ontario Workman*'s editor wrote a few months later, "and that, therefore, the obtaining of shorter hours of labor would prove not a blessing but a curse to those who secured them." Ibid., 26 September 1872, 4. A decade later, labour spokespersons were still lashing out at these charges that "the time saved

from labor will be oftener spent in the saloon and the corner grocery, indulging in the fascination with cards and stimulating drinks." *Labor Union*, 10 March 1883, 1.

17 *Globe*, 15 February 1872, 4.
18 *Spectator*, 29 January 1872, 2. For similar arguments in Britain, see Cross, *Quest for Time*, 29.
19 *Spectator*, 31 January 1872, 2.
20 Globe, 15 February 1872, 4.
21 *Spectator*, 29 January 1872, 2; *Globe*, 15 February 1872, 4; *Ontario Workman*, 9 May 1872, 5.
22 *Ontario Workman*, 18 April 1872, 4.
23 *Globe*, 15 February 1872, 4.
24 *Spectator*, 29 January 1872, 2. US workers had emphasized the importance of time to enable full citizenship as far back as the 1830s. Roediger and Foner, *Our Own Time*, 19–42.
25 *Ontario Workman*, 23 May 1872, 5.
26 Ibid., 18 April 1872, 4.
27 *Globe*, 15 February 1872, 4.
28 *Ontario Workman*, 9 May 1872, 5. For further discussion of this theme, see Burr, *Spreading the Light*, 127–35.
29 *Globe*, 15 February 1872, 4; *Ontario Workman*, 2 May 1872, 1.
30 *Spectator*, 12 February 1872, 2. These themes also resonated through the US shorter-hours campaigns dating back to the 1830s. Roediger and Foner, *Our Own Time*, 41, 99.
31 *Ontario Workman*, 9 May 1872, 5; Kealey and Palmer, *Dreaming of What Might Be*. In 1883 Hamilton's *Palladium of Labor* launched a series of article entitled "Our Social Club," which gave a graphic example of the appropriate form of mental cultivation. *Palladium of Labor*, 8 September 1883, 1.
32 *Labor Union* (Toronto), 27 January 1883, 4.
33 *Palladium of Labor*, 21 February 1885, 1.
34 Canada, House of Commons, *Journals*, 45 (1909–10), Appendix, Part 3 ("Proceedings of a Special Committee on Bill No. 21, 'An Act Respecting Hours of Labour on Public Works,' Comprising Reports, Evidence and Correspondence, December 9, 1909 – May, 1910"), 328.
35 Ibid., 614.
36 Ibid., 617, 620, 622, 642, 643, 646, 661, 662, 670, 676, 678, 679, 680, 688, 689.
37 Canada, House of Commons, *Debates*, 1909–10, 5922.
38 F.S. Spence, "Shorter Hours: An Important Public Question" (Canadian Institute for Historical Microreproductions, no. 28918). 3. See also for

Palladium of Labor, 12 January 1884, 2; 22 November 1884, 2; 20 December 1884, 2; 10 January 1885, 1.

39 Craig Heron, ed., *The Workers' Revolt in Canada, 1917–1925* (Toronto: University of Toronto Press 1998).

40 Ruth Frager, *Sweatshop Strife: Class, Ethnicity, and Gender in the Jewish Labour Movement of Toronto, 1900–1939* (Toronto: University of Toronto Press 1992).

41 *Globe* (Toronto), 23 March 1872, 2.

42 Canada, Royal Commission on the Relations of Labour and Capital, *Report: Evidence – Ontario*, 85, 147, 156–7, 203, 243, 303, 393, 440 (quotation), 456–7, 463, 510 (quotation), 550–1 (quotation), 813–14, 843, 948–9, 960, 1003, 1040, 1181–2.

43 *Canadian Lumberman*, April 1893, 7. For similar comments from the same paper, see ibid., 1 November 1881, 8; September 1892, 6; February 1896, 4.

44 Canada, House of Commons, *Journals*, 45 (1909–10), Appendix, Part 3, 169 (quotation), 171, 174, 182 (quotation).

45 Ibid., 190.

46 Ibid., 480, 487, 497, 524, 569, 585.

47 *Globe*, 15 February 1872, 4.

48 Canada, Royal Commission on the Relations of Labour and Capital, *Report: Evidence – Ontario*, 85, 156–7 (quotation), 463.

49 Canada, House of Commons, *Journals*, 45 (1909–10), Appendix, Part 3, 333; see also 335.

50 Ibid., 659.

51 Canada, National Industrial Conference of Dominion and Provincial Governments with Representative Employers and Labour Men, *Official Report of Proceedings and Discussions* (Ottawa: King's Printer 1919), 81.

52 Margaret Westley, *The Remembrance of Grandeur: The Anglo-Protestant Elite of Montreal* (Montreal: Libra Expression 1990); Michael Bliss, *A Canadian Millionaire: The Life and Business Times of Sir Joseph Flavelle, Bart., 1858–1939* (Toronto: Macmillan 1978); Heron, *Lunch-Bucket Lives*, 24–8; Sven Backert, *The Moneyed Metropolis: New York City and the Consolidation of the American Bourgeoisie, 1850–1896* (Cambridge: Cambridge University Press 2001).

53 *Palladium of Labor*, 18 August 1883, 2.

54 Rodgers, *Work Ethic*, 94–124; Tom Lutz, *Doing Nothing: A History of Loafers, Loungers, Slackers, and Bums in America* (New York: Farrar, Straus, and Giroux 2006), 141–7; E. Anthony Rotundo, *American Manhood: Transformations in Masculinity from the Revolution to the Modern Era* (New York: Basic Books 1993), 185–93; Michael Kimmel, *Manhood in America: A Cultural History* (New York: Free Press 1996), 134–5.

55 Steven M. Gelber, *Hobbies: Leisure and the Culture of Work in America* (New York: Columbia University Press 1999).
56 See the letters and testimony presented to the parliamentary committee on the eight-hour bill in 1910; Canada, House of Commons, *Journals*, 45 (1909–10), Appendix, Part 3.
57 *Ontario Workman*, 26 September 1872, 4; 23 January 1873, 1; 8 May 1873, 5; see also 15 May 1873, 3; 5 June 1873, 5.
58 *Palladium of Labor*, 1 September 1883, 1.
59 Heron, "Factory Workers."
60 *Palladium of Labor*, 21 February 1885, 1.
61 *Labor Union*, 10 February 1883, 1.
62 *Palladium of Labor*, 3 April 1886, 1.
63 Craig Heron, *Lunch-Bucket Lives: Remaking the Workers' City* (Toronto: Between the Lines 2015); Cross, *Quest for Time*, 70.
64 Tim Cresswell, *The Tramp in America* (London: Reaktion 2001); Richard Wormser, *Hoboes: Wandering in America, 1870–1940* (New York: Walker and Company 1994); Frederick Feied, *No Pie in the Sky: The Hobo as American Cultural Hero in the Works of Jack London, John Dos Passos, and Jack Kerouac* (New York: Citadel Press 1964).
65 Mark Leier, *Where the Fraser River Flows: The Industrial Workers of the World in British Columbia* (Vancouver: New Star Books 1990); Ross McCormack, "Wobblies and Blanket Stiffs: The Constituency of the IWW in Western Canada," in W.J.C. Cherwinski and G.S. Kealey, eds., *Lectures in Canadian Labour and Working-Class History* (St John's and Toronto: Committee on Canadian Labour History and New Hogtown Press 1985), 115–26; Joyce L. Kornbluh, ed., *Rebel Voices: An I.W.W. Anthology* (Ann Arbor: University of Michigan Press 1968), 71–2; https://en.wikipedia.org/wiki/Hallelujah,_I'm_a_Bum (quotation).
66 Robert Weir describes how the Knights of Labor struggled to control the expressive excesses of their membership at the Order's social events; Weir, *Beyond Labor's Veil: The Culture of the Knights of Labor* (University Park: Pennsylvania State University Press 1996), 277–319. See Also Craig Heron and Steve Penfold, *The Workers' Festival: A History of Labour Day in Canada* (Toronto: University of Toronto Press 2005), 118–25.
67 Jim Phillips, "Poverty, Unemployment, and the Administration of the Criminal Law: Vagrancy Laws in Halifax, 1864–1890," in Philip Girard and Jim Phillips, eds., *Essays in the History of Canadian Law, Volume III: Nova Scotia* (Toronto: University of Toronto Press 1990), 128–62; David Bright, "Loafers Are Not Going to Subsist on Public Credulence: Vagrancy and the Law in Calgary, 1900–1914," *L/LT* 36 (Fall 1995),

37–58; "Regulations against Idleness," Privy Council Order 815, 4 April 1918.

68 Gary Cross sees this discursive retreat as early as the 1880s in Britain and France; *Quest for Time*, 59–60.

69 LAC, R1176–0-0-E (Commission to Inquire into and Report upon Industrial Relations in Canada), Minutes, 2296–7; National Industrial Conference, *Official Report of Proceedings*, 72–3.

70 National Industrial Conference, *Official Report of Proceedings*, 59.

71 Heron, *Lunch-Bucket Lives*, 229–70.

72 In 1888 William C. Teague, an Ottawa printer, argued: "My opinion is that a man can do as much in nine hours' continuous work as he can in ten hours' continuous work." Canada, Royal Commission on the Relations of Labour and Capital, *Evidence – Ontario* (Ottawa: Queen's Printer 1889), 1181–2.

73 Canada, House of Commons, *Debates*, 1909–10, 7 May 1909, 5914, 5921; 9 December, 1253.

74 Melissa Turkstra, "Christianity and the Working Class in Early Twentieth Century English Canada" (PhD dissertation, York University 2005).

75 National Industrial Conference, *Official Report of Proceedings*, 72–3.

76 Ibid., 72–3, 88–9.

77 Canada, House of Commons, *Journals*, 45 (1909–10), Appendix, Part 3, 661. For earlier arguments in the same vein, see the Hamilton *Standard*, quoted in *Ontario Workman*, 24 October 1872, 5; ibid., 12 December 1872, 5.

78 National Industrial Conference, *Official Report of Proceedings*, 53–6.

79 Ibid., 55–6

80 Ibid., 67.

81 That was the argument of the minority report from the Royal Commission on Industrial Relations, which was signed by two employers. The employers' group at the National Industrial Conference insisted that the federal government should appoint a commission to "undertake investigations as to the adaptability of the hours of labour principles of the Peace Treaty to the different industries of the country." Ibid., x.

82 Ibid., 60–1. Labour Minister Mackenzie King hired Shortt to conduct a study for working hours for the 1910 parliamentary committee on the eight-hour day, and the Nova Scotia government recruited Magill to head up its Commission on Hours of Labour in 1908. Both presented arguments about the unfeasibility of shorter hours.

83 E. Ingles, "Legal Limitation of Hours of Work to Not More Than Eight on the Day and Forty-Eight in the Week," *Canadian Congress Journal* (hereafter *CCJ*), April 1925, 46.

84 *CCJ*, February 1927, 26.
85 James Naylor and Tom Mitchell, "The Prairies: The Eye of the Storm," in Heron, ed., *Workers' Revolt*, 216n7.
86 *CCJ*, November 1934, 18; June 1935, 24; November 1935, 21; *Labor Review*, June 1937, 181–2.
87 Canada, House of Commons, *Debates*, 1935, 1671.
88 Benjamin Kline Hunnicutt, *Work Without End: Abandoning Shorter Hours for the Right to Work* (Philadelphia: Temple University Press 1988); Shirley Tillotson, "Time, Swimming Pools, and Citizenship: The Emergence of Leisure Rights in Mid-Twentieth-Century Canada," in Robert Adamoski, Dorothy Chunn, and Robert Menzies, eds., *Contesting Canadian Citizenship: Historical Readings* (Toronto: Broadview Press 2002), 203–4.
89 *Labour Research*, December 1949, 3.
90 *CCJ*, July 1932, 15.

WATCHING FOR PREY

Chapter Five

Labour and Liquor

For a century before the 1920s, Canadians debated the merits of curtailing alcohol consumption. From the 1850s onwards, most temperance advocates wanted to completely shut down the "Liquor Traffic" by legally prohibiting the production and sale of alcoholic beverages. Although plenty of drinking men in working-class communities opposed prohibition, the most articulate voices of the labour leadership at the turn of the century were far more likely to be abstainers. The shift in the larger temperance movement to legislated coercion made these workers uneasy, however, and gradually labour drifted away from the "dry" alliance. By the end of the First World War, after many years of deep division, the Canadian labour movement ultimately became one of the leading forces in opposition to prohibition.

Reaching that position had been a tortuous path. In the last third of the nineteenth century, many working-class leaders were committed teetotallers who, in their search for working-class respectability, worried about the impact of alcohol and alcoholism on working-class family households and on a drinker's ability to join in any collective working-class struggle. Some craft unions had actively promoted sobriety. The Brotherhood of Locomotive Engineers had staked out what was perhaps the most militant position with its motto of "Sobriety, Truth, Justice and Morality" and constitutional provisions for expelling habitual drunkards, whose names were published in its monthly journal. In 1892 the railway brotherhoods went a step further and organized a "white-button" movement in parallel with the Woman's Christian Temperance Union's white-ribbon campaign, to encourage railway workers to display their sobriety with pride. To discourage

Temperance cartoon. *Pioneer*, 26 December 1920

their members' drinking and raise their organizations' respectability in middle-class eyes, many labour groups moved their meetings out of taverns and thus turned their backs on the European practice of linking organized workers' movements and working-class popular culture in cafes and taverns. Instead, early in the twentieth century, Canada's city-based unions would begin to pool their money to build their own halls, known as "Labour Temples."[1]

These concerns had reached their highest form of expression in the Knights of Labor. In 1884 the Knights' weekly newspaper in Hamilton, the *Palladium of Labor*, had summed up that movement's perspective on "The Fight for Temperance":

> The working classes do not probably drink more than others, but they experience its effects more. The expense of drink that would not be appreciably felt by a merchant or professional man will keep the laborer destitute and rob his family of all the comforts and sometimes of the necessaries of life. The habit is fatal to independence and self-control. The workingman who spends a large portion of his wages in liquor is obliged to live from hand to mouth, and often to go into debt. He is absolutely at the mercy of his employer who, knowing that he has no savings to fall back upon, often takes advantage of his necessities and compels him to accept low wages. Drinking fosters habits of irresolution and instability. It has been the cause of the ignominious failure of many a movement on the part of workingmen which otherwise had fair prospect of success. It is in every way bad and any movement which tends to its suppression should have the cordial sympathy of Labor Reformers.[2]

The Knights officially supported temperance as part of their effort to promote a new culture of assertive, collective working-class respectability (in contrast to middle-class individualism), and barred from membership any "person who either sells or makes his living by the sale of intoxicating drink" – meaning, primarily, saloon-keepers (bankers, lawyers, stockbrokers, and professional gamblers were the only others on the prohibited list). Sobriety could be a goal for those wanting to change the direction of the new capitalist economy as much as for those who directed it. In 1886 the Knights' Grand Master Workman, Terence V. Powderly, penned a pledge for the Order's members, which he claimed some 100,000 members took within six months:

> I am a Knight of Labor. I believe that every man should be free from the curse of slavery, whether that slavery appears in the shape of monopoly,

> usury or intemperance. The firmest link in the chain of oppression is the one I forge when I drown my manhood and reason in drink. No man can rob me of the brain God has given me unless I am a party to the theft. If I drink to drown grief, I bring grief to my wife, child and sorrowing friends. I add not one iota to the sum of human happiness when I invite oblivion over the rim of a glass.[3]

Nevertheless, the Order entered the fray with great caution. Around its members swirled demeaning middle-class discourses about working-class degradation that made them uncomfortable. The *Palladium* warned, "The attempt of employers to dictate as to the personal habits of their workmen so long as the latter do not incapacitate themselves for work by excess ought to be sternly resisted." In his testimony before the Royal Commission on the Liquor Traffic, a Knights leader in Montreal bristled at the disparaging comments of a witness who had preceded him: "I do not like to see such prejudice shown against the working class and their organizations." Moreover, temperance was a divisive issue within working-class communities, because so many working men scoffed at the prospect of giving up their glass of beer and their social life in the saloon. Even teetotalling wage-earners worried that state repression of drinking violated fundamental personal liberties.[4]

Rather than merge into existing temperance groups, then, the Knights developed their own angle on temperance. In contrast to the individualism of the middle-class temperance cry, they argued that a strong organization of temperate working men could establish independence and dignity for workers and usher in a new oppositional culture of working-class respectability. In the pages of the *Palladium of Labor*, Phillips Thompson looked forward to "the new direction" that abstinence "would give the thoughts and aspirations of the toilers. They would have more time and more inclination for mental culture." According to Thompson, the workers "would learn to place their hopes in the future, and to take their share, well and worthily in the struggle for equal chances." Temperance thus became only part of a larger vision of the "nobler and holier" place of working people in a reformed industrial society. The issue had been appropriated and recast as a tool in the battle for working-class emancipation.[5]

In practical terms the Knights demanded a high standard of deportment among their members. As one Montreal Knight explained, the Order insisted that members

> must be dressed neat and tidy, must not be seen on the streets drunk or they are liable to be expelled, and the result is that men get into the habit of coming to our meetings, they dress better, and the fact of spending money to get dress prevents them from going to the saloons, and their families are better off. Thousands of women ... say that their husbands were never so good as since they joined the order of the Knights of Labour.

The Knights also organized their own wholesome entertainment to bring both men and women into booze-free settings, from picnics and dances to public lectures. This, they hoped, would appeal to working-class wives and daughters and strengthen the men's cultural ties to their households, rather than to saloons.[6]

The Knights leadership also took tentative steps towards an alliance with the mainstream temperance movement. By the mid-1880s, their local newspapers were promoting the benefits of taking the pledge and giving verbal support to efforts to limit saloon licences and even to full-fledged prohibition under the Scott Act. The fledgling Trades and Labor Congress of Canada, in which the Knights played a leading role, attempted to bridge the divide in the labour movement with a resolution in 1883 that "any practical legislation tending to reduce the consumption of intoxicating liquor" would meet with its "hearty approval." Officers of the national Dominion Alliance for the Total Suppression of the Liquor Traffic made a pitch to the 1886 Congress convention and saw the 1883 resolution renewed. Behind these moves lay an effort in the mid-1880s to build an electoral coalition of Labour Reformers and prohibitionists, which the Congress also endorsed. This brief, fragile alliance brought a reformist mayor, William Howland, to office in Toronto in 1886, and a Labour-Prohibitionist candidate, William Garson, won a seat in the Ontario legislature the next year. Otherwise there was little to show for this collaboration in Ontario, and the same was apparently true in British Columbia.[7]

Nor was there any clear sign that the prohibitionists had much interest in labour's wider goals. The WCTU's US leader, Frances Willard, had made a well-publicized claim that workers needed to learn to manage their wages better rather than demanding higher wages. Willard eventually retracted her comment and worked hard in the late 1880s and early 1890s to cement an alliance between her organization and the labour movement, though no such overtures came from the Canadian WCTU. The Knights' alternative vision of temperance seemed to have been sacrificed to narrow electoralism. In the 1890s some labour figures attempted to work with shifting clusters of social "regenerators," which included radical prohibitionists such as WW Buchanan, editor of the *Templar*, a temperance newspaper, and many of whom would merge into the new Canadian Socialist League in 1899. But these new political currents lacked the Knights' numerical strength and distinctive working-class perspective.[8]

For much more complex reasons than their views on alcohol, the Knights had declined after the late 1880s, and a new North American labour movement based more narrowly on craft unionism slowly coalesced around the new American Federation of Labor (AFL) and its smaller, weaker Canadian counterpart, the Trades and Labor Congress of Canada. Although many former Knights moved over into it, this new labour movement never tried to rearticulate the same coherent vision of working-class temperance. Indeed, the AFL told the WCTU in 1897 that it did not see prohibition as essential to workers' emancipation, and a year later the Trades and Labor Congress of Canada voted down a prohibition resolution (that same year Winnipeg's unions apparently kept a temperance float out of their Labour Day parade, but made room for some brewery wagons). According to a 1901 survey, a block of nine of the thirty-nine leading international craft unions (including railwaymen, sailors, tailors, and typographers) still strongly opposed the saloon, and several more were at least somewhat negatively inclined. But those craft unionists whose livelihood was tied to the liquor traffic (especially brewers, bartenders, coopers, cigarmakers, musicians, and teamsters) and those who believed that their heavy labour required beer as a refreshment (such as the glassworkers) were staunch opponents of prohibition.[9]

The Federation tried to respect this division of opinion by avoiding any clear policy statements on booze. Similarly, when the Dominion Alliance pushed Toronto's Independent Labor Party to take a stand in 1911, a prominent labour man urged the party to steer clear: "We have in our party men who are utterly opposed to any restriction on the liquor traffic," he said, "and we cannot give the Alliance a favorable reply without antagonizing a large body of our members."[10]

Deepening Ambivalence

Few labour leaders in Canada spoke out in defence of drinking or of saloons before the war. Even though some unions had made it clear that they wanted nothing to do with prohibition, the dominant craft-union movement in the pre-war period had set a public course of responsible action to win acceptance by employers and the state, and it had no intention of risking its credibility or respectability by openly allying with the liquor traffic. This position represented more than pure opportunism; many union activists were still cast in the earnest, morally upright mould of the late nineteenth century. Indeed, like Hamilton's Allan Studholme, the lone labour member of the Ontario legislature from 1906 to 1919, several individuals responded positively to the overtures of Social Gospellers to participate in reform alliances, notably in the various provincial Social and Moral Reform Councils launched after 1907, where they rubbed shoulders with prohibitionists for a few years (but generally and eventually drifted away). For the drys, the most prominent voice within international unionism was the widely read Reverend Charles Steltzle, a former machinist turned independent Presbyterian minister, whose writings on a labour-oriented Social Gospel appeared regularly in Canadian labour newspapers. In 1909, when the AFL's annual convention met in Toronto, Steltzle called a mass meeting to launch an anti-saloon fellowship within the Federation, where some prominent international union leaders defended prohibition. Thanks to the efforts of AFL president Samuel Gompers, no such organization emerged. Nonetheless, before leaving home in Britain, some recent immigrants might also have come into contact with the Trade Union and Labour Officials' Temperance Fellowship, organized in 1905 to rally the considerable number of teetotallers in the British labour movement.[11]

Even on the far left, teetotalism was remarkably common, as it was on the European and British left in the early twentieth century. To be sure, socialists typically blamed capitalism for drunkenness and saw no need for special organization or public policy to deal with this issue because it would disappear under socialism. As socialist Colin McKay wrote in 1901:

> The clergy inveigh, halfheartedly, against the liquor traffic. They ought to see that it is a necessity concomitant of the profit-mongering system, which will continue just as long as the motive principle of industry is private profit, because it affords an easy method of amassing wealth. Under the system of socialism, where industry was carried on for public welfare, not individual aggrandizement, the liquor traffic would disappear, because nobody would have any interest in prosecuting it.

In a similar vein, the socialists' leading Canadian mouthpiece, the *Western Clarion*, argued two years later: "Provide the workingmen with clean, cheerful homes and the means of intellectual culture and they will stop drinking bad whiskey in filthy and malodorous saloons." In the BC legislature, Socialist MLA James Hawthornthwaite proposed a popular socialist alternative to the liquor traffic in the form of municipal ownership of the drink trade modelled on the Scandinavian "Gothenburg System," but no government was prepared to go near that approach in the pre-war period.[12]

Many men in the Socialist Party of Canada not only rejected temperance as a reformist middle-class ploy that deflected attention from the anti-capitalist cause, but also linked a tough version of working-class masculinity to the struggle for a new world. They objected in particular to the WCTU's multipronged attack on masculine amusements. Their scorn for prohibition was as searing as for any other threats to gender privilege, including women's suffrage. Yet some socialist women spoke out for controls on men's drinking, including British Columbia's widely read socialist journalist Merrill Burns, and many in the growing Finnish socialist community, which organized its own temperance societies. Once the Social Democrats had split away from the Socialist Party of Canada, their newspaper, *Cotton's Weekly*, regularly published sympathetic views of prohibition penned by the editor, William Cotton, or his sister Mary Cotton Wisdom. One of the country's most prominent socialists (and vice-president of the Trades and Labor Congress of Canada), Toronto's Jimmy Simpson, appeared on many dry platforms before and during the war.[13]

The women among these anti-booze socialists tended to rest their case on the plight of neglected or abused wives and children. The men more often argued that alcohol undermined collective working-class struggle. By the end of the war, British Columbia's R.P. ("Parm") Pettipiece was thundering:

> Drink will break a strike sooner than anything else except hunger ... The wage slave that tries to drown the misery of daily toil and poverty in "booze" is hopeless. He can be neither organized [nor] educated and it will require a sober, organized and educated working class to emancipate itself from wage slavery.[14]

Organized labour was nonetheless caught in a deepening dilemma in the early twentieth century. Most of the North American labour movement (outside the socialist organizations) had shifted their discourses around wage labour away from a condemnation of "wage slavery" based on the ideal of the independent producer. In doing so they had moved to demands for "fair" wages, or "a living wage," that would permit breadwinners to provide for their families all necessities and at least some luxuries. By insisting on a high-wage economy and shorter hours of labour (in contrast to the "degraded" workers among "uncivilized races" elsewhere in the world), Canadian and US labour leaders made a case for a kind of working-class consumerism, including spending on leisure pursuits. Yet they also expressed more than a whiff of disapproval of the commercialized mass culture on which workers were spending their spare change. Both labour and socialist spokespeople often seemed troubled that the saloon, roller rink, or vaudeville house appealed to baser, more hedonistic instincts and failed to uplift the worker.[15]

The leadership's view of culture was more rooted in long-standing notions of working-class self-improvement through prudent, educational forms of recreation: reading, attending lectures or debates, listening to musical concerts, and participating in the collective social life of workers' movements. When they undertook to organize an annual workers' festival on Labour Day (first celebrated in the 1880s and then as a legal holiday beginning in 1894), they emphasized sober, orderly respectability in their parades and earnest, wholesome fun in their public lectures, sports programs, band concerts, and picnics – all within the range of what has come to be known as "rational" recreation. The country's first May Day celebrations, which began in Montreal in 1906, were even more sober versions of parading and speech-making.[16]

Many labour leaders apparently still shared the earlier concerns of craft unionists and Knights of Labor that the increased leisure resulting from their demands for shorter hours posed problems as well as opportunities for workers. Unionists who showed up drunk to the Labour Day parade might be fined by their local, and beer was often officially banned from the annual picnics. Some locals supplied it nonetheless, and unionists got their own supplies from private flasks and nearby saloons, until tighter provincial liquor laws had put an end to these public pleasures by the middle of the First World War. The discomfort of some of the labour leadership – and the widening gulf between their notions of appropriate leisure activities and the real world of working-class popular culture – was evident in an interview in Toronto with an unnamed "prominent laborite" standing amid the bustle of activity outside a bar on Yonge Street in 1913. It was a shame that the authorities were allowing the bars to remain open on Labour Day, this man declared, "in view of the weakness of many who might better have been with their families spending the nickels on innocent and educative entertainment at the [Canadian National] Exhibition." The steady decline of labour-sponsored Labour Day festivities in the decade before the war reflected in part how working men were voting with their feet and seeking out their own amusements.[17]

Still, the scepticism about booze and its place in a rapidly emerging world of commercialized mass culture did not push these labour and socialist figures comfortably into the arms of the prohibition movement. Ever since the days of the Knights of Labor several key points of disagreement in analysis and strategy had lingered on. They hinged on the extent to which working men should bear the brunt of blame and repressive public policy. These were fundamental class issues that pitted the narrowly focused middle-class prohibitionists against the generally more flexible working-class temperance advocates. One central issue was coercion. As far back as 1877, a prominent Toronto labour leader, John Hewitt, had "strongly advocated the use of moral suasion, but was opposed to coercive legislation in any movement that would rob a man of his rights." Several years later a Montreal Knight had a similar concern: "I do not think that any particular body of men should say what the other should take." Another had insisted that prohibition would not work: "I believe people have to be educated up to anything before they can receive it quickly, quietly and satisfactorily. Whenever too much restriction is forced on them they will rebel against it, and naturally seek other channels in order to secure what they think they have been improperly and unfairly deprived of."[18]

Many labour voices, preferring persuasion to compulsion, concentrated on promoting moderation and providing alternatives (such as meetings of the Knights of Labor or local unions, or the public libraries that the labour movement was backing in this period). Eventually many were drawn to the antiprohibitionist campaign's emphasis on individual rights – an emphasis, ironically, most often proclaimed by Conservative politicians whom labour rarely supported – and bristled at the middle-class WCTU's rhetoric as attacks on their manhood and male privileges.

There was also a key disagreement about cause and effect. While the Dominion Alliance or the WCTU saw the core of the problem in the individual weakness of the drunkard, unionists were increasingly more likely to see drunkenness as resulting from poverty rather than causing it. A Montreal Knight told the Royal Commission on the Liquor Traffic that "long hours and poverty do more than anything else to cause drunkenness." A decade later, Southern Ontario's regional labour paper, the *Industrial Banner*, explained:

> The best substitute for the saloon is the home, and a better one cannot be proposed. The trade union aims to make the home beautiful and attractive through improving the environment of the toiling masses, by shortening the work-day and obtaining a wage that will enable the husband and father to clothe his wife and children decently, have pictures on the wall, carpets on the floor and music in the home.

In 1911 an Independent Labor Party member in Toronto insisted: "Give the workingman sufficient money to enable him to make his house a home and then he will stop drinking." Labour leaders resented the indifference or hostility of prohibitionists to this larger struggle. At the same meeting in 1911, one speaker stated, "The Dominion Alliance has done nothing to strike at the social and industrial evil which in a great measure causes intemperance." Another argued, "If they came over to our side and advocated industrial reform they would do more for temperance than if they sought any amount of legislation."[19]

More and more often, even dedicated temperance supporters within the labour movement were also critical of the class bias involved in shutting down working men's saloons but leaving the rich men's private clubs and well-stocked wine cellars untouched. Studholme denounced any legislation that kept "the glass from the workingman," but allowed "the rich man to have his highball." Nor was it fair that "the rich man could get drunk and be taken home in an auto or put to bed until he sobers up at the club, while the workingman when he got a little too much was thrown out on the street to be picked up by a patrol wagon."[20]

The ever narrower focus of the post-1900 prohibitionists on the evils of the working-class saloon and their relative indifference to the older temperance approaches of moral suasion and mutual support left the dry voices in working-class communities with no comfortable space in the anti-booze crusade. Ultimately, there were far more abstainers than prohibitionists in working-class communities, but they were soon drowned out by the rising chorus of wet voices in working-class Canada.

The Rise of the Wets

As the debate over prohibition intensified at the beginning of the First World War, some prominent labour leaders expressed support. The

Brotherhood of Locomotive Engineers, the bedrock of dry unionism, endorsed it in 1915. The same year, the Saskatoon Trades and Labor Council unanimously supported the Saskatchewan government's move to close barrooms and introduce government dispensaries. The editor of *Alberta Labor News*, Elmo Roper, insisted, "From an economic or humanitarian standpoint, progressive Labor's stand must be uncompromisingly against booze in any shape or form." In keeping with printers' union teetotalism, Halifax's typographical union declared prohibition would be of "inestimable benefit to the working class and to society."[21]

For the first time, however, the wet unions mobilized an outspoken resistance movement. Since well before the war, the brewery workers' union in the United States had been leading the charge. Generally (and ironically, considering that they had a staunchly socialist leadership), the US union worked in close alliance with the brewing companies, whose national organization funded full-time organizers to work with labour and supplied a steady stream of articles for the labour press. Through the national organization the companies also provided funds for anti-prohibition campaigns, often waged under the banner of Trade Union Liberty Leagues or Wet Leagues. With the threat of prohibition in Canada rising by 1915, the brewery workers rallied others, such as bartenders and cigar-makers, whose jobs were at risk, and reached out to other unions, which began to show public support.

Some six hundred bartenders, brewery workers, cigar-makers, and restaurant and hotel employees gathered in Toronto's Labor Temple that year to proclaim their opposition to restrictions. Several months later they put their support behind the Personal Liberty League, an anti-prohibition organization. In March 1916 Ontario's *Industrial Banner* reported, "During the past few weeks several of the most influential central labor bodies in the province have voiced the sentiment that it would be detrimental to the best interests of the general public to put prohibition into effect at the present time." In Manitoba the bartenders' union took the lead in forming an alliance with brewers and hotel-owners in the oddly named Manitoba Prohibition League, and they brought in the well-known US civil rights lawyer, Clarence Darrow, to highlight civil libertarian arguments. During Alberta's referendum campaign in 1915, both the Lethbridge and Calgary trades and labour councils denounced prohibition. The Alberta Federation of Labor proclaimed its almost unanimous opposition to the measure. Darrow also did a speaking tour around that province for labour.[22]

A few months later Vancouver's brewery workers pulled together a British Columbia Workers' Equal Rights Association to resist that province's new legislation, and trades and labour councils in all the leading cities formally denounced the law. A delegation from the Cumberland miners' union local arrived at the B.C. premier's door carrying a petition with six thousand signatures and insisted that they needed beer to be able to endure their work. Nationally, delegates to the 1915 convention of the Trades and Labor Congress of Canada voted to end its affiliation with the Social Service Council of Canada (formerly the Moral and Social Reform Council), in part because of the council's pro-prohibition position. The sprinkling of labour men who appeared on prohibitionist platforms – such as Vancouver printer R.H. Neelands and Toronto socialist Jimmy Simpson – could not counterbalance the general impression of growing labour opposition.[23]

With prohibition in place, the main councils and federations of the labour movement across the country moved cautiously on a potentially divisive issue in a time of national emergency. In some places, disagreements were too sharp for labour bodies to take any position.[24] Yet the campaigns of resistance to prohibition never completely stopped. By the end of the war, labour's anti-prohibition coalition was broadening out to include many more unionists. The mainstream of the Canadian labour movement began to lobby governments for the return of the working men's favourite beverage – beer with a stronger alcoholic content than the "near beer" available in hotels under prohibition. They also argued for the return of light wine, which few Anglo-Celtic workers drank but would no doubt have been appreciated by many European immigrants and some Québécois. They abandoned the liquor drinker indeed, worried out loud about the increasing consumption of liquor once the saloons closed – and sidestepped the issue of public drinking. The whole focus of the subsequent campaign was on bringing back a heartier beer. Ontario unions took the lead. In September 1916 the Toronto District Trades and Labor Council brought to the national Trades and Labor Congress convention a resolution that called on the TLC's Ontario executive to ask the province's government to permit the retail sale of light wines and beers, to hold a referendum on such beverages, and to allow local option for municipalities that voted for them. After lengthy debate, in which labour's dry voices fought back forcefully, the resolution was carried "by a large majority." That Ontario had not conducted a plebiscite before imposing prohibition gave a sharper edge to the province's labour leaders' concerns. In December and again in January 1918, the Ontario executive took this message into their annual meeting with Premier William Hearst and his cabinet, but got a bluntly unsympathetic response. The following spring, a much more substantial mobilization got underway. Trades and labour councils in Windsor, London, Brantford, Hamilton, Toronto, Kingston, and Ottawa brought large delegations to a rally at the Toronto Armouries on 2 March 1918, where they agreed to a resolution demanding 2.5 per cent beer. The campaign slogan was to be: "If you are going to make it, make it fit to drink." A parade of some five thousand working men and war veterans then formed up behind a pipe band and banners (which included the shipbuilders' threat of "No Beer – No Boats") and marched through the streets to the provincial legislature to meet the premier and his cabinet. When Hearst again rejected the men's request, he was greeted with "hoots and shouting" and had to beat a hasty retreat behind police barricades as angry workers surged forward.[25] Meanwhile the New Brunswick and Alberta federations of labour were making no more headway with their respective governments. Early in 1919, a labour delegation's pro-beer arguments did help to convince the Quebec premier to hold a referendum on beer and wine.[26]

By this point the momentum had reached Ottawa. The issue was raised when the new Unionist government headed by Sir Robert Borden summoned fifty-four labour leaders for a conference on "war problems" in January 1918. Avoiding "the merits or demerits of beer as an ordinary beverage," those in attendance eventually decided "that inasmuch as some men considered it a necessity, and it did not need any food grains to produce, and that it might possibly prevent some men from freely changing their place of employment," they asked the government to reconsider its recently announced order-in-council aimed at shutting down the liquor traffic as a wartime emergency.[27]

On 15 April the country's leading unionists were back in Ottawa for the annual presentation of the Trades and Labor Congress resolutions to the federal cabinet. This time they requested that the government amend the wartime prohibition measure to allow 2.5 per cent beer to be made, imported, and sold across the country. They noted that "twenty-five large labor organizations" had endorsed the measure. The cabinet minister assigned to respond was none other than the staunch "banish-the-bar" crusader from the pre-war Ontario Liberal Party, Newton W. Rowell, who had joined the Unionist government in Ottawa a few months earlier. He made it clear that the alcohol content had been established by the wartime provincial legislation, and that the government had no intention of interfering with standards set by the provinces. The next fall, with only "about forty dissenting votes," the Congress endorsed the action of the Ontario executive and for the first time called on all federal and provincial governments to legalize the production and sale of stronger beer. The Congress executive presented this proposal to the federal government in February 1919, along with a petition signed by thousands of workers from across the country, but returned home empty-handed. They were no more successful a month later in a special meeting with the cabinet to consider the resolution.[28]

South of the border, Sam Gompers, a former cigar-maker who liked saloons, had been speaking out against prohibition. Gompers, the head of the international labour movement to which most Canadian unionists were connected, carefully distinguished his personal views from those of the American Federation of Labor, which was still officially neutral on the question. Once the prohibitionist Eighteenth Amendment to the US Constitution had been approved, he urged President Woodrow Wilson to exempt beer and wine, but, despite the president's personal support, neither Congress nor the Democratic Party would cooperate. The Volstead Act, which was passed over Wilson's veto as the enabling legislation for the Eighteenth Amendment, included beer and wine as unacceptable intoxicating beverages. Soon thousands of workers in and around New York City were actively considering staging a national general strike for their beer. In June 1919 the AFL convention finally passed a resolution opposing the Eighteenth Amendment.[29]

By the time nearly a thousand delegates arrived in Hamilton for the annual convention of the Trades and Labor Congress in September 1919, 1,500 labour organizations across the country (out of some 1,900) had endorsed the Congress leadership's demand for stronger beer (even the Winnipeg Women's Labor League had expressed support). At that meeting, Congress president Tom Moore reviewed the many efforts made to convince federal and provincial governments to make the beer available, and delegates passed a new resolution demanding government action. This labour campaign became a prominent feature of the wet advertising campaign in the Ontario prohibition plebiscite underway that fall.[30]

Arguably, Ontario workers had the best chance of getting back their lost rights, since in October 1919 a new Farmer-Labour government swept to power in the provincial election. Ontario's provincial federation of labour, then known as the Labor Educational Association of Ontario, passed a resolution the following spring in support of "a good palatable beer of sufficient alcoholic strength." Hamilton's labour member, George Halcrow, was a consistent "wet" voice in public discussions. Yet on this issue (as on the question of the eight-hour working day), Ontario's labour movement got no help from the dominant Farmer element in the coalition. Farmer leaders were committed temperance men and prohibition supporters. The one effort to get the government to hold a referendum on making beer and wine available was defeated in the house. Labour organizations in other provinces were no more successful in their lobbying with their provincial governments.[31]

Then again, the demand for alcohol was not on the agendas of the more left-wing unionists and radical working-class organizations emerging at the end of the war. The left still insisted that prohibition was not a central issue in the workers' struggle for emancipation from capitalist exploitation. "We realize that the two old parties, the Siamese twins of capitalism, will continue to make the liquor question a paramount issue to the exclusion of more fundamental matters being pressed by Labor," the manifesto of Toronto's Labour Representation Political Association proclaimed in 1923. "But we warn the workers not to be divided and side-tracked." It was more in keeping with Tom Moore's more cautious, anti-radical leadership that he kept a high public profile in the postwar campaigns of the mixed-class anti-prohibition groups, the Citizens' Liberty League and Moderation League, pushing for the stronger beer that he said had been endorsed by many labour conventions as a realistic demand within the existing social system.[32]

Arguing for Beer

The arguments raised in this campaign for the working man's beer had a familiar ring, but also some new twists. Initially, much of the labour objection to the wartime prohibition crusade centred on the economic consequences, especially the unemployment that would result. The country was in the grips of a severe depression from 1913 to 1915, and labour leaders later told provincial and federal governments that the new legislation had forced "thousands engaged in the brewing and allied industries" out of work. This was one of the key arguments in the Toronto unionists' arsenal used to win over support for their resolution at the Trades and Labor Congress convention in 1916. It appealed to the labour movement's traditions of mutual support: "Now that the positions of these workers were in jeopardy it was the duty of the Congress to go to their assistance." The bartender's union itself made an impassioned pitch for help in saving their livelihood.[33]

Once prohibition was in place and the campaign shifted to bringing back the working man's beer, the focus became the beverage and its importance, not the saloons where it had long been consumed. BC miners argued that "men who had to labor for the most part under ground were called upon to endure the strain of the most arduous and strenuous nature," and that "the solid properties of beer to a large extent counterbalanced loss of energy from the physical tax endured." The quality of the "near beer" on sale in hotels under prohibition legislation was roundly denounced. From the steps of the Ontario legislature, speakers declared it was "horrid, sickening and damaging" to the constitution and "unhealthy, unwholesome, indigestible and nauseating to the drinker." A month later, Moore told the federal cabinet that "men who take two or three drinks detrimentally affect their stomachs." Labour spokespersons and the labour press continued to complain that the former beer drinkers were turning to whisky when they could not get their favoured brew. Moore attempted to shock the Ontario government with the claim that "deaths were resulting through drinking of wood alcohol and other stimulants." Moreover, the most likely source of this booze was a medical doctor, who was "apparently making a fortune at 'one dollar per.'"[34]

The message could also take a patriotic, imperialist turn. In 1918 the Alberta Federation of Labor reminded the provincial government that the strength of beer requested was "similar to the war beer of Great Britain." The TLC delegation to Ottawa early in 1919 even gave their concerns a racist twist when they argued that "if Canada is to attract British immigration, instead of the unsatisfactory alien immigration of the past, the laws of the Dominion must be such as commend themselves to possible immigrants." They warned that "the tide of immigration would turn to Austalia, where prohibition has not been spoken of, unless the palatable beer is conceded to the workers of the Dominion." BC miners even argued that the "physical inferiority of the Asiatic races" could be explained by the lack of alcohol in their diet.[35]

Labour journalists reminded working-class readers that prohibition had little to offer any workers. "Life and death to the working class is not a question of beer or no beer," the *BC Federationist* thundered. Repeatedly, moreover, labour spokespersons denounced what they believed to be a glaring class bias in regulations that cut off a working man's glass of beer but allowed a rich man to import his liquor – "class legislation pure and simple." The *Citizen* noted that working people could not stock their cellars with booze as the wealthy had, and that they were being treated as though they could not be trusted to drink in moderation. According to a leader of the Ontario bricklayers, it was "a direct attempt to take away the comfort and pleasure of the worker more than of the leisured and privileged class." An Ontario electrical worker saw even more sinister designs behind the new legislation:

> Prohibition is affirmed in general by those who have reason to continue the exploitation of the masses. No thought is given to the matter as to the right or wrong of it, but it is urged – and it is urged in general – because of economic efficiency. In other words, because if enacted it will bring greater profits to the manufacturer, the financier, and the capitalist generally. Prohibitory legislation as to what one eats or drinks is the earmark of a servile State and therefore in antagonism to working-class interests.

The *BC Federationist* argued that prohibition "merely voices the material aspirations of one group of capitalists as opposed to another ... One group believes workers will be rendered more productive – therefore more profitable – by being denied opportunity to consume alcoholic liquors. The material interest of the other group lies in the profit to be derived from the sale of alcoholic liquor."[36]

Increasingly, to justify their demands for an end to the dry regime, labour leaders used the same language of "democracy" that was fuelling so many other parts of the workers' "revolt" that spread across the country in the years after 1917. The agitation for the right to a particular kind of leisure activity was part of the expansive working-class agenda for a fuller social citizenship in postwar society. As they were doing with so many other issues, labour's wet voices took the wartime rhetoric and recast it for a working-class agenda. Fred Craig, a plumber, rose in the Nova Scotia Federation of Labor convention and explained:

> My reasons for enlisting in the cause of temperance reform is chiefly to endeavour to bring back to Nova Scotia that birthright that is mine; the liberty to think and the freedom to enjoy the privileges that were my forefather's and have been denied to me and the rest of liberty loving Nova Scotians, under legislation placed on the statute books of this province due to the hysteria of war so prevalent during the dark days of 1915–1916.

Clifford Dane, a radical metalworker from New Glasgow, made a similar argument: "It was not constitutional to take away a man's right without giving him a voice in the matter." The Charlottetown Laborers' Protective Union declared prohibition "a violation of British fair play." At the 1919 Trades and Labor Congress convention, an American visitor had delegates cheering when he denounced prohibition as "an infringement on the rights of the men and contrary to the very idea of democracy."[37]

All these efforts by organized labour to end the bone-dry regime seemed to resonate among much larger numbers of Canadian working men and women. The prim, teetotalling working-class masculinity of the pre-war years had apparently been largely eclipsed by a version that had quietly taken root in working-class saloons in that same period, and that was finally ready to defend publicly their right to drink responsibly and moderately. The plebiscite results in 1919–21 revealed solid wet majorities in working-class communities in Canadian cities. As Ontario's new Farmer premier, E.C. Drury, settled into office at the end of 1919, he was reminded of this fact in private correspondence from many people, including the following:

> You may think other matters will overshadow the question of prohibition, that the talk about it will die out, if you have that idea, dismiss it. The people are discontented at so many prohibition laws, possibly in the country around which you farm ideas may be different, but get the ideas of the workers in the Cities, in the Towns, get the ideas of the great majority and you will see that prohibition of the People's liberty is not favoured.

When William Ivens, the popular Labour MP, called a meeting to convince workers at the Canadian Pacific's Weston Shops not to vote down prohibition in 1923, only two hundred of the two thousand workers showed up, and even these heckled him heavily. When the US dry orator "Pussyfoot" Johnson tried to speak in Windsor, he was shouted down and retreated to the Detroit ferry under police escort and a hail of rocks and eggs.[38]

The return of thousands of soldiers from overseas had swelled the ranks of the wet camp considerably. Alcohol consumed in sociable spaces had been central to their military experience. In England their free time had been filled with drunken binges in nearby pubs until the army set up wet canteens inside their camps. Behind the front lines in France, both officers and enlisted men had become accustomed to gathering in bars in the mess or in neighbouring towns, where some inevitably developed a serious alcohol dependency. Back in Canada, veterans' organizations had jumped into the thick of the fight for beer. The largest, the Great War Veterans' Association, sent delegations to provincial governments to demand the return of the "real stuff," in place of near beer, and they gave active support to the Citizens' Liberty and Moderation leagues, in which their leading officers were often prominent.[39]

Canada's working men, then, had struggled hard to fit their concerns into the great debates over booze in the late nineteenth and early twentieth centuries. Given that overwhelmingly the labour leaders who spoke out were male wage-earners, the perspective of working-class housewives and daughters was rarely heard. The issue was highly divisive in working-class Canada and consequently, after the decline of the Knights of Labor, was generally avoided by labour councils at all levels, just as they kept religion out of their business. On the one hand, there was a strong current of teetotalism, especially among labour leaders, which, despite its concerns about the evils of drinking, was increasingly estranged from mainstream prohibitionism. On the other hand were the drinkers, who generally remained silent before the war but found their voices once prohibition was in place.

Windsor's Robert Potts was undoubtedly right when he told the large crowd outside the Ontario legislature in 1918 that "workers resented the imputation that there was no difference between the drunkard and the man who wanted to refresh himself at the end of the day's work with a glass of beer." By the end of the war, the great majority of unions and the bulk of working-class voters, both men and women, had marginalized the dry voices among them and loudly rejected prohibition as a form of unjust, class-biased legislation. Working-class drinkers were finally coming out of the closet.

They undoubtedly felt more confident to take a stand as broader moderationist and libertarian campaigns, led by highly respectable upper-class figures, for the first time defended the right to drink in moderation, but the campaign for the working man's beer had its own momentum flowing from indignation at yet another affront to workers' rights and aspirations. This was as close as labour would come at any point after the 1880s to articulating a distinctive agenda for a public policy on alcohol consumption – an admittedly limited one at that, which never broached the possibility of public ownership, as some labour activists and socialists were doing on the other side of the Atlantic. Booze was thus swept up in the class politics of the workers' revolt in Canada at the end of the war. The difficulties that working-class leaders had in getting governments to respond to their concerns about stronger beer reflected the defeat of that wider class mobilization by the early 1920s. After that point, the workers' perspective was submerged in the more bourgeois moderationist campaigns, and the political initiative fell to the old parties, especially the Tories.[40] Unions and veterans' organizations nonetheless played an active role in the campaigns that ultimately replaced prohibition with government-controlled liquor stores in all provinces but Prince Edward Island by 1930. Everywhere but the Maritimes, moreover, workers had access to a glass of beer in a public drinking place by 1935.

Notes

1 *The Yeas and Nays Polled in the Dunkin Act Campaign in Toronto, Carefully Prepared with Official Returns, with Introductory Remarks and Extracts of Speeches Delivered during the Campaign* (Toronto: Leader Steam Job Printing Office 1877), vi, xv, xvi–xvii; Ronald Morris Benson, "American Workers and Temperance Reform, 1866–1933" (PhD dissertation, University of Notre Dame 1974), 35–94; Christina Burr, *Spreading the Light: Work and Labour Reform in Late-Nineteenth-Century Toronto* (Toronto: University of Toronto Press 1999), 14–31; W. Scott Haine, *The World of the Paris Café: Sociability among the French Working Class, 1789–1914* (Baltimore: Johns Hopkins University Press 1999); Susanna Barrows, "'Parliaments of the People': The Political Culture of Cafés in the Early Third Republic," in Susanna Barrows and Robin Room, eds., *Drinking: Behavior and Belief in Modern History* (Berkeley: University of California Press 1991), 87–97; H. Julia Roberts, "Taverns and Tavern-Goers in Upper Canada, the 1790s to the 1850s" (PhD dissertation, University of Toronto 1998).

2 *Palladium of Labor* (Hamilton) (hereafter *POL*), 12 January 1884.

3 Canada, Royal Commission on the Liquor Traffic in Canada, *Minutes of Evidence* (Ottawa: S.E. Dawson 1895), Vol. 2, 359–61; Gregory S. Kealey and Bryan D. Palmer, *Dreaming of What Might Be: The Knights of Labor in Ontario, 1880–1900* (Toronto: New Hogtown Press 1987); M.P. Sendbuehler, "Battling 'The Bane of Our Cities': Class, Territory, and the Prohibition Debate in Toronto, 1877," *UHR* 22, no. 1 (October 1993), 31–3; Benson, "American Workers and Temperance Reform," 150–86 (quotation by Powderly); Samuel Walker, "Terence V. Powderly, the Knights of Labor, and the Temperance Issue," *Societas* 5, no. 4 (Autumn 1975), 279–93. Nova Scotia's leading labour movement, the Provincial Workmen's Association, incorporated the same principles into its ideological framework. Ian McKay, "'By Wisdom, Wile, or War': The Provincial Workmen's Association

and the Struggle for Working-Class Independence in Nova Scotia, 1879–97," *L/LT* 18 (Fall 1986), 13–62.

4 *POL*, 12 January 1844, 1 (quotation by paper); Royal Commission on the Liquor Traffic, *Minutes of Evidence*, Vol. 2, 360, 369 (quotation by Knight); Brian Paul Trainor, "Towards a Genealogy of Temperance: Identity, Belief, and Drink in Victorian Ontario" (PhD dissertation, Queen's University 1993); Kealey and Palmer, *Dreaming of What Might Be*; Walker, "Terence V. Powderly, the Knights of Labor, and the Temperance Issue"; David Brundage, "The Producing Classes and the Saloon: Denver in the 1980s," *LH* 26, no. 1 (Winter 1985), 29–52.

5 *POL*, 12 January 1884, 1 (quotation). In Finland in the late nineteenth century the emerging labour movement similarly used temperance as a unifying force in working-class struggle and actually organized a "drinking strike" in 1898; workers were numerically dominant in the country's temperance movement; see Irma Sulkunen, "Temperance as a Civic Religion: The Cultural Foundation of the Finnish Working-Class Temperance Ideology," *Contemporary Drug Problems* 12, no. 2 (Summer 1985), 267–85. Similarly, in Sweden, where drinking was associated with bourgeois immorality, the temperance movement was overwhelmingly proletarian and closely linked to labour, socialist, and universal-suffrage movements; Madeleine Hurd, "Liberals, Socialists, and Sobriety: The Rhetoric of Citizenship in Turn-of-the-Century Sweden," *International Labor and Working-Class History* 45 (Spring 1994), 44–62.

6 Royal Commission on the Liquor Traffic, *Minutes of Evidence*, Vol. 2, 374; Palmer, *Working-Class Experience*, 127–32; Robert E. Weir, *Beyond Labour's Veil: The Culture of the Knights of Labor* (University Park: Pennsylvania State University Press 1996).

7 *POL*, 12 January 1884, 1; Trainor, "Towards a Genealogy of Temperance," 190–250 (quotation); Darren Ferry, "'To the Interests and Conscience of the Great Mass of the Community': The Evolution of Temperance Societies in Nineteenth-Century Central Canada" (paper presented to the Canadian Historical Association, Annual Meeting 2003); Desmond Morton, *Mayor Howland: The Citizens' Candidate* (Toronto: Hakkert 1973); Carlos A. Schwantes, *Radical Heritage: Labor, Socialism, and Reform in Washington and British Columbia, 1885–1917* (Seattle: University of Washington Press 1979), 34.

8 Walker, "Terence V. Powderly, the Knights of Labor, and the Temperance Issue"; Gene Howard Homel, "'Fading Beams of the Nineteenth Century': Radicalism and Early Socialism in Canada's 1890s," *L/LT* 5 (Spring 1980), 9–32; W. Craig Heron, "Working-Class Hamilton, 1895–1930" (PhD dissertation, Dalhousie University 1981), 588–91.

9 Benson, "American Workers and Temperance Reform," 253–6; Nuala McGann Drescher, "Organized Labor and the Eighteenth Amendment," *LH* 8, no. 3 (Fall 1967), 280–99; C. Mark Davis, "I'll Drink to That: The Rise and Fall of Prohibition in the Maritime Provinces, 1900–1930" (PhD dissertation, McMaster University 1990), 206; Ruth Bordin, *Women and Temperance: The Quest for Power and Liberty, 1873–1900* (Philadelphia: Temple University Press 1981), 104–8; *Star* (Toronto), 19 September 1898, 1.

10 *Globe* (Toronto), 4 December 1911, 8 (quotation).

11 Nancy Christie and Michael Gauvreau, *A Full-Orbed Christianity: The Protestant Churches and Social Welfare in Canada, 1900–1940* (Montreal and Kingston: McGill-Queen's University Press 1996), 208–10; Craig Heron, "Allan Studholme," *Dictionary of Canadian Biography, Vol. 14, 1911 to 1920* (Toronto: University of Toronto Press 1998), 976–80; Trades and Labor Congress of Canada, *Report of the Proceedings of the Annual Convention* (hereafter TLCCP), 1907, 37; 1908, 9–10; 1909, 62–8; 1911, 95–6; 1914, 94–6; 1915, 78, 84, 105–6; 1916, 117–18; Drescher, "Organized Labor and the Eighteenth Amendment," 188–9; Stephen G. Jones, "Labour, Society, and the Drink Question in Britain, 1918–1939," *Historical Journal* 30, no. 1 (March 1987), 114–19; J.B. Brown, "The Pig or the Stye: Drink and Poverty in Late Victorian England," *IRSH* 17 (1973), 389–95.

12 Chris Waters, *British Socialists and the Politics of Popular Culture, 1884–1914* (Manchester: Manchester University Press 1990); James S. Roberts, "Alcohol, Public Policy, and the Left: The Socialist Debate in Early Twentieth Century Europe," *CDP* 12, no. 2 (Summer 1985), 309–30; James S. Roberts, *Drink, Temperance, and the Working Class in Nineteenth-Century Germany* (Boston: George Allen and Unwin 1984), 83–108; Jan De Lint, "Anti-Drink Propaganda and Alcohol Control Measures: A Report on the Dutch Experience," in Eric Single, Patricia Morgan, and Jan De Lint, eds., *Alcohol, Society, and the State. Vol. 2: The Social History of Control Policy in Seven Countries* (Toronto: Addiction Research Foundation 1981), 87–102; Ian McKay, ed., *For a Working-Class Culture in Canada: A Selection of Colin McKay's Writings on Sociology and Political Economy, 1897–1939* (St John's: Canadian Committee on Labour History 1996), 9, 34–8, 66 (quotation), 101; Mimi Ajzenstadt, "Medical-Moral Economy of Regulation: Alcohol Legislation in B.C., 1871–1925 (PhD dissertation, Simon Fraser University 1992)," 94 (quotation); John Albert Hiebert, "Prohibition in British Columbia" (MA thesis, Simon Fraser University 1986) 54.

13 Janice Newton, *The Feminist Challenge to the Canadian Left, 1900–1918* (Montreal and Kingston: McGill-Queen's University Press 1995), 22–4, 29–36, 145; Varpu Lindstrom-Best, "Finnish Socialist Women in Canada,

1890–1930," in Linda Kealey and Joan Sangster, eds., *Beyond the Vote: Canadian Women and Politics* (Toronto: University of Toronto Press 1989), 211; Sulkunen, "Temperance as a Civic Religion"; Sakari Sariola, "The Finnish Temperance Movement in the Great Lakes Area of the Midwest," *CDP* 12, no. 2 (Summer 1985), 287–307; Hurd, "Liberals, Socialists, and Sobriety"; Gene Howard Homel, "James Simpson and the Origins of Canadian Social Democracy" (PhD dissertation, University of Toronto 1978).

14 Robert A. Campbell, *Demon Rum or Easy Money: Government Control of Liquor in British Columbia from Prohibition to Privatization* (Vancouver: UBC Press 1991), 30 (quotation). Toronto's John W. Bruce, the socialist plumber, had similar concerns: "A sober and studious working class are the best asset of the nation, and if the workers ever hope to liberate themselves from the bonds of wage slavery, it will only be when they themselves are strong and free from the destructive influence of intoxicating liquor." *Pioneer* (Toronto), 3 October 1919, 1. Out of the East Coast, the radical leader of Cape Breton's coal miners, J.B. McLachlan, was equally caustic: "I hate the liquor traffic with a whole hearted hatred because I have seen used over and over again to dash the hopes of working men when they are on the eve of doing something for themselves." He fought hard against an effort to pass a resolution in favour of abolishing prohibition at the first Nova Scotia Federation of Labor convention in January 1919 and continued to carry his concerns into the pages of his popular newspaper, the *Maritime Labor Herald*, in the early 1920s. Davis, "I'll Drink to That," 206–9 (quotation at 207); see also Margaret J. Strople, "Prohibition and Movements of Social Reform in Nova Scotia, 1894–1920" (MA thesis, Dalhousie University 1974) 155–6; David Frank, *J.B. McLachlan: A Biography* (Toronto: James Lorimer 1999).

15 Lawrence B. Glickman, *A Living Wage: American Workers and the Making of Consumer Society* (Ithaca, NY: Cornell University Press 1997); Weir, *Beyond Labor's Veil*; Waters, *British Socialists and the Politics of Popular Culture.*

16 Craig Heron and Steve Penfold, *The Workers' Festival: A History of Labour Day in Canada* (Toronto: University of Toronto Press 2005).

17 Ibid., 129 (quotation).

18 *Yeas and Nays*, xv (quotation by Hewitt); Royal Commission on the Liquor Traffic, *Report*, 376–7 (quotation by Knights); *Herald* (Hamilton), 6 March 1913, 5.

19 *POL*, 12 January 1994, 1; 31 May 1884, 1; Royal Commission on the Liquor Traffic, *Minutes of Evidence*, vol. 2, 360–1, 371, 373 (quotation), 744–5; *Industrial Banner* (hereafter *IB*), January 1906, 2 (quotation), April

1912; *Herald*, 4 April 1912, 13; 31 March 1914, 5; *Globe*, 4 December 1911, 8 (quotation).

20 *Labor News* (Hamilton) (hereafter *LN*), 19 June 1914, 4 (quotation); Decarie, "Something Old, Something New …: Aspects of Prohibitionism in Ontario in the 1890s," in Donald Swaison, ed., *Oliver Mowat's Ontario* (Toronto: Macmillan 1972), 158, 167; Davis, "I'll Drink to That," 208; Benson, "American Workers and Temperance Reform," 260–1. For similar tensions between prohibitionists and labour in New Zealand, see A.R. Grigg, "Prohibition, the Church, and Labour: A Programme of Social Reform, 1890–1914," *New Zealand Journal of History* 15, no. 2 (October 1981), 135–54. In a parallel development, Black temperance supporters in the United States felt increasingly uncomfortable linked to a movement that became overtly racist in the US South; see Denise Herd, "Ambiguity in Black Drinking Norms: An Ethnohistorical Interpretation," in Linda A. Bennett and Genevieve M. Ames, eds., *The American Experience with Alcohol: Contrasting Cultural Perspectives* (New York: Plenum Press 1985), 149–70.

21 Strople, "Prohibition and Movements of Social Reform," 156 (quotation by printers); Benson, "American Workers and Temperance Reform," 270–3; J.M. Bumsted, ed., *Documentary Problems in Canadian History, Vol. 2: Post-Confederation* (Georgetown, ON: Irwin-Dorsey 1969), 195 (quotation); Suzanne Morton, *Ideal Surroundings: Domestic Life in a Working-Class Suburb in the 1920s* (Toronto: University of Toronto Press 1995), 71.

22 Decarie, "Prohibition Movement," 294–5; *IB*, 10 March 1916, 2 (quotation); John Herd Thompson, "The Voice of Moderation: The Defeat of Prohibition in Manitoba," in S.M. Trofimenkoff, ed., *The Twenties in Western Canada* (Ottawa: National Museum of Man 1972), 170–90; Robert Erwin McLean, "A 'Most Effectual Remedy': Temperance and Prohibition in Alberta, 1875–1915" (MA thesis, University of Calgary 1979), 122–3; James Gray, *Booze: The Impact of Whisky on the Prairie West* (Scarborough, ON: New American Library of Canada 1972), 79; *Canadian Annual Review of Public Affairs* (Toronto), 1916, 519; Forbes, "Prohibition and the Social Gospel," 76.

23 Hiebert, "Prohibition," 74–6; Campbell, *Demon Rum or Easy Money*, 28–33; Hallowell, *Prohibition in Ontario*, 19; Pinno, "Temperance and Prohibition," 64–5; TLCCP, 1915, 106–7; Benson "American Workers and Temperance Reform," 261–2, 274–81; Drescher, "Organized Labor and the Eighteenth Amendment."

24 The trades and labour councils in Hamilton in 1916 and Vancouver in 1920 voted to remain neutral. When Nova Scotia unionists took up the question early in 1919, a bitter two-hour debate ensued before a compromise

resolution emerged. In New Brunswick a stalemate developed when Moncton's labour council refused to allow the provincial federation of labour to endorse a partial repeal of prohibition. And some labour figures continued to appear on prohibitionist platforms – notably a few prominent BC socialists who had abandoned the wet camp. *Sun* (Vancouver), 8 October 1920, 5; Davis, "I'll Drink to That," 261; Allen, *Social Passion*, 267–9.

25 TLCCP, 1916, 148–52 (quotation at 152); 1918, 49, 58; *Globe*, 30 September 1916, 7; 4 March 1918, 1, 9; *Telegram* (Toronto), 4 March 1918, 14; *Herald* (Hamilton), 4 March 1918, 10; *LN* 8 March 1918, 1.

26 *Gazette* (Montreal), 9 April 1919, 4.

27 TLCCP, 1918, 18.

28 Ibid., 1918, 26–7, 30, 112–13 (quotation at 113); 1919, 32–3; *Globe*, 16 April 1918, 13; *Spectator* (Hamilton), 6 February 1919, 1.

29 Drescher, "Organized Labor and the Eighteenth Amendment," 292–9; Benson, "American Workers and Temperance Reform," 286–95.

30 TLCCP, 1919, 32–3, 60, 73, 81; 1924, 57; 1925, 71, 73, 158; 1926, 77, 156; 1927, 74, 76, 167; Newton, *Feminist Challenge*, 82.

31 Hallowell, *Prohibition in Ontario*, 101, 148–9 (quotation); *Canadian Annual Review*, 1922, 590–1. At least one of Halcrow's ILP colleagues in the legislature had doubts about this issue and objected to "any man adopting the beer keg as an emblem, and he didn't believe that the people would vote for the man with the beer keg on his shoulder. "The beer and wine question should not be brought into the Labor movement," he argued in 1923. *LN*, 23 February 1923, 1.

32 Hallowell, *Prohibition in Ontario*, 148–9 (quotation).

33 TLCCP, 1916, 148–52; 1918, 26–7 (quotation), 58 (quotation).

34 *Star*, 5 December 1916, 17; *LN*, 8 March 1918, 1 (quotations by Ontario labour speaker); 21 June 1918, 2; 18 October 1918, 2; TLCCP, 1918, 27 (quotation by Tom Moore). Halifax's labour weekly, the *Citizen*, ran a series of articles by C.E. Popplestone, a French and German professor at the University of New Brunswick, who hammered away at the ineffectiveness and hypocrisy of prohibition and the growth of illicit production and bootlegging.

35 *Spectator*, 6 February 1919, 1 (quotation by TLC delegation); Ajzenstadt, "Medical-Moral Economy," 212 (quotation by BC miners' union).

36 Hiebert, "Prohibition in British Columbia," 75 (quotations by BC paper); *Free Press* (London), 18 October 1919, 12 (quotation by bricklayer); David, "I'll Drink to That," 259–63; Strople, "Prohibition and Movements of Social Reform," 156–9, 173; Campell, *Demon Rum or Easy Money*,

29–31; Thompson, "Voice of Moderation," 183; Thompson, "Prohibition Question," 89; TLCCP, 1916, 148; *Globe*, 30 September 1916, 7; *Herald* (Hamilton), 2, 4 March 1918, 10; *Spectator*, 6 February 1919, 1; *LN*, 8 March 1918, 1; 21 June 1918, 1; 18 October 1918, 2; *New Democracy* (Hamilton), 29 April 1920, 2; *IB*, 28 May 1920, 4; *Star*, 5 December 1916, 1, 17; *Canadian Annual Review*, 1916, 523; Benson, "American Workers and Temperance Reform," 274–6.

37 Heron, "Contours of a Workers' Revolt," in this volume; Davis, "I'll Drink to That," 259–62 (quotations by Craig, Dane, and Charlottetown union); *Spectator*, 24 September 1919, 11 (quotation by US visitor).

38 Hiebert, "Prohibition in British Columbia," 107; Stretch, "From Prohibition to Government Control," 18; Pinno, "Temperance and Prohibition," 159; Johnston, *Drury*, 155 (quotation by letter-writer); Thompson, "Prohibition Question," 100; C.H. Gervais, *The Rumrunners: A Prohibition Scrapbook* (Thornhill, ON: Firefly Books 1980), 59.

39 Morton, *When Your Number's Up*, 26, 109, 239.

40 *Telegram*, 4 March 1918, 4 (quotation); *Gazette*, 9 April 1919, 4; Jones, "Labour, Society, and the Drink Question."

6,500
NO WAGE CUTS! FOR OUR TEACHERS!
NO SCHOOL ON MAY 1st
JOIN THE PIONEERS
Always Ready
SMASH

Chapter Six

Into the Streets

For many decades, large groups of Canadian workers have been reaching out to grab public attention with large, colourful festivals. They have often brought the normal life of a community to a halt to focus attention on working people, their dignity, their respectability, and their importance to society, and at the same time their aspirations for a better world. There have been a variety of these events: International Women's Day on 8 March, Workers' Remembrance Day on 28 April, May Day on 1 May, Davis Day (or Miners' Memorial Day) in Nova Scotia on 11 June, and Labour Day on the first Monday in September. All have been occasions when large numbers of workers in many parts of the country moved out into the streets and parks of their own town and cities to make a great public spectacle.

We need to take these moments of working-class organizing seriously, first, because they tell us a lot about what organized workers in particular periods of Canadian history wanted out of life and how determined they were to get it through working-class solidarity; and second, because they are the most widespread form of collectively created working-class culture that ever appeared in Canada. For the workers who organized them, these festivals were great cultural events in their communities. They were local events without national or regional coordination, planned and built by local unions and other workers' groups. They carefully chose their costumes and regalia, they produced striking works of art that travelled through the streets, they arranged themselves purposefully into highly symbolic marching formations, and they organized various forms of entertainment. The "art" involved

May Day march, Toronto, 1934. City of Toronto Archives, *Globe and Mail* 33191 was simple, sometimes crude, but it was always colourful and engaging. It wasn't always entirely original – it often borrowed heavily from many familiar forms of public celebration. But labour organizers gave them a particular working-class twist. Museums have rarely shown much interest in this kind of popular artistry. Most of the floats, costumes, banners, and placards were not made to last and have largely vanished. Today little survives outside old photographs.

So I want to take you back into the streets of Canadian cities at various points over the past 150 years.[1] Our focus will be on Labour Day, the oldest and most persistent of these festivals. In June 1894 the Canadian House of Commons passed legislation making the first Monday in September a statutory holiday to be known as Labour Day. There were only three other non-religious celebrations on the statute books at that point – New Year's Day, Victoria Day, and Dominion Day. Labour Day thus became the only legal public holiday in Canada devoted to the interest of a specific class or group. Canadian labour leaders had been arguing for this legislation since the mid-1880s. In reality, legalizing this labour festival only confirmed what had already become an established event on the local holiday calendar in several Canadian cities and towns. Nova Scotia coal miners in the old Provincial Workmen's Association had first organized a celebration in the summer of 1880. Two years later, the Toronto labour movement held the first celebration in the rest of the country (a few weeks before the first held in the United States in New York City), and most leading industrial towns and cities had similar events by the early 1890s.[2] They mostly got their inspiration from south of the border, though similar festivals had already been launched in Australia and New Zealand a few years earlier. The informal celebration of Labour Day that started in New York in 1882 spread across the United States, and won legal recognition from several states by the late 1880s.[3]

One question inevitably lurks behind this story: why do we have Labour Day in September while in Europe and many other countries the annual labour celebrations are on May Day in the spring? There is a popular myth in the modern labour movement that Canadian and US workers rejected May Day in favour of Labour Day. That isn't true, at least not initially. In fact, the first May Day was declared in 1886 in the United States in the same working-class upsurge that created the demand for a labour festival in the fall. The American Federation of Labor, which was just getting started as the national voice of labour in the United States, called for a "day of revolt – not of rest" on 1 May 1886 to demand the eight-hour day for wage-earners. It continued to call for such annual spring protests until the turn of the century. Beginning in 1890, European socialists and anarchists copied the US example and embraced May Day as an occasion to demonstrate for shorter hours and political demands. May Day, then, was a day of protest, Labour Day one of celebration. In practice, the major difference was that, until the 1920s, the European May Day was a voluntary, one-day work stoppage often launched in defiance of government edict and the wrath of employers. It was not a government-sanctioned holiday there until the 1920s. In North America, May Day would definitely become the preferred event among left-wingers after the turn of the century. But at the beginning, no such polarization existed.[4]

The Craftsmen's Spectacle

The decision to launch Labour Day was part of something bigger in the world of labour in the 1880s. Far more workers than ever before were organizing themselves into aggressive, class-conscious movements. They were drawing together a broad range of workers into new craft unions, local assemblies of a big new organization known as the Knights of Labor, local trades and labour councils, the first independent labour political campaigns, and, beginning in 1886, the Trades and Labor Congress of Canada, labour's national organization. Across North America, this became known as the "Great Upheaval." Like so much else in this "Upheaval," the new workers' festival marked a major shift in the consciousness of many wage-earners. They were no longer willing to live in a quiet, respectful relationship with paternalistic employers. They had come to believe that they had separate interests in industrial capitalist society that had to be promoted and defended.[5]

The labour leaders who campaigned for a Labour Day overtly challenged class boundaries in both space and time. First, they confronted the definition of what was considered "public" and how public space should be used, and they demanded that it be democratized by giving workers full, equal, independent access. Particularly with their colourful parades, they created a public festival that rejected roles for workers as mere spectators to upper-class pageantry and instead brought large numbers of working people into the main streets of industrial centres to celebrate the social value, the respectability, and the determination of unionized workingmen. And, second, these men fought for release from the pressures of work in capitalist industry and for expanded leisure time. They demanded another day off work to push back the increasingly rigid boundaries between waged labour and "free" time. In this sense, the demand for an official labour holiday was part of the much broader campaign for shorter working hours that had begun in the 1870s – first the nine-hour, then the eight-hour day.[6]

There were several parts to official Labour Day celebrations. They usually began in the morning with a parade, and then moved into a public park for some combination of track-and-field events, baseball or lacrosse matches, horse races, band concerts, and family picnics. The centrepiece of the day, however, was undoubtedly the parade. Here was the public face that organized workingmen wanted to present to their fellow citizens, and that undoubtedly drew far more attention than any other part of the day's festivities. Early in the twenty-first century, that may seem surprising. We don't see that many parades these days, and we don't take them all that seriously unless they are large (such as the quarter of a million people who paraded in Toronto's Days of Action in 1996). But back in the nineteenth century there were lots of them, and they were taken quite seriously. Street processions were used to highlight public holidays, religious occasions, ethnic events, election campaigns, funerals, the arrival of circuses, and much, much more.[7] Why was that?

People lived closer together in much smaller towns and cities where they could easily walk across town. A parade could catch the attention of most of the population, since it didn't pass far from most people's doorsteps. It was more complicated than that, however. These weren't loose or chaotic events – they were carefully structured and thoughtfully organized. Walking through the streets was a public statement, and marchers presented themselves in particular ways to make sure that the townsfolk got the message they were trying to convey. A parade was an important mode of communicating with fellow citizens. The rich and powerful, for example, put on a show of pageantry that was intended to make people respect them and accept a world in which they were dominant. Every time the governor-general came to town, he passed through the streets with appropriate aristocratic pomp and ceremony. Some other parade-organizers wanted to make fun of the rich and powerful, and dressed up in outrageous costumes to put on a different kind of show for spectators (they often called themselves Calithumpians or Polymorphians). Still others took to the streets to protest – from charivaris (against newly-weds) to spontaneous marches of angry strikers, including some of the first generation of Nova Scotia coal miners.[8] Most paraders, however, were more orderly and proper, since organizers wanted to impress their fellow citizens with their own respectability and the respectability of their cause. That included the first organizers of labour parades in the nineteenth century. They took the respectable road, but nonetheless put their own working-class stamp on it.

The first unionists who organized parades made use of what were then called "trades processions," a ceremonial tradition that stretched back through generations to the marches organized by craft guilds in early modern Europe. Here in nineteenth-century British North America, master craftsmen and early industrialists in a particular trade often led their journeymen and apprentices through the streets as part of larger civic celebrations. When the crafts began to splinter into capitalist employers and waged workers, the new craft unions adopted many of the "ancient" symbols of the craft. They too were often incorporated into public ceremonies, such as the large annual parades on Saint Jean-Baptiste Day in Quebec.[9] In the 1860s and 1870s, however, craftworkers in Canada began to break away and hold their own street processions as part of their first struggles for rights and recognition, including the famous march for a nine-hour day in Hamilton, Ontario, in 1872.[10] They used the form of the older trades procession for these new marches. When they began to organize Labour Day celebrations, labour leaders merely incorporated and expanded this new form of independent labour parading.

Above all the Labour Day parade was intended to show the massed strength of the local labour movement, to convince everyone that workers were well organized and united. Yet it was also to convey the meaning of the movement to the workers' families, neighbours, and fellow citizens. The first Labour Day organizers were particularly concerned to show off the respectability of workingmen. They wanted to ensure that workers could lift their heads proudly and march through the main streets of the town or city as full citizens, without scorn or condescension, and with respect for their valuable contributions to the evolving urban industrial society. In the process they also implied what in their eyes constituted the legitimate elements of this society.[11]

The most visible step towards respectability came when workingmen shed grubby overalls and aprons and strode forth in their best shirts, ties, jackets, and hats. Although some wore special outfits to symbolize their particular trade, they never marched in their actual working clothes. They also insisted on full public acceptance by marching along the main avenues of the towns and cities, not merely in the working-class districts where they lived.

To give you a flavour of how carefully workers thought about this issue of respectability, let me take you inside the meeting hall of the Halifax printers' union in the evening of 15 June 1889. The members had been summoned to a special meeting to hear the report of the Labour Day Committee that they had elected two weeks earlier. First, they examined and debated sample badges and sashes and decided which to order, at the steep cost of 75 cents each. They then agreed on the flags to be carried, and voted to get a horse for their marshal and a carriage for elderly members. Head gear was more controversial. The committee recommended bowler hats, but an amendment in favour of tops hats ("beavers") resulted in a tied vote. The president cast the deciding vote in favour of bowlers. The next year, the same sharp division of opinion brought another tied vote, but this time the president opted for top hats. Voting to allow apprentices to join them and not to carry canes in the procession also sparked deep disagreements. In both cases the members reversed the votes at the next regular meeting. These were all decisions of great significance to these craftworkers and not to be taken lightly. The distinctive costume of Halifax printers had thus been set. The silk hats, dark clothes, and white gloves and ties that they wore for many years to come suited these "aristocrats" of labour, who regularly headed the Halifax parade.[12]

You could see the respectability in the very structure of the Labour Day parades themselves. Like so many other parade-makers in the period, labour leaders took military processions as their model. Each Labour Day parade was headed by a marshal mounted on a horse, most often followed by a contingent of mounted policemen or uniformed firemen. All participants marched in disciplined and orderly formation to the beat of the marching bands. Yet copying the powerful had its limits. Despite the debts to military conventions, the militia itself, with all its pomp, hierarchy, and weaponry, was never invited to participate in these early years. Nor were the clergy – these were secular events.

Instead, the parade-makers were quite prepared to highlight workers' identities as citizens in a democratic country. They often invited the mayor and alderman to ride in carriages near the head of the parade, as the popularly elected representatives of the people. They declared their citizenship by carrying the Union Jack at many points in the procession, though in many English-Canadian cities it was often paired with the Stars and Stripes in a bold declaration of international solidarity. In Quebec parades the flag most often displayed was the French tricolour.

Craftsmen were more than citizens, however. They were producers who worked with their hands. And their parade organizers aspired to artistic representation of the distinct and "ancient" traditions of specific trades and the values and practices they carried forward into the new industrial period. Craftworkers unfurled beautiful silk banners with striking symbolic depictions of their craft and its central symbols, along with slogans declaring universal principles – "Unity Founded on Equity Is the Strongest Bond of Society," or "By Diligence or Perseverance We Overcome All Things," or the ever-popular *Labor Omnia Vincit* ("Labour Conquers All"). By the turn of the century, these banners often had slogans and allusions to current concerns, such as shorter hours. More of these messages were also appeals to consumers to buy goods marked with the union label or to support the early closing of retail shops. The artistry and mythology also started to fade, and they more often contained simply the names and numbers of the union locals with a simple emblem of an international union.

In most Labour Day parades, skilled workmen also carried on the tradition of putting their craftsmanship itself on display as a kind of street theatre. Some proudly carried the tools of their trade or the products of their labour. Others showed off the equipment they worked with: the longshoremen had huge ship models, the firemen brought out their glittering wagons and apparatus, the electrical workers showed off their blazing electrified floats, and so on. Most fascinating for the crowds were the more animated floats that showed craftworkers at work – what late-nineteenth-century journalists liked to call "allegorical cars" – printers manning printing presses, cigarmakers and bakers making their products and tossing them to the crowds, barbers shaving faces or cutting hair, building tradesmen constructing tiny houses, metalworkers putting on dazzling displays of sound and light with their small furnaces and hot iron, and much more. Some of these exhibitions of workmanship were set up on floats bearing a company name. Companies were, in fact, invited to put floats in the parades. But employers were not invited to march with their workers. These were parades of wage-earners.

Not just any wage-earners, however. Above all else, Labour Day in its infancy was a celebration of craft unionism. It flourished only where craftworkers had reached sufficient numbers and a sufficient sense of injustice in their workplaces to organize successful unions. Here, then, was a crucial ingredient in the working-class definition of respectability. These men were not just scrubbed, sober, and orderly – they were organized, determined, and proud of their collective independence from their employers' paternalistic, authoritarian control.

The exclusiveness of the craft organizations was clear to all those who watched them march by. At a minimum, each contingent of paraders had special badges and sometimes colourful sashes. More striking were the uniform-like costumes that individual unions wore and that set them apart as an occupation. This kind of costuming both accented the tight bonds among the group of marchers and set them apart from their audience. A Labour Day parade was not a spontaneously participatory event; there were no calls for onlookers to join in. It was a spectacle to be watched and admired and to convey important lessons.

Most striking, perhaps, was what was missing from this presentation of "Labour." Rarely did less skilled wage-earners find their way into the parades before the First World War. As a result, these were preponderantly parades of white anglophones and francophones, inaccessible to African Canadians, native Canadians, and the newcomers from southern and eastern Europe and Asia, who increasingly filled the jobs at the bottom of the occupational ladder and who were rarely unionized before the First World War. The only blacks and indigenous peoples who appeared were essentially clowns.

Wage-earning women were included somewhat more often, though they were still generally rare sights. Typically they sat in their finest clothes waving safely and primly from union carriages or automobiles. Generally, as paraders, they were constrained both by the masculine aura of military-style processions and by the nineteenth-century bourgeois standards of feminine respectability that frowned on women walking in the street.[13] Otherwise women were used as symbols of some higher principles, playing the role of a classically draped symbolic figure, such as Liberty or Britannia. No floats or carriages in these early Labour Day parades ever recognized the work women did in the household. Similarly, children typically found a role only as symbols or ornaments on floats, not as wage-earners.

It is clear, then, that these processions were affirmations of respectable white working-class "manhood" – from the pride in manual strength and craft skill to the clear message that these men were the breadwinners of their families who did not need other family members in the paid workforce. In the words of an Ottawa labour columnist, Labour Day was the "practical recognition of brotherhood and fatherhood."[14]

These determined craft unionists were upset at how the first generations of industrial capitalists had disrupted their workplace customs and routines. In the face of those changes on the job, they were vigorously re-asserting the dignity of the respectable workingman, the wage-earning craftworker. And that meant standing tall against the use of cheaper labour to degrade their crafts, including women and children, and defending their role as breadwinners for their families.

However angry they were with the new age of industrial capitalism, Labour Day marchers nonetheless generally kept their processions polite. In May Day demonstrations in western Europe, the marchers carried a petition to state authorities, but the Labour Day parade in Canada and the United States was not intended as an overt act of protest. Parading through the streets on a labour holiday was nonetheless intended as a quietly political act aimed at publicizing their positive alternative to the apparent degradation of work that this labour movement offered.

Challenges

Labour Day processions seem to have been popular with the broader public. Well into the early 1900s, the parades and other official Labour Day activities got front-page coverage in local newspapers. Shopkeepers readily strung up coloured bunting along the parade route, and thousands of spectators turned up on the sidewalks each year to watch and often to applaud or cheer particular union contingents. Certainly the parade-makers had public support for continuing their annual processions. Yet, within a few years into the twentieth century, the parades were in trouble in many communities. They were held less frequently or cancelled completely in many places in the decade before the First World War. Even where they still appeared on city streets every year, they often dwindled in size and lost their sparkle. Unions' participation in Labour Day parades began to decline, along with the quality of the performance. Journalists in many places reported the diminishing numbers of floats and uniforms. Everywhere unions began to ignore the call to participate, and those that did sometimes had to threaten fines for members who failed to appear for the march. Many trades and labour councils eventually cancelled their processions to concentrate on sports and entertainment, or gave up holding any kind of event at all. In most of western Canada, Labour Day parades died out forever with the First World War. Only Toronto,

Ottawa, and Montreal had regular annual parades well into the twentieth century.

What had gone wrong? The deteriorating of the parading tradition often reflected what has been called the "crisis of the craftsman."[15] The first Labour Day parades had always drawn most of their energy from the buoyancy and confidence of local craft unions, and the revival of these organizations across the country at the turn of the century had temporarily re-invigorated the celebrations. Within a few years, however, these unions were increasingly on the defensive in the face of employer hostility and state indifference. In fact, the foundations of craft unionism were under systematic attack. Many of these skilled men witnessed their role in industrial production destroyed or diminished in what has been called the Second Industrial Revolution. Fewer workers probably felt the craftworker's independent pride in their contribution to industry. A good many may have been more interested in escaping work than in celebrating it. In this context, craft unions often could ill afford the time and money to prepare for a parade that seemed to be doing little to strengthen their positions in the community. Many Canadian unionists seemed to quietly abandon the expectations of the earnest Labour Day pioneers that public displays of pride and determination could make much difference to the ongoing battles for the well-being of workingmen.

In many cases where the parades survived, they frequently lost their earnestness and took on a more commercial flavour as fundraising efforts for local trades and labour councils. They also lost much of their original working-class vitality. With the emergence of more mass-production labour processes, it was increasingly difficult to present small tableaux of workers practising their trade on the back of a wagon. Reporters across the country noted with regret the disappearance of the "allegorical cars" showing craftworkers at work. More and more, the parades relied for their colour and attractiveness on the company-sponsored floats, carriages, and cars. These had been woven through or tacked on at the end of the parade, but now they became more prominent. Perhaps the most remarkable example of this growing commercialization cropped up in Toronto's parade in 1933, a year in which local craft unionists had begged for company floats to sustain the parade. The T. Eaton Company was one of the city's most anti-union employers and soon to be exposed in the Royal Commission on Price Spreads for its harsh treatment of its employees. That year it nonetheless sponsored an elaborate float in the city's Labour Day procession carrying three symbolic figures of "Inspiration," "Achievement," and "Labor" over the banner "The Reward of Labor."[16] This kind of commercialization would continue.

Relying on commercial content to guarantee enough sparkle in the spectacle, Labour Day parades began to lose some of their distinctiveness and perhaps to suffer by comparison with some other parading events, notably Eaton's own Santa Claus Parade, inaugurated in 1905. The union content was certainly watered down. Ultimately, these commercialized parades became increasingly a form of civic boosterism. Municipal government added their support with regular contributions of firefighting equipment and floats from various works departments.

Moreover, labour leaders found other voices trying to define the meaning of this holiday. Local newspapers almost invariably published editorials and editorial cartoons reflecting on workers and work, local clergymen preached "Labour Sermons" on the day before the festivities, and politicians addressed Labour Day crowds. These community commentators liked to congratulate labour leaders on their accomplishments, but more often to lecture them on the need for sober restraint and cooperation with their bosses. They liked to take the occasion to trumpet how well off workers now were (the respectable marchers in the parades were cited as proof) and therefore how far they were from being European-style fire-breathing revolutionaries. They also used the apparent prosperity to emphasize how healthy the local economy must be. But they also tried to generalize the meaning of "labour" beyond unionized workers. They either focused simply on all blue-collar workers, or argued that "we are all workers" and therefore should not give any prominence to unionists. By the early 1900s, then, the meaning of Labour Day was quickly shifting beyond the confines intended by its founders.

By the 1920s, moreover, as advertising became more sophisticated, prominent local firms placed large ads in daily newspapers on the Saturday before Labour Day with glowing text and often powerful visual imagery to praise the contributions of the blue-collar worker and sometimes to hint at the importance of social peace, high productivity, and cooperative industrial relations. These ads, however, never mentioned unions. Elsewhere in the same papers, workers were encouraged to buy any number of products to make Labour Day worthwhile.

Rank-and-file workers also began to redefine Labour Day themselves by turning the day off work into a time for private pleasures, rather than public celebrations. Here was the inner tension built into Labour

Day from the start. Workers might simply spend the day relaxing at home, or more often enjoy an outing with family, friends, or perhaps lodge brothers. The growing leisure industries soon began to offer cultural products to be consumed on the holiday. So the speeches, concerts, and sporting events that Labour Day organizers laid on for unionists and their fellow citizens had to compete with family picnics and outings to the beach, spectator sports, vaudeville and movies, boat or train excursions out of the city, and, by the 1940s, long weekends away in the family car. Reports on labour parades got overwhelmed by reports on holiday traffic.

Parades were also reaching far fewer people. Cities were much bigger, and working-class families were moving out of the old downtown core. They also watched movies and listened to the radio, and used such mass media as their way to know and understand the world. Who needed parades any more? The official Labour Day program arranged by local labour leaders simply got lost. The same thing, of course, was happening to all public holidays by the early twentieth century, but it must have been especially demoralizing for the Labour Day organizers.

By the First World War, then, you would find Labour Day parades as regular events only in larger cities – mostly capital cities and metropolitan centres. The parades were much weaker, more sporadic, or non-existent in more thoroughly industrial communities where unions' strength had been undermined and where civic celebrations seemed less vibrant. Labour festivals in small-town Nova Scotia and Quebec were rare, and in the many small southern-Ontario factory towns they appeared only occasionally. In western Canada they had disappeared completely by 1920.

Marching to Different Tunes

The fate of Labour Day was also caught up in the internal politics of the labour movement. Some groups of workers turned their backs on the existing Labour Day events and redirected working-class parading traditions into new celebrations that reflected the aspirations of their new workers' movements.

The first group was the radicals.[17] After the turn of the twentieth century, socialists began to scoff at the claim that the Labour Day program did much to further the workers' cause. The editor of the *Western Clarion* referred to the holiday as "Slave Day," and said the parade was nothing but a "display of toadyism."[18] Gradually they turned to

May Day as the preferred workers' festival, in line with the pattern of socialist movements in other countries. The first May Day parade in Canada was staged by Montreal's socialists in 1906, and by the First World War these events were drawing thousands of people into Montreal's streets every spring. There were similar events in Port Arthur/Fort William, but elsewhere in Canada, until the early 1920s, May Day celebrations seemed to be limited mainly to indoor meetings with lots of speeches. In the 1920s, the Communists took over May Day celebrations and made them a major event on their organizational calendar. They organized parades or public meetings in cities from Glace Bay to Vancouver, including the largest Prairies centres. In the 1920s May Day parades could draw as many as 3–4,000 marchers in some cities. In the 1930s participation reached peaks of 15,000 in Vancouver and 25,000 in Toronto. These parades blossomed into major working-class cultural events on many city streets in Ontario and western Canada.

Before the Second World War, May Day parades had some similarities with Labour Day events, but many more sharp divergences. Marchers still put on their best suits and marched in quasi-military formation. But they emphasized their common working-class identity rather than highlighting occupational differences with badges, sashes, uniforms, and special outfits. The parade organizers drew in a broader range of working-class participants than the craft unions of the past had done, including radical political organizations, ethnic groups, industrial unionists, unemployed workers, women, and children.

May Day processions were intensely serious and overtly didactic and generally relied on less subtle symbolism than Labour Day processions. Floats were far less common until the mid-1930s, and, where they appeared, were generally simple satire or melodramas of social realism, rather than the old occupational tableaux. At various times in Vancouver, for example, marchers dragged along an effigy of the mayor reading the Riot Act during the relief-workers' strike and a replica of a relief-camp bunkhouse on wagons, while an anti-fascist float portrayed "a white-garbed girl, representing B.C. democracy, bound and menaced by a pair of masked brown shirts with swastika arm bands."[19] The few bands that might be used invariably played the "Internationale" or "The Red Flag," rather than popular marching music. Marchers commonly chanted slogans and sang revolutionary and labour songs as they moved along, sometimes led by choirs.

Banners fluttering over their heads were generally covered with words, not allegorical symbols – either the name of the marching contingent or, more commonly, a variety of slogans denouncing capitalism and inspiring action. The red flag was always carried as well, in preference to the Union Jack or the Stars and Stripes, and nothing upset local authorities more. Some municipalities passed bylaws requiring a Union Jack in every parade. Police regularly seized red flags from marchers (in 1924 paraders in Montreal responded to this police harassment by flourishing hundreds of small red flags).

None of these symbols resonated with local community leaders and their boosterist aspirations in the way that the earlier Labour Day parades had. No local firms ever contributed commercial floats or wagons. No daily newspapers published favourable reports. On the contrary, May Day was constructed by politicians and newspapermen as an explicit threat to the social order. Marchers faced regular police harassment. Large crowds nonetheless turned out to watch.

These spring festivities retreated somewhat during the Second World War and returned for a few years after the war in a few centres, notably Vancouver. But they withered in the subsequent Cold War period, along with the radical organizations that has sponsored them. They would be revived once again in the 1960s and 1970s in Montreal and western Canada.

Meanwhile, alongside May Day, a distinctly different workers' festival had been developing in Quebec. There the Catholic unions dominated by the clergy created a new festival centred on its patron saint, St Joseph. In Montreal and Quebec their celebrations were held on the Sunday before Labour Day, when major sermons usually delivered outdoors by prominent church leaders drove home the message that workers should obey their bosses and avoid strikes. The processions centred on the churches dedicated to St Joseph, and Catholic clergy presided over the solemn occasion. Clergy and lay people also marched with the unionists. By 1938 10,000 people were reported to be participating in this ritual in Montreal (alongside some 20,000 in the secular Labour Day parade the next morning).

Clowns and Clenched Fists

It might seem, then, that Labour Day parading had declined into bland commercialism or in some cases been eclipsed by new, more vigorous forms of celebration. Yet, by the First World War, this old workers' festival had been around long enough to become something of a labour tradition that could be revived where it had died out or resuscitated where it had lost its lustre. That is exactly what happened in many parts of central and eastern Canada whenever militancy and radicalism surged up again in working-class communities – notably at the end of the First World War, briefly in the 1930s, after the Second World War, and again in the 1960s and 1970s. (The 1970s was actually a significant decade in the history of Canadian workers' festivals: May Day and Davis Day were both revived, International Women's Day marches were launched, and Labour Day got more militant.)

Many of the older elements remained in the post–Second World War parades[20] – the marching bands, floats, special uniforms, quasi-military formations, and the general attempt to highlight the respectability and value of working people to local industry and community life. Some of the commercialization remained intact as well. To grab more public attention, Labour Day organizers added features that were appearing in such other processions as the old circus parades or the newer Santa Claus parades. Clowns became increasingly common by the 1940s. More striking were the beauty pageants to choose a Miss Labour Day or Labour Day Queen, and the many scantily clad young women who were used as majorettes or as nothing more than sexual baubles on union floats – a far cry from the gender politics of the earlier parades.

The imagery of the displays in the revived parades also looked different from those of the early craftworkers' processions. They had simpler industrial motifs than the old elaborate craftworkers' banners and often incorporated the name of their employer (which may well have supplied the float). Where the old craft unions had organized on a city-wide basis, the locals of new industrial unions focussed on a single enterprise and identified strongly with its products. The labour processes in these workplaces were also now less often on display. Floats were now more likely to show industrial products or machinery rather than tools of the trade or craftsmanship in action. Workers on these company floats wanted to emphasize their importance to industrial production in the firms they worked for, and the gains they had won through collective bargaining.

The participants were also changing. Far more of them were less-skilled workers enrolled in industrial, rather than craft, unions. The most noticeable newcomers were the growing numbers of women. The revival of unions in the late 1930s and early 1940s brought many more women into the streets, this time as full-fledged marchers. The dramatic shift in female employment during the Second World War gave them still more space in these parades, often marching in the special uniforms they wore on the job. Some of the women marched in their familiar capacity as domestic manager, but with a new militant spirit, such as the Ladies' Auxiliary of Mine-Mill Local 598, which headed the 1946 parade in Sudbury, and the Housewives Consumers' Association, which joined the Toronto parade carrying rolling pins and demanding price control on bread. Of course, these women had to try to assert themselves as workers to be taken seriously alongside the more sexist imagery mentioned above.

The revived parades after each World War rippled with new industrial militancy and political radicalism. Most were staged at moments of surging union strength and intensified industrial conflict, and usually marchers were shaking an angry fist of collective strength and solidarity. The Labour Day parade that had once been a simple declaration of respectability and social and moral worth was thus recast more and more often as defiant street theatre connected to specific current struggles on the job or, more broadly, to newfound union strength and determination. The post–Second World War parades in particular bristled with placards and arm bands announcing demands raised on their picket lines. By the 1970s, moreover, newly organized public-sector workers, including teachers and nurses, were bringing their new organizational energy to the marches.

These events also became more overtly political. By the 1940s labour's demands for new legislation to regulate collective bargaining and to establish some social security, notably old-age pensions and socialized health care, were splashed across many banners and floats. The dampening effect of the Cold War and the new bureaucratization of labour relations drained off some of this anger for much of the next twenty years, but it never disappeared completely. By the late 1960s the political tone was once again unmistakable, and in the 1970s and 1980s it was not uncommon for parade organizers to announce a theme for the whole parade, such as the 1976 fight against wage and price controls or the 1988 fight against free trade with the United States.

The new themes in the postwar parades often brought in the socialist-realist allegories that had appeared in May Day parades. The cartoon figure of the capitalist in top hats and tails appeared from time to time. By the 1960s and 1970s paraders were regularly using imagery of death, with figures standing around coffins, to symbolize the destruction of labour rights, from injunctions to wage controls. They also set up prison bars to highlight the constraints on labour action or even the imprisonment of labour leaders.

Of course, these sharp political messages were mixed into the same parades that included clowns and beauty queens. This dual spirit of celebration and defiance epitomized the new Labour Day parades of the postwar era. The willingness to weave the fanciful and frivolous into these events can be read as a new part of the working-class vision – one that insisted on a place for humour and fantasy in a society driven by the frenzied pace of wage labour. There was also some clear convergence in the parading "traditions" built separately on Labour Day and May Day. And, as May Day revived in some cities in Quebec and the West in the 1960s and 1970s, the forms of the two parades were more similar than ever before.

Now, of course, both sets of parades had to find a working-class audience that had dispersed in many directions and used many other modes of mass communication beyond street processions and picnics. By the 1960s and 1970s, more and more local labour movements gave up the parades, and stuck to smaller-scale fun in a local park. Labour Day marches have nonetheless survived in some cities. Thousands of working people, mostly in Ontario, apparently still believe that taking to the streets once a year will remind others that they are part of a movement united in pursuing common concerns and that they will not abandon hope of achieving them. In that sense, while their impact may be more limited, the spirit of the Labour Day pioneers is still alive and well.

Notes

1 For a fuller treatment of the issues discussed here, see Craig Heron and Steve Penfold, *The Workers' Festival: A History of Labour Day in Canada* (Toronto: University of Toronto Press 2005).

2 *Trades Journal* (Springhill/Stellarton), 17 August 1881, 3; 13 September 1882, 2; *Globe* (Toronto), 24 July 1882, 6; 4 August 1883, 2; *Herald* (Halifax), 3 August 1888, 3; 9 July 892, 3; *Acadian Recorder* (Halifax), 23 July 1889, 3; 18 July 1890, 3; *Morning Chronicle* (Halifax), 20 July 1891, 1; *Advertiser* (London), 6 September 1892, 5; *Spectator* (Hamilton), 4 August 1883, 1; *Palladium of Labor* (Hamilton), 11 August 1883, 1, 6; 18 August 1883, 1; *Journal* (Ottawa), 30 August 1890, 6; *Gazette* (Montreal), 7 September 1886, 3; 3 September 1889, 5; Bryan D. Palmer, *Culture in Conflict: Skilled Workers and Industrial Capitalism in Hamilton, Ontario, 1860–1914* (Montreal and Kingston: McGill-Queen's University Press 1979), 57; Eugene Forsey, *Trade Unions in Canada, 1812–1902* (Toronto: University of Toronto Press 1982), 293–9, 302, 311–12, 317–18, 320, 330–1, 335, 339.

3 Bert Roth, "Labour Day in New Zealand," in John E. Martin and Kerry Taylor, eds., *Culture and the Labour Movement: Essays in New Zealand Labour History* (Palmerston North, New Zealand: Dunsmore Press 1991), 304–14; Andrew Reeves, *Another Day, Another Dollar: Working Lives in Australian History* (Carleton North, Australia: McCullough Publishing 1988), 74–105; Michael Kazin and Stephen J. Ross, "America's Labor Day: The Dilemma of a Workers' Celebration," *JAH* 78, no. 4 (March 1992), 1294–1323.

4 Philip S. Foner, *May Day: A Short History of the International Workers' Holiday, 1886–1986* (New York: International Publishers 1986); Maurice Dommanget, *Histoire du premier mai* (Paris: Éditions de la Tête de Feuilles 1972); Georges Seguy, *1er mai: Les 100 printemps* (Paris: Messidor/Éditions sociales 1989); Michelle Perrot, "The First of May 1890 in France: The Birth of a Working-Class Ritual," in Pat Thane, Geoffrey Crossick, and Roderick Floud, eds., *The Power of the Past: Essays for Eric Hobsbawm* (Cambridge, U.K.: Cambridge University Press 1984), 143–71; Andrea Panaccione, ed., *May Day Celebration* (Venice: Marsilio Editori 1988).

5 Forsey, *Trade Unions in Canada*; Gregory S. Kealey and Bryan D. Palmer, *Dreaming of What Might Be: The Knights of Labor in Ontario, 1880–1900* (Toronto: New Hogtown Press 1987); Ian McKay, "'By Wisdom, Wile, or War': The Provincial Workmen's Association and the Struggle for Working-Class Independence in Nova Scotia, 1879–97," *L/LT* 18 (Fall 1986), 13–62; Bryan D. Palmer, *Working-Class Experience: Rethinking the History of Canadian Labour, 1800–1991* (Toronto: McClelland and Stewart 1992), 117–54.

6 John Battye, "The Nine-Hour Pioneers: The Genesis of the Canadian Labour Movement," *L/LT* 4 (1979), 25–56; Palmer, *Culture in Conflict*, 125–52; David R. Roediger and Philip S. Foner, *Our Own Time: A History of American Labor and the Working Day* (London: Verso 1989).

7 Peter G. Goheen, "Symbols in the Streets: Parades in Victorian Urban Canada," *UHR* 18, no. 3 (February 1990), 237–43; Peter G. Goheen, "The Ritual of the Streets in Mid-19th-Century Toronto," *Environment and Planning D: Society and Space* 11, no. 2 (April 1993), 127–45; Peter G. Goheen, "Parading: A Lively Tradition in Early Victorian Toronto," in Alan Baker and Gideon Biger, eds., *Ideology and Landscape in Historical Perspective* (New York: Cambridge University Press 1992), 330–51; Peter G. Goheen, "Negotiating Access to Public Space in Mid-Nineteenth Century Toronto," *JHG* 20, no. 4 (1994), 430–49; Susan G. Davis, *Parades and Power: Street Theatre in Nineteenth-Century Philadelphia* (Berkeley: University of California Press 1986); Mary Ryan, "The American Parade: Representations of the Nineteenth-Century Social Order," in Lynn Hunt, ed., *The New Cultural History* (Berkeley: University of California Press 1989), 131–53; Bonnie

Huskins, "Public Celebrations in Victorian Saint John and Halifax" (PhD dissertation, Dalhousie University 1990); Michael Cottrell, "St. Patrick's Day Parades in Nineteenth-Century Toronto: A Study in Immigrant Adjustment and Elite Control," *HS/SH* 49 (May 1992), 57–73; Gregory S. Kealey, *Toronto Workers Respond to Industrial Capitalism, 1867–1892* (Toronto: University of Toronto Press 1980), 115–23; Remi Tourangeau, *Fêtes et spectacles du Québec: Région du Saguenay-Lac-Saint Jean* (Quebec: Nuit Blanche Éditeur 1993); Doug A. Mishler, "'It Was Everything Else We Knew Wasn't': The Circus and American Culture," in Ray B. Browne and Michael T. Marsden, eds., *The Cultures of Celebrations* (Bowling Green, OH: Bowling Green State University Popular Press 1994), 127–44.

8 Bryan D. Palmer, "Discordant Music: Charivaris and Whitecapping in Nineteenth Century North America," *L/LT* 3 (1978), 5–62; James M. Cameron, *The Pictonian Colliers* (Halifax: Nova Scotia Museum 1974), 141–3.

9 Huskins, "Public Celebrations," 176–217; Forsey, *Trade Unions in Canada*, 10–13, 311; Palmer, *Culture in Conflict*, 56–7.

10 Battye, "Nine-Hour Pioneers."

11 The following discussion on early Labour Day parades is based on reports in newspapers in cities across the country from the 1880s to the 1910s; for more detail, see Heron and Penfold, *Workers' Festival*, 41–79.

12 Public Archives of Nova Scotia, MG 20, Halifax Typographical Union Records, Vol. 332, 15 June, 6 July 1889; 5 July 1890.

13 Bonnie Huskins, "The Ceremonial Space of Women: Public Processions in Victorian Saint John and Halifax," in Janet Guidlford and Suzanne Morton, eds., *Separate Spheres: Women's Worlds in the Nineteenth Century Maritimes* (Fredericton: Acadiensis Press 1994).

14 *Journal* (Ottawa), 2 September 1899, 2.

15 Craig Heron, "The Crisis of the Craftsman: Hamilton's Metalworkers in the Early Twentieth Century," *L/LT* 6 (Autumn 1980), 7–48.

16 *Globe* (Toronto), 5 September 1933, 1.

17 For more detail on these parades, see Heron and Penfold, *Workers' Festival*, 166–90.

18 *Western Clarion*, 10 September 1904, 1; 9 September 1905, 1; 10 September 1906, 1; 10 September 1910, 1.

19 *Sun* (Vancouver), 2 May 1935, 1; 2 May 1938, 20.

20 For more detail on these postwar parades, see Heron and Penfold, *Workers' Festival*, 193–269.

PART THREE

Getting Organized

FEDERAL ELECTION

REGISTER!

SEPTEMBER 24th TO SEPTEMBER 30th

VOTE LABOR

HEAPS, A. A. X

Polling Day, October 29th

REMEMBER—Mark Your Ballot With a X

Chapter Seven

Labourism and the Canadian Working Class

Labourism has been the neglected child of the Canadian left. Between the 1880s and the 1920s workers frequently appeared in electoral campaigns across Canada as "Labour" candidates; yet for most of the past half-century this movement has languished in a dimly lit corner of Canadian intellectual inquiry, while historians and social scientists lavished attention on its ideological stepsisters, angry agrarianism, saintly Fabianism, and feisty Marxism.[1] Recently the flood of new research into individual working-class communities in Canada in the late nineteenth and early twentieth centuries has brought to light the particular histories of several local Labour parties. This essay will attempt to draw together this scattered research, to outline how, where, and when labourism strode onto the political stage, and to scrutinize its ideological complexion more carefully. The purpose of this exercise is to suggest that labourism was a distinct ideological form in Canadian politics, resembling but differing from agrarian populism, contemporary liberalism, and socialism, and the brand of social democracy which emerged after 1930. It was, moreover, the main ideological current in independent working-class politics east of the Rockies before 1920, and thus deserves to be rescued from its relative obscurity and neglect.

I

The social composition of this political movement needs clarification first. Before the latter part of the First World War, when Canadians from

Election poster, Winnipeg. From Leo Heaps, *Rebel in the House* varied social backgrounds began to jump aboard the labourist bandwagon, there is no doubt that this was a thoroughly proletarian movement. With few exceptions it was blue-collar workers who peopled the Labour parties' executive posts, ran as party candidates, and edited and wrote for the many local labour newspapers which supported the movement.[2] More specifically, however, labourism was the political expression of a distinct layer of the working class – the skilled workers in manufacturing, construction, and mining, who might be referred to collectively as craftworkers.[3] The leadership and active membership of the labourist cause came almost entirely from this group of printers, carpenters, plumbers, cigarmakers, moulders, coal miners, and so on. In fact, there was usually a great overlap in personnel between the local craft-dominated trades and labour council or the district miners' organization and the same community's Labour Party. (Unlike the British experience,[4] however, trades councils rarely sponsored political candidates directly. Until the end of the war, Canadian Labour parties, like trade unions, were individual membership organizations.)[5]

It is central to an understanding of labourism in Canada to recognize this specific social base on which it was built. As we will see, the ideological hues of the movement would reflect the world view of the skilled worker. But its social composition also helps to explain its two-stage development. First, craftpersons had to be detached from their traditional party allegiances, especially from the Liberal Party, a process which was well underway by the early 1900s. But then the skilled workers' new political vehicle had to harness broader support within the whole Canadian working class. They regularly proclaimed that their parties were open to all wage-earners, organized and unorganized, and often gave their rhetoric a populist twist by appealing to the vaguely-defined "masses." Winning that broader support, however, was a much slower process, which began to succeed only at the end of the First World War, when unusual wartime conditions made many more Canadian workers receptive to the craftworkers' appeal.

The pre-war record at the polls was bleak. Three Labour candidates were elected to the House of Commons before the war – Ralph Smith, Arthur Puttee, and Alphonse Verville – but each slid quickly into the Liberal caucus.[6] The only labourists elected to any provincial legislatures were Allan Studholme, who rode out of a bitter street railway strike in Hamilton in 1906 into a thirteen-year term in the Ontario house, and Donald McNab, who spent only a few months in the Alberta legislature in 1909.[7] (The only other proletarian parliamentarians outside the old parties before 1914 were three socialist MLAs in the British Columbia house and one in Alberta).[8]

The problem was not simply that the Liberal and Conservative parties had put down deep roots into elements of the working class,[9] but, more importantly, that there was a growing disillusionment and cynicism with electoral politics which was translating into much lower turnouts at the polls in many cities.[10] Increasingly the labourists' chances of electoral success depended on being able to mobilize these political abstainers.

The great breakthrough came towards the end of the First World War. The tendency of so many writers to focus on J.S. Woodsworth and on the House of Commons has obscured both the real gains labourists had made by the end of the war and the decentralized, community-based orientation of the movement. During these years scores of workers won seats as independent labour candidates on municipal councils and school boards and in provincial legislatures across the country.[11] These men and women were typically nominated by autonomous local organizations, most often called Independent Labor Parties. Typically too, these little parties initially had short lives and had to be rebuilt for each new electoral assault. But by the end of the First World War virtually every industrial community in the country had one. By this point, the local Labour parties were developing more permanence between elections, with social and educational programs to keep the labourist fires burning and to draw in new members.[12] Some of the newcomers were women, who shattered the male dominance of these organizations in Ontario and the West by creating their own Women's Labor Leagues and Women's Independent Labor Parties.[13] Numerous community-based labour weeklies proclaimed the message of the labourist cause.[14]

Only when there were enough of these local parties with sufficient vitality and strength would they federate at the provincial level. The first attempts at provincial organization in Ontario and Manitoba occurred in 1907, with limited, brief success,[15] but after 1916 more coherent provincial Labour parties with common platforms began to appear – the Independent Labor Parties of Nova Scotia and Ontario, the Quebec section of the Canadian Labor Party, the Dominion Labor Parties on the Prairies, and the Federated Labor Party in British Columbia.[16] Local organizations became branches of the provincial party, and in some cases the head office dispatched literature and speakers to help build the movement. Yet for election campaigns the organizational initiative remained with the local branches. National federation never took place in any real sense: the so-called Canadian Labor Party first created in 1917 was never more than a paper organization uniting regional and local efforts, and its few national meetings took place simply as offshoots of Trades and Labor Congress conventions. This was, in short, a highly decentralized political movement, reflecting the equally decentralized organization of the entire labour movement in the period.[17]

The upsurges of labourist organizing between the 1880s and the 1920s mark moments of more generalized class-conscious activity within the working class. First, they invariably took place in periods of burgeoning trade union strength (and, by the same token, political activity receded when unions were weak or on the defensive). And second, labourist interventions into local politics invariably occurred in the context of intensifying industrial conflict, reflecting many accumulating resentments and a recognition of common interest across occupational lines. There were four distinct phases: the mid-to-late 1880s, the early 1900s, the half decade before the war, and, finally, the years of most aggressive militancy, 1916–20. The turn to politics was seldom a swing away from the industrial battleground, but rather an attempt to broaden and intensify the same conflict into a unified class initiative.[18]

II

Establishing these patterns in the occurrence of labourist politics is not so difficult, but attempting to analyse the ideological dimensions of the movement can be a frustrating task. Like activists in the British Labour Party, but unlike those in many European socialist parties or even in large parts of the Socialist Party of America, these working-class politicians usually preferred to discuss issues of practical and immediate importance and seldom presented lengthy or lofty statements of their perspective on the world. It was quite common to hear labourist candidates promising simply "a square deal" for workers. Consequently any attempt to examine the elusive frame of reference of Canadian labourism must penetrate a thick fog and piece together many scattered fragments from men and women who often revealed annoyingly contradictory tendencies in their thinking. We must bear in mind that this was not an intellectualized doctrine, but more like an inclination and a set of political impulses which proceeded from some common ground. It was the politics not of ideologues but of practical people moving outward from their economic struggles. In the words of one historian of the parallel movement in Australia, they "proceeded from the particular to the general – to a collection of ethical catch-cries, subject to an infinity of interpretations."[19]

This ideological woolliness should not lead us to assume, however, that labourist politicians could see no further than a few limited reforms in the interest of organized labour, as Martin Robin has suggested. To dismiss them as "reformists" is also too easy and too imprecise: we need to ask in what specific ways they differed from other reformists of the period (and there were many varieties). Likewise, labelling them simply North American "populists," as Paul Phillips has done, is equally ambiguous, and, more important, ignores the striking similarities with labourism in Britain, Australia, and New Zealand.[20] It is possible, I think, to find a coherence and a consistency in the issues raised, the planks hammered into party platforms, and the rhetoric rolling down from the hustings across the country, and thus to see labourism as a distinct ideological form in the world of the Canadian working class.

Labourist political ideas owed less to books than to experience, especially experience in the world of work. These skilled workers were wage-earners, but they retained something of the mode of work that had preceded them in the evolution of capitalist production processes – that of the artisan and the "independent collier." Craftworkers exercised a degree of shop-floor autonomy and took responsibility for exercising complex manual tasks without compulsion from employers.[21] In the language of the theorist, they had yet to make the complete transition from "formal" to "real" subordination on the job. Even in the early twentieth century, these workers held on in the pockets of industry where their traditional skills still enjoyed some integrity. Their libertarian style of work, their rugged shop-floor equality, the self-respect and pride in accomplishment, and the spirit of comradeship, nourished in the workshop, construction site, or mine and reinforced in their craft unions, were all carried outward to social and political relationships in the wider community.

Not surprisingly, then, these people, like the artisans and *sans-culottes* of the more distant past, were the bearers of the natural rights traditions that flowed from the great democratic revolutions of the seventeenth and eighteenth centuries. Labourism, in fact, owed its greatest ideological debts to nineteenth-century Radicalism, of both the British liberal and American republican varieties. This form of working-class politics in Britain and her settler dominions had followed a course from Tom Paine and the English Jacobins, through the early nineteenth-century struggles for parliamentary reform and the tumultuous Chartist agitations, and, by the 1860s, into the Radical wing of that dynamic Victorian reform coalition, the Gladstonian Liberal Party.[22] In the United States a democratic radicalism with similar sources in the American Revolution eventually flowed into the Republican Party in the Civil War era.[23] And when Wilfrid Laurier finally knit together a coherent national Liberal Party in Canada by the 1890s, there was a recognized place for organized workers alongside the francophones, farmers, Catholics, and corporate capitalists in the Liberal alliance.[24] It is important to recognize that nineteenth-century Liberalism was a coalition of diverse ideological tendencies; a working-class radical, for example, was no Benthamite.[25]

The working-class Radicals who operated on the left wing of Canada's Liberal Party – men like Nanaimo miner Ralph Smith, Toronto printer Daniel O'Donoghue, Hamilton engineer Edward Williams, and Springhill, Nova Scotia, newspaper editor Robert Drummond – were prominent trade union leaders who regularly asserted working-class rights and concerns and expected action from party leaders.[26] In the 1880s the independent spirit of these skilled workers was producing the first quasi-independent organizing on the edge of official Liberalism, a phenomenon known as Liberal-Labourism, or, more commonly, Lib-Labism. Party leaders kept these Lib-Lab workers on a loose leash and then tugged into party caucuses any of those who were elected.[27] As long as Liberal administrations continued to make friendly gestures towards this working-class constituency – as they continued to do most assiduously in the Maritimes and Quebec, and on the Prairies – the Liberal alliance could be held intact. But at regular intervals it had to absorb the seismic shock waves of industrial conflict. Craft unions often looked in vain for substantial support from Laurier and his provincial counterparts in their increasingly bitter battles with hostile employers. With flourishes of anger and frustration, Radicalism would then move outside the Liberal Party to become labourism. This first wave of disillusionment prompted the organization of independent electoral organizations in the 1880s, like the Workingmen's Political Club of Cape Breton, the People's Political Party of Kingston, the Hamilton Labor Political Association, the London Workingmen's Association, and the Workingmen's Party on Vancouver Island, often as offshoots of the Knights of Labor.[28] By the turn of the century the craftworkers' patience was again evaporating. TLC conventions around 1900 heard loud denunciations of Liberal perfidy, and a new crop of local Labour parties began to spring up: Independent Labor Parties in Cape Breton, Winnipeg, and Vancouver, le Parti ouvrier de Montreal, the Canadian Labor League in Toronto, and the Workingmen's Political Association in Hamilton.[29] "Il faut aller en Chambre et au Conseil et adopter nous-mêmes les reformes dont nous avons besoin," argued Montreal printer J.A. Rodier in denouncing Liberal inaction. After another lull, similar voices were heard in the pre-war years. "Let us quit begging from the present politicians and political parties for what is our just due," a Saint John worker wrote in 1910; "organize our own party, elect our own men, and we can expect then, and only then, to remedy the evils that are confronting us today."[30]

Of course, these dramatic departures did not make all labourists impervious to renewed Liberal blandishments. Many electoral saw-offs were arranged across the country to keep labourists and Liberals from competing for votes (usually, to be sure, in constituencies where the Liberals were particularly weak). Whenever Labour organizations languished, individuals in the movement tended to drift back, and socialists continually denounced the labourists as tools of the Liberals.[31] Men like Smith, Puttee, and Verville had not travelled such a great ideological distance from the Liberal Party that returning to the fold was impossible.[32] Rank opportunism should never be overlooked in these cases; yet it seems that principled working-class Radicals were prepared to pursue their goals either on the left wing of the Liberal Party or through a Labourist party, depending on the responsiveness of the Liberals. At the same time, however, by the early 1900s there was no going back for growing numbers of politically conscious skilled workers. They were convinced of the strategic wisdom of cutting their links with mainstream Liberalism permanently, especially since well before the war they could point to shining examples of independent labourism in Britain and Australia. When William Lyon Mackenzie King approached Allan Studholme, Ontario's lone Labour MLA, for support for the Liberals in 1908, he was firmly informed that for men like Studholme Lib-Labism was finished: "Labor men have lost all faith in party men and are determined to have their own class on the floor of the house so as to have some say in making the laws they have to live under."[33] Studholme's unswerving independence during his thirteen years in the legislature testified to this new labourist determination to go it alone.

Ideologically, however, labourists seldom strayed far from their Radical roots. The hallmark of the Radical tradition had been an analysis which "saw privilege and political inequality as the root of social evils."[34] The Halifax labour paper, the *Citizen*, captured the essence of labourist politics when it urged workers in 1919 to "take their places in the army of reconstruction that is someday going to storm the citadel of vested rights and privilege."[35] Like generations of artisans before them,[36] these workers were Canada's foremost champions of parliamentary democracy. Political life, they believed, should be thoroughly re-invigorated with proportional representation, referenda, a more democratic franchise which included women,[37] the abolition of that house of "privilege," the Senate (and its provincial counterparts, the legislative councils), and the sweeping away of all property qualifications and election deposits.[38] In their idealized, liberal view of the state, they argued that all citizens should have full access to a neutral apparatus which could serve an undefined common good. Here was the purest legacy of Jacobin democracy.

The craftworkers' commitment to libertarian and egalitarian democracy was deeply troubled by the corruption, mismanagement, and authoritarianism that they saw in the Canadian state by the end of the war. They were disturbed by national registration and conscription, which, they feared, foreshadowed industrial compulsion. Many resented the imposition of prohibition. Most were appalled by the suppression of radical organizations and trade union rights in the fall of 1918, and, even if they did not support the OBU, denounced the suppression of the Winnipeg General Strike. The Halifax *Citizen* greeted the news of the arrest of the strike leaders with the cry that "Prussianism is in power in Canada." Increasingly the labourists seized on the wartime rhetoric of defending democracy and turned it back on the country's political leaders. Immediately after the war, it seems, they concluded that the mantle of true defenders of democratic traditions had fallen to the "masses," especially workers and farmers. The legacy of Radical liberalism was theirs alone to preserve.[39]

At the same time that they promoted and defended individual liberties, however, they vigorously asserted a prickly class-consciousness in politics. "Capital shall not press a crown of thorns on Labor's brow," the Hamilton *Labor News* thundered during the 1919 provincial election campaign. "Capital shall not crucify Labor on a cross of gold."[40] Yet it was not the mere existence of rampant capitalist power that irked these men, but rather the exclusiveness and unchecked tyranny of that power: "the classes versus the masses," as they often phrased it in its Gladstonian idiom. What they demanded was simply the right for working people to the full promise of liberal democracy, to be able to share power with other social groups, including capital. "The upper and middle classes have, in the past been represented by men of their choosing, and from their own ranks," the Grand Master of the Provincial Workmen's Association in Nova Scotia, Thomas Johnston, reasoned in 1886. "The workingmen claim the privilege of naming a candidate from among themselves to represent, in parliament, the class to which they belong, and all classes."[41] A quarter of a century later a Hamilton ILP activist exhorted his fellow moulders to independent political action by urging that their goal should be "to cultivate and consolidate the whole of the masses when by aggressive but not dominant action labor may have its fair share of what is due to them who are toiling." Many of the local and regional Labour parties made the right to participate in a wartime government a central theme of their 1917 federal election campaigns.[42]

In fact, representation in official political life seemed to become an end in itself for Labourists – the right to be there in legislative halls to present the working-class perspective. Allan Studholme and the many municipal Labour representatives spent the bulk of their time in parliamentary deliberations simply passing comment on the impact of legislative measures and state programs on workers. Labourists were undeniably class-conscious, but did not view the liberal-democratic state as an instrument for the working-class majority.

This attempt to create an independent political base for workers actually paralleled the emergence of a more professional, bureaucratic unionism at the turn of the century: both represented efforts by craftsworkers to solidify formal, institutionalized niches for workers in monopoly-capitalist society. Their goal seemed to be to carry their new bureaucratic model of collective bargaining into the political sphere, in the hopes of avoiding bitter industrial conflict. A piece of election rhetoric from the 1919 provincial campaign in Hamilton is revealing in this regard. A *Labor News* writer explained to working-class voters:

> This is not a contest of personalities. It is a contest for a principle. It is literally a contest between the capitalist and the laborer. The man who labors has in his hands the power to bring his employer to terms on a reasonable basis. It is a power much more to be prized than that gained by strikes. It is a power which places the integrity of the workingman on a par with the capitalist. And when the capitalist realizes beyond a doubt that the workingman is in possession of equal legislative rights as himself,

then, and only then, will he consider the rights of his employees in actual earnestness.[43]

Thus the liberal heritage of equal rights for individuals would assure equal rights for classes. It was through this class-conscious participation in the Canadian state that the working class could then press for the specific reforms of working conditions that filled up Labourist platforms, especially at the municipal and provincial levels (proper inspection of workplaces, abolition of subcontracting and child labour, weekly payment of wages, and so on). From this point, of course, labourism was only a stone's throw from the agrarian-inspired notion of "group government," expounded in the West by that pivotal figure in the farmer-labour connection, William Irvine.[44] Significantly, the collaboration between farmers' and workers' organizations across the country seems to have been typically joint and concurrent sponsorship of the same candidate by each "group," rather than fusion into a single party.[45] Their interests remained separate and distinct.

These class-conscious waters were thoroughly muddied, however, by various pronouncements of labourist spokespersons that suggested labour's commitment to public service, not class identity. Ontario's future Minister of Labour, Walter Rollo, for example, promised in his 1914 election campaign "to legislate in the interests of all the people, and not a favored few," and Hamilton's new ILP municipal office-holders emphasized to a victory rally in 1919 that "primarily they intended to legislate for the best interests of the community wholly – not class."[46] In the same vein, Montreal's Gustave Francq wrote: "Le contrôle de l'État doit être le fait du concours de tous et non d'une classe ou d'un caste."[47] And Cape Breton's A.R. Richardson argued that "no class should be barred from having a say in the government of their country."[48] The same perspective was carried into the Ontario Farmer-Labour government, and after four years the Labour MLAs' hesitation to press working-class demands left them with virtually no record to defend. No real breakthroughs were made in social welfare legislation, and the legislated eight-hour day remained an unfulfilled dream.[49]

The labourist critique of Canada's political system, after all, emphasized domination by capitalist and other manipulative interests, and these craftsworker-politicians were not about to propose a further perversion of liberal democracy by imposing their own "class rule." Their campaigns, therefore, were contradictory appeals to class solidarity and community service, as in the following 1914 report of Rollo's stump oratory:

> The [Labour] party stood for legislation for the masses and not the classes, and would not fail to support any move which would benefit the community. It did not seek merely to advance legislation solely beneficial to Labor, but the time had come when Labor should be regarded in a higher light than it was by the men who occupy seats in the house at present.[50]

The strong emphasis in labour's Radical baggage on the "brotherhood of man" and community of interest among citizens evidently overrode the experience of class divisions in capitalist society. In the ringing words of labourist campaign rhetoric in 1911: "The working class was the only class that was not a class – it was the nation."[51] Perhaps Wayne Roberts is right to dub this ideology "radical rotarianism."[52]

The labourist faith in liberal-democratic parliamentarianism, naturally enough, also included a commitment to gradualism. "To obtain a perfect state of society when everything shall be changed at a given time, even altho[ugh] a majority are in favor of it, seems to me impossible," wrote one of Hamilton's most prominent labourist politicians, George Halcrow, in 1916.[53] Gradualism was well established in the labourist tradition (and, we should recall, in the pre-Bolshevik Marxist tradition in Britain and Canada,)[54] in part because of the craftworkers' libertarian sensitivity to freedom from coercion, and in part because of the long series of small victories that craftsworkers believed they had won, in a piecemeal fashion, within industrial capitalist society. They had built up their many institutions of self-defence, especially their unions, to consolidate a small space for themselves in that society, and could countenance no abrupt changes that threatened those gains.[55] Moreover, industrial capitalist society in Canada, as in Britain, rarely presented itself as a rigid, immovable monolith that seemed to require a sudden, cataclysmic overthrow. In the early twentieth century it was only the wartime convergence of economic and political oppression that would push many labourists as close to outright rejection of capitalism as they ever ventured. Even then, the limited political perspective evident both in the Winnipeg General Strike and in the Ontario ILP's performance in the Farmer-Labour government tell us that, however many of them began to see a substantially new social order on the horizon, they still expected to get there by gradual steps.

The same Radical heritage also framed the labourist view of economic relationships and the state's role in adjusting them. In general they saved their harshest criticisms for the monopolists and the middlemen – the evil forces of economic "privilege" – who interfered with the productive life of the country and threatened working-class living standards. While they might lambaste individual industrialists for their heartlessness, Labour leaders seldom questioned their right to exist in an idealized society. The "single tax" on unimproved land values hung on in labourist platforms well into the twentieth century as a solution to social problems.[56] Besides "landlordism," the villains most commonly attacked were utility monopolies (gas, electricity, telephone, railway, and so on) and the unscrupulous but elusive "profiteer" who gouged the consumer.[57] The only public ownership planks in their platforms were aimed at utilities and, by the war, banks and some natural resource industries.

This limited critique is not surprising, given the social composition of this labourist movement. These were preponderantly people with traditional manual skills who carried into the early twentieth century some of the artisanal consciousness of the independent producer. From this perspective, an entrepreneurial industrialist was a co-producer, facing the same enemy in the economic "parasites" who lived off the honest toil of the "producing classes." In 1909 Ontario's regional labour paper, the *Industrial Banner*, argued that "the merchant, the mechanic, and the small manufacturer" were all victims of the same oppressive system: "The trouble lies in the fact that both employed and employer are chained fast in the grasp of an unjust and unworkable social system, which is the producer of the gigantic trusts and combines that are crippling the merchant, bankrupting the small manufacturer and pauperizing the masses."[58]

The hardy "producer" consciousness that lay behind this particular demonology rested not only on the assumption of common "parasitic" enemies, but also on an element of respect and admiration towards the accomplishments of one's fellow "producers." Labourism contained a strong belief in advancement according to merit – meaning implicitly, through manual or mental proficiency and honest labour. "Character, not wealth, should be the test of citizenship," the *Industrial Banner* insisted in 1904; and a few years later Allan Studholme regretted that "money was given preference to brains."[59] These craftworkers knew the social value attached to their own manual skills that they worked so assiduously to develop and defend, and they always insisted on wage differentials that recognized their exalted status over helpers and labourers. Their view of a liberal-democratic society was egalitarian in the sense of opposing privileged access to power and wealth, but they were quite prepared to accept some limited degree of hierarchical stratification, with industrialists well up the ladder, as long as the differentiation was honestly earned on the basis of merit. This perspective helps to explain the deference that was so marked among numerous craftworker-politicians towards many of Canada's economic and political leaders.[60] Yet the craftsworkers believed this advancement should be open to all, and the free, compulsory education for which they all campaigned would facilitate that kind of equal opportunity for all.[61] They demanded, in addition, that the Canadian civil service should be recruited only on the basis of merit, not patronage. A meritocratic perspective within labourism, then, fed the "producer" consciousness.

This strain within labourist ideology had taken shape in an earlier stage of Canadian capitalist development – one which was rapidly disappearing by the 1890s – in which the skilled worker had still been assured a respected place in industrial society, and in which community solidarity to promote industrial growth in single towns and cities had been a crucial dynamic.[62] As anachronistic as it seemed in the early twentieth-century context of continental and transnational corporations, this "producer" mentality remained an important element in the political thinking of those skilled workers who still held on in the nooks and crannies where their craft skills were still valued. At the same time, of course, it also contributed a strong dose of pride and dignity to working-class politics and thus strengthened the class-consciousness of the movement.

An idealized view of the state and a naive perspective on political economy, however, were complemented by an equally old-fashioned, but nonetheless potent, moral sensitivity, a concern to infuse political life with principles of natural justice (a concern, of course, that often contrasted with the dominant faith of nineteenth-century political economists). Labourist rhetoric in this period rippled with appeals to "fairness." The Greater Toronto Labor Party, for example, urged new members in 1917 to "dissociate … from the old party affiliations and play the game fair,"[63] and promises of a "square deal" were heard repeatedly. To be "unfair" seemed to mean to violate customary standards for living and working, especially the notions of social equality and honest toil as the basis of social worth. In all social and political relations, they expected citizens to treat each other equitably, honestly, and impartially, and there were frequent invocations of the "golden rule." We have already seen that there were "fair" and "unfair" ways of accumulating wealth – diligent labour versus parasitic draining of wealth produced by others' labour. From this perspective, exploitation was, fundamentally, immoral.

Similarly the labour movement had long ago encapsulated this notion of equity and justice in social relationships with the old adage, "a fair day's work for a fair day's wage."[64] Their experience, however, had taught them that political measures were necessary to buttress "fair" employment practices – like abolishing subcontracting and prison labour, stemming the tide of immigrants who flooded the labour market, and barring Asians or women and children from jobs, all to prevent unfair degradation of the craftsmen's work experience. A legislated minimum wage was also necessary to maintain fair wages for the unskilled. "Fair wage" clauses in government contracts would set the appropriate tone for all employment. Equity also demanded equal pay for men and women on the same jobs, although not a word was uttered about the relegation of women to low-wage job ghettos. Most particularly, it was to standards of natural justice that labourists appealed when they demanded a legally sanctioned eight-hour day: it was not fair to work men and women for excessive lengths of time and thus deprive them of a full life as citizens and family members. As the *Industrial Banner* argued in 1912:

> Long hours of labor have a tendency to stifle the intellect, to impair the energy and the vital organs of the body, and to reduce the opportunity for physical and mental improvement. The reduction of the hours of labor to eight out of each twenty-four, only six days per week, in all branches of industry is a stepping stone to a higher state of civilization.[65]

Both Alphonse Verville and Allan Studholme repeatedly introduced eight-hour-day bills in their respective houses in the decade before the war,[66] and the postwar Labour programs all highlighted this demand.

The same moral criteria also inspired the small package of welfare measures in the labourists' platforms. Society, they argued, had an obligation to maintain those who could not support themselves by their own labour – the old, the sick, the unemployed, and the single mothers, all of whom deserved pensions, and the victims of industrial accidents, who deserved compensation. They did not, however, campaign for broad programs of income subsidy for the poor in general.

They seemed, on the whole, too suspicious of state intervention into social life,[67] and preferred self-help and self-improvement through individual and cooperative activity on a voluntary basis – from temperance, to technical education, to trade unionism. Being an independent, self-disciplined, respectable worker meant leaning on no one for material support, least of all the state. Some British historians have detected in this attitude a hint of condescension and implicit criticism of the unskilled labouring poor.[68] In the same vein Canadian labour publications sometimes carried moralistic scorn for those among the less skilled who refused to defend their "manhood" through collective self-help.[69] Throughout the period under discussion, the moral fibre that labourists expected of all citizens included self-reliance, mutual assistance, and community responsibility.

III

Historians' discussions of labour's moral sensitivity invariably short circuit to the pervasive influence of the Christian faith, especially Methodism. Diverse writers have suggested that this religious influence was vitally important either in establishing the moral basis of working-class politics,[70] or in blunting class-consciousness and radicalism by encouraging notions of the "brotherhood of all men," along with an analytical fuzziness that contrasts with the "scientific" socialism of the European labour movement.[71] Both positions seem to have been overstated, though we know too little at this stage about the actual role of the church in Canadian workers' lives to be able to reach firm conclusions. For example, we do not yet know how many workers went to church, or how often, aside from the stray outcries of clergymen who feared for the souls of the godless masses.[72] We do have hints that, like so many other institutions by the early twentieth century, many Protestant congregations had distinct class colourations and therefore may have reinforced a sense of class identity rather than undermining it. Moreover, historians have often encountered the angry barbs thrown from labourist ranks at the official churches for their insensitivity to workers' needs.

We might well ask if religion was the only source of morality. Did appeals to the "brotherhood of man" descend from Jesus Christ or from Tom Paine? Were moral critiques drawn from the Bible or from the great Romantic critics of mainstream political economy, especially Thomas Carlyle, John Ruskin, and William Morris, whose impact on

British working-class leaders was so profound? Or were they picked up second-hand from England's irrepressible ethical socialist, Robert Blatchford, publisher of the *Clarion*, whose work was widely read in Canada?[73] Arguably, the small minority of clergymen who had joined the labourist cause by the early 1920s have drawn far more attention to the religious context than its real impact on working-class politics deserves.

Yet there is no denying that various labour leaders were church-goers and revealed an evangelic cast of mind, with their emphasis on such forms of personal moral regeneration as temperance.[74] Certainly religious imagery runs through much labourist rhetoric. The president of the Winnipeg Labor Party in 1899 believed the movement originated in "an upper room in Jerusalem,"[75] while twenty years later a "Working Woman" in Sydney declared: "We want a little bit of heaven on earth, just the same as the monied fellows … We want true religion; the brotherhood of man the world over."[76] About the same time a man from Temiskaming on the Ontario ILP speakers' circuit indicated his readiness to speak on "The Democracy of Moses."[77] Nor can we ignore the flourishing Labour Churches in western Canada after the war, though we might want to re-examine them in the light of Fred Tipping's claim that it "was a misnomer to call them churches. They held no religious dogma … Many, if not all of the sermons were economic in character rather than religious."[78]

The crucial question remains whether working-class leaders got their politics from Christianity, or turned to a common cultural reservoir to express their politics. After all, religious metaphors were the common coin of public discourse in Canada. Some of these women and men undoubtedly found their personal political inspiration in religion, but ultimately to see the social gospel as the driving force behind labourist politics seems to be putting the cart before the horse. First and foremost, what brought these men and women into this political movement was the material reality of their unsatisfactory experience as workers in capitalist society. For the devout among them, religious faith helped to validate and discipline their struggles for a better world. On the whole, however, the mode of thinking that appeared in the pages of the labour press and on the hustings in labourist campaigns reflected much more often the secular influence of working-class liberalism. Religious imagery might be invoked to inspire alternative social visions that little else in popular culture could summon up, but it was the doctrine of the "rights of man" that underlay the message.

Much of the confusion arises from the presence of working-class leaders on platforms with crusading churchmen and other "Progressives" or "New Liberals," like Samuel Chown or William Lyon Mackenzie King. For labourists there were evidently some practical advantages in these alliances for securing specific reforms, like a day of rest on Sunday, mothers' allowances, or favourable labour legislation. But the differences that set these workers apart from their middle-class allies were at least as striking as their areas of agreement. The strong libertarian, democratic basis of labourism contrasted sharply with the Progressives' elitist preference for professional expertise and their eagerness to meddle with the child-rearing practices or leisure pursuits of the working class.[79] Perhaps most important, labourists usually stood alone in defending what they considered the pivotal institution of working-class life, the trade union.[80] Whatever their willingness to cooperate, these workers were neither Progressives nor New Liberals.

There were other allies available, however. Alongside labourism, an alternative working-class ideology had been flourishing since the 1890s. Marxist socialism had appeared first in the Socialist Labor Party and then, after 1904, in the Socialist Party of Canada. The particular brand of Marxism that became dominant in Canada drew first on the rigid formulations of the American theoretician Daniel De Leon, and then on the SPC's own west-coast ideologues of "impossibilism." In the pages of the socialist press, party theoreticians poured scorn on economic struggles as a waste of time, and on street corners across the country, workers were treated to soap-box denunciations of the "labour fakirs" in the craft-union movement.[81]

Labourist craftworkers consequently developed a deep distrust and dislike for socialists and their doctrine. In an age of relentless challenges from ruthless corporate employers,[82] skilled workers placed defence of their workplace organizations above all else, and the ceaseless attacks from the left on these craft unions created a virtually unbridgeable gulf between socialism and labourism. The craft unionists' continental leader, Samuel Gompers, summed up their resentment in a letter to a Canadian correspondent: "It is not Socialism that we have been called on to combat, but the pernicious activity of Socialists who seem to have made it their particular mission in life to either dominate or destroy the trade unions. They defame and assassinate the character of men who dare to defend their convictions and who stand for the organization of trades unions." One of Canada's leading craft unionists, John Flett, who had supported socialism within the TLC a decade earlier, likewise lashed out in 1907: he and his fellow unionists objected "to being maligned by these men who call themselves Socialists and who shout their doctrines at us from every soap-box on the street corner."[83] British visitors like Keir Hardie and Ramsay MacDonald were astonished at the bitterness and mutual hostility between the two camps, and Winnipeg's Arthur Puttee lamented to them his inability to bring about the equivalent of the British labour alliance of 1900 known as the Labour Representation Committee.[84] Outside of the militant mining communities of Nova Scotia, Alberta, and British Columbia, therefore, Marxist socialism remained a marginal phenomenon in the Canadian working-class experience, largely owing to its doctrinal rejection of trade unionism.[85]

Something of a thaw appeared in socialist attitudes after a large group, including most of the central Canadian membership, split away to form the Social Democratic Party of Canada in 1911. In several Canadian cities labourists and Social Democrats worked out a degree of electoral cooperation just before the war, though not without some occasional backsliding into mutual recrimination.[86] Some of the main architects of this new socialist-labourist collaboration were an assortment of working-class radicals who were ethical socialists rather than hard-boiled Marxists, and who had had difficulty finding a natural home in Canadian political life since the turn of the century.

In Britain their counterparts worked through a socialist society known as the Independent Labor Party, whose chief spokesmen were Keir Hardie and Ramsay MacDonald. The British ILP propagated a brand of ethical socialism with a more transcendent vision (the "co-operative commonwealth") than the somewhat more narrow-minded labourists, but without the analytical rigour and hard-nosed scepticism of the Marxists.[87] In the 1890s Canada's ethical socialists had spawned numerous little societies and clubs, including the short-lived Winnipeg Labor Party, before consolidating in the Canadian Socialist League.[88] But intensifying industrial conflict had left these men and women on the sidelines, and after the decline of the CSL at the turn of the century, men like New Brunswick's H.H. Stewart, Toronto's James Simpson, Winnipeg's Fred Tipping, and, above all, the energetic William Ulric Cotton, publisher of the popular socialist paper *Cotton's Weekly*, had held an uncomfortable position on the right wing of the SPC. Eventually, however, they had found more room to manoeuvre in the SDP, especially in larger cities like Toronto and Winnipeg.[89]

During the war the sectarian spirit retreated still further, and many Social Democrats joined the labour parties, especially after the SDP was banned in 1918 and former party members began to part company over affiliation with the Third International. In Cape Breton the miners' radical leader J.B. McLachlan became an official and a candidate for Nova Scotia's ILP. In Montreal Marxists like Michael Buhay, Richard Kerrigan, and Albert Saint-Martin participated in the Quebec section of the Canadian Labor Party. In Toronto the veteran socialist Jimmy Simpson helped to weld together an ILP-SDP alliance whose mouthpiece was the *Industrial Banner.* In Hamilton the socialists' leading light, Fred Flatman, plunged into ILP work, eventually assuming the editorship of the local *Labor News* in 1918–19. In Winnipeg the alliance of socialists and labourists was perhaps most thoroughly developed, but even in British Columbia the original theorist of dogmatic "impossibilism," E.T. Kingsley, was active in the province's Federated Labor Party.[90]

The significance of this wartime development in the history of Canadian working-class politics should not be underestimated. For the first time on a national scale, working-class liberalism had linked up with elements of Marxist and ethical socialism in a dynamic alliance, which, under the old label of labourism, provided the ideological dimension of the unprecedented postwar upsurge of the Canadian working class. The presence of the radicals within the house of labour by the end of the war helped to sharpen the focus of the movement's analysis and to give the rhetoric a more visionary quality. The new Cape Breton ILP formally set its sights on "the working class ownership and democratic management of all the social means of wealth production and distribution at the earliest possible date." British Columbia's Federated Labor Party likewise promised "the collective ownership and democratic operation of the means of production," and the Manitoba party declared its goal was the "transformation of capitalist property into social property, with production for use instead of for profit." Even the cautious Ontario ILP incorporated a plank calling for "the democratic control of industry," and by the fall of 1919, was hailing the arrival of the "New Democracy."[91] In Halifax an aging socialist stirred a Labor Party meeting in 1919 with his cry that "this was no time for small things, but a time for old men to have dreams and young men to have visions."[92] The hard-core labourists were often tugged along by these more articulate socialists, but all working-class leaders were actually being pushed from below by the discontent of Canadian workers by the end of the war. Not only did the war experience generate dissatisfaction with soaring living costs, profiteering, and government mismanagement, as well as unleashing a powerful new rhetoric of democracy and public service; it also provided the economic security of full employment at high wages which gave workers a more secure base from which to launch their battles.[93] It was clearly the surging working-class confidence, aggressiveness, and self-consciousness which encouraged socialists and labourists to bury the hatchet and cooperate in building unified working-class parties.

By 1919, however, the strength of that alliance, and of the millennial quality of labourist politics, varied across the different regions of the country. The extent to which working-class politicians moved towards a thorough-going rejection of industrial capitalism seemed to depend on the political economy of the region. The most cautious could generally be found in Ontario's manufacturing centres. There a series of campaigns, stretching back over at least two decades had drawn them into some kind of working partnership with the industrialists who employed them. Most of the organized workers in manufacturing could be found in the consumer-goods industries, where intensifying competition had encouraged an alliance between bosses and workers in the form of the union label, first introduced in Canada in the 1890s. Most union-label employers expected the unions in their shops to promote the sale of the firms' clothing, cigars, beer, stoves, or whatever, to working-class shoppers; and the Ontario labour movement had obliged with local Union Label Leagues in several industrial centres.[94] In a similar fashion, many local craft-union leaders had been swept up into the municipal boosterism that characterized southern Ontario manufacturing towns in the early twentieth century. Promoting new industry meant expanding job prospects for workers in construction as well as in manufacturing. The most dramatic form of this sort of campaign was the "public power" movement, which united the labour movement and the local manufacturers across southwestern Ontario in a struggle against the huge private utilities corporations.[95]

The real cement of this alliance with manufacturers, however, was the tariff issue. Through their political mouthpiece, the Conservative Party, Ontario's industrialists repeatedly terrorized the province's workers with apocalyptic scenarios of unemployment and starvation if the Canadian market were opened to unfettered foreign competition. In virtually every federal election campaign, working-class voters were rallied to the defence of the region's industrial life against would-be agents of destruction, whether free-trade Liberals or militant farmers. Soon after the war, the Ontario ILP was thrown into turmoil over the tariff question. The Hamilton branches led a successful fight to overturn a free-trade resolution at a party convention in 1920.[96] Thus, however militant they may have become in asserting workers' rights in the political arena, these Ontario labourists were committed to helping their employers survive in the uncertain climate of the postwar economy. Some labour papers in the region even rallied to the Canadian Manufacturers' Association's "Buy Canadian" campaign, once again to help save workers' jobs. These concerns inevitably drove a wedge into the always fragile relations with the Ontario farmers' movement, which was opposed to tariff protection. In the Maritimes a somewhat similar pattern unfolded in many of the smaller, crisis-ridden communities of the region, with the added twist of regional discontent against a common enemy, central Canada. By the early 1920s some labourist leaders were drifting into the Maritime Rights movement, the political expression of hard-pressed small business operators of the east, while the labourist Halifax *Citizen* similarly boosted the cause of regional rights.[97]

This particular alignment of the "producing classes" that emerged in Ontario and parts of the Maritimes had few counterparts in the West. Manufacturing was an insignificant part of the economy west of the Lakehead, which was dominated by resource extraction and transportation industries. For the most part, owners of the means of production were either independent farmers or powerful corporations, which had no need for collaboration with their employees to strengthen or maintain their market position. The urban craftsworkers who promoted labourism in the West were preponderantly in the building trades and in the repair and maintenance departments of the transportation sector, notably Winnipeg's huge railway yards and related contract shops.[98] The bitter, often violent confrontations between workers and their corporate bosses in the mining, forest, and transportation industries helped to breed the most radical forms of socialism in the country – as they did in the coal-mining regions of Nova Scotia at roughly the same time.[99] Countervailing patterns of cooperation between capital and labour to defend industry, especially the Conservatives' tariff campaigns, never had the bite they had in southern Ontario. Moreover, the peculiarities of the western political economy also bred a bumptious movement of independent commodity producers against sundry monopolists and middlemen.[100] Dialogue between the western farmer and labour movements began before the war, and the cooperation of these "producers" helped to send William Irvine to Ottawa as

Calgary's Labour MP in 1921.[101] These regional contrasts clearly suggest that the "producer" ideology of the skilled workers was quite an ambivalent phenomenon.

Whatever the regional variations, however, labourism had collapsed as a significant force in Canadian politics by 1925. The waning membership of the various parties and their increasingly dismal performance at the polls reflected the final defeat of the craftworker in Canadian industry. Technological and managerial innovations had already transformed craft jobs or pushed craftworkers to the margins of the work world, and the severe economic slump of the early 1920s allowed employers to eliminate the last major strongholds of craft unionism outside printing and construction. The Winnipeg General Strike was only one of the most dramatic of numerous battles lost across the country.[102] The self-confidence and optimism which had swelled up in the ranks of Canadian workers during the war quickly turned to demoralization and defensiveness once the wartime prosperity disappeared. Labourist politics languished without the full union treasuries which had funded their efforts, and the aggressive class consciousness that had provided the momentum.

In this context of weakness, labourism underwent two important changes. The first was a disintegration of the socialist-labourist unity that had been so marked in the 1917–20 period. The policy of collaboration had caused uneasiness on both sides from the start and could not survive the disagreement over appropriate industrial tactics that brought the OBU into existence. More and more labourist craftworkers drew the line at industrial unionism and full-scale socialism. In Nova Scotia the ILP began to splinter in the early 1920s. In Montreal Gus Francq raged against the left both in his newspaper, *Le Monde Ouvrier*, and in a pamphlet, *Bolchevisme ou Syndicalisme, lequel?*, published in 1919. In Toronto and Hamilton the more cautious labourists drew back from the alliance with the socialists, and James Simpson was forced into a successful libel suit by his political foes in the Toronto labour movement. In Manitoba the Dominion Labor Party split, and the socialists formed a new Independent Labor Party. Probably most devastating in the long run was the withdrawal of TLC backing for the labourist movement by 1921, on the grounds that the socialist presence had become too strong.[103]

Across the country, moreover, most of the Marxist socialists were gravitating to the emerging North American Communist movement by 1920, and the old sectarian hostilities to labourism re-emerged.

The efforts of the new Workers' Party to rebuild the links after 1922 by using the federated structure of the Canadian Labor Party proved largely fruitless, since most of the labourist remnants had withdrawn by 1925.[104] The ethical socialists who remained – including Simpson and John Buckley in Toronto, Sam Lawrence in Hamilton, and Ernest Steeves in Vancouver – and the non-Communist Marxists, many of them Jewish Social Democrats, regrouped in the late 1920s and welcomed the creation of the CCF in 1933.[105] Many more of the old-style labourists, however, retained their scepticism about a "cooperative commonwealth" and held aloof from the new party throughout the 1930s. Labour MP Humphrey Mitchell, for example, Mackenzie King's future minister of labour, refused to join, as did his political organization, the Central Hamilton ILP.[106] Even Winnipeg's Labour MP A.A. Heaps was uneasy in the new social-democratic organization.[107] Only the upsurge of industrial unionism in the 1940s brought the CCF its coveted trade union base.[108]

The second change was more subtle but no less significant in the long term. For their electoral battles in the early 1920s, the beleaguered labourist craftworkers turned more often for candidates to the articulate middle classes who had drifted into their political camp towards the end of the war. In 1920 Manitoba's new Labour caucus included the former clergymen A.E. Smith and William Ivens, and the next year, among the Labour candidates for the federal house were the Reverends William Irvine of Calgary, J.S. Woodsworth of Winnipeg, and E.J. Etherington of Hamilton. Later in the 1920s, of course, middle-class men like M.J. Coldwell, Stanley Knowles, and T.C. Douglas would follow the same path into the labourist fold.[109] They brought a new emphasis on the spirit of the social gospel, but also, especially in the person of J.S. Woodsworth, a strong dose of Fabianism. This new national spokesman for the movement had been inspired by the British Labour Party's new program of 1918, a solidly Fabian document,[110] and his public utterances would place increasing emphasis on social planning – an element which had never been strong in pre-war labourism. In fact, he became the fragile link between the labourism of the past and the group of young Fabian intellectuals who formed the League for Social Reconstruction in 1932 and who made him their honorary president. Ultimately the Fabian emphasis meshed more easily with the highly centralized, more bureaucratic unionism that emerged under the CIO banner in the 1930s and 1940s, than it did with the remnants of craft unionism.

IV

Labourism, then, was a diffuse, unsystematic ideology, but one with clearly identifiable characteristics that set it apart from other currents on the Canadian left. Like agrarian populism, it levelled an anti-monopoly, "producerist" critique at capitalist society, but its program expressed the concerns of wage-earners, not independent commodity producers. Like middle-class Progressives, labourists sought a wide range of immediate social reforms, but put much greater emphasis on independent working-class self-help through trade unionism. Like their socialist contemporaries, the men and women of the labourist movement bristled with class consciousness, but generally had not accepted the need for the fundamental transformation of capitalist society that both the Marxists and the ethical socialists demanded. And like the social democrats of the CCF, the labourists envisaged an orderly, gradualist process of social and political change; yet they shied away from a greatly expanded economic role for the state and never proposed the centralized planning role projected by later Fabian intellectuals. Labourism remained, for the most part, the direct heir of nineteenth-century working-class liberalism.

However inchoate, the labourists shared a loose consensus about what a properly constructed society ought to look like. It was a vision of a decentralized society of small-scale production, where social and political power were widely diffused, where citizens were not far separated in social status, were treated equally under the law, and enjoyed equal opportunities, and where self-reliance, voluntary association, and mutual assistance would be more important than state coercion. For an anonymous proletarian poet in 1905, all these ingredients went into "The Workman's Ideal":

> What does the workman want? He wants his own,
> His honest share of what his hands produce;
> He craves no charity and begs no bone
> But only asks for freedom from abuse.
>
> What does the workman want? He wants good will,
> But not at the cost of justice and of life;
> Not if it means that he must need be still
> While others rob his babies and his wife.

What does the workman want? He wants fair play
And equal rights and equal chance for all
And privilege for none to steal and slay
Or force his weaker brother to the wall.

What does the workman want? He wants the right
Against the vain traditions of the law,
Against the sophistries of age and might,
Against religion's oft mistaken awe.

The workman wants the reign of common sense;
He wants the true democracy of man.
Nor any patronage nor all pretense
Will hold him long to any other plan.

The common welfare is the workman's goal,
The common use of all the common wealth
The common rights of every common soul
And common access to the springs of health.

And every man a workman by and by,
His own employer, his own king and priest,
Nor any rich or poor, nor low or high,
When all the world's monopolies have ceased.[111]

Labourism was the political expression of skilled men and women who worked with their hands and thus made "honest toil" the touchstone of their value system; it was also the politics of people who cherished the personal freedoms that the great struggles for popular democracy in the British political system had brought. In its narrowest, probably most common form, this meant the freedom to be left alone. Certainly it involved a suspicion of too much intervention into their lives by either their employers or the state. In its more aggressive manifestations, however, freedom became the right to full participation in all aspects of social and political life. The bitterness at the exclusion of the working class from this full life prompted labourists' most militant, class-conscious flourishes. Despite the individualistic thrust of the liberal heritage, they wanted to raise the whole working class to full equality. In contrast to contemporary and latter-day denunciations of their conservatism and opportunism, the record of labourist political activity in Canada reveals men and women who were principled, on the whole, but all too often simply naive. Their outlook on social and economic relations, in particular, was rooted in a world which was fast disappearing by the early twentieth century. Yet it was precisely their outrage at how the emerging monopoly capitalist society violated their more old-fashioned sensibilities that gave their politics its cutting edge. The war brought the craftworkers' outrage to its sharpest point. Bitter industrial conflict and political chicanery pushed labourism as far to the left as it could go. The new alliance with socialism that emerged during the war gave labourist politics a clearer focus and helped to crystallize the admittedly vague alternative vision of society that had always lain buried in the ideological fuzziness. If these working-class politicians were not always fundamentally at odds with capitalism, they were certainly opposed to the version of it that was reshaping Canadian society. This was not a revolutionary challenge, but it was a resistance movement.

The brake on any further radicalization of labourism was precisely the force which set this brand of politics in motion – an unswerving commitment to craft unionism. In 1919, just as at the turn of the century, labourists faced a new left-wing attack on their most highly prized class institutions, this time from the industrial unionists in the OBU. They quickly recoiled from their wartime alliance. Gradualism and restraint surfaced again, and the weakness of labourist ideology and practice as a tool for the wider working class became apparent. The halting, lacklustre performance of the labourists in the Farmer-Labour government – the only situation where they had substantial legislative power – revealed the deep ambiguities in their thinking, particularly the tension between asserting working-class interests and governing in the interest of all classes. The British Labour Party would reveal the same problem during its terms in office.[112]

For those in search of the articulate, visionary proletarian voices of the past, the labourists will almost inevitably appear muddled, uninspiring, often annoyingly narrow-minded, at least in comparison with many of their working-class counterparts in the socialist movement, who usually exhibited remarkable erudition, analytical skills, and eloquence. Yet, to be fair, we should recognize a salient feature of Canadian labourism. As a movement it reasserted a faith in radical democracy in the face of political corruption and manipulation and, perhaps more importantly, in the face of new elitist theories of the state that were modelled on the private corporation.[113] This rigorously democratic ethos, along with the decentralized, community-based focus and the more limited use of the state to right social wrongs, was eclipsed by subsequent movements on the Canadian left, both Fabian and Communist.[114] Without casting any heroic mantle over these working-class politicians who have settled into such ill-deserved historical obscurity, we owe them some respect for trying to keep alive the legacy of "liberty, equality, and fraternity."

Notes

1 Most often labourism appears in hasty, often inaccurate first chapters of books on the Co-operative Commonwealth Federation, or as faint background to the biographies of early CCF leaders like J.S. Woodsworth or William Irvine; e.g., Kenneth McNaught, *A Prophet in Politics: A Biography of J.S. Woodsworth* (Toronto: University of Toronto Press 1959); Anthony Mardiros, *William Irvine: The Life of a Prairie Radical* (Toronto: James Lorimer 1979). Norman Penner totally ignores labourism in Canada in *The Canadian Left: A Critical Analysis* (Scarborough: Prentice-Hall 1977). The only sustained treatment of the movement nationally remains Martin Robin's book-length study of labour radicalism before 1930, *Radical Politics and Canadian Labour, 1880–1930* (Kingston: Industrial Relations Centre, Queen's University 1968), which is heavy on institutional development at the provincial and federal levels, but quite light on analysis of social and ideological developments.

2 W. Craig Heron, "Working-Class Hamilton, 1895–1930" (PhD dissertation, Dalhousie University 1981), 586–713; Michael J. Piva, "The Toronto District Labour Council and Independent Political Action: Factionalism and Frustration, 1900–1921," *L/LT* 4 (1979), 119; Jacques Rouillard, "L'action politique ouvrière, 1899–1915," in Fernand Dumont et al., eds., *Idéologies au Canada français, 1900–1929* (Quebec: Presses de l'Université Laval 1974), 267–312; Robert Babcock, "Labour, Socialism, and Reform Politics in Portland (Me.) and Saint John (N.B.), 1895–1914" (paper presented to the Canadian Historical Association Meeting, 1980), 48. Winnipeg seems to have been something of an exception; that city's ILP did have a minority of middle-class members in the decade before the war. A. Ross McCormack, *Reformers, Rebels, and Revolutionaries: The Western Canadian Radical Movement, 1899–1919* (Toronto: University of Toronto Press 1977), 89–92; Allen Mills, "Single Tax, Socialism, and the Independent Labour Party of Manitoba: The Political Ideas of F.J. Dixon and S.J. Farmer," *L/LT* 5 (1980), 38–9.

3 Such a typology of labour activists inevitably needs some qualification. By no means all craftsworkers participated in this movement: for the aloofness of bricklayers and certain waterfront crafts, see Wayne Roberts, "Artisans, Aristocrats, and Handymen: Politics and Trade Unionism among Toronto Skilled Building Trades Workers, 1896–1914," *L/LT* 1 (1976), 111–13; Ian McKay, "Class Struggle and Mercantile Capitalism: Craftsmen and Labourers on the Halifax Waterfront, 1850–1902," in Rosemary Ommer and Gerald Panting, eds., *Working Men Who Got Wet* (St John's: Maritime History Group, Memorial University 1980), 287–320. Even more important, by the First World War, labourist ranks included some important groups of semi-skilled workers, like street railwaymen and longshoremen. What united them all, however, was some degree of workplace autonomy: less skilled workers had joined the craft union movement after winning their own forms of job control through union regulation. In any case, skilled workers certainly seem to have remained numerically predominant in the movement and most influential in shaping and articulating its ideology.

4 See, for example, Ross McKibbon, *The Evolution of the Labour Party, 1910–1924* (London: Oxford University Press 1974).

5 Le Parti ouvrier de Montréal, however, allowed union affiliation after 1908.

6 Robin, *Radical Politics*, 48–53; Robert H. Babcock, *Gompers in Canada: A Study in American Continentalism before the First World War* (Toronto: University of Toronto Press 1974), 70–1; A.R. McCormack, "Arthur Puttee and the Liberal Party: 1899–1904," *CHR* 51, no. 2 (June 1970), 141–63; Rouillard, "Action politique ouvrière," 276–81, 291–4.

7 Heron, "Working-Class Hamilton," 606–19; Charles Allen Seager, "A Proletariat in Wild Rose Country: The Alberta Coal Miners, 1905–1945" (PhD dissertation, York University 1981), 229–30.

8 Seager, "Proletariat in Wild Rose Country," 231–4; McCormack, *Reformers, Rebels, and Revolutionaries*, 28–32, 62–4.

9 Wayne Roberts, "Studies in the Toronto Labour Movement, 1896–1914" (PhD dissertation, University of Toronto 1978), 473–508; Rouillard, "Action politique ouvrière," 283; Babcock, "Labour, Socialism, and Reform Politics," 14–22; Seager, "Proletariat in Wild Rose Country," 202–71; Heron, "Working-Class Hamilton," 491–584.

10 Heron, "Working-Class Hamilton," 493–508; Michael J. Piva, "Workers and Tories: The Collapse of the Conservative Party in Urban Ontario, 1908–19, *UHR* 3–76 (1977), 23–9.

11 Canada, Department of Labour, *Labour Organization in Canada* (Ottawa: King's Printer), 1917–25. For detailed studies of the postwar municipal

success, see David Frank, "Company Town/Labour Town: Local Government in the Cape Breton Coal Towns, 1917–1926," *HS/SH* 27 (1981), 177–96; J.E. Rea, "The Politics of Class: Winnipeg City Council, 1919–45," in Carl Berger and Ramsay Cook, eds., *The West and the Nation: Essays in Honour of W.L. Morton* (Toronto: McClelland and Stewart 1976), 232–49; Geoffrey Ewen, "Labour Political Action in Quebec, 1917–1929" (unpublished paper, York University 1983); Heron, "Working-Class Hamilton," 638–97.

12 Paul MacEwan, *Miners and Steelworkers: Labour in Cape Breton* (Toronto: Samuel Stevens Hakkert 1976), 18; Anthony MacKenzie, "The Farmer-Labor Party in Nova Scotia" (MA thesis, Dalhousie University 1969), 48–50; Rouillard, "Action politique ouvrière," 277–83; Piva, "Factionalism and Frustration," 120; Heron, "Working-Class Hamilton," 588–628; McCormack, *Reformers, Rebels, and Revolutionaries*, 77–97; Robin, *Radical Politics*, 62–91, 104–18.

13 Star Rosenthal, "Union Maids: Organized Women Workers in Vancouver, 1900–1915," *BC Studies* 41 (1979), 36–55; Veronica Strong-Boag, "The Girl of the New Day: Canadian Working Women in the 1920s," *L/LT* 4 (1979), 153; Norman Penner, ed., *Winnipeg 1919: The Strikers' Own History of the Winnipeg General Strike* (Toronto: James Lorimer 1973), 74; Heron, "Working-Class Hamilton," 459–70.

14 Russell Hann, et al., comps., *Primary Sources in Canadian Working-Class History, 1860–1930* (Kitchener: Dumont Press 1973), 109–10.

15 Robin, *Radical Politics*, 79–91; Babcock, *Gompers in Canada*, 155–82.

16 Robin, *Radical Politics*, 119–59; David Frank, "The Cape Breton Coal Miners, 1917–1926" (PhD dissertation, Dalhousie University 1979), 301–5; MacKenzie, "Farmer Labor Party"; D. James Naylor, "The Independent Labor Party in Ontario" (unpublished paper, York University 1982); Alfred Charpentier, "Le mouvement politique ouvrier de Montréal (1883–1929)," in Femand Harvey, ed., *Aspects historiques du mouvement ouvrier au Québec* (Quebec: Boréal Express 1973), 162–4; McCormack, *Reformers, Rebels, and Revolutionaries*, 143; McNaught, *Prophet in Politics*, 91–6; Mardiros, *Irvine*, 59–62, 78; Dorothy G. Steeves, *The Compassionate Rebel, Ernest Winch and the Growth of Socialism in Western Canada* (Vancouver: J.J. Douglas 1977), 37.

17 The centre of action of Canadian labour before the 1930s was not in the TLC, as so many writers have assumed, but in the local trades councils, where the common interests of the working class were promoted on a week-to-week basis. Recognizing this fact, the One Big Union made city labour councils its basic structural units. David J. Bercuson, *Fools and Wise*

Men: The Rise and Fall of the One Big Union (Toronto: McGraw-Hill Ryerson 1978), 178.

18 Gregory S. Kealey, *Toronto Workers Respond to Industrial Capitalism, 1867–1892* (Toronto: University of Toronto Press 1980), 175–253; Sharon Reilly, "The Provincial Workmen's Association of Nova Scotia, 1879–1898" (MA thesis, Dalhousie University 1979), 51–106; Paul Phillips, *No Power Greater: A Century of Labour in British Columbia* (Vancouver: BC Federation of Labour and Boag Foundation 1967), 1–84; Stuart Marshall Jamieson, *Times of Trouble: Labour Unrest and Industrial Conflict in Canada, 1900–66* (Ottawa: Queen's Printer 1968), 62–191; Craig Heron and Bryan D. Palmer, "Through the Prism of the Strike: Industrial Conflict in Southern Ontario, 1901–14," *CHR* 58 (1977), 423–58; MacEwan, *Miners and Steelworkers*, 9–90; Ian McKay, "Strikes in the Maritimes, 1901–1914" (unpublished paper, Dalhousie University 1980).

19 Ian Turner, *Industrial Labour and Politics: The Labour Movement in Eastern Australia, 1900–1921* (Canberra: Cambridge University Press 1965), 20.

20 Robin, *Radical Politics*, 294; Paul Phillips, "Power Politics: Municipal Affairs and Seymour James Farmer, 1909–1924," in A.R. McCormack and Ian Macpherson, eds., *Cities in the West: Papers of the Western Canada Urban History Conference* (Ottawa: National Museums of Canada 1975), 160.

21 Kealey, *Toronto Workers*, 53–97; Bryan D. Palmer, *A Culture in Conflict: Skilled Workers and Industrial Capitalism in Hamilton, Ontario, 1860–1914* (Montreal and Kingston: McGill-Queen's University Press 1979), 71–96; Roberts, "Toronto Labour Movement"; Frank, "Cape Breton Coal Miners"; Ian McKay, "Workers' Control in Springhill, 1882–1927" (paper presented to the Canadian Historical Association Meeting, 1981); Craig Heron, "The Crisis of the Craftsman: Hamilton Metal Workers in the Early Twentieth Century," *L/LT* 6 (1980), 7–48.

22 E.P. Thompson, *The Making of the English Working Class* (Harmondsworth: Penguin 1968); L.J. Prothero, *Artisans and Politics in Early Nineteenth Century London: John Gast and His Times* (London: Dawson 1979); Geoffrey Crossick, *An Artisanal Elite in Victorian Society: Kentish London, 1840–1880* (London: Croom Helm 1978), 199–242; John Vincent, *The Formation of the Liberal Party, 1857–1868* (London: Constable 1966), 76–82; Royden Harrison, *Before the Socialists: Studies in Labour and Politics, 1861–1881* (London: Routledge and Kegan Paul 1965); Trygve R. Tholfson, *Working Class Radicalism in Mid-Victorian England* (London: Croom Helm 1977).

23 Eric Foner, *Free Soil, Free Labor, Free Men: The Ideology of the Republican Party Before the Civil War* (New York: Oxford University Press 1970); David

Montgomery, *Beyond Equality: Labor and the Radical Republicans, 1862–1872* (New York: Knopf 1967); Alan Dawley, *Class and Community: The Industrial Revolution in Lynn* (Cambridge, MA: Harvard University Press 1976), 194–219; Leon Fink, *Workingmen's Democracy: The Knights of Labor and American Politics* (Urbana: University of Illinois Press 1983), 3–17.

24 Frank Underhill ignored the working-class presence in his survey of the Victorian Liberal Party in Canada; see *In Search of Canadian Liberalism* (Toronto: Macmillan 1960), 3–20. The social base of the Canadian Liberal Party at the end of the nineteenth century has never been systematically analysed, but can be pieced together from various secondary sources. See, for example, Oscar Douglas Skelton, *Life and Letters of Sir Wilfrid Laurier* (abridged edition, 2 vols., Toronto: McClelland and Stewart 1965), Vol. 2, 1–27; Ross Harkness, *J.E. Atkinson of the Star* (Toronto: University of Toronto Press 1963); H. Blair Neatby, *Laurier and a Liberal Quebec: A Study in Political Management* (Toronto: McClelland and Stewart 1973); Ramsay Cook, *The Politics of John W. Dafoe and the Free Press* (Toronto: University of Toronto Press 1963); Paul Douglas Stevens, "Laurier and the Liberal Party in Ontario, 1887–1911" (PhD dissertation, University of Toronto 1966), 1–191; Brian P.N . Beaven, "A Last Hurrah: Studies in Liberal Party Development and Ideology in Ontario, 1878–1893" (PhD dissertation, University of Toronto 1981).

25 See R.V. Clements, "British Trade Unions and Popular Political Economy, 1850–75," *Economic History Review*, 2nd series, 14 (1961), 93–104.

26 Kealey, *Toronto Workers*, 124–53, 216–36, 254–73; Reilly, "Provincial Workmen's Association," 72–85; Babcock, *Gompers in Canada*, 157; McCormack, "Puttee," 156–7. This emphasis on Liberal craft-union leaders is not meant to diminish the importance of working-class Conservatives in the Canadian labour movement, especially in the 1870s (see Kealey, *Toronto Workers*, 124–71). But a willingness to work within the Tory traditions of elitism, deference, and loyalism set these men apart ideologically from working-class liberals. They also seem to have been numerically less important by the turn of the century.

27 In Nova Scotia the dominant Lib-Lab figure, Robert Drummond, was rewarded with a seat in the province's appointed legislative council. Reilly, "Provincial Workmen's Association."

28 Ibid., 87; Gregory S. Kealey and Bryan D. Palmer, *Dreaming of What Might Be: The Knights of Labor in Ontario, 1880–1900* (Cambridge: Cambridge University Press 1982), 204–47; Phillips, *No Power Greater*, 13–15.

29 Trades and Labor Congress of Canada, *Proceedings* (Ottawa), 1900–1906; MacEwan, *Miners and Steelworkers*, 17–18; McCormack, *Reformers, Rebels,*

and Revolutionaries, 77–84; Robin, *Radical Politics*, 49–61; Rouillard, "Action politique ouvrière," 269–75; Roberts, "Toronto Labour Movement," 355–7; Gene Howard Homel, "James Simpson and the Origins of Canadian Social Democracy" (PhD dissertation, University of Toronto 1978), 195–6; Heron, "Working-Class Hamilton," 594–600.

30 Quoted in Rouillard, "Action politique ouvrière," 272; Babcock, "Labour, Socialism, and Reform Politics," 46.

31 McCormack, *Reformers, Rebels, and Revolutionaries*, 90–6. After the final collapse of the movement in the 1920s, several former labourist politicians found their way back into the left wing of official Liberalism, including men like northern Ontario's Peter Heenan and Arthur Roebuck, former ILP members of the Ontario legislatures who ended up in Liberal cabinets. See H. Blair Neatby, *William Lyon Mackenzie King, 1924–1932: The Lonely Heights* (Toronto: University of Toronto Press 1963), 173; Neil McKenty, *Mitch Hepburn* (Toronto: McClelland and Stewart 1967), 60.

32 Montreal's leading labourist spokesman, Gustave Francq, even argued in 1916 that the Labor Party's programme was simply the old Liberal Party program long-since abandoned. Geoffrey Ewen, "The Ideas of Gustave Francq as Expressed in *Le Monde Ouvrier / The Labour World*" (MA thesis, University of Ottawa 1981), 96–7.

33 LAC, William Lyon Mackenzie King Papers, Vol. 11, p. 9558 (Studholme to King, 6 October 1908).

34 Crossick, *Artisan Elite*, 240.

35 Quoted in MacKenzie, "Farmer-Labor Party," 68.

36 See Thompson, *Making*, 84–203; Prothero, *Artisans and Politics*, 73–155, 267–327; Harrison, *Before the Socialists*, 137–209.

37 Before the war Allan Studholme was Ontario's foremost champion of women's right to vote and hold office. Heron, "Working-Class Hamilton," 613–14.

38 The platforms of the various Labour parties can be found in: MacEwan, *Miners and Steelworkers*, 18; MacKenzie, "Farmer-Labor Party," 54, 69; Babcock, "Labour, Socialism, and Reform Politics," 48; Charpentier, "Mouvement politique ouvrier," 165–7; Rouillard, "Action politique ouvrière, " 288–96; Piva, "Factionalism and Frustration"; Naylor, "Independent Labor Party," 11–12; Heron, "Working-Class Hamilton," 594–697; McCormack, *Reformers, Rebels, and Revolutionaries*, 77–97; Mardiros, *Irvine*, 59–60; *Labour Organization in Canada, 1919–21*.

39 MacKenzie, "Farmer-Labor Party," 72; Frank, "Cape Breton Coal Miners," 301–5; Heron, "Working-Class Hamilton," 638–41; Robin, *Radical Politics*, 119–77.

40 *Labor News* (Hamilton) (hereafter *LN*), 10 October 1919.
41 Labour Canada Library, Provincial Workmen's Association, "Minutes of Proceedings and Other Documents," 1 (1879–89), April 1886, 107.
42 *International Molders' Journal* 49 (1913), 1048 (emphasis added); Heron, "Working-Class Hamilton," 639–40; Robin, *Radical Politics*, 119–37. By the same logic the Hamilton Women's ILP decided they had a right to be involved in the National Council of Women.
43 *LN*, 10 October 1919.
44 See Irvine's *The Farmers in Politics* (Toronto: McClelland and Stewart 1976 [1920]); Mardiros, *Irvine*; C.B. Macpherson, *Democracy in Alberta: Social Credit and the Party System* (Toronto: University of Toronto Press 1962). The similarities to agrarian populist ideology should not blind us to important differences. As Macpherson has argued, farmers were independent commodity producers with a limited understanding of the world of wage-earners. This fundamental difference would make relations between the two movements difficult in most parts of the country, as workers and farmers split over such key issues as the eight-hour day and the tariff.
45 Mardiros, *Irvine*, 109–10; MacKenzie, "Farmer-Labor Party," 27–32, 77–108; Naylor, "Independent Labor Party," 38; Heron, "Working-Class Hamilton," 645–6.
46 *LN*, 13 November 1914, 3 January 1919.
47 Quoted in Ewen, "Francq," 103.
48 Quoted in Frank, "Cape Breton Coal Miners," 355.
49 Naylor, "Independent Labor Party," 60; Robin, *Radical Politics*, 219–36.
50 *Herald* (Hamilton), 16 November 1914.
51 Ibid., 6 December 1911.
52 Roberts, "Toronto Labour Movement."
53 *LN*, 30 June 1916.
54 McCormack, *Reformers, Rebels, and Revolutionaries*, 53–76.
55 See John Saville, "The Ideology of Labourism," in Robert Benewick, R.N. Berki, and Bhikhu Parekh, eds., *Knowledge and Belief in Politics: The Problem of Ideology* (London: Allen and Unwin 1973), 219–22; E.P. Thompson, "The Peculiarities of the English," *Socialist Register*, 1965, 343–4.
56 Ramsay Cook, "Henry George and the Poverty of Canadian Progress," *HP* 1977, 142–57; James K. Chapman, "Henry Harvey Stuart (1873–1952): New Brunswick Reformer," *Acadiensis* 5 (1972), 92–4; Mills, "Dixon and Farmer"; Heron, "Working-Class Hamilton," 678–9; *Labour Organization in Canada*, 1919, 57; 1920, 52–4; 1921, 51.
57 Rouillard, "Action politique ouvrière," 294–5; Heron, "Working-Class Hamilton," 678–9.

58 *Industrial Banner* (hereafter *IB*), August 1909; see also Rouillard, "Action politique ouvrière," 295–7.
59 *IB*, October 1904; *Herald* (Hamilton), 3 April 1912.
60 In 1912, for example, Allan Studholme made a crucial distinction between "two kinds of honor" in criticizing his fellow Hamilton MLA, the wealthy industrialist John S. Hendrie. "The political honor was to beat the other fellow at his game at any hazard, with cards up his sleeve and the dice loaded," he said. "The business honor of the honorable gentleman was unquestioned." *LN*, 22 March 1912.
61 Leon Fink has correctly noted that this individualistic streak lacked the aggressive competitiveness of "the possessive individualism that anchored the world of the workers' better-off neighbours." *Workingmen's Democracy*, 12.
62 See, in particular, T.W. Acheson, "The Social Origins of Canadian Industrialism: A Study in the Structure of Entrepreneurship" (PhD dissertation, University of Toronto 1971). On the early forms of the "producer" ideology, see Lillian Gates, "The Decided Policy of William Lyon Mackenzie," *CHR* 40, no. 3 (September 1959), 185–208; Palmer, *Culture in Conflict*, 97–122; Kealey, *Toronto Workers*, 154–71.
63 Quoted in Naylor, "Independent Labor Party."
64 For an extended discussion of the implications of this phrase, see Richard Hyman and Ian Brough, *Social Values and Industrial Relations: A Study in Fairness and Equality* (Oxford: Blackwell 1975).
65 *IB*, September 1912.
66 Heron, "Working-Class Hamilton," 610; Rouillard, "Action politique ouvrière," 292–4.
67 In this sense, the legacy of Tom Paine persisted. See Prothero, *Artisans and Politics*, 29; Thompson, *Making*, 100–2; and, from another perspective, Henry Pelling, *Popular Politics and Society in Late Victorian Britain* (London: Macmillan 1968), 1–18, 61–81. The influence of Gompersite unionism was equally strong, however; see William M. Dick, *Labor and Socialism in America: The Gompers Era* (Port Washington: Kennikat Press 1972).
68 Prothero, *Artisans and Politics*, 328–32; Fred Reid, *Keir Hardie: The Making of a Socialist* (London: Croom Helm 1978), 177–84.
69 See, for example, Heron, "Crisis of Craftsman," 44.
70 Most particularly, Richard Allen, *The Social Passion: Religion and Social Reform in Canada, 1914–28* (Toronto: University of Toronto Press 1973); see also Nelson Wiseman, "An Historical Note on Religion and Parties on the Prairies," *JCS* 16 (1981), 109–12.

71 Most outlandishly, Tom Nairn, "The English Working Class," in Robin Blackburn, ed., *Ideology in Social Science: Readings in Critical Social Theory* (London: Fontana 1972) 187–206.

72 The 1901 Census of Canada gives a rare chance to compare stated religious affiliation and church attendance. Christopher Armstrong and H.V. Nelles used these statistics to calculate that within Toronto's five largest religious faiths, only a third of the adherents were church members, and that the Protestants had much lower rates of membership than the Roman Catholics. See *The Revenge of the Methodist Bicycle Company: Sunday Streetcars and Municipal Reform in Toronto, 1883–1897* (Toronto: Peter Martin Associates 1977), 183. On religion in general, see Eric Hobsbawm, "Religion and the Rise of Socialism," *Marxist Perspectives* 1 (1978), 14–33.

73 Stuart Macintyre, *A Proletarian Science: Marxism in Britain, 1917–1933* (Cambridge: Cambridge University Press 1980), 50; Stanley Pierson, *British Socialists: The Journey from Fantasy to Politics* (Cambridge: Harvard University Press 1979); McCormack, *Reformers, Rebels, and Revolutionaries*, 78; A. Ross McCormack, "British Working-Class Immigrants and Canadian Radicalism: The Case of Arthur Puttee," *CES* 10 (1978), 26–7.

74 Allen, *Social Passion*, 13–15, 82–103; Fred Tipping, "Religion and the Making of a Labour Leader," in Richard Allen, ed., *The Social Gospel in Canada* (Ottawa: National Museums of Canada 1975), 63–5; McCormack, "British Working-Class Immigrants," 22–37; Heron, "Working Class Hamilton," 615–18.

75 Quoted in McCormack, "Puttee," 151.

76 *Canadian Labor Leader* (Sydney), 13 April 1918.

77 Naylor, "Independent Labor Party," 19–20. For an extended discussion of this sort of imagery, see Herbert G. Gutman, "Protestantism and the American Labor Movement: The Christian Spirit in the Gilded Age," in Gutman, *Work, Culture, and Society in Industrializing America: Essays in American Working Class and Social History* (New York: Knopf 1977), 79–117.

78 Tipping, "Religion," 80. The ex-clergymen who had joined the movement were no longer seen as religious figures either. See McNaught, *Prophet in Politics*, 158–9; Mardiros, *Irvine*, 76–7; Reginald Whitaker, "Introduction," to Irvine, *Farmers in Politics* (1976 ed.), xvi.

79 For a sampling of these elitist schemes of social engineering, see Paul Rutherford, ed., *Saving the Canadian City: The First Phase, 1880–1920* (Toronto: University of Toronto Press 1974).

80 See, for example, Reginald Whitaker, "The Liberal Corporatist Ideas of Mackenzie King," *L/LT* 2 (1977), 153–8.

81 See McCormack, *Reformers, Rebels, and Revolutionaries*, 53–76; Robin, *Radical Politics*, 44–61, 79–103; Penner, *Canadian Left*, 40–76; Carlos Schwantes, *Radical Heritage: Labor, Socialism, and Reform in Washington and British Columbia, 1885-1917* (Seattle: University of Washington Press 1979), 103–83; George T. Troop, "Socialism in Canada" (MA thesis, McGill University 1922), 10–42; David Frank and Nolan Reilly, "The Emergence of the Socialist Movement in the Maritimes, 1899–1916," *L/LT* 4 (1979), 84–114; Roberts, "Toronto Labour Movement," 357–64; Heron, "Working-Class Hamilton," 649–56.

82 It is worth noting that British and European craftworkers, who tended on the whole to have better relations with socialists, were not encountering the same systematic, hostile attacks from capitalists that were shattering the North American trade union movement.

83 Quoted in Babcock, *Gompers in Canada*, 160, 172. Babcock lays too much blame for the socialist-labourist strife at the door of Sam Gompers and his AFL henchmen. Canadian craft unionists developed their own sensitivity to attacks on their industrial organizations without waiting for orders from Washington.

84 McCormack, "British Working-Class Immigrants," 31–3.

85 Paradoxically, however, several militant socialists played important roles as individuals in the trade union movement. See Homel, "Simpson"; Roberts, "Toronto Labour Movement"; Babcock, "Labour, Socialism, and Reform Politics," 39–41; McCormack, *Reformers, Rebels, and Revolutionaries*, 56–7.

86 Roberts, "Toronto Labour Movement," 417–25; Piva, "Factionalism and Frustration," 123–4; McCormack, *Reformers, Rebels, and Revolutionaries*, 92–7.

87 Henry Pelling, *The Origins of the Labour Party, 1880–1900* (Oxford: Clarendon Press 1965), 99–168; Stephen Yeo, "A New Life: The Religion of Socialism in Britain, 1883–1896," *HW* 4 (1977), 5–56.

88 Gene Howard Homel, "'Fading Beams of the Nineteenth Century': Radicalism and Early Socialism in Canada's 1890s," *L/LT* 5 (1980), 7–32; Roberts, "Toronto Labour Movement," 333–40; McCormack, *Reformers, Rebels, and Revolutionaries*, 77–84; Heron, "Working-Class Hamilton," 588–93; Frank and Reilly, "Socialist Movement," 87; Chapman, "Stewart," 84–5; Gerald Henry Allabee, "New Brunswick Prophets of Radicalism: 1890–1914" (MA thesis, University of New Brunswick 1972), 13–50.

89 Homel, "Simpson," 565–714; McCormack, *Reformers, Rebels, and Revolutionaries*; Tipping, "Religion," 74–7; Leo Heaps, *The Rebel in the House: The Life and Times of A.A. Heaps, M P* (London: Niccolo 1970), 1–7; Edward M. Penton, "The Ideas of William Cotton: A Marxist View of Canadian Society (1908–14)" (MA thesis, University of Ottawa 1978).

90 Frank, "Cape Breton Coal Miners, " 301–5; MacKenzie, "Farmer-Labor Party," 33–76; Fred Thompson, "A Rebel Voice: Fred Thompson Remembers Halifax, 1919–20," *This Magazine* 12 (1978), 8; Charpentier, "Mouvement politique ouvrier," 161–5; Ewen, "Labour Political Action," 14–20; Naylor, "Independent Labor Party"; Heron, "Working-Class Hamilton," 659–66; McCormack, *Reformers, Rebels, and Revolutionaries*, 143; Steeves, *Compassionate Rebel*, 37; McNaught, *Prophet in Politics*, 119–37; Ian Angus, *Canadian Bolsheviks: The Early Years of the Communist Party of Canada* (Montreal: Vanguard 1981), 3–26; Elizabeth Ann Taraska, "The Calgary Craft Union Movement" (MA thesis, University of Calgary 1975), 56.

91 Frank, "Cape Breton Coal Miners," 304–5; Phillips, *No Power Greater*, 71; *Labour Organization in Canada*, 1919, 51; 1920, 52.

92 Thompson, "Rebel Voice," 8.

93 Bercuson, *Fools and Wise Men*, 1–86; McCormack, *Reformers, Rebels, and Revolutionaries*, 118–64; Robin, *Radical Politics*, 619–53; Heron, "Working-Class Hamilton," 638–49.

94 Roberts, "Toronto Labour Movement"; Heron, "Working-Class Hamilton," 87–9.

95 See H.V. Nelles, *The Politics of Development: Forests, Mines, and Hydro-Electric Power in Ontario, 1849–1941* (Toronto: Macmillan 1974), 215–306; Heron, "Working-Class Hamilton," 536–44.

96 Heron, "Working-Class Hamilton," 527–36; Paul Craven and Tom Traves, "The Class Politics of the National Policy, 1872–1933," *JCS* 14 (1979), 14–38.

97 MacKenzie, "Farmer-Labor Party," 137–88; Ernest R. Forbes, *The Maritime Rights Movement, 1919–1927: A Study in Canadian Regionalism* (Montreal and Kingston: McGill-Queen's University Press 1979); Babcock, "Labour, Socialism, and Reform Politics," 35–6.

98 Paul Phillips, "The National Policy and the Development of the Western Canadian Labour Movement," in A.W. Rasporich and H.C. Klassen, eds., *Prairie Perspectives 2* (Toronto: Holt Rinehart and Winston 1973), 41–62.

99 David Jay Bercuson, "Labour Radicalism and the Western Industrial Frontier, 1897–1919," *CHR* 57, no. 2 (June 1977), 154–75; Frank and Reilly, "Socialist Movement"; Frank, "Cape Breton Coal Miners"; Donald Macgillivray, "Industrial Unrest in Cape Breton, 1919–1925" (MA thesis, University of New Brunswick 1971). Bercuson has exaggerated the differences in radicalism between Nova Scotia's miners and those in western Canada, as the work of Frank and Macgillivray indicates.

100 The many studies of western farmers ' movements include: L.A. Wood, *A History of the Farmers' Movements in Canada* (Toronto: University of Toronto Press 1974); W.L. Morton, *The Progressive Party in Canada* (Toronto: University of Toronto Press 1950); Macpherson, *Democracy in Alberta*; R.J. Brym, "Regional Social Structure and Agrarian Radicalism in Canada: Alberta, Saskatchewan, and New Brunswick," *CRSA* 15 (1978), 339–51; J.F. Conway, "Populism in the United States, Russia, and Canada: Explaining the Roots of Canada's Third Parties," in J. Paul Grayson, ed., *Class, State, Ideology, and Change: Marxist Perspectives on Canada* (Toronto: Holt Rinehart and Winston 1980), 305–21; P.R. Sinclair, "Class Structure and Populist Protest in Western Canada," *JCS* 1 (1975), 1–17.
101 Mills, "Dixon and Farmer"; Mardiros, *Irvine*.
102 Jamieson, *Times of Trouble*, 164–213.
103 MacKenzie, "Farmer-Labor Party," 137–88; Ewen, "Francq," 37–9, 98–9; Ewan, "Labour Political Action," 24–46; Piva, "Factionalism and Frustration," 126–7; Heron, "Working-Class Hamilton," 669–75; Mills, "Dixon and Farmer," 48–9; McNaught, *Prophet in Politics*, 147–53; Heaps, *Rebel in the House*, 56; Robin, *Radical Politics*, 237–67.
104 Angus, *Canadian Bolsheviks*, 27–127; William Rodney, *Soldiers of the International: A History of the Communist Party of Canada, 1919–29* (Toronto: University of Toronto Press 1968), 28–106; Robin, *Radical Politics*, 237–67.
105 Robin, *Radical Politics*, 262–3, 268–73; Steeves, *Compassionate Rebel*, 70–84; John M. McMenemy, "Lion in a Den of Daniels: A Study of Sam Lawrence, Labour in Politics" (MA thesis, McMaster University, 1965); Rae, "Politics of Class," 232 ; David Lewis, *The Good Fight: Political Memoirs, 1909–1958* (Toronto: Macmillan 1981), 29–30; Ewen, "Labour Political Action," 46–71; McNaught, *Prophet in Politics*, 204–14, 255–77; Gerald Caplan, *The Dilemma of Canadian Socialism: The CCF in Ontario* (Toronto: McClelland and Stewart 1973), 22–4 ; Walter Young, *The Anatomy of a Party: The National CCF, 1932–61* (Toronto: University of Toronto Press 1969), 21–8; Doris French Shackleton, *Tommy Douglas* (Toronto: McClelland and Stewart 1975), 59–70; George Hoffman, "The Saskatchewan Farmer-Labor Party, 1932–1934: How Radical Was It at Its Origins?" in D.H. Bocking, ed., *Pages from the Past: Essays on Saskatchewan History* (Saskatoon: Western Producer Prairie Books 1979), 210–24.
106 McMenemy, "Lion in a Den of Daniels," 37.
107 Heaps, *Rebel in the House*, 137–9.
108 Young, *Anatomy of a Party*, 77–8, 82–90; Penner, *Canadian Left*, 213–16; Irving Martin Abella, *Nationalism, Communism, and Canadian Labour: The*

CIO, the Communist Party, and the Canadian Congress of Labour, 1935–1956 (Toronto: University of Toronto Press 1973), 66–85.

109 A.E. Smith, *All My Life: An Autobiography* (Toronto: Progress Books 1949), 64–70; McNaught, *Prophet in Politics*, 145–53; Mardiros, *Irvine*; Heron, "Working-Class Hamilton," 667; Shackleton, *Douglas*, 58–70. Besides these clergymen the labourist tickets included several doctors. *Labour Organization in Canada*, 1921, 55–6.

110 McNaught, *Prophet in Politics*, 92–7.

111 *IB*, May 1905.

112 See Ralph Miliband, *Parliamentary Socialism: A Study in the Politics of Labour* (London: Merlin Press 1973).

113 See, for example, John C. Weaver, "Efficiency and Order: Samuel Morley Wickett and the Urban Progressive Movement in Toronto, 1900–1915," *Ontario History* 69 (1977), 218–34; and Nelles, *Politics of Development*, 489–95.

114 See Allen Mills, "*The Canadian Forum* and Socialism, 1920–1934," *JCS* 13 (1978), 11–27; Michiel Horn, *The League for Social Reconstruction: Intellectual Origins of the Democratic Left in Canada, 1930–1942* (Toronto: University of Toronto Press 1980); Angus, *Canadian Bolsheviks*.

Chapter Eight

The Great War, the State, and Working-Class Canada

Wars in the modern world are never merely military campaigns. They are rare moments that allow national states to mobilize the resources and collective will of their citizenry to a degree seldom, if ever, attempted during peacetime. The self-interest that drives the capitalist economy and the social relations within it are challenged by new ideologies of self-sacrifice and national service. At the same time, longstanding social antagonisms can be inflamed by the unusual economic, social, and political conditions of wartime society. In some countries revolutions have erupted. In Canada the First World War eventually disrupted the dynamics of pre-war working-class life and provided new pressures and opportunities that would fuel large-scale working-class organization, resistance, and radicalization across the country. It turned out to be quite a "Great War" of class forces on the home front.[1]

The Great War in Canada

The European war that erupted in the late summer of 1914 never extended to Canadian soil, but Canadians nonetheless found it a profoundly disruptive event. Although it galvanized the country into a single national purpose and revitalized a sagging economy, it also transformed the role of the state and unleashed a new flood of protest from many sectors of Canadian society.

Munitions production in Toronto during the First World War.
City of Toronto Archives, James 851

For Canadian industrialists, their employees, and thousands of primary producers, war would eventually become an economic godsend. Initially, however, it deepened the depression that had hung over the country since 1913 by restricting access to foreign capital and by disrupting some vital trade and commerce. Economic recovery was slow and uneven across the country. British officials delayed placing orders for military supplies in Canada because of worries about the ability of the Dominion's manufacturers to produce to the exacting specifications required. The cost and complications of retooling for uncertain war production gave many industrialists pause before they took war contracts. Not until mid-1915 did the increasing orders for food, lumber, munitions (mostly shells), uniforms, and other supplies for British and French troops bring fuller employment for factory workers in central Canadian cities, where the bulk of these contracts were filled. Eventually Canada supplied a huge proportion of the ammunition that the Allies fired at the enemy.

Other sectors of the economy got a similar boost. Miners began to feel the heavier demand for their labour power by early 1916. On the east and west coasts and on the Great Lakes, new shipbuilding operations drew together large new workforces. Prairie farmers quickly expanded their acreage in response to the voracious European demand for Canadian wheat. Certainly by the end of 1916, although construction and a few other sectors were still stagnant, unemployment had dried up virtually everywhere in the country. As more people found jobs, consumer spending at home also took off. The wartime boom nonetheless reinforced longer-term patterns of uneven development in the Canadian capitalist economy. The Maritime provinces shared least in the prosperity, while Ontario and Quebec probably enjoyed the most benefits. Manufacturing and agriculture got a far greater boost than most resource industries. On the whole, though, the massive death and destruction under way in Europe allowed the Canadian economy to surge to unprecedented heights of production and profit.[2]

First and foremost, of course, the war was a military event. Before the war, the dominant strain of English-Canadian nationalism had been "imperialism" – a passionate identification with the Empire – and the previous half-decade had seen a flurry of military preparedness (militia reforms, cadet training, and the like) under the frenetic Minister of Militia, Colonel Sam Hughes. As the loyal administration of a colonial state within the British Empire, Robert Borden's Conservative government responded to Britain's declaration of war by organizing a contingent within the British armed forces known as the Canadian Expeditionary Force. What began as a jaunty little adventure that was expected to end by Christmas became more than four agonizing years of carnage and destruction. More than six hundred thousand Canadians would eventually don the khaki uniform of the Canadian Armed Forces during the First World War, while fifty thousand more served in other allied armies. In all, roughly a third of the male population at military age enlisted. Nearly one in ten did not return from the battlefields. Thousands more limped back with physical and psychological wounds.[3]

Initially, the federal government tried to carry out its responsibilities for the war effort overseas and at home with as much voluntary and philanthropic organization as possible. Private individuals and organizations took on responsibilities for recruitment (and, to some extent, equipping) of individual battalions, pro-war propaganda, munitions production, resource coordination, and assistance for soldiers' families and returned veterans.[4] Newspaper editors, Protestant clergymen, and school teachers whipped up jingoistic fervour. Local voluntary recruiting leagues organized parades and nabbed men for the army. Branches of the Canadian Patriotic Fund solicited donations to support soldiers' families. Women's organizations knitted socks for the men in the trenches. Schoolchildren collected scrap metal. Women volunteered to replace men in traditionally male jobs. At every turn in their daily lives, Canadians were exhorted to buy war bonds.[5] The passions aroused occasionally boiled over into violent attacks on German-Canadians and other "aliens,"[6] but, on the whole, this was an orderly national moral crusade. Pacifists and others opposed to the war, especially radical labour leaders, were overwhelmed and isolated. The pre-war resolutions of the Trades and Labor Congress calling for a general strike in the event of war were quietly shelved. Even such traditionally cautious French Canadian leaders as Sir Wilfrid Laurier and Henri Bourassa pledged their support for the cause. Few noticed the quiet indifference to all this hoopla in the Maritimes, Quebec, and much of the rural countryside generally.[7]

Wartime propaganda initially emphasized Canadian obligations to the British Empire, but calls for private sacrifice and public service increasingly highlighted a fight against "Prussianism" or "Kaiserism," and the "great war for democracy." Paradoxically, by the end of 1916 such rhetoric stood in increasingly sharp contrast to life on the home front. Voluntarism was giving way to state compulsion and authoritarian restriction of civil liberties. The sweeping War Measures Act had made such moves possible since 1914, and some measures dated that far back. A press censor monitored and hectored the country's newspaper editors to avoid revealing such evidence of social discontent as strikes. (A press blackout became one of the more effective devices for undermining the first major wartime munitions strike.) Within the country's eastern-European immigrant communities, many men were loosely and often inaccurately branded "enemy aliens" and interned or ordered to register each week with local police departments. Despite their lack of love for the Austro-Hungarian Empire, Ukrainians probably felt the fullest weight of these measures. The Dominion Police and Royal North West Mounted Police also recruited spies to report on labour activities that looked threatening to the war effort. In 1916 strikes in war-related industries were brought under the regulatory mechanisms of the Industrial Disputes Investigation Act (IDIA), the pre-war federal labour legislation that required workers and their bosses in resource, transportation, and utilities industries to submit their demands to compulsory conciliation before initiating strikes or lockouts.[8]

In the first two years of the war, the state moved cautiously in expanding its traditionally limited role. In 1917, however, it became sharply more interventionist. The Director of Public Information took over coordination of propaganda activities. Most shocking for French Canadians, farmers facing labour shortages, and socialist labour leaders – all of whom were decidedly cool to this imperialist war – was the government announcement in 1916 that registration of all manpower would be necessary to deal with labour shortages at home and in the trenches. The National Service Board was put to work registering and classifying the country's workforce. Amid the steady pressure of rising casualty rates and imperial demands for more soldiers in the trenches, full-scale military conscription followed the next year. The state even invaded Canadians' leisure time. Beer drinkers found their supply cut off by provincial prohibition legislation in 1916 and 1917 and eventually by federal action in March 1918 – all in the name of a more efficient war effort. Everyone had to adjust their clocks in an unpopular new scheme, known as "Daylight Saving," aimed at more efficient use of light. Early in 1918 the federal government even went so far as to pass the "Anti Loafing Act," which required adult males to make themselves available for wage-earning work or face criminal prosecution. A series of orders-in-council in September and October 1918 brought the heaviest repressive legislation, which outlawed several radical labour organizations (and their newspapers) and banned strikes. By this point the cabinet had become accustomed to ruling by order-in-council.[9]

The state had also entered into unprecedented economic regulation, though never on the scale that it would in the Second World War. As much as possible it recruited help from the private sector, rather than expanding the civil service. The Imperial Munitions Board, established late in 1915 to replace the much-maligned Shell Committee in administering war contracts, was like its predecessor a committee of industrialists and experts. The board set new standards for coordination of production across the country's metalworking plants, with centrally controlled inspection and factory-administration guidelines in some six hundred firms by 1917. The board also set up its own production facilities, known as National Factories, to manufacture shells, explosives, aircraft, and ships. In 1917 the federal government moved much more decisively into the economy: it established a Board of Grain Supervisors, a Coal Controller, a Canadian Wool Commission, and a Natural Resources Commission, and made its first moves to take over the floundering railways that would become the Canadian National Railways in 1919.

Meanwhile, public outrage over wartime "profiteering" had not been placated by orders-in-council denouncing hoarding and price gouging or by the introduction of direct taxation in the form of a business war-profit tax in 1916 and a "temporary" income tax the next year. The government therefore appointed a Cost-of-Living Commissioner in 1917 to investigate and report on price inflation (though not to prosecute). The food controller also undertook to investigate food prices; in 1918 its work was transferred to a Food Board with powers to fix prices and control supplies. Concerns about labour shortages brought campaigns to recruit more farm labour and eventually the creation of a nationally coordinated Employment Service of Canada. A new federal ministry was charged with the reintegration of returned soldiers into Canadian life. The War Trade Board created in February 1918 had sweeping powers to effect centralized coordination of the private-enterprise economy.[10]

As Canadian capitalists took on administrative roles in many of these new bodies, traditional liberal conceptions about the separation of capital and the state were eclipsed by a growing fascination with some kind of corporatist state (denounced on the left in Britain as the "servile state"). State institutions would more directly sustain the capitalist economy, and the principles of efficiency and managerial expertise – the hallmarks of what is often called pre-war "progressivism" – would prevail over narrow party spirit. The recently established National Research Council seemed a promising example of this new notion of capitalist collaboration within the state. The Board of Commerce, appointed in 1919 to deal with soaring price inflation, was another.[11]

It was the Conservative Party that presided over this more activist state apparatus at the national level and in five provinces at the beginning of the war (Nova Scotia, Quebec, Saskatchewan, and Alberta were the exceptions). The war did not eliminate the easy morals that had so often characterized Tory administrations. Sam Hughes and the "minister of elections," Robert Rogers, made sure that Tory supporters were well rewarded with jobs, commissions, and contracts, turning the war into what historian John English has called "a massive Conservative rally." By the end of 1915 newspapers were regularly publishing stories about the misuse of patronage and the serious flaws in military training and equipment. Abandoning the party truce, the Liberal opposition repeatedly attacked the government's apparent favouritism, corruption, and general mismanagement, especially in the distribution of war contracts through the hastily improvised Shell Committee, which was dissolved in November 1915. From press, pulpit, and Canadian Club auditoriums, the public outcry against narrow party allegiances grew louder.

The Conservatives eventually responded by creating the coalition Union government in October 1917. In the emotion-charged re-election campaign that followed, the Unionists rallied the country to the war effort, the Empire, and the Anglo-Saxon "race," and denounced their opponents with unprecedented rhetorical venom. The cynical, flagrantly corrupt procedures of that election – which included giving the vote to all soldiers and (for the first time) all their female relatives and taking it away from all those who had arrived from enemy countries since 1902, regardless of naturalization – were probably the most blatant example of the Tory willingness to give democracy short shrift. In December the Unionist forces won a smashing victory (outside Quebec) that consolidated the Tory hegemony and marginalized official Liberalism within national politics until after the war was over.[12]

Many other traditional threads of Canadian Toryism – elitism, imperialist jingoism, and bigotry, in particular – found their fullest expression in this context of single-minded national commitment. Official intolerance of ethnic minorities flourished. Anti-French sentiment once again broke through into Ontario politics, as the English-Canadian majority in the federal Parliament endorsed the provincial government's move to curb francophone schooling in 1916. Manitoba followed Ontario's example the same year. In the 1917 federal election French Canadians faced vicious attacks from Unionist candidates for their resistance to military conscription.[13] The government's campaign also fanned the growing resentment against European immigrants. Not surprisingly, 97 per cent of the 152 Unionists elected were white Anglo-Canadian Protestant males from prosperous business or professional backgrounds.[14]

By 1917 workers were not alone in raising questions about the longer-term implications of wartime developments. The combination of war-induced moral fervour, strong inducements to subordinate private to public concerns, and popular outrage at the unsavoury practices of business and the state tore loose many groups of Canadians from their traditional social and ideological moorings and opened wide-ranging, intense debate about "reconstruction" in postwar society. Numerous social movements presented their own agendas and competing visions, most of them projecting little confidence in the existing political and economic institutions. The moral energies of the Protestant churches' "social gospel," which had spilled over into patriotic passion for the war effort, were now focused as never before on the social and moral purification of Canadian society. Prohibition was the moral reformers' great wartime triumph, but they looked for more. In 1918 the Methodist Church of Canada went so far as to announce its commitment to production based on "co-operation and service" rather than "competition and profits."[15] Many of the women involved in these campaigns were delighted that politicians were finally won over to the justice of giving them the right to vote in most provinces and at the federal level in 1918.[16] Intellectuals from many backgrounds looked for new solutions to the moral crisis; indeed, seldom had Canada seen such an outpouring of books prescribing remedies for all that ailed industrial capitalist society in Canada.[17] The farmers gave a far angrier edge to this ferment. Throughout rural Canada they were organizing against the erosion of their incomes and way of life, once again placing Canadian tariff policies at the centre of their demonology.[18] Veterans soon joined the chorus of angry voices. Returning from the trenches with their various scars and resentments, they became another volatile new force in Canadian society and politics – a force that found expression in spontaneous crowd action in the streets and, more persistently, through new organizations such as the Great War Veterans' Association.[19] All of this political turmoil spilled over into the months after the Armistice, when the restraints set by cries of support for the military effort had lifted. For many Canadians, much was at stake in 1919–20.

The third year of the war, then, proved a turning point, with the shift from voluntarism to more authoritarian state intervention, the growing popular uneasiness about private enterprise, the divisive political crisis over conscription, the take-off of retail price inflation, and the increasing demoralization and disaffection of a war-weary population. It was in this broad context that the workers' revolt began to take shape in Canada.

Fuelling a Revolt

In the first two years of the war, working-class Canada showed considerable support for the war effort – sending sons to war, buying war bonds, holding back "selfish" demands. But by 1917 workers' cynicism about the Great War was growing. A spirit of revolt was in the air, primarily as a result of the war's impact on working-class life.

The war economy had certainly shifted the balance of class forces in Canadian labour markets. At the outbreak of hostilities in 1914, Canadian workers had already suffered through more than a year of prolonged lay-offs, short time, and wage cuts in the deepest economic slump yet seen in the twentieth century. "There have been other periods of depression in times gone by," the executive of the British Columbia Federation of Labor noted that summer, "but there has never been one so extensive and so entirely devoid of promise of improvement for years to come, as the present one." Similarly gloomy comments were heard across the country. Many city councils had to face large demonstrations of jobless workers demanding "work or bread." It is not surprising, then, that the first military recruits were often the unemployed, particularly recent British immigrants. Indeed, during the early stages of the war few sections of Canadian society provided more soldiers than the labour movement. By the end of 1915 incomplete returns from unions in Canada showed that some thirteen thousand union members – one in twelve – had already enlisted. In many cases there was clearly more than patriotism motivating the decision to go to war. The sting of widespread unemployment and hunger "conscripted" many. Since enlistment entitled the families of the recruits to support from the Canadian Patriotic Fund, and held the possibility of improving their eligibility for relief payments, many unemployed workers regarded overseas service as a means of providing for loved ones. As James McVety, president of the Vancouver Trades and Labor Council, reported in November 1914, 'Many of the families of the men who enlisted were so hard up that relief had to be given almost before the names were hardly dry on the enlistment roll."[20]

Unemployment soon disappeared, however, as a result of both military recruitment and opportunities in the quickening industrial economy, especially munitions. The closing of immigration prevented the replenishment of pools of labour in the traditional way, and employers taxed their ingenuity to find workers and hold on to them. By the end of 1916 the Imperial Munitions Board was pushing employers to hire women workers for the shell plants. Perhaps thirty-five thousand ultimately worked in munitions. During the next year male labour shortages also brought women into such traditionally male jobs as bank teller and streetcar conductor. Far more of these female wage-earners were married than ever before, though single women still predominated.[21] Youngsters were similarly pulled out of school and retired workers from old-age homes in the search for more wage-earners.[22] "Enemy aliens" were also shipped from internment camps to industrial centres where their labour was needed. European immigrants in general found their way into much better jobs than had been available to them in the ethnically stratified pre-war labour markets, which had typically left them on the lowest rungs of the occupational ladder.[23]

Free from the haunting fear of unemployment and bottomless poverty, Canadian workers showed a new confidence by 1916 that was in sharp contrast to their desperation in the pre-war slump. At home, working-class families in Canada began to feel the relief from economic insecurity that the bigger wage packets brought into their households. Families that had been doubled up in rented accommodation could now afford to rent their own places. They ate more meat. Player pianos and victrolas appeared in more working-class parlours. Some savings went into war bonds.[24] This was a familiar pattern from pre-war years – families taking advantage of economic upturns to clear away debts and take a few steps towards improving their living standards before another depression forced them back into a much more pinched existence.[25] On the job, wage-earners also revived time-worn means of using the tighter labour market to their advantage. They could risk a cockier manner and thumb their noses at their foremen's efforts to get them to work harder. They could take an afternoon off work to enjoy a ball game or a movie, or even a move to another job, where the boss was probably willing to pay still higher wages to get help.

They could even discuss unions more openly. "Employment is so easily obtained that workmen change from one occupation to another for no apparent reason," Nova Scotia's factory inspector reported in 1917, "and employers complain that it is impossible to enforce discipline in their factories." The same year, a Cominco official wrote from the other end of the country, "Workers have been absolutely independent, knowing that if they were fired from one job they could get another immediately." Toronto's John Inglis Company complained that it was "[a]lmost impossible to co-operate with present class of help as they appear to be getting too much money and don't want to work," while Hamilton's National Steel Car plant bemoaned the difficulty "to get our men to average 9 hours a day. It is not a question of too little money with them, but the trouble is they have too much. The surplus amount allows them to take a great deal more time off than they ordinarily would." Another manufacturer later complained, "Taking a day off was a frequent occurence for many men who were receiving double, possibly treble, what they had ever done before." By the end of the war, according to a government study, "Turnover was universally high, many employers stating that 30 per cent of their staff was floating. Absence was also abnormal, amounting to 5 per cent per day and often running as high as 10 per cent."[26]

These would hardly seem to be the conditions to promote a revolt. In fact, during 1915–16 most wage-earners seemed more interested in making hay while the sun shone. Although union membership increased gradually and workers staged some significant confrontations (notably the 1916 strikes in the Thetford asbestos mines, Montreal shipyards, Hamilton munitions plants, Cobalt silver mines, and Alberta coal fields),[27] two features of working-class activity in the period predominated: the mobilization of as many able-bodied members of the household as possible to bring in wages; and the remarkable labour turnover, as workers jumped from job to job in search of better wages and less oppressive working conditions.

Yet the wartime boom was unsettling for workers at home and on the job. First, the newfound prosperity was soon threatened in many working-class households by the retail price inflation that began a dizzying four-year ascent in 1917. Canadian workers had already faced sharp price increases before the war, especially in the 1912–13 period, but no one could remember prices rising as fast or as high as they did in this new inflationary burst. An average weekly food basket for a family of five that had cost $10.11 at Christmas 1916 was fetching $12.25 the next Christmas (a jump of 20 per cent), and the addition of fuel, lighting, and rent brought the total increase to 31 per cent. By December 1918 the cost of this family budget had leaped by 46 per cent over the 1916 level and, at the peak of the inflationary spiral in July 1920, by 82 per cent. At that point the food basket cost a whopping 128 per cent more than it had on the eve of the war in 1914. (The European belligerents had much higher inflation rates, though Britain's was only moderately higher at 158 per cent; the United States was slightly lower at 115 per cent, and Australia and New Zealand fell well behind at 94 and 67 per cent respectively.)[28] Almost every day, Canadian newspapers splashed stories across their front pages about the high cost of living, or "H.C.L." At a conference of international unionists held in 1917, delegates worried that Canadian workers were confronting a "serious depression of their standard of living occasioned by the increase in the price of necessities of life."[29] The problem was that wages were not keeping pace. All recent attempts to determine working-class income in Canada in this period have pointed to serious erosion of real wages after 1917 (although all these studies are marred by the use of the only available data, namely, the hourly wage rates of relatively skilled men, rather than their actual take-home pay or the earnings of the less skilled).[30]

Here was a family-based issue that irked the working-class housewife as much as her wage-earning husband.[31] Searching angrily for explanations for this injustice, workers invariably suspected that shady, unscrupulous profiteers were at work – in the words of the Regina trades council, "feasting on the nation's suffering" and "fattening on our soldiers' blood."[32] Such highly publicized scandals as the revelations about the super-profits of pork-packer Sir Joseph Flavelle generated a deepening hostility towards the leading figures of Canada's business establishment. "Having been engaged in recording Canadian political events for the past quarter century," one veteran Conservative politician cautioned Prime Minister Borden in the wake of the Flavelle controversy, "I can truly say that I never before met with such wide spread [*sic*] *rage* over any other scandal."[33] In households and workplaces across Canada, deference to captains of finance and industry came unhinged as news of alleged corporate profiteering spread. As the federal government's numerous initiatives failed to curb the continuing price inflation through 1920, resentment at unknown profiteers who threatened rising working-class income raged across working-class dinner tables throughout the country. "The authorities have had enquiry after enquiry made but they only show more clearly the gravity of the evil," a Montreal commissioner reported in 1919. "The masses understand nothing, they are driven mad for no remedy comes from anywhere."[34] This "madness" had prompted the Trades and Labor Congress, in 1917, to call for an end to "gambling in foodstuffs by speculators" and to propose controls on (even the nationalization of) food-processing plants, coal mines, and railways.[35] From all parts of the country came demands for the "conscription of wealth" as well as, or in preference to, the conscription of people (the new income tax was the government's reluctant and extremely limited response).[36] Workers also confronted the rising cost of living with a measure of self-help. Co-operative stores blossomed across the country – at least nineteen in British Columbia, more than one hundred on the Prairies, twenty in Ontario, and thirteen in the Maritimes – many of them in working-class communities.[37]

Workers became even more fearful about their household finances after the Armistice, when many lost their jobs in munitions work and unemployment rose steeply across the economy in the early months of 1919. In March unions reported levels of joblessness among their members that had not been seen since the end of 1915. Somewhat fuller employment returned during the next year and a half, broken by some slackness in the winter of 1919–20. Uncertainty hung over most industries, however, until the great crash in the winter of 1920–1, when enterprises closed or curtailed production drastically and thousands of wage-earners were thrown out of work.[38] These could be the conditions that would allow employers to get the upper hand again, as they always had in previous economic downturns. So, through the lurching uncertainties and instability of the postwar era, wage-earners and their families looked anxiously into the future and grasped at ways to build more collective economic security into their lives.

The wartime boom also had a disruptive effect on the capitalist workplace. In most industries employers accelerated production in order to meet the pressing demands for goods. Particularly in manufacturing, the high-volume production and the general labour shortage encouraged employers to cut costs and reorganize work to a degree unimaginable in the more limited pre-war markets. Workers in the busy clothing industry felt these pressures.[39] In munitions thousands of untrained workers were recruited to run narrowly specialized machines on piecework – a process soon known as "dilution" of the crafts. The trend towards mass production that had begun at the turn of the century – the Second Industrial Revolution – was accelerating.[40] Craftsmen, especially in the metalworking plants, recognized that the prolonged attack on their crafts had intensified.[41] They resented losing more of the control they had long exercised over the labour process. Their craft pride was also offended by the erosion of the status hierarchy in their workplaces. The skilled workers who had so far survived the Second Industrial Revolution, such as the machinists, and those who had emerged within new work processes, such as the steelworkers, were disgruntled to see untrained, transient men (and sometimes women) taking home previously unimaginable wages earned on high-volume piecework, while their more skilled, longer-service workmates who set up and maintained the machinery enjoyed far smaller increases. The gap between skilled and unskilled was narrowing to the apparent detriment of the craft worker. "It is true that young girls, with no experience … [got] higher wages for doing soft snaps than skilled mechanics whose labor was indispensable to the proper carrying on of the work received," one workman blustered in 1917.[42] "The majority of the men on the plant did not share in these high wages, because they were kept in their old positions of skill and responsibility in order that the whole plant might continue to operate successfully," Nova Scotia steelworkers complained three years later.[43]

The concern about disruptions in established workplace hierarchies extended to more workers as Europeans and Asians gained access to labour markets previously closed to them. To meet the chronic shortage of labour, many employers intensified the recruitment of non-Anglo Canadian labour that they had begun before the war.[44] Now they drew in more European peasant-labourers from the resource industries of the north and west into the heavy secondary manufacturing of central and eastern Canada. The federal government even obliged by shipping interned enemy aliens, mostly non-Austrian citizens of the Austro-Hungarian Empire, to some large corporations short of less skilled labour, including railways, coal mines, and steel mills. In 1917 the *Canadian Annual Review* noted that "the labour shortage everywhere [has] resulted in the employ of Austrian and German aliens in works of all kinds – the Imperial Munitions Board, the Lindsay Arsenal and many munitions and other industrial plants."[45] Many Anglo-Canadian wage-earners were outraged. The press heaped fuel on the fires of resentment with regular reports of high wages among these workers. White, English-speaking commentators also resuscitated pre-war fears of cultural degeneration they believed they saw in the immigrants' crowded boardinghouse lifestyle, ignoring the reality that many of these men were simply biding their time until the re-opening of immigration allowed them to return to Europe or Asia.

By the end of 1917 returning soldiers had become the loudest and most belligerent critics of the employment of "interlopers" and "enemy aliens," terms applied loosely to Europeans of many different backgrounds. Over the next two years the veterans often took to the streets to attack the men they alleged were stealing their jobs and to demand that the government intern or deport them. Early in 1919 there were violent assaults on eastern European immigrants in Calgary, Drumheller, Winnipeg, Port Arthur, Sudbury, and Halifax. Employers also felt the wrath of their workers, who demanded that the "enemy aliens" be fired. Many companies complied to varying degrees. By 1919 this nativistic backlash was simmering in every part of the country where southern and eastern Europeans or Asians were working in large numbers.[46]

The huge strike wave that swept over all parts of the country after 1916 was also fed by the unflinching refusal of employers to deal with their workers collectively. In strike after strike, workers ended up on the picket lines because their bosses would not discuss the demands presented to them by workers' representatives. Capitalists dug in their heels to prevent wartime conditions from introducing any permanent changes in power relations in their enterprises. Workers who saw their employers profiting handsomely from big war contracts found their intransigence unfair and unacceptable: this was the issue that would ignite some of the biggest strikes in 1919, including the Winnipeg General Strike.

Part of what made these issues of shop-floor politics so unusually intense and widespread was the way in which the state was implicated, particularly the Borden government. Here was an administration that seemed to have lost its right to rule. For the thousands of families whose menfolk were dying in the trenches, grief mingled with bitterness at the apparent ineptitude and corruption in the prosecution of the war. Those working on the home front were no less outraged. The government had imposed rigid, authoritarian controls, from prohibition to national registration to restraints on strikes. It seemed to be protecting profiteers (the best known, Flavelle, was head of the Imperial Munitions Board). It offered no sympathy to workers who locked horns with their employers (indeed, in restraining strikes by means of the Industrial Disputes Investigation Act, it seemed to be tying the hands of unionists). And it refused to involve labour representatives in its wartime deliberations, in contrast to well-publicized initiatives in Britain and the United States.[47]

The creation of the Union government late in 1917 temporarily shored up the state's crumbling legitimacy, but the apparent insensitivity to working-class concerns continued into the postwar period. Many workers in Quebec and in the West were horrified by the heavy-handed use of the Military Service Act to impose conscription. Huge demonstrations and bloody riots broke out in the streets of Quebec.[48] In British Columbia draft dodgers were harassed and chased through the woods. Thousands of Vancouver unionists stopped work on 2 August 1918 to protest the fatal shooting of the fugitive draft dodger and radical unionist Albert "Ginger" Goodwin.[49] The orders-in-council introduced in September and October 1918 to repress radical organizations and ban strikes were the final straw. Protest meetings against such attacks on civil liberties helped to radicalize the labour movement still further in cities as politically diverse as Toronto, Winnipeg, and Vancouver.[50]

The problem for this government was that the war had created new expectations of public morality among the mass of the population. Since 1914 workers had been urged to remember the men in the trenches and the cause they were allegedly fighting for and to hold their personal desires in check for the great crusade against "Kaiserism." From pulpits and street corners, on billboards and slips in their pay packets, workers had been asked to follow the banner of public service and self-sacrifice, ideals not often proclaimed in a capitalist society organized fundamentally on the basis of self-interest. By 1917 it appeared that many capitalists, especially their employers, were not showing the right spirit of self-denial. Nor were politicians and state officials themselves. In 1917 the constraining power of patriotic pro-war rhetoric began to fade and a deepening cynicism about the war effort spread. The last time patriotism was used to effect was in the 1917 federal election, but the elitism of the Union government and the flagrant electoral abuses left a foul odour.

A few months later the Imperial Munitions Board's director of labour reported a 30 per cent drop in productivity in war plans; "all the enthusiasm and all the idea that munitions are vitally essential had gone out of the minds of the workpeople," he noted, "and ... today they take the War, and the work related to it, as they take the sunrise – an incident of the day."[51] That summer the government's own security adviser, Montreal lawyer C.H. Cahan, reported that workers' discontent stemmed from "the weakening of the moral purpose of the people to prosecute the war to a successful end," a deepening awareness of "the bloody sacrifices and irritating burdens entailed by carrying on the war," and the growing belief that the Union government is failing to deal effectively with the financial, industrial, and economic problems growing out of the war."[52] The country had been saturated with the rhetoric of service and the noble goal of fighting to defend "democracy," and workers now bitterly threw these words back at those in power. In 1918 Sydney's labour paper stated, "The people of Cape Breton have suffered too dearly on the fields of Flanders and at home to be ruled by an autocracy [in the local steel plant]."[53] Western labour leaders similarly viewed the government's draconian labour legislation in the fall of 1918 as "Prussianism at home."[54] Democracy had become the new touchstone of industrial relations and politics.

Workers and their leaders could take heart that other Canadians – farmers, clergymen, intellectuals, veterans, women, and more organized groups – had similar concerns. Labour activists were also increasingly aware that they were part of an international working-class ferment. In scattered parts of the globe workers were challenging established political and economic power with bold new programs, and they were winning. Almost every day, there appeared in the press stories of massive strikes in Britain, Europe, and the United States. Canadian labour papers reported favourably on the British shop stewards' movement and "Triple Alliance" (of coal miners, railwaymen, and transport workers), as well as on the new industrial unionism in Australia, especially the One Big Union. Labour Party breakthroughs in Australia also attracted much attention, as did the decision of England's revitalized Labour Party early in 1918 to transform its program from a weak labourist project into an overtly socialist vision.[55] These international working-class challenges were further legitimized when delegates at the postwar peace conference in Paris felt compelled to issue a set of principles governing industrial relations that guaranteed workplace standards and rights to organize.[56]

The pockets of socialist activists across Canada received even more inspiration from Russia's fragile new experiment in workers' power. Some of the European immigrant communities, especially the Ukrainians, Russians, Jews, and Finns, were particularly excited about the new radicalism in Eastern Europe. The Edmonton socialists even named their new newspaper *The Soviet* early in 1919. For socialists in Canada, Russia was a shining example rather than an ideological reservoir, since Bolshevik theoretical work had scarcely touched North America at this stage. The left in Canada soon found surprisingly large audiences for its efforts to educate Canadian workers on the emerging soviet system. Montreal's Tom Cassidy spoke for many long-time socialist activists in crowing that, since the Bolshevik revolution, Canadian workers were far more interested in socialism than in "the days when we stood out on the bald prairies howling and lonesome like a native coyote."[57] What many Canadian workers drew from the Bolshevik experience was a boundless belief that what could be yearned and struggled for could also be achieved. For one Winnipeg labourer, the Russian example promised a resolution of all working-class problems: "equal rights for men and women, no child labor, no poverty, misery and degradation, no prostitution, no mortgages on farms, no revolting bills for machinery to keep peasants poor till the grave, no sweatshops, no long hours of heavy toil for a meagre existence but an equal opportunity for all, a life made worth living with unlimited possibilities to all, aided by splendid machinery to make [the] earth a real paradise where nothing but happiness can prevail ... this is Bolshevism."[58] The Canadian government's decision to send troops to join the military invasion of the Soviet Union in 1919 brought cries of protest from the left of the Canadian workers' movements. Labour newspapers and socialist rallies regularly drew connections between all these dramatic international developments and the aspirations of Canadian workers.

The workers' revolt in Canada at the end of the First World War, then, was not the desperate cry of a downtrodden and poverty-stricken proletariat. Rather it grew out of a newfound confidence in working-class power, a profound sense of injustice, and a determination that society could run differently. It was fuelled by a volatile mixture of those factors that had prompted working-class resistance in Canada for more than half a century and some special wartime conditions. Labour struggles over living standards in working-class households and wage-earners' rights on the job were hardly new. But the prosecution of the war and the (mis)management of the wartime economy, which gave the national state such prominence, had unified many previously fragmented struggles around the country and given them some common focus. Wartime ideals, especially the fight for democracy, had also injected into public debate in Canada and abroad a moral fervour that piqued workers' imagination and heightened their expectations about the future. Old ways of viewing (and justifying) social relationships in capitalist society were dissolving. The wartime convergence of material and ideological forces thus facilitated the creation of the most broad-based, anticapitalist workers' movements that had ever appeared in Canada. And, as the revolt took shape, workers inspired each other; the remarkable success of working-class mobilization in the final years of the war bred a heady confidence in the potency of workers' collective action.

The Limits of a Labour Movement

In 1914 working-class organizations in Canada were in no shape to face the shock waves that the Great War would send through Canadian society. They included two distinct and often hostile camps on the industrial front: craft unionism and industrial unionism. At the turn of the century the craft unionists had hitched their star firmly to the new, narrowly focused, bureaucratically structured "international" unions based in the United States and affiliated with the American Federation of Labor (AFL). For the most part, the craft unionists sought from their employers nothing more than a regularized contractual relationship that would protect their craft status and workplace power, in return for labour peace and wage stability.[59] Despite an effort at revival in the prewar boom, the craft unionists had been driven out of most of the major urban industries. Local trades and labour councils across the country nonetheless still tried to represent the collective interests of these skilled workers. Their national organization, the Trades and Labor Congress of Canada (TLC), continued to pose as the central "House of Labour" in the country, despite its acceptance of the autonomy of the big internationals and of the right of the American Federation of Labor to mediate jurisdictional disputes, and despite its weakness in the Maritimes and the West.

In those regions in particular, many workers had turned to new industrial unions that signed up everyone in one workplace. Some leaders of these organizations hoped to rally Canadian workers for a general assault on the capitalist system. In western Canada some of them had organized for the colourful Industrial Workers of the World, which had been launched in 1905 and had made its greatest impact among more transient workers in the region between 1909 and 1912.[60] Less flamboyant versions of industrial unions put down roots among coal miners, longshoremen, textile and clothing workers, and a few other groups, and just before the war led these workers out in some of the biggest, most bitter strikes in living memory.[61] Employers attacked the new unions with the same tactics they had used against the craftsmen – strike-breakers, special police, industrial spies, and blacklists.

By 1914 industrial unions had carved out a place for themselves within the various workers' movements in the country, but few of them had much numerical strength or bargaining clout. Nor had they overcome the divisions along lines of race and ethnicity and gender; both craft and industrial unionists were predominantly white, male, anglophone, and francophone Canadians. In Quebec the Roman Catholic clergy were promoting a less aggressive form of unionism based on clerical supervision of the workers' movement and Franco-Catholic solidarity across class lines, but by 1914 they too had only limited success to report.[62]

There were further splits in the Canadian workers' movement by the outbreak of the war. Industrial struggles had become rigidly separated from political campaigns, and, within the realm of independent working-class politics, two ideological tendencies – labourism and socialism – confronted each other. Both groups had a tiny handful of their standard-bearers elected to provincial legislatures and municipal councils, but their overall impact on Canadian politics was extremely limited.[63] Although the workers' movements in Canada had undergone some important changes in structure and ideology since the turn of the century, by 1914 they were still fragmented by occupation, industry, locality, race and ethnicity, gender, and ideology. Within working-class communities they represented an extremely limited force (the 166,000 unionists reported in 1914 amounted to barely 10 per cent of all wage-earners in the 1911 census and were confined principally to railways, coal mining, and skilled urban trades). Their economic and political power had been shattered by employers' attacks and the devastating depression of 1913–15. Traditions of solidarity had been either seriously weakened by these assaults or not yet fully developed in communities overwhelmed with newcomers.

Some of the first stirrings of a collective working-class response to the new wartime conditions came from craft-union officials, particularly the Trades and Labor Congress of Canada. The new importance of the Canadian state put pressure on the Congress to intervene as the major working-class lobbying agency at the national level. For this task the organization had only two permanent officers: the president since 1910, former British Columbia miner and socialist James Watters, and the secretary since 1900, printer Paddy Draper, once described as a "straight line 'pure and simple' trade unionist."[64] Rounding out the Congress executive were three additional members, elected by convention, who remained on staff with their respective unions (provincial executives also maintained relations with their respective governments). In its dealings with the state, the Congress confined itself strategically to traditional lobbying methods, eschewing any attempts at mass mobilization to advance its claims. Its officers preferred personal correspondence and private meetings, asserting the urgency of concessions by the state and capital lest rank-and-file militancy escalate beyond union officials' restraining capacities.[65] Labour's lobby, however, proved ineffectual. As Borden confided to his diary, the Congress's annual meetings with the federal cabinet took on an inert ritual of their own. After both the 1914 and 1915 meetings, the prime minister noted that the views expressed by Watters and Draper were both moderate and sensible, and his own cautious, non-committal response brought an end to their consideration for another year.[66] Labour's inability to lobby its way to redress would be part of the alchemy of the rising working-class revolt.

During the first three years of the war, the Congress's weakness was starkly exposed by its failure to make a dent on government policy in three prime areas of concern. First, the Congress pressed the Borden government repeatedly to alleviate the hardship of early wartime unemployment through more generous relief programs and an expansion of public works. It got neither.[67] Second, as the war economy took off in 1915, the Congress and its affiliates spent over a year pleading with the Borden government and the Imperial Munitions Board to impose fair wage clauses on military production in order "to protect our people from extortion on the one hand and grinding poverty on the other."[68] Instead, Ottawa extended the discredited Industrial Disputes Investigation Act to wartime industries, thereby imposing compulsory conciliation against strike attempts by discontented workers. Across the country labour's frustration at this outcome was vented not only at the government but also at the Congress leadership, condemned by the Toronto District Labor Council for not exercising "the proper vigilance and care … when a measure of the character referred to has been allowed to become law." At the TLC convention in September 1916, a majority of delegates voted for the act's repeal. Over the next two years, however, the federal government turned ever more frequently to IDIA boards, special royal commissions, roving labour department troubleshooters, and threats of coercion under the War Measures Act (seldom actually used) to head off strikes and maintain industrial peace.[69]

Third, the Congress failed to influence the conduct of the war itself, an issue that proved highly divisive within the house of labour. Before 1914 no representative body in Canadian society had developed a stronger anti-war position than the Congress. In 1913 it had even reaffirmed its willingness to call a general strike in the event of hostilities. Canadian labour, however, proved no more capable of preserving its pacifist principles than its European counterparts. At its September 1914 convention, the Congress reiterated its abhorrence of war but voted to support a war effort now characterized not as an internecine conflict among the capitalist classes of Europe, but as a principled struggle pitting British and French democracy against German autocracy. The organization's position was not so surprising. Most unionists undoubtedly supported the Allied cause at this point; nor could there be any doubt that to persist with resistance might result in mass arrests, possibly culminating in an outright ban on unions. Besides, support for the war might enhance unions' legitimacy with both government and employers. A similar resolution in support of "the cause of freedom and democracy" passed in 1915, though this time with a larger chorus of dissent.[70]

The creation of the National Service Board in October 1916 to undertake a compulsory national workforce registration placed the Congress leadership in a delicate position. Not only was labour characteristically excluded from board representation, but the whole procedure appeared to be at odds with the 1915 Congress resolution that emphatically declared "unchangeable opposition to all that savours of conscription." Many in the labour movement regarded registration as a prelude to military conscription and regimentation at work. Yet, after meeting with Borden in December and receiving his word that registration was unconnected to any specific plans for conscription, the Congress executive issued a statement recommending that all affiliated workers complete their registration forms. Labour leaders in Quebec and the West immediately denounced the statement. When conscription was introduced the following spring, Borden noted cheerfully that Canada's house of labour would mount only ritualistic opposition to the measure it had decried for years. "They were very receptive and good natured," he observed after meeting with the Congress executive, "but we may have a good natured tilt with them as they said."[71]

The Congress leaders were clearly attempting to barter their services to the state in return for recognition. Thus, immediately after signing on for registration, they urged Borden to bring a labour representative into the cabinet. (Watters had already begun quietly promoting himself for the job, to the prime minister's great exasperation.)[72] A campaign of resistance to military conscription was more important as leverage in pressing for greater recognition of organized labour by the Borden government. Accordingly, the summer of 1917 witnessed the

Congress's most energetic anti-government campaign yet. In early June it convened a four-day conference to discuss problems confronting the labour movement. Delegates from across the country, representing eighty different affiliated unions, participated in wholesale condemnation of the Imperial Munitions Board, the high cost of living, and conscription itself. The Congress leadership stepped up the call for labour representation in policy development and demanded that wealth be conscripted before lives. Yet once conscription received parliamentary assent, the Congress executive faithfully fell into line, recommending to the September 1917 convention that Canadian labour not oppose the government's forced call to arms. At this point, however, they faced a large minority in opposition, which unleashed a torrent of passionate rhetoric against conscription and in favour of a general strike against the policy.[73] In this context, it is not surprising that the Congress leadership endorsed the creation of a Canadian Labor Party as a safer channel into which to direct this working-class anger over state policy.

Borden's government also sensed the dangers in continuing to ignore or deflect the labour leadership. As the December 1917 federal election approached, appointing a labour minister seemed essential to conferring greater legitimacy and workers' support on the new Union cabinet and its labour policies. Borden's choice was inspired. Gideon Robertson was Canadian vice-president of one of the country's consistently "safe and sane" railway brotherhoods, the Order of Railroad Telegraphers. He already sat in the Senate and privately admitted to Borden to having "done all possible since 1914 to maintain industrial peace in Canada, which is essential to efficient results in our war work." He promised "to support [the Borden government's] war policy, [and] to promote industrial peace in Canada." Robertson's appointment to the cabinet as minister without portfolio was followed by a decided shift in state labour policy, no doubt inspired by the new tripartite structures recently introduced by the American government. In January 1918 four cabinet ministers held extensive discussions with fifty-six labour leaders carefully selected by Congress officials from forty different unions. For the first time, labour received representation on a host of state regulatory bodies and, most important, the Labour Sub-Committee of the cabinet's Reconstruction and Development Committee. Moreover, the Congress executive triumphantly informed its affiliates, all such labour appointees would have to be recommended by, or acceptable to, "the recognized heads of our movement." As a symbol of the new openness to labour, AFL President Samuel Gompers was invited to address Parliament. According to James Watters, the war showed "the necessity of co-operation, not alone on the actual field of battle, but in every industrial activity associated with the prosecution of the war … Competition has, therefore, given place to co-operation – co-operation between the State and Capital and Labor." Here were the terms of the social contract that labour leaders hoped to establish. In exchange for their commitment to harmonious workplace relations and production, these officials expected the quid pro quo of reciprocal recognition from the state and capital.[74]

Pursuing such a course inevitably drove Canada's top union leadership towards intensified commitment to the government's industrial agenda. The Congress endorsed a second registration campaign for a further inventory of the country's labour force. More important, labour officials accepted the government's apparent commitment to conciliation of industrial disputes (including some of their proposed amendments to the IDIA) and worked assiduously to prevent strikes. Union staff and structures were mobilized to restrain working-class militancy. In two critical sectors – coal mining and shipbuilding – unions participated in tripartite forums with employers and state officials to discuss means of averting strikes and boosting production.[75] A national strike of 30,000 railway shop workers was averted only by the threats of charter revocation from international headquarters. The use of the "big stick," as one labour paper termed it, brought compliance from the Canadian bargaining committee representing the rail workers and the imposition of a collective agreement patterned on a recent American rail settlement.[76] In a number of instances, such international union directives against strike action in Canada were prompted by a direct federal government appeal. Watters himself became something of a roving troubleshooter acting on government request to curb militancy, as in the Nova Scotia steel industry in the spring of 1918.[77] In the same year, on at least three occasions during 1918 Gideon Robertson called on AFL President Sam Gompers and Secretary Frank Morrison to prevent strikes of Cape Breton coal miners and British Columbia shipbuilders and electrical workers.[78]

During 1918, however, it became apparent that the state was dictating the terms of its rapprochement with labour and that the new relationship produced no demonstrable advances in state labour policy. In fact, in both its legislative and employer roles, the federal government showed renewed intransigence in its dealings with labour. Although it announced a policy endorsing unionization that summer, the government provided no enforcement mechanisms and, in fact, enacted its most coercive labour legislation of the war during 1918 – first the infamous "Anti-Loafing Act" in April and then the orders-in-council out lawing radical organizations and banning strikes in the fall. On none of these measures was labour consulted. An order-in-council in July announcing the terms of employment that workers had a right to expect, including collective bargaining, lacked any enforcement mechanism and therefore had no significant impact on labour relations in the country. The Trades and Labor Congress leadership had been incorporated into the state apparatus not to shape policy, but to enhance the legitimacy of coercive measures deemed necessary by the Borden government.

Nor did the new ties to the Congress transform the federal government's treatment of its own employees. Public-sector employees had been particularly victimized by wartime inflation. At the federal level wage restraint was the byword of a government straining to meet its wartime expenditures. Indeed, federal intransigence in the face of wage appeals from letter carriers brought western Canada to the brink of a massive general strike in the summer of 1918. When a paltry government wage offer was rejected in July, letter carriers went off the job in six centres, and within forty-eight hours widening strike action left twenty centres with no mail service. In contrast to their coverage of most other wartime strikes, the country's press was uniformly sympathetic to the aggrieved strikers. The *Calgary Herald* branded Ottawa "utterly careless and lacking in the first principles of common decency as employers."[79] When letter carriers in thirteen western cities rejected a new settlement negotiated by their leaders, the postmaster general instructed local postmasters to begin hiring strike-breakers and served notice that all strikers would be dismissed unless they returned to work within twenty-four hours. Several unions in the West threatened sympathy strikes, and a settlement was quickly negotiated to restore mail service by 1 August.[80] The 1918 postal strike revealed two problems that confronted labour officialdom in its new relationship with the state – first, persistent tendencies to intransigence and coercion in state labour policies and, second, a union membership no longer willing to accept its leadership's restraining hand. The workers' movements that were taking shape across the country would not be tied down to the narrow project of corporatist accommodation among state, labour, and capital. "The fact is they have got beyond our control," one union official lamented in the summer of 1918.[81] Despite the machinations of national labour leaders in and around Ottawa, workers wanted a labour movement that was more flexible, more militant, and often more radical: it was a challenge as much to their established leadership as to capital and the state.

The Iron Fist and the Velvet Glove

The Canadian state never flinched in the face of the escalating, widely based labour revolt. However much the legitimacy of the Borden government had been undermined in the popular mind, state institutions in Canada had not crumbled as they had in Germany, Austria-Hungary, or Russia, and political leaders and officials moved quickly to fashion new tools of statecraft to curb the working-class challenge. The federal government shared business fears about the postwar economy and the need for restraint on labour demands. Borden told a national audience in September 1919 that the challenge was to foster greater production, efficiency, and cooperation in industry while avoiding measures that would "drive away capital, restrict industry or hinder development." But the government's concerns were also political. Now guided in its response to the revolt by the rigidly conservative Arthur Meighen, the government recoiled in horror at the size and radical overtones of the workers' movements in Canada, especially those in the West. Since September 1918, when a secret report on mushrooming radicalism in Canada crossed the cabinet's desks, politicians and state officials had been aware that more was at stake than wages and working conditions. The secret security apparatus of the Dominion Police and the Royal North-West Mounted Police was strengthened to allow the placement of spies inside labour organizations. The spectre of Bolshevik-style revolutions hung over the cabinet table as these agents' reports inflated the radical undercurrents in strike settings where workers took direction from leaders with a long-term anti-capitalist agenda. According to the labour minister, the government was also deluged with "insistent inquiries and requests … that something be done immediately or that Bolshevism may prevail, property and life held lightly, and the country be destroyed." Although it still hoped to direct workers' aspirations into safe channels until the normal market mechanisms of peacetime could tame them, the government was even more determined to show that radical options were not necessary and would not be tolerated.[82]

The infamous orders-in-council in September 1918 – the first effort to stifle the new radicalism, especially in the immigrant communities and in the West generally – had been followed by several arrests. "Alien" internment and press censorship (now aimed at socialist, not anti-war, ideas) continued for more than a year after the Armistice. The secret security reports advised that the spirit of revolt was continuing to spread in all parts of the country. The Western Labour Conference of March 1919 seemed particularly menacing. In this context, the well-established machinery of industrial conciliation was set aside in favour of blunt coercion. Winnipeg workers became the first postwar strikers to confront the full state arsenal of weapons for strike-breaking and repressing radicalism. Troops and "special" police were deployed to harass strikers and to take back control of public space. Arrests were made under a hastily legislated measure for deporting immigrants ("alien" or British) who were deemed seditious. (The strike leaders were ultimately tried under pre-existing criminal law against seditious conspiracy; immediately after the strike, the Criminal Code's definition of sedition was broadened through the addition of the infamous Section 98.)

Winnipeg's workers were not the last to face such measures. In a similar effort to control the streets, the military clamped down on all public working-class gatherings during the subsequent Vancouver general strike. Four years later in Sydney, steelworkers were hit with similar military and legal repression, as were the Nova Scotia miners in 1925, this time at the hand of the provincial government. After crushing the Winnipeg strike, the federal government collaborated in the anti-radical Red Scare that businessmen and conservative journalists were promoting across the country. The workers' revolt had thus pushed the state to create more powerful, centralized mechanisms for combatting radicalism than had existed in pre-war Canada.[83]

Borden's government was astute enough to realize that repression alone could have backfired had the outrage it prompted unified all labour leaders in opposition. It therefore made conciliatory gestures to the voices of caution and moderation in the labour movement. First, in the spring of 1919 a royal commission on industrial unrest – chaired by Justice T.G. Mathers and including Trades and Labor Congress President Tom Moore and another reliable union leader, John Bruce – visited twenty-eight centres across the country to allow for an airing of grievances and a show of official concern, just at the height of militancy within the workers' revolt. In September there occurred the most remarkable public dialogue ever held between capital, labour, and the state – the National Industrial Conference. Convened in the

Senate Chamber in Ottawa, this tripartite domestic peace conference was modelled on a similar gathering in Britain a few months earlier: a labour representation of eighty-eight "responsible" men and women, carefully handpicked by the TLC leadership, faced an equal number of employers (chosen by the Canadian Manufacturers' Association and assorted trade associations) and thirty-four public representatives nominated by the government.

The results of both the royal commission and the conference were inconclusive. Neither body straightforwardly endorsed the eight-hour day or the right to organize and bargain collectively. Both endorsed industrial councils but never clarified whether these were to include unions. Precisely the same stand-off on important issues developed when the government sent representatives of labour and capital to the recently established International Labour Organization. Within a year these conciliatory gestures were no longer felt to be necessary, and labour requests that the industrial conference be reconvened were politely ignored. Having beaten labour into submission on the picket lines, neither capital nor the state felt the need for concessions in the name of stability. Fifty years later John Bruce recalled his experience with the Mathers Commission as "one of the bitterest lessons that ever I learned about political chicanery."[84]

The Great War transformed the social relations of production in Canada. Workers gradually developed a measure of material and ideological confidence in wartime society, but also the grounds for a deep-seated sense of injustice. Their outrage was vented at shadowy profiteers, intransigent employers, and, to an unprecedented degree, an insensitive state. The national labour leadership never managed to defend workers' interests effectively and fell victim to the national government's determined efforts to derail the workers' revolt. These common features of the Great War experience in working-class Canada were played out in particular ways in each region of the country. Overall, something quite fundamentally new and different was happening in working-class Canada between 1917 and 1925.

Notes

1 On the impact of war on the home front, see Arthur Marwick, *War and Social Change in the Twentieth Century: A Comparative Study of Britain, France, Germany, Russia, and the United States* (London: Macmillan 1974); Paul Fussell, *The Great War and Modern Memory* (New York: Oxford University

Press 1975); Jay Winter, *The Great War and the British People* (Cambridge: Harvard University Press 1987); Modris Eksteins, *Rites of Spring: The Great War and the Birth of the Modern Age* (Toronto: Lester and Orpen Dennys 1989); Daphne Read, ed., *The Great War and Canadian Society: An Oral History* (Toronto: New Hogtown Press 1978).

2 Adam Shortt, "Economic Effects of War upon Canada," Royal Society of Canada, *Transactions*, 3rd ser., 10 (1916), 65–74; R.T. Naylor, "The Canadian State, the Accumulation of Capital, and the Great War," in R.T. Naylor, ed., *Dominion of Debt: Centre, Periphery, and the International Economic Order* (Montreal: Black Rose Books 1985), 61–108; Kenneth Norrie and Douglas Owram, *A History of the Canadian Economy* (Toronto: Harcourt Brace Jovanovitch 1991), 411–40; John Herd Thompson, *The Harvests of War: The Prairie West, 1914–1918* (Toronto: McClelland and Stewart 1978), 50–6.

3 The course of the Canadian military effort can be followed in Desmond Morton and J.L. Granatstein, *Marching to Armageddon: Canadians and the Great War* (Toronto: Lester and Orpen Dennys 1989). The plight of the Canadian soldier in this war is sensitively treated in Desmond Morton, *When Your Number's Up: The Canadian Soldier in the First World War* (Toronto: Random House 1993).

4 J.A. Corry, "The Growth of Government Activities in Canada, 1914–1921," *CHAAR*, 1940, 63–73.

5 On social life in Canada during the war, see Read, ed., *Great War and Canadian Society*.

6 For example, coal miners in western Canada's District 18 of the United Mine Workers used a strike in 1915 to get "enemy aliens" removed from the mining operations where they worked. In April 1917 the office of a German newspaper was ransacked in Regina. Donald Avery, "Ethnic and Class Tensions in Canada, 1918–1920: Anglo-Canadians and the Alien Worker," in Frances Swyripa and John Herd Thompson, eds., *Loyalties in Conflict: Ukrainians in Canada during the Great War* (Edmonton: Canadian Institute of Ukrainian Studies, University of Alberta 1983), 80, 89. See also Barbara Wilson, *Ontario and the First World War, 1914–1918* (Toronto: University of Toronto Press 1977), lxx–lxxxiv.

7 Thomas P. Socknat, *Witness against War: Pacificism in Canada, 1900–1945* (Toronto: University of Toronto Press 1987), 43–59.

8 Allan L. Steinhart, *Civil Censorship in Canada during World War I* (Toronto: University of Toronto Press 1986); Curtis Johnson Cole, "The War Measures Act, 1914: Aspects of Emergency Limitation of Freedom of Speech and Personal Liberties in Canada, 1914–1919" (MA thesis, University of Western Ontario 1980); Jeff Keshen, "All the News That Was Fit to Print: Ernest

J. Chambers and Information Control in Canada, 1914–19," *CHR* 73, no. 3 (September 1992), 315–43; Myer Siemiatycki, "Munitions and Labour Militancy: The 1916 Hamilton Machinists' Strike,' *L/LT* 3 (1978), 131–52; Peter Melnycky, "The Internment of Ukrainians in Canada," in Swyripa and Thompson, eds., *Loyalties in Conflict*, 1–24; Gregory S. Kealey, "State Repression of Labour and the Left in Canada, 1914–1920: The Impact of the First World War," *CHR* 73, no. 3 (September 1992), 281–314.

9 Corry, "Growth of Government Activities"; David Edward Smith, "Emergency Government in Canada," *CHR* 50, no. 4 (December 1969), 429–48; Thompson, *Harvests of War*, 27–44; Joseph Boudreau, "Western Canada's 'Enemy Aliens' in World War One," *Alberta Historical Review* 12, no. 1 (Winter 1964), 1–9; Swyripa and Thompson, eds., *Loyalties in Conflict*; Anthony W. Rasporich, *For a Better Life: A History of Croatians in Canada* (Toronto: McClelland and Stewart 1982), 75–92; Paul Craven, *An "Impartial Umpire": Industrial Relations and the Canadian State, 1900-1911*(Toronto: University of Toronto Press 1980); J.L. Granatstein and J.M. Hitsman, *Broken Promises: A History of Conscription in Canada* (Toronto: Oxford University Press 1977), 22–104; R.E. Spence, *Prohibition in Canada* (Toronto: Ontario Branch of the Dominion Alliance 1919); Gerald Hallowell, *Prohibition in Ontario, 1919–1923* (Toronto: Ontario Historical Society 1972), 7; Ernest R. Forbes, "Prohibition and the Social Gospel in Nova Scotia," in E.R. Forbes, *Challenging the Regional Stereotypes: Essays on the Twentieth-Century Maritimes* (Fredericton: Acadiensis Press 1989), 13–40; Craig Heron, "Daylight Savings Comes to Hamilton," *Spectator* (Hamilton), 26 October 1979; Nolan Reilly, "The General Strike in Amherst, Nova Scotia, 1919," *Acadiensis* 9 (1980), 56–77.

10 Corry, "Growth of Government Activities"; Smith, "Emergency Government in Canada"; Robert Craig Brown and Ramsay Cook, *Canada, 1896–1921: A Nation Transformed* (Toronto: McClelland and Stewart 1974); R.D. Cuff, "Organizing for War: Canada and the United States during World War I," in R.D. Cuff and J.L. Granastein, eds., *Ties That Bind: Canadian-American Relations in Wartime from the Great War to the Cold War* (Toronto: Samuel Stevens Hakkert and Company 1977), 3–20; Desmond Morton and Glenn Wright, *Winning the Second Battle: Canadian Veterans and the Return to Civilian Life, 1915–1930* (Toronto: University of Toronto Press 1987).

11 James Hinton, *The First Shop Stewards' Movement* (London: George Allen and Unwin 1973); Doug Owram, *The Government Generation: Canadian Intellectuals and the State, 1900–1945* (Toronto: University of Toronto Press 1986); Mel Thistle, *The Inner Ring: The Early History of the National*

Research Council of Canada (Toronto: University of Toronto Press1966); Tom Traves, *The State and Enterprise: Canadian Manufacturers and the Federal Government, 1917–1931* (Toronto: University of Toronto Press 1979), 55–70; James Struthers, *No Fault of Their Own: Unemployment and the Canadian Welfare State, 1914–1941* (Toronto: University of Toronto Press 1983), 16–43.

12 John English, *The Decline of Politics: The Conservatives and the Party System, 1901–1920* (Toronto: University of Toronto Press 1977), 88–221; Robert Craig Brown, *Robert Laird Borden: A Biography, Vol. 2, 1914–1937* (Toronto: Macmillan 1980).

13 Elizabeth Armstrong, *The Crisis of Quebec, 1914–1918* (Toronto: McClelland and Stewart 1974 [1937]).

14 English, *Decline of Politics*, 136–203; Brown, *Robert Laird Borden*, 83–125; Roger Graham, *Arthur Meighen: A Biography, Vol. 1, The Door of Opportunity* (Toronto: Clarke Irwin 1960), 145–210; Granatstein and Hitsman, *Broken Promises*, 70–83.

15 Michael Bliss, "The Methodist Church and World War I," *CHR* 49, no. 3 (September 1968), 213–33; Richard Allen, *The Social Passion: Religion and Social Reform in Canada, 1914–1928* (Toronto: University of Toronto Press 1973), 63–103; Thompson, "'Beginning of Our Regeneration': The Great War and Western Canadian Reform Movements," *HP* 1972, 227–45; James H. Gray, *Booze: The Impact of Whiskey on the Prairie West* (Toronto: New America Library 1972); Hallowell, *Prohibition in Ontario.*

16 Catherine Cleverdon, The *Woman Suffrage Movement in Canada* (Toronto: University of Toronto Press 1950); Carol Lee Bacchi, *Liberation Deferred?: The Ideas of the English-Canadian Suffragists, 1877–1918* (Toronto: University of Toronto Press 1983).

17 See, for example, J.O. Miller, ed., *The New Era in Canada: Essays Dealing with the Upbuilding of the Canadian Commonwealth* (Toronto: J.M. Dent and Sons 1917); Salem Bland, *The New Christianity, the Religion of the New Age* (Toronto: University of Toronto Press 1973 [1920]); William Irvine, *The Farmers in Politics* (Toronto: McClelland and Stewart 1920); William Lyon Mackenzie King, *Industry and Humanity: A Study in the Principles Underlying Industrial Reconstruction* (Toronto: University of Toronto Press 1973 [1918]); Stephen Leacock, *The Unsolved Riddle of Social Justice* (London: J. Lane 1920); R.M. MacIver, *Labor in the Changing World* (Toronto: E.P. Dutton 1919). For a discussion of this intellectual ferment, see Owram, *Government Generation*, 80–106.

18 Thompson, *Harvests of War*; W.L. Morton, *The Progressive Party in Canada* (Toronto: University of Toronto Press 1950); Louis Aubrey Wood, *History of*

Farmers' Movements in Canada (Toronto: Ryerson Press 1920); W.R. Young, "Conscription, Rural Depopulation, and the Farmers of Ontario, 1917–1919," *CHR* 53, no. 3 (September 1972), 289–320.

19 Morton and Wright, *Winning the Second Battle*; Morton, *When Your Number's Up*, 253–75.

20 *BC Federationist*, 3 July 1914; Myer Siemiatycki, "Labour Contained: The Defeat of the Rank and File Workers' Movement in Canada, 1914–1921' (PhD dissertation, York University 1986), 10–15; Patricia Roy, "Vancouver: 'The Mecca of the Unemployed,' 1907–1929," in Alan Artibise, ed., *Town and City: Aspects of Western Canadian Urban Development* (Regina: Canadian Plains Research Centre 1981), 400–2; Diane Matters, "Public Welfare Vancouver Style, 1910–1920," *JCS* 14 (Spring 1979), 3–15; David Schulze, "The Industrial Workers of the World and the Unemployed in Edmonton and Calgary in the Depression of 1913–1915," *L/LT* 25 (Spring 1990), 47–76; Michael Goeres, "Disorder, Dependency and Fiscal Responsibility: Unemployment Relief in Winnipeg, 1907–1942" (MA thesis, University of Manitoba 1981), 39; Avery, "Ethnic and Class Tensions," 80; W. Craig Heron, "Working-Class Hamilton, 1895–1930" (PhD dissertation, Dalhousie University 1981), 206; Michael J. Piva, *The Condition of the Working Class in Toronto, 1900–1921* (Ottawa: University of Ottawa Press 1978), 76–82; Claude Larivière, *Albert Saint-Martin, militant d'avant-garde (1865–1947)* (Laval: Éditions Albert Saint-Martin 1979), 109–18; Geoffrey Ewen, "Quebec: Class and Ethnicity," in Craig Heron, ed., *The Workers' Revolt in Canada, 1917–1925* (Toronto: University of Toronto Press 1998), 87–143; Canada, Department of Labour, *Labour Organization in Canada*, 1915, 17; UBC Archives, Vancouver Trades and Labor Council Minutes, 19 November 1914; Morton and Granatstein, *Marching to Armageddon*, 7–8; Morton, *When Your Number's Up*, 278–9. According to Morton's calculations, nearly two-thirds of the Canadian Expeditionary Force counted in March 1916 had been manual workers.

21 Enid M. Price, "Changes in the Industrial Occupations of Women in the Environment of Montreal during the Period of the War, 1914–1918" (MA thesis, McGill University 1919); Ceta Ramkhalawansingh, "Women during the Great War," in Janice Action et al., eds., *Women at Work: Ontario, 1850–1930* (Toronto: Women's Press 1974), 261–307; Graham S. Lowe, *Women in the Administrative Revolution: The Feminization of Clerical Work* (Toronto: University of Toronto Press 1987); Linda Kealey, "Women and Labour during World War I: Women Workers and the Minimum Wage in Manitoba," in Mary Kinnear, ed., *First Days, Fighting Days: Women in Manitoba History* (Regina: Canadian Plains Research Centre 1987), 76–99;

James Naylor, *The New Democracy: Challenging the Social Order in Industrial Ontario, 1914–15* (Toronto: University of Toronto Press 1991), 13; Piva, *Condition of the Working Class*, 40–3; Heron, "Working-Class Hamilton," 388–90.

22 Terry Copp, *The Anatomy of Poverty: The Condition of the Working Class in Montreal, 1897–1929* (Toronto: McClelland and Stewart 1974), 56; Piva, *Condition of the Working Class*, 40–3; Craig Heron, "The High School and the Household Economy in Working-Class Hamilton, 1890–1940," *HSE* 7, no. 2 (Fall 1995), 217–59; Heron, "Working-Class Hamilton," 29.

23 Michael Bliss, *A Canadian Millionaire: The Life and Business Times of Sir Joseph Flavelle, Bart., 1858–1939* (Toronto: Macmillan 1978); David Carnegie, *The History of Munitions and Supply in Canada, 1914–1918* (London: Longmans, Green 1925); Avery, *"Dangerous Foreigners"*; Andrij Makuch, "Ukrainian Canadians and the Wartime Economy," in Swyripa and Thompson, eds., *Loyalties in Conflict*, 69–78; Heron, "Working-Class Hamilton," 319–24; and Craig Heron, *Working in Steel: The Early Years in Canada, 1883–1935* (Toronto: McClelland and Stewart 1988), 140.

24 Heron, "Working-Class Hamilton," 237–8.

25 See Bettina Bradbury, *Working Families: Age, Gender, and Daily Survival in Industrializing Montreal* (Toronto: McClelland and Stewart 1993); Jane Synge, "The Transition from School to Work: Growing Up Working Class in Early Twentieth Century Hamilton, Ontario," in K. Ishwaran, ed., *Childhood and Adolescence in Canada* (Toronto: McGraw-Hill Ryerson 1979), 249–69; Jane Synge, "Self-Help and Neighbourliness: Patterns of Life in Hamilton," in Irving Abella and David Millar, eds., *Canadian Workers in the Twentieth Century* (Toronto: Oxford University Press 1978), 97–104; Copp, *Anatomy of Poverty*; Piva, *Condition of the Working Class*; Heron, "High School and the Household Economy."

26 Nova Scotia, Factories' Inspector, *Report*, 1917, 6; Naylor, *New Democracy*, 34; Siemiatycki, "Labour Contained," 111; LAC, MG 30, A16 (Sir Joseph Flavelle Papers), Vol. 2, File: Department of Labour, Basil Magor to J. Flavelle, 7 June 1916; "The Industrial Slacker," *Canadian Foundryman* 9, no. 5 (May 1918), 105; Piva, *Condition of the Working Class*, 106; Carnegie, *History of Munitions and Supply*, 252–3; Heron, "Working-Class Hamilton," 238–9; Heron, *Working in Steel*, 114–16.

27 Ewen, "Quebec: Class and Ethnicity"; Brian F. Hogan, *Cobalt: Year of the Strike, 1919* (Cobalt, ON: Highway Book Shop 1978), 24–31; Siemiatycki, "Munitions and Labour Militancy"; Allen Seager, "A Proletariat in Wild Rose Country: The Alberta Coal Miners, 1900–1945" (PhD dissertation, York University 1981).

28 *LG*, September 1917, 736–7; January 1918, 48–9; August 1919, 1004–5; July 1921, 972. Calculations of percentages are ours.
29 Canada, Department of Labour, *Labour Organization in Canada* (Ottawa: King's Printer), 1917, 38–9.
30 R.T. Naylor, "Canadian State," 83–7; Piva, *Condition of the Working Class*, 27–59; Copp, *Anatomy of Poverty*, 30–43; Eleanor A. Bartlett, "Real Wages and the Standard of Living in Vancouver, 1901–1929," *BC Studies* 51 (Autumn 1981), 57; Joseph Harry Sutcliffe and Paul Phillips, "Real Wages and the Winnipeg General Strike: An Empirical Investigation" (unpublished paper); Glen Makahonuk, 'Class Conflict in a Prairie City: The Saskatoon Working-Class Response to Prairie Capitalism, 1906–1919,' *L/LT* 19 (Spring 1987), 98–100; Heron, *Working in Steel*, 139.
31 See Frank, "The Miner's Financier: Women in the Cape Breton Coal Towns, 1917," *Atlantis* 8, no. 2 (Spring 1983), 137–43.
32 Quoted in A. Ross McCormack, *Reformers, Rebels, and Revolutionaries: The Western Canadian Radical Movement, 1899–1919* (Toronto: University of Toronto Press 1977), 127.
33 Bliss, *Canadian Millionaire*, 329–62; LAC, MG 26, H 1(a) (Sir Robert Borden Papers), Northrup to Borden, 21 July 1917.
34 Quoted in Copp, *Anatomy of Poverty*, 134.
35 Canada, Department of Labour, *Labour Organization in Canada*, 1917, 38–9; McCormack, *Reformers, Rebels, and Revolutionaries*, 121–3.
36 Martin Robin, *Radical Politics and Canadian Labour, 1880–1930* (Kingston: Industrial Relations Centre, Queen's University 1968); McCormack, *Reformers, Rebels, and Revolutionaries*, 128–9.
37 Ian MacPherson, *Each for All: A History of the Co-operative Movement in English Canada, 1900–1945* (Toronto: McClelland and Stewart 1979), 63–6. Working-class consumer co-ops are discussed in Craig Heron and George De Zwaan, "Industrial Unionism in Eastern Ontario: Gananoque, 1918–1921," *OH* 77, no. 3 (September 1985), 169, 172; and Heron, "Working-Class Hamilton."
38 *LG*, 1919–20.
39 Mercedes Wells Steedman, "Female Participation in the Canadian Clothing Industry, 1890 to 1940" (PhD dissertation, University of London 1990); Ewen, "Quebec: Class and Ethnicity"; Heron, "Working-Class Hamilton," 422.
40 In the decade before the war many of Canada's new corporate employers, both domestic and foreign, had begun to reorganize their work processes with more centralized, authoritarian managerial structures and new labour-saving technology. The transformation of

their workplaces was most evident in such central Canadian cities as Montreal, Toronto, and Hamilton, where trend-setting American managerial styles had their greatest impact, but was far from complete in most industries by the outbreak of the war. Heron, *Working in Steel*; Craig Heron, "The Second Industrial Revolution in Canada, 1890–1930," in Deian R. Hopkin and Gregory S. Kealey, eds., *Class, Community, and the Labour Movement: Wales and Canada, 1850–1930* (Aberystwyth, Wales: Llafur and Canadian Committee on Labour History 1989); Craig Heron and Bryan D. Palmer, "Through the Prism of the Strike: Industrial Conflict in Southern Ontario, 1901–1914," *CHR* 58, no. 4 (December 1977), 423–58; Ian McKay, "Strikes in the Maritimes, 1901–1914," *Acadiensis* 13 (1983), 3–46; Lowe, *Women in the Administrative Revolution*; Robert Armstrong, "The Quebec Asbestos Industry: Technological Change, 1878–1929," in Duncan Cameron, ed., *Explorations in Canadian Economic History: Essays in Honour of Irene M. Spry* (Ottawa: University of Ottawa Press 1985), 189–210; Duncan Stacey, *Sockeye and Tinplate: Technological Change in the Fraser River Canning Industry, 1871–1912* (Victoria: British Columbia Provincial Museum 1982); Richard Rajala, "Managerial Crisis: The Emergence and Role of the West Coast Logging Engineer, 1900–1930," in Peter Baskerville, ed., *Canadian Papers in Business History* (Victoria: Public History Group 1989), 101–27; Richard Rajala, "The Rude Science: A Social History of West Coast Logging, 1890–1930" (MA thesis, University of Victoria 1987); Logan W. Hovis, "Technological Change and Mining Labour: Copper Mining and Milling Operations at the Britannia Mines, British Columbia, 1898–1937" (MA thesis, University of British Columbia 1986); Robert Babcock, "Saint John Longshoremen during the Rise of Canada's Winter Port, 1895–1922," *L/LT* 25 (Spring 1990), 15–46; John Bellamy Foster, "On the Waterfront: Longshoring in Canada," in Heron and Storey, eds., *On the Job*, 181–308; Mercedes Steedman, "Skill and Gender in the Canadian Clothing Industry, 1890–1940," ibid., 152–76; Hugh Tuck, "Union Authority, Corporate Obstinacy, and the Grand Trunk Strike of 1910," *HP* 1976, 175–92; Herbert Marshall, Frank Southard, Jr, and Kenneth W. Taylor, *Canadian American Industry: A Study in International Investment* (Toronto: McClelland and Stewart 1976 [1936]).

41 Heron, "Crisis of the Craftsman"; Wayne Roberts, "Toronto Metal Workers and the Second Industrial Revolution, 1889–1914," *L/LT* 6 (Autumn 1980), 49–72.

42 *Industrial Banner* (Toronto), 7 September 1917, 43.

43 Quoted in Heron, *Working in Steel*, 140.

44 Avery, *"Dangerous Foreigners"*; Andrij Makuch, "Ukrainian Canadians and the Wartime Economy," in Swyripa and Thompson, *Loyalties in Conflict*, 70; Wickberg, ed., *From China to Canada.*

45 Makuch, "Ukrainian Canadians and the Wartime Economy," 71; Peter Melnycky, "The Internment of Ukrainians in Canada," in Swyripa and Thompson, eds., *Loyalties in Conflict*, 14–15; Desmond Morton, *The Canadian General: Sir William Otter* (Toronto: Hakkert 1974), 343; Avery, *"Dangerous Foreigners,"* 32.

46 Edmund Bradwin, *The Bunkhouse Man: A Study of Work and Pay in the Camps of Canada, 1903–1914* (Toronto: University of Toronto Press 1971 [1928]); Robert F. Harney, ed., *Gathering Place: Peoples and Neighbourhoods of Toronto, 1834–1945* (Toronto: Multicultural History Society of Ontario 1978); Bruno Ramirez, *On the Move: French Canadians and Italian Migrants in the North Atlantic Economy, 1860–1914* (Toronto: McClelland and Stewart 1991); Heron, *Working in Steel*; Avery, "Ethnic and Class Tensions," 79–98; Avery *"Dangerous Foreigners,"* 73–89; McCormack, *Reformers, Rebels, and Revolutionaries*, 121; Heron, "Working-Class Hamilton," 320–7; Wickberg, ed., *From China to Canada*, 120–2; Ian McKay, "The 1910s: The Stillborn Triumph of Progressive Reform," in E.R. Forbes and D.A. Muise, eds., *The Atlantic Provinces in Confederation* (Toronto and Fredericton: University of Toronto Press and Acadiensis Press 1993), 222.

47 Robin, *Radical Politics and Canadian Labour*; McCormack, *Reformers, Rebels, and Revolutionaries*, 122–3.

48 Provencher, *Québec sous la loi des mesures de guerre*; Armstrong, *Crisis of Quebec*; Ewen, "Quebec: Class and Ethnicity."

49 Susan Mayse, *Ginger: The Life and Death of Ginger Goodwin* (Madeira Park, BC: Harbour Publishing 1990); Derek Hanebury, *Ginger Goodwin: Beyond the Forbidden Plateau* (Vancouver: Pulp Press 1986).

50 James Naylor, "Southern Ontario: Striking at the Ballot Box," in Heron, ed., *Workers' Revolt*, 144–75; Robin, *Radical Politics and Canadian Labour*, 163–9; McCormack, *Reformers, Rebels, and Revolutionaries*, 152–4.

51 LAC, MG 30 (Sir Joseph Flavelle Papers), A16, Vol. 38, File 1918–19, March Irish to Flavelle, 20 June 1918.

52 Quoted in Robin, *Radical Politics and Canadian Labour*, 165.

53 Quoted in Heron, *Working in Steel*, 142.

54 Quoted in Bercuson, *Fools and Wise Men*, 71.

55 Ibid., 75–8.

56 The leadership of the Winnipeg General Strike made much of this declaration. See Norman Penner, *Winnipeg 1919: The Strikers' Own Story of the Winnipeg General Strike* (Toronto: James Lorimer), 40–1; Ian McKay and

Suzanne Morton, "The Maritimes: Expanding the Circle of Resistance," in Heron, ed., *Workers' Revolt*, 43–86.

57 Public Archives of Manitoba, Robert Russell Papers, Cassidy to Stephenson, 19 January 1919.

58 McCormack, *Reformers, Rebels, and Revolutionaries*, 139–43 (quote at 141); Avery, *"Dangerous Foreigners,"* 70–6; Peter Krawchuk, *The Ukrainian Socialist Movement in Canada, 1907–1918* (Toronto: Progress Books 1979); Edward W. Laine, "Finnish Canadian Radicalism and Canadian Politics: The First Forty Years, 1900–1940," in Jorgen Dahlie and Tissa Fernando, eds., *Ethnicity, Power, and Politics in Canada* (Toronto: Methuen 1981), 94–112.

59 Robert H. Babcock, *Gompers in Canada: A Study in American Continentalism before the First World War* (Toronto: University of Toronto Press 1974).

60 McCormack, *Reformers, Rebels, and Revolutionaries*; Mark Leier, *Where the Fraser River Flows: The Industrial Workers of the World in British Columbia* (Vancouver: New Star Books 1990).

61 Ian McKay, "Industry, Work, and Community in the Cumberland Coalfields, 1948–1927" (PhD dissertation, Dalhousie University 1983); Paul MacEwan, *Miners and Steelworkers: Labour in Cape Breton* (Toronto: Samuel Stevens Hakkert and Company 1976); Seager, "Proletariat in Wild Rose Country"; Foster, "On the Waterfront"; Jacques Rouillard, *Les travailleurs du coton au Québec, 1900–1915* (Montreal: Les Presses de l'Université du Québec 1974); Steedman, "Female Participation in the Canadian Clothing Industry."

62 Jacques Rouillard, *Les syndicats nationaux au Québec de 1900 à 1930* (Quebec: Les Presses de l'Université Laval 1979).

63 Robin, *Radical Politics and Canadian Labour*; McCormack, *Reformers, Rebels, and Revolutionaries*; Frank and Reilly, "Emergence of the Socialist Movement"; Krawchuck, *Ukrainian Socialist Movement*; Laine, "Finnish Canadian Radicalism"; Ruth Frager, "Radical Portraits: The Roots of Socialism in Toronto's Immigrant Jewish Community, 1900–1939" (unpublished paper, Department of History, McMaster University); Craig Heron, "Labourism and the Canadian Working Class," *L/LT* 13 (Spring 1984), 45–76.

64 Wisconsin State Historical Society, American Federation of Labor Papers, Flett to Gompers, 3 October 1916.

65 Siemiatycki, "Labour Contained," 51–6.

66 LAC, MG 26, H 1(a), Borden Diaries, 5 June 1914; 15 June 1915.

67 Siemiatycki, "Labour Contained," 25–8.

68 LAC, MG 30, A16, Watters to Borden, 22 November 1915.

69 LAC, Toronto District Trades and Labor Council, Minutes, 6 April 1916; Siemiatycki, "Munitions and Labour Militancy"; Tucker, "World War I and the Post-War Labour Revolt."

70 Canada, Department of Labour, *Labour Organization in Canada*, 1914, 18–19; Socknat, *Witness against War*, 37; Trades and Labor Congress of Canada (TLC), *Proceedings*, 1914, 20; 1915, 14, 91.

71 TLC, *Proceedings*, 1915, 15; LAC, MG 26, H 1(a), Borden Diaries, 21 May 1917.

72 Siemiatycki, "Labour Contained," 153–4.

73 Ibid., 155–8.

74 LAC, MG 26, H 1(a), Robertson to Borden, 23 August 1917; Watters and Moore, "To Organized Labor in Canada" (undated circular); TLC, *Convention Booklet*, 1918.

75 *Herald* (Halifax), 26 February 1918; *Machinists' Monthly Journal*, May 1918, 455.

76 *Labor News*, 26 July 1918.

77 Craig Heron, "The Great War and Nova Scotia Steelworkers," *Acadiensis* 16, no. 2 (Spring 1987), 17.

78 Siemiatycki, "Labour Contained," 216–17.

79 *Calgary Herald*, 23 July 1918.

80 Siemiatycki, "Labour Contained," 203–4.

81 *Telegram* (Toronto), 23 July 1918.

82 Canada, National Industrial Conference, *Official Report of Proceedings and Discussions* (Ottawa: King's Printer 1919), 6; Graham, *Arthur Meighen*, 211–44; S.W. Horrall, "The Royal North-West Mounted Police and Labour Unrest in Western Canada, 1919,' *CHR* 61, no. 2 (June 1980), 169–90; Kealey, "State Repression of Labour"; Canada, Senate, *Debates*, 2 April 1919, 194.

83 Mitchell, "'To Reach the Leadership of This Revolutionary Movement': A.J. Andrews, the Canadian State, and the Suppression of the Winnipeg General Strike," *Prairie Forum* 18, no. 2 (Fall 1993), 239–55; David J. Bercuson, *Confrontation at Winnipeg: Labour, Industrial Relations, and the General Strike* (Kingston and Montreal: McGill-Queen's University Press, 2nd ed., 1990), 115–75; Don Macgillivray, "Military Aid to the Civil Power: The Cape Breton Experience in the 1920s," in Don Macgillivray and Brian Tennyson, eds., *Cape Breton Historical Essays* (Sydney: University College of Cape Breton 1980); David Frank, "The Trial of J.B. Mclachlan," *HP* 1983, 208–25; Allen Seager and David Roth, "British Columbia and the Mining West: A Ghost of a Chance," in Heron, ed., *Workers' Revolt*, 231–67. On federal collaboration in the Red Scare, see Canada, Department of

Labour, *Information Respecting the Russian Soviet System and Its Propaganda in North America* (Ottawa: King's Printer 1920). Before the war radicalism that seemed menacing was simply repressed in an ad hoc fashion. Local municipal police forces would simply lock up soapbox socialists who caused a seditious nuisance. Any combination of large-scale militancy and radicalism would generally result in the mobilization of the militia to occupy the streets. Leier, *Where the Fraser River Flows*; Schulze, "Industrial Workers of the World"; Frank and Reilly, "Emergence of the Socialist Movement," 89–90; McCormack, *Reformers, Rebels, and Revolutionaries*, 105–7; Heron, "Working-Class Hamilton," 654–5; Morton, "Aid to the Civil Power."

84 Canada, Royal Commission on Industrial Relations, *Report* (Ottawa: King's Printer 1919) (the unpublished testimony is available at LAC); Canada, National Industrial Conference, *Report*; Siemiatycki, "Labour Contained," 355–67; Naylor, *New Democracy*, 188–214; James Naylor, "Workers and the State: Experiments in Corporatism after World War One," *SPE* 42 (Autumn 1993), 28–35; Larry G. Gerber, "United States and Canadian National Industrial Conferences of 1919: A Comparative Analysis," *Labor History* 32, no. 1 (Winter 1991), 42–65; J.G. Hucul, "Canada and the International Labour Organization" (MA thesis, University of Windsor 1984); LAC, John Bruce Papers, Interview, 30 March 1963.

I'D HATE
LIKE HELL
TO BE A SCAB

Chapter Nine

Contours of a Workers' Revolt

The great appear great to us because we are on our knees. Let us rise!

W.A. Pritchard[1]

Rarely in the history of capitalist society do workers stand poised to overthrow the social system in which they live and work. More limited hopes and horizons generally frame their lives. Workers may harbour an intense sense of injustice but feel powerless to achieve redress. They may grumble fatalistically. They may have come to believe that as workers they have no right to expect more from their society. Or they may channel their anger and aspirations into daily trench warfare over terrain marked by more immediate, and more modest, objectives. It takes a major rupture in the material underpinnings of their daily experience and in their understanding of the way the world works – their "common sense" – to fashion a new and shared conviction that their subordinate status within capitalist society must and can change. Then masses of workers may suddenly rise boldly to assert a new place for themselves within transformed relations of production, politics, and social life generally. Capitalists, politicians, and others in positions of authority cannot ignore them. It then takes a grinding destruction of the bases of working-class strength in everyday life and an erosion of that heady new ideological openness to force workers back into compliance and resignation to their subordinate fate.

In the four years after 1916, workers in Canada developed a remarkably assertive sense of purpose and power – their society could be different and their actions could transform it. The war launched Canadian

Demonstration in Toronto, 1919. City of Toronto Archives, James 2543 workers on a trajectory of escalating demands and expectations. By the mid-1920s, however, labour's upsurge had been snuffed out across the country. The rise and fall of the workers' revolt followed a distinctive rhythm in each region, but there were key features that emerged in all major industrial centres. The purpose of this essay is to examine country-wide patterns in the revolt and its defeat.

The Workers' Challenge, 1917–1920

The most visible manifestation of the emerging workers' revolt was the wave of strikes that began after 1916 – a clear indication that the more individualistic drifting and shifting of the preceding two years was moving towards more collective responses and longer-range concerns about postwar society. As the research of Douglas Cruikshank and Gregory Kealey indicates,[2] the 218 strikes recorded for 1917 involved more than 50,000 workers, twice the previous year's total and far more than in any single year since the turn of the century. Moreover, militancy paid off. Aside from those in the coalfields, most of the few big confrontations of 1916 had resulted in failure, but the following year strikers were successful in an unprecedented 40 per cent of their strikes and settled for compromises in another 20 per cent; employers got clear victories in only 19 per cent of strikes.[3] Strikers were also more regularly jumping the gun on the slow procedures of the Industrial Disputes Investigation Act by engaging in illegal strikes.[4] The annual total of strikers had doubled by 1919, when nearly 150,000 workers marched out in 427 strikes. In 1920 the number of strikes peaked at 457, though the number of strikers dropped by half. Over the four-year period 350,000 wage-earners participated in strikes in Canada, distributed remarkably evenly across the country: 17 per cent in the Maritimes; a fifth in each of Quebec, the Prairies, and British Columbia; and a quarter in Ontario. More than a third of strikes were in manufacturing and a quarter in mining; three out of five strikers in this period were in these two sectors. Within manufacturing, the metal trades, shipbuilding, and clothing and textiles were flashpoints; together they constituted 44 per cent of strikes and more than half the strikers in that sector. In all parts of the country but the Maritimes, the peak of this strike wave was in mid-1919; however, the rate of militancy's decline varied across regions. In particular, after the crushing of the Winnipeg General Strike, workers on the Prairies retreated from the picket lines much more quickly than elsewhere in the country.

Workers were not simply striking; they were also rapidly banding together into unions. There can be no doubt that the various workers' organizations that appeared across the country between 1917 and 1925 constituted a mass popular movement of wage-earners throughout most of urban Canada. At the end of 1915 union membership reported to the federal Department of Labour bottomed out at just over 140,000, and during the next year rose to only 160,000, still below the totals for 1913 and 1914. By the end of 1917, however, it was just shy of 205,000 and then leaped to almost 250,000 in 1918. Yet the most spectacular increase was recorded in 1919, when total reported union membership in Canada reached 378,000, the highest to that point in Canadian history. That high-water mark held through 1920, when only five thousand members were lost from the total union rolls.[5] These official figures for 1919–20 amount to just under 18 per cent of the non-agricultural workforce counted in the 1921 census, a historic peak in union membership up to that point. Yet, as the labour department admitted, these totals are undoubtedly low since many unions did not submit membership statistics and the reporting was at the end of the year, well after the great defeats in the spring and summer of 1919. A reasonable estimate is that at least one worker in five took out a union card. Probably well more than one in four passed through a union in these years, a level comparable to that of the mid-1940s. The dramatic increase in membership after 1918 and the many demands for union recognition in the industrial battles of this period point to the change in working-class consciousness that had set in by the end of the war. Workers were not simply trying to win immediate demands; they were turning to unions to solidify wartime gains and to prevent a return to the insecurity and indignity of the pre-war era. "If we don't do something we will get our heads taken off after this great war is over," a Gananoque unionist warned.[6]

Initially, the growth in union membership primarily revived pre-war patterns of organization. The first to put their unions back on their feet were craft unionists, especially the metalworkers in the munitions plants and shipbuilding yards, and coal miners in the East and West.[7] Union locals then began to appear among the less skilled workers who also had a record of organizing – street railwaymen, teamsters, longshoremen, and the like. By 1918, however, workers who had never before shown much interest in unions were signing up. Among the new union members were factory workers in resource processing plants in British Columbia and mass-production plants in southern Ontario, Quebec, and Nova Scotia; loggers in the West and northern Ontario; unskilled workers of various kinds; clerical workers in several cities; and public-sector workers at all three levels of government, including municipal labourers, policemen (in ten cities), firemen, teachers, and letter carriers.[8] In fact, public-sector strikes were often the most controversial and menacing to dominant social relations.[9] Wage-earners in all parts of the country, in large cities and small towns, were entering the house of labour. Women were found in growing numbers among the unionized and even on union executives, although in a role subordinate to that of men.[10] There was also more ethnic diversity in many of these unions, especially those in the mass-production and resource industries, from Sydney steel mills to Thetford asbestos mines to Toronto meatpacking factories to Trail smelters. A number of unions were organized primarily along ethnic or racial lines – for example, the Chinese Shingle Weavers' Union and Japanese Camp and Mill Workers' Union in British Columbia, the Finnish loggers in northern Ontario, the Jewish clothing workers in Montreal and Toronto, the black sleeping-car porters on the CPR, and the Italian construction labourers in several cities.[11] Some of these workers were inspired by the Russian Revolution; many more rode a wave of ethnic self-consciousness and assertiveness as political change convulsed their homelands.[12] Whatever their inspirations, all these workers were eager to confront the oppression and exploitation they experienced as wage-earners in Canada.

Joining a union in this period was no passive process under the manipulative control of union bureaucrats. The established labour leaders were overwhelmed by the flood of new members who eagerly signed their union cards with little prompting and by the restlessness and combativeness of rank-and-file unionists in all parts of the country. Labour officials tried frantically to cool this ardour as it reached the boiling point in many workplaces. Often the workers ignored their leaders completely and pressed on with bold demands and direct action. "At the foundation of all this agitation is the general restlessness and dissatisfaction," the national government's security chief warned. "The greater number of labour men, and probably the community as a whole, are in an uncertain, apprehensive, nervous and irritable temper. Perhaps these agitators are but the foam on the wave."[13] Montreal machinist J.O. Houston captured both the spirit and trajectory of working-class mobilization: "More and more each worker is doing his own thinking, is becoming his own intellectual, and to the extent that this is so he is placing less and less trust in labour leaders. He is looking for neither a Moses nor a Saviour. All the Sammy Gompers are doomed. His new representative will be an instrument to perform a specific act decided upon by the rank and file of an industrial organization."[14]

Rank-and-file activism and solidarity soon forged a qualitatively different labour movement. More than ever before, divisions between workers seemed to be giving way to a remarkable spirit of working-class unity and class consciousness. As we have seen, organizational structures became more flexible in devising imaginative experiments readily adapted to immediate needs and conditions. In addition to less exclusivist craft unionism and more widespread industrial unionism, there was an innovative, all-inclusive "community unionism" that touched many centres with weak or non-existent union traditions, and in some cases, a small, diverse local workforce close to primary production. Across the country the objective was the same: to mobilize greater numbers in common cause. Before the middle of 1919, the great majority of these new unions were affiliated with international organizations headquartered in the United States. At the same time, Canadian branches everywhere found new ways to work together with other union locals while maintaining considerable independence from their American parents. District councils linked up locals of some of the larger unions, and many locals federated across occupational lines into more cooperative local, district, and provincial bodies. For the most part, it was the local trades and labour council or district miners' organization that played the active coordinating role of drawing together and speaking for the local wage-earning population. In many cities trades councils sponsored, directly or indirectly, local labour newspapers that were produced independently of the international union publications, and that grew in number from four in 1914 to seventeen by 1919 and became important forums of information on local issues, international labour news, and debate about evolving strategies.[15] Some radicals even began to envisage the trades councils as the new base of the labour movement.[16] Whatever their political cast, the councils reflected the decentralized, community-based focus of most of the workers' movements in these years.

The new spirit of solidarity and working-class consciousness was evident in action as well as organization. The best-known example, the general sympathy strike, was widely discussed and began to appear in many parts of the country in 1918. It had mass popular support when it got its first major tests in Winnipeg and Amherst, Nova Scotia, in May 1919. As sympathy strikes spread across the West in response to the repression of the Winnipeg strikers, the radical leadership could do no more than place itself at the head of a burst of solidarity and militancy that was largely beyond its control.[17]

In this context of militancy and confrontation, the thousands of new unionists quickly grew impatient with some of their more cautious leaders.[18] Although most of the existing labour leaders held on to their old power bases, they had to face an emergent cadre of feistier, more radical leaders in the new union locals: Pictou County's Clifford Dane, Cape Breton's J.B. McLachlan, Montreal's Tom Cassidy, Gananoque's Gordon Bishop, Toronto's Jack MacDonald, Hamilton's Fred Flatman, Winnipeg's R.B. Russell, Regina's Joseph Sambrook, Calgary's R.J. Tallon, Edmonton's Joe Knight, the Crows Nest Pass's Phillip Christophers, and Vancouver's Jack Kavanagh.[19] Among the best-known female militants were Helena Gutteridge in Vancouver, Amelia Turner in Calgary, Sarah Johnston-Knight in Edmonton, Helen Armstrong in Winnipeg, Mary McNab in Hamilton, and Rose Henderson in Montreal.[20] These were the men and women who chaired meetings, helped organize new unions, led strikes, edited labour newspapers, and generally tried to awaken workers to wider visions of a reconstructed society after the war. Many were local socialists who after years of conflict with the existing labour leadership had found a receptive ear among the increasingly militant workers. They were more popular partly because, as socialists, they had reassessed their long-standing reservations about industrial action and were undertaking, among themselves, an ideological renewal that reflected lessons learned from the massive militancy of Canadian workers in the period.[21] Ironically, the socialist parties to which they belonged made fewer adjustments in their formal programs and continued their narrow emphasis on socialist education and propaganda.

The workers' movements that took shape in the 1917–20 period were rooted first and foremost in industrial action. They followed in the long Anglo-American tradition of struggling for their goals primarily (though not exclusively) in the workplace, as opposed to the European tradition of forging a broader assault on an illiberal, authoritarian state through some kind of socialist party. It was powerful unions and tough bargaining with employers that held out the most promise for shoring up the male breadwinner's family wage and guaranteeing his dignity and relative independence in the workplace. Many radicals in this period put special emphasis on organizing the working class for confrontations at the point of production. Yet, apart from some voices in the West Coast logging camps,[22] few were espousing genuine "syndicalism" – that European brand of radicalism that rejected radical social change through electoral politics in favour of the revolutionary potential of direct action on the picket line. Canadian historians have too often applied the label loosely to cover various forms of radical rhetoric in favour of tough-minded industrial unionism.[23] Even in western Canada, the One Big Union was led by socialists who saw the value of solid industrial organization in mobilizing the working class but never imagined a general strike as anything more than the most militant form of exerting working-class power for immediate goals, whether in workplace negotiations or in confronting the government over specific grievances.[24] Despite the hysterical claims at the time, the general strikes in eastern and western Canada never involved any attempted seizure of state power. And there was no "return to politics" after some kind of syndicalist interlude. In fact, the class solidarity of the picket line and the union hall started overflowing into Canadian politics in industrial centres across the country as early as 1917. Immediate issues had become so politicized in any case that the distinction between the two spheres of activity must have seemed increasingly obscure.

In a period of great experimentation and fluidity of working-class organization, the precise form of independent working-class politics could have been an open question. In 1917 James Simpson, the socialist vice-president of the Trades and Labor Congress, proposed that the labour movement respond to the introduction of conscription by organizing workers' and soldiers' councils similar to Russian soviets (and to some new organizations in Britain at that time, as Simpson must have learned during his three-month visit that year).[25] But before the middle of 1919, outside some limited socialist circles (especially the eastern European radicals who were inspired by the Russian Revolution),[26] that idea generally fell on deaf ears. Anglophone and francophone labour leaders of all stripes were thoroughly constitutionalist in their political orientation, and the vehicle chosen in working-class communities across the country was the independent labour party. Well before the Trades and Labor Congress of Canada put out its call for a Canadian Labor Party in the fall of 1917, many union leaders had taken the initiative in organizing such a party in their own communities. These local labour parties, which always remained completely separate from their union structures, soon began to federate into loosely structured provincial political organizations, though never into an official national labour party. By organizing speakers' bureaus, distributing literature, and generally acting as a clearing house for debate and strategizing, the provincial parties provided important coordination of political organizing and education. The political wing of the workers' movements in this period nonetheless remained highly decentralized, with the local city-based parties retaining the power to nominate their own candidates and run their own campaigns.[27]

The 1917 federal election marked the first major foray of independent labourism, but, under the heavy torrents of Unionist jingoistic hysteria, most of the thirty-five labour candidates lost their deposits (even though the Laurier Liberals stepped aside for thirteen of them).[28] More successful were efforts at the municipal level in several industrial centres. Handfuls of labour representatives were also elected to provincial legislatures in 1919–20 – two each in New Brunswick and Quebec, three in British Columbia, four in Nova Scotia, eleven in Manitoba, and the same number in Ontario, where they entered the country's first Farmer-Labour government.[29] That coalition was only the most visible of its kind. In an electoral system in which wage-earners were outnumbered by independent commodity producers, the independent labour parties were motivated to look for political allies among the organized farmers. In some constituencies containing smaller urban centres, fusion candidates had the support of both groups, but generally the workers and farmers kept their own distinct organizations.[30] The other group that labour parties had to learn to work with were the returned soldiers, who were being pulled in different political directions as they pursued a better deal for themselves and their families. While officers tried to direct their men's anger against the new radicalism of the period, in some parts of the country a more proletarian, left-of-centre faction responded favourably to labourist proposals of electoral cooperation, one example of which was the Canadian Union of Ex-Servicemen, known as CNUX.[31] The labour parties themselves also began to attract disaffected middle-class citizens, including the famous "social gospellers" J.S. Woodsworth, William Ivens, William Irvine, and A.E. Smith.[32] Yet, unlike the situation in the British Labour Party in this period and the Cooperative Commonwealth Federation in the 1930s, no radicalized middle-class intelligentsia moved into key roles in the parties.[33] On the whole, the leadership and membership of the various independent labour parties across Canada remained predominantly working-class.

The local labour parties became remarkably lively, relatively non-sectarian forums for discussion and debate about pressing concerns in working-class life and the most appropriate strategies for organizing. Until the middle of 1919 a rare ideological openness, fluidity, and tolerance prevailed among the labourists, single-taxers, socialists, and sundry freethinkers who joined the parties. Each local branch tended to have a slightly different ideological emphasis that fell somewhere between the old pre-war working-class liberalism known as "labourism" and unadulterated Marxist socialism.[34] Generally, these organizations had shifted considerably further to the left than their pre-war counterparts – a shift owing largely to the presence of committed socialists or a regular dialogue with members of the main socialist parties (especially the Social Democrats, who had now carved out a primarily educational role for themselves within the political wing of the workers' movements). Across the country the labourist-socialist alliance expressed itself through more visionary rhetoric and more ambitious programs aimed at, in the words of the Cape Breton ILP, "the working class ownership and democratic management of all the social means of wealth distribution at the earliest possible date," or, at least, in the words of the Ontario and Quebec labour parties, "the industrial freedom of those who toil and the political liberation of those who for so long have been denied justice."[35]

As the federal government's Royal Commission on Industrial Relations (the Mathers Commission) discovered on its cross-country trek in the spring of 1919, many workers shared in the search for a new vision.[36] In the words of Calgary postal worker Clifford Nichols, "the worker has gotten enormous ideals and he is determined to work them out."[37] The "common sense" that had guided most workers' lives for so long had been shattered in the wartime crucible. As they looked to a future in which things would be different, workers across the country were receptive to a variety of voices that called for more working-class dignity, independence, and material well-being, and that proposed more power for them to influence decisions that affected their lives on the job, as citizens, and in society more generally. For some, these demands were part of a revolutionary project that would sweep away capitalist society and replace it with a democratically managed workers' republic; for others, they were the harbingers of social reforms that would democratize government and soften the impact of market forces. But the distinction between reform and revolution was frequently blurred in the millennial rhetoric of the period (how many hopes and dreams were hung on, for example, the oft-repeated slogans "production for use" and "New Democracy"?). Political distinctions were also blurred by the commitment of virtually all political factions to orderly social change through some combination of mass industrial action and parliamentarism.

At all points along the political continuum, the new vision was about workers' power. It was a revolt against the kind of subordination that workers had hitherto known in Canadian capitalist society, against the elitist, authoritarian, and paternalistic ways in which business and the state had grown accustomed to ruling in Canada. It was an affirmation of working-class pride in their role as producers and a deep sense of natural justice captured in the constitutional preamble of Toronto's Domestic Workers' Association (chartered as Local 599 of the Hotel and Restaurant Employees International Alliance), which proclaimed its belief in "the natural right of those who toil to enjoy to the fullest extent the wealth created by their labor, realizing that under the changing conditions of our times it is impossible for us to obtain the full reward of our labor except by United action."[38] If the whole social system was not to be replaced, it would have to be drastically democratized. "Democracy" meant reforms to guarantee that political institutions were not in the tight, exclusive grasp of other classes. Political platforms bristled with long-sought-after reforms: the abolition of property qualifications and election deposits for candidates; the scrapping of the Senate and its provincial equivalents; proportional representation in legislatures; and popular democracy through referendums, initiative, and recall. Privilege should be removed from the economy by placing railways, public utilities, banks, and natural resources under public ownership and democratic management. The state should also intervene to soften the effects of an unrestrained market on workers, in the form of mothers' allowances, old-age and veterans' pensions, and health and unemployment insurance. In contrast to later versions of social democracy, there was no call for state bureaucracies and rule by experts. Working-class redress was not to be achieved by proxy. Fundamentally, the workers' revolt was a movement rooted in notions of rank-and-file mobilization, autonomy, and democracy. In place of the traditional authority of bosses, politicians, and even union officials, working-class organization and action would be the surest safeguard of Canadian labour's interests.

In large part what was at stake was the contested meaning of democratic citizenship as workers strove to articulate their own sense of citizenship and nationhood within the British political and cultural heritage. As they invoked the traditions of British rights and justice, for which they believed the war had been fought and the peace treaty signed, they could more easily make common cause with returned soldiers and challenge both the undemocratic examples of "Kaiserism" and the postwar capitalist efforts to define citizenship more narrowly as a matter of "loyalism." "We, brought up under British laws, thought that the fight for political freedom had been fought and won ... [but] the fight is on!" the *Western Labor News* announced in the midst of the Winnipeg General Strike. For these workers, democratic citizenship brought broad entitlements within the body politic. The Union Jack itself became a contested symbol. For Peterborough's Labour Day parade in 1919, the moulders decorated their float with "a bull dog in a setting of Union Jacks and a sign announcing, "What We Have We'll Hold."[39]

At the same time, the "industrial democracy" so often demanded would mean much more working-class power on the job. Organized wage-earners used their unions to confront their employers with demands not only for immediate changes in the terms of their employment (especially higher wages) but also for a formalization of the union-management relationship that would give them greater decision-making authority in the workplace.[40] A huge proportion of the strikes in the period that did not formally include the demand for union recognition resulted from employers' refusal to deal with union leaders and the demands they carried from their members. By the end of the war many union leaders, confident of workers' labour-market leverage, were turning to the state for support and demanding that the once-despised Industrial Disputes Investigation Act (which now covered all munitions work) be used to compel their bosses to pay attention to their concerns. Union requests for boards of conciliation poured into the federal Department of Labour, as did demands for royal commissions to investigate various industries.[41] The department's Fair Wages Officers became roving conciliators sent into scenes of simmering industrial conflict. This state involvement, along with the urgent labour shortages and the unflinching determination of unionized workers, convinced reluctant employers in several sectors and all regions to agree to some kind of regular collective-bargaining arrangement. In steel, meat packing, rubber, textiles, and pulp and paper, the agreements were generally informal and tenuous.[42] Workers and their employers on the railways, in urban construction and printing, in Nova Scotia and Alberta coal mining, and in the Toronto and Montreal clothing industries devised more elaborate agreements, with signed contracts and grievance and arbitration structures.[43] "Industrial legality" became one concrete mechanism sought by many local union leaders in their campaign for "industrial democracy."

Determining the most appropriate negotiating structures provoked considerable debate and ideological disagreement. Many union leaders, including the Trades and Labor Congress executive, supported the single-enterprise industrial councils proposed by the British government's Whitley Committee – a model involving equal numbers of management and union representatives. This notion of collective bargaining was challenged on two fronts. Employers preferred the so-called Colorado Plan (developed for the Rockefellers by William Lyon Mackenzie King) because it involved no unions from outside the enterprise.[44] Radicals, for their part, advocated a soviet-style council, described by a Victoria printer as an agreement in which "the employer does not appear, he is pitched overboard, and the people themselves take control of the industry."[45] Cape Breton's workers had some of the country's most elaborate plans for workers' self-management presented to them in their local labour paper in the early 1920s.[46] Visions of some kind of workers' control of production began to assume a mass resonance.

The strike weapon, and especially the sympathy strike, could also be used to advance political goals. Radical propaganda promoted the general strike as an effective response to both the challenge of postwar reconstruction and for such political outrages as the repressive orders-in-council of 1918, the brutal crushing of the Winnipeg General Strike the following spring, the arrogance of Montreal's unelected city administration in 1920, and the heavy-handed use of troops against Sydney steelworkers in 1923.[47] The mass general strike and the increasing interest in strikes as political weapons set this working-class upsurge dramatically apart from most of its predecessors in Canada.

The single demand that probably rolled up most of the aspirations of the workers' movements in this period was for a shorter workday. In 1919 a quarter of strikes incorporated this issue, far more than ever before or since.[48] The One Big Union was prepared to launch a general strike across the West over the issue.[49] Labour leaders raised it in every forum of discussion – especially the Mathers Commission and the National Industrial Conference in September 1919 – and labour representatives carried it into the provincial legislatures.[50] Most often the demand was for an eight-hour day, though the western labour movement and radicals elsewhere in the country wanted only six hours. The demand for a shorter workday served many functions: it encapsulated the desire for greater independence from the rigours of intensified work in mines and mills of Canadian industry; it held out the promise of minimizing unemployment by spreading around available work; it raised the possibility of a fuller social, recreational, and political life for wage-earners, a prospect first introduced in the shorter-hours campaigns of the 1870s and 1880s; and it could touch a responsive chord among middle-class sympathizers. By 1919 several groups of workers had convinced their employers to shorten their hours of work, though no legislature would yet touch the issue.[51]

Overall, then, workers were united in the search for greater economic security, on-the-job independence and power, political influence, and overall dignity for the working class. In that sense, the vision of a different kind of society at the heart of the workers' revolt was greater than the sum of its individual parts. The democratizing vision behind all these demands nonetheless incorporated important distinctions within the working class itself. This imaginative vision was conceived primarily by white, English-speaking men (especially married men) whose manhood was deeply enmeshed in their status as breadwinners for their families. Throughout the language of the workers' revolt their notion of entitlement assumed male dominance of public life and the dependence of women and children on their men. Most working-class leaders continued to believe that the best place for women was tending the home fires while their menfolk earned the family's wages. Yet these same leaders gave more help to women who wanted to unionize than had ever been extended before, allowed a few into leadership roles, and welcomed small bands of committed working-class housewives into a special supportive relationship within the workers' movements with their own Women's Labor Leagues and Women's Independent Labor Parties. Female activists used this separate space provided for them, along with the greater public receptiveness to gender equality that had flowed from the granting of voting rights to women during the war, to push for a wider social and political role – one that recognized their participation in both the men's world of production and the domestic realm of reproduction. The main thrust of their activities nonetheless remained a working-class variant of what has become known as "maternal feminism," in this case a central concern with family and community needs.[52] Similarly, labour leaders carried an image of the typical worker as not only male but also white and English-speaking. Yet while they still suspected the European newcomers as a potential threat to their "skilled" status in the workplace and to their expectations of a "British" standard of living, they willingly gave them union membership cards.[53] Distinctions and prejudices did not disappear during the workers' revolt, but they were certainly eroded.

By 1919 most Canadians of any class would have been aware that something profoundly different was afoot in working-class Canada. They could even see it from their windows. The new assertive class consciousness brought a new use of urban space. The "constitutionalism" of the revolt included the rights to free speech and association and to open assembly. Instead of keeping to the confined paths of their individual daily lives, workers used the public spaces of their towns and cities for parades, mass picnics and sporting events, huge educational forums featuring guest speakers, and spontaneous gatherings for particular protests. Since their towns and cities had few facilities built to hold large numbers, they took control of streets, parks, theatres, and churches. In reasonably compact urban centres where most workers still got around by foot or on streetcars, the working-class crowd was an aggressive force to be reckoned with. Strikes would become massive community events as working-class families extended their long-standing patterns of mutual support out of their neighbourhoods and into picket-line support, collective action against strike-breakers, or sympathy strikes. Workers thus became a much more publicly visible force in Canada's urban centres.[54]

The Workers' Defeat, 1919–1925

The workers' revolt had emerged in full form by the spring of 1919, and maintained much of its momentum across the country for at least another year. (In the eastern and western coalfields, the buoyancy lasted through 1922.) Yet, as early as the spring of 1919, the severe limitations on the workers' movements were becoming evident. From that point onward, workers were on the defensive. By 1922 most of their gains had been lost almost everywhere outside the coalfields. Strikes were defeated, union locals lost members and often disintegrated, provincial federations collapsed, independent labour parties expired, and the spirit of hope and determination drained away. The decline and fall of such a major social force was a complex process. In part, as so many Canadian historians have argued, the momentum of the revolt was sapped by ideological disagreements between a right and a left that had serious consequences for the strategic direction of the movements. To a much greater extent, however, the workers' revolt foundered on the hard, inhospitable rocks of the Canadian economy, class formation, and state.

Workers never get to choose the terrain on which they confront capital or the state. By 1919 a variety of capitalists had already made some decisions about the location and structure of their enterprises and the kind of workforce they would need. At the same time, the larger market forces continued to set constraints on what kind of working-class resistance would be possible. In Canada the industrial capitalist economy was fragmented into a myriad of widely separated projects in capital accumulation that followed quite different rhythms of development and crisis. The many isolated parts of the resource economy struggled to secure a space in highly competitive markets, the manufacturers cowered behind their tariff walls, and the transportation industries tried to survive on the success of the others. After the war each of these sectors, and their many subsectors, faced its own agonizing readjustment. Every capitalist economy contains this diversity, but Canada's seemed to be an exaggerated version, not least because of the vast distances that separated industrial activity but even more because of the various sectors' disarticulated links to the larger international economy that were unconnected to each other. Here was a good part of the explanation for the regionalism that ran through the workers' movements, as it did through the rest of Canadian society. Yet none of the regions itself had a single industrial pattern. So, despite their efforts at solidarity, wage-earners found themselves divided by the fragmented, uneven structure of the Canadian economy and drawn into the ideological framework of regional politicians and businessmen who had their own agendas for coping.

Reinforcing those divisions was the unevenness of working-class power within the production processes of the various industries. While this different leverage was partly a matter of the skill content of jobs and workplace independence of wage-earners, skilled workers usually had the additional advantage of ethnic and sexual homogeneity. Once again, these were for the most part structural characteristics of particular occupations that emerged from that process of capitalist planning and organizing. But, by the First World War, occupational identities of skilled, white, English-speaking (and many French-speaking) male wage-earners bore the stamp of long-standing fights to preserve their shop-floor power, independence, and self-esteem. The occupational groups at the forefront of the workers' revolt – coal miners, metal trades workers, and "frontier labourers" – had each fashioned a version of the distinctive muscular, masculine working-class culture that was idealized in the visual arts of the period, whether art nouveau or socialist realism.[55] This reservoir of resistance was not available to wage-earners made vulnerable by their limited skills or by their gender or ethnic identity. The weaker participation of factory workers in the workers' revolt is not surprising given that skills had been drastically reduced or eliminated in many factories, while the skills that survived were industry-specific and tied closely to occupational mobility inside individual firms. This was also where female and non-Anglo-Celtic labour had often been integrated into the least skilled jobs and lacked the social sanctions enjoyed by the skilled male breadwinners. These were also workers with little accumulated history of mobilization in their own defence. What is remarkable about the working-class revolt in this period is the extent to which these vulnerable workers participated aggressively, and to which the better placed workers often reached out to offer them support. However, occupational and ethnic differences, in combination with the industrial fragmentation of the country, made holding together a broad-based revolt a formidable task.

However much workers in all parts of the country shared common aspirations and similar patterns of organizing in the 1917–25 period, the various working-class movements that emerged faced very different opportunities and obstacles. The consciously decentralized nature of the movement made coordination of these distinct struggles extremely problematic. Canada had an archipelago of isolated industrial centres between which it was difficult to maintain regular, informed communication among the various workers' movements. The failure of western radicals to make common cause with their comrades east of the Lakehead was one of the best indicators. National labour institutions in Canada were weak, and national debate and the bonds of national solidarity were never fully developed.

Differences based on gender and ethnicity further divided Canadian workers. The white, anglophone and francophone male wage-earners who marched in the front ranks of the workers' revolt remained ambivalent about the role of women in the workforce and labour movement. "There is no doubt that the women are being exploited by the manufacturers," wrote a machinists' union official in 1917, "and their use in the munitions factories has been the cause of reducing the wages of men shell operators."[56] Despite women's enhanced role in working-class organizing, the patriarchal mould of the working-class family had certainly not been broken. On the contrary, a central goal of the workers' revolt of 1917–25 was to defend the household economy that had been the bedrock of working-class life in Canada for more than half a century and of the husband-father's role as chief breadwinner.[57] Working men took their families on labour picnics and welcomed them onto mass picket lines, yet the vast sea of men's faces that fill up photographs of labour meetings taken during the Winnipeg General Strike suggest how thoroughly male the public life of the workers' movements still was.[58] Even the radical left had a heavily male-centred, productionist focus that left little room on its agenda for the female half of the working class.[59]

Not all men were welcome, however. Anglo-Canadian wage-earners had often been highly suspicious of capitalists' use of non-Anglo-Celtic and non-white immigrants as cheap labour in many industries and feared a direct threat to their status and earnings within the rapidly changing capitalist labour process. As a result, Anglo-Canadian and other workers eyed each other cautiously and often resentfully in ways that suggested that the elements that employers had drawn together into a workforce had not yet congealed into a full community of working-class solidarity, especially considering the continuing transiency of so many of the non-Anglo-Celtic "sojourners." Three vigorous counterpoints to the workers' revolt stood out in the 1917–20 period: the French Canadians' blistering anger over their forced participation in the "English" war; rising Anglo-Canadian hysteria about European "enemy aliens," accompanied by demands (spearheaded by the veterans) for their expulsion from industry;[60] and the revival of anti-Asian agitation in British Columbia. The two exclusionary campaigns, which led to the immigration restrictions of 1920, must have sown deep bitterness in immigrant urban enclaves. Many labour leaders refused to be associated with such nativist activities and appealed for tolerance and working-class brotherhood. But the ethnic fissures did not disappear. The French kept their distance from the Jewish and English-Canadian radicals in Montreal.[61] Rarely were European immigrants as well integrated into the rising workers' movements as they would be in the CIO period. They were virtually never found within the ranks of the labour parties in this period (although left-wing elements in some eastern European communities maintained contact with radical socialists). The Asians, who were so numerous in West Coast industries, were completely shut out.[62] Not until the 1930s and 1940s, when the endless waves of sojourners and newcomers stopped and the working-class communities stabilized somewhat, would the ethnic divides start to close. In the meantime, the wage-earning members of many ethnic groups were drawn into rising cross-class nationalism within their own communities in Canada, especially in Quebec and in many European immigrant ghettoes in central and western Canada. These ethnic divisions had different dimensions in each region, and, aside from the West Coast anti-Asian animus, they may not have amounted to the same wall of hostility that rose up in the United States as hundreds of thousands of blacks moved north in this period.[63] But they did deflect some of the energy of the workers' revolt along paths that weakened class-conscious solidarity.

In addition to overcoming internal fragmentation and division, working classes in industrial capitalist societies sought to situate themselves within a larger configuration of classes. In most industrialized countries outside Britain, they found themselves in a minority, and the Canadian class structure was essentially no different. Unless the workers' movements opted for the Bolshevik model of seizing power and imposing the dictatorship of the proletariat, as few Canadian labour leaders suggested before 1920, they had to find political allies. In Canada labour leaders attracted, or maintained a friendly dialogue with, disaffected elements of the urban middle class whose influence could be great but whose numbers were not large. In fact, aside from such celebrated exceptions as J.S. Woodsworth, most of the middle class either stood uncomfortably aloof from the workers' revolt or participated in attempts to contain or repress it. The white-collar workers who organized their own unions, especially teachers and civil servants, generally kept their distance from the rest of the labour movement.[64] Even the country's most celebrated suffragist, Nellie McClung, nervously opposed the Winnipeg General Strike.[65] Most social gospellers began looking for some mechanisms for reconciling the warring camps of capital and labour.[66]

In most industrialized countries in the period, the largest other class was usually some version of independent commodity producers, whether peasants or commercial farmers. At the end of the war, farmers were still by far the largest and electorally most powerful element in Canada, at least east of the Rockies. They posed the same "agrarian question" that perplexed working-class movements throughout the world. As we have seen, in their relationship with workers, farmers were, at best, ambivalent allies and, at worst, strong hindrances. They occasionally sniped at the militancy, showed limited concern about the mass working-class unemployment of the early 1920s, and refused to support labour's most prized legislative measures, most notably the eight-hour day.[67] But this rural population posed an even thornier problem. People in the rural world of early-twentieth-century Canada often shaded over from independent primary producer to wage-earner, bringing far more uncertainty about their quasi-proletarian status and far less commitment to urban-based movements.[68] Much of the logging, fishing, and construction industries rested on their labour. Some undertook remarkable organizational campaigns on an unprecedented scale – the Fishermen's Protective Union of Newfoundland under William Coaker and the Lumber Workers' Industrial Union in British Columbia, in particular.[69] But most rural workers remained outside the workers' revolt or were only tangentially connected. The same point could be made about Indigenous peoples, especially on the West Coast.[70] Canadian capitalism would not be seriously challenged on this front.

Beyond calling for unity and solidarity, the leaders of Canadian workers' movements rarely reflected on the structural constraints of economic, regional, sexual, and ethnic fragmentation and isolation of Canadian workers. Probably pondering such dilemmas was a luxury the immediate organizational exigencies did not allow them. Whatever theorizing they did drew not from the specifics of the Canadian social formation but rather from the thinking of labourists or Marxists elsewhere. In this sense they were clearly disadvantaged in the face of corporate capital and the state in Canada, whose existence rested on their ability to overcome that kind of fragmentation and to integrate diverse parts of the social formation. By the end of the First World War, workers confronted highly centralized corporations with national or continental networks of organization and a national state with a remarkably strong executive branch (much more aggressive as a result of its interventionist wartime experience). The workers' movements were thus overwhelmed by powerful forces that were better able to manoeuvre in the difficult Canadian setting. Whatever the structural constraints, the real crisis facing wage-earners came from the aggressive resistance of employers who dug in their heels against workers' demands, and the state, which set out to undercut the radical potential of the workers' movements. Both employers and the state followed a course of crushing the militants and radicals and then appealing to "safe and sane" wage-earners and, if necessary, their leaders.

The surest indication of unprecedented class conflict in postwar Canada was the extent to which both capital and labour mobilized to assert their interests. The economic dislocations and instability rampant across Canada in the immediate aftermath of hostilities drove both to new extremes in attitude and organization. In 1919–20 the prospect of a renewed rivalry with both European and American industry (the return of "competitive competition again," in the telling redundancy of one BC manufacturer)[71] convinced many Canadian employers that the viability of their operations was now at stake. Capitalists across the country worried that markets for the products of their vastly expanded productive apparatus were disappearing, that price inflation had made them uncompetitive (especially in terms of labour costs), that the creation of many new unions limited their ability to alter wages and labour processes (perish the thought of an eight-hour day!), and that the free-trade sentiments of the powerful new farmers' movements would threaten their tariff protection. At a more general level, they sensed that a large mass of the population had come out of the war with a cynical, if not openly hostile, view of corporate dominance over Canadian social and economic life. Capitalists had not only to secure the subordination of the working class but also to restore the legitimacy of their hegemony more generally.

After the Armistice employers launched a concerted offensive of union-busting and wage-cutting in an effort to reclaim ground conceded to labour under extraordinary wartime circumstances. Workers in virtually all the twenty-eight cities visited by the Royal Commission on Industrial Relations in the spring of 1919 complained of extensive firing and blacklisting of union supporters since the end of the war.[72] Many of the protracted (and ultimately defeated) strikes of the postwar era were marked as much by capitalist intransigence as by labour's militancy. In 1920 workers won less than one strike in five, and employers were clear winners in a third – a dramatic reversal of the strike outcomes in 1917–18. From 1921 to 1924 close to half these confrontations ended on employers' terms, to which could be added many of those strikes whose outcomes were classified as "Indefinite" (27 per cent in 1920, 24 per cent in 1921, and 20 per cent in 1922).[73] The decisive defeats came at different points in each industry and region. The collapse of the Winnipeg General Strike and the various sympathy strikes marked the beginning of the end in urban centres across the West. The defeat of the prolonged metal trades strikes in several Canadian cities in 1919 was devastating, but for most manufacturing industries in Ontario, Quebec, and Nova Scotia the major symbolic defeats did not arrive until mid-1920. The shipyard strikes of that year were catastrophes for organized labour in several parts of central and eastern Canada. Even the solidly entrenched printers' unions were dealt a crippling blow in their unsuccessful struggle for the forty-four-hour week.[74] Sydney steelworkers did not meet their Waterloo until 1923, and coal miners in Cape Breton and Alberta held on for two more years.[75] The final confrontation of Cape Breton's miners and corporate bosses in 1925 was as bitter, brutal, and devastating as any in the whole period under study.

As the many studies of strikes in the period have revealed, a common pattern emerged almost everywhere. Companies forced a strike by refusing to negotiate and then frequently hired strike-breakers, often from professional strike-breaking operations such as the Pinkerton or Thiel detective agencies. As defeated workers drifted back, employers blacklisted local union militants to drive them out of town; some even installed spies on the shop floor to watch for potential trouble-makers. Little of this activity was carried out under the defiant "open shop" banner that American capitalists were unfurling at this time,[76] but the outcome was the same. Anti-union tactics became much easier to implement in the context of a rapidly declining economy. The 16.5 per cent unemployment rate among unionized workers in the spring of 1921 was destroying their leverage in the labour market.[77] Nearly universal wage cuts of 10–20 per cent in the early months of that year met with little resistance. By the end of 1922 the Department of Labour's statistics showed over 100,000 fewer union members than at the 1919 peak – a loss of 27 per cent.[78]

As workers were taught the lesson that militancy and unionism would not be tolerated, many corporations tried to sweeten the medicine with a package of welfare reforms for their employees to promote loyalty and dedication to the individual firm rather than to the working class. Out of corporate boardrooms cascaded safety plans, lunch rooms, company magazines, recreation programs, and pension and insurance plans. To workers who were once again facing economic insecurity, the pension and insurance plans were far more attractive than patronizing programs aimed at constructing a "corporate family." In a few large plants, corporations also responded to the call for "industrial democracy" with industrial councils (made up of equal numbers of management and employee representatives) in which issues arising in the workplace could be addressed. Company executives quickly found they had to deflect their employees' attempts to discuss wages and hours, and the councils rapidly dissolved into toothless forums for debate on safety and recreation issues.[79] Probably only a small minority of Canadian wage-earners ever enjoyed any crumbs from the table of welfare capitalism in any case.

At the same time, capitalists launched a campaign to re-legitimize their dominant role in Canadian society. In addition to publicizing their corporate welfarism,[80] they sought a common enemy against which workers and the broader population could be rallied. Industrialists contributed heavily to propaganda that tried to terrorize Canadians into believing that the democracy they had just fought for was endangered by blood-thirsty Bolshevists. Lurid, full-page advertisements informed newspaper readers of the "alien" quality of the workers' revolt. A Canadian-made, employer-funded movie called *The Great Shadow* depicted Bolshevik subversion of labour struggles in a shipyard (several companies supplied free tickets for their employees).[81] Some capitalists even bought the support of conservative labour leaders by funnelling money to them secretly and by supporting such red-baiting newspapers as the Ottawa-based *Canadian Labor Press*.[82]

The various (mostly rural) forces threatening the tariff structure could be constructed as another common enemy. The most powerful corporate capitalists threw their support behind Sir John Willison's Canadian Reconstruction Association, the statesmanlike public face of capital that highlighted the benefits of corporate welfarism and built broader support for the tariff.[83] Eventually, the Tories held onto most of industrialized Ontario in the 1921 federal election, as they had in 1911, by exploiting working-class fears of job loss in a free-trade economy.[84] In Quebec the Catholic Church provided another successful alternative in the form of Catholic unionism, which preached worker-employer harmony (within a framework of Catholic values) and began to mushroom in size and influence in 1919. Quebec's employers were pleased.[85] Finally, in the East, local employers placed themselves at the head of a new Maritime Rights movement in the early 1920s.[86] In each case workers' anger and insecurity were deflected into class-collaborationist channels, though only once their industrial militancy had been crushed.

The Canadian state made no effort to curb the attacks on workers and their organizations. On the contrary (as we saw in chapter 5), politicians and state officials had moved decisively to repress and undermine working-class militancy and radicalism. They turned loose against radical leaders their secret-service spies, federal troops, and new criminal-law and immigration legislation, as well as their blandishments of more moderate leaders with a royal commission and a National Industrial

Conference. The federal government offered no solid inducements or protection for working-class organization.

At this point the structure of Canadian federalism played its complicated role in mediating class relations. Workers' movements across the country had directed much of their political energy into provincial politics, wherein resided many of the constitutional responsibilities for such worker concerns as the eight-hour day. That meant battling on nine different fronts. Provincial governments had been the first to respond to the general unrest in the population after 1916, and several administrations (especially those run by reform-minded Liberals) had used such measures as minimum-wage legislation and mothers' allowances to try to buy back some legitimacy for the social and political system.[87] Some provincial politicians, such as Ontario's Henry Cody, looked to longer-term means of restoring the legitimacy of the social order with increased schooling for adolescents to inculcate appropriate notions of "citizenship," as did the National Conference on "Character Education" held in Winnipeg in October 1919.[88] Each of these moves by the provincial branches of the Canadian state reinforced the regional particularities in the timing and rhythms of the workers' revolt. Since no federal election was called until 1921, workers' movements were not able to confront the national Borden government directly on the hustings until after the revolt had lost most of its momentum.

It is against this agonizingly difficult backdrop of structural constraint and repressive counter-attack that we must assess the splits that had opened up within the labour leadership by the spring of 1919. Once again, they hit each region at different moments. Yet this was fundamentally a divergence between left and right, not East and West. In every region of the country labour leaders were engaging in heated debate about the appropriate industrial and political working-class response to the new resistance that the revolt was facing. While the left urged escalation, the right called for a retreat. The major points of disagreement concerned the most appropriate form of union organization, the link with the international unions centred in the American Federation of Labor, and the willingness of the workers' movements to show more aggressiveness in pursuit of their goals. Since the middle of the war, labour leaders had argued over these issues, and, as we saw, those who constituted the movements' national voice in the Trades and Labor Congress of Canada had always counselled and practised restraint. The confrontation came to a head at the 1918 Congress convention, where a minority report denouncing the executive's cozy relations with the government sparked a furious debate about the directions of the labour movement. A set of militant tactical resolutions was defeated and a more conservative slate, headed by carpenters' union organizer Tom Moore, was elected to the Congress executive. Moore had been a solid supporter of conscription and a central figure in the rapprochement with the Borden government in 1918. The defeat for the left at the 1918 convention was not simply a matter of the East overpowering the West (fifty-one easterners joined twenty-nine westerners on the losing side, against a majority of three from the West and eighty-one from the East). It was quite significant, however, that the western delegates constructed the defeat in regional terms. They chose to minimize the evidence of support for their position east of the Lakehead and to use a Western Labour Conference as a springboard for reconstruction of the whole labour movement. Then, in the early spring of 1919, they moved decisively towards secession with the creation of the One Big Union.[89]

That spring well-established craft union leaders in most major cities began to consider the risks associated with the widening solidarity and political radicalism. In the western conferences leading up to the formation of the One Big Union, there were dissenting voices. J.H. McVety in Vancouver, David Rees in Fernie, Alfred Farmilo in Edmonton, Alex Ross in Calgary, and Ernie Robinson in Winnipeg all opposed withdrawing from the international unions to form the One Big Union. The Calgary labour movement was lukewarm about this new experiment, while the Edmonton trades council stayed out altogether.[90] In southern Ontario and Montreal the more entrenched craft union leaders were not prepared to see their organizations disrupted by surging notions of industrial unionism.[91] All these men were still looking to the state and capital for the legitimacy and recognition they believed caution and moderation would bring. Their strategy was to raise the threat of labour unrest and to present themselves as the restraining force that would curb militancy and radicalism. In an address to the Canadian Manufacturers' Association in February 1919, Tom Moore was reported to have advised his audience that "the responsible, intelligent trades unionist was the capitalist's strongest bulwark, if only a friendly co-operation were extended to him, since the trade unionist, and indeed, the worker fully realized that the downfall of the capitalist, and the cessation of the work in the factory spelled his own idleness and possible starvation."[92] (Moore later insisted that he had referred to unions as "*civilization's* strongest bulkwark"; misquote or not, his message was clear.) The same concern with cementing an accord with the state and capital explains the enthusiastic participation of the craft union leadership in the National Industrial Conference.[93]

By the end of 1919, the fluidity of the previous two years had evaporated, and positions on the right and left were hardening. In the wake of the OBU breakaway, the Canadian branches of the international unions threw themselves into a campaign to win back the West and to prevent any further secessions. The more conservative craft union leaders steadily withdrew their support for the more experimental organizational forms and practices that had blossomed alongside the normal channels of international union procedure. They insisted on the honouring of contracts negotiated with individual employers. (This abiding faith in "industrial legality" discouraged various groups of wage-earners from joining larger struggles.)[94] They used the disciplinary power of their organizations to curb unauthorized sympathy or general strikes. In many cases they seriously undermined local struggles by curtailing solidarity actions by their members. By rejecting cooperation and amalgamation of crafts and rigorously defending individual craft jurisdiction and rights, these union officials undoubtedly robbed less skilled workers of leadership, resources, and negotiating strength. Over the next two years the leading figures in the craft union movement distanced themselves from the main currents of the workers' revolt. They also opened a rhetorical barrage against the left in general, using some of the existing labour newspapers as well as the new *Canadian Labor News*, the *Edmonton Free Press*, and, from the end of 1919, *New Democracy*. By 1921 the leaders of the Trades and Labor Congress even refused to endorse the independent labour candidates who were running in that year's federal election. These craft unionists settled solidly into the cautious, complacent, apolitical mould that had been developed in the Gompersite American Federation of Labor and would not wander far from those moorings until the Second World War.[95]

Facing these men across the increasingly bitter political battlefield were a variety of militants and radicals who, as we have seen, were spread across the country. Region does not help explain their location as much as industry, occupation, ethnicity, and the recent history of industrial relations in their respective communities. Some were based in the older male occupations with long traditions of workplace pride and independence and recent success in confronting their employers, especially the coal miners and the highly skilled railway shopcraft workers.[96] Others had a solid following in the newly organized unions of semi-skilled and unskilled workers, notably in mass production, resource processing, and water transport.[97] Also providing some ginger were clusters of European-born socialists who were found in logging, mining, and clothing production.[98] The radicals' success depended on the strength of the local unions in their respective industries and on the established power of the international craft union leadership in the local labour movement. AFL-style craft unions were much weaker in the Maritimes and the West, where they had never put down as deep roots and had always had to coexist with bumptious industrial unions, usually most solidly based in mining.[99] They were also somewhat weaker in Quebec, where their insensitivity to francophones had limited their impact (the AFL finally appointed a bilingual organizer for the province in 1918).[100] Southern Ontario was the heartland of this cautious brand of unionism and the headquarters of a solid cadre of full-time labour officials – business agents, organizers, Canadian vice-presidents, and the leading officials of the Trades and Labor Congress of Canada – who were committed to the link with the AFL and industrial legality in collective bargaining. Their caution was more than a slavish mimicking of an American model; it was also the product of experience in a harshly anti-union climate that had kept unions out of Ontario's major industries since the turn of the century. The craft unionists' prominence and strength in the region's labour movement rested in large part on the lack of a substantial industrial union movement based in the province's many factories until the end of the war. Those industrial unions that eventually did emerge in cities like Toronto and Hamilton were latecomers and remained extremely fragile. The craft unionists greeted them with coolness and some apprehension.[101]

The divisions in the labour leadership went beyond the right-left tensions. The radicals themselves were divided on the issue of staying with the international unions. The great majority of westerners voted to leave and form the One Big Union. In central and eastern Canada, this strategy had its supporters.[102] (Because unions in these regions generally refused to hold referendums on secession, it is impossible to gauge the precise amount of support for the OBU.) However, most militant leaders in central and eastern Canada opted to remain within the international union movement. The left within the workers' movement was therefore divided at a crucial moment. By the end of 1919 the radicals' secessionist project in the West had foundered. East of the Lakehead those who remained in the mainstream labour movement became increasingly isolated. Only in the Maritimes did they maintain a leadership role, which persisted until 1923.

Beset by failures and a heavily repressive environment, many socialist militants began to gravitate towards the emerging Communist movement. The old Social Democratic Party had disintegrated soon after the state's iron heel came down on it late in 1918. Socialists from the party's right wing (notably James Simpson in Toronto) settled into independent labour party work. At the same time, feistier members of its left wing joined forces with a handful of revolutionary socialists and radical members of some Eastern European immigrant groups, some of whom had already begun clandestine propaganda early in 1919. In the heat of state repression and the general Red Scare, this new pro-Bolshevik left had both an underground life for theorizing and strategizing and a public forum for revolutionary education and unbridled attacks on the dominant labour leadership. Many of the militant sparkplugs from the workers' revolt – including Jack MacDonald in Toronto, Fred Flatman in Hamilton, Annie Buller in Montreal, and J.B. McLachlan in Cape Breton – were drawn to this emerging movement, as were many European-born socialists. In May 1921, at a secret meeting in a barn outside Guelph, the underground Communist Party of Canada was founded, uniting all these revolutionary socialists east of Manitoba. Its public face, the Workers' Party of Canada, emerged in February 1922. In the West the aging Socialist Party of Canada eventually disintegrated as branches left to join the Workers' Party. Branches of a few local labour parties in such places as Halifax and Fernie followed suit. Ironically, shortly after its founding the Communist Party, in line with the new direction of the Third International in Moscow, began to favour the politics of coalition over sectarian attacks on the established labour institutions and their leaders. The Workers' Party affiliated with the Canadian Labor Party, and individual Communists directed their energies back into locals of international unions, the trades councils, and the Trades and Labor Congress. However, the craft union leadership was unwelcoming, and by the late 1920s most Communists had been expelled from unions for their agitation.[103] The left, then, had also been unable to meet the challenge of the crisis facing workers after 1919. At that critical moment, the radicals' flamboyant sectarianism may have sometimes been unrealistic, but it was the divisive issue of secession from the mainstream international labour movement, combined with the ideological hardening that had taken place in the context of the well-orchestrated Red Scare, that deprived the radicals of the credibility and effectiveness that would have allowed them to take a larger role.

A substantial number of activists from the workers' revolt chose to embrace neither narrow craft unionism nor Communism. The minority of non-Communist socialists left behind after the splits in the old socialist parties continued to find common cause with the handfuls of still committed labourists. Most of their political energy was devoted to maintaining the local labour parties. But the 1921 federal election, called in the depths of the postwar depression when most of the momentum of the workers' revolt had already been destroyed, was the final death knell for these socialists. They struggled on, but, with only two representatives in the House of Commons, without a majority in any provincial legislature, and thoroughly compromised in the Ontario Farmer Labour government,[104] they had little to show for their efforts. Their constituency rapidly vanished. For several years in the mid-1920s they worked with the Communists in a revived Canadian Labor Party, but with no significant success. A handful of labour representatives would hang on in city councils, provincial legislatures, and Parliament, partly on the basis of personal popularity and probity, and a decade later would help to launch a new social-democratic party, the Cooperative Commonwealth Federation.[105]

By the mid-1920s labour leaders from all these political camps must have looked back in sober dismay at the opportunities that had been lost. In the years between 1917 and 1920 a massive number of Canadian workers had become part of a great collective groping for a new kind of society. With the limited resources available in working-class neighbourhoods across the country, they had united in countless ways to show their determination to change the lot of workers in Canada. They had pursued their goals in a constitutionalist fashion through the existing institutions of society, especially unions and political parties, rather than armed insurrection, but their open-ended vision of working-class power had nonetheless carried radical dimensions and potential that did not escape the notice of bourgeois leaders. The workers had never been given the opportunity to carry their planning and dreaming far forward into the postwar era because Canadian capitalists would not consider the shift in power that even the mildest reforms implied, and because those in control of the state had shared this apprehension about a more powerful working class. When the crunch had come, the workers' revolt had failed to transcend the great diversity and structural weaknesses of the Canadian working class. Workers in every part of the country, in almost every occupational group, had participated in the revolt, but they had failed to coalesce (sometimes even at the local level) into an effective, coherent force able to withstand the crippling attacks of capital and the state and the enervating impact of unemployment. In this moment of crisis the leadership of the workers' movements had fragmented into three distinct currents according to their divergent readings of how to respond – cautious craft unionism, revolutionary Communism, and social-democratic parliamentarism – none of which managed to capture the dynamism, mass mobilization, and ideological and strategic diversity of the early stages of the revolt.

Meanwhile, thousands of workers on the defensive by 1920 had begun to lose their optimism that working-class movements could deliver the "New Democracy." The spirit of class solidarity had quietly faded away. Workers accepted what they could get from employers willing to hire them, abandoned their unions lest membership get them fired, and stopped voting for labour candidates (if they voted at all). Fearful caution and cynicism, if not fatalism, had settled in.

The long-term impact was devastating for the Canadian working class. For the next twenty years, despite some determined efforts in the 1930s, workers did not come close to regaining the collective power they had summoned up in 1917–20. Although unions did not disappear (total union membership by the mid-1920s had not, in fact, tumbled to the pre-war lows), they were for the most part marginal to Canadian industrial life. Most industrial corporations could confidently expect to operate in a "union-free" environment. Canadian political life would take some time to recover from the various postwar crises, but in working-class communities voter absenteeism or traditional Liberalism and resurgent Toryism were predominant by 1925. The moment when the Canadian capitalist system faced one of its most serious challenges in the country's history had clearly passed.[106]

The legacy of the workers' revolt would nonetheless endure. The most negative part of this legacy concerned working-class organization. The lessons of the period had left labour activists of all political stripes sceptical about the ideological and organizational fluidity of the revolt. Craft unionists, social democrats, and Communists hardened permanently into their own increasingly rigid views of the most appropriate forms of working-class mobilization. The survivors of the revolt also shaped the options for the future. Rather than the imaginative organizational flexibility for uniting workers in the 1917–20 period, the feeble torch that was passed on to the next generation of militants in the 1930s was two variants of cautious, rigid, bureaucratic organization – namely, the AFL's craft unionism and the narrower industrial unionism promoted by the United Mine Workers and the clothing unions. Both regarded challenges to capitalist property rights or its attendant industrial legality as anathema. Labour leaders would use their control of trade unionism to ensure that working-class aspirations were confined to issues of "reconcilable class differences," leaving industry controlled by capital and unions controlled by their officers.[107]

On a more positive note, the working class had undoubtedly carved out a somewhat larger place in Canadian public life. Canadian politicians could never again ignore the concerns of workers to the extent they had in the past. A small residue of social legislation remained on the statute books,[108] and a handful of labour parliamentarians at all three levels of the state would continue to voice workers' concerns. J.S. Woodsworth' s success in extracting an old-age pension plan from Mackenzie King in 1926 was the most impressive example.[109] Moreover, in some parts of the country where the revolt was not buried beneath the suffocating blankets of Maritime Rights, francophone nationalism, or industrial protectionism, the struggles of 1917–20 were not forgotten and would be used to rally workers in future battles. It seems that the mass strikes (such as those in Winnipeg and Cape Breton) that had drawn workers into direct confrontation with the armed might of the state, rather than simply mobilization through the ballot box, had etched the deepest memories.

The working class in Canada would indeed rise up again a quarter-century later. The form of the new workers' movements would be as different as this one had been from its predecessors in the 1880s, but workers' renewed aspirations for economic security, independence, and dignity would make clear that they were not prepared to remain on their knees forever.

Notes

1 Quoted in Doug Smith, *Let Us Rise! An Illustrated History of the Manitoba Labour Movement* (Vancouver: New Star Books 1985), 1.

2 Douglas Cruikshank and Gregory S. Kealey, "Canadian Strike Statistics, 1891–1950," *L/LT* 20 (Fall 1987), 85–145; Gregory S. Kealey, "The Parameters of Class Conflict: Strikes in Canada, 1891–1930," in Deian R. Hopkin and Gregory S. Kealey, eds., *Class, Community, and the Labour Movement: Wales and Canada, 1850–1930* (Aberystwyth: Llafur and Canadian Committee on Labour History 1989), 213–48. Their statistics provide the basis for the following discussion.

3 Bob Russell's analysis of wartime strikes assumes that a compromise was a loss for strikers, but in this period it was more likely that gaining any ground, even if less than they wanted, was a major accomplishment for workers. Bob Russell, *Back to Work? Labour, State and Industrial Relations in Canada* (Scarborough: Nelson 1990), 140–52.

4 Bob Russell calculates that nearly three-quarters of strikes in 1917–18 and two-thirds in 1920 were illegal. Russell, *Back to Work?* 161–3.

5 Canada, Department of Labour, *Labour Organization in Canada* (Ottawa: King's Printer), 1914–20. A careful reading of these labour department reports makes clear that the totals were rough estimates and undoubtedly underestimated union membership. Tables that broke the statistics down by province reveal that generally about a third of the locals failed to report their membership. The department then filled in the holes "from department records and other sources" (ibid., 1919, 243).

6 Quoted in Craig Heron and George De Zwaan, "Industrial Unionism in Eastern Ontario: Gananoque, 1918–1921,' *OH* 77, no. 3 (September 1985), 167.

7 Myer Siemiatycki, "Munitions and Labour Militancy: The 1916 Hamilton Machinists' Strike," *L/LT* 3 (1978), 131–52; Marine Workers and Boilermakers Industrial Union, Local No. 1, Marine Retirees Association, *A History of Shipbuilding in British Columbia* (Vancouver: Marine Retirees Association 1977), 10–20; David Frank, "The Cape Breton Coal Miners, 1917–1926" (PhD dissertation, Dalhousie University 1979); Allen Seager, "A Proletariat in Wild Rose Country: The Alberta Coal Miners, 1905–1945" (PhD dissertation, York University 1981); Canada, Department of Labour, *Organization in Canada*, 1916–20.

8 Siemiatycki, Myer, "Labour Contained: The Defeat of a Rank and File Workers' Movement in Canada, 1914–1921" (PhD dissertation, York University 1986); Gregory S. Kealey, "1919: The Canadian Labour Revolt," *L/LT* 13 (Spring 1984), 11–44; Craig Heron, *Working in Steel: The Early Years in Canada, 1883–1935* (Toronto: McClelland and Stewart 1988); James Naylor, *The New Democracy: Challenging the Social Order in Industrial Ontario* (Toronto: University of Toronto Press 1991); John Tait Montague, "Trade Unionism in the Canadian Meatpacking Industry" (PhD dissertation, University of Toronto 1950); Gil Schonning, "Union-Management Relations in the Pulp and Paper Industry in Ontario and Quebec, 1914–1950" (PhD dissertation, University of Toronto 1955); Stanley Scott, "A Profusion of Issues: Immigrant Labour, the World War, and the Cominco Strike of 1917," *L/LT* 2 (1977), 54–78; Gordon Hak, "British Columbia Loggers and the Lumber Workers' Industrial Union, 1919–1922," *L/LT* 23 (Spring 1989),

67–90; Ian Radforth, *Bushworkers and Bosses: Logging in Northern Ontario, 1900–1980* (Toronto: University of Toronto Press 1987); Anthony Thomson, "'The Large and Generous View': The Debate on Labour Affiliation in the Canadian Civil Service, 1918–1928," *L/LT* 2 (1977), 108–36; Bruce McLean, *"A Union amongst Government Employees": A History of the B.C. Government Employees Union, 1919–1979* (n.p. 1979); Greg Marquis, "Police Unionism in Early-Twentieth-Century Toronto," *OH* 81, no. 2 (June 1989), 109–28; Greg Marquis, "The History of Policing in the Maritime Provinces," *UHR* 19, no. 1 (October 1990), 94; Bill Doherty, *Slaves of the Lamp: A History of the Federal Civil Service Organizations, 1865–1924* (Victoria: Orca Book Publishers 1991); and the regional essays in Craig Heron, ed., *The Workers' Revolt in Canada, 1917–1925* (Toronto: University of Toronto Press 1998).

9 Gregory S. Kealey, "Parameters of Class Conflict," 225–6.

10 Linda Kealey, "'No Special Protection – No Sympathy': Women's Activism in the Canadian Labor Revolt of 1919," in Hopkins and Kealey, eds., *Class, Community, and the Labour Movement*, 134–59; Linda Keealey, "Women's Labour Militancy in Canada, 1900–1920" (Paper presented to the Canadian Historical Association, Annual Meeting, Kingston 1991); Patricia Roome, "Amelia Turner and Calgary Labour Women, 1919–1935," in Linda Kealey and Joan Sangster, eds., *Beyond the Vote: Canadian Women and Politics* (Toronto: University of Toronto Press 1989), 89–117; Elaine Bernard, "Last Back: Folklore and the Telephone Operators in the 1919 Vancouver General Strike," in Barbara K. Latham and Roberta J. Pazdro, eds., *Not Just Pin Money: Selected Essays on the History of Women's Work in British Columbia* (Victoria: Camosun College 1984); Elaine Bernard, *The Long Distance Feeling: A History of the Telecommunications Workers Union* (Vancouver: New Star Books 1982), 50–71; Mary Horodyski, "Women and the Winnipeg General Strike of 1919," *Manitoba History* 11 (Spring 1986), 28–37; Marie Campbell, "Sexism in British Columbia Trade Unions, 1900–1920" in Barbara Latham and Cathy Kess, eds., *In Her Own Right: Selected Essays on Women's History in B.C.* (Victoria: Camosun College 1980), 167–86; Christine Smillie, "The Invisible Workforce: Women Workers in Saskatchewan from 1905 to World War II," *Saskatchewan History* 29, no. 2 (Spring 1986), 62–79; Ruth Frager, "No Proper Deal: Women Workers and the Canadian Labour Movement, 1870–1940," in Linda Briskin and Linda Yanz, eds., *Union Sisters: Women in the Labour Movement* (Toronto: Women's Press 1983), 44–64.

11 Donald Avery, *"Dangerous Foreigners": European Immigrant Workers and Labour Radicalism in Canada, 1896–1932* (Toronto: McClelland and Stewart 1979); Gillian Creese, "Class, Ethnicity, and Conflict: The Case of Chinese and Japanese Immigrants, 1880–1923," in Rennie Warburton and David

Coburn, eds., *Workers, Capital, and the State in British Columbia: Selected Papers* (Vancoucer: UBC Press 1988), 55–85; Radforth, *Bushworkers and Bosses*, 110–19; Orest T. Martynowych and Nadia Kazymyra, "Political Activity in Western Canada, 1896–1923," in Manoly R. Lupul, ed., *A Heritage in Transition: Essays in the History of Ukrainians in Canada* (Toronto: McClelland and Stewart 1982), 85–107; Edgar Wickberg, ed., *From China to Canada: A History of Chinese Communities in Canada* (Toronto: McClelland and Stewart 1982), 130; Jacques Rouillard, "Les travailleurs juifs de la confection à Montréal (1910–1980)," *L/LT* 8/9 (Autumn/Spring 1981–2), 253–9; Ruth Frager, *Sweatshop Strife: Class, Ethnicity, and Gender in the Jewish Labour Movement of Toronto, 1900–1939* (Toronto: University of Toronto Press 1992), 35–54; Agnes Calliste, "Sleeping Car Porters in Canada: An Ethnically Submerged Split Labour Market," *CES* 19, no. 1 (1987), 1–20.

12 Jean Burnet, with Howard Palmer, *"Coming Canadians": An Introduction to a History of Canada's Peoples* (Toronto: McClelland and Stewart 1988); Harney, *Italians in Canada* (Toronto: Multicultural History Society of Ontario 1978), 20–2; John E. Zucchi, *Italians in Toronto: Development of a National Identity, 1875–1935* (Montreal and Kingston: McGill-Queen's University Press 1988); Henry Radeki, with Benedyckt Heydenkorn, *A Member of a Distinguished Family: The Polish Group in Canada* (Toronto: McClelland and Stewart 1976); David Montgomery, "Immigrants, Industrial Unions, and Social Reconstruction in the United States, 1916–1923,' *L/LT* 13 (Spring 1984), 101–15.

13 Quoted in Gregory Kealey, "1919," 39.

14 International Association of Machinists, *Bulletin* (Winnipeg), August 1918.

15 In 1914 there were four labour papers: Vancouver's *BC Federationist*, Winnipeg's *Voice*, Hamilton's *Labor News*, and Toronto's *Industrial Banner*. By mid-1919 all but the *Voice* were flourishing and had been joined by the *Citizen* (Halifax), the *Eastern Federationist* (New Glasgow), *Workers' Weekly* (Stellarton), the *Union Worker* (Saint John), *Le Monde Ouvrier* (Montreal), *L'Unioniste* (Quebec City), the *Canadian Labor Press* (Ottawa), the *Labor Leader* (Toronto), *New Democracy* (Hamilton), the *Herald* (London), the *Western Labor News* (Winnipeg), the *Confederate* (Brandon), the *Searchlight* (Calgary), and the *Edmonton Free Press*. Canada, Department of Labour, *Labour Organization in Canada*, 1919, 295.

16 At the famous 1918 convention of the Trades and Labor Congress of Canada, radicals failed to win majority support for their proposal that the officials at this level should be consulted by the government, not the officers of international unions. The One Big Union later made these bodies the centre of its organizational structure. Martin Robin, *Radical*

Politics and Canadian Labour, 1880–1930 (Kingston: Industrial Relations Centre, Queen's University 1968), 161; David J. Bercuson, *Fools and Wise Men: The Rise and Fall of the One Big Union* (Toronto: McGraw-Hill Ryerson 1978), 149.

17 Siemiatycki, "Labour Contained," 279–325; Ross McCormack, *Reformers, Rebels, and Revolutionaries: The Western Canadian Radical Movement, 1899–1919* (Toronto: University of Toronto Press 1977), 145–6; David J. Bercuson, *Confrontation at Winnipeg: Labour, Industrial Relations, and the General Strike* (Montreal and Kingston: McGill-Queen's University Press, 2nd ed. 1990); Nolan Reilly, "The General Strike in Amherst, Nova Scotia, 1919," *Acadiensis* 9 (1980), 56–77; Gerald Friesen, "'Yours in Revolt': Regionalism, Socialism, and the Western Canadian Labour Movement," *L/LT* 1 (1976), 139–57.

18 Among the discredited or ignored were Nova Scotian miners' leader John Moffatt, the aging Quebec Lib-Lab MP Alphonse Verville, prominent Hamilton labour journalist Sam Landers, Winnipeg's venerable Arthur Puttee, Alberta miners' leader David Rees, and Vancouver's J.H. McVety and W.R. Trotter. Paul MacEwan, *Miners and Steelworkers: Labour in Cape Breton* (Toronto: Samuel Stevens Hakkert and Company 1976), 46; Geoffrey Ewen, "Quebec: Class and Ethnicity," in Heron, ed., *Workers' Revolt*, 87–143; W. Craig Heron, "Working-Class Hamilton, 1895–1930" (PhD dissertation, Dalhousie University 1981); McCormack, *Reformers, Rebels, and Revolutionaries*, 137–64; Bercuson, *Fools and Wise Men*, 65–7.

19 Craig Heron, "Great War and Nova Scotia Steelworkers," *Acadiensis* 16, no. 2 (Spring 1987), 2–34; David Frank, "The Cape Breton Coal Miners, 1917–1926" (PhD dissertation, Dalhousie University 1979); Heron and De Zwaan, "Industrial Unionism," 170–1; Ian Angus, *Canadian Bolsheviks: The Early Years of the Communist Party of Canada* (Montreal: Vanguard Press 1981), 66–9; Heron, "Working-Class Hamilton," 251–9; Bercuson, *Fools and Wise Men*, 65–8; Akers, "Rebel or Revolutionary? Jack Kavanagh and the Early Years of the Communist Movement in Vancouver, 1920–1925," *L/LT* 30 (Fall 1992), 9–44.

20 Susan Wade, "Helena Gutteridge: Votes for Women and Trade Unions," in Latham and Kess, eds., *In Her Own Right*, 187–204; Linda Kealey, "'No Special Protection'"; Roome, "Amelia Turner and Calgary Labour Women"; Horodyski, "Women and the Winnipeg General Strike"; Heron, "Working-Class Hamilton," 380–489.

21 Peterson, "Revolutionary Socialism and Industrial Unrest in the Era of the Winnipeg General Strike: The Origins of Communist Labour Unionism in Europe and North America," *L/LT* 13 (Spring 1984), 115–32; Angus, *Canadian Bolsheviks*, 3–62; Friesen, "'Yours in Revolt.'"

22 Gordon Hak, "British Columbia Loggers and the Lumber Workers Industrial Union, 1919–1922," *L/LT* 23 (Spring 1989), 67–90.

23 Robin, *Radical Politics and Canadian Labour*, 170–7; McCormack, *Reformers, Rebels, and Revolutionaries*, 143–5; Bercuson, *Fools and Wise Men*, 83 (but see also his rethinking of this subject in "Syndicalism Sidetracked: Canada's One Big Union," in Marcel van der Linden and Wayne Thorpe, eds., *Revolutionary Syndicalism: An International Perspective* [Aldershot, UK: Scolar Press 1990], 221–36).

24 On this point the interpretations of the western revolt by Gerald Friesen and Larry Peterson are more convincing; see Friesen, "'Yours in Revolt,'" 145–7; Larry Peterson, "The One Big Union in International Perspective: Revolutionary Industrial Unionism, 1900–1925," *L/LT* 7 (Spring 1981), 53–8. See also Akers, "Rebel or Revolutionary?" 19–20.

25 Robin, *Radical Politics and Canadian Labour*, 130; Ken Coates, ed., *British Labour and the Russian Revolution: The Leeds Conference, A Report from the Daily Herald.* (Nottingham, UK: Russell Press n.d. [1917]).

26 McCormack, *Reformers, Rebels, and Revolutionaries*, 142; Angus, *Canadian Bolsheviks*, 27–48; Peter Krawchuk, *The Ukrainian Socialist Movement in Canada, 1907-1918* (Toronto: Progress Books 1979); Roseline Usiskin, "The Winnipeg Jewish Radical Community: Its Early Formation, 1905-1918," in Jewish Historical Society of Western Canada, *Jewish Life and Times: A Collection of Essays* (Winnipeg: Jewish Historical Society of Western Canada 1983), 155–68.

27 Craig Heron, "Labourism and the Canadian Working Class," *L/LT* 13 (Spring 1984), 48–9.

28 Howard A. Scarrow, *Canada Votes: A Handbook of Federal and Provincial Election Data* (New Orleans: Hauser Press 1962), 28–9.

29 Canada, Department of Labour, *Labour Organization in Canada*, 1917–20.

30 Anthony MacKenzie, "The Farmer-Labour Party in Nova Scotia" (MA thesis, Dalhousie University 1969); Margaret Watson, "The United Farmers of Ontario and Political Co-operation with the Independent Labour Party, 1919–1923" (Unpublished paper, York University 1984); James Naylor, "Ontario Workers and the Decline of Labourism," in Roger Hall et al., eds., *Patterns of the Past: Interpreting Ontario's History* (Toronto: Dundurn Press 1988), 278–300; Anthony Mardiros, *William Irvine: The Life of a Prairie Radical* (Toronto: James Lorimer 1979).

31 Akers, "Rebel or Revolutionary?" 24.

32 Kenneth McNaught, *A Prophet in Politics: A Biography of J.S. Woodsworth* (Toronto: University of Toronto Press 1959); Richard Allen, *The Social Passion: Religion and Social Reform in Canada, 1914–1928* (Toronto:

University of Toronto Press 1973); Mardiros, *William Irvine*; Jaroslav Petryshyn, "From Clergyman to Communist: The Radicalization of Albert Edward Smith," *JCS* 13, no. 4 (Winter 1978–9), 61–71; Tom Mitchell, "From the Social Gospel to 'The Plain Bread of Leninism': A.E. Smith's Journey to the Left in the Epoch of Reaction after World War I," *L/LT* 33 (Spring 1994), 125–51.

33 Michiel Horn, *The League for Social Reconstruction: Intellectual Origins of the Democratic Left in Canada, 1930–1942* (Toronto: University of Toronto Press 1980).

34 Labourism was a brand of working-class liberalism that challenged political privilege, undemocratic practices, economic monopoly, and the exclusion of workers from social and political power, but stopped short of a full-scale assault on the capitalist system. Heron, "Labourism and the Canadian Working Class."

35 Quoted in Frank, "Cape Breton Coal Miners," 304–5; Canada, Department of Labour, *Labour Organization in Canada*, 1919, 57.

36 Gregory Kealey, "1919," 11–15; Siemiatycki, "Labour Contained," 279–325.

37 LAC, Royal Commission on Industrial Relations, Evidence, Calgary, 3 May 1919.

38 *Globe* (Toronto), 20 March 1919.

39 Chad Reimer, "War, Nationhood and Working-Class Entitlement: The Counter-hegemonic Challenge of the Winnipeg General Strike," *PF* 18, no. 2 (Fall 1993), 219–37 (quotation on 231); *Examiner* (Peterborough), 2 September 1919; Naylor, *New Democracy*; Ian McKay and Suzanne Morton, "The Maritimes: Expanding the Circle of Resistance," in Heron, ed., *Workers' Revolt*, 43–86; Tom Mitchell and James Naylor, "The Prairies: In the Eye of the Storm," ibid., 176–230.

40 Wages were an issue in 46 per cent of the strikes in 1917, 44 per cent in 1918, 39 per cent in 1919, and 45 per cent in 1920. Gregory Kealey, "Parameters of Class Conflict," 240.

41 Ben M. Selekman, *Postponing Strikes: A Study of the Industrial Disputes Investigation Act of Canada* (New York: Russell Sage Foundation 1927), 168–78. The device of the royal commission was used, for example, in the Toronto and Hamilton munitions industry and Cobalt silver mining in 1916, and the Nova Scotia coal and steel industries several times after 1916. Myer Siemiatycki, "Munitions and Labour Militancy: The 1916 Hamilton Munitions Strike," *L/LT* 3 (1978), 131–52; Brian F. Hogan, *Cobalt: Year of the Strike 1919* (Cobalt, ON: Highway Book Shop 1978); MacEwan, *Miners and Steelworkers*; Heron, "Great War and Nova Scotia Steelworkers."

42 Heron, *Working in Steel*, 141–2; Schonning, "Union-Management Relations in the Pulp and Paper Industry"; Montague, "Trade Unionism in the Canadian Meatpacking Industry"; Naylor, *New Democracy*, 51–3, 209–10.

43 Stephen G. Peitchinis, *Labour-Management Relations in the Railway Industry* (Ottawa: Queen's Printer 1971), 104–12; Naylor, *New Democracy*, 185–8; Sally Zerker, *The Rise and Fall of the Toronto Typographical Union, 1832–1972* (Toronto: University of Toronto Press 1972), 178–204; Ian McKay, *The Craft Transformed: An Essay on the Carpenters of Halifax, 1885–1985* (Halifax: Holdfast Press 1985), 68–73, McKay, "Industry, Work, and Community"; Seager, "Proletariat in Wild Rose Country"; Michael Brecher, "Patterns of Accommodation in the Men's Garment Industry in Quebec, 1914–1954," in H.D. Woods, ed., *Patterns of Dispute Settlements in Five Canadian Industries* (Montreal: Industrial Relations Centre, McGill University 1958), 89–186.

44 Bruce Scott, "'A Place in the Sun': The Industrial Council at Massey-Harris, 1919–1939," *L/LT* 1 (1976), 158–92; Naylor, *New Democracy*, 159–88; Victor Levant, *Capital and Labour: Partners? Two Classes – Two Views* (Toronto: Steel Rail Press 1977), 9–36; F.A. McGregor, *The Fall and Rise of Mackenzie King, 1911–1919* (Toronto: Macmillan 1962).

45 LAC, Royal Commission on Industrial Relations, Evidence, Victoria, Phil Smith, 26 April 1919.

46 David Frank, "Contested Terrain: Workers' Control in the Cape Breton Coal Mines in the 1920s," in Craig Heron and Robert Storey, eds., *On the Job: Confronting the Labour Process in Canada* (Montreal and Kingston: McGill-Queen's University Press 1986), 114–18.

47 McCormack, *Reformers, Rebels, and Revolutionaries*, 146, 165–6; Ewen, "Quebec: Class and Ethnicity"; James Naylor, "Southern Ontario: Striking at the Ballot Box," in Heron, ed., *Workers' Revolt*, 144–75; Don Macgillivray, "Military Aid to the Civil Power: The Cape Breton Experience in the 1920s," in Don Macgillivray and Bryan Tennyson, eds., *Cape Breton Historical Essays* (Sydney: University College of Cape Breton Press 1980), 95–109.

48 Gregory S. Kealey, "Parameters of Class Conflict," 40.

49 Bercuson, *Fools and Wise Men*, 85.

50 MacEwan, *Miners and Steelworkers*, 71–2; Naylor, *New Democracy*, 193–4.

51 See Bryan D. Palmer, *A Culture in Conflict: Skilled Workers and Industrial Capitalism in Hamilton, Ontario, 1860–1914* (Montreal and Kingston: McGill-Queen's University Press 1973); Gregory S. Kealey and Bryan D. Palmer, *Dreaming of What Might Be: The Knights of Labor in Ontario, 1880–1900* (New York: Cambridge University Press 1982). The issue of shorter hours within workers' movements has been the subject of much fascinating

recent research. See David R. Roediger and Philip S. Foner, *Our Own Time: A History of American Labor and the Working Day* (New York: Verso 1989); Gary A. Cross, *A Quest for Time: The Reduction of Work in Britain and France* (Berkeley: University of California Press 1989); Gary A. Cross, ed., *Worktime and Industrialization: An International History* (Philadelphia: Temple University Press 1988); Benjamin Kline Hunnicutt, *Work without End: Abandoning Shorter Hours for the Right to Work* (Philadelphia: Temple University Press 1988).

52 Joy Parr, *The Gender of Breadwinners: Men, Women, and Change in Two Industrial Towns, 1880–1950* (Toronto: University of Toronto Press 1990), 149–52; Linda Kealey, "'No Special Protection'"; Roome, "Amelia Turner and Calgary Labour Women"; Naylor, *New Democracy*, 129–55; Campbell, "Sexism in British Columbia Trade Unions"; Varpu Lindstrom-Best, *Defiant Sisters: A Social History of Finnish Immigrant Women in Canada* (Toronto: Multicultural History Society of Ontario 1988), 147–55; Lindstrom-Best, "Finnish Socialist Women in Canada, 1890–1930," in Kealey and Sangster, eds., *Beyond the Vote*, 196–216; Lindstrom-Best and Allen Seager, "*Toveritar* and Finnish Canadian Women, 1900–1930," in Christianne Harzig and Dirk Hoerder, eds., *The Press of Labor Migrants in Europe and North America, 1880s to 1930s* (Bremen, Ger.: Labor Migration Project, Labour Newspaper Preservation Project, Universität Bremen 1985), 243–64; Steve Penfold, "'Have You No Manhood in You?': Gender and Class in the Cape Breton Coal Towns, 1920–1926," *Acadiensis* 23 (Spring 1994), 21–44.

53 Scott, "A Profusion of Issues"; Allen Seager, "Class, Ethnicity, and Politics in the Alberta Coalfields, 1905–1945," in Dirk Hoerder, ed., *"Struggle a Hard Battle": Essays on Working-Class Immigrants* (De Kalb: Northern Illinois University Press 1986), 304–24; Heron, *Working in Steel*, 135.

54 Bercuson, *Confrontation at Winnipeg*; Penner, ed., *Winnipeg 1919*; Horodyski, "Women and the Winnipeg General Strike"; Suzanne Morton, "Labourism and Economic Action: The Halifax Shipyards Strike of 1920," *L/LT* 22 (Fall 1988), 67–98; Naylor, *New Democracy*; Heron and De Zwaan, "Industrial Unionism in Eastern Ontario"; Ewen, "Quebec: Class and Ethnicity."

55 See Rosemary Donegan, "The Iconography of Labour: An Overview of Canadian Materials," *Archivaria* 27 (Winter 1988–9), 35–56.

56 Quoted in Heron, "Working-Class Hamilton," 388–9.

57 Joy Parr has appropriately dubbed this collective defence of the family wage "social fathering" and "breadwinner unionism." Parr, *Gender of Breadwinners*, 149–50.

58 See photos in Penner, ed., *Winnipeg 1919*, and J.M. Bumstead, *The Winnipeg General Strike of 1919: An Illustrated History* (Winnipeg: Watson Dwyer

1994). Even the large Central Strike Committee had only two female members.

59 McKay and Morton, "The Maritimes: Expanding the Circle of Resistance"; Ruth Frager, "Class and Ethnic Barriers to Feminist Perspectives in Toronto's Jewish Labour Movement, 1919–1939," *SPE* 30 (Autumn 1989), 143–66; Frager, *Sweatshop Strife.*

60 The "Reconstruction Policy" of the Greater Toronto Labor Party called on the government to "tax all Aliens and enemy aliens very heavily; immigration after the War to be of friendly Aliens only for a definite period." *Canadian Annual Review* (Toronto), 1918, 343.

61 Ewen, "Quebec: Class and Ethnicity."

62 Allen Seager and David Roth, "British Columbia and the Mining West: A Ghost of a Chance," in Heron, ed., *Workers' Revolt*, 231–67.

63 See, for example, William M. Tuttle, *Race Riot: Chicago in the Red Summer of 1919* (New York: Atheneum 1970).

64 The BC Provincial Service Association affiliated with the Trades and Labor Congress but refused to join the Victoria Trades and Labor Council. McLean, *"A Union amongst Government Employees,"* 5, 15. See also Thomson, "'Large and Generous View'"; Glen Makahonuk, "Masters and Servants: Labour Relations in the Saskatchewan Civil Service, 1905–1945," *PF* 12, no. 2 (Fall 1987), 257–76.

65 Candice Savage, *Our Nell: A Scrapbook Biography of Nelly McClung* (Saskatoon: Prairie Books 1979), 142–3.

66 Allen, *Social Passion*, 104–96.

67 Naylor, "Ontario Workers and the Decline of Labourism"; David Patrick Yeo, "Alliance Unrealized: Farmers, Labour, and the 1919 Winnipeg General Strike" (MA thesis, University of Calgary 1986); David Patrick Yeo, "Rural Manitoba Views the Winnipeg General Strike," *PF* 14, no. 1 (Spring 1989), 23–36. On the general topic of rural workers, see Daniel Samson, ed., *Contested Countryside: Rural Workers and Modern Society in Atlantic Canada, 1800–1950* (Fredericton: Acadiensis Press 1994).

68 This important feature of the Canadian social formation has had far too little attention from Canadian historians, especially in English Canada. For some discussion, see McKay and Morton, "The Maritimes: Expanding the Circle of Resistance"; Ewen, "Quebec: Class and Ethnicity"; Normand Séguin, "L'économie agro-forestière: Genèse du développement au Saguenay au 19e siècle," in Normand Séguin, ed., *Agriculture et colonisation au Québec: Aspects historiques* (Montréal: Boréal Express 1980), 159–64; René Hardy and Normand Séguin, *Forêt et société en Mauricie: La formation de la région de Trois-Rivières, 1830–1930* (Montréal: Boréal Express 1984); Everett

C. Hughes, *French Canada in Transition* (Chicago: University of Chicago Press 1943); Bruno Ramirez, *On the Move: French-Canadian and Italian Migrants in the North Atlantic Economy, 1860–1914* (Toronto: McClelland and Stewart 1991); José Igartua, "Worker Persistence, Hiring Policies, and the Depression in the Aluminum Sector: The Saguenay Region, Quebec, 1925–1940," *HS/SH* 43 (May 1989), 9–34 ; Radforth, *Bushworkers and Bosses;* Joy Parr, "Hired Men: Ontario Agricultural Wage Labour in Historical Perspective," *L/LT* 15 (Spring 1985), 91–103; John Herd Thompson, "Bringing in the Sheaves: The Harvest Excursionists, 1890–1929," *CHR* 59, no. 4 (December 1978), 467–89; Donald Avery, "Canadian Immigration Policy and the 'Foreign' Navvy, 1896–1914," in Michael S. Cross and Gregory S. Kealey, eds., *The Consolidation of Canadian Capitalism, 1896–1929* (Toronto: McClelland and Stewart 1983), 47–73; L. Anders Sandberg, "Dependent Development, Labour, and the Trenton Steel Works, Nova Scotia, c. 1900–1943," *L/LT* 27 (Spring 1991), 127–62; James Sacouman, "Semi-Proletarianization and Rural Underdevelopment in the Maritimes," *CRSA* 17 (1980), 232–45; Leo Johnson, "Precapitalist Economic Formations and the Capitalist Labour Market in Canada, 1911–1971," in James E. Curtis and William G. Scott, eds., *Social Stratification: Canada* (Scarborough: Prentice-Hall 1979), 89–104; Rolph Knight, *Stump Ranch Chronicles and Other Narratives* (Vancouver: New Star Books 1977).

69 Ian D.H. McDonald, *"To Each His Own": William Coaker and the Fishermen's Protective Union in Newfoundland Politics, 1908–1925* (St John's: ISER Books 1987); Hak, "British Columbia Loggers."

70 Rolph Knight, *Indians at Work: An Informal History of Native Labour in British Columbia, 1858–1930* (Vancouver: New Star Books 1978); Arthur J. Ray, *The Canadian Fur Trade in the Industrial Age* (Toronto: University of Toronto Press 1990).

71 LAC, Royal Commission on Industrial Relations, Evidence, Vancouver, J.J. Coughlin, 29 April 1919.

72 Siemiatycki, "Labour Contained," 249.

73 Gregory S. Kealey, "Parameters of Class Conflict," 241.

74 Zerker, *Rise and Fall of the Toronto Typographical Union*, 178–204; Allen, *Social Passion*, 175–96.

75 Heron, "Great War and Nova Scotia Steelworkers"; Seager, "Proletariat in Wild Rose Country"; Frank, "Cape Breton Coal Miners"; Don Macgillivray, "Industrial Unrest in Cape Breton, 1919–1925" (MA thesis, University of British Columbia 1971); MacEwan, *Miners and Steelworkers*; McKay and Morton, "The Maritimes: Expanding the Circle of Resistance."

76 Naylor, *New Democracy*, 188–214.

77 *LG*, May 1921, 709; June 1921, 817.

78 Two years later total reported union membership had fallen by a further 17,000 to 260,000. Canada, Department of Labour, *Labour Organization in Canada*, 1921, 257; 1924, 10.

79 Scott, "'A Place in the Sun'"; Naylor, *New Democracy*, 188–214; Parr, *Gender of Bread winners*, 39–49; Allen Seager, "A New Era for Labour? Canadian National Railways and the Railway Worker, 1919–1929," *JCHA* 1992, 171–96; Heron, *Working in Steel*, 98–111; Margaret McCallum, "Corporate Welfarism in Canada, 1919–1939," *CHR* 71, no. 1 (March 1990), 46–79.

80 Heron, *Working in Steel*, 105.

81 Peter Morris, *Embattled Shadows: A History of Canadian Cinema, 1895–1939* (Montreal and Kingston: McGill-Queen's University Press 1978), 67–9; Naylor, *New Democracy*, 199. The Red Scare deserves fuller research; see Avery, *"Dangerous Foreigners"*; Donald Avery, *Reluctant Host: Canada's Response to Immigrant Workers, 1896–1994* (Toronto: McClelland and Stewart 1995); Theresa Catherine Baxter, "Selected Aspects of Canadian Public Opinion on the Russian Revolution and Its Impact in Canada, 1917–1919" (MA thesis, University of Western Ontario 1973); Elliott Samuels, "Red Scare in Ontario: The Reaction of the Ontario Press to the Internal and External Threat of Bolshevism, 1917–1919" (MA thesis, Queen's University 1971); Joseph Boudreau, "The Enemy Alien Problem in Canada, 1914–1921" (PhD dissertation, University of California 1964); W.R. Askin, "Labour Unrest in Edmonton and District and Its Coverage by the Edmonton Press: 1918–19" (MA thesis, University of Alberta 1973). On the same campaign in the United States, see Robert K. Murray, *Red Scare: A Study in National Hysteria, 1919–1920* (New York: McGraw Hill 1964).

82 Naylor, *New Democracy*, 199–201.

83 Ibid.; Naylor, "Workers and the State"; Tom Traves, *The State and Enterprise: Canadian Manufacturers and the Federal Government, 1917–1931* (Toronto: University of Toronto Press 1979), 15–28.

84 Naylor, *New Democracy*; Heron, "Working-Class Hamilton," 522–59.

85 Jacques Rouillard, *Les syndicats nationaux au Québec de 1900 à 1930* (Québec: Les Presses de l'Université Laval 1979); Ewen, "Quebec: Class and Ethnicity."

86 Ernest R. Forbes, "The Rise and Fall of the Conservative Party in the Provincial Politics of Nova Scotia, 1922–1933" (MA thesis, Dalhousie University 1967); Ernest R. Forbes, *The Maritimes Rights Movement, 1919–1927: A Study in Canadian Regionalism* (Montreal and Kingston: McGill-Queen's University Press 1979); McKay and Morton, "The Maritimes: Expanding the Circle of Resistance."

87 Margaret McCallum, "Keeping Women in Their Place: The Minimum Wage in Canada, 1910–1925," *L/LT* 17 (Spring 1986), 29–59; Linda Kealey, "Women and Labour during World War I: Women Workers and the Minimum Wage in Manitoba," in Mary Kinnear, ed., *First Days, Fighting Days: Women in Manitoba History* (Regina: Canadian Plains Research Centre 1987), 76–99; Elizabeth Jane Campbell, "'The Balance Wheel of the Industrial System': Maximum Hours, Minimum Wages, and Workmen's Compensation Legislation in Ontario, 1900–1939 (PhD dissertation, McMaster University 1980); Peter Oliver, "Sir William Hearst and the Collapse of the Ontario Conservative Party," in Peter Oliver, ed., *Public and Private Persons: The Ontario Political Culture, 1914–1934* (Toronto: Clark Irwin 1975).

88 Craig Heron, "The High School and the Household Economy in Working-Class Hamilton, 1890–1940," *HSE* 7, no. 2 (Fall 1995), 217–59; Tom Mitchell, "'The Manufacture of Souls of Good Quality': Winnipeg's 1919 Conference on Canadian Citizenship, English-Canadian Nationalism, and the New Order after the Great War," *JCS* 31, no. 4 (Winter 1996–7), 5–28.

89 Siemiatycki, "Labour Contained"; Robin, *Radical Politics and Canadian Labour*; Bercuson, *Fools and Wise Men*; Friesen, "'Yours in Revolt,'"141. Gregory Kealey presents slightly different figures for the 1918 vote (a minority of fifty-eight easterners and thirty-two westerners versus a majority of three westerners and ninety-seven easterners), but notes that the pattern remains the same. The West sent only 45 of the 440 delegates to the 1918 convention, which was held in Quebec City. Kealey, "1919," 36.

90 Bercuson, *Fools and Wise Men*; David Bright, "Bonds of Brotherhood? The Experiences of Labour in Calgary, 1903–1919" (MA thesis, University of Calgary 1990); David Bright, "'We Are All Kin': Reconsidering Labour and Class in Calgary, 1919," *L/LT* 29 (Spring 1992), 59–80.

91 Naylor, *New Democracy*; Ewen, "Quebec: Class and Ethnicity."

92 *Canadian Labor Press*, 1 March 1919.

93 Siemiatycki, "Labour Contained."

94 Ewen, "Quebec: Class and Ethnicity"; Naylor, "Southern Ontario: Striking at the Ballot Box."

95 Robin, *Radical Politics and Canadian Labour*; Siemiatycki, "Labour Contained"; Naylor, *New Democracy.*

96 Frank, "Cape Breton Coal Miners"; Seager, "Proletariat in Wild Rose Country"; Bercuson, *Confrontation at Winnipeg*; Bercuson, *Fools and Wise Men*; and the regional essays in Heron, ed., *Workers' Revolt*.

97 Naylor, *New Democracy*; Ewen, "Quebec: Class and Ethnicity"; Heron, *Working in Steel.*

98 Radforth, *Bushworkers and Bosses*; Allen Seager, "Finnish Canadians and the Ontario Miners' Movement," *Polyphony* 3 (Fall 1981), 35–45; Seager, "Class, Ethnicity, and Politics"; Hogan, *Cobalt*; Rouillard, "Les travailleurs juifs"; Frager, *Sweatshop Strife.*

99 McKay, *Craft Transformed*; Frank, "Cape Breton Coal Miners"; MacEwan, *Miners and Steelworkers*; Heron, "Great War and Nova Scotia Steelworkers."

100 Ewen, "Quebec: Class and Ethnicity"; Jacques Rouillard, *Histoire du syndicalisme Québécois: Des origines à nos jours* (Montréal: Boréal 1989), 134.

101 Craig Heron and Bryan D. Palmer, "Through the Prism of the Strike: Industrial Conflict in Southern Ontario, 1900–1914," *CHR* 58, no. 4 (December 1977), 423–58; Heron, "Working-Class Hamilton"; Naylor, *New Democracy.*

102 In Amherst, Nova Scotia, the local labour movement affiliated with the OBU, as did its counterpart in Carleton Place, Ontario, and several northern Ontario miners' and loggers' organizations. In Montreal, Toronto, Hamilton, and a few smaller towns in southern Ontario, small groups of socialist militants set up local OBU units and set out to compete with the established local leadership for working-class support. Fred Flatman expanded the circulation of his Hamilton paper *New Democracy,* which became the eastern mouthpiece for the OBU. Reilly, "General Strike in Amherst"; Bercuson, *Fools and Wise Men*; Naylor, *New Democracy,* 64–71.

103 Angus, *Canadian Bolsheviks*, 63–80; William Rodney, *Soldiers of the International: A History of the Communist Party of Canada, 1919–1929* (Toronto: University of Toronto Press 1968); Ivan Avakumovic, *The Communist Party in Canada: A History* (Toronto: McClelland and Stewart 1975), 1–53; Tim Buck, *Yours in the Struggle: Reminiscences of Tim Buck,* edited by William Beeching and Phyllis Clarke (Toronto: NC Press 1977), 89–140; Louise Watson, *She Was Never Afraid: The Biography of Annie Buller* (Toronto: Progress Books 1978), 1–20; Catherine Vance, *Not by Gods, But By People: The Story of Bella Hall Gauld* (Toronto: Progress Books 1968), 1–45; Avery, *"Dangerous Foreigners,"* 116–23; Frank, "Working-Class Politics"; Akers, "Rebel or Revolutionary?"; Peter Campbell, "'Making Socialists': Bill Pritchard, the Socialist Party of Canada, and the Third Intrernational," *L/LT* 30 (Fall 1992), 45–63; John Manley, "'Preaching the Red Stuff': J.B. McLachlan, Communism, and the Cape Breton Miners, 1922–1935," *L/LT* 30 (Fall 1992), 65–114; Craig Heron, "Frederick J. Flatman," *Dictionary of Hamilton Biography, Vol. 3, 1925–1939* (Hamilton: Dictionary of Hamilton Biography 1992), 52–7.

104 Naylor, "Ontario Workers and the Decline of Labourism."

105 McNaught, *Prophet in Politics*; Leo Heaps, *Rebel in the House: The Life and Times of A.A. Heaps, M.P.* (London: Niccolo Publishing 1970); Dorothy G. Steeves, *The Compassionate Rebel: Ernest Winch and the Growth of Socialism in Western Canada* (Vancouver: J.J. Douglas 1960), 70–92; Mardiros, *William Irvine*, 109–204; Walter Young, *The Anatomy of a Party: The National CCF, 1932–1961* (Toronto: University of Toronto Press 1969), 2–37; Gerald Caplan, *The Dilemma of Canadian Socialism: The CCF in Ontario* (Toronto: McClelland and Stewart 1973), 7–18; Ivan Avakumovic, *Socialism in Canada: A Study of the CCF-NDP in Federal and Provincial Politics* (Toronto: McClelland and Stewart 1978), 11–70.

106 Bryan D. Palmer, *Working-Class Experience: Rethinking the History of Canadian Labour, 1800–1991* (Toronto: McClelland and Stewart 1992), 214–67.

107 Ian McKay has developed this argument more fully in "Industry, Work, and Community," 800–28; *Craft Transformed*, 55–144; and (with Michael Earle), "Introduction: Industrial Legality in Nova Scotia," in Michael Earle, ed., *Workers and the State in Twentieth Century Nova Scotia* (Fredericton: Acadiensis Press 1989), 9–23.

108 Marion Findlay, "Protection of Workers in Industry," in W.P.M. Kennedy, ed., *Social and Economic Conditions in the Dominion of Canada* (Philadelphia: American Academy of Political and Social Science 1923), 254–66.

109 McNaught, *Prophet in Politics*, 215–20.

PART FOUR

A Gendered World

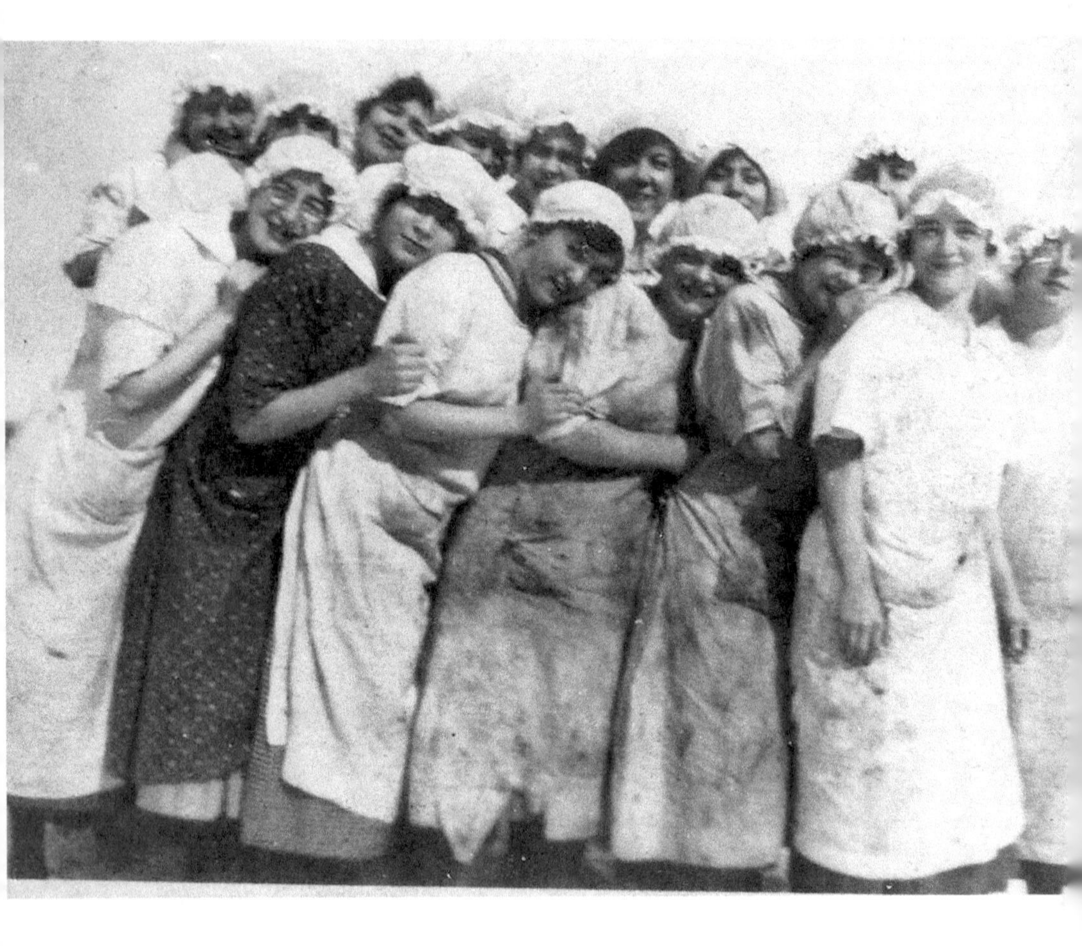

Chapter Ten

Working Girls

They streamed out of factories. They crowded into street cars. They lined up to get into the movie theatres. They wiggled and twisted wildly across dance floors. They frolicked on beaches. They made their way more soberly up church steps. They strolled sedately through streets and parks. No one could miss the ever larger numbers of young "working girls" out and about in the public spaces of an industrial city in the early twentieth century. Over the half century before the Second World War, they got bolder and more assertive, and their public behaviour often provoked controversy. The distinctively working-class femininity they were expressing operated within the patriarchal framework of their domestic and public experience that set the limits of most possibilities in their lives. But working-class women pushed back repeatedly at the frontiers of their oppression and in many ways recast their place in working-class communities.

In this essay, our window on young working-class women is Hamilton, Ontario, between the 1890s and the 1930s. This large factory city is best known for its heavy industries producing primary steel and metal goods, but, until the middle of the twentieth century, it also provided industrial employment for thousands of women, especially in several large primary cotton and knitting mills. In 1911 half the female wage-earners in Hamilton worked in factories, and seven out of ten of those punched a clock in a clothing or textile mill (three out of four by the end of the 1930s).[1]

Women workers at Proctor and Gamble in Hamilton.
School of Labour Studies Collection, LS22

Jobs

Young girls from working-class households learned to balance the conflicting needs of helping with the domestic labour (especially child care if they were older), attending elementary school, and finding time for friends on the street corner. Few stayed in school beyond age fifteen, and a majority moved quickly into full-time work.[2] A large number did unpaid work in their family household, but many of those not counted in the workforce at a specific moment would probably have worked for wages at some point in the eight to ten years between school and marriage. Almost all still found jobs in female ghettoes that were extensions of women's work in the home or allegedly involved specifically female attributes, even inside "heavy" industry, where they could be found in small numbers, for example, making nails and screws or winding electrical coils.[3]

Alongside factory work, roughly one female worker in six or eight continued to work in trade, mainly retail sales, throughout the period. But the category of domestic service that had absorbed so many girls and young women for so many decades dropped off steadily (except for a brief resurgence in the deep depression of the early 1930s).[4] The small size of the middle class in the city meant fewer households wanted to hire this kind of worker,[5] but in the early twentieth century Hamilton's young women were also just as scornful of the work as their counterparts throughout urban Canada.[6]

Two other job opportunities were slowly opening up to absorb some single working-class women – nursing and clerical work.[7] In many cases, the new recruits for these jobs were middle-class daughters with the necessary schooling and polish as well as the desire for good pay. Indeed, for these women, office work and nursing, along with teaching, became the main occupational outlets.[8] In contrast, a *Spectator* reporter concluded from his interviews with wage-earning women in 1919 that "many intelligent, wholesome and sensible girls" had been held back from a nursing career by "a question of social standing."[9] For the better clerical jobs, parents had to be willing to cover the costs of their daughters' prolonged schooling and thus forego her earnings. This was a luxury that only the families of better-paid, more regularly employed skilled workers could afford. They typically relied much less heavily on their children's contributions to the household economy. Yet less-well-paid, low-end office work did not require as much training, and girls from blue-collar households flocked into the city's private business schools and high-school commercial courses in the 1920s and 1930s, suggesting that this was an increasingly attractive option.[10]

In each of the census years between 1911 and 1941, the average weekly earnings of female workers in Hamilton were only half that of the average male worker, and many earned even less. The difference had little to do with the scarcity of their skills in the labour market – textile knitters often had to be imported, for example, but never earned anything close to comparably skilled men. The issue was simply that they were female and had to accept a "woman's wage."[11] Typically the average female wage-earner in Hamilton suffered less unemployment than a male, especially in the 1930s, probably because, on the whole, the manufacturing industries in which the city's women worked were less unstable than the male-dominated metalworking industries.[12] In 1920 the Ontario government enacted a new minimum-wage law for women, but the rates varied by industry and in general merely confirmed existing wage levels.[13] The gendered inequities of the workplace payroll were merely reinforced and, in fact, given legal sanction.[14]

Almost nothing in their engagement with specific labour processes gave working girls the basis on which to build a gender identity rooted in wage-earning. Some took pride in the skills they exercised – at a sewing or knitting machine or a typewriter, for example – but rarely did managers acknowledge them. Most did simple, numbingly repetitive, enervating work on light machinery or in packing departments. Like virtually all working-class wage-earners, they had to rely on the strength and dexterity of their young bodies in their work – from good eyesight to strong backs to their often-noticed "nimble fingers." The justification for all this, which most women no doubt accepted,[15] was that they had no future in the paid workplace and were destined for unpaid work in their own family households. That was also the excuse for the paltry wages they were paid. As they punched the time clock at the end of the day, they also stepped out into terrain where their public behaviour was rigorously scrutinized for its potential violations of appropriate feminine decorum. These were all conditions that deprived young women of the same independence that their male counterparts were developing at the same age.

Before the First World War, "working girls" could expect no substantial support from the preponderantly male craft-union movement. In the few unionized industries in which women worked, most of them remained unorganized, or, like the local garment and shoe workers, were hived off into their own locals. There their vulnerability as low-wage workers and limited sojourn in the paid workforce (or in one workplace) undermined their effectiveness. The local United Garment Workers' leader, Sam Landers, liked to refer to the home as women's "natural sphere" and decried how business had drawn women out of that sphere, how in some trades they even outnumbered men. The first (and only) women to appear at a Hamilton Trades and Labor Council meeting before the First World War – representatives of the female workers at McPherson's shoe company – were a cause for surprised comment.[16]

In most of the pre-war years, women remained peripheral to the garment workers' organization in Hamilton, as they were to almost all other unions in the city. When the entire garment industry erupted in a mass strike for two weeks in April 1913, however, hundreds of the women signed up and proved themselves effective picketers. But the settlement that the male leadership imposed on them ignored their concerns, and they soon abandoned the union. A new wave of organizing at the end of the war, this time in the more progressive, industrially organized Amalgamated Clothing Workers Union, drew many female garment workers into the fold, included some on the local's executive, and brought more direct attention to women's wages. But the union's accomplishments were short-lived, as employers struck back and broke the organization in another general strike of the local industry in 1921.[17]

Meanwhile, since the turn of the century, small female-dominated work groups had ignored union affiliations and challenged unacceptable management initiatives with spontaneous, short-lived strikes of their own. Between 1929 and 1933 women in three of Hamilton's large textile plants – Canadian Cottons, Hamilton Cotton, and Mercury Mills – built on this more informal tradition of collective protest and saw their initial confrontations quickly spread across each plant and draw in the entire workforce. Their battles became prolonged, militant battles in which new unions emerged, sometimes with help from Communist activists. Like all other collective workplace struggles in Hamilton in the period, however, the strikes were defeated.[18] "Working girls" could look back half a century and see no sustained results in building a workplace culture of formal solidarity among their workmates.

Off the Job

Within these constraints, some opportunities did arise. As a greater number of working girls shunned jobs in domestic service, they worked more fixed hours with more clearly defined free time, and their status as wage-earners within their families often earned them the right to spend some of that leisure time and some small part of their earnings outside the home. Many working-class women later looked back on this phase of their lives as a time of greater freedom and fun. Domestic burdens might lighten up somewhat for some, especially if another sister was staying home. That sense of entitlement could vary between different ethnic groups – young Jewish women seemed to have a particularly strong leverage within their culture, Italians somewhat less so – but most working-class daughters preferred to gain some distance from the small domestic spaces and close supervision of the family circle.[19] For some, plunging into a social life beyond the home was a form of rebellion against the constraints of domesticity and, in certain cases, against abusive relationships with parents.[20] By the First World War, moreover, hundreds who had apparently migrated to the city on their own in search of work were living in boarding houses far from the direct oversight of parents (although landladies invariably kept an eye on them, and moral reformers watched them anxiously). Still, most young working women seemed to recognize that their attachment and commitment to their families were paramount – this was particularly though not exclusively so for those in the European immigrant households – and few made a complete break.[21] Those who were able to keep a small part of their wages for their own use had some time and income for enjoying a few pleasures of their own. In contrast to most of their middle-class counterparts, they turned the streets and other public sites into spaces for private socializing.[22]

Many working girls drifted between jobs in search of more satisfying or better-paid work,[23] but everywhere they seemed to develop the close bonds with workmates that, for instance, percolated up onto the picket lines of strikes like that of the city's garment workers in 1913 or textile workers in 1929 and 1933. To some extent these relationships were a coping strategy in the face of degrading work situations. Like many other wage-earners, they cooperated at work to help each other out. They told stories, joked and teased each other, sang songs, discussed novels, and chatted and gossiped intimately.[24] They had a lot in common – most of them were single and ranged in age from mid-teens to their mid-twenties. As a result of the informal recruitment processes, it was not unusual to have sisters or friends from the neighbourhood working nearby.[25] Knowing that in most cases their future lay in domestic labour as wives and mothers, they shared a fascination with romance and courtship. When corporate employers began to design recreational programs for their female workers towards the end of the First World War, they tried to build on these workplace practices of sociability.[26]

In many cases, the workplace friendships overflowed into lively fun off the job.[27] As investigators in many cities at the time and several writers more recently have noted, the feminine cultural practices they developed proclaimed a sense of entitlement, dignity, and pride that differed considerably from what men developed on the job. They turned away from the harshness and indignities of their wage-earning experiences and focused on leisure time in the present, particularly on aspirations to be well dressed and attractive, to enjoy some immediate pleasures, and to express their sexuality in the company of men. In the only novel written about working women in this period by a Hamilton author, Mabel Burkholders's *The Course of Impatience Carningham*, the young heroine tells an upper-class questioner that she wants what one recent historian argues was every working girl's aspiration – to become "a beautiful lady."[28] These young women turned modest consumerism to their own ends, and tried to shape their feminine identities as "ladies" through the cheap goods and amusements they purchased for pleasure. They were more active agents than passive victims, and made fullest use of the limited consumerist resources available to them to fashion an agenda of public possibilities – in short, to dream.[29] In the process their young bodies became the main vehicle for expressing femininities that were distinctively working class, and that in many ways pushed at the boundaries of prescribed gender expectations.

Looking attractive, and especially dressing well, were central. Before the First World War, investigators into working girls' lives across the continent repeatedly found them willing to forego other essentials – street-car fare and even occasionally lunch – to be able to buy fancy dresses, elegant high-heeled shoes, and, above all, flamboyant hats, which feature prominently in photographs of young women in the prewar period and caused great consternation within theatre audiences. In the interwar period their head gear became simpler but still essential.[30] Escaping from the family cycle of hand-me-downs must have been an important assertion of independence.[31] Their clothing tastes ran to the flashy, gaudy, and outlandish, in stark contrast to the more restrained middle-class dress standards. As a result, in the perceptive words of one historian, "they staged a carnivalesque inversion that undermined middle-class efforts to control the definition of 'lady.'"[32] Such styles probably also challenged the conventions of mothers from peasant backgrounds in Southern and Eastern Europe, as their daughters tried to adapt to North American standards.[33] Here was the most visible way for working girls to assert that they had not been ground down by wage labour – this was especially so when they actually wore the prized clothing to work.

Nothing upset clergymen and moralistic commentators more than did working girls' fascination with "finery."[34] Even Sam Landers, the prim (teetotalling) editor of the local *Labor News* and former garment workers' organizer, had the gall to suggest in 1912 that "more girls go astray as a result of vanity and pride in desiring costly clothes, jewelry, etc., that an honest livelihood cannot afford." Staking a claim to social entitlement on the basis of allegedly "frivolous" female consumer practices was far outside the framework of mainstream labour-movement thinking, and indeed threatened the carefully constructed imagery of the family home tended by a virtuous wife that unionists were using in their public postulations. The "rising of the women" in Hamilton's clothing industry in 1913 revealed how they could indeed base their militancy on quite different concepts of femininity. In any case, the charges of wild spending were generally exaggerated. Despite the clothing industry's new output of cheaper, mass-produced garments, young working-class women must have found their limited incomes allowed few plunges into much extravagant consumerism. Shopping for clothing could be a popular outing, but many made or altered their own clothes or had their mothers make them. In contrast to their middle-class counterparts, they could rarely afford to indulge in the emerging culture of department stores, which was so overtly aimed at female consumers from the middle class. By whatever means, however, working girls unquestionably struggled to dress in a way that would put on a fine display.[35]

In the decade before the war the debate about the styles of this "finery" heated up. Critics thought that much of it was too provocative and "immodest." By the end of the war the controversies had focused on shortening skirts, plunging necklines, "georgette waists," "peek-a-boo blouses," bobbed hair, and the growing use of cosmetics to enhance a young woman's features.[36] In 1921 the police admitted that they had no intention of following an Alabama precedent of forcibly scrubbing off the make-up on young women in the streets, but a year later so many adolescent school girls were applying "powder and paint" that a major conference of youth workers was convened to discuss whether this constituted "dirt" that, by law, a girl could be ordered to wash off. Tolerance triumphed, and over the next few years the "flapper" style of short skirts and short hair similarly took hold.[37] When in 1924 a female evangelist denounced the local YWCA for allowing girls to wear "dresses up to their knees," a young woman had the confidence to rise in the gallery and defend the organization and its young members. Tighter, one-piece bathing suits that exposed more flesh also appeared on Hamilton beaches in the 1920s, and, by the end of the decade, beauty contests had emerged to legitimize these trends. By this point, young working women could also look to the movies for models of flamboyant self-presentation as a strategy for social success.[38]

Looking good was a public performance, not a private act. Girls and young women were staking a larger claim to being allowed to enjoy themselves in the public spaces outside their own households. For many, starting in early adolescence, that meant boldly promenading along the streets together in the evening. In the decade before the First World War, the police and the Children's Aid Society inspector announced crack-downs on what appeared to be a new practice among young girls (dubbed "linewalkers") of "spending a couple of hours every night on the principal streets." "The practice has become so common as to be conspicuous on the down-town streets and other public places," a reporter noted in 1911. "The YWCA and the Salvation Army officials are agreed that the street walking habit amongst the young girls of Hamilton is very bad and has gotten beyond all bounds," another paper reported a year later. A by-law forbade youngsters under sixteen from being on the streets unaccompanied after 9 p.m., and the police were prepared to march these late-night offenders home to their parents. Girls found out and about too often could soon be labelled "incorrigible" and brought into police court (though few were). But the police never seemed to have been able to stamp out the practice, and some linewalkers were far from submissive. The *Spectator* reported in 1910 that "many of the female sex who have been asked to move … have most indignantly refused to be 'bossed' by a man." A *Times* columnist noted, "The toney stare, the indignant look, the muttered words of rebellion and the sarcastic shrug of the shoulders must be aggravating." By the early 1920s, many of these girls in the street were also spotted lighting up cigarettes (probably a little later than boys were seen doing the same).[39]

Young girls set out on these promenades to enjoy each other's company, but the real point of "walking the line" was to meet and flirt with boys or men – to "mash" them, in the street vernacular. Men and boys lounging on street corners regularly engaged in suggestive repartee with the passing crowds of females (and sometimes even physically assaulted them). These wandering clusters of young women may have given each other some protection but also the courage and skills to negotiate their encounters with males in public places.[40]

The week-long centennial carnival sponsored by the city in August 1913 showcased this increasingly controversial "sparking" in the street. Crowds took over whole downtown streets in various modes of merry-making. "Hundreds of girls who invariably walk the streets with chins tilted disdainfully at angles not conducive to spine restfulness, laughed gaily when tickled under the chins by gay Lotharios – and thought nothing of it," the *Spectator* reported. The male aggressors were using small feather dusters known as "ticklers." Many girls fought back with showers of confetti and ticklers of their own. Clusters of them stood on street corners "gently tapping the male folk as they passed by." An alderman grumpily suggested that some of them should be spanked. Newspaper reporters saw women wearing buttons and ribbons with such provocative slogans as "No Introduction Needed," "See Me Alone," "I Have My Eyes on You," "Single, but Willing to Be Married," and "Kiss Me – I'm a Bear." Some who thought that men had gone too far punched, slapped, or kicked them or walloped them with an umbrella. But, on the whole, these interactions seemed tolerant and good-natured. On the last night of these "riotous frivolities," in true carnival spirit, an impromptu parade of cross-dressed men and women entertained the crowds. "Yes," said the *Times*, "Mabel, Katie and Vera were Willies, Jims and Johns last night." It was this kind of behaviour that prompted the police magistrate to muse a few years later that "the girls do most of the courting nowadays."[41]

Space for Us

The venues for this heterosexual sparking expanded beyond the street corner, especially for girls reaching their later teens. With commercialized sites of more respectable pleasure proliferating after the turn of the century – notably amusement parks, train and steamship excursions, and vaudeville and movie houses – the owners consciously reached out to women with their elegant decor and morally sound programming. Indeed, the presence of women was supposed to be a guarantee of respectability, though vaudeville-house managers noticed plenty of female interest in the scantily clad bodies of male acrobats or strong men. Women appeared in particularly large numbers in movie houses, which were cheap and relatively safe. Working girls often arrived together in the early evening, or a bit later on the arm of a beau. "We'd go to the show for five cents, get popcorn, and later a bag of chips wrapped in newsprint," one woman remembered. "If you got uptown early enough and had the money, you could take in two features in one night, and many young people did," other old-timers recalled. All these new amusement sites were free from parental supervision and allowed young women a considerable degree of intimacy with men.[42]

Other commercial spaces, notably skating rinks and dance halls, appealed specifically to young adult courtship. Ice skating had a long history in a city with sub-zero winters and a large frozen harbour. Several indoor rinks were also opened to attract paying customers over a longer stretch of the cooler months. Roller skating first took hold only in the 1880s, but by the first decade of the next century the city's three roller rinks were attracting thousands of patrons every year.[43] The owners of these large venues for ice and roller skating provided live bands and organized special events – novelty acts, skating competitions, and "fancy-dress" or "rube" carnivals – which became spectacles to be viewed from the balcony. By the 1920s women skaters regularly paid a quarter for admission. Once the skaters were inside, the lyrics in local ragtime composer Charlie Wellinger's song "Come with Me for a Roller Skate" advised a man to "Put your arm round her waist," and "Twixt the turns whisper sweet words of love!"[44]

Public dancing was probably the fastest growing and most controversial activity among the youth of working-class Hamilton before the First World War. People here and in most other towns and cities had been dancing for generations, usually as part of kin or community celebrations, such as weddings, civic holidays, lodge socials, or union-sponsored balls.[45] But something new emerged in the early twentieth century – a commercialized space for unchaperoned young people to gather and practice much more sexually provocative dance steps. These spaces included dance pavilions at such summertime resorts as Grimsby Beach. In 1906, when the city's licencing laws were overhauled, the licence inspector reported no dance halls within the city limits. Three years later there was one, and in 1912 only two. But the next year he collected fees from seven and in 1914 ten. A decade later there were nineteen.[46]

A dance craze had exploded in every major city across North America in the decade before the war, as thousands of young people learned to do the so-called "animal dances" – the turkey trot, the bunny hug, the grizzly bear, and so on – along with the sensual tango, the more restrained fox trot, and eventually the Charleston, all to the beat of the new ragtime music.[47] When Hamilton staged its centennial celebration in 1913, the downtown streets filled up every night with young dancers showing off their skills at these new steps, and the *Herald* reported that it was becoming "quite popular at all band concerts" for young couples to start dancing behind the band stand.[48] In 1917 the city saw its first jazz performers, imported from New York, and soon this new music was animating many dances. By the 1920s a working girl could get into a dance hall for a quarter, though higher prices at some venues signalled a more socially exclusive clientele.[49]

This so-called tough dancing involved close body contact, fast pace, and various shakes and shimmies that hinted strongly at sexual intercourse. No other popular amusement gave young women such an open outlet for sexual expression. As a pastime devoted to dramatic, expressive use of the body, this kind of dancing was at the outer edge of respectability for young women, and, at least until the 1920s, the commercial dance hall attracted mainly working-class youth. Typically young women arrived with female friends and used the setting to find a companion of the opposite sex for the evening (once going steady, it seems, couples were less likely to frequent a dance hall). Here was where a young woman's flamboyant "finery" could pay off, and where she could hone her skills at flirtation and "mashing." Indeed, this was a site where, in defiance of parental expectations and middle-class or ethnic norms, a young working-class woman could exercise an unusual degree of control over her interactions with men, rejecting or changing partners, perhaps outclassing them with her dancing skills, or choosing to dance with other women instead. On the darkened sidelines, she might enjoy hugs and kisses with an attractive beau, but leave with her girlfriends.[50]

Not surprisingly, the dance hall was quickly constructed as roughly the female equivalent of the most morally suspect male-dominated space, the saloon. In 1913 a telephone operator was fired for dancing the tango at a company tea party, and the next winter both the YMHA and the Hamilton Tigers, the city's football team, banned it from their social events. Several dance-hall owners called their businesses "dance academies" to try to soften the moral scorn, but, whatever the label, bodies still twisted and gyrated across the polished dance floor in the same ways. So many of the city's young women ignored the prudes and embraced the dance craze that in 1919 the local YWCA decided it had to make a historic break with its past policy and allow mixed dancing (and card playing) during social evenings. Since "the girls get these amusements outside," the board concluded, it would be better to hold onto them "under proper supervision." The same year Mercury Mills, a large plant filled with working girls, welcomed some 800 young men and women for a dance held in the new addition to its factory. A decade later, striking textile workers at Canadian Cottons filled an evening with dancing. Although a new city by-law in 1924 banned girls under sixteen from entering dance halls and required women to be accompanied by an escort, working girls had found a new environment within the growing world of commercial amusements for asserting independence and expressing desire.[51]

Shorter hair, layers of make-up, more daring necklines, open smoking, exuberant dancing – for growing numbers of Hamilton's working girls, these abrupt changes in public behaviour had begun by the early 1920s to shape a new working-class femininity. At that point a major change in public policy took some of them one step further away from the prim confines of turn-of-the-century feminine identity. In 1919 voters in a province-wide referendum confirmed that a wartime measure to shut down all retail sales of beverage alcohol, including in all saloons, would continue indefinitely into the postwar period. Until the Ontario government retreated to a less draconian liquor-control policy in 1927, social drinking was forced into the shadows, where bootleggers and "blind-pig" operators provided single bottles for home consumption or small private spaces for consumption with others. Before prohibition, women rarely appeared in saloons, but in the 1920s the male dominance of social drinking was under attack. Not only were many of the neighbourhood bootleggers women, but now some young women joined boyfriends or spouses in the unregulated space of the blind pig or at the hotel dance hall with flasks in their pockets. Some of the many new immigrants in the city from England and Scotland might have starting drinking back home, where, before the war and even more so after, women joined in pub life much more regularly than they did on this side of the Atlantic. In 1932 the anti-prohibitionist Moderation League organized an unofficial referendum among factory workers across southern Ontario on selling beer by the glass, and three Hamilton plants with preponderantly young, female workforces voted 80 per cent in favour.[52]

When in 1934 Ontario legislation permitted the opening of beer parlours (known as "beverage rooms"), women could not be waitresses (or sit behind the cash register, even if they were owners or the wives of owners),[53] but in each establishment they were allowed to enter a separate beverage room for "ladies and escorts." These were roughly the same size as the men-only rooms and during the 1930s filled up during peak periods of drinking each week. Photographic evidence reveals that no particular effort was made to make ladies' beverage rooms more attractive to women – they were just as starkly unadorned and uninviting as the men's side – but the regulations tried to maintain some moral decorum by allowing men to enter only in the company of women. Although they could visit beverage rooms in Ontario with female friends, the administrative regime assumed that, as in the dance halls, women were accompanied by, and under the protection of, men, their "escorts."[54] This was part of a broader pattern of inclusion of women in formerly all-male events. In 1930 the *Spectator* had reported "a goodly attendance of ladies" with male companions at boxing matches in recent years.[55]

Many women who frequented these drinking places seemed to enjoy their alcohol as much as their male mates and friends, and were often among the raucous crowds leaving the place at closing time. One man reported that "some women seem to make a practise [*sic*] of being in these Beverage rooms sometime afternoon and nights looking for fellows to buy them beer." In 1935 one worried wife wrote about the Hotel Mart: "On a Saturday night when they have an orchestra the place is overrun with drunken women and men dancing a drunken orgie [*sic*]." Even young, under-aged women slipped in, it seems. One of many reports on female minors came from a father concerned about conditions at the Vulcania Hotel: "My girl, at seventeen, and her chums can go in there and have all the beer they want, although their ages are very apparent." When confronted with a similar charge, the owner of the Dog and Gun Hotel stated that such young girls came from the nearby Tuckett's Tobacco factory. Some young women were anything but demure: when the owner of the Gurry Hotel refused to serve some "young ladies," they called him "some very unpleasant names" and slapped and kicked him before being thrown out. The inspector occasionally reported on female drunks, like the one who staggered out of the Genesse Hotel one night in 1936 and "lay on the sidewalk in a very drunken condition." Occasionally women were even involved in their own fights. In 1935 a brawl erupted outside the Hotel Mart, in which women were described as drunk, "using filthy hotel staff language," and "screeching, hollering and cursing" along several city streets. Some such women were barred from particular beverage rooms by the owners. In a few hotels, women evidently used the ladies' beverage rooms as a space for offering their services as prostitutes, though this seems to have required the connivance of the hotel staff.[56] Although certainly far from all, or even most, young working-class women entered a beverage room, a public space had opened that enabled the more daring among them to expand the range of more outlandish, transgressive possibilities.

As more and more young working women found new ways to express themselves by using their bodies in unconventional ways – from promenading to dancing to getting drunk – many also began to turn to somewhat less controversial activities: sports. The first sport to take off among them was basketball, which began at the YWCA in 1908 and became so popular across the city by 1919 that a Hamilton team competed in the finals of the Ontario Ladies Basketball Association. The following year a well-publicized girls' basketball league included teams from several churches, the Oliver Chilled Plow works, and the YWCA.[57] When the courts were closed for the summer, many working girls headed out to playing fields to play softball. In 1920 teams from eight large factories and a war veterans' women's auxiliary drew good crowds to local baseball diamonds, and the winning team from Imperial Cotton had their picture prominently displayed on the sports page of the *Spectator*.[58] As non-contact sports, both these games escaped some of the moral outrage about potential dangers to their reproductive capacity.[59]

Women also began to get involved in their own track-and-field events. A women's section of the Hamilton Olympic Club (formed in 1926) gave many the chance to practise and to make strong showings in international Olympic competitions from 1928 on and in a meet organized alongside the British Empire Games played in Hamilton in 1930.[60] The amateur athletes who played these sports not only had a new outlet for energetic physical activity, but became acclaimed heroines for much larger numbers of female spectators. Working-class women seemed far less restrained by the physical expressiveness involved, or by the controversies over scanty sports attire, excessive competitiveness, male coaching, and general "masculinizing" influences.[61] In the interwar period, then, a young working woman could incorporate a love of strenuous bodily exertion into an acceptable feminine identity.

Local sport stars like Olympic hurdler Betty Taylor might inspire working girls, but these young women also had a larger reservoir of brazen femininity available to them. The blossoming popular culture that targeted young working women provided a host of female images and role models that reinforced their audacity in pushing the limits of permissible femininity. Alongside bevies of provocative chorus girls, the vaudeville and movie circuits highlighted many female "stars," often brash, aggressive, stylishly sensual figures, who legitimized women's active presence in the public sphere – women as diverse as Mary Pickford and Theda Bara, and, later, Greta Garbo, Marlene Dietrich, and Mae West. These stars were featured in the local newspapers' theatre columns and advertisements, and developed a following of loyal fans. Advertisers took advantage of this public adoration by using stars to promote their soaps or face creams. On stage and screen (and later on radio), featured performers often portrayed independent women with courage, biting wit, and active sexual appetites. Sometimes they boldly cross-dressed to play male roles, or put on blackface to sing comical "coon songs" or to act out outlandish slapstick comedy. Others won the label of "vamps" for their steamy performances. Still others entered a circus ring, vaudeville stage, or movie set to handle snakes or wild animals, or displayed their scantily clad, well-muscled female bodies in spectacular, gender-bending acrobatic turns. (Sometimes men played these same roles in drag.)[62]

All female performers had to struggle with deep-seated assumptions that such eroticized public spectacles made them little more than prostitutes, but they were able to embrace a new respectability provided by their bosses, who had turned these venues into sites of wholesome family entertainment. These showmen made efforts to contain the women's performances within acceptable bounds of female behaviour and to publicize their good characters and dedication to home and family. But the women's bold, unconventional public lives nonetheless suggested the possibility in the early twentieth century of new feminine identities beyond the dominant images of frailty, passivity, and domesticity. Some female entertainers, including circus star Josie DeMott Robinson and movie heroine Mary Pickford, pushed the implications of their public presence still further by actively supporting campaigns to give women the vote. A young woman who summoned up the pluck to jump up onto the stage in some east-Hamilton theatre's amateur night may have secretly yearned for escape to this exciting world of female expressiveness (as fan culture encouraged them to do). Certainly moral reformers worried obsessively about the power of popular amusements to stimulate the social and sexual imagination of girls and young women.[63]

Those anxious moralists could take some comfort from considering how most poorly paid or seasonally employed working girls could afford only limited contact with the new commercial pleasures.[64] Even with male companions, they might stick to simple pastimes. In 1907 a *Spectator* reporter found many couples simply ambling on the edge of the city in the evening. "We used to go walking – that was the only entertainment we had," the daughter of a wire-drawer later recalled. In cold weather this couple simply met in the corner grocery store.[65]

Generally, however, young women looked to their beaus to pay for outings. One man remembered courting his wife through numerous amusements, which he must have paid for: "We'd go to a dance on Saturday night. And in the summer we'd go on the Moonlights [cruises]. We'd go down to Grimsby with two bands on there and stop in Grimsby for an hour. They had games and all that sort of thing."[66]

Relying on men to pay their way could open up major risks for young women. In the intimacy of the dance floor or the darkened movie theatre, men might well demand sexual favours in return, and trading sex for access to commercial entertainment could taint a working girl's reputation and, of course, possibly result in an unwanted pregnancy. Across North America such women were labelled "charity girls" and "occasional" prostitutes. As early as 1891, a local Anglican clergyman told the Ontario Prison Reform Commission: "They are not admitted to society unless they are well dressed; they are not even admitted into church unless they are well dressed. It takes all they can do to earn enough to keep them and they must steal or misconduct themselves for the clothes they wear." A quarter-century later, when a female store clerk was charged with stealing shirt-waists and petticoats from the department store where she worked, she argued that theft was an alternative to immorality. "There are loads of girl clerks in this city who are kept by men," she insisted. "They feel that they are forced to accept that support, but I have not and will not stoop to that sort of thing." Moral reformers assumed that such tendencies led to a quick, slippery slope into full-fledged prostitution, particularly among girls who were tempted by a "soft, easy" life rather than hard work. One front-page newspaper story in 1913 told of a policeman who had encountered a young woman leaving a brothel. The officer said the woman claimed "she was not receiving enough wages and had to put on some style at work." Since there was never a census of sex workers, it is impossible to know how many cash-strapped working girls stepped over this line, but, for worried moral activists, it was the blurring of the boundaries between precocious flirting and serious soliciting that sounded alarm bells.[67]

Of course, many young women avoided all these controversial pleasures and their alleged dangers. Fatigue at the end of a working day and lack of money often held them back. Parents also set limits, because they both expected help with domestic labour and worried about sexual dangers. Some ethnic groups were much more protective of their daughters. Many Southern Italian parents insisted that their daughters had to be chaperoned by brothers, though younger siblings may have escaped this surveillance.[68] An adolescent girl had to negotiate her leisure time away from the family and her curfew, and often found a mother waiting up for her on a Saturday night. Landladies in boarding houses could also be watchful. Yet, since she was rarely chaperoned, a young working-class woman probably had more relative freedom to step out than her middle-class counterpart in the city.[69]

Some young women would not have participated in all this burgeoning popular culture by choice. Perhaps they were uncomfortable with the loose morality associated with public amusements and concerned about their reputations. In many cases, their "escape" from the demands of their lives was into novels. "The fiction shelves are greatly patronized by girls of the working classes," Hamilton's chief librarian stated in 1919. "Many girls who might otherwise be looking for amusement on the streets and in dance halls were provided with plenty of thrills at home by the stories of Robert W. Chambers, Arthur B. Reeves, and other writers of the class that forms an irresistible attraction to most lovers of light fiction." Only a small percentage of the population used the public library, however. In 1920, as the population topped 100,000, fewer than 18,000 people held library cards. Most of the library's collection was in the main downtown building, and, although the working-class east end got its own small branch in 1908, it was poorly stocked and uninviting. By the 1920s two small outlets in that district served mostly children, and even the new building opened with great fanfare in 1932 had pathetically little on its shelves. It was closed three years later in a civic cost-cutting move, amidst a flurry of protest from unions and workers' political organizations.[70]

Beyond the library were the dime novels. These mass-produced, often serialized, formulaic tales of romance and thrilling adventure, often involving working-class women escaping the clutches of bourgeois or aristocratic fiends, were not the earnest, didactic books focusing on character development that were favoured by middle-class readers. Nor did they highlight industrial conflict or political confrontation as men in the labour movement might have expected. Young women could nonetheless find fascinating heroines from their own class – women who demonstrated their resourcefulness, triumphed over adversity, and asserted their own brand of "ladyhood." It is hard to know how widely read this literature became. Probably, as in the United States, there was a market for dime novels, which then circulated from hand to hand at lunch breaks on the job, where discussion of their plots and characters could be lively.[71]

Looking back from the 1930s, then, single working girls could marvel at how much had changed in working-class Hamilton since the days of their mothers or grandmothers. They had a few more job options and more free time, though no better pay. They were still expected to help out with domestic labour at home. Yet, after work, among their friends, they were able to cultivate a much more expansive recreational life as new socializing rituals and commercial amusements welcomed them. Working girls had begun pushing back constraints on their public behaviour in the decade before the First World War, and the partial blurring of gender prescriptions during that war, including most symbolically the granting of the right to vote, had engendered more confidence.[72] By the interwar period they could wear provocative clothing and make-up, go to movies, dance, smoke, drink, play energetic sports, and much more without arousing much moral outrage. If she wanted to, a working girl could cultivate some defiant, flamboyant ways of displaying and using her body to assert a distinctively working-class femininity. The distance between such behaviour and the more restrained deportment of shyer or more religiously inclined young women – between what had once been designated the "respectable" and the "rough" – had certainly narrowed.

Safer Paths

Working-class girls were objects of concern in early-twentieth-century industrial centres. Their parents certainly tried to keep them close to home, both to help out with the domestic labour and to avoid risks to the girls' (and their families') reputation for moral probity. Elementary school teachers, who kept them under strict supervision for several hours every weekday, segregated them from boys in schoolyards and physical-education programs, sent them off to "domestic science" classes every week to learn proper domestic skills, and taught them key elements of their feminine identities. Various external agencies tried to corral working-class girls into structured activities in their play time that would reinforce the elementary school's messages about female domesticity and moral purity. The Sunday schools were probably the most pervasive.[73] Outside home and school, these girls also attracted the attention of leading women's organizations, who set themselves the task of helping to shape the femininity of working-class girls in appropriate ways. The most prominent was the Young Women's Christian Association, whose Hamilton branch had a long history of reaching out to girls and young women in their free time after school and work. Their success, however, was limited.

The moral reformers' best hope, it seems, was to find activities that would divert young women from the lurking dangers of commercial amusements and predatory men. The various churches made consistent efforts to create mid-week programming for young women, including, where possible, those from working-class families. Unmarried women made up a much larger percentage of church members in the city than did their bachelor brothers, and on week nights they found their way to meetings of groups such as the Girls' Friendly Society in the north-end St Luke's Anglican, the Sunbeam Circle at the east-end Calvin Presbyterian, or the Junior Catholic Women's League at the St Patrick's Girls' Clubhouse. They also joined in with the mixed-gender choirs and Bible classes. Their churches' social program provided many working girls with their main source of weekly recreation and conviviality, particularly before the First World War. Some three-quarters of the single women at Calvin Presbyterian Church, for example, had factory jobs.[74]

The WCTU had also set up distinct branches for evangelically inclined young women, though they seem to have attracted mainly middle-class participants, in rapidly declining numbers. In the 1890s the main work of these young women in Hamilton as elsewhere was to instruct children in temperance principles and domestic responsibilities, but, in the early 1890s and again at the turn of the century, they tried, with little success, to interest working girls in meetings of their own. The image of prim, self-restrained femininity that the WCTU promoted was increasingly out of step with the new lifestyles of young working women. After optimistically reporting in 1901 that they had "just commenced work among 'working girls,'" the Hamilton branches admitted a year later that the reading room they had opened for them in the east end "was not appreciated by those whom it was intended to help" and the project was abandoned.[75] The more socially aloof Independent Order Daughters of the Empire also tried to set up a girls' club in the east end in 1911, with classes in dramatic dancing and first aid, but ended up a year later simply running a small boarding house and dining room for recently arrived British working girls, which had only sixteen boarders in 1914 and closed in 1920.[76]

Among the non-denominational agencies, the YWCA had the longest, most ambitious track record. From its founding, its core clientele were white-collar office and retail workers ("business girls"), most of them from middle-class families. But, from time to time in the two decades before the First World War, the Y gingerly reached out into the unfamiliar world of what was coming to be known as the "industrial girl." Staff occasionally approached factory managers to take out memberships for all their female employees, sent special invitations to working girls to attend evening social events, and hired an "extension" or "industrial" secretary to visit working-class girls. Evidently few responded, and fewer returned.[77] It was not hard to see why coaxing working-class girls into the Y's premises could be unsuccessful. Sweeping through the tastefully furnished YWCA downtown headquarters were the city's leading ladies, who not only ran the Y, but also used the place for meetings of many of the clubs and associations they ran. Around them flowed the larger numbers of middle-class young women who could afford the membership fees, the relatively costly boarding fees, and the special outfits or equipment for particular programs. This was hardly a welcoming environment for more proletarian "ladies."

If they wouldn't come to the downtown building, perhaps they would be more interested in something closer to their own neighbourhoods. At the Y's north-end branch, it tried to drum up interest in a small lunchroom for local working girls in 1897, and eight years later invited local factory girls to weekly Saturday-night socials and then to short-lived Sunday evening prayer meetings at this satellite branch. Small turnouts quickly killed the projects. Over the next decade the organizers made repeated attempts to pull together a club for wage-earning girls, though the weekly attendance seldom reached as high as twenty-five before, in September 1917, the faltering branch was quietly shut down.[78] That year the Y shifted its focus eastward and put a new emphasis on organizing industrial girls into self-governing clubs in a new east-end branch. The girls once again showed limited interest.

Like the Christian churches at the same time, the YWCA wanted to position itself as a mediator of class tensions in postwar Canada.

Addressing the recreational needs of working girls more effectively would stave off more menacing social and political projects being discussed and promoted in the period. "Canada is at the cross-roads," one local official warned; "it is our work to see that all girls have a chance to develop along the right lines."[79] Y officials were also conscious that the arrival of votes for women since 1916 had raised new challenges for women in the public sphere, and began to refer to their work as training for "citizenship."[80] Yet after conducting a special survey in Hamilton, the head of the Y's national Industrial Department reported in 1920 that the local Y was reaching only "the girls of a better class" and not the estimated 5,300 young women employed in factories. "The churches do not provide any recreational program for these girls," she reported, "their enjoyment being practically limited to dance halls and movies." She stressed the need "to compete with these amusements, indirectly raising the standard of enjoyment, and bringing in better influences."[81]

In 1920 the Y decided to invade the east-end factories themselves. With the blessing of plant managers, once a week the Y's staff and volunteers, including some twenty-five young middle-class women, began visiting working girls in their lunch hours in a few of the largest east-end plants. They entertained the women with musical programs and held sing-songs. Managers at Mercury Mills and the Imperial Cotton Company, in particular, welcomed these visits as enhancements of their own blossoming welfare-capitalist programs. Of the roughly 600 working girls whom the Y said it was in touch with, however, only tiny numbers accepted invitations to weekly social and devotional meetings at the main Y building.[82]

Some two years later the east-end project reopened in a spacious room over a bank under the name of the Blue Triangle Club, which still did not catch fire until the national office loaned its industrial secretary, Berta Hamilton, to study and then run the eat-end operation in the city. Hamilton[83] moved quickly to expand the programs and outreach of the Blue Triangle Club. Young women could join specialized clubs to do gymnastics, play basketball, swim, or set off on a hike, practise dancing, acting, or singing, and learn dressmaking, home nursing, basketry, or even lip-reading. Married women started their own club, as did a group of British immigrant domestics. Sunday afternoon sing-songs and thinly attended evening services kept alive the devotional theme. The industrial secretary also worked with social-welfare agencies to get help for girls in financial trouble. An in-house branch of the city's Workers' Educational Association did not get off the ground, but a study group on economics did.[84]

Berta Hamilton stressed the draw of a club for working girls, rather than a straightforward effort to get them to take out Y memberships, especially since so many could not afford the fifty-cent fee. Each of the clubs elected a representative to an executive of the Blue Triangle Club. Her vision of the Y program in the east end was unquestionably a community centre, and she quickly helped to shepherd into existence a completely new building in the east end. The branch opened in spring 1925 with live-in staff, and within three years it could report nearly 700 members in classes and clubs. Independent groups were encouraged to hold their meetings in the building as well, and dances drew in good numbers of non-members every Saturday night. The choral, drama, and debating clubs, public lectures, concerts, and plays, lending library, card and dance parties, and other programs in this new Y outpost, mostly run by self-governing clubs, strongly resembled the work of settlement houses that reached into working-class neighbourhoods across North America.[85]

Before the war, all these church and interdenominational projects had thought of their work as an evangelical alternative to theatres and dance halls.[86] Typically they had offered working girls heavy doses of earnest singing around a piano, Bible study and prayer, or such didactic activities as guided reading or sewing and cooking classes, organized in an overtly patronizing way. Some young women, especially the churchgoers, might have been temperamentally and morally inclined to such pastimes, but the reluctance of the great majority of working girls to attend regularly after exhausting days on the job was understandable. The YWCA's landmark decision to allow dancing and cards in 1919 signalled some change in how to confront the new commercialized culture of working girls, as did the new self-governing clubs that followed. Yet the core of the Y's thinking was still that Hamilton's working girls were culturally deprived, that their home and neighbourhood environment gave them nothing of value. East-end Y workers argued that, unless "these girls from unattractive homes can come to spend the evening in proper and attractive surroundings," they would be "left to find their pleasure on the street."[87] They seemed particularly uneasy about the family life of European immigrants and not surprisingly drew in few women from these households.[88]

The upper-class board members and middle-class staff were also never completely comfortable with factory work for young women (when the depression left many of them jobless in the 1930s, the Y's answer was to offer classes in domestic science to refashion them into employable servants).[89] Board members and staff assumed that the girls' jobs could endanger their future reproductive capacities and, in the short term, stimulate too much interest in exciting after-work fun. "Girls do not deliberately choose recreation and companionship which will exert a degenerative influence against them physically and morally," a 1924 fund-raising appeal argued. "But music, excitement and gayety make a strong appeal to a girl whose daily occupation is colorless." Since "commercial interests" had "seized upon the need of the girl for pleasure and friends," the Y had to offer the recreation she needed with "kindly and understanding supervision, and introducing other wholesome interests into her life."[90] YWCA board members continued to harbour suspicions that these young women should not be expected to look after themselves,[91] and resented the independence of first the Blue Triangle Club and then the east-end branch, as well as the development of programs that had not been centrally approved, notably regular Saturday-night dances.[92]

Working girls themselves had mixed feelings about the Y and its programs. Most stayed away. Perhaps they were unable to afford the membership fees,[93] or perhaps they were suspicious of the organization's motives. "Everywhere is the concealed fear that the Association is trying to better the industrial girl," one Y worker wrote in the organization's national magazine, "and the industrial girl does not welcome the betterment."[94] Some did evidently join, particularly to use the swimming pool and the basketball court, and to enjoy the Saturday night dances (the devotional meetings were never as popular).[95] For them, the Y was simply one of a range of cultural resources that they could tap into in their neighbourhoods. The new postwar emphasis on self-government among Y members also gave them more scope to speak out more independently. In 1924 the girls of the Blue Triangle Club demanded (and got) representation on the Y's Industrial Committee, and two years later the Pioneer Club, which claimed to represent the east-end membership there, tried (unsuccessfully) to get the Dominion Council to hold a national conference of "industrial girls" the following summer.[96] When the cornerstone was laid for the new east-end branch, a working girl from the Blue Triangle Club wrote enthusiastically in a *Spectator* article that she and her friends were finally "being given a chance to express themselves as individuals instead of being regarded [as] just one class, Industrials." She saw them as "the future voters of the city" who "know from first hand their industrial needs, so therefore need to mix socially with other members of their class and discuss from equal positions the tangle and disorder of conditions in industry at the present time."[97]

That writer might have been Janey English, who was emerging as a prominent voice among the Y's east-end members and a symbol of the independent working-class femininity that was blossoming in this branch of the association. She had migrated to Hamilton from Lancashire, England, in 1923, and, although married, found a job as a weaver at the Hamilton Cotton Company. She joined classes of the Workers' Education Association and the Blue Triangle Club, and became what the *Spectator* called "the guide, philosopher, and friend" to a group of "young folks at the very start of their working career" – a group known as the Glad Girls' Club. In 1925 she became the first Canadian chosen to attend an eight-week summer program for working-class women at Bryn Mawr College in the United States. That experience apparently radicalized her to some extent – "the 'Truth' stood out in blazing letters," she later wrote to a friend – and the next winter she participated in special Industrial History classes taught at the East End Y. Yet, although a self-styled "Radical," she remained an active member of the predominantly working-class Laidlaw Presbyterian Church – just the sort of sincerely religious young woman the Y hoped to attract. She worked closely with Berta Hamilton, but, after that official's departure, found herself and her fellow members in the east end drawn into what she called a "war" with patronizing staff and board members. Even after she had been elected president of the Blue Triangle Club in 1926, she charged that, although "factory girls were never expected to think by a certain class of people," they "do know what they want and say so."[98]

Out in the same working-class neighbourhoods where the YWCA's new east-end members lived were other women who shared Janey English's energy and enthusiasm for social betterment, but who had hitched their stars to unions rather than to a preponderantly bourgeois women's organization. In the years after 1917, the men who had always assumed that unionists were exclusively male were changing their attitudes and behaviour slowly and reluctantly. Union meetings held in smoke-filled halls at late hours were not welcoming for many working girls, but they showed up in good numbers at union dances, card games, and picnics.[99] The local United Textile Workers and Amalgamated Clothing Workers unions made room for some of them within their executives.

One was Mary McNab, whom the *Industrial Banner* accurately described in 1918 as "one of the coming leaders in the women's labor movement." The year before she had poured the organizational acumen and reformist zeal that she had learned in church and YWCA work into a union organizing campaign for clothing workers, and soon became the new local's business agent. She went on to active roles in the local Independent Labor Party, the Ontario Independent Labor Party (of which she was vice-president by 1919), the Women's Independent Labor Party, and the Women's Educational Federation of Ontario, often speaking from podiums at election rallies. In 1919 she spoke out against the indifference of organizations like the National Council of Women. "What do they know of the working girl?" she asked ("with withering scorn," a journalist noted). "The only ones who can look after such girls' interests are either from the girls themselves or those who have at some time or other actually worked with them." She used such arguments to advocate joining the National Council "so that working women might be represented by people of their own class." When she declared in 1921 that "the woman of today has new ideals, new moral conceptions, new methods of action, the justice of which has given her the courage of her convictions," she was describing the new current of working-class feminine identity that was taking hold by the early 1920s.[100]

By that decade, then, growing numbers of young working women were participating in the recreational programs offered to them by churches, women's groups, corporate employers, and unions. Some were undoubtedly more comfortable in these safely supervised environments. Others may have simply taken advantage of facilities not available to them elsewhere in working-class Hamilton to have fun with their friends, especially those who filled the numerous church and company baseball and basketball teams.[101] Yet some, like Janey English and Mary McNab, negotiated a feminine identity that incorporated elements of the earnest, respectable, Christian emphasis of these programs, but gave them a particular working-class meaning. A more confident, class-conscious independence could flourish, however uncomfortably, within institutions that expected more deference and conformity to a more circumscribed notion of womanhood. The YWCA's new direction after the First World War was a belated attempt to come to terms with the ways in which by the 1920s young working-class women in Hamilton had fashioned a new range of cultural and gender identities.

A New Womanhood

In the 1930s as much as in the 1890s, a girl still evolved into a woman knowing that the household and domestic responsibilities would be the core of her life. Her still limited job prospects and income continued to reinforce her economic dependence. She was still subject in various ways to regulation by legal and social institutions. Yet what is equally striking is how young working girls found ways to assert some spunky independence. In choosing to avoid work as domestic servants, they gave themselves more space for leisure in the public sphere, and many took full advantage of the new commercial outlets for recreation. Indeed, they used their limited power as consumers to shape their highly performative public behaviour. Some also turned to voluntary institutions that had adapted their programming to their needs, notably the churches and the East End YWCA. What emerged was a new continuum of respectability that allowed large numbers of working-class women to participate in public activities to the degree that they were comfortable and still be "ladies." By 1920, far more thus found ways to express a more assertive femininity through their own combinations of flamboyant clothing, make-up, bobbed hair, dancing, movie-going, sports, smoking, drinking, and sexual experimentation, alongside church work, union participation, or the rites of citizenship in political activity. There could still be a wide gap between the women who oriented primarily to their churches and those who patronized beer parlours, but the gap between them seems to have narrowed over the period. In the process, these women shaped versions of distinctive working-class femininity that they knew, and regularly declared through their patterns of socializing, were not identical to those of their middle-class counterparts.

Notes

1 *Census of Canada* (Ottawa: King's Printer) (hereafter CC), 1911, Vol. 6, 306–17; 1941, Vol. 7, 196–201.

2 In 1921 56 per cent of Hamilton's sixteen-year-old girls were working full-time and 64 per cent of seventeen-year-olds.

3 As with men, recruitment came through informal channels of personal connection. A woman who started at Tuckett's tobacco plant in the 1920s recalled that managers who needed extra hands simply asked their workers if they had sisters looking for jobs. The Imperial Cotton Company similarly prided itself on family recruitment. Workers' Arts and Heritage Centre (hereafter WAHC), Interview with Lil Seager; *Fabricator* (Hamilton), April 1921, 10–11; August 1921, 4. Joan Sangster found similar practices in Peterborough. Sangster, *Earning Respect: The Lives of Working*

Women in Small-Town Ontario, 1920–1960 (Toronto: University of Toronto Press 1995), 52.

4 In 1911 census-takers found just over 1,000 women who identified themselves as domestic servants, making up almost one in seven female wage-earners; by 1941, despite the doubling of the city's population, the figure was still only about 1,200, comprising only one in twenty women workers. *CC*, 1911, Vol. 6, 307; 1941, Vol. 6, 246.

5 In 1911 only 24 per cent of gainfully employed women in Hamilton worked in "domestic and personal service," compared to 42 per cent in Vancouver, 39 per cent in Winnipeg and Ottawa, 33 per cent in Montreal, and 27 per cent in Toronto. In 1931 fewer than 12 per cent of Hamilton's working women were domestic servants and in 1941 only 6.5 per cent. For Vancouver the comparable figures were 15 and 14 per cent, for Winnipeg 19 and 17 percent, for Toronto 13 and 10 per cent, and for Montreal 15 and 16 per cent. *CC*, 1911, Vol. 6, 250, 262, 276, 286, 296, 306; 1931, Vol. 7; 1941, Vol. 6. Calculations are mine.

6 *Herald* (Hamilton) (hereafter *HH*), 10 May 1913, 7 (quotation); *Spectator* (Hamilton) (hereafter *HS*), 25 February 1905, 11 (quotation); 20 September 1919, 17 (quotation); 6 May 1920, 27; *LL*, 28 January 1921, 4; Jane Synge, "Changing Conditions for Women and Their Consequences in Hamilton and Its Rural Environs, 1900–1930: An Empirical Study Based on Life History Interviews" (Paper presented to the Working Sexes Symposium, University of British Columbia 1976), 18; Dawn Sebire, *A Woman's Place: The History of the Hamilton Young Women's Christian Association* (Hamilton: YWCA n.d. [c. 1991]), 98–106; Craig Heron, Shea Hoffmitz, Wayne Roberts, and Robert Storey, *All That Our Hands Have Done: A Pictorial History of the Hamilton Workers* (Oakville: Mosaic Press 1981), 57; Lloyd G. Reynolds, *The British Immigrant: His Social and Economic Adjustment in Canada* (Toronto: Oxford University Press 1935), 48; Marilyn Barber, *Immigrant Domestic Servants in Canada* (Ottawa: Canadian Historical Association 1991). On the preference of working women for other than domestic work and upper-class women's difficulty in finding or holding onto them, see *Industrial Banner* (hereafter *IB*), April 1899, 4; *HH*, 18 April 1911, 1; 16 May 1911, 4; 19 September 1912, 1; 12 June 1916, 4; 20 April 1918, 3; *HS*, 24 August 1910, 12; 14 January 1920, 13; 21 January 1920, 1; 29 November 1920, 8; 15 November 1934 (clipping in Hamilton Public Library [hereafter HPL] scrapbook); Ontario, Trades and Labour Branch, *Report* (King's Printer), 1917, 21; 1918, 26; 1919, 22; National Council of Women of Canada, *Women of Canada: Their Life and Work* (Ottawa: National Council of Women 1975 [1900]), 108; Jean Thomson, *The Conditions of Female Labour in Ontario* (Toronto: University of

Toronto 1892), 19; Hamilton Local Council of Women, *Fifty Years of Activity, 1893–1943* (Hamilton: Local Council of Women 1944); Wayne Roberts, *Honest Womanhood: Feminism, Femininity, and Class Consciousness among Toronto Working Women, 1893–1914* (Toronto: New Hogtown Press 1976), 13–16; Genevieve Leslie, "Domestic Service in Canada, 1880–1920," in Janice Acton et al., *Women at Work: Ontario, 1850–1930* (Toronto: Women's Press 1974), 71–125. By the First World War, "mistresses" had come to rely mostly on British immigrants, as well as more use of day labour rather than live-in servants. African-Canadian women were also always available in small numbers, since they generally found most other doors to employment closed to them. If the economy slumped, factory workers might turn to domestic work, though, as a local government official noted in 1921, they would "insist on sleeping at home." In the 1930s the YWCA organized classes to better train young women for this work and opened a Home Service Training Centre under a federal youth-training program. But few women were drawn to this belated effort to raise the status of a difficult, unattractive job. Ontario, Commission on Unemployment, *Report*, 168; *HS*, 20 September 1919, 17; 6 May 1920, 27; Marilyn Barber, "The Women Ontario Welcomed: Immigrant Domestics for Ontario Homes, 1870–1930," in Michael J. Piva, ed., *A History of Ontario:Selected Readings* (Toronto: Copp Clark Pitman 1988), 144–60; Adrienne Shadd, *The Journey from Tollgate to Parkway: African Canadians in Hamilton* (Toronto: Natural Heritage Books 2010); Dionne Brand, "We Weren't Allowed to Go into Factory Work Until Hitler Started the War," in Peggy Bristow, ed., *"We're Rooted Here and They Can't Pull Us Up": Essays in African Canadian Women's History* (Toronto: University of Toronto Press 1991), 171–91.

7 *CC*, 1911, Vol. 6, 306–17; 1921, Vol. 4, 400–19; 1931, Vol. 7, 180–91; 1941, Vol. 7, 196–201, 796–808. The nineteen women hired into clerical jobs at city hall during the war stayed on. *HH*, 7 April 1919, 1.

8 Synge, "Changing Conditions for Women," 19–24.

9 *HS*, 20 September 1919, 17.

10 Future MP Ellen Fairclough was a fairly typical example of the young female worker who moved out of local commercial schooling into clerical work in a series of offices. Ellen Louks Fairclough, *Saturday's Child: Memoirs of Canada's First Female Cabinet Minister* (Toronto: University of Toronto Press 1995), 25–35.

11 For comparison of male and female earnings, see *CC*, 1921, Vol. 3, 150, 152, 154; 1931, Vol. 5, 20, 61, 63; 1941, Vol. 6, 236–47. A cigarmakers' union leader admitted in 1919 that women were never paid the same as men. LAC, R1176–0-E (Commission to Inquire into and Report upon

Industrial Relations in Canada, Minutes), Vol. 4, 2403. When fifteen blanket weavers at Porritts and Spence struck in 1923, the manager admitted that "we could not replace them," but noted they were earning only eighteen to twenty dollars a month. LAC, R224–0-4-E (Department of Labour, Strikes and Lockouts Files), Vol. 331, File 23 (51). In 1919 the *Spectator* reported, "There is no place in Hamilton of any kind where the self-supporting single woman, no matter what her business, can find suitable accommodation of a home variety at a reasonable figure." *HS*, 6 September 1919, 15. Some teenaged girls earned little or nothing when they were learning a job; see ibid., 15 October 1921, 13. "The female wage allowed women to survive," Alice Kessler-Harris notes; "the male wage suggested a contribution to national economic well-being." *A Woman's Wage: Historical Meanings and Social Consequences* (Lexington: University of Kentucky Press 1982), 19. On women workers and workers' compensation in this period, see Robert Storey, "From Invisibility to Equality? Women Workers and the Gendering of Workers' Compensation in Ontario, 1900–2005," *L/LT* 64 (Fall 2009), 79–87.

12 Craig Heron, *Lunch-Bucket Lives: Remaking the Workers' City* (Toronto: Between the Lines 2015), Table 24.

13 Eric Tucker, *Administering Danger in the Workplace: The Law and Politics of Occupational Health and Safety Regulation in Ontario, 1870–1914* (Toronto: University of Toronto Press 1990); Kessler-Harris, *Woman's Wage*, 33–56; Margaret E. McCallum, "Keeping Women in Their Place: The Minimum Wage in Canada, 1910–1925," *L/LT* 17 (Spring 1986), 29–59; Linda Kealey, "Women and Labour during World War I: Women Workers and the Minimum Wage in Manitoba," in Marty Kinnear, ed., *First Days, Fighting Days: Women in Manitoba History* (Regina: Canadian Plains Research Centre, University of Regina 1987), 76–99; Jenny Lee, "The Redivision of Labour: Women and Wage Regulation in Victoria, 1896–1903," in Susan Magarey et al., *Debutante Nation: Feminism Contests the 1890s* (St Leonards, Australia: Allen and Unwin 1993), 27–38; Susan Lehrer, *Origins of Protective Labor Legislation for Women, 1905–1925* (Albany: State University of New York 1987).

14 Ontario, Minimum Wage Board, *Report* (Toronto: King's Printer), 1921–40; *HS*, 5 October 1921, 10; 25 October 1921 13.

15 As late as 1929 Florence Custance, a Communist organizer, regretted that a major obstacle to organizing wage-earning women was "the fact that women do not take wage-earning seriously. To them it is only a temporary necessity, a means of living just before getting married and after, just to meet a temporary difficulty." University of Toronto Library, Rare Books

and Special Collections, Kenney Papers, Box 2, F. Custance, "Our Tasks among Women."

16 Ruth Frager, *Sweatshop Strife: Class, Ethnicity, and Gender in the Jewish Labour Movement of Toronto* (Toronto: University of Toronto Press 1992), 111.

17 Heron, *Lunch-Bucket Lives*, 278–81, 285–6, 291–2.

18 Ibid., 296–302.

19 This process of trying to balance family responsibility with the desire to use some earnings on fun had a long history; see Bettina Bradbury, *Working Families: Age, Gender, and Daily Survival in Industrializing Montreal* (Toronto: McClelland and Stewart 1993), 144–9; Christine Stansell, *City of Women: Sex and Class in New York, 1780–1860* (Urbana: University of Illinois Press 1987), 53; Susan Porter Benson, *Household Accounts: Working-Class Family Economies in the Interwar United States* (Ithaca: Cornell University Press 2007), 70–6. On Jewish women, see Frager, *Sweatshop Strife*, 150–1; Susan A. Glenn, *Daughters of the Shtetl: Life and Labor in the Immigrant Generation* (Ithaca: Cornell University Press 1990), 8–49.

20 Jane Synge, "Family and Community in Hamilton" (Unpublished manuscript, John Weaver Collection, McMaster University), chapter 5.4; Carolyn Strange, *Toronto's Girl Problem: The Perils and Pleasures of the City, 1880–1930* (Toronto: University of Toronto Press 1995), 136–7.

21 Donna Gabacchia, "Immigrant Women: Nowhere at Home?" *Journal of American Ethnic History* 10, no. 4 (Summer 1991), 68–71; Miriam Cohen, *Workshop to Office: Two Generations of Italian Women in New York City, 1900–1950* (Ithaca: Cornell University Press 1992), 10–11; Elizabeth Ewen, *Immigrant Women in the Land of Dollars: Life and Culture on the Lower East Side, 1890–1925* (New York: Monthly Review Press 1985), 109.

22 Jane Synge's working-class interviewees from Hamilton explained that they rarely brought friends home. Her middle-class subjects said they were discouraged from socializing with friends at sites of popular culture. Synge, "Family and Community," chapters 3.1; 6. See also Beth L. Bailey, *From Front Porch to Back Seat: Courtship in Twentieth-Century America* (Baltimore: Johns Hopkins University Press 1989), 17–19.

23 Ontario, Commission on Unemployment, *Report*, 170–1.

24 Alice Klein and Wayne Roberts, "Besieged Innocence: The 'Problem' and Problems of Working Women – Toronto, 1896–1914," in Janice Acton et al., eds., *Women at Work: Ontario, 1850–1930* (Toronto: Canadian Women's Educational Press 1974), 211–59; "Videre," "A Little Independence: Factory Girls, 1912," in Irving Abella and David Millar, eds., *The Canadian Worker in the Twentieth Century* (Toronto: Oxford University Press 1978), 167–78; Sangster, *Earning Respect*, 97–106; Kathy Peiss, *Cheap Amusements:*

Working Women and Leisure in Turn-of-the-Century New York (Philadelphia: Temple University Press 1986), 45–55; Nan Enstad, *Ladies of Labor, Girls of Adventure: Working Women, Popular Culture, and Labor Politics at the Turn of the Twentieth Century* (New York: Columbia University Press 1999); Leslie Woodcock Tentler, *Wage-Earning Women: Industrial Work and Family Life in the United States, 1900–1930* (New York: Oxford University Press 1979), 58–80; Glenn, *Daughters of the Shtetl*, 132–66. These practices would continue after the Second World War; see Pamela Sugiman, *Labour's Dilemma: The Gender Politics of Auto Workers in Canada, 1937–1979* (Toronto: University of Toronto Press 1994), 81–7.

25 Lil Seager started working at Tuckett Tobacco in 1923 and found many people related to each other, including her sisters. "That's what I've often thought about Tuckett's," she recalled years later. "We were family." WAHC, Interview with Lil Seager.

26 Heron, *Lunch-Bucket Lives*, 258–9.

27 Pat Bird, "Hamilton Working Women in the Period of the Great Depression," *Atlantis* 8, no. 2 (Spring 1983), 125–36; WAHC, Interviews with Lil Seager, Florence Fisher.

28 Mabel Burkholder, *The Course of Impatience Carningham* (Toronto: Musson Book Company [1911]), 14; Enstad, *Ladies of Labor, Girls of Adventure*. A former working woman in Peterborough told Joan Sangster that to be treated with respect on the job was to be treated "like ladies." Sangster, *Earning Respect*, 105. For a discussion of the treatment of "working girls" in Canadian fiction in this period, see Lindsey McMaster, *Working Girls in the West: Representations of Wage-Earning Women* (Vancouver: UBC Press 2008), 44–87.

29 Nan Enstad follows Walter Benjamin in arguing that these women tried to actualize the "wish images" embedded in the products they purchased and thus opened up their "utopian" possibilities. *Ladies of Labor, Girls of Adventure*, 68–9, 82. On this more positive possibility for the woman's (unfairly low) wage see Kessler-Harris, *Woman's Wage*, 26–9.

30 *Times* (Hamilton) (hereafter *HT*), 24 August 1917, 1; Peiss, *Cheap Amusements*, 67; Roberts and Klein, "Besieged Innocence," 211; Christina Bates, "Shop and Factory: The Ontario Millinery Trade in Transition, 1870–1930," in Alexandra Palmer, ed. *Fashion: A Canadian Perspective* (Toronto: University of Toronto Press 2004), 113–38; Sangster, *Earning Respect*, 89; Frances Swyripa, *Wedded to the Cause: Ukrainian-Canadian Women and Ethnic Identity, 1891–1991* (Toronto: University of Toronto Press 1993), 63–4; Glenn, *Daughters of the Shtetl*, 160–6; Ewen, *Immigrant Women*, 69–71; Cohen, *Workshop to Office*, 70–2; Benson, *Household Accounts*, 69–70;

John Beaumont, "English View of the Canadian Factory Girl," *Canadian Textile Journal*, November 1911, 285–6. In 1910 the *Herald* reported that "a number of young men who are in the habit of attending the various picture shows" did not think that signs requesting women to remove their hats were adequate and intended to petition theatre managers to ask them to enforce the rule. One manager admitted that "when approached in regard to the matter the greater number of the ladies got angry and left the theatre." *HH*, 28 March 1910. The demand for these hats meant that the next year census-takers counted 299 milliners in Hamilton; Bates, "Shop and Factory," 132.

31 Sangster, *Earning Respect*, 89.

32 Enstad, *Ladies of Labor, Girls of Adventure*, 10; see also Sarah Berry, *Screen Style: Fashion and Femininity in 1930s Hollywood* (Minneapolis: University of Minnesota Press 2000), xxiii.

33 Ewen, *Immigrant Women*, 71, 197–202; Cohen, *Workshop to Office*, 70–2.

34 Community leaders within particular ethnic groups could be scathing about young women's fondness for fine clothing; see Swyripa, *Wedded to the Cause*, 92–102. See also David Monod, *Store Wars: Shopkeepers and the Culture of Mass Marketing, 1890–1939* (Toronto: University of Toronto Press 1996), 113–14.

35 *LN*, 27 September 1912, 2 (quotation); Enstad, *Ladies of Labor, Girls of Adventure*; Peiss, *Cheap Amusements*, 62–7; Stansell, *City of Women*, 127; Mercedes Steedman, *Angels of the Workplace: Women and the Construction of Gender Relations in the Canadian Clothing Industry, 1890–1940* (Toronto: Oxford University Press 1997); Synge, "Family and Community," chapters 3.1, 3.6; *HH*, 26 July 1924, 7 (for observations drawn from interviews with young women living in the YWCA residence); Ewen, *Immigrant Women*, 70–1; Cynthia Wright, "'The Most Prominent Rendezvous of the Feminine Toronto': Eaton's College Street and the Organization of Shopping in Toronto, 1920–1950" (PhD dissertation, University of Toronto 1993); Ann Schofield, "Rebel Girls and Union Maids: The Woman Question in the Journals of the AFL and IWW, 1905–1920," *FS* 9, no. 2 (Summer 1983), 335–58. The Ontario government's 1923 film on factory girls' health, *Her Own Fault*, depicts a young woman "wasting" her lunch break by racing off to find a bargain in a clothing sale.

36 *HH*, 10 December 1919, 1; 17 March 1920, 1; 23 March 1920, 1; 28 May 1920, 7.

37 *HH*, 9 February 1921, 1; 25 March 1922, 1; 24 August 1923, 1; *HS*, 28 March 1922, 1; Veronica Strong-Boag, *The New Day Recalled: Lives of Girls and Women in English Canada, 1919–1939* (Toronto: Copp Clark Pitman 1988),

14–15. The decision-making meeting involved the school principal, two school inspectors, the Children's Aid Society inspector, and the chair of the school board.

38 *HH*, 26 May 1924, 3 (quotation); Angela J. Latham, "Packaging Woman: The Concurrent Rise of Beauty Pageants, Public Bathing, and Other Performances of Female Nudity,'" *JPC* 29, no. 3 (Winter 1995), 149–67; Patrizia Gentile, "Queen of the Maple Leaf: A History of Beauty Contests in Twentieth Century Canada" (PhD dissertation, Queen's University 2006), 119; Berry, *Screen Style*. For the contrast between women's pre-1920s bathing costumes on Hamilton's beaches and what they sported later, see Dorothy Turcottte, *The Sand Strip: Burlington/Hamilton Beaches* (St Catharines, ON: Stonehouse Publications 1987), 51–2; Brian Henley, *Hamilton Back Then* (Burlington: North Shore Publishing 1998), 51.

39 *HH*, 12 October 1909, 1 (quotation); 1 October 1910, 20; 15 March 1911, 1 (quotation); 30 March 1911, 1; 29 August 1910, 1; 17 September 1912, 5 (quotation); 23 March 1914, 1; 5 December 1915 (quotation); 25 October 1920; 17 November 1920, 1; *HS*, 9 January 1907, 12; 26 July 1900, 8; 6 October 1900, 8; 19 November 1910, 1 (quotation); 28 December 1920, 15; HPL, J. Brian Henley, "Hamilton in Ragtime," 17 July 1976 (quotation); Tamara Myers, *Caught: Montreal's Modern Girls and the Law, 1869–1945* (Toronto: University of Toronto Press 2006), 46–8; Peiss, *Cheap Amusements*, 57–9.

40 Stansell, *City of Women*, 99.

41 All this promenading and parading was created spontaneously by young people, and none of it was part of the centennial's official program. *HH*, 12 August 1913, 1; 13 August 1913, 1, 11; 15 August 1913, 3; 18 August 1913, 4; *HS*, 18 August 1903, 1, 7; 19 August 1903, 1; 21 August 1903, 1, 3; 12 August 1913, 1 (quotation); 16 August 1913, 4; 18 August 1913, 1, 5, 6; *HS*, 14 August 1920, 19 (quotation); *HT*, 12 August 1913, 1; 13 August 1913, 4 (quotation); 18 August 1913, 4 (quotation); *Star* (Toronto), 21 August 1903, 1. The thousands of British immigrants who arrived in Hamilton in this period would have been familiar with these youthful street activities, since British investigators continued to note them right through the interwar period; see Andrew Davies, *Leisure, Gender, and Poverty: Working-Class Culture in Salford and Manchester, 1900–1939* (Buckingham, Eng.: Open University Press 1992), 96–108.

42 Shelley Stamp, *Movie-Struck Girls: Women and Motion Picture Culture after the Nickelodeon* (Princeton: Princeton University Press 2000), 10–40; M. Alison Kibler, *Rank Ladies: Gender and Cultural Hierarchy in American Vaudeville* (Chapel Hill: University of North Carolina Press 1999), 30–1,

46–54; Lauren Rabinovitz, *For the Love of Pleasure: Women, Movies, and Culture in Turn-of-the-Century Chicago* (New Brunswick, NJ: Rutgers University Press 1998), 117–18; Synge, "Family and Community," chapter 3.6 (quotation); Laurence Murphy and Philip Murphy, *Tales from the North End* (Hamilton: Authors 1981), 213 (quotation).

43 The first roller rink, the Palace, burned down in 1903. Five years later there were three: the Armory, the Britannia, and the Alexandra. Normally they closed in late May for the summer, and a seasonal operation opened in Mountain View Park. *HS*, 15 June 1907, 24; 21 May 1909, 14; *HH*, 18 January 1908, 13; Margaret Houghton, "The Alexandra: Roller Skaters Packed the Hall," in Margaret Houghton, ed., *Vanished Hamilton, II* (Burlington, ON: North Shore Publishing 2006), 17–18; Brian Henley, *The Grand Old Buildings of Hamilton* (Hamilton: The Spectator 1994), 114–15; Lynne Marks, *Revivals and Roller Rinks: Religion, Leisure, and Identity in Late-Nineteenth-Century Small-Town Ontario* (Toronto: University of Toronto Press 1996), 129–30.

44 *HS*, 17 March 1905, 20; 5 February 1907, 12; 12 February 1907, 12; 15 February 1907, 12; 25 October 1907, 20; 13 January 1908, 12; 7 April 1909, 14; 5 November 1909, 16; 9 March 1910, 14; 15 March 1910, 12; 26 February 1916, 16; 28 November 1930, 4; 25 November 1932, 10; LAC, "Sheet Music from Canada's Past," www.collectionscanada.gc.ca (quotation).

45 Bryan D. Palmer, *A Culture in Conflict: Skilled Workers and Industrial Capitalism in Hamilton, Ontario, 1860–1914* (Montreal and Kingston: McGill-Queen's University Press 1979), 55–9; Peiss, *Cheap Amusements*, 90–3. Such sponsored dances continued, of course; see, for example, a blacksmiths' union dance noted in *LN*, 29 November 1912, 1.

46 *HS*, 9 June 1910, 12; "Report of the License Inspector," Hamilton City Council, *Minutes* (Hamilton), 1906–14; *HT*, 3 September 1917, 1; *HH*, 16 December 1921, 1. In 1915 a recruiting rally in Gore Park was disrupted by the pounding piano of a third-floor dance hall nearby. *HH*, 24 August 1915, 1. Canadian dance halls have not yet been subjected to the careful research that their US counterparts have attracted; see, in particular, Randy D. McBee, *Dance Hall Days: Intimacy and Leisure among Working-Class Immigrants in the United States* (New York: New York University Press 2000).

47 Peiss, *Cheap Amusements*, 93–7; David Ewen, *The Life and Death of Tin Pan Alley: The Golden Age of American Music* (New York: Funk and Wagnalls 1964), 179–87.

48 *HH*, 11 August 1913, 3; 16 August 1913, 1; *HS*, 12 August 1913, 20; 15 August 1913, 1; 18 August 1913, 5. A few months later a newspaper report

suggested that "Hamilton society" had only acknowledged these dances during 1913. *HH*, 5 January 1914, 1, 12. The Savoy Theatre was soon running amateur tango contests. *HH*, 30 October 1914, 10.

49 *HS*, 20 November 1920, 14; 26 November 1921, 16; 29 November 1924, 32; 26 November 1926, 30; 24 November 1928, 15; 7 October 1929, 4; 4 November 1932, 4; *HT*, 31 August 1917, 16; 3 September 1917, 4. Multicultural History Society of Ontario, ITA-0884-VIO; WAHC, Interview with Lil Seager; Synge, "Family and Community," chapter 6. By the end of the war, some Hamilton hotels, notably the Royal and the Royal Connaught, were organizing public dancing and dance classes in a cabaret environment for more upper-class youth. *HT*, 31 August 1917, 16; 3 September 1917, 8; *HH*, 2 September 1922, 19; *Canadian Hotel Review* December 1933, 4, 19; Mark Miller, *Such Melodious Racket: The Lost History of Jazz in Canada, 1914–1949* (Toronto: Mercury Press 1997), 49–50. Katrina Srigley's study of female leisure working-class Toronto in the 1930s found clear distinctions among particular dance halls based on the entrance fee and therefore the clientele. Katrina Penelope Srigley, "Working Lives and Simple Pleasures: Single, Employed Women in a Depression-Era City, 1929–1939" (PhD dissertation, University of Toronto 2005), 242–50. One large Hamilton family, the Washingtons, were regularly performing jazz by the 1930s. Shadd, *Journey from Tollgate to Parkway*, 238.

50 McBee, *Dance Hall Days*, 82–114.

51 *HT*, 12 January 1914, 1; *HS*, 20 December 1919, 36; 16 November 1923, 1; *HH*, 27 January 1914, 3; 20 February 1924; 1 April 1924, 1; 7 April 1924, 3; 4 February 1929; Hamilton YWCA Archives (hereafter HYWCAA), Minute Books, 11 February 1919 (quotation); Sebire, *Woman's Place*, 85; WAHC, Interview with Lil Seager; Jean Casey, "Community Recreation in the Y.W.C.A." Canadian Council on Social Work, *Proceedings*, 1930, 221–3; Linda J. Tomko, *Dancing Class: Gender, Ethnicity, and Social Divides in American Dance, 1890–1920* (Bloomington: Indiana University Press 1999); Peiss, *Cheap Amusements*, 93–114. In October 1920 the *Spectator* ran ads for the Alexandra Academy, the Sharples Academy, and the Bluebird Academy; *HS*, 20 October 1920, 14. For criticism, see, for example, *HH*, 24 April 1911, 1; 19 August 1912, 5; 24 March 1913, 1; 1 September 1913, 1; 5 January 1914, 12; 25 February 1914, 1. The YWCA's new openness did not mean that there were many dances held there. Late in 1921 a delegation from the Big Sisters' organization prompted a board discussion about "having regular dances in the building, oftener than we have had formerly, in order primarily to get in touch with these girls who are under the patronage of the Big Sisters." But three years later board members were

still expressing scepticism about social evenings that included dancing. HYWCAA, Minute Books, 16 December 1921 (quotation), 13 March 1924.

52 *HS*, 28 May 1920, 22; 10 October 1924, 5; 9 January 1925, 5; 2 May 1925, 5; 10 August 1925, 5; McBee, *Dance Hall Days*, 131; Davies, *Leisure, Gender, and Poverty*; David W. Gutzke, "Gender, Class, and Public Drinking in Britain during the First World War," *HS/SH*, 27, no. 54 (November 1994), 367–91; Archives of Ontario (hereafter AO), RG 3–8-0–226 (Liquor Control Operation, 1932). In the 1920s, although an active Methodist, the young clerical worker (and future MP) Ellen Fairclough, later wrote that she "drank a beer or two." Fairclough, *Saturday's Child*, 33. In the late 1890s a local hotel-owner had experimented with barmaids, brought in from England, but this brief experiment was never repeated, and in fact became illegal in Ontario in 1907 and again in 1934. *HS*, 18 March 1961, 30; Craig Heron, *Booze: A Distilled History* (Toronto: Between the Lines 2003), 112, 289, 407n.53.

53 AO, RG 36–8, Box 329, 27 July 1942.

54 Dan Malleck, *Try to Control Yourself: The Regulation of Public Drinking in Post-Prohibition Ontario, 1927–44* (Vancouver: UBC Press 2012), 162–76; Heron, *Booze*, 288–92. The Hamilton inspector pressured any holdouts among hotel-keepers to add a ladies' room, and only two still refused. AO, RG 36–8, Box 133, Fischer's (then known as the New Commercial), 8 July 1935; Box 155, Grand, 6 July 1935; Box 390, Wellington, 13 May 1943. A curious anomaly in the LCBO regulations was the ban on female membership in the licensed clubs. The issue blew up first in 1935 when the Germania Club, which had always had a mixed membership, was ordered to stop serving beer to women. Most clubs had women's auxiliaries, but, even when they held their own meetings and socials on club premises, they were not allowed to have beer. The board was only willing to sanction monthly or bi-weekly "social evenings" or "ladies' nights." The women evidently chafed under this restraint, especially as the wartime conditions gave them new opportunities and responsibilities. The secretary of His Majesty's Army and Navy Veterans' Society wrote in 1940 that there was "a little agitation on the part of some members or perhaps I should say probably a little spurring on by their women folk asking us to write you … to have a little more freedom in this connection." He noted that wives and daughters had joined the "various auxiliary forces, some of them are in uniform," and "the circumstances to day are just a little different to ordinary time and perhaps the women have some right to expect a little more of us than heretofore." The board refused to change its policy. AO, RG 36–8, Box 420, Canadian Legion No. 7, 18 October 1941,

3–6 April 1943, 11 April 1945, 28 February 1949; Box 426, Canadian Legion No. 56, 4 October 1940, 17 November 1940, 22 November 1941; Box 452, Army and Navy Veterans in Canada, 1941; Box 460, British Imperial Club, 26 February 1941; Box 463, Canadian Pensioners' Association of the Great War, 27 November, 4 December 1934, 21 May 1940, 3 December 1941; Box 474, Her Majesty's Army and Navy Veterans' Society, 1, 15 May 1939, 13–15 November 1940, 17 November 1941; Box 483, Old Contemptibles' Association, 7 June 1939, 28 April 1942, 20 September 1946; Box 502, Veterans Service League, 14 May 1943. In 1949 the LCBO restricted the number of ladies' nights per month to three.

55 *HS*, 30 January 1930, 28.

56 Ibid., Box 18, Armory, 22 March 1936, 26, 30 March 1938, 4 December 1940, 16 June 1942, 14 March 1943; Box 28, Bayview, 20 December 1937, 27 January 1943; Box 44, Britannia (formerly Vulcania), 3 April, 22 May 1940; Box 61, Cecil, 9 November 1942, 7 February 1948; Box 93, Corktown (formerly Gurry), 18 April 1938; Box 133, Fischer's (formerly New Commercial), 25 February, 15 March, 14 April, 23 June, 3–10, 17 November 1937, 25 March 1938; Box 142, Genesse, 27, 30 June 1936; Box 269, Old City (formerly Dog and Gun), 30 May 1938; Box 155, Grand, 6 July 1935, 30 August 1941; Box 169, Homeside, 19 June 1942, 7–10 September 1945; Box 178, Iroquois (formerly Dominion), 18 September 1941; Box 519, Whitmore (formerly Mart), 29 July, 16 September 1935, 20 October 1936, 22 March 1938.

57 HYWCAA, Minute Books, 8 March 1908; Bruce Kidd, *The Struggle for Canadian Sport* (Toronto: University of Toronto Press 1996), 98; *HS*, 7 February 1920, 20; 9 February 1920, 14; 12 February 1920, 23; 17 February 1920, 19; 19 February 1920, 18; 28 February 1920, 20, 21; 1 March 1920, 18; 2 March 1920, 19; 4 March 1920, 18; 8 March 1920, 19; 11 March 1920, 18; 19 March 1920, 26; 20 March 1920, 24; 1 April 1920, 268 April 1920, 23; 16 April 1920, 24; 19 April 1920, 18; 23 April 1920, 28. Margaret Lord, a leader of women's sports in Hamilton, told Bruce Kidd that basketball was the "sport of entry" into other athletics for most girls. *Struggle for Canadian Sport*, 101.

58 *HS*, 21 May 1920, 31; 25 May 1920, 20; 27 May 1920, 20; 31 May 1920, 16; 9 June 1920, 24; 14 June 1920, 18; 25 June 1920, 20; 26 June 1920, 26; 28 June 1920, 18; 29 June 1920, 16; 6 July 1920, 18; 10 July 1920, 20; 12 July 1920, 14; 14 July 1920, 21; 20 October 1920, 20; *Hamilton Harvester Bulletin* (Hamilton), July 1920, 35; WAHC, Interview with Florence Fisher. The teams came from factories with large female work forces, including Imperial Cotton, Zimmerknit, Chipman Holton, Eagle Knitting, and American Can. The number of company-sponsored girls' softball teams declined during the 1920s. By 1930 there seemed to be only two, which

competed with teams from other Ontario cities. *HS*, 18 December 1926, 25; 29 May 1930, 28.

59 Helen Lenskyj, "Femininity First: Sport and Physical Education for Ontario Girls, 1890–1930," in Morris Mott, ed., *Sports in Canada: Historical Readings* (Toronto: Copp Clark Pitman 1989), 187–200. When a group of women in the east-end working-class suburb of Homeside formed a football (soccer) club, they had few competitors and played mainly exhibition matches, including one against a group of war amputees, which was intended to be more comedy than serious sport. *HS*, 27 May 1920, 20; 19 June 1920, 30; 27 August 1920, 23; 1 September 1920, 21.

60 *HS*, 4 February 1930, 18; 17 February 1930, 16; 21 February 1930, 27; Kidd, *Struggle for Canadian Sport*, 108, 112, 129, 131, 139; Ivan Miller, ed., *Centennial Sports Review, Hamilton Canada: Sports over the Century* (Hamilton: Centennial Sports Committee 1967); Cathy Macdonald, "Hamilton's Hurdler – Betty Taylor," *Canadian Woman Studies* 4, no. 3 (May 1983), 19–21; Helen Lenskyj, "We Want to Play … We'll Play: Women and Sport in the Twenties and Thirties,' *CWS* 4, no. 3 (May 1983), 15–18.

61 Miller, ed., *Centennial Sports Review*; Strong-Boag, *New Day Recalled*, 31; Kidd, *Struggle for Canadian Sport*, 107–8. "My mother never approved my involvement in sport," Margaret Lord, a middle-class teacher, told Bruce Kidd repeatedly. Ibid., 140.

62 Kibler, *Rank Ladies*, 55–170; Ewen, *Immigrant Women*, 218; Janet M. Davis, *The Circus Age: Culture and Society under the American Big Top* (Chapel Hill: University of North Caroline Press 2002), 82–141.

63 Davis, *Circus Age*, 89; Stamp, *Movie-Struck Girls*, 37–40; Berry, *Screen Style*, 22–30.

64 *HS*, 13 May 1907, 3; Synge, "Family and Community," chapter 5.4. In 1924 a *Herald* reporter concluded from interviews with young women living in the YWCA residence that those earning twelve dollars a week (which was roughly the average female weekly wage at that point) would likely have no more than fifty cents of that sum for entertainment (twenty-five dollars a year). *HH*, 26 July 1924, 7.

65 Synge, "Family and Community," chapter 3.1 (quotation).

66 Ibid.

67 Ontario, Commissioners Appointed to Enquire into the Prison and Reformatory System of Ontario, *Report* (Toronto: Warwick and Sons 1981), 271 (quotation); *HH*, 27 January 1913, 1 (quotation); 13 November 1916, 1 (quotation); Strange, *Toronto's Girl Problem*, 120–4; Peiss, *Cheap Amusements*, 53–5; McBee, *Dance Hall Days*, 106–13; Bailey, *From Front Porch to Back Seat*, 25–56.

68 Enrico Cumbo, *The Italian Presence in Hamilton: A Social History: 1870–2000* (N.p.: Author, n.d.); Enrico Cumbo, "'As the Twig Is Bent, the Tree's Inclined': Growing Up Italian in Toronto, 1905–1940" (PhD thesis, University of Toronto 1995), 27–31; Ewen, *Immigrant Women*, 210–14.

69 Synge, "Family and Community," chapter 5.4; *HS*, 18 March 1969; Peiss, *Cheap Amusements*, 67–72.

70 Ontario, Department of Education, *Report* (Toronto), 1911–19; *HS*, 1 February 1915, 5; 20 September 1919, 18 (quotation); *HH*, 30 January 1920, 13; *Clarion*, 2 February 1937, 1; HPL, Our Heritage Scrapbook, Vol. 3, 65; J. Katherine Greenfield, *Hamilton Public Library, 1889–1963: A Celebration of Vision and Leadership* (Hamilton: Hamilton Public Library 1989), 36, 43, 47–8, 66, 69–72.

71 Enstad, *Ladies of Labor, Girls of Adventure*, 17–83.

72 Joan Sangster, "Mobilizing Women for War," in David Mackenzie, ed., *Canada and the First World War: Essays in Honour of Robert Craig Brown* (Toronto: University of Toronto Press 2005), 157–93.

73 Each year, the Methodist deaconesses ran a special summer camp for working-class children (and their mothers) and held large Christmas parties for as many as 350 youngsters. Methodist Church, Board of Management of the Toronto Deaconess Home and Training School, *Annual Report*, 1900–20, in United Church Archives, Methodist Church (Canada), Toronto Conference, Deaconess Board of Management, 78.101C, Box 4.

74 In 1914 the local Presbyterians reported 976 females among the 1,522 members of the Presbytery's young people's societies (only half of whom were communicants), but these figures lumped together Hamilton participants with those in several other cities, including Niagara Falls. In her study of working women in Peterborough, Joan Sangster also found many whose social networks operated through particular churches, as did Katrina Srigley in Toronto. *HS*, 29 April 1910, 7; *HH*, 16 April 1924; Presbyterian Church of Canada Archives, 1977–3014, Box 2, 3 March 1914, 13; Melissa Turkstra, "Christianity and the Working Class in Early Twentieth Century English Canada" (PhD dissertation, York University 2005), 274–9; Edward Arthur Warwick Smith, "Working-Class Anglicans: Religion and Identity in Victorian and Edwardian Hamilton, Ontario," *HS/SH*, 36, no. 71 (May 2003), 132, 143; Fairclough, *Saturday's Child*, 21–3, 30–1; Sangster, *Earning Respect*, 90; Srigley, "Working Lives and Simple Pleasures," 223–31. The Girls' Friendly Society was founded in Britain in 1874 and spread across the empire as a religiously based structure for drawing together deferential working-class women with their aristocratic "betters"; Brian Harrison, "For Church, Queen and Family: The Girls'

Friendly Society, 1874–1920," *Past and Present* 61 (November 1973), 107–38. For a case study of a young woman whose social life revolved around her local Baptist Church, see Catherine Gidney, "The Dredger's Daughter: Courtship and Marriage in the Baptist Community of Welland, Ontario, 1934–1944." *L/LT* 54 (Fall 2004), 129–31, 136–7.

75 AO, F 885, Ontario WCTU, Annual Reports, 1890, 1892, 1897, 1898, 190, 192. On the steady decline of the YWCTU branches after 1900, see Cook, *"Through Sunshine and Shadows": The Woman's Christian Temperance Union, Evangelicalism, and Reform in Ontario, 1874–1930* (Montreal and Kingston: McGill-Queen's University Press 1995), 154–94. A new east-end YWCTU, known as the Maple Leaf Y, formed in 1911, may have had a more working-class membership, but it had folded by the end of the First World War. AO, F 885, Ontario WCTU, Annual Reports, 1917–18; *Canadian White Ribbon Tidings*, 1 November 1911, 1 June 1913, 1 May 1917.

76 Imperial Order Daughters of the Empire, Municipal Chapter Archives, Minutes, 6 May, 3 June, 7 October, 4 November, 2 December 1910; 3 February, 19 April, 5 May, 2 June, 6 October, 3 November, 1 December 1911; 5 January, 7 June, 4 October, 6 December 1912; 3 January, 3 March, 7 March 1913; 28 October 1914.

77 HYWCAA, Minute Books, 4 May, 6 December 1904; 14 February, 5 December 1905; 4 January 1906; 2 June 1908; 4 March 1911; 13 October 1913; Diana Pedersen, "'Keeping Our Girls Good': The Young Women's Christian Association of Canada, 1870–1920" (MA thesis, Carleton University 1981), 143. HYWCAA, Minute Books, 31 January 1907, 16 August, 12 September, 114 November, 12 December 1911; 28 May, 12 July, 8 October, 12 November 1912, 8 April, 8 July 1913; 10 March 1914; 1 June, 12 June, 12 September 1917

78 HYWCAA, Minutes Books, 4 October, 6 December 1904; 3 January, 14 February, 7 March, 5 December 1905; 6, 20 March, 1 May, 17 July 1906; 2 June, 17 September, 2 November, 8 December 1908; 2 February 1909; 15 November 1910; 17 January, 17 February, 4 March, 18 April, 16 August, 14 November, 12 December 1911; 9 January, 23 January, 6 February, 2 April, 14 May, 10 September, 12 November 1912; 8 April, 11 November 1913; 14 December 1915; 11 January, 14 March, 10 May 1916; 13 February, 13 March, 10 April, 11 September 1917; *HS*, 9 October 1897, 3; *HT*, 27 September 1893 (in HPL, YWCA Scrapbook); Sebire, *Woman's Place*, 76–8.

79 Pedersen, "Keeping Our Girls Good," 159–60; Turkstra, "Christianity and the Working Class"; HYWCAA, Minute Books, 25 September 1923.

80 HYWCAA, Minute Books, 13 January 1920. In fundraising for expansion, east-end employers were prime targets; see ibid., 5 March, 15 April 1924; 11 February, 9 November 1926.

81 HYWCA, Minute Books, 23 March 1920. The emphasis on clubs in national YWCA discussions dated back to 1910. Pedersen, "Keeping Our Girls Good," 148.

82 HYWCAA, Minute Books, 5 October, 9 November, 14 December 1920; 11 January, 8 February, 8 March, 12 April, 19 May 1921; 10 January, 14 February, 16 February, 22 May, 12 December 1922. The noon-hour meetings seem to have fallen off during the economic slump of the early 1920s, but revived late in 1924. Ibid., 13 January 1925.

83 HYWCAA, Minute Books, 16 February, 11 April, 22 May, 14 November 1922.

84 Ibid., 8, 17 May, 11 September, 25 September, 13 November, 11 December 1923; 8 January, 12 February (quotation), 19 February, 26 February, 5 March, 11 March, 13 March, 25 March, 7 April, 15 April, 8 May, 27 May, June, 17 July, 6 August 1924, 30 September, 14 October 1924; 11 May, 9 November 1926; 10 January, 3 November, 13 December 1927; *HS*, 6 January 1919, 15; 3 August 1920; *HH*, 21 May 1919, 2; 23 May 1922, 8; 8 December 1923, 6; January 1924; 21 January 1924; 16 February 1924, 6; 20 February 1924, 7; 28 February 1924, 7; 12 April 1924, 7; 5 July 1924; 22 November 1925.

85 HYWCAA, Minute Books, 10 January, 11 February, 14 May 1929; *HH*, 22 November 1928; Casey, "Community Recreation"; Sebire, *Woman's Place*, 83–96.

86 See, for example, YWCA Archives, 3 September 1907, 4 February 1908, 17 November 1911, 26 January 1915.

87 HYWCAA, Minute Books, 5 March 1924 (quotations).

88 The discomfort with these new immigrants peeked through in the directors' deliberations; see HYWCAA, Minute Books, 19 February, 30 September 1924. Discussion about starting some kind of "Canadianization" program never went anywhere.

89 HYWCAA, Minute Books, 19 March, 14 April 1931; 11 September, 13 November, 11 December 1934; 17 September 1935. In 1934 the national YWCA developed a "Nine-Point Plan" for upgrading domestic service to encourage more single unemployed women to take it up. Sabire, *Woman's Place*, 97–106.

90 *HS*, clipping in HYWCAA scrapbook.

91 In 1916 the YWCA's national magazine published a disparaging assessment: "In many ways these girls are still childish in their attitude, but at the same time they are sensitive and jealous of their rights as self-supporting grown-ups. Their mental calibre is limited and their power of concentration weak, so diversity in the evening's programme

is necessary." Quoted in Pedersen, "Keeping Our Girls Good," 150. For similar attitudes in other industrial centres, see Sangster, *Earning Respect*, 91; Suzanne Morton, *Ideal Surroundings: Domestic Life in a Working-Class Suburb in the 1920s* (Toronto: University of Toronto Press 1995), 137.

92 The east-end work was supervised by a board committee known as the Industrial Committee, which in October 1924 was substantially expanded with non-board representatives, in recognition of the special needs of the working-class clientele the new branch would be working with. At a heated special meeting of the board a few months later, which had been called to discuss the increasing tension between the east-end and main branches, one board member declared that "the crux of the situation is in the fact that the Industrial Secretary [Berta Hamilton] and Committee refuse to recognize the authority of the Board of Directors." Two months later, Hamilton resigned. HYWCAA, Minute Books, 14 October 1924; 16 March, 6 June, 23 June 1925.

93 Berta Hamilton and a board member on the Industrial Committee were emphatic about poverty as a deterrent to membership among east-end young women; HYWCAA, Minute Books, 13 January, 10 February 1925.

94 Quoted in Pedersen, "Keeping Our Girls Good," 144.

95 In 1922, for example, the local Y's Industrial Committee reported that the young women from the Imperial Cotton Company wanted swimming and basketball classes, and those from the Moodie, Eaton, and Chipman-Holton plants came in primarily for basketball practice. HYWCAA, Minute Books, 9 May, 12 December 1922. For similar attitudes, see Sangster, *Earning Respect*, 91–2.

96 HYWCAA, Minute Books, 11 November 1924; 9 February 1926.

97 *HS*, 16 August 1924, 2.

98 *HS*, 23 May 1925, 2; 22 July 1925; HYWCAA, Minute Books, 28 April 1925, 13 April 1926; Sebire, *Woman's Place*, 93–6.

99 *Advance*, 26 October 1917, 5; 9 December 1921, 1; *New Democracy* (Hamilton), 31 December 1919, 2.

100 *Advance*, 28 December 1917, 7; *IB*, 11 October 1918, 2 (quotation); *HH*, 22 October 1919, 5; *HS*, 8 May 1920, 13; *LN*, 25 April 1919, 1 (quotation); 7 May 1920, 1; 23 December 1921, 1; *ND*, 7 April 1921, 1; Mary MacNab, "Woman's Place in Citizenship," *ND*, 5 September 1921, 2 (quotation). Hamilton's teachers had their own flash of militancy late in 1919, when, to get higher salaries, they collectively threatened to resign en masse. The protest quickly petered out. *Labor Leader* (Toronto), 12 December 1919, 1.

101 Pedersen, "Keeping Our Girls Good," 153.

Chapter Eleven

Boys Will Be Boys

"Men are but boys grown up." So began a reporter's wry account of the "carefree abandon" and "carnival spirit" that he had seen among working-class men and boys the night before in a local urban festival in 1913.[1] Most contemporaries would undoubtedly have agreed that many elements of a working man's boyhood shone through in his adult behaviour. A century later, as writers ponder the historically specific features of working-class manhood, it is arguably useful to pick apart that reporter's old aphorism and consider more closely the construction of working-class masculinities over the life-course of proletarian males.

This article takes up that challenge, and argues that, long before individual working men embraced the identity of breadwinner and head of family, they had learned and practised how to be "masculine" in home, school, street, workplace, and pleasure site. The result was a complex bundle of contradictory attitudes and practices in which the processes of class, ethnic/racial, and gender formation were closely interwoven. The article also suggests that working-class masculinities were not fixed, static, or universal, but shaped in specific ways in different contexts and subject to challenges and re-negotiation over time. Here we will consider the period between the 1890s and the 1930s in a major North American factory town – a time and a place of dramatic reconstruction of working-class life and of new forms of male experience.

Boys at Hamilton Beach. Hamilton Public Library

Masculinities

Writers who take seriously the notion that gender dynamics have been crucial to human history have not always agreed on how to fit men into the story. The use of the often over-generalized, trans-historical concept of "patriarchy" to denote the domination of men over women (and children) has been eclipsed in much of the work on gender history in recent years, but can never be completely displaced. Instead it has proven more useful to incorporate an understanding of the exercise of patriarchal power, authority, and privilege into a more flexible, dynamic, historically contingent analysis of gender relations. That approach has characterized an outpouring of new writing on "masculinities." As with women's history, it is now clear that "innate" biological differences explain relatively little, since the patterns of gender relations have varied so widely over time. Rather, we can more usefully conclude that men and women have participated in processes of constructing gender as processes of socially and culturally defined expectations, behavioural practices, and institutional arrangements. These emerge from dynamic relationships between the sexes historically, in which men have justified and enforced their positions of power, authority, and privilege in different periods. In the best of the new literature on masculinities, there has been a serious effort to move beyond popular essentialist assumptions about masculinity as some timeless, universal, testosterone-induced behavioural traits, the limited theoretical notion of a simple "sex role" comprised of character traits that are learned and performed, and the simplified notion of an ideology through which men are constructed. Masculinity is best seen as a complex expression of male practices, consciousness, and cultural representation developed in specific contexts in constant interaction with subjects gendered as female and with other men (and boys).[2]

Of course, the picture gets more complicated when other forms of oppression and exploitation based on class, ethnicity/race, and nationality are brought into the picture. The most compelling analyses see all four as simultaneous and mutually interactive, so that women and men relate to each other from distinct class and ethnic/racial situations and citizenships. We must therefore deal with different masculinities, each of which is integrally linked to other parts of a man's identity. At any given moment in most societies, there is a "hegemonic" masculinity that attempts to articulate and organize appropriate male behaviour and to rationalize male power. It is articulated by dominant elites, and disseminated and reinforced through the structures of their power. Within the same society, there may also be a number of "subordinate" masculinities, which share some part of the dominant form but develop their own dynamics. All of this means that there is nothing fixed or eternal about "manhood" or "manliness"; rather these expressions of male identity are unstable, contradictory, and constantly being renewed and reconstructed.[3]

Historians have recently written a good deal about masculine identities among working-class males within households, wage labour, and community associations.[4] Rarely, however, have they linked these spheres of activity or followed a male's evolution through them over his life cycle, from boyhood to prolonged bachelorhood to breadwinning.[5] Nor have many studies paid much attention to the centrality of the body in almost all aspects of the male working-class experience – applying muscular strength on the job, coping with the heat and grime of the workplace, suffering crippling injury or illness (at any age, but especially in middle and old age), eating for nourishment (often on limited income), drinking for pleasure (and to get drunk), playing demanding sports, performing sexually, fighting with and violently assaulting others, and swaggering, shouting, whistling, singing, swearing, belching, and farting in deliberately performative ways.[6] Working-class male bodies were the source of claims to class pride within demeaning wage labour, gender superiority over allegedly weaker women, and, in an age of imperialist excess, racial triumph over the "lesser breeds." Their bodies had to be developed to meet the social demands put on them (what R.W. Connell has called "body-reflexive practices") in contrast to the expectations of women's bodies, and became the clear measure of achievement (successful laborer, athlete, lover, or happy drunk) and the visible sign of failure (weakness, malnutrition, dismemberment, disease, degenerate drunkenness, death). Working men literally wore themselves out in pursuit of their masculinity.

These analytical concerns, then, shape the following discussion of the making of male working-class identity. Since these are questions best addressed in a specific time and place, the paper focuses on the gender dynamics of working-class life in one large Canadian industrial community, Hamilton, Ontario, in the half-century before the Second World War. By 1930 it was the country's fifth largest city and third largest manufacturing centre and the most heavily dependent on factory employment. In contrast to the industrial diversity of the late nineteenth century, its large new plants specialized in heavy metal products, including primary steel, and textiles, both primary cotton and knit goods. Thousands of newcomers arrived in the city after 1900 (and often left after only short sojourns), some from the Ontario countryside, many from England and Scotland, and, for the first time, growing numbers from southern and eastern Europe, particularly Italy and Poland. The city grew by leaps and bounds from 50,000 at the turn of the century to 100,000 just before the First World War, to over 150,000 in the 1930s. Over the same half-century, it would be hard to call this a "union town," since, by the outbreak of the First World War, the local labour movement had been shattered and marginalized within the "Second Industrial Revolution" underway in city factories, a trajectory not substantially reversed in the brief burst of organizing at the end of the war and more sporadically in the late 1920s and 1930s. Permanent unionization of the big plants would not arrive until the end of the Second World War. In the meantime, a vigorous local Independent Labor Party held seats in the Ontario Legislature from 1906 to 1923, and (under the new banner of the Cooperative Commonwealth Federation) in the mid-1930s, and frequently won municipal offices after 1916.[7]

Many adult men in Hamilton after 1900 would not have grown up in the city, but the thousands who came from cities in the British Isles before the First World War and during the 1920s would have had broadly similar experiences of growing up working class and male. Those who migrated from the Canadian countryside and the much smaller number from peasant communities in continental Europe would also have learned similar ways of being male, though, among the latter groups, the structure of local agriculture, the weaker role of state schooling, and a large place for the Catholic Church would have made a considerable difference.[8]

Home

Before he took up a full-time wage-earning job, a boy in working-class Hamilton learned what it meant to be male at home, in school, and on the street.[9] At home, he might regularly hear homilies from his parents on what was expected of him, or get stern lectures on his failure to measure up (decades later, interviewees would remember their working-class parents as strict disciplinarians), but he probably picked up much more by watching and doing. He grew up within a family where his father must have seemed a somewhat shadowy, distant figure who disappeared from the household for more than ten hours a day, six days a week, and got special care and concern from his mother when he returned home each evening. He got the right to rest from his labours in the evenings and on days off and might also take off one or more nights a week to meet up with other men – in a lodge or union meeting, sports field, ethnic club, political rally, or saloon. Men interviewed years later remembered relatively little emotional interaction with their working-class fathers. "We were afraid of dad, and we'd go to mother for consolation," one recalled; "we had just undying respect for him."[10]

A boy would notice early on that, like most of the other mothers in the neighbourhood, his "mum" never seemed to stop working and did not participate much in the wider world that his father seemed to roam through, beyond her regular trips up the street to corner stores and perhaps to church on Sunday. She was a crucial figure of nurture and admonition in his life, but he could not have missed how fundamentally dependent the whole family was on his father's regular breadwinning. The boy would have seen his mother's relief when his father handed over his pay packet (some dads, of course, held back part of their wages); her worries if he had not brought home enough to pay all the bills; her anxiety if he was injured, seriously ill, or laid off (as usually happened at some point every year and ever more frequently as the business cycles of the first third of the twentieth century lengthened and deepened);[11] or her anger and resentment if he squandered any of his earnings on his personal pleasures (like excessive drinking). At some point, the boy may even have seen a drunken man in the neighbourhood abusing his family or heard about a wife taking her ne'er-do-well husband to court for non-support. Many fathers could be petty tyrants in their own homes, expecting their wives and children to accommodate their every whim. In any of the lengthening stretches of unemployment and underemployment, the boy might also have faced the unpredictable moodiness brought on by his father's wounded pride at having to let his wife look for some waged work or applying for relief. Being a man, the boy saw, meant shouldering a huge obligation to look after a family, but also reaping some clear privileges and respect not available in the same forms to females, as well as the right to exercise more power and authority within the family.[12]

He would also learn early in his childhood that working-class family members were all expected to contribute to the collective upkeep of the family, but that males and females did different work. He saw his mother juggling a set of demanding domestic tasks. He saw his sisters recruited to assume more and more of this work (or even to do it all if mother was sick or died). At a young age he might have to help his mother, but there would likely come a point in his boyhood when he would not be expected to do laundry or cook meals. Once he could be trusted, he would be sent regularly on errands in the neighbourhood, his first independent forays into life beyond the household. If the family was in difficult straits, there could also be foraging expeditions for firewood or coal.[13]

In a still sharper sexual division of labour, a boy would almost certainly be expected to help his father with odd bits of work around the house. Being a worker, he would see, meant hard physical labour for everyone, but being a man meant leaving most of the domestic tasks to the females in the family and concentrating on the "men's work" around the household and in the paid workforce. To be a man was in large part not to be a girl or a woman. The slow process of extracting himself from household tasks and his mother's supervision probably extended into his teens and could no doubt be conflict ridden (the number and age of sisters and his place in the birth order could be crucial).[14] He must also have been steadily more aware that all this manual labour at home, as well as the work he would be expected to take up one day like his father, required developing strength and dexterity. A man had to rely heavily on his body.

School

Working-class parents doubtless had a story or an aphorism for every occasion to teach their children right from wrong,[15] but, with fathers gone so long each day and mothers weighed down with domestic drudgery, they seemed ready to hand over their offspring to others for more regular instruction in morality, discipline, and practical academic skills. Young boys thus found themselves led off first to a local Sunday school and then to the neighbourhood elementary school. There they were expected to learn how to behave properly and to pick up basic literacy and numeracy. In this process they came under the supervision and tutelage of others with agendas that could be quite different from their parents', particularly the schools' middle-class teachers.

Overall, Hamilton's workers, like others on both sides of the Atlantic, had mixed feelings about clergymen and institutional churches, but many working-class parents also seemed to believe that their young offspring needed a good grounding in Christian morality. The city's Sunday schools drew in thousands of children each year, especially in the distinctively working-class Christian congregations that were appearing in several neighbourhoods.[16] Typically boys left at an early age, however, partly no doubt recognizing that more women than men were church-goers. Indeed, withdrawing from church activity became part of the gendered division of labour that they were learning, in this case reflecting the mother's special responsibility for nurturing the spiritual health of the family.[17]

Meanwhile, by age six, most boys and girls also left the family household every weekday morning to spend several hours in the more rigidly structured atmosphere of an elementary schoolroom. In contrast to the late-nineteenth-century period,[18] most working-class families in Hamilton were committed to more-or-less full-time schooling for their children by the early 1900s. The number of full-time wage-earners under age fourteen dropped sharply in the 1890s, under the combined pressure of the 1886 Ontario Factory Act, the province's 1891 compulsory school attendance legislation, and the 1893 Children's Protection Act (aimed at "neglected and dependent" children found on the streets). Plenty would still slip through the new truant officer's net, and, even as late as the First World War, several local firms were charged with hiring children under age. Yet by the early 1900s most boys and girls were in classrooms fairly regularly from September through June.[19] Few stayed beyond age fourteen to attend the city's one high school.[20] In 1921, an economically depressed year, two out of three sixteen-year-old boys had full-time jobs, as did four out of five seventeen-year-olds. That year, a new provincial Adolescent Attendance Act kicked in, requiring them to stay two years longer. In the interwar years, the great majority left at age sixteen, typically after a short spell in the new commercial and technical high schools (a much smaller proportion stayed on in the academic stream).[21]

During those eight-to-ten years in school, working-class boys were presented most forcefully with the exemplary hegemonic masculinity that they were expected to embrace. They sat in the same classrooms with girls, usually under the direction of a female teacher, but their academic program divided them by gender for special "manual training" classes and physical education in the form of military drill. The school curriculum and the annual Empire Day celebrations each spring also encouraged boys to identify strongly with the glories of the British Empire.[22] The lessons of imperial adventure that saturated their spellers and readers and the rituals of Anglo-Celtic hegemony that the schools staged (including, after 1912, a military cadet program in the senior grades of elementary schools)[23] could certainly have fired their imaginations and helped to shape their identity as white males. The actors at the centre of imperial triumphs were all men – soldiers, sailors, hunters, explorers, and so on – and their highly performative, often violent acts of courage, duty, and self-sacrifice were presented as models of sterling manhood. They cut a swathe along colonial frontiers where there were no women but plenty of inferior "races" to be subdued. To varying degrees, then, Hamilton's Anglo-Canadian boys learned an aggressive virility and a sharper sense of gendered and racial superiority that could seep into their after-school play and begin to frame not only their consciousness of Empire, but also their attitudes to small local African-Canadian and Chinese populations and their response to the new immigrants from southern and eastern Europe moving into the city in much larger numbers in the decade before the First World War. The children of those European newcomers, however, would have shared little of this racialized gender-building. They were almost invariably sent to Catholic "separate" schools that segregated them from Anglo-Canadian children. The ethnic divide that was opening up in the local working-class population started young.[24]

Other lessons were less inspiring for working-class boys. They found little in the curriculum that resonated with their home life. Their readers sometimes spoke to them about poverty, for example, but made it seem inevitable, acceptable, even ennobling, but certainly insurmountable, except through individual self-improvement and nose-to-the-grindstone hard work. Most of the academic content of their schooling placed far more value on mental than manual work and on the development of white-collar careers, and was too abstracted from the experience of their families to have much relevance to these youngsters.[25] Above all, the rote learning and strict classroom discipline taught conformity and obedience. Boys learned how to follow orders and to behave in an orderly fashion, respect property, exhibit good manners, and maintain personal hygiene.[26] Severe corporal punishment was inflicted on rowdy or disobedient boys to drive home the behavioural norms.[27] The schools seemed to want boys to accept that working-class manhood meant deference to authority and expertise and to the superiority of book-based knowledge (and of those professionals who had accreditation for spending many years reading them) over practical know-how learned through daily experience. Small wonder that when the school bell rang, boys were happy to escape to the life of the streets.

Streets

Gangs of boys in working-class Hamilton regularly caught public attention.[28] They were variously dubbed "wayward," "rowdy," "rough," and "tough," and, in their worst forms, "ruffians" and "hoodlums" (though rarely "street Arabs," the nineteenth-century label, or "hooligans," the term used in Britain by the early twentieth century). A gang was simply a cluster of boys or adolescents, usually close to the same age, who separated themselves from the direct oversight of parents, teachers, employers, or police. Some had more or less fixed memberships, probably (though not necessarily) a charismatic leader, and perhaps a name for themselves (some called themselves "clubs"); others hung out together for no more than an evening or two. In these gangs, boys developed patterns of behaviour among themselves and in relation to structures of authority that provided excitement and added to their emerging manhood strong streaks of solidarity and defiance. Invariably this involved using their young bodies boldly and aggressively in highly performative, transgressive ways. It is impossible to know whether all boys joined some kind of gang, but their high visibility must have been a constant pole of attraction and inspiration for boys in every working-class neighbourhood – what a local Congregational minister called "the supremacy of the 'gang' passion."[29]

Their games encouraged a relentless competitiveness (and probably perpetual insecurity) – from craps to informal team sports that brought respect for physical strength and athletic prowess to elaborate make-believe fantasies – military warfare, cops-and-robbers chases, or Wild West confrontations – waged with simple makeshift toy weapons. Others could involve challenges to budding masculine honour that could only be met in fist fights. Gangs regularly challenged each other over turf or reputation, but also confronted property owners, shopkeepers, policemen, and others over the limits of acceptable urban behaviour.[30]

Struggles over space were never ending. Gangs regularly appropriated street corners as their rallying points, where, among themselves, they might engage in roughhouse jostling and horseplay, shoot craps, concoct adventures with any nearby street activity, or simply stand around talking. On this informal public stage, they also played to larger audiences of others who used the streets. With cigarettes dangling from their lips, they struck defiant poses, shouted, bragged, practised their profanities, and insulted passers-by.[31] Gangs seldom stood still for long, however. They might head off along sidewalks in cocky, four-abreast formation, or ramble through public parks, vacant lots, or empty fields, or down to the waterfront to enjoy the water (or ice) of Hamilton's large harbour.[32] As new urban development appropriated this natural play space and the new city parks prohibited boyish rowdiness, they defiantly invaded private backyards, railway tracks, and industrial lands, inciting the wrath of property owners and night-watchmen.[33] An abandoned house, a shuttered boathouse, an unlocked warehouse, or a crude shed constructed by gang members themselves as a "clubhouse" could become a hideaway for more secretive activities, especially smoking, gambling, and occasionally drinking.[34] Some boys also broke into schools and churches and damaged the furnishings in apparent defiance of the moral authority of these institutions.[35] In their early teens, some gangs moved indoors into pool rooms and cigar stores.[36] They also scraped together the pennies for a cheap seat in nickelodeons or vaudeville and movie theatres, and hooted, applauded, and jeered at the performances.[37] Moral reformers were probably right to conclude that the slap-stick comedians, gunslinging cowboys, and sneering gangsters became models of bravado and defiance in their games in the streets (new Ontario legislation in 1911 barred children under fifteen from attending without adult accompaniment).[38]

Wherever they went, petty pilfering seems to have been common (if not universal) and intended for the boys' own consumption, not family coffers. Some theft was for immediate enjoyment – stealing fruit from an orchard, or more boldly snatching some from stands in front of stores or in the central market. Sometimes, boys broke into shops to get tobacco, food, or candy. Other thefts evolved out of the boys' endless scavenging for small objects to be sold quickly for cash either to other boys or to the city's numerous second-hand junk shops. They used the money to buy cigarettes, to pay off gambling debts, or to enjoy such hedonistic pleasures as pork pies, fruit cakes, or ice cream – luxuries that their families probably could rarely afford to provide. The occasional thefts of bicycles and wagons and, after the First World War, of automobiles for joy-rides reflected a similar yearning for pleasures denied them by limited family incomes. Only a few of these boys seem to turn occasional pilfering into more systematic theft, which throughout the period remained by far the most common charge laid in court against boys under age sixteen.[39]

Group solidarity also emboldened many to engage in taunts and physical assaults with stones or snowballs (or frozen horse droppings).

Their targets might be other gangs or specific individuals (such as an elderly black man), and sometimes property, such as passing trains, street lights, or store windows. Much of this vandalism could appear to be aimlessly destructive, but some assaults seemed to be escalations of verbal battles with proprietors who challenged them or tried to stop their play.[40] Gangs also played pranks of various kinds (such as greasing street car tracks) and disrupted such sedate public events as outdoor band concerts.[41]

Sometimes all this boyish exuberance and mischief expanded beyond the street corners or empty lots of a single neighbourhood. Once a year on Halloween, in particular, working-class boys enjoyed remarkable tolerance from the law and the public for a full night of city-wide riotous revelry and outrageous pranks (pulling down fences, tearing off steps and shutters, overturning outhouses, and much more) – "the annual saturnalia of questionable fun," as the Hamilton *Spectator* dubbed it.[42] This ancient spirit of "misrule" could erupt at other times as well, when working-class boys became the cutting edge of larger crowd activities across the city, both celebratory and contestative. Boys' exuberance and rowdiness punctuated election-night celebrations, public holidays, and the special summer carnivals held in 1889, 1903, and 1913 (the last in honour of Hamilton's centennial), when they tossed confetti and talcum powder, tickled total strangers under the chin with small feather dusters (known as "ticklers"), and deafened them with their horns.[43] Similarly, during a turbulent street railway strike in 1906, boys and youths emerged regularly as daring instigators, bringing into play their familiar forms of aggression and subversion.[44]

Gangs apparently included no girls (though some might hang around the edges), and in various ways these boys turned a misogynist gaze on females. Young women often complained about being mocked, ridiculed, and even assaulted in public spaces. Sometimes these attacks extended to young couples, whose public courting might prompt loud laughter, profanities, or the tossing of projectiles. Around these gangs of adolescent boys hung a collective ambivalence (or even resistance) to heterosexual courtship and bonding.[45]

Working-class boys and teens, then, flexed their public bravado as a form of resistance to oppression, a determination to establish a sense of self-worth in the face of the indignities of economic scarcity and the many-sided efforts to subordinate, tame, and silence them. Their insults, fights, pranks, and vandalism were not private, individualized acts, but rather were staged in a context where their behaviour would have the support and approval of others, mostly their peers, whose judgment could affirm their identity as working-class males.

What galled the city's authority figures was the remarkable independence of these boys. At the turn of the century, their predominant response was still repression.[46] With help from the new truant officer, police attempted to send rowdy youth home or to school, and, when necessary, marched them into police court.[47] Most working-class parents wanted their children to avoid trouble with the law, and the most street-wise boys seemed to come from those families where parental control was loosest. Occasionally, parents asked the magistrate to declare their son "incorrigible" and to send him to the Victoria Industrial School at Mimico (thirty miles away near Toronto).[48] After 1894, the new local Children's Aid Society could bypass parents of these "neglected" children altogether and demand legal custody, before farming them out to foster homes.[49] Hamilton was extremely slow, however, to set up a special court for the re-labelled "juvenile delinquents" and the associated system of paroles, made possible under 1908 federal legislation. Only in 1923 did the city finally establish a formal Juvenile Court, with the newly formed Big Brothers as legal parole agents for boys. More informally, school principals, store managers, welfare officials, individual policemen, and parents turned over to the Big Brothers boys who "because of their delinquencies and anti-social behavior, presented problems to the community," and by the late 1930s the association was handling more than 500 boys a year.[50]

Meanwhile, in the decade before the First World War, Hamilton businessmen, professionals, and their wives had founded numerous organizations with programs addressed at what they called the "boy problem." Rather than relying on the coercive power of the law, they aimed at distracting boys from the thrill of the streets and preventing the drift into juvenile delinquency. In contrast to previous child-savers, they focused on the body more than the mind and looked for ways to deflect boyish exuberance into safer channels with more direct adult supervision, and in the process to nurture a new form of more responsible manhood. The Christian churches encouraged local congregations to create boys clubs and sports teams with vigorous mid-week recreational programs that harnessed the "gang instinct,"[51] the Young Men's Christian Association overcame some of its reluctance to work with boys, rather than just young men, and launched a small east-end branch in 1907,[52] and in 1910 Hamilton got its first Boy Scout troop aimed at making boys aged twelve through eighteen "loyal, helpful, friendly, courteous, kind, obedient, cheerful, thrifty, and clean."[53]

A year earlier, a group of the city's leading citizens organized the Hamilton Playgrounds Association to provide a well-equipped, supervised space for pre-adolescent youngsters in working-class neighbourhoods during the summer months.[54]

The impact of all these interventions into working-class boys' street life was limited before 1920. Truancy work was spotty, and the local police court still had no special provisions for young law-breakers. There were only four playgrounds in a city of 100,000, and, like the Sunday Schools and Boy Scouts, the youth workers there had trouble holding onto older boys. The Scouts had collapsed by 1914, without drawing in many non-Anglo or working-class boys (the fact that the first Scout commissioner was the principal of the city's elite boys' college and that uniforms cost a boy a whopping $5 must have deterred their participation).[55] The YMCA's programs of physical exercise, business education, and evangelical fellowship also reached primarily a white-collar, middle-class clientele, and the east-end branch never attracted many boys before closing its doors in 1918.[56] Moreover, "misrule" now sometimes included small-scale guerilla warfare with the new institutions established to tame these boys – invasions of playgrounds after hours or rowdiness on church teams, for example.[57]

The interwar period, however, saw a considerably increased intervention into the street life of working-class boys, who were spending far more time under the supervision of middle-class adults. The new school-attendance law backed up by more rigorous enforcement kept them in their classrooms regularly till age sixteen (and beyond) and discouraged employers from hiring them. The new Juvenile Court and its parole system also kicked in to handle problem cases more effectively. Probably far more important, boys' playtime was invaded much more aggressively. The number of city playgrounds grew quickly from four to seventeen, and in 1931 the city finally took them over. The membership in the reorganized Scouts (and Cubs) climbed quickly from 150 in 1921 to 1,253 two years later. The Big Brothers expanded their outreach to boys who had no contact with the courts, and made recreation programs the predominant thrust of their work in Hamilton. By the 1930s they were running twenty-two basketball teams, thirty hockey teams, a baseball league of sixty teams, and an East End Boys' Club of some 150 members. Even the east-end branch of the Independent Labor Party had a youth wing in the 1920s (which reconstituted itself as the Marxian Youth Group in the early 1930s and organized a baseball team, dances, and debating forums). Perhaps the long-term result of all these initiatives was to direct much more boyish energy and aggression into organized sport.[58]

Yet many boys could participate in such weekly events and keep their older street life intact. Some may have simply moved their neighbourhood associational patterns indoors to make better use of the sports facilities. Others no doubt kept their distance. One boy's response to his encounter with the playgrounds program in the 1920s was probably common: "After two days, I had had enough. They called this recreation and to me it was only school transposed to an outside setting and no more interesting than what went on inside ... With my friends, I took off for more interesting pursuits in our tree house."[59] For such boys, the street corner doubtless remained a regular training ground for the long-familiar independence, defiance, and subversion of working-class boyhood. That behaviour continued to be splashed across the silver screen in Hal Roach's ever-popular "Little Rascals/ Our Gang" films of the 1920s and 1930s.

Throughout the period under discussion, then, boys in working-class Hamilton continued to celebrate personal freedom and group solidarity and picked up some important, often apparently contradictory attitudes and behaviours – intense loyalty, aggressive display, personal toughness, competitiveness, the importance of peer recognition through performance, and the disowning of any "feminine" tendencies. These patterns of association were more fenced in by new youth programs, but not fundamentally undermined. Middle-class boys might share some of the exuberant playfulness, but their world of play in this period was bounded more strictly by bourgeois conventions about appropriate behaviour and flowed more regularly into the supervised realm of formal boys' organizations. They also generally had less incentive to rebel against systems of authority over which they would eventually be taking control. In contrast, working-class boys struggled to make their fun with limited resources and a deepening recognition about their long-term subordination. And, unlike their middle-class counterparts who made no significant contribution to their family's upkeep, they were constantly aware that this street life had to be balanced with a deeply rooted obligation to contribute to their family economies.[60]

Work

Long before they reached their teens, boys in working-class families took responsibility for earning some income, either to contribute to the family coffers, or to pay for their own small pleasures. Full-time work under age twelve was fast disappearing, but, from time to time, they could earn pennies for doing odd jobs for individuals or other families. In the summer they might pick berries or even work briefly in local canning factories. Some took on the more demanding year-round part-time jobs of delivering groceries, selling newspapers, shining shoes, or setting up pins in bowling alleys. Newsboys were certainly the most visible of these young wage-earners in the more free-wheeling "street trades" and the most likely to be truants from school and active participants in the street culture.[61]

Before the 1920s, leaving school at the legal age of fourteen generally led to finding full-time wage labour relatively soon. Parents knew that teenaged boys had more employment options and higher earning potential than daughters. Boys were expected to turn over all their earnings to their mothers (and hoped for a little spending money in return). Frequent bouts of joblessness for young wage-earners, especially between the wars, may have allowed more time with old friends on the street corner, but most boys probably found themselves torn between their deeply ingrained sense of responsibility to the mutuality of the working-class family and the unfettered excitement of the street life with their friends – a personal dilemma that would plague some of them for years to come.[62]

This was a major turning-point in a boy's life. Like his father, he was now part of a man's world beyond the household. Yet the world of wage-labour could be deeply contradictory for the working-class youth. On one hand, he had come to expect that he had finally made it – that productive work done here would give him the independence and respect as a full-fledged man, whose earnings would be useful to himself and his family and would guarantee his power within the domestic sphere and beyond. Henceforth he would insist on his "right" to work. On the other, he found himself in a setting that immersed him in potentially hazardous dirt and smoke, that subjected his body to muscle strain, mental stress, and the ever-present danger of accidents, and that demanded subservience to rigid authority that constantly intimidated and demeaned him.[63] Lots of these young workers were entering workplaces in the early twentieth century with rapidly changing work routines. Many well-established trades, especially in the city's all-important metal-working plants, were under attack, and even the new skills created within mass production were only grudgingly recognized by corporate managers. Almost none of the trades had an active apprenticeship program after 1900, and, although a few large corporations tried to re-invent the practice through the local technical school after 1910, the programs involved only a tiny handful of boys. Pride in skill was harder to build in a new environment of cost-cutting front-office managers, roving efficiency experts, and bullying foremen. Proportionally, many more men were expected to learn to operate specialized machinery quickly and effectively under much closer, more rigid supervision that assumed such workers should be give no more responsibility or autonomy than wayward children. The intensified work routines amid the vast array of new technology were also getting more dangerous, and workplace injuries mounted.[64] Layered onto these sensitivities about skill and safety were new concerns about ethnicity and race. White Anglo-Celtic skilled men watched nervously as their employers recruited newcomers from southern and eastern Europe to cheapen their labour costs, speed up production, and otherwise disrupt what English-speaking workers understood to be the norms of their workplaces. For their part, the European newcomers eagerly took what new jobs were available to them in mass-production plants and resented the exclusionary practices they faced.[65]

It was clearly an ongoing struggle for a young working man to buttress the beleaguered basis of his masculinity in the workplace. Much of that experience was mediated by his relations with his workmates. Gradually he learned the routines and expectations of the particular occupation he was settling into, and the ways in which the men around him constructed a particular masculine pride in the skills or strength demanded of that job. This was a process worked out only among men and boys, since, unless he started in one of the textile, tobacco, or food-processing plants, he would encounter no women or girls on the job. He would soon come to appreciate the different kinds of masculine behaviour demanded in different workplaces – the steady hand, quick eye, and meticulous care of the typographer, the intense exertion and subtle know-how of the molder, the muscular strength and keen eye of the rolling-mill hand, or the labourer's reservoir of stamina to lift, heave, and tote for hours on end. Doing each job well and winning the respect of the others in his work group engendered many variants of working-class masculinity.

A boy thus learned that a man grounded his masculinity in his contributions to the upkeep of a family, but also in his ability to feel pride in his skills and respect from his workmates. They formed small, tight-knit work groups on the shop floor that provided regular sociability, reliable companionship, often boyish playfulness and practical jokes during the working day, and mutual support and collusion in the face of management authority, bonds that might carry over into after-work fun. At the same time, these informal social relations on the shop floor could also be competitive, especially as recruitment for the semi-skilled jobs in the company's internal labour markets, and, for various reasons, might explode into the same kind of angry quarrels or fisticuffs that the feistier young men displayed in their "free time" outside the plant.[66] In fact, shop-floor relations among male wage-earners of all ages strongly resembled the street life of boys.

The male solidarities on the shop floor could also provide the energy and organizational base of spontaneous strikes or longer-term efforts to create unions. Labour leaders were most often older, married men, who shaped much of the official rhetoric of their organizations around the demands of breadwinners, but unions also drew in earnest, determined young men who turned the toughness of the shop-floor culture into militancy and learned to express the bonds of solidarity as "brotherhood." Among the more radical among them, their masculine identities provided a language of overtly class-based "manhood" that cast withering scorn on the alleged "effeminacy" of non-unionists or strikebreakers. In many ways, however, others carried over the narrow, local focus of the neighbourhood street gang and the occupational work group. They rarely included the new immigrant workers in their union-building projects, and made little space for women, arguing passionately against the employment of married women.[67]

Breadwinner-unionism spoke for few younger workers because they did not rush into marriage. Throughout the period, most waited until their mid to late twenties. As a result, young men in Hamilton (as in most other Canadian cities) commonly had up to ten years of wage-earning before marrying.[68] Most did not move out of their parents' home, and most were still expected to contribute to the family coffers. As the young man entered his early twenties, his earnings could quickly reach the average wage for his whole occupational group. So, like his father, he could take pride in being a provider for his parents and siblings. In some households, a young working man might even do better than his father if the older man's trade was being eroded by the industrial transformations underway, or if he suffered from frailties or disabilities that hindered his wage-earning capacities. How much of this income a young man turned over to his family and how much he got to keep was a subject of ongoing negotiation and inevitable conflict.

Yet parents must have conceded him more spending money as a guarantee that he would not leave home completely.[69]

Whether as a part of family strategizing, a form of resistance to family obligations, a search for adventure, or simply frustration with local employment prospects, some young men took off on their own to look for work or better wages somewhere else in North America. Many washed up in Hamilton on such a quest and boarded with other families, in some cases in larger boarding houses in the growing European immigrant community. Most probably sent home at least some of their wages. A certain comradeship could develop among these young men on the road. These young transient workers were the most likely to have coins jingling in their pockets, though even those living at home probably had enough spending money to allow for some personal indulgences. Their sisters never had as much mobility, financial independence, or freedom from domestic responsibilities.[70]

Pleasure

In the early twentieth century, then, young men in working-class Hamilton enjoyed a lengthy space within their life cycle where their responsibilities to their family households were diminishing, their workplace identities were solidifying, their disposable income was rising, and, while under their parents' roof or in a cheap boarding house, their living expenses were limited. This material reality gave them opportunity – and the privilege – to participate in a vibrant leisure-time culture of young bachelorhood – one that had roots in the pre-industrial world of artisans and resource-industry workers, but which over the nineteenth century had been expanding to include more men drawn into full-time wage-earning within industrial capitalism. Bachelor pleasures could, of course, be severely constrained by small, unstable incomes and ten-to-twelve-hour days of physically exhausting labour, perhaps on shift work. Many young workers likely still worked on Saturday afternoons and, at best, had only their evenings, Sundays, and public holidays to enjoy their bachelorhood. The federal government's 1906 Lord's Day Act also restricted how they could spend their weekly day off.[71]

Bachelor life built on the solidarities and practices that such men had developed at a younger age with other boys, and was largely acted out in the public spaces of the city, rather than the privacy of households. The "gang spirit" carried over particularly vigorously into team sports.

Young men regularly played pick-up games of baseball, hockey, sometimes football, and, among the many new British immigrants, soccer. They joined teams in church and industrial leagues in large numbers and, if good enough, moved into the professional or semi-professional circuits to represent Hamilton in regional or national leagues. They were also enthusiastic spectators (if they were lucky enough to get a half-holiday on Saturday, when most games were played; otherwise they kept in touch with local and continental contests through the sports pages of the daily press and, by the late 1920s, radio broadcasts). The dramatic confrontations between contending teams in both amateur and professional games could symbolize fundamental antagonisms in these spectators' lives – "between good and evil, between the privileged and the underprivileged, between the local and the foreign," as anthropologist Thomas Dunk suggests. From the sidelines, they identified so closely and emotionally with the players and might surge onto the field to disrupt play or challenge officials' rulings. The stars of these events emerged as paragons of a working-class manliness that valued bodily strength, aggressive competitiveness, and gang-like teamwork. By the 1920s, commercialized team sports in which they worked had become mass entertainment.[72]

In working-class Hamilton, young men also still liked watching other men pummel each other in a boxing ring – a fascination not always shared by the police, who intervened frequently to uphold the 1881 federal ban on prize fights. Entrepreneurial promoters increasingly packaged boxing matches as carefully controlled (sometimes corrupt) spectacles for mass consumption. After years of viewing or joining in street fights, they could appreciate the muscled, half-naked pugilists who competed in amateur union bouts or prize fights as minor heroes of remarkable strength, athletic prowess, and courage, who defended their honour with dramatically ritualized violence and swaggering braggadocio, in contrast to the more restrained, "gentlemanly" boxing encouraged by the likes of the YMCA by the turn of the century.[73] Like many other spectator sports, including the more elite horse racing, these events also widened young workers' opportunities for gambling.[74]

Young men often organized themselves into independent social and sporting "clubs."[75] But companies, unions, churches, and other groups also tried to harness those energies to their own projects. Agencies of moral reform, in particular, both churches and the YMCA, never relented in trying to redirect this young maleness into a more restrained, overtly Christian form of "muscular" masculinity, but proportionally the young men who participated in this earnest social and recreational life seem to have been a distinct minority among their peers.[76]

The part-time militia – Canada's "citizen army" – also reached out to the city's young men to link recreational life and war. Before 1914 the response was limited in working-class Hamilton,[77] but, over the next four years, the Canadian Expeditionary Force soaked up thousands of young, unmarried men from Hamilton, whose experience, if they survived the trenches, became a fusion of the hegemonic ideologies of imperial masculinity and the plebeian comradeship of the enlisted men they trained and fought with. The desperate struggles to avoid being killed and the bitter resentments at poor food and equipment, rats and lice, officers' incompetence, politicians' corruption, and much more, punctuated by the horrors of forays into "No Man's Land," forged intense bonds of loyalty among enlisted men at the Front and an occasional willingness to resist or subvert military authority. Behind the lines, they smoked, drank, gambled, and womanized together, played baseball and other sports, and attended music-hall-style concerts and variety shows, where the humour was regularly risqué and anti-authoritarian. Back in Canada, after demobilization, many displayed the visible price their bodies had paid for imperial valour in the form of wounds or missing limbs. Many more tried to keep the spirit of boyish comradeship alive in a variety of veterans' organizations, which, besides lobbying for their interests, opened clubhouses and sponsored numerous social and cultural events. Some hung out more informally in small, disconsolate groups in old haunts. For most able-bodied working men from their late teens through their mid-thirties during the 1910s (and for many more who did not serve), the war experience of homosocial life and expressiveness through the body would have sharpened the edges of a working-class masculinity based in prolonged bachelorhood.[78]

Both before and after the war, a lot of the time working-class bachelors spent together lacked any formal structure but continued such public rituals of boyhood as street-corner lounging, dramatic fist fights, and visits to pool rooms or the cheap seats of vaudeville and movie theatres. Eventually, at the end of their teens, they also began to congregate in saloons.[79] Each week in the early 1900s, especially after work on Saturday, thousands of Hamilton's male wage-earners crowded into these so-called "working men's clubs" to enjoy the conviviality of shared drinks with workmates or neighbours. They participated in rituals of male bonding symbolized by "treating" (buying rounds of drinks) and nourished a boyish freedom from control. Standing beneath pictures of scantily clad women and scenes of hunting and sporting events, they chatted and argued about sports, jobs, politics, women, and much more, and blithely denounced authority and ridiculed pretense. They could smoke, spit, swear, whistle, sing, tell off-colour jokes, laugh loudly and shout, and generally ignore the civilizing constraints of domesticity. Some saloon patrons became boisterous, potentially violent heavy drinkers, who roamed between hotel bar-rooms, extending the stage for their loud performances onto the street and not uncommonly ending up in fights (and perhaps police court). The great majority of these were single men. Yet, not all drinkers were drunks. Methodist and Presbyterian investigators put the label of "intoxicated" on only 12 per cent of the 1,775 Hamilton drinkers they tallied up in the city's saloons in the last hour before closing one Saturday night in 1913. Most men apparently restrained their consumption, and went home no more than a bit tipsy. In the mock-elegant setting of the bar-room, with its gleaming mahogany and giant mirrors, young working men could construct their socializing patterns there as perfectly respectable. Informally and collectively, they were taming their time and space apart with the "boys," hoping to hold onto such an important, but controversial, realm of autonomous working-class masculine expression.[80]

These alcohol-soaked sites of male sociability were nonetheless closed in province-wide prohibition in 1916. Over the next decade, social drinking had to retreat into the shadows of bootleggers' "dives" and private homes, drunks lost their public stage for their swaggering braggadocio, and, unless brewed at home, alcohol became prohibitively expensive amidst the prolonged postwar unemployment (lasting in Hamilton until at least 1926). Alcoholic beverages went back on sale in government-controlled liquor stores and brewers' warehouses in 1927 and then in 1934 in tightly regulated "beverage rooms" (elsewhere known as "beer parlors"). In these deliberately austere establishments, patrons could not stand up with drinks, eat food, play games, sing, or watch any entertainment. Yet the wage-earners who flocked in quickly recreated many of the associational patterns of the old-time saloons. In particular, the many serious drunks still seemed to be the froth on a much larger sea of moderation among working-class drinkers.[81]

Inevitably there were considerable numbers of young men who avoided all these public sites of expressive bachelor culture. Some probably consciously spurned the moral laxness of this mode of relaxing and turned to more "wholesome" activities in church programs, including the well-attended Sunday-afternoon men's meetings that some clergymen organized. Some took evening courses at the new Hamilton Technical School, until that program was gradually wound down in favour of adolescent education. For young men in more skilled trades, there was an occupational and class culture to be found in union and left-wing halls, including serious meetings, stirring speeches and lectures, and engaging reading material.[82] Many more young men found new counter-attractions in commercially run leisure sites. Here, however, they were more likely to be moving beyond the homosocial and looking to spend time with women.

Marriage

The transition from a wholly male associational life to one involving females must have been awkward for young workers. However it happened, somehow most young men began to reach out across the social gulf, and, at some stage, to spend time with girls as "dates" and potential sexual partners and, eventually, as spouses.

Most young wage-earners were unlikely to see females at work, and, even in plants that employed women and girls, they generally had completely different jobs in distinct departments. They might have struck up acquaintanceships with "working girls" walking to and from work, but they would have had to run the gamut of misogynist cat-calls and jeering at young heterosexual couples that other boys and young bachelors bellowed out from street corners. In contrast to middle-class practices, working-class courtship was certainly a public process. The streets provided some highly ritualized contact between groups of young men and young women, who enjoyed more freedom from parental supervision and domestic responsibility during their wage-earning years. Girls promenading together along the sidewalks often used cheeky banter to provoke playful interaction with gangs of boys or men. There were also more respectable, though also public settings for striking up relationships with young women, including church-sponsored religious and recreational activities.[83]

Undoubtedly, however, young working-class men could most easily meet members of the opposite sex in the commercialized leisure spots. Generally they could afford the small admission charges to dance-halls, roller or skating rinks, ball parks, cruise boats, amusement parks, and vaudeville and movie theatres, all of which were becoming more numerous and heavily patronized after the turn of the century.[84] In an extension of street flirtations, they might visit these sites with male friends and pick up female companions, or they might invite one to join them on such an outing.[85] After the First World War, in fact, women were venturing much more confidently into public sites of recreation and entertainment, either with female friends or male companions. In the 1920s, moreover, the more adventurous might take their dates to the city's many small "blind pigs" or invite them to share a flask while out dancing or skating. Certainly by the time the new "beverage rooms" opened in 1934, government policy assumed that women wanted to be included in public drinking and designated restricted areas for "ladies and escorts." Boisterous, bachelor-driven patterns of male socializing thus coexisted cheek by jowl with a newer companionate, heterosexual leisure.[86]

By that point, the practices of "dating" were reflected in and reflective of the romanticized images of heterosexual coupling beaming out of movie screens across the city.[87] There, and in the sophisticated advertising splayed across newspapers, magazines, and billboards, young men saw representations of masculine ideals in dress and comportment, most of which did not draw on working-class experience, but which did appeal to the performative dimension of their public lives. Some working-class bachelors no doubt indulged in buying products to look the part,[88] but probably more young men borrowed skills for successful behaviour from media stars and honed them for performance on their heterosexual outings.[89]

Many bachelors also engaged in sex with women (and perhaps with men, though the city never seems to have developed the visible homosexual communities of metropolitan centres such as New York or Toronto in this period). However limited their actual sexual knowledge, they tended to act out an understanding of their own sexuality that assumed that they were driven by almost uncontrollable, "natural" lustful passions different from those of females, that aggression might be necessary (as in other social relationships), and that they had a right to be the dominant partner. If they reached adulthood before the 1920s, they would have faced stern hegemonic discourses that encouraged them to exercise self-control, preferably abstinence, but after the First World War the frequent films and lectures on venereal disease organized by public-health authorities made sexuality a much more public issue with less moralism and more medical science.[90] The movies' silver screen also regularly legitimated more expressive sexual lifestyles. Some men simply sought out the few downtown brothels, a practice that became much more visible when so many soldiers arrived back from the trenches of the First World War infected with venereal diseases.[91] Alternatively, they might look for quiet spaces to be alone with their dates, where they might expect some sexual favours in return for treating their girlfriends to a dance or a movie. Eventually, "going steady" might well assume some degree of regular consensual sex between partners, on the assumption that marriage would follow. Some young men assumed they had a right to bypass such negotiations and simply forced themselves on their sexual partners in what could amount to rape, especially if they construed their prey as "bad" or "loose." It was not always easy to draw the line between persistent pressure on a woman to have sex and outright sexual assault, as many court cases revealed (virtually all of them involving working-class males), and many men apparently expected their partners to set the limits.[92] Needless to say, all these practices of male working-class sexual pleasure outside marriage flew in the face of hegemonic bourgeois conventions about sexuality (and the draconian Criminal Code of Canada enacted in 1892). They nonetheless became a training ground for the patriarchal power relations involved in intimacy with women throughout their adult lives.

A significant minority of men – one in ten over age thirty-four in the interwar period – seemed to prefer to linger in this bachelor world, avoiding long-term heterosexual commitment (sustained in popular culture by the lone cowboy, the unattached gangster, the hard-boiled private detective, or such comedic confirmed bachelors as W.C. Fields or Laurel and Hardy). The city's old-age home housed many elderly versions of these working men. At some point in their mid-twenties, however, the great majority of Hamilton's young working men made a decision to marry. Setting up a new household and starting a family brought serious breadwinning responsibilities and expectations that a man would turn his back on the excesses of bachelorhood. In practice, over their married lives, working-class men seem to have fallen somewhere along a continuum of behaviour. At one extreme, if they had not already done so, they withdrew completely from the rowdiness and carousing of young adulthood. They dutifully turned over their wages to their wives and replaced hedonism with thrift and delayed gratification. The already stern legal regime that buttressed a man's breadwinning responsibilities got even tougher through new legislation in the early 1920s to nail a man down to his children and his parents. These working men also tended to stay home in their leisure time, focusing their energies on household tasks, and took their families on excursions to local parks or beaches on special occasions. They might also be open to a more companionate social life with their wives, as the spread of card parties and the new mixed beverage rooms attested. It was this family focus that gave their sporadic unionizing efforts their ethical edge, and local labour struggles often highlighted the language of breadwinning.[93]

At the other extreme, a man who remained restless and unwilling to accept the domestic constraints of being a husband and father might have a life punctuated with frequent drunkenness, gambling, absenteeism from work, or violent behaviour. Some fell into seriously debilitating heavy drinking. In 1909–10, a third of Hamilton's court cases for drunkenness involved married men. All too often, it seems, they could create havoc with family finances and sometimes attacked their wives and children. Every week women brought abusive husbands to police court on charges of assault or non-support.[94]

Between the extremes of home-bodies and drunkards, however, many married working-class men might maintain some middle ground where they took the occasional opportunity to enjoy the all-male camaraderie of their bachelor haunts. A weekly stop at a saloon or bootlegger's "blind pig" or an afternoon in a ball park might be enough. Less frequent all-male hunting and fishing expeditions could become rituals of the "rougher" masculinity as well.[95] All these men might also participate in the apparently more sedate homosocial culture of fraternal societies, unions, or veterans' organizations. They still found some time for the "boys."

Conclusion

Growing up male in working-class Hamilton, then, involved a layering of experiences over time that produced distinctive class-based gender identities. Early in life, a boy learned the privileges of his gender superiority over the females in his life and sharply differentiated himself from them, but also ran up against the structures of class and ethnic or racial subordination – in particular the economic scarcity that limited everything from his play space to his job prospects to his adult recreational options, and the authority figures who controlled and contained his behaviour, from parents to teachers to policemen to bosses. Within these confines, he and his young male friends developed a cluster of often contradictory masculine practices that defined them as emergent working men. In contrast to middle-class men (who turned to muscle-building as compensation for their non-manual work), young male wage-earners took pride in using their bodies to express themselves in virtually all parts of their lives – in heavy manual labour, in physically demanding play (whether sports or drinking), in arguments and fights, in sexual conquests – generally undertaken as some kind of exuberant performance in a public setting. In boyhood, adolescence, and bachelorhood, moreover, they participated to varying degrees in collective practices of class, ethnic/racial, and gender solidarity and of defiance of authority and bourgeois morality. Working-class boys learned to be loud, lewd, and cocky. So much of that behaviour was dismissed with a shrug in the essentialist phrase "boys will be boys."

To be sure, there were tamer versions of this masculine identity – perhaps boys who stayed in school a bit longer, liked to read or play a musical instrument more than throw stones at neighbours' cats, embraced religion more fervently, avoided the pool room and the saloon, took up trades that demanded sober concentration, deferentially accepted the authority of foremen, or later emerged as activists in the local labour movement. Beyond individual personality differences, this kind of divergence undoubtedly rested in large part on the material resources that a particular working-class family could muster as the boy was growing up – the greater the scarcity, the less likely a boy would be to aspire to such modest respectability, particularly if he belonged to a systematically disadvantaged ethnic or racial group. Yet all boys and men in working-class Hamilton shared to some degree the profoundly contradictory tendencies between self-indulgent irresponsibility and deeply ingrained commitments to collective solidarity owed to family and workmates. In the end, working-class men constructed their masculine identities largely as survival mechanisms. They enjoyed the privileges of being men, and used them to create their own cultural oases, but, aside from the few who were quickly targeted as "incorrigible" boys, chronic drunks, or vagrants, they still had to pitch in to help sustain their families and still punched the clock in a capitalist workplace each day.

A lot of these practices dated back to the first encounters with industrial capitalism. But the half-century before the Second World War saw significant changes in the lives of working-class males that brought about a perceptible reconstruction of their gender identities by the 1920s and 1930s. In particular, they faced new forms of institutional regulation in schools, workplaces, streets, and military trenches, the commercialization of many of their pleasures, and new independence and assertiveness in the public sphere among the women of their communities. Working-class males responded to all these challenges and renegotiated their identities in a variety of ways. While the street-corner lounging, loutish drunkenness, and sexual assaults suggest plenty of continuity of old patterns of boyish bachelorhood into the interwar period, the explosion of youthful team sports, the sedateness of most public drinking places, the companionate socializing with girls and women, and the serious unionizing efforts suggested a taming of the rougher edges. The essential power dynamics of patriarchy had not been dissolved, but the forms through which they operated had been reshaped. Working men in Hamilton, as elsewhere, continued to struggle with their dual experience as dominators and dominated.

Notes

1 *Spectator* (Hamilton) (hereafter *HS*), 15 August 1913, 1.

2 I have been most influenced by Robert W. Connell's work, especially *Masculinities* (Berkeley: University of California Press 1995); see also John Tosh, "What Should Historians Do with Masculinity? Reflections on Nineteenth-Century Britain," *HW* 38 (Fall 1994), 179–202.

3 Connell, *Masculinities*, 67–86; Blye Frank, "Hegemonic Heterosexual Masculinity," *SPE* 24 (Autumn 1987), 159–70; John Tosh, "Hegemonic Masculinity and the History of Gender," in Stefan Dudink, Karen Hagerman, and John Tosh, eds., *Masculinities in Politics and War: Gendering Modern History* (Manchester: University of Manchester Press 2004), 41–58.

4 See, for example, Ava Baron, ed., *Work Engendered: Toward a New History of American Labor* (Ithaca: Cornell University Press 1991); Bettina Bradbury, *Working Families: Age, Gender, and Daily Survival in Industrializing Montreal* (Toronto: McClelland and Stewart 1993); Roger Horowitz, ed., *Boys and Their Toys? Masculinity, Class, and Technology in America* (New York: Routledge 2001); Thomas W. Dunk, *It's a Working Man's Town: Male Working-Class Culture in Northwestern Ontario* (Montreal and Kingston: McGill-Queen's University Press 1991); Lisa Fine, *The Story of Reo Joe: Work, Kin, and Community in Autotown, USA* (Philadelphia: Temple University Press 2004); Lynne Marks, *Revivals and Roller Rinks: Religion, Leisure, and Identity in Late-Nineteenth-Century Small-Town Ontario* (Toronto: University of Toronto Press 1996); Keith McClelland, "Masculinity and the "Representative Artisan" in Britain, 1850–80," in Michael Roper and John Tosh, eds., *Manful Assertions: Masculinities in Britain since 1800* (London: Routledge 1991), 74–91; Gunther Peck, *Reinventing Free Labor: Padrones and Immigrant Workers in the North American West, 1880–1930* (New York: Cambridge University Press 2000), 117–57.

5 For an early contribution to masculinity studies that did address the process of growing up male (though not historically), see Andrew Tolson, *The Limits of Masculinity* (London: Tavistock Press 1977).

6 Performance as an element in relationships of subordination has been explored by, among others, Peter Bailey, "'Will the Real Bill Banks Please Stand Up?': Towards a Role Analysis of Mid-Victorian Working-Class Respectability," *JSH* 12, no. 2 (Summer 1979), 336–51; James C. Scott, *Domination and the Arts of Resistance* (New Haven: Yale University Press 1990); Judith Butler, *Gender Trouble: Feminism and the Subversion of Identity* (New York: Routledge 1999).

7 W. Craig Heron, "Working-Class Hamilton, 1895–1930" (PhD thesis, Dalhousie University 1981).

8 Jane Synge, "Family and Community in Hamilton" (in McMaster University, Department of History, John Weaver Collection [hereafter Weaver Collection]), chapter 4.

9 The following discussion is necessarily based on fragmentary evidence drawn from scattered personal accounts (especially interviews conducted separately by Jane Synge, Wayne Roberts, and Peter Archibald, all of McMaster University, and researchers at the Multicultural History Society of Ontario and the Workers' Arts and Heritage Centre), middle-class observations (including newspaper reports), and various statistical compilations.

10 Synge, "Family and Community," chapters 3.2, 3.4, 3.5.

11 Heron, "Working-Class Hamilton," 26–33.

12 The gendering of household labour is discussed a greater length in my *Lunch-Bucket Lives: Remaking the Workers' City* (Toronto: Between the Lines 2015), which draws, in part, on Jane Synge, "The Transition from School to Work: Growing Up Working Class in Early 20th Century Hamilton, Ontario," in K. Ishwaran, ed., *Childhood and Adolescence in Canada* (Toronto: McGraw-Hill Ryerson 1979), 249–69; Jane Synge, "Young Working Class Women in Early 20th Century Hamilton – Their Work and Family Lives," in A.H. Turritin, ed., *Proceedings of the Workshop Conference on Blue-Collar Workers and Their Communities …* (Toronto: York University 1976), 137–45; Jane Synge, "Immigrant Communities – British and Continental European – in Early Twentieth Century Hamilton, Canada," *Oral History* 4, no. 2 (Autumn 1976), 38–51; Jane Synge, "Family and Community," chapter 3.4; Peter Archibald, "Distress, Dissent, and Alienation: Hamilton Workers in the Great Depression," *UHR* 21, no. 1 (October 1992), 3–32; Peter Archibald, "Small Expectations and Great Adjustments: How Hamilton Workers Most Often Experienced the Great Depression," *CJS* 21,

no. 3 (Summer 1996); Donald A. Garvie, *Growing Up in the City* (Dundas, ON: Darm Publishing n.d.); Laurence Murphy and Philip Murphy, *Tales from the North End* (Hamilton: Authors 1981).

13 Synge, "Family and Community," chapter 3.2; Workers' Arts and Heritage Centre Archives, Workers' City Project Interviews (hereafter WAHC Interviews), Florence Fisher, Floyd Read; Multicultural History Society of Ontario (hereafter MHSO), ITA-0982-PAS (interview with Donna Pasquale, 13 April 1983); Murphy and Murphy, *Tales from the North End*, 122–8; Peter Hunter, *Which Side Are You On, Boys?: Canadian Life on the Left* (Toronto: Lugus Productions 1988), 6.

14 Synge, "Family and Community," chapter 3.3.

15 Jane Synge's interviewees remembered their parents' strong desire to instill a sense of obedience, respectful behaviour, and "decency." Ibid., chapter 3.3.

16 *Acts and Proceedings of the Presbyterian Church in Canada*, 1901; *Journal of the Proceedings of the Diocese of Niagara* (Hamilton), 1910, 114; 1921, 126; *Minutes of the Annual Conference of the Methodist Church*, 1906, 1921; *Baptist Year Book*, 1920, 296–7. Synge, "Family and Community," chapter 3.3.

17 Melissa Turkstra, "Social Christianity and the Working Class in English Canada, 1900–1930" (PhD thesis, York University 2005), chapter 4; Michael Gauvreau, "'[F]actories and Foreigners': Church Life in Working-Class Neighbourhoods in Hamilton and Montreal, 1890–1930" (unpublished paper); Murphy and Murphy, *Tales from the North End*, 53; Patricia Dirks, "Serving Church and Nation: Methodist Sunday Schools in Canada's Century," Canadian Methodist Historical Society, *Papers*, 1995, 46–62; Enrico Carlson Cumbo, "Salvation in Indifference: Gendered Expressions of Italian-Canadian Immigrant Catholicity, 1900–1940," in Nancy Christie, ed., *Households of Faith: Family, Gender, and Community in Canada, 1760–1969* (Montreal and Kingston: McGill-Queen's University Press 2002), 205–33.

18 Ian E. Davey, "Educational Reform and the Working Class: School Attendance in Hamilton, Ontario, 1851–1891" (PhD thesis, University of Toronto 1975).

19 *HS*, 25 March 1901, 8; 15 May 1905, 10; Craig Heron, "The High School and the Household Economy in Working-Class Hamilton, 1890–1940," *HSE* 7, no. 2 (Fall 1995), 217–59.

20 In 1901 only 663 of the city's 5,500 young people aged fifteen to nineteen were enrolled in the Hamilton Collegiate Institute, and only 56 more in the equivalents of grades 8 and 9 in the Catholic system. Heron, "High School and the Household Economy," 225–8.

21 Ibid.

22 There were dissenting voices in working-class Hamilton on imperialism and militarism. See, for example, *Labor News* (hereafter *LN*), 12 January 1912, 2.

23 Robert Stamp, "Empire Day in the Schools of Ontario: The Training of Young Imperialists," *JCS* 8, no. 3 (August 1973), 32–42; Desmond Morton, "The Cadet Movement in the Moment of Canadian Militarism, 1909–1914," ibid. 13, no. 2 (Summer 1978), 56–68; Mark Moss, *Manliness and Militarism: Educating Young Boys in Ontario for War* (Toronto: Oxford University Press 2001); Tosh, "What Should Historians Do with Masculinity?" 196 (quotation); Hamilton, Board of Education, *Minutes* (Hamilton), 2 May 1912, 69; 7 November 1912, 131; 11 February 1932, 55–6, 271–3; 8 June 1933, 175; 4 October 272; 12 October 1933, 252; 6 February 1934, 55–6; Ontario, Department of Education, *Annual Reports* (Toronto), 1913–1934; Donald M. Oliphant, comp., *Hess Street School* (Hamilton: Aggus 1974), 24. The cadet program was abruptly and permanently shut down in 1934.

24 Moss, *Manliness and Militarism*, 61–89; John Tosh, "Imperial Masculinity and the Flight from Domesticity in Britain, 1880–1914," in Timothy P. Foley et al., *Gender and Colonialism* (Galway: Galway University Press 1995), 76–7. Catholic children from Italian and Slavic immigrant families were taught in a separate floor of St Ann's School, which was given the name of St Stanislaus School, with its own staff and playground. Diane Brandino, "The Italians of Hamilton, 1921–1945" (MA thesis, University of Western Ontario 1977), 102–3.

25 Bernd Baldus and Meenz Kassam, "Make Me Truthful, Good, and Mild: Values in Nineteenth-century Ontario Textbooks," *CJS* 21, no. 3 (Summer 1996), 327–40; George S. Tomkins, *A Common Countenance: Stability and Change in the Canadian Curriculum* (Scarborough: Prentice-Hall Canada 1986).

26 Synge, "Family and Community," chapter 3.3; Murphy and Murphy, *Tales from the North End*, 61. One woman told Jane Synge that her working-class mother expected perfect marks in "Attendance," "Punctuality," and "Conduct."

27 Oliphant, comp., *Hess Street School*, 36–9.

28 Street gangs were certainly not completely new urban formations in the early twentieth century. See Bryan Hogeveen, "'Can't You Be a Man?': Rebuilding Wayward Masculinities and Regulating Juvenile Deviance in Ontario, 1860–1930" (PhD thesis, University of Toronto 2003).

29 J.K. Unsworth, *The Church and the Boy* (n.p. [Hamilton] 1903) (CIHR No. 80639), 4. The following discussion links the scattered Hamilton evidence to other contemporary and later studies, including William Byron Forbush, *The Boy Problem* (Boston: Pilgrim Press 1907): J. Adams Puffer, *The Boy and His Gang* (Boston: Houghlin Mifflin 1912); Frederic M. Thrasher, *The Gang:*

A Study of 1,313 Gangs in Chicago (Chicago: University of Chicago Press 1926); Kenneth H. Rogers, *Street Gangs in Toronto: A Study of the Forgotten Boy* (Toronto: Ryerson Press 1945); Neil Sutherland, *Growing Up: Childhood in English Canada from the Great War to the Age of Television* (Toronto: University of Toronto Press 1997), 227–8, 238–42; David Nasaw, *Children of the City: At Work and At Play* (Garden City, NY: Anchor Press 1985); Stephen Humphries, *Hooligans or Rebels?: An Oral History of Working-Class Childhood and Youth, 1889–1939* (Oxford: Basil Blackwell 1982), 174–208; Andrew Davies, "Youth Gangs, Masculinity and Violence in Late Victorian Manchester and Salford," *JSH* 32, no.2 (Winter 1998), 349–69.

30 *HS*, 13 June 1900, 8; 26 July 1900, 8; 14 August 1900, 8; 7 May 1901, 8; *Herald* (Hamilton) (hereafter *HH*), 28 February 1914, 1; Murphy and Murphy, *Tales from the North End*, 155–75.

31 Ontario, Commissioners Appointed to Enquire into the Prison and Reformatory System of Ontario, *Report* (Toronto: Warwick and Sons 1891) (hereafter Ontario Prison Commission), 251, 264; *Hamilton Times* (hereafter *HT*), 10 July 1893, 8; *HS*, 14 October 1908, 4; 9 March 1909, 10; 8 April 1909, 7; *HH*, 10 May 1910, 1; 30 March 1911, 1; 10 March 1923, 1; 23 March 1923, 1; Hamilton Public Library, Special Collections (hereafter HPL), RG 10, Series S (Board of Police Commissioners, Minutes), 31 May 1912.

32 Murphy and Murphy, *Tales from the North End*, 75–88, 105, 155–75.

33 *HT*, 9 August 1913, 13; *HS*, 5 June 1900, 8; 2 September 1901, 8; Ontario Prison Commission, 260, 269, 280–1, 308, 309; *HH*, 23 May 1913, 4; T.J. Newlands, "The History and Operation of Hamilton's Parks," *Wentworth Bygones* 9 (1971), 9–15; John James Halcrow, "Burlington Bay as I Remember It," ibid., 56–61; HPL, RG 18, Series A (Board of Parks Management, Minutes), 1900–40; Murphy and Murphy, *Tales from the North End*, 101, 235–6; Ken Cruikshank and Nancy B. Bouchier, "*Dirty Spaces*: Environment, the State, and Recreational Swimming in Hamilton Harbour, 1870–1946," *SHR* 29 (1998), 59–76.

34 *HS*, 5 January 1900, 8; 31 March 1900, 8; 6 July 1900, 8; 23 July 1900, 8; 24 July 1900, 8; 7 January 1930, 7. In 1909, 80 out of 91 juveniles brought to the police court were listed as "intemperate." Nancy A. Nagy, "Juvenile Deliquency in Hamilton: 1895 and 1909" (unpublished paper in Weaver Collection), 7.

35 *HT*, 10 July 1893, 8; *HS*, 31 March 1900, 8; 19 June 1900, 6.

36 *HS*, 1 March 1901, 10; Methodist Church of Canada, Department of Temperance and Moral Reform, and Presbyterian Church of Canada, Board of Social Service and Evangelism, *Report of a Preliminary and General Social Survey of Hamilton* (n.p. [Hamilton] 1913), 18.

37 HPL, RG 10, Series S, 7 November 1906, 17 October 1912.
38 *HS*, 9 September 1910, 1; 28 October 1910, 16; *HH*, 22 October 1910, 6; 4 November 1910, 1; 28 June 1911, 12; *HT*, 5 July 1910, 1; 12 September 1910, 6; 21 October 1910, 1; 22 October 1910, 6. Film exhibitors were furious about the ban on young movie-goers "since their audiences were for the most part children." *HH*, 11 March 1911, 8.
39 Ontario Prison Commission, 269, 271, 281, 290; *HS*, 12 January 1900, 8; 17 January 1900, 8; 1 February 1900, 8; 20 February 1900, 8; 23 March 1900, 8; 1 May 1900, 8; 15 May 1900, 8; 26 May 1900, 8; 29 May 1900, 8; 30 May 1900, 8; 31 May 1900, 8; 4 June 1900, 8; 11 September 1900, 8; 19 September 1900, 8; 15 December 1900, 8; 15 March 1910, 8; 28 June 1920, 7; 3 July 1920, 7; 22 July 1920, 7; 27 July 1920, 12; 2 January 1930, 7; 10 January 1930, 7; 13 January 1930, 7; 24 January 1930, 7; 19 February 1930, 7; 4 March 1930, 7; 28 November 1930, 7; *HT*, 10 July 1893, 8; 28 September 1912, 1; Murphy and Murphy, *Tales from the North End*, 66, 100, 106, 162–3; Garvie, *Growing Up*, 12; Big Brothers' Association Archives, Board of Directors, Minutes, 4 March, 2 December 1935; HPL, RG 10, Series A (Police Department, Annual Reports), 1920–31.
40 Garvie, *Growing Up*, 20; *HS*, 22 June 1900, 8; 24 August 1900, 8; 13 November 1900, 3; 25 November 1900, 8; 16 January 1901, 8; 6 May 1901, 8; 1 November 1907, 1.
41 *HS*, 18 June 1920, 7; see also 25 August 1910, 10; *HH*, 20 July 1917; Murphy and Murphy, *Tales from the North End*, 90. This aggression and violence never seems to have reached the level of intensity in Hamilton that it did in East London, Manchester, Birmingham, or Glasgow in the same period. Humphries, *Hooligans or Rebels?*, 174–6; Davies, "Youth Gangs, Masculinity and Violence."
42 *HS*, 1 November 1898, 1; 1 November 1907, 1; 1 November 1919, 1; 2 November 1925; 1 November 1929, 6, 7; Garvie, *Growing Up*, 28 (quotation); Nicholas Roger *Halloween: From Pagan Ritual to Party Night* (New York: Oxford University Press 2000), 56–62.
43 *Toronto Star*, 21 August 1903, 1; *HS*, 12 March 1891, 2; 18 August 1903, 1, 7; 19 August 1903, 1; 21 August 1903, 1, 8; 27 October 1908, 7; 12 August 1913, 1, 20; 15 August 1913, 1, 7, 14; 16 August 1913, 1; 18 August 1903, 5; Garvie, *Growing Up*, 25–6.
44 *HS*, 6 November 1906, 1, 6; 7 November 1906, 1; 8 November 1906, 10; 9 November 1906, 1, 9; 16 November 1906, 1; 24 November 1906, 1, 6, 16.
45 *HS*, 30 July 1900, 8; 9 March 1909, 10; 8 April 1909, 7; *HT*, 23 March 1911, 1; 12 August 1913, 1.
46 See the Hamilton evidence in Ontario Prison Commission, 245–311; Hogeveen, "'Can't You Be a Man?'"

47 This was a forum for handling wayward boys – scarcely any girls appeared in police court. John C. Weaver, *Crimes, Constables, and Courts: Order and Transgression in a Canadian City, 1816–1970* (Montreal and Kingston: McGill-Queen's University Press 1995).

48 Ontario Prison Commission, 252, 253, 263, 270, 293; *HS*, 17 August 1900, 8; 4 September 1900, 8; 11 October 1900, 8; 21 January 1901, 8; 22 January 1901, 8; 26 March 1901, 8; 8 May 1901, 8; Cathy Wever, "Crime and Punishment in Hamilton: Jelfs and Social Control" (unpublished paper in Weaver Collection), 9–11; Paul W. Bennett, "Taming 'Bad Boys' of the 'Dangerous Class': Child Rescue and Restraint at the Victoria Industrial School, 1887–1935," *HS/SH* 21, no. 41 (1988), 71–96.

49 *HS*, 23 January 1894, 31 January 1894, 23 February 1894, 30 January 1901, 31 December 1902, 18 December 1903, 29 June 1904, 2 February 1910, 27 September 1910, 25 November 1922 (clippings in HPL, Children's Aid Society Scrapbook); Penney Benner, *100 Years for Children, 1894–1994: The Children's Aid Society of Hamilton-Wentworth, "Celebrating 100 Years for Children"* [Hamilton 1994].

50 HPL, Rotary Club of Hamilton, Minutes, 1917–20; ibid., RG 10 Series A (Police Department Records), 1920–31; *HH*, 2 February 1921, 9; *HS*, 5 June 1920, 15; 2 February 1921, 3; 26 January 1925, 2; 22 January 1927, 13; Hamilton Board of Education, *Minutes*, 1921, 67–8; Big Brothers Association Archives, Board of Directors, Minutes, 1929–39; Big Brothers Association of Hamilton, *Annual Report*, 1936, 2; 1937, 2; 1939, 6–8; Canadian Welfare Council, *A Study of the Community Fund and Its Member Agencies in Hamilton, 1937* (Ottawa: Canadian Welfare Council 1937), 97–100.

51 Murphy and Murphy, *Tales from the North End*, 65–6; David Howell and Peter Lindsay, "Social Gospel and the Young Boy Problem, 1895–1925," in Morris Mott, ed., *Sports in Canada: Historical Readings* (Toronto: Copp Clark Pitman 1989), 220–33; Patricia Dirks, "'Getting a Grip on Harry': Canada's Methodists Respond to the 'Big Boy' Problem," Canadian Methodist Historical Society, *Papers* 1990, 67–82.

52 Murray G. Ross, *The Y.M.C.A. in Canada: The Chronicle of a Century* (Toronto: Ryerson Press 1951), 194; David I. Macleod, *Building Character in the American Boy: The Boy Scouts, YMCA, and Their Forerunners, 1870–1920* (Madison: University of Wisconsin Press 1983); HPL, Archives File, Young Men's Christian Association – East End, Minutes; M. Lucille Marr, "Church Teen Clubs, Feminized Organizations? Tuxis Boys, Trail Rangers, and Canadian Girls in Training, 1919–1939," *HSE* 3 no. 2 (Fall 1991), 249–67.

53 *HH*, 2 February 1910, 1, 4; 25 November 1920, 12 (quotation); *HT*, 12 March 1910, 1; Patricia Dirks, "Canada's Boys – An Imperial or National Asset? Responses to Baden-Powell's Boy Scout Movement in Pre-War Canada" (paper presented to the British World Conference, Calgary 2003); Moss, *Manliness and Militarism*, 115–17.

54 Hamilton Playgrounds Association, *Souvenir Number: An Historical Review* [Hamilton: n.p. 1931]; *HT* 13 July 1916, 7.

55 *HH*, 26 February 1910, 10; 26 October 1912, 8; *HS*, 11 May 1916, 8; J.O. Springhall, "The Boy Scouts, Class, and Militarism in Relation to British Youth Movements, 1908–1930," *IRSH* 17 (1972), 3–23; David I. Macleod, "Act Your Age: Boyhood, Adolescence, and the Rise of the Boy Scouts of America," *JSH* 16, no. 2 (Winter 1982), 3–20.

56 See, for example, HPL, Archives File, YMCA – East End, Minutes, 9 November, 6 December 1915; 10 January, 7 February, 6 March, 10 April, 8 May, 12 December 1916.

57 *HT*, 4 February 1911, 1; HPL, Hamilton Playgrounds Association, Chief Supervisor, General Report, 1919–25; see also *HT*, 11 February 1910, 11; Canadian Conference on Charities and Correction, *Proceedings*, 1911, 48; HPL, Rotary Club of Hamilton, Minutes, 1921; Murphy and Murphy, *Tales from the North End*, 65–6. For similar episodes of Boy Scout rowdiness, see HPL, Soldiers' Aid Commission, Minutes, 10 April 1919.

58 Heron, "High School and the Household Economy"; Hamilton Playgrounds Association, *Souvenir Number*; *HH*, 21 January 1922, 4; 14 November 1923, 11; HPL, Hamilton Chamber of Commerce, Minutes, 7 December 1920, 106; HPL, Rotary Club of Hamilton, Minutes, 13 March 1919; Canadian Welfare Council, *Study of the Community Fund*, 97–100; Hunter, *Which Side Are You On, Boys?*, 9–32; Murphy and Murphy, *Tales from the North End*, 194, 210.

59 Garvie, *Growing Up*, 12.

60 Synge, "Family and Community," chapter 6; E. Anthony Rotundo, "Boy Culture: Middle-Class Boyhood in Nineteenth-Century America," in Mark C. Carnes and Clyde Griffen, eds., *Meanings for Manhood: Constructions of Masculinity in Victorian America* (Chicago: University of Chicago Press 1990), 15–36; Macleod, *Building Character*.

61 WAHC Interviews, Florence Fisher, Fred Purser, Ken Withers; Synge, "Family and Community," chapter 3.6; Murphy and Murphy, *Tales from the North End*, 159; Hunter, *Which Side Are You On, Boys?*, 5; *HH*, 30 March 1911, 1.

62 Heron, "High School and the Household Economy"; Synge, "Family and Community," chapter 3.6; Synge, "Transition from School to Work," 254–6, 258.

63 Tolson, *Limits of Masculinity*, 47–51.

64 Craig Heron, "The Crisis of the Craftsman: Hamilton's Metal Workers in the Early Twentieth Century," *L/LT* 6 (Autumn 1980), 7–48; Heron, "Working-Class Hamilton," 78–287; Heron, *Working in Steel*, 33–111; *Census of Canada*, 1921, Vol. 4, 400–9. Between 1916 and 1920 in Wentworth County, where Hamilton was by far the dominant industrial centre, 70 workers were killed on the job, 1,334 were permanently disabled, and 15,111 temporarily laid up by their injuries. Ontario, Workmen's Compensation Board, *Annual Reports* (Toronto), 1917–20.

65 Heron, "Working-Class Hamilton," 289–378; Heron, *Working in Steel*, 74–87, 94–7, 118–24; Peck, *Reinventing Free Labor*.

66 See, for example, *HS*, 3 February 1920, 16; 14 December 1920, 18.

67 Heron, "Working-Class Hamilton," chapters 2–5; Todd McCallum, "'Not a Sex Question'? The One Big Union and the Politics of Radical Manhood," *L/LT* 42 (Fall 1998), 15–54.

68 Ontario, Secretary and Registrar General, *Report*, 1890–1924 (there are no published breakdowns by city after this date); *Census of Canada*, 1921, Vol. 2, 184–5; 1931, Vol. 3, 136–7; 1941, Vol. 3, 122 (calculations of percentages are mine). Before 1921, the published census data for Hamilton did not include marital status by age group.

69 *Census of Canada*, 1921, Vol. 3, 142, 153–4; Synge, "Transition from School to Work"; Synge, "Young Working Class Women"; Synge, "Family and Community," chapter 3.6.

70 Enrico Cumbo, "Italians in Hamilton, 1900–40," *Polyphony* 7, no.2 (Fall/Winter 1985), 28–36; Synge, "Immigrant Communities"; Heron, "Working-Class Hamilton," 288–342. In 1921 female cotton workers earned an average of only $10 a week, and clothing workers less than $12. *Census of Canada*, 1921, Vol. 3, 154.

71 Sharon Meen, "The Battle for the Sabbath: The Sabbatarian Lobby in Canada, 1890–1912" (PhD thesis, University of British Columbia 1979); Paul Laverdure, *Sunday in Canada: The Rise and Fall of the Lord's Day* (Yorkton, SK: Gravelbooks 2004).

72 *HH*, 8 September 1908, 8; 8 March 1910, 8; 26 March 1910, 8; 4 April 1910, 9; 7 April 1910, 8; 8 April 1910, 12; 19 April 1910, 9; 2 May 1910, 9; 3 May 1910, 8; 11 May 1910, 1, 11; 17 June 1910, 16; 13 September 1910, 4; 15 April 1911, 17; 12 June 1911, 8; 24 June 1912, 8; 25 January 1913, 1; 1 February 1913, 1; 28 March 1913, 16; 19 May 1913, 5; 20 April 1914, 10; 28 June 1916, 8; 1 August 1917, 13; 24 September 1918, 10; *HS*, 15 July 1926, n.p.; *LN*, 12 April 1912, 1; 27 September 1912, 3; 1 November 1912, 1; 31 July 1914, 1; 6 August 1915, 2; 30 April 1920, 4; Murphy and Murphy, *Tales from the*

North End, 88, 182, 188–9, 194–201; Alan Metcalfe, *Canada Learns to Play: The Emergence of Organized Sport, 1807–1914* (Toronto: McClelland and Stewart 1987), 26, 54–65, 163–72; Dunk, *It's a Working Man's Town*, 65–100 (quotation at 88).

73 *HH*, 9 March 1910, 8; 22 April 1910, 11; 2 June 1910, 11; 3 June 1910, 1; 17 June 1910, 1; 8 July 1910, 5; 22 February 1911, 1; 24 February 1911, 1; 27 February 1911, 1; 28 February 1911, 1; 2 March 1911, 1; 17 March 1911, 1; *HS*, 12 March 1901, 10; 16 March 1901, 12; *Industrial Banner* (London), May 1906, 4; *Amalgamated Journal*, 12 May 1921, 8; HPL, Central ILP Minutes, 10, 24 March, 12, 29 April 1922; Murphy and Murphy, *Tales from the North End*, 191–4. For the masculine identities cultivated in and around boxing rings, see Elliott J. Gorn, *The Manly Art: Bare-Knuckle Prize Fighting in America* (Ithaca: Cornell University Press 1986).

74 Crap-shooting also remained an immensely popular form of gambling. HPL, RG 10, Series A, 1905, 1909, 1911, 1912, 1915; Canada, Royal Commission in Racing Inquiry, *Report* (Ottawa: King's Printer 1920), 38–44; Murphy and Murphy, *Tales from the North End*, 47–50, 175–9. Between 1907 and 1912 nearly two-thirds of those caught gambling were under age thirty. Tom Irwin, "Moral Order Crime in Hamilton: 1907–1912" (unpublished paper, in Weaver Collection).

75 Hunter, *Which Side Are You On, Boys?*, 9; Murphy and Murphy, *Tales from the North End*, 85–8, 155, 179–81.

76 Single men made up only 7 per cent of the membership of the predominantly working-class congregation at Calvin Presbyterian between 1910 and 1925. Turkstra, "Social Christianity and the Working Class," chapter 4; see also Addison, "Life and Culture," 52, 63–4; Smith, "Dialectics of Faith," 255; Gauvreau, "'[F]actories and Foreigners.'"

77 Mike O'Brien, "Manhood and the Militia Myth: Masculinity, Class and Militarism in Ontario, 1902–1914," *L/LT* 42 (Fall 1998), 115–41.

78 Desmond Morton, *When Your Number's Up: The Canadian Soldier in the First World War* (Toronto: Random House 1993); David Englander and James Osborne, "Jack, Tommy, and Henry Dubb: The Armed Forces and the Working Class," *Historical Journal* 21, no. 3 (September 1978), 593–621; J.G. Fuller, *Troop Morale and Popular Culture in the British and Dominion Armies, 1914–1918* (Oxford: Clarendon Press 1990); Graham Dawson, *Soldier Heroes: British Adventure, Empire, and the Imagining of Masculinities* (London: Routledge 1994). Nearly two-thirds of the CEF had been manual workers, roughly four out of five were bachelors, and nearly seven out of ten were under thirty. One in eight who served overseas in the CEF died, and another one in three was wounded. Morton, *When Your Number's Up*, 181, 278–9.

79 The ensuing discussion draws on my article "The Boys and Their Booze: Masculinities and Public Drinking in Working-Class Hamilton, 1890–1946," *CHR* 86, no. 3 (September 2005), 411–52.

80 That was the spirit behind the Canadian labour movement's campaign to roll back prohibition of alcoholic beverages immediately after the First World War. See Craig Heron, *Booze: A Distilled History* (Toronto: Between the Lines 2003), 213–32.

81 Heron, "Boys and Their Booze."

82 Turkstra, "Social Christianity and the Working Class," chapter 4; Gauvreau, "'[F]actories and Foreigners'"; Heron, "High School and the Household Economy"; Heron, "Working-Class Hamilton."

83 Synge, "Family and Community," chapters 3.1, 5.4; *HH*, 1 October 1910, 20; 29 August 1911, 1; 17 September 1912, 1; 23 March 1914, 1; *HS*, 19 November 1910, 1; 17 January 1925, 5; Garvie, *Growing Up*, 8; Karen Dubinsky, *Improper Advances: Rape and Heterosexual Conflict in Ontario, 1880–1929* (Chicago: University of Chicago Press 1993), 117; Adam Givertz, "Sex and Order: The Regulation of Sexuality and the Prosecution of Sexual Assault in Hamilton, Ontario, 1880–1929" (MA thesis, Queen's University 1992), 40–5; Cruickshank and Bouchier, *"Dirty Spaces,"* 66–7.

84 On dancing and popular music, see *HS*, 12 August 1913, 20; 18 August 1913, 5; *HH*, 1 September 1913, 1; 2 September 1913, 1; 4 January 1914, 12; 5 January 1914, 1; 24 January 1914, 1; 5 February 1914, 1; 25 February 1914, 1; 28 February 1914, 1; 30 October 1914, 10; 16 September 1916, 9; 16 January 1918, 1; 16 December 1921, 12; 2 September 1922, 19; *HS*, 20 December 1919, 36; *HT*, 31 August 1917, 13; 3 September 1917, 4; 4 September 1917, 11; 13 September 1917, 11; Mark Miller, *Such Melodious Racket: The Lost History of Jazz in Canada, 1914–1949* (Toronto: Mercury Press 1997), 49–50, 95, 128, 130–1, 137, 139, 142. Local amusement parks are discussed in Dorothy Turcotte, *The Sand Strip: Burlington/Hamilton Beaches* (St Catharines: Stonehouse Publications 1987), 32; Brian Henley, *Hamilton: Our Lives and Times* (Hamilton: Hamilton Spectator 1993), 64–5.

85 Synge, "Family and Community," chapter 5.4.

86 Carolyn Strange, *Toronto's Girl Problem: The Perils and Pleasures of the City, 1880–1930* (Toronto: University of Toronto Press 1995); Kathy Peis, *Cheap Amusements: Working Women and Leisure in Turn-of-the Century New York* (Philadelphia: Temple University Press 1986); Heron, "Boys and Their Booze"; Heron, *Booze*.

87 Virginia Wright Wexman, *Creating the Couple: Love, Marriage, and Hollywood Performance* (Princeton: Princeton University Press 1993).

88 Mark A. Swiencicki, "Consuming Brotherhood: Men's Culture, Style, and Recreation as Consumer Culture, 1880–1930," *JSH* 31, no.4 (Summer 1998), 773–808: Lizabeth Cohen, *Making a New Deal: Industrial Workers in Chicago, 1919–1939* (New York: Cambridge University Press 1990), 144–5.

89 Kevin White, *The First Sexual Revolution: The Emergence of Male Heterosexuality* (New York: New York University Press 1993), 100; cf. David Fowler, *The First Teenagers: The Lifestyle of Young Wage-Earners in Interwar Britain* (London: Woburn Press 1995), 116–33.

90 George Chauncey, *Gay New York: Gender, Urban Culture, and the Making of the Gay Male World, 1890–1940* (New York: Basic Books 1994); Stephen Maynard, "'Horrible Temptations': Sex, Men, and Working-Class Male Youth in Urban Ontario, 1890–1935,' *CHR* 78, no.2 (June 1997), 191–235; White, *First Sexual Revolution*, 84–6; *Canadian White Ribbon Tidings*, 1 May, 1 July 1910; Michael Bliss, "'Pure Books on Avoided Subjects': Pre-Freudian Sexual Ideas in Canada," *HP*, 1970, 89–108; Jay Cassel, *The Secret Plague: Venereal Disease in Canada, 1838–1939* (Toronto: University of Toronto Press 1987); Lesley A. Hall, *Hidden Anxieties: Male Sexuality, 1900–1950* (London: Polity Press 1991), 15–62; Givertz, "Sex and Order"; Dubinsky, *Improper Advances;* Karen Dubinsky and Adam Givertz, "'It Was Only a Matter of Passion': Masculinity and Sexual Danger," in Kathryn McPherson, Cecilia Morgan, and Nancy M. Forestall, eds., *Gendered Pasts: Historical Essays in Femininity and Masculinity in Canada* (Toronto: Oxford University Press 1999), 65–79.

91 *HS*, 31 December 1895, 8; 1 April 1901, 8; 20 June 1904, 10; 6 November 1906, 12; 20 April 1914, 16; *HH*, 16 February 1909, 1; 13 March 1911, 1; 7 November 1912, 3; 27 January 1913, 1; 9 January 1914, 1; 20 April 1914, 14. The local police magistrate (whose term ran from the 1890s to the 1920s) preferred a policy of tolerance of properly run brothels over complete repression, and the police chief was only interested in shutting down "objectionable" places; *HH*, 1 January 1909, 1; 23 January 1912, 4; 20 April 1914, 14. By 1925 the Hamilton General Hospital's VD clinic was treating nearly 6,000 men. Ontario, Provincial Board of Health, *Annual Report*, 1920, 228; 1921, 325–8; 1922, 262–3; 1923, 388–9; 1926, 15; Cassel, *Secret Plague*.

92 *HT*, 15 July 1916, 1; *HS*, 14 August 1920, 19. Carolyn Strange, "From Modern Babylon to a City Upon a Hill: The Toronto Social Survey Commission of 1915 and the Search for Sexual Order in the City," in Roger Hall, William Westfall, and Laurel Sefton MacDowell, eds., *Patterns of the Past: Interpreting Ontario's History* (Toronto: Dundurn Press 1988), 255–77; Dubinsky, *Improper Advances*, 33, 74–7, 134–8; Lori Chambers, "Courtship, Condoms, and 'Getting Caught': Working-Class Sexual Behaviour

in Ontario, 1921–1969" (paper presented to the Canadian Historical Association meeting, 1995); John D'Emilio and Estelle Freedman, *Intimate Matters: A History of Sexuality in America* (New York: Harper and Row 1988), 256; White, *First Sexual Revolution*, 15; Givertz, "Sex and Order," 107–48; Dubinsky and Givertz, "'It Was Only a Matter of Passion.'"

93 James Snell, "'The White Life for Two': The Defence of Marriage and Sexual Morality in Canada, 1890–1914," *HS/SH* 16, no. 31 (1983), 111–28; Jane Ursel, *Private Lives, Public Policy: 100 Years of State Intervention in the Family* (Toronto: Women's Press 1992), 102, 143–5, 341; Murphy and Murphy, *Tales from the North End*, 31–9; Alf Ready, *Organizing Westinghouse: Alf Ready's Story*, ed. Wayne Roberts (Hamilton McMaster University Labour Studies Program 1979); Joy Parr, *The Gender of Breadwinners: Women, Men, and Change in Two Industrial Towns, 1880–1950* (Toronto: University of Toronto Press 1990); Steven Penfold, "'Have You No Manhood in You?': Gender and Class in the Cape Breton Coal Towns, 1920–1926," *Acadiensis* 23, no. 2 (Spring 1994), 21–44.

94 Heron, "Boys and Their Booze."

95 Lisa M. Fine explores these practices in "Rights of Men, Rites of Passage: Hunting and Masculinity at Reo Motors of Lansing, Michigan, 1945–1975," *JSH* 33, no.4 (Summer 2000), 805–23.

PRISON BARS
CANNOT
CONFINE IDEAS
HUDSON'S
BAY

Chapter Twelve

Male Wage-Earners and the Canadian State

A male worker meets many faces of the state. Few of them seem friendly. One afternoon, he is handed a leaflet advising him that his union's negotiators have met with a provincial mediator but have been unable to work out a settlement. The next morning he joins a picket line where he confronts a phalanx of policemen trying to keep the company's gates open. By angrily resisting the police, he is arrested and meets in succession the jail keepers and then the judge, who fines him heavily and orders him to stay away from the picket line. Arriving home that night, he sees on television the stern face of the premier deploring the picket-line violence and the inconvenience to the public. His daughter informs him that her teacher had made similar comments at school. Eventually opening his mail, he finds a letter from the workers' compensation board rejecting his long-standing claim for help as a result of a back injury at work. As the strike drags on for several weeks, he lines up first in the unemployment insurance office and then at the welfare department trying to convince tightfisted administrators that he needs help in paying his rent and feeding his family. The next spring, he will curse more loudly than usual the taxes he has to pay to support these various state apparatuses.

These many faces of the Canadian state are not always closely connected and, on occasion, can even present contradictory messages. Yet there is an overall consistency in their approach to workers in Canada that allows us to sketch a collective portrait. In doing so, we enter into the hotly contested terrain of theories of the state. Most Marxists agree

Parade in Winnipeg 1919. Library and Archives Canada, C 37329 that the state in a capitalist society plays a role that facilitates the process of capital accumulation and the maintenance of capitalist power. The debate is over precisely how to conceptualize that role. It is not argued that the state is directly at the beck and call of capitalists, or that its activities are shaped purely in response to expressed capitalist concerns. Rather, the institutions, policies, and programs of the capitalist state evolve with some autonomy, though always within a broad consensus that private ownership of the means of production and the subordination of other classes to the dominant capitalist class are good for society. State activity tends to promote capital accumulation directly (through tariffs, development of the infrastructure, tax write-offs, and so on), but also works to legitimize the social order in the eyes of the citizenry. In particular, it encourages the consent of subordinated classes to their place in the structure of wealth and power and attempts to keep all social conflicts within acceptable bounds. State officials can rarely claim any particular clarity of social vision – often their activity amounts to little more than political opportunism by governing parties – but sometimes they play a creative role in identifying and attempting to eliminate the sources of major social tensions.[1]

In Canadian history the state has had to deal with workers as a problem for both accumulation and legitimization. First, they had to be marshalled into a well-stocked capitalist labour market if industrial development (and thus capital accumulation) were to proceed in the country. Second, as one of the two major subordinate classes in Canada (alongside the once much larger numbers of independent commodity producers), the working class has not always "consented" to the terms of its subordination and has posed repeated challenges to the structure of accumulation. Over the past 150 years the Canadian state has intervened in workers' lives in an ongoing, dynamic process of anticipating and responding to their activity. Initially that intervention reflected a concern with controlling individual workers, but by the last quarter of the nineteenth century, industrial militancy and working-class political pressure prompted more vigorous state action. The focus of this discussion will be primarily on male wage-earners, for the simple reason that during most of the period under examination public life has been defined as a masculine sphere from which women were almost completely excluded. The state, in the person of male politicians, judges, civil servants, and so on, helped to define women's appropriate role as "private" and domestic, and to circumscribe tightly the female wage-earning experience.[2]

The first workers whose behaviour brought state attention were those at the dawn of large-scale capitalist development in Canada who appeared unwilling to integrate themselves compliantly into an emerging capitalist society. As colonial officials noted with consternation in the first half of the nineteenth century, many seemed more interested in the independence of backwoods farming than in making themselves available for regular wage-earning. State land-granting policies were subsequently tightened up to make land less accessible and thus to create a pool of landless labour that incipient industrialists could employ.[3] When potential workers continued to flow into the rural hinterland or out of the country, the state undertook to promote and facilitate extensive immigration, especially from Britain, Europe, and Asia.[4] In later years, the problem was mainly the supply of sufficient numbers of skilled workers. Despite some pioneering programs in technical education aimed at upgrading Canadian labour to meet changing economic needs in the early twentieth century, it was not until 1960 that Canada moved decisively (though never completely) away from immigration as the main mechanism for meeting new skill requirements, and introduced much more elaborate vocational training programs in a vastly expanded public education system.[5] Throughout its history the Canadian state has thus taken a major role in establishing and maintaining the capitalist labour market.

Men and women might be coaxed and cajoled into making their labour power available to Canadian employers, but, as newcomers to capitalist social relations, they often resisted the self-discipline expected in a bourgeois social order. Concerned merchants, industrialists, lawyers, clergymen, and others in the upper and middle classes believed that many workers were too often drunk and disorderly, too resistant to the punctuality of clock time, and too ready to avoid the discipline of the capitalist labour market by living off charity or crime. Alongside voluntaristic campaigns to encourage personal moral regeneration such as evangelical Protestantism and temperance, and intellectual "improvement" through mechanics institutes and the like, they promoted a variety of state initiatives, beginning as early as the 1830s and 1840s, designed to reshape the attitudes and behaviour of this first generation of Canadian workers into a form compatible with and supportive of capitalist development – that is, industry, diligence, sobriety, punctuality, and general respect for property. New laws appeared to restrict and even criminalize a wide range of public behaviour, especially leisure activities – from Sunday observance to controls on ball playing in the streets to restrictions on the sale and consumption of alcohol.[6] New professional police forces appeared in many towns to curb inappropriate social and moral behaviour, and police courts became colourful new arenas for punishing recalcitrant workers.[7] In the early twentieth century the state stepped up its moral regulation with such experiments as complete prohibition of liquor and the censorship of movies – creating in the process some of the most straight-laced urban cultures in the western world.[8]

Paralleling these repressive initiatives were efforts to reform rather than simply punish workers who resisted orderly self-discipline. State-funded charitable institutions were reorganized to teach the poor new habits for the new age. The Kingston Penitentiary was opened with a great flourish as a reformatory for criminals, and "lunatic asylums" similarly promised to cure the disruptive behaviour of those designated insane. Perhaps most important, beginning at mid-century, a state-run public school system emerged to begin inculcating the new discipline and "correct" knowledge at an early age.[9] Most of these institutions ran into difficulties as the zeal of the reformers dissolved into the narrow-mindedness of the administrators, and as workers continued to elude or subvert their influence (e.g., by sending their older children out to work rather than to school). The regular influx of new workers from non-industrial backgrounds threw up the same problems for successive generations of social engineers in Canada. Many new programs were launched in the early twentieth century to accomplish essentially the same old goals, notably through a more far-reaching compulsory school system and the growing fields of social work and public health.[10] A wide range of state institutions still works away at restraining the disruptive behaviour of individual workers (absenteeism, alcoholism, drug abuse, and so on) and instilling the appropriate self-restraint. It is, in part, the extension of state activities into these areas of moral regulation that has prompted some writers to talk about state formation as "cultural revolution."[11]

Few of these initiatives touched workers directly on their jobs. It was judges who set the first and most important parameters for workers' behaviour in a capitalist workplace. Through their evolving interpretation of the common law, British jurists and their colonial cousins implemented the concept of the contract of employment between workers and employers ("masters and servants"), which could be enforced in the courts. Central to this notion was the assumption that the two parties to the contract participated equally and freely in forming the contract, just as any two parties might in arranging any other kind of contract. Yet, in practice, employers normally had the upper hand in these deals. Not only could they frequently rely on competition in a well-stocked labour market to keep down wages, but what they got from workers in return for the payment of wages was open-ended service, obedience, and loyalty. Judges readily supported this employer control over his worker with legal sanctions. In Canada West the legislature strengthened the judge's hand with a Masters and Servants Act in 1847 and later with similar legislation governing railway employees. Until 1877, then, a disobedient worker in Canada could be a criminal.[12]

A set of assumptions and structures that insisted on treating workers as individuals in a capitalist labour market ran into difficulties, however, when the workers responded with collective assertions of their own needs and concerns. First, they challenged their employers on the jobs with strikes and other disruptions of production and, occasionally, disturbed public order. By the late nineteenth century, many were joining increasingly well-organized unions to carry out these workplace confrontations. Canadian workers also had political rights in a liberal-democratic state that forced politicians to take heed of their concerns lest their disaffection lead them towards political options that threatened the status quo. These industrial and political challenges thus prompted some creative statecraft to prevent collective resistance from disturbing the central processes of capitalist accumulation in Canada, and to restore workers' consent to their subordination within the social order.

These were pressures felt throughout the western world, but state intervention in the lives of Canadian workers took its characteristic shape from two overriding considerations: the particular structure of the Canadian state itself, and the relative weakness of workers' movements in Canada. The Canadian state developed within the liberal-constitutionalist mould established in Britain by the mid-nineteenth century. Politicians and state officials kept close touch with policy initiatives within the British state and frequently adopted these as models for Canadian legislation. The legal systems were closely integrated through the common law and the final appellate jurisdiction of the Judicial Committee of the Privy Council (until 1950). But state structures and policy evolved according to the specific economic and social conditions of the Canadian context, notably a heavy emphasis on resource export and the proximity of a powerful southern neighbour, the United States. Particularly important for considering the state's policies towards workers were strong regional divisions, which were entrenched in the British North America Act and strengthened by the courts in subsequent decades. Through their constitutional responsibility for "property and civil rights," the provinces got the power to legislate in labour relations (scarcely imagined in 1867) and thus eventually produced an uneven legal patchwork reflecting major regional differences in industrial structure and development and in working-class power. All workers have not been treated the same in Canada.

Within Canadian capitalist society, moreover, workers' movements remained relatively weak within industrial life and thus within the body politic. Workers had difficulty holding together permanent organizations for a variety of reasons. They faced seriously divisive forces. A relatively small working population was strewn across a vast expanse of land in small clusters of industrial activity that varied significantly between regions and shared few common concerns. The contrast between the many craftsmen in the factory towns of Ontario and Quebec and the miners and transportation workers in the West is probably the most striking. Workers in each region often had more regular contact and affinity with their counterparts south of the American border than with other Canadian workers far across the country. Even within their own workplaces and communities workers faced forces that undermined the potential for solidarity and collective action. Transiency was one problem. The widespread seasonality of production and employment, especially in the resource industries, and the frequent booms and busts of the business cycle in most sectors of the Canadian economy prompted many workers to move on, either to another city or region or out of the country altogether. Transiency must also be seen within a context of intense competition for jobs within frequently over-stocked labour markets, particularly as a result of heavy immigration. Furthermore, over the past century and a half, the Canadian working class has gone through a series of major recompositions resulting from the transplantation and wholesale reorganization of production processes and from new recruitment practices. The Canadian state facilitated these transformations through state-sponsored research on science and technology, tax incentives for "modernizing" plants, and so on.[13] These changes dissolved pre-existing patterns of cohesion at the workplace, and required workers to learn new modes of solidarity and community within new mixes of occupation, ethnicity, race, and gender.

Canadian employers added to Canadian distinctiveness by striking a vigorous anti-union posture from the start. In the large and important sectors of the Canadian economy based on resource extraction and semi-processing for export, two groups of employers with considerable political clout – farmers and resource corporations – were determined to keep down labour costs on the products that had to compete internationally. They therefore insisted on heavy immigration to stock the labour market and resisted any concessions to labour. These concerns were shared by those provincial governments, such as that of Nova Scotia, whose tax revenues rested heavily on royalties from resource extraction. At the same time, many manufacturers imitated American models of powerful, large-scale corporations, which used mass-production techniques to help them escape heavy reliance on scarce, high-priced skilled workers, and adopted aggressive union-busting practices.

Under these circumstances, few unions in Canada survived in the century before the Second World War, huge sectors of industry remained untouched by unions, and the first substantial labour parties appeared only at the end of the First World War and died quickly.[14] Even where workers were able to organize, they most often felt outnumbered: the Canadian working class was a minority within the total social structure until after the Second World War, when the number in the previously largest class, the independent commodity producers, began to decline precipitously.[15] As a minority, workers could more easily be ignored within the political process. All these particular features of the Canadian situation produced a set of state policies towards the working class with predominantly repressive and miserly overtones.

Meeting the Challenge of Militancy

Militancy erupted in Canadian workplaces from the earliest days of capitalist employment. In the mid-nineteenth century camp labourers, miners, and other groups of workers often organized themselves informally but effectively in defence of common interests and traditional practices that they believed their employers had violated. The state's only involvement in these frays was repressive: whenever crowd action seemed threatening to social peace, or likely to succeed, troops were sent in to put down the "riot."[16] By mid-century, journeymen craftsmen in the larger towns and cities had also begun to organize, though they created more permanent, and more respectable, craft societies whose tactics were less riotous.[17] While some employers came to terms with these new organizations informally, many were still unwilling to tolerate any collective efforts to effect the terms or conditions of employment. The workers' tactics of striking and picketing brought criminal prosecutions, and the very existence of a union was construed in some circles as an illegal conspiracy in restraint of trade under the common law, although, in Halifax and Toronto at least, no workers were ever successfully prosecuted purely for membership in a union.[18]

It is worth emphasizing that the state's first repressive framework for dealing with organized workers was never completely dismantled. New elements were simply grafted on, although often fitting uncomfortably. Judges continued to uphold the primacy of the contract of employment until the Second World War, when new collective-bargaining legislation was passed that superseded the common law. But the postwar jurisprudence in labour law still tried to keep the key concepts of the individual employment contract alive in the new collective-bargaining regime.[19] Similarly, the armed force of the state was mobilized repeatedly in industrial disputes involving mass pickets and displays of strong working-class consciousness, usually in order to allow employers to maintain production with scab labour. The militia was sent into numerous struggles, especially in the resource, transportation, and construction industries, including the Sydney steel strikes of 1904 and 1923, the coal miners' strikes in Nova Scotia in 1909–11 and on Vancouver Island in 1912–14, and numerous street railway strikes across the country. These troops rolled into their last strike in Stratford, Ontario, in 1933, but by that time the Royal Canadian Mounted Police and provincial police forces had taken over this responsibility, often acting as little more than goon squads in the service of anti-union employers. Sydney steelworkers met these toughs in 1923, as did Lockeport fishery workers in 1939 and the women striking at Fleck Manufacturing in small-town Ontario in 1978.[20] Frequently, it should be noted, the use of armed force backfired, in that wider sympathy for the strikers and anger at the state violence spread through the community and boosted the workers' morale.

Repression also took on a political dimension. It was never uncommon for local police forces to dispense with free speech and break up street-corner meetings of radical workers,[21] and, after socialism became a matter of international politics in 1917, the federal government became much more deeply involved in the battle to prevent the spread of radical ideas in Canada. During the First World War the Borden government developed a network of spies to report on working-class radicals and militants, and after the war consolidated this espionage work in a permanent new branch of the RCMP.[22] During the Winnipeg

General Strike, the federal government also introduced an amendment to the Criminal Code to outlaw radical activities, which allowed for the prosecution of strike leaders in Winnipeg and, in 1931, for the banning of the Communist Party and the jailing of its leaders.[23] While the Mackenzie King government repealed this draconian measure in 1936, it used the War Measures Act five years later during the Second World War to outlaw communist activity and to intern the party's leaders.[24] Also, throughout the period from the First World War to the Cold War, immigration policy was used to expel foreign-born radicals from their working-class communities, where they were seen to be dangerous troublemakers.[25] The racist overtones of conflating "foreigner" with "radical" also served to divide workers and discourage the development of a cohesive class consciousness. The Criminal Code thus remained a potent resource for repressing working-class resistance.

Workers in Canada, therefore, had good reason to see the state as a set of frequently hostile institutions. They were not deterred, however, from coalescing, as early as the 1850s, 1860s, and 1870s into occupationally based unions and cross-occupational councils, federations, and congresses. They developed structures of solidarity, often stretching across the 49th parallel, which allowed them to sustain more effective battles with employers, although most unions had a tenuous and brief existence before the Second World War. In the face of persistent militancy from these organized workers, successive administrations at the federal and provincial levels soon learned that outright repression alone would not work. Smashing workers' organizations might only breed deeper resentment and more serious industrial or political challenges to the existing order. It was necessary to cultivate the consent of organized workers to their subordinate status within capitalist society. The Canadian state therefore set out to find a new framework for tolerating but tightly regulating union activity. Four times in Canadian history the state intervened with a legal restructuring of industrial relations. Each time the new regime so established was a response to workers' demands for better negotiating relationships with their employers, but the state's response never took the precise form labour wanted. Each time the government's intention was to use state regulation to channel the exercise of collective working-class power so as to limit its destructive impact on capital accumulation and the larger social order. Unions were to be placated with some formal recognition and increased responsibility, but the basically repressive intent was evident in the repeated efforts to restrict the use of the strike weapon. While the state took these initiatives in the interests of stabilizing the capitalist system, this was not always with the complete agreement of all capitalists; often, in fact, there was considerable resistance until employers discovered how the new regime could work to their benefit. The Canadian state thus had a semi-autonomous role in alleviating class conflict.

The first explosion of working-class organizing peaked in 1872 when craft unionists in several central Canadian towns and cities launched the nine-hours movement and thus brought the legal ambiguities regarding workers' organizations to a head. The Toronto printers, who took the lead in striking for shorter hours, found their leaders arrested for criminal conspiracy in restraint of trade at the instigation of the bellicose George Brown and his fellow employing printers. Before they came to trial, however, Brown's wily political foe in Ottawa, Sir John A. Macdonald, brought the prosecutions to an end with a new Trade Unions Act. Macdonald's coup was a brilliant political manoeuvre for shoring up working-class support for his party and its emerging policy of stimulating industrialization. Yet there was little substance to this apparently dramatic stroke freeing unions from the criminal taint. The Tories had borrowed an elaborate legislative package enacted in Britain the year before, which was much more restrictive in intent than some latter-day commentators have assumed. Unions were to be tolerated legally only if they formally registered. Moreover, under a Criminal Law Amendment Act passed as part of the package, their activities in striking and picketing were to be restrained just as harshly as they had been under the common law. The few cases heard under this new legislation in the mid-1870s continued the repression that had been imposed over the previous twenty years. In short, legal recognition within this new regime would come at the cost of any effective power to confront employers. This first attempt to place a legal straightjacket on Canadian unions failed, however, when unions refused to register under the Trade Unions Act, and when a persistent labour movement used its limited political clout to win federal laws in 1876–7 permitting non-obstructive picketing and decriminalizing breaches of the contract of employment.[26] Henceforth, the legislatures assumed that workers and their bosses could proceed with "private ordering" of the employment relationship without the criminal sanction. In practice, the courts no longer entertained the notion that unions were criminal conspiracies, but refused to recognize them in common law.

Over the last quarter of the nineteenth century, the Canadian state made no dramatic new departures to curb industrial militancy beyond making available mediation services, which were seldom used. In 1888 Nova Scotia introduced the country's first compulsory arbitration legislation, but it proved unworkable and was quietly abandoned.[27] The explanation for this inactivity undoubtedly lies in the general weakness of organized labour in late-nineteenth-century Canada and the regular failure of so many of the strikes launched in the period (in contrast to the growing web of collective bargaining spreading through several British industries).[28] An overstocked labour market and capitalist intransigence were restraining militancy quite adequately without any help from the state. By the early 1900s, however, industrial conflict was escalating quickly in many parts of the country, most alarmingly on the railways and in mining communities that were closely tied to the government's economic development plans. The Canadian judiciary became much more active in penalizing militant strike activity in civil actions under common law, especially in the wake of the Taff Vale decision in Britain, which allowed employers to sue unions for damages and encouraged similar actions in Canadian courts. British unionists got legislative relief from this legal constraint in 1906, when the new Labour Party exerted its increased parliamentary pressure on the Liberals, but, in the absence of any comparable labour representation, no Canadian provincial legislature made a similar move in this period except in British Columbia, where a socialist MLA with the balance of power managed to push a measure through the house in 1902.[29]

The potential dissonance between state institutions became more evident when the federal government passed the federal Conciliation Act in 1900 and thereby declared, in contrast to the courts' union-busting animus, a willingness to use mediation to promote industrial peace. In fact, implicitly the federal government was announcing its predominance over the provinces in dealing with industrial conflict (though not other matters of labour policy) in the national interest – a role that would last for half a century with only a minor interruption in the mid-1920s. The architect of what was to become the second major state initiative into containing workers' industrial power was the young deputy minister of labour (and chief conciliator under the 1900 legislation), William Lyon Mackenzie King. Building on the already emerging practice of the federal government, King's solution to the "labour problem" took the form of compulsory conciliation. This was embodied in special legislation for railway workers in 1903, and then in the Industrial Disputes Investigation Act of 1907, which remained the most important Canadian legislation governing industrial conflict until 1944.

The law required workers and employers in resource, transportation, and utilities industries to postpone strikes or lockouts until a three-person board of conciliation had heard the issues, deliberated, and issued a report, and until an appropriate "cooling-out" period had allowed the two sides to consider the report and to feel the weight of public opinion. Jumping the gun could make a party liable to criminal prosecution, though the government virtually never used that penalty. Despite the rhetoric about the restraining power of public disapproval, in practice the boards were expected to work more quietly to mediate a settlement of the dispute without issuing a report – indeed, often by threatening to expose the parties' positions to public scrutiny if they did not settle. The advantage of this new set of procedures was clearly that production would continue without disruption while some settlement was attempted. Unfortunately, many workers found that the delays could undermine the momentum that new unions built up and that employers were still free to dismiss union leaders and in various ways prepare for a strike. During the First World War, the act was extended to cover all munitions workers and eventually any unionized workforce. Paradoxically, many union leaders came to support this compulsory conciliation law by the end of the war for its implicit support of recognition from employers. In 1925 the Industrial Disputes Investigation Act was successfully challenged in the Judicial Committee of the Privy Council as beyond the federal government's constitutional powers, but most provinces soon enacted legislation allowing the law to be extended into their jurisdiction. At the outbreak of the Second World War all war-related industries once again came under the act.[30]

The third major state initiative designed to contain collective working-class activity arose out of the dramatic wave of union organizing and militant strikes that peaked in 1943 and that threatened to overflow into support for the social-democratic Cooperative Commonwealth Federation. Early in 1944 the Mackenzie King government passed an order-in-council, PC 1003, which introduced a set of procedures for recognizing union representatives and guaranteeing that employers would have to sit down with them at a bargaining table. Like some parallel initiatives at the provincial level in the same period, this emergency legislation borrowed several of its essential provisions from the Wagner Act passed in the United States in 1935, especially the creation of a labour relations board to oversee union representatives' certification and to monitor "unfair labour practices," but it never formally recognized unions and built in numerous constraints on aggressive union organizing techniques. The act also incorporated the key concepts and practices of the Industrial Disputes Investigation Act, including the compulsory conciliation procedures. It took a huge wave of successful strikes immediately after the war to convince state officials to make the legislation a permanent feature of postwar Canadian industrial relations, this time, however, decentralized to the provinces.

The new structures assumed that labour and capital would continue to work out most of their differences and the contents of their agreements on their own – the state guaranteed no specific outcome. Backed by a federal government promise to stimulate a full-employment economy, organized workers were expected to be able to wrench significant concessions from their corporate employers. But the state had tied unions' hands in numerous ways. Most important was the severe restriction on the right to strike. Not only did workers have to wait out the familiar "cooling-off" period during and after conciliation before they could strike, but they were also forbidden to strike for union recognition or during the lifetime of a collective agreement, when disputes were to be settled by a grievance-arbitration system. The traditional forms of direct action that workers had used spontaneously to resist management pressure on the job were now to be replaced by slower, more impersonal, more bureaucratic procedures that were most often controlled by lawyers and wrapped in a mystifying new legal language. Sympathy strikes were now mostly impossible, since workers' contracts bound them to stay on the job, and, as employers and labour relations boards soon insisted on single-plant bargaining units, workers' collective power was divided into tiny, isolated fragments across the country. The Winnipeg General Strike could never again happen legally. And there was now less chance of the rapid leftward politicization that so often resulted from major strike waves, when workers had found common cause in shared and parallel struggles.[31]

This new regime of tightly structured industrial legality took deep root in the mass-production, resource, and transportation industries, and between 1965 and 1975 was extended to public-sector workers, including Nova Scotia provincial government employees.[32] Cracks had begun to appear by that point, however, as new generations of workers facing tougher management, disruptive technological change, and rapid retail price inflation found the system too cumbersome and insensitive to their concerns. A massive explosion of militancy across the country in the decade after 1965, sometimes in defiance of union officials and generally spearheaded by newly unionized public-sector workers, reached unprecedented proportions that were allegedly surpassed internationally only by Italy.[33] In 1975 the Canadian state made its fourth major structural effort to constrain workers' collective power. The wage control program introduced that year by the federal government and supported by all the provinces, along with a simultaneous turn to tight-money monetarist policies, inaugurated a new era of curbing working-class incomes and constraining workers' collective power. Federal and provincial governments also undermined workers' bargaining strength by deliberately stimulating unemployment and weakening the "safety net" of social security programs. They disrupted and limited collective bargaining with increasingly frequent use of back-to-work legislation and other controls on public-sector unions. Following the example of Nova Scotia's so-called Michelin Bill, which undercut union organizing drives in the province's new tire plants, some provinces made moves in the 1980s to weaken permanently unions' legal room to manoeuvre. Workers have not found, in general, that their organizations were attacked and destroyed on the model of American union-busting, but that their unions have nevertheless been severely weakened in the Canadian industrial relations system.[34]

In Canadian history, also, state regulation rather than repression of unions has been a policy applied only to the most organized and most vocal, excluding large groups of workers who were less well organized, who were more vulnerable to employer retaliation, or who were employed in areas considered too sensitive. Until late in the twentieth century, domestic servants and farm labourers were explicitly exempted from collective-bargaining legislation in most jurisdictions in deference to upper-class householders and farmers. These workers consequently remained enmeshed in private, patriarchal work relations with little or no recourse to state assistance. Fishermen were another group of vulnerable workers facing legal restraints. In Nova Scotia, once they had begun to organize collectively to resist their abjectly dependent status as producers and wage-earners, the courts excluded them from the collective-bargaining regime in 1947 on the grounds that they were "co-adventurers" with the corporations controlling the fishing industry and therefore not employees under collective-bargaining legislation.[35] And employees of the federal and provincial governments were consistently denied collective-bargaining rights until the 1960s and 1970s, when new legislation generally still limited their right to strike or to negotiate over such important issues as job classifications or pensions.

Since the mid-1970s, moreover, these workers have had even those limited rights drastically reduced.

To win the widest possible support for new forms of labour regulation, the state began in the early twentieth century to justify its intervention with some definition of the "public interest" separate from the interests of the specific workers involved. Mackenzie King was an early ideological architect of a distinct public interest in labour relations, in practice in the operations of the Industrial Disputes Investigations Act, and in long-winded theory in his *Industry and Humanity*.[36] By the 1970s and 1980s the state's public-interest rhetoric had turned nastier, describing unionized workers as greedy, selfish, and threatening to the economic well-being of all Canadians. The highly fragmented structures of postwar collective bargaining that isolated the struggles of individual groups of workers and inhibited sympathetic actions of solidarity made it harder for workers to link their immediate interests with those of a larger public (some public-sector workers have been struggling to make these connections in recent years, most notably the beleaguered postal workers).[37]

At the same time, the Canadian state has regularly reached out to managers and union leaders to deepen their commitment to industrial peace. During the twentieth century the Canadian state added to its new forms of regulation some programs to encourage new managerial methods aimed at promoting harmony between workers and bosses. Before the First World War, Mackenzie King's Department of Labour publication the *Labour Gazette* broadcast the early, scattered experiments in company-welfare programs for workers, and after the war that department actively promoted the expansion of such management "with a human face." Department officials also pushed another King solution to labour problems, developed for the Rockefeller interests in the United States – the industrial council of employee and employer representatives in one workplace, which was to discuss issues without the conflictual relations brought by unions. Half a century later, federal and provincial governments began to promote a program with a similar goal, most often known as "Quality of Working Life," which encouraged worker participation in low-level decision-making on the shop floor. New provincial and federal legislation introduced in the 1970s and 1980s also sought to promote the settlement of disputes regarding occupational health and safety in committees outside the framework of collective bargaining. In practice, of course, these programs were exercises in convincing workers to reduce or abandon their own class interests in the face of their employers' need for more productivity and profitability. Relative to other approaches to working-class militancy, however, these state initiatives to encourage workplace harmony had an extremely limited impact.[38]

Ultimately more important were the Canadian state's efforts to cultivate the support of apparently trustworthy, responsible labour leaders who seemed to share a common interest in industrial peace. Almost invariably these have been the bureaucrats of the labour movement – full-time officials and staff concerned about the respectability and political and financial stability of their organizations. Most often these men (and more recently women) have also been politically cautious and resistant to any radicalism and militancy that emerged within their unions. In Nova Scotia the coal miners' unions produced a series of these men – Robert Drummond in the 1890s, John Moffat in the 1910s, Silby Barrett from the 1920s to the 1940s.[39] The headquarters of international unions and the executive offices of the Trades and Labour Congress of Canada were often fertile breeding ground for such unionists. They usually had a clear enough sense of their independent union interests that they seldom became complete dupes of politicians or civil servants, but they were generally willing to cooperate in any new state framework that guaranteed them and their organizations recognition and some semblance of power. Since the Second World War many of these union leaders have been social democrats who have looked longingly at the active role of their counterparts under social-democratic administrations in western Europe.

Since the turn of the twentieth century, federal and provincial departments of labour have most often been the agencies for building these relationships with reliable union bureaucrats. Mackenzie King was among the first to cultivate union leaders when he strung together his network of *Labour Gazette* correspondents across the country after the creation of the federal Department of Labour in 1900. Since King's day as well, state officials have courted the leaders of "legitimate" unions and excluded from their embrace the heads of more radical or militant organizations. As secretary of a 1903 royal commission on industrial conflict in British Columbia, King penned the first denunciation of irresponsible radicalism, making charges that would be repeated in ever more vigorous forms against the One Big Union and Communist-led unions from the 1920s to the 1950s.[40] Yet, despite the flirtations with individual union bureaucrats, formal experiments in corporatist integration of labour leaders were rare in Canadian history, probably because so few Canadian capitalists would sit down with unionists and because unions were so comparatively weak before the Second World War. After refusing to involve union leaders in any significant wartime administrative bodies, Robert Borden's government made a stab at a corporatist solution to labour unrest in 1919 when it convened a large National Industrial Conference of labour, employer and "public" representatives, intended to advise the government on labour policy and carefully chosen to exclude any "reds." It resolved nothing and was never reconvened.[41]

For the next half-century, labour leaders continued to complain that they were excluded from all significant advisory and administrative boards beyond those narrowly focussed on such specific labour matters as unemployment insurance. In 1962 the Nova Scotia government gestured in a corporatist direction when it began to respond to the advice of the privately sponsored Joint Labour-Management Study Committee.[42] Thirteen years later, federal Labour Minister John Munroe sponsored a short-lived tripartite Canadian Labour Relations Council in 1975 seeking solutions to some of the major problems that had cropped up in the industrial relations system. But the next year, when the Canadian Labour Congress leadership proposed European-style tripartite bodies to engage in social and economic planning, federal officials gently deflected such ideas into new discussions of some more limited kind of corporatism, which soon involved the Business Council on National Issues. The CLC and the Business Council eventually launched the bipartite National Labour Market and Productivity Centre in 1984 with federal government support. In the same period, labour leaders joined businessmen on several departmental committees for long-range economic forecasting. However, as a major state solution to labour-relations problems, corporatism never really got off the ground in the 1970s and 1980s. Constitutional power over industrial relations is too spread out through the provinces for national structures to have any real impact. Moreover, neither capital nor labour had a central organization with the mandate to carry out the negotiations that would be necessary to make such a system work. In any case, most capitalists seemed more interested in a get-tough approach to organized labour, rather than in polite dialogue with union bureaucrats.[43] Federal officials nonetheless have never underestimated the importance of seeking a friendly rapport with labour leaders who were uncomfortable with militancy and who craved some political recognition for themselves and their organizations.

Their commitment to the legitimacy of the social order could help to discipline their membership.

Overall, then, the Canadian state's response to collective working-class resistance in the workplace has been repressive regulation. Union organizing and striking were consistently hampered by court and military repression until they appeared to threaten serious disruption of production processes, public order, or workers' faith in the capitalist system in general. At the first seriously menacing point, in the early 1900s, the federal government began to put together a subtler alternative that tried to promote industrial peace through interventionist mediation. Federal labour officials subsequently played a key role in industrial relations through the first half of the twentieth century, often in the face of continuing belligerence from courts and provincial administrations (witness Mackenzie King's discomfort at the heavy-handed use of militia and police force in Sydney in 1923, which prompted him to set up a royal commission to investigate). The legal recognition that the federal government granted to unionized workers was nonetheless always highly restrictive in that it tightly constrained both the use of the strike weapon and the scope for broadening workers' struggles beyond a particular workplace. These forms of regulation were introduced most often when workplace militancy and the overall labour movement seemed unusually powerful, notably in 1907 and 1944, but when unions lacked sufficient real strength to press successfully for legislation more favourable to the workers' interests. Other state initiatives to encourage personnel management policies or corporatist integration of union bureaucrats were too sporadic and limited in their impact to change the fundamentally repressive pattern of state action against working-class organization and workplace struggles in Canada.

The Politics of Labour

One of the ironies of a liberal-democratic capitalist society is that workers have more egalitarian rights in the political than the economic sphere. Of course, unlike their counterparts in the United States, Canadian male workers did not enjoy full electoral rights at the dawn of industrial capitalism in the mid-nineteenth century. It would take steady pressure to win the right to vote and hold office for all white men (generally by the turn of the century), women (during and after the First World War, though not until 1940 in Quebec), and Asians (in the late 1940s in British Columbia).[44] Nor, given the defeat of the 1837–8 insurrections, could workers appeal to any specific revolutionary traditions within Canada such as existed in several European countries and in the United States to guarantee the "rights of man." However, as "free-born Englishmen," Anglo-Canadian workers had some idea that they had a right to influence state policy (even if most often they cynically denied that their voice had any impact and often did not bother to vote – the most industrialized parts of the country have seen abysmally low voter turnouts at several points in the twentieth century).[45]

Politicians who controlled the elected branches of the state had to pay at least some attention to placating working-class voters, lest they vote for the opposition or, worse yet, form a new party of their own with an anti-capitalist ideology and program. The latter possibility was generally strongest when the size, power, and anger of the labour movement was on the rise.[46] Typically in such circumstances, a royal commission or special investigation was set in motion to indicate sympathy without definite commitment. Ultimately, modest reforms became an alternative to both the untrammelled capitalist labour market and the bogey of socialism.[47] Legislation intended to ameliorate the working and living conditions of workers and their families was introduced in spurts that corresponded to upsurges of labour organizing and militancy – the 1880s, the 1910s, the 1940s, and the mid-1960s through mid-1970s. The Tories made a few sympathetic gestures in the 1870s,[48] but for several decades, it was mainly Liberal administrations that took the reform initiative. In fact, the Liberals' success in placating labour leaders in Nova Scotia, Quebec, and the Prairies in the early twentieth century helped to delay the emergence of a substantial labour party in most of these regions until the First World War, and enabled them to tug back the independent-minded Liberal-Labour types (the "Lib Labbers"). Seldom could direct representatives of the labour movement or labour parties carry their own legislative program through a Canadian legislature. Before the Second World War, Canadian labour parties were directly involved in provincial governments only in Ontario from 1919 to 1923 and, marginally, in Alberta from 1921 to 1935. The postwar record was slightly better but still limited: the CCF's breakthrough into government in Saskatchewan in 1944 was not matched until 1969 in Manitoba and 1971 in British Columbia.[49] Small wonder, then, that Canada's "social wage" has remained much more limited than that in most other advanced capitalist countries (excepting the United States and Japan) and that postwar federal governments preferred the indirect approach of the Keynesian full-employment economy to a European-style welfare state.

The measures introduced by all these administrations covered many aspects of workers' lives, especially occupational health and safety, minimum wages, shorter hours and paid holidays, and other employment standards, as well as such income-security measures as mothers' allowances, unemployment insurance, pensions, health insurance, and so on. Most of it differed from the regulatory measures discussed above in that it attempted to intervene in the contract of employment to limit an employer's freedom of action, either by forbidding certain employment practices or by providing alternative forms of income to that available purely through wages. For the most part, however, such legislation did not constrain capital nearly as much as state regulation–bound labour.

In each case, labour was usually first to put such reform issues on the political agenda. Without much working-class representation in the legislatures, however, the eventual legislation often reflected some departure from labour's stated goals. Almost invariably some substantial body of capitalists opposed the measures, and politicians were wary about upsetting business sentiment too profoundly. But key business leaders did occasionally recognize that more economic and social stability might well result from laws easing workers' conditions. Once workers were organized and mobilized successfully enough to be taken seriously, two forces generally shaped the outcome of demands for this kind of legislation: the convergence of diverse social interests on a particular demand, and the ideology of the labour movement itself.

Other groups often shared an interest in a particular reform for quite different reasons. Labour's demands were only part of the chorus of concern about the impact of rapid industrialization and urbanization. For example, upper- and middle-class activists, especially the women, were particularly anxious to protect idealized notions of fragile femininity and precious childhood that seemed to be threatened in the new factories and sweatshops. They found common cause with labour leaders, who operated on their own patriarchal views of women and children (and fears about the erosion of their own skills), but were also concerned about the degradation and exploitation of labour evident in the patterns of women's employment. The factory acts of the 1880s and the minimum-wage legislation of the early 1920s both reflected this combination of interests.[50] In a similar way, the unemployment insurance scheme that emerged in 1941 bore the stamp not only of labour demands, but also of bankers' and politicians' concerns about the solvency of municipal governments required to dole out relief during the depressions.[51]

Once the legislative initiative was underway, the intervention of capitalist lobbyists could be crucial in limiting the scope of reform, to prevent it from dramatically threatening capital-accumulation processes. Through such pressure the factory acts were tamed to prevent officious inspectors from disrupting production. The Canadian Manufacturers' Association seems to have bungled similar attempts to shape Ontario's workers' compensation legislation just before the First World War, but in Nova Scotia the corporate fish-packers managed to get their workers out from under the protection of such legislation in 1928.[52] Also, the actual administration of the acts, which generally lay beyond any direct democratic control, could alter the effect of a law from the original intention. The reluctance of factory inspectors to prosecute employers for violating the factory acts and the turn-of-the-century violations of the Alien Labour Act were glaring examples.[53] Similarly, any legislation that involved payments to workers – workers' compensation, old-age pensions, unemployment insurance, and so on – was marked by the suspicions of working-class "pauperism" that had dominated charity and social-welfare administration since the early nineteenth century. As a result, economic assistance to workers often came wrapped in means tests and other demeaning red tape and was invariably kept well below normal earnings from wages. Industrial discipline (the "work ethic"), based on the threat of poverty, was not to be undermined by these programs. The treatment of the working-class victims of the 1917 Halifax explosion provides a good example of the suspicions workers had to confront when they applied for relief.[54]

The residue that accumulated on the statute books from these initiatives was particularly constraining for women workers. Only in the 1970s did women begin to challenge the assumption built into most legislation that men should earn a "family wage" on which the women, relegated to the domestic sphere, should be dependent. Much of the early labour legislation was primarily concerned with restricting the employment of women, setting special hours and other working conditions for them. The first minimum-wage boards similarly reinforced women's limited labour-force participation by pegging female wages far below those of men. The limited mothers' allowances introduced in the 1920s and the "baby bonus" in the 1940s were income supplements paid only for mothering responsibilities. Other welfare schemes were structured on the assumption of the family wage.

It must be said, however, that the ultimate shape of this labour legislation also reflected what the labour movement expected from the state. Perhaps the most important difference between Canadian and many continental European unions in the nineteenth century was that, like their British and American counterparts, they won some limited freedom to operate in capitalist society without the sponsorship of a socialist party. Labour leaders thus came to believe that amelioration of working-class life was possible through the slow and fragmented processes of union organizing (especially craft unions) and negotiations with employers – in short, collective self-help. In effect, they promoted a form of working-class liberalism that maintained a rigid separation of state and civil society. The American Federation of Labor, to which so many Canadian craft unionists hitched their stars at the turn of the twentieth century, was led by men committed to winning labour's battles solely through industrial action without state intervention. The Catholic labour movement that had taken shape in Quebec by the end of the First World War was similarly dedicated to voluntarism, rather than state action. In the early twentieth century, many Canadian craft unionists were more ambivalent. It was their frustrations with the "unfair" lopsidedness of the state's support for capital, especially in the courts, that pushed these men into an independent political stance, first on the edge of the Liberal Party (as "Lib-Labbers"), and then in Independent Labour Parties. These labourists were most often craft unionists who urged democratization of government (through an unrestricted franchise, proportional representation, abolition of the Senate, and so on), but they remained slightly suspicious of the state. They still put more faith in free association of workers, and fair, voluntary agreements with capitalists within the general rule of law, than they did in any fundamental transformation of capitalist social and economic structures. Their calls for state intervention were generally limited to demands for legislation to curb monopolies and other sources of ill-deserved and privileged power, to protect voluntary union activity, and to support those incapable of supporting themselves – women and children, the sick and aged, the unemployed.[55] The heyday of labourism was over by the 1920s, and Canadian craft unionists henceforth followed the preference of the AFL and the Catholic unions for keeping a distance from politics.

There has seldom been complete ideological unanimity in the House of Labour. Two other political tendencies, Marxism and social democracy, attempted to win over Canadian unionists. Compared to labourism, both were advocates of a larger social vision and of a more active role for the state in working-class liberation. In contrast to the labourists (whom they regularly denounced), the early Marxists' analysis of workers' problems brought them to the conclusion that capitalism had to be replaced with some version of a socialist society controlled and managed by workers themselves. These radicals attempted to convince their fellow unionists that politics mattered much more than narrow union interests, and that the state could be an effective instrument for ending workers' exploitation and oppression by seizing control of the means of production, distribution, and exchange. Before the First World War, the Marxists in the Canadian labour movement were members of small socialist parties, who found their strongest support in coal mining towns, where a handful of them were elected to seats in the British Columbia and Alberta legislatures. Elsewhere their influence was minimal.[56] For a brief period at the end of the First World War these radicals found much wider audiences within the general working-class revolt of the period, notably in the One Big Union, and helped to sharpen the vision of workers' movements.[57] For the next forty years, it was the Communists who carried the banner of Marxism in the labour movement under the inspiration of the Soviet Union and the always-shifting Bolshevik road to social transformation. They had a significant, though fluctuating following, through their leadership of the Workers' Unity League in the early 1930s, and later some of the CIO unions, but the repression of the Cold War era pushed them to the margins of the labour movement.[58] Today their political heirs can be found within the minority opposition caucuses in the provincial federations and the Canadian Labour Congress.

The social democrats first emerged as a distinct political tendency in the 1920s and in 1933 coalesced into the Cooperative Commonwealth Federation. They were slower to win a following in the labour movement, but by the 1940s were engaged in a head-to-head confrontation with the Communists for control of the new industrial union movement in Canada. By the early 1950s they had manoeuvred themselves into command of most of the large new labour organizations in the country. In the CCF, social-democratic labour leaders were junior partners in a formal alliance with radicalized professionals, other middle-class Canadians, and, in the West, farmers. Initially their program shared with the Communists a moral rejection of capitalism and projected a stirring vision of an alternative society based on considerable state ownership, centralized planning, and extensive social-security programs. Their soaring popularity during the Second World War that so frightened Mackenzie King was based on their calls for an extensive "welfare state" to take the insecurity out of workers' lives. By the time of the creation of the New Democratic Party in 1961, the social democrats had jettisoned nationalization and extensive state planning in favour of Keynesian regulation of the economy and concentrated on a package of reforms for making capitalism more humane.[59] The dominance of social-democratic politics in the postwar labour movement and the partial implementation of a social-democratic program (often by the Liberals) nonetheless created an expectation of "social rights" to economic security guaranteed by the state that went beyond the concepts of "liberty, equality, and fraternity" carried forward from the eighteenth-century revolutions by the old labourists. The modern labour movement was thus loud in its defence of the social programs that late-twentieth-century Canadian governments seemed so eager to slash.

Yet Canadian unionists never lost the old suspicion of the state. Social-democratic politicians envisioned major social change proceeding only through elections and parliamentary acts, and major social policy being set by elites of enlightened experts. Workers would benefit from this kind of society, but only as passive recipients. The politicians recognized workers' right to organize and bargain collectively, but assumed that these rights would be subordinated to centrally planned incomes policies (all three NDP governments supported wage controls in the mid-1970s). That statist perspective inevitably created tensions with the labour leadership, which remained suspicious of too much state intervention in industrial relations, preferring voluntarism and free association for both unions and private enterprise corporations (the unions participating in the New Democratic Party have repeatedly used their power to curb left-wing enthusiasm for public ownership). They are also still prepared to use more direct action in the form of strikes than social-democratic politicians are normally comfortable with; hence the often chilly relations between provincial labour movements in Manitoba, Saskatchewan, and British Columbia and their New Democratic governments in the 1970s. More importantly, the NDP's failure to elect a national government, or a provincial government in some provinces, left the labour movement little choice but to continue its emphasis on industrial action (or, in a few cases, tripartism).

The Canadian labour movement also never abandoned its patriarchal assumptions about women workers. It was probably the first social group to raise the demand of women's right to vote and run for office, but male workers collaborated in the creation of protective legislation for women and the defence of the family wage. Only in the 1970s and

1980s did women workers begin to break down some of these prejudices among their fellow unionists.

The politics of labour, then, has been a mixed bag. Not only has labour seldom been close enough to state power to carry out its own agenda and thus has seen its concerns watered down and twisted in unanticipated ways, but the mainstream Canadian labour movement has never completely abandoned the labourist faith in voluntarist relationships outside the state as the most appropriate way to improve workers' conditions. Labour still harbours some uneasiness about too much state intervention. Limitations in the scope of the labour legislation that entered the state books reflected at least in part labour's limited focus on freedom of association for workers' organizations and on the economic well-being of working-class families attacked by crises with which they were unable to cope on their own. More radical alternatives that envisioned aggressive state action to transform Canadian society into a workers' republic were jettisoned in the Red Scares that followed each world war. The defeat of radicalism within the labour movement was reinforced by state repression and by the creation of tightly controlled, fragmented collective-bargaining structures, which limited the political solidarity that could grow out of industrial struggles. Labour's ideological caution developed in a position of beleaguered weakness, as capital used its considerable power to undermine a series of labour movements and to blunt their political achievements, and as the state quite effectively constrained the exercise of collective working-class power in industrial life.

In the end, then, Canadian workers have most often encountered the state as a check or deterrent on their individual and collective behaviour. It was certainly not neutral in the fundamental conflicts that erupted in industrial capitalist society. The many branches of the Canadian state have not always marched in lock-step in their approach to the "labour problem" – the courts and the legislatures have often followed their own tunes, and the various provincial administrations have dallied and straggled according to their own rhythms. But, on balance, the institutions of the Canadian state saw the "labour problem" as one of order, not equity or justice. The overriding concern was always the efficient functioning of capitalist industry in Canada, especially its labour markets and labour processes. Workers' ability to organize collectively and challenge the terms of their subordination in Canadian capitalist society was consistently restricted by state action, and consequently their ability to mobilize political movements to use the state for their own interests was severely limited. Where workers organized they were carefully regulated to avoid serious disruptions; otherwise they were left to work out the best deals they could through uncertain private negotiations with their employers. The only state programs intended to improve workers' living and working conditions directly were those introduced under pressure from labour and its occasional allies, and, owing to labour's industrial and political weakness and ideological ambivalence, those remained incomplete and comparatively parsimonious. The state thus remained more a stern disciplinarian than a kindly paternalist for the Canadian working class.

To suggest that workers found the state in Canada fundamentally constraining is not to suggest that those workers have been consistently on the verge of open revolt, held in check only by coercion. The existence of repressive mechanisms, the historical memory of their use, and the thorough extinction of alternative possibilities can limit expectations, whether through fear or fatalism; but repression alone is never very successful. Coercion, to be most effective, must interact with positive reassurances of good intentions from politicians and others that are aimed at making workers feel comfortable with their place in the social order (though in Canada the payoff for workers' compliance has been a lower "social wage" than in most industrialized countries). Workers' consent also reflects the successful inculcation of normative values, beliefs, and habits of deference by the schools, the mass media, and other agencies. The unequal divisions of power and wealth in capitalist society and the appropriately limited expectations for workers come to seem natural and inevitable. The particular blend of coercion and consent that emerged in Canadian state practice has thus helped to give the working class its own "Canadian identity."

Notes

1 See Leo Panitch, "The Role and Nature of the Canadian State," in Panitch, ed., *The Canadian State: Political Economy and Political Power* (Toronto: University of Toronto Press 1977), 3–77; Paul Craven, *"An Impartial Umpire": Industrial Relations and the Canadian State, 1900–1911* (Toronto: University of Toronto Press 1980), 157–207; and, for a review of much of the debate over theories of the state, Bob Jessop, *The Capitalist State* (Oxford: Oxford University Press 1982).

2 A full discussion of the state and the Canadian working class would have to address the impact of the unpaid domestic work carried out by women,

especially the work of reproduction, including state intervention through schooling, public health, child welfare work, medical regulation, and much more beyond the scope of this paper.

3 Leo A. Johnson, "Land Policy, Population Growth, and Social Structure in the Home District, 1793–1851," in J.K. Johnson, ed., *Historical Essays on Upper Canada* (Toronto: McClelland and Stewart 1975), 32–57; Gary Teeple, "Land, Labour, and Capital in Pre-Confederation Canada," in Teeple, ed., *Capitalism and the National Question in Canada* (Toronto: University of Toronto Press 1972), 43–66. Note that encouraging the development of a "free" labour market did not prevent the continuation of "unfree" indentured labour where labour shortages required it, notably among young farm workers and Chinese labour in British Columbia. See Joy Parr, *Labouring Children: British Immigrant Apprentices to Canada, 1869–1924* (London: Croom Helm 1980); Edgar Wickberg, ed., *From China to Canada: A History of the Chinese Communities in Canada* (Toronto: McClelland and Stewart, 1982).

4 Norman MacDonald, *Canada: Immigration and Colonization, 1841–1903* (Toronto: Macmillan 1966); Donald Avery, *"Dangerous Foreigners": European Immigrant Workers and Labour Radicalism in Canada, 1896–1932* (Toronto: McClelland and Stewart 1979); Freda Hawkins, *Canada and Immigration: Public Policy and Public Concern* (Montreal and Kingston: McGill-Queen's University Press 1972).

5 Robert Miles Stamp, "The Campaign for Technical Education in Ontario, 1876–1914" (PhD dissertation, University of Toronto 1970); and *The Schools of Ontario, 1876–1976* (Toronto: University of Toronto Press 1982); Donald MacLeod, "Practicality Ascendant: The Origins and Establishment of Technical Education in Nova Scotia," *Acadiensis* 15, no. 2 (Spring 1986), 53–92.

6 J.R. Burnet, "The Urban Community and Changing Moral Standards," in Michiel Horn and Ronald Sabourin, eds., *Studies in Canadian Social History* (Toronto: McClelland and Stewart 1974), 298–325; Christopher Armstrong and H.V. Nelles, *The Revenge of the Methodist Bicycle Company: Sunday Streetcars and Municipal Reform in Toronto, 1888–1897* (Toronto: Peter Martin Associates 1977).

7 Nicholas Rogers, "Serving Toronto the Good: The Development of the City Police Force, 1834–84," in Victor Russell, ed., *Forging a Consensus: Historical Essays on Toronto* (Toronto: University of Toronto Press 1984), 116–40; Paul Craven, "Law and Ideology: The Toronto Police Court, 1850–80," in David Flaherty, ed., *Essays in the History of Canadian Law, Volume 2* (Toronto: University of Toronto Press 1982), 248–65; Allan Greer, "The Birth of the Police in Canada" (paper presented to the interdisciplinary workshop "Social Change and State Formation in British North America, 1830–1870," 1989).

8 E.R. Forbes, "Prohibition and the Social Gospel in Nova Scotia," in Samuel D. Clark et al., *Prophecy and Protest: Social Movements in Twentieth-Century Canada* (Toronto: Gage Educational Publishing 1975), 62–86; Gerald A. Hallowell, *Prohibition in Ontario, 1919–1923* (Ottawa: Ontario Historical Society 1972); Malcolm Dean, *Censored! Only in Canada: The History of Film Censorship – The Scandal Off the Screen* (Toronto: Virgo Press 1981).

9 Judith Fingard, "The Relief of the Unemployed Poor in Saint John, Halifax, and St. John's, 1815–1860," in P.A. Buckner and David Frank, eds., *Atlantic Canada before Confederation: The Acadiensis Reader, Volume One* (Fredericton: Acadiensis Press 1985), 190–211; Dan Francis, "The Development of the Lunatic Asylum in the Maritime Provinces," ibid., 245–60; Richard B. Splane, *Social Welfare in Ontario, 1791–1893* (Toronto: University of Toronto Press, 1965); Susan E. Houston and Alison Prentice, *Schooling and Scholars in Nineteenth-Century Ontario* (Toronto: University of Toronto Press 1988); Bruce Curtis, *Building the Educational State: Canada West, 1836–1871* (London, ON: Althouse Press 1988).

10 See, for example, Neil Sutherland, *Children in English-Canadian Society: Framing the Twentieth-Century Consensus* (Toronto: University of Toronto Press 1976).

11 Philip Corrigan and Derek Sayer, *The Great Arch: English State Formation as Cultural Revolution* (Oxford: Blackwell 1985); Curtis, *Building the Educational State.*

12 Harry J. Glasbeek, "The Contract of Employment at Common Law," in John Anderson and Morley Gunderson, eds., *Union-Management Relations in Canada* (Don Mills: Addison-Wesley 1982), 47–77; Paul Craven, "The Law of Master and Servant in Mid-Nineteenth Century Ontario," in David H. Flaherty, ed., *Essays in the History of Canadian Law: Volume 1* (Toronto: University of Toronto Press 1981), 173–211; Paul Craven and Tom Traves, "Dimensions of Paternalism: Discipline and Culture in Canadian Railway Operations in the 1850s," in Heron and Storey, eds., *On the Job*, 49–52.

13 I have discussed these factors at greater length elsewhere: see "On the Job in Canada" (co-authored with Robert Storey), in Heron and Storey, eds., *On the Job*, 3–46; "Labourism and the Canadian Working Class," *L/LT* 13 (Spring 1984), 45–76; *Working in Steel: The Early Years in Canada, 1883–1935* (Toronto: McClelland and Stewart 1988); "The Second Industrial Revolution in Canada, 1890–1930," in Deian Hopkin and Gregory S. Kealey, eds., *Class, Community, and the Labour Movement in Canada and Wales, 1890–1930* (Aberystwyth and St John's: Llafur and the Committee on Canadian Labour History 1989); "The Great War and Nova Scotia Steelworkers," *Acadiensis* 16, no. 2 (Spring 1987), 3–34.

14 For a brief sketch of the fortunes of Canadian unions, see Craig Heron, *The Canadian Labour Movement: A Short History* (Toronto: James Lorimer 1989).
15 Leo A. Johnson, "The Development of Class in Canada in the Twentieth Century," in Teeple, ed., *Capitalism and the National Question*, 141–84.
16 Ruth Bleasdale, "Class Conflict on the Canals of Upper Canada in the 1840s," *L/LT* 7 (Spring 1981), 9–39; C.B. Fergusson, *The Labour Movement in Nova Scotia before Confederation* (Halifax: Public Archives of Nova Scotia 1964), 19–21; James M. Cameron, *The Pictonian Colliers* (Halifax: Nova Scotia Museum 1964), 141–3; K.G. Pryke, "Labour and Politics: Nova Scotia at Confederation," *HS/SH* 6 (November 1970), 33–5; Bryan D. Palmer, "Labour Protest and Organization in Nineteenth-Century Canada, 1820–1890," *L/LT* 20 (Fall 1987), 62–7.
17 Eugene Forsey, *Trade Unions in Canada, 1812–1902* (Toronto: University of Toronto Press 1982).
18 Pryke, "Labour and Politics," 34–40; Paul Craven, "Workers' Conspiracies in Toronto, 1854–72," *L/LT* 14 (Fall 1984), 49–70. In both Britain and the United States, the courts were slowly working out a legal distinction between the mere existence of a workers' organization, which was tolerable, and its activities in interfering with other workers' fulfillment of their contract of employment, which was not. See Henry Phelps Brown, *The Origins of Trade Union Power* (New York: Oxford University Press 1986), 23–44; Christopher L. Tomlins, *The State and the Unions: Labor Relations, Law, and the Organized Labor Movement in America, 1880–1960* (New York: Cambridge University Press 1985), 32–59.
19 Glasbeek, "Contract of Employment."
20 Desmond Morton, "Aid to the Civil Power: The Canadian Militia in Support of Social Order, 1867–1914," in Horn and Sabourin, eds., *Studies in Canadian Social History*, 417–34; Desmond Morton, "Aid to the Civil Power: The Stratford Strike of 1933," in Irving Abella, ed., *On Strike: Six Key Labour Struggles in Canada, 1919–1949* (Toronto: James Lorimer 1974), 79–92; Donald MacGillivray, "Military Aid to the Civil Power: The Cape Breton Experience in the 1920s," in MacGillivray and Brian Tennyson, eds., *Cape Breton Historical Essays*, 95–109; Heron, *Working in Steel*, 154–6; Jim Green, *Against the Tide: The Story of the Canadian Seamen's Union* (Toronto: Progress Books 1986), 68–70; Julie White, *Women and Unions* (Ottawa: Canadian Council on the Status of Women 1980), 95–103.
21 David Frank and Nolan Reilly, "The Emergence of the Socialist Movement in the Maritimes, 1899–1916," in Robert J. Brym and R.J. Sacouman, eds., *Underdevelopment and Social Movements in Atlantic Canada* (Toronto: New Hogtown Press 1979), 89–90; A. Ross McCormack, *Reformers, Rebels,*

and Revolutionaries: The Western Canadian Radical Movement, 1899–1919 (Toronto: University of Toronto Press 1977), 105–7; W. Craig Heron, "Working Class Hamilton, 1895–1930" (PhD dissertation, Dalhousie University 1981), 654–5.

22 S.W. Horrall, "The Royal North-West Mounted Police and Labour Unrest in Western Canada, 1919," *CHR* 61, no. 2 (June 1980), 169–90.

23 David Jay Bercuson, *Confrontation at Winnipeg: Labour, Industrial Relations, and the General Strike* (Montreal and Kingston: McGill-Queen's University Press 1974), 163–75; Lita-Rose Betcherman, *The Little Band: The Clashes between the Communists and the Political and Legal Establishment in Canada, 1928–1932* (Ottawa: Deneau 1981).

24 Reg Whitaker, "Official Repression of Communism during World War II," *L/LT* 17 (Spring 1986), 135–66.

25 Avery, *Dangerous Foreigners*; Barbara Roberts, "Shovelling Out the 'Mutinous': Political Deportation from Canada before 1936," *L/LT* 18 (Fall 1986), 77–110.

26 John Battye, "The Nine-Hour Pioneers: The Genesis of the Canadian Labour Movement," *L/LT* 4 (1979), 25–56; Donald Creighton, "George Brown, Sir John A. Macdonald and the 'Workingman,'" in *Towards the Discovery of Canada: Selected Essays* (Toronto: Macmillan 1972), 174–93; Gregory S. Kealey, *Toronto Workers Respond to Industrial Capitalism, 1867–1892* (Toronto: University of Toronto Press 1980), 124–53; Craven, *Impartial Umpire*, 167–74.

27 Ian McKay, "'By Wisdom Wile or War': The Provincial Workmen's Association and the Struggle for Working-Class Independence in Nova Scotia, 1879–97," *L/LT* 18 (Fall 1986), 46–9; Margaret E. McCallum, "The Mines Arbitration Act, 1888: Compulsory Arbitration in Context," in P. Girard and J. Phillips, eds., *Essays in the History of Canadian Labour Law, Volume 3* (Toronto: University of Toronto Press 1989).

28 C.J. Wrigley, ed., *A History of British Industrial Relations, 1875–1914* (Amherst: University of Massachusetts Press 1982).

29 Craven, *Impartial Umpire*, 196–207.

30 Craven, *Impartial Umpire*; Jeremy Webber, "Compulsion and Consent in Canadian Labour Law: Canada's Choice of Conciliation over Arbitration, 1900–1907" (paper presented to the York University Advanced Research Seminar on Labour and Law in the Commonwealth, 1989); Judy Fudge, "Voluntarism and Compulsion: The Canadian Federal Government's Intervention in Collective Bargaining from 1900 to 1946" (PhD dissertation, Oxford University 1987).

31 Laurel Sefton MacDowell, "The Formation of the Canadian Industrial Relations System during World War Two," *L/LT* 3 (1978), 175–96; Jeremy

Webber, "The Malaise of Compulsory Conciliation: Strike Prevention in Canada during World War II," in Bryan D. Palmer, ed., *The Character of Class Struggle: Essays in Canadian Working Class History* (Toronto: McClelland and Stewart 1986), 135–59; Judy Fudge, "Voluntarism and Compulsion: The Canadian Federal Government's Intervention in Collective Bargaining from 1900 to 1946" (paper presented to the Australian-Canadian Labour History Conference, Sydney, 1988); Peter J. Warrian, "'Labour Is Not a Commodity': A Study of the Rights of Labour in the Canadian Postwar Economy, 1944–48" (PhD dissertation, University of Waterloo 1986); Heron, *Canadian Labour Movement.*

32 Allen Ponek, "Public-Sector Collective Bargaining," in Anderson and Gunderson, eds., *Union Management Relations*, 343–78; Anthony Thomson, "The Nova Scotia Civil Service Association, 1956–1967," *Acadiensis* 12, no. 2 (Spring 1987), 81–105; Anthony Thomson, "From Civil Servants to Government Employees: The N.S.G.E.A., 1967–1973," in Michael Earle, ed., *Workers and the State in Twentieth Century Nova Scotia* (Fredericton: Acadiensis Press 1989), 217–40.

33 Heron, *Canadian Labour Movement.*

34 David A. Wolfe, "The Rise and Demise of the Keynesian Era in Canada: Economic Policy, 1930–1982," in Michael S. Cross and Gregory S. Kealey, eds., *Readings in Canadian Social History, Volume 5: Modern Canada, 1930–1980's* (Toronto: McClelland and Stewart 1984), 46–78; Allan M. Maslove and Gene Swimmer, *Wage Controls in Canada, 1975–78: A Study in Public Decision Making* (Montreal: Institute for Research on Public Policy 1980); Leo Panitch and Donald Swartz, *The Assault on Trade Union Freedoms: From Consent to Coercion Revisited* (Toronto: Garamond 1988).

35 E. Jean Nisbet, "'Free Enterprise at Its Best': The State, National Sea, and the Defeat of the Nova Scotia Fishermen, 1946–1947," in Earle, ed., *Workers and the State*, 171–90

36 Craven, *Impartial Umpire.*

37 R.A. Sample, "Struggle '88: Postal Workers' Vision of an Improved Canada Post," *CD* 23, no. 1 (January/February 1989), 33–6.

38 Craven, *Impartial Umpire*, 101–5; Bruce Scott, "'A Place in the Sun': The Industrial Council at Massey-Harris, 1919–1929," *L/LT* 1 (1976), 158–92; James Naylor, "The New Democracy: Class Conflict in Industrial Ontario, 1914–1925" (PhD dissertation, York University 1988), 373–442; Don Wells, *Soft Sell: "Quality of Working Life" Programs and the Productivity Race* (Ottawa: Canadian Centre for Policy Alternatives 1986); Victor Levant, *Capital and Labour: Partners? Two Classes – Two Views* (Toronto: Steel Rail 1977).

39 McKay, "Wisdom, Wile, or War"; Paul MacEwan, *Miners and Steelworkers: Labour in Cape Breton* (Toronto, 1976); Michael Earle and Hebert Gamberg, "The United Mine Workers and the Coming of the CCF to Cape Breton," in Earle, ed., *Workers and the State*, 85–108.
40 Craven, *Impartial Umpire*; David Jay Bercuson, *Fools and Wise Men: The Rise and Fall of the One Big Union* (Toronto: McGraw-Hill Ryerson 1978); Whitaker, "Official Repression"; Green, *Against the Tide.*
41 Naylor, "New Democracy," 443–504.
42 C.H.J. Gilson and A.M. Wadden, "The Windsor Gypsum Strike and the Coming of the Joint Labour-Management Study Committee: Conflict and Accommodation in the Nova Scotia Labour Movement, 1957–1979," in Earle, ed., *Workers and the State*, 191–216.
43 Roy J. Adams, "The Federal Government and Tripartism," *RI/IR* 37, no. 3 (1982), 606–17; K.G. Waldie, "The Evolution of Labour-Government Consultation on Economic Policy," in W. Craig Riddell, ed., *Labour-Management Cooperation in Canada* (Toronto: University of Toronto Press 1986), 151–201; Don Wells, "Ontario's Quality of Working Life Centre Dies, but Co-optation of Labour Thrives," *CD* 22, no. 7 (October 1988), 26–7.
44 Norman Ward, *The Canadian House of Commons: Representation* (Toronto: University of Toronto Press 1950); Catherine Cleverdon, *The Women's Suffrage Movement in Canada* (Toronto: University of Toronto Press 1950); W. Peter Ward, *White Canada Forever: Popular Attitudes and Public Policy toward Orientals in British Columbia* (Montreal and Kingston: McGill-Queen's University Press 1978).
45 See, for example, Michael J. Piva, "Workers and Tories: The Collapse of the Conservative Party in Urban Ontario, 1980–19," *UHR* 3-76 (1977), 23–30; Heron, "Working-Class Hamilton," 493–508.
46 Heron, "Labourism"; MacDowell, "Formation of the Canadian Industrial Relations System."
47 The International Labour Organization, created at a peak of labour unrest in 1919, was supposed to be the worldwide rallying point for this reformist alternative, but Canadian governments ignored most of the ideal labour standards enunciated there. John Mainwaring, *The International Labour Organization: A Canadian View* (Ottawa: Labour Canada 1986).
48 Pryke, "Labour and Politics," 48–53; Kealey, *Toronto Workers*, 124–72.
49 Heron, "Labourism"; Naylor, "New Democracy," 312–72; Anthony Mardiros, *William Irvine: The Life of a Prairie Radical* (Toronto: James Lorimer, 1979); Ivan Avakumavic, *Socialism in Canada: A Study of the CCF-NDP in Federal and Provincial Politics* (Toronto: McClelland and Stewart 1978).

50 Lorna F. Hurl, "Overcoming the Inevitable: Restricting Child Factory Labour in Late Nineteenth Century Ontario," *L/LT* 21 (Spring 1988), 87–122; Margaret McCallum, "Keeping Women in Their Proper Place: The Minimum Wage in Canada, 1910–25," ibid., 17 (Spring 1986), 29–58. On the specifically working-class notions of womanhood, see Bettina Bradbury, "Women's History and Working-Class History," ibid., 19 (Spring 1987), 35–6.

51 James Struthers, *No Fault of Their Own: Unemployment and the Canadian Welfare State, 1914–1941* (Toronto: University of Toronto Press 1983).

52 Eric Tucker, "Making the Workplace 'Safe' in Capitalism: The Enforcement of Factory Legislation in Nineteenth Century Ontario," *L/LT* 21 (Spring 1988), 45–86; Eric Tucker, "The Determination of Occupational Health and Safety Standards in Ontario, 1860–1982: From the Market to Politics to ... ?" *McGill Law Journal* 29 (March 1984), 260–311; Michael J. Piva, "The Workmen's Compensation Movement in Ontario," *OH* 67 (March 1975), 39–56; Fred Winsor, "'Solving a Problem': Privatizing Workers' Compensation for Nova Scotia's Offshore Fishermen," in Earle, ed., *Workers and the State*, 68–84.

53 Avery, *Dangerous Foreigners*, 32–3.

54 Suzanne Morton, "The Halifax Relief Commission and Labour Relations during the Reconstruction of Halifax, 1917–1919," in Earle, ed., *Workers and the State*, 47–67.

55 Heron, "Labourism."

56 Frank and Reilly, "Socialist Movement"; McCormack, *Reformers, Rebels, and Revolutionaries.*

57 Gregory S. Kealey, "1919: The Canadian Labour Revolt," *L/LT* 13 (Spring 1984), 11–44; Heron, "Labourism."

58 Norman Penner, *Canadian Communism: The Stalin Years and Beyond* (Toronto: Methuen 1988).

59 Walter D. Young, *The Anatomy of a Party: The National CCF, 1932–61* (Toronto: University of Toronto Press 1969); Irving M. Abella, *Nationalism, Communism, and Canadian Labour: The CIO, the Communist Party, and the Canadian Congress of Labour, 1935–1956* (Toronto: University of Toronto Press 1973); Desmond Morton, *NDP: Dream of Power* (Toronto: Hakkert 1974).

PART FIVE

Doing History

Chapter Thirteen

Workers in the Camera's Eye

The 1840s saw the emergence of two distinct but related social forces in British North America. On the one hand, the first industrialists began pulling together workforces in coal mining, metal-working, textile production, saw milling, and much more, where men, women, and even children settled into regular wage-earning and eventually began to coalesce into a distinct social class. The First Industrial Revolution was born, and along with it the first working class.[1] On the other, as part of the new mechanized, more scientifically based industry, the new craft of photography arrived, so that by the 1850s there were many new photo studios opening in cities and towns across British North America down the street from the burgeoning industrial enterprises.[2] For generations afterward, the relationship between Canada's working-class population and this new mode of pictorial representation remained complex.

Although social historians in Canada have been using photographs in their published work since at least the 1970s, they have seldom subjected them to the same level of critical scrutiny that they devote to other sources.[3] Historians have rarely interrogated the source of those images, the purposes and conditions of their creation, or their initial use. Instead, they most often hunt down pictures to "illustrate" their text after they finished writing. There has also been a fondness for "pictorial" histories, in which the images are expected to speak for themselves, as more-or-less direct reflections of the past.[4] By extension, museums and other heritage groups have made photographs a central part of their exhibition practice, often, again, without critical engagement with their history as artefacts.[5]

Photographers at Queen's Park. City of Toronto Archives, file 1244, item 3548

A distinct literature on Canada's photographic history emerged within the field of art history, much of it created by archivists, but most of those studies have focused on specific photographers or archival collections, or on historical images themselves, often assembled by subject matter.[6] Less attention has been paid to the social and cultural context of photographic production more generally within Canadian society.[7]

These issues are of particular salience when the human subjects of photographs are subordinate groups within Canadian society, who were often the focus of picture-taking by outsiders and who had limited direct access to photographic technology themselves until well into the twentieth century. The relationship between First Nations and photographic production has received a good deal of attention,[8] but the same cannot be said for working-class Canadians. The most penetrating analysis was Allan Sekula's essay on a Cape Breton photographer,[9] but it stands virtually alone, despite the enormous growth in the scholarship on working-class history over the past thirty years. What is needed is a social history of photographic production and a cultural interpretation of the meaning of such images. How did photography help to shape the history of the Canadian working class? This essay offers some preliminary mapping.

Conceptualizing Photography

A camera has always been a mechanical device that records what its lens is facing when the shutter is opened. Unlike painting (which can be created purely out of imagination), the subject was indeed there in front of the lens, and what emerged, in its earliest days, was often called a "mirror image." That process has given photography its status as a scientifically sound method for recording "reality" and established its claim to "truthfulness." Yet, the camera has always had an operator, who made important decisions about what subjects to record (and what not to bother recording), what angle and perspective to take, how to frame the image, how to prepare subjects for the picture-taking with appropriate lighting, posture, and/or theatrical staging, and whether to alter the image later during developing. That camera-person thus shaped the photographic image that resulted, often following the long-running conventions of the fine arts. The image was frequently expected to convey something more profound than simply surface features of the subject – such as beauty, character, and emotion. Moreover, human subjects or sponsors of photography might negotiate with the photographer over what kind of image to create. The picture would subsequently appear in any of various formats where it communicated to larger audiences – a picture frame, album, book, newspaper, magazine, or poster – often with a caption or textual contextualization, which helped to shape the impact of the image on its spectators. Those frozen moments of time thus immediately became woven into specific kinds of memory. Spectators who viewed the images, at the time and much later, did not merely look at them, but in fact read them as a kind of text, open to multiple interpretations and re-assessments. For all its undoubted scientific rigour, then, photography has been a highly social process of cultural construction, of representation and communication. It has never existed completely independently, but can only be appreciated in the material and cultural contexts within which it was created and practised.[10]

Photographers

An extensive history of photography around the world has documented the technological innovations and business practices of the nineteenth-century practitioners of what was initially a craft. In Canada that story is still partial and incomplete; the only attempt at a general history stops in 1920.[11] Who was taking these pictures?

For more than a decade after the invention of photography in 1839, amidst some technological diversity, picture-taking was dominated by a complex process that produced one-off images known as daguerreotypes. In the 1850s a new "collodion" wet-plate process allowed for the easier production of negatives and thus the multiple reproduction of images on paper. A parallel innovation put photographic images on small, thin metal sheets, known as "tintypes." All these technical processes were cumbersome and slow and limited images to stationary objects. In the late 1870s, the industry was shaken up with the introduction of commercially manufactured dry-plate negatives that made camera work considerably more flexible and allowed for the development of smaller, more portable cameras, though heavy glass plates were still necessary for developing. Then in 1888 George Eastman unveiled his new Kodak camera, which contained a roll of film that could be sent in for commercial developing (or, with the right skills, processed at home). Henceforth cameras became steadily easier to handle.[12]

In the first half-century of photographic production, practitioners required a thorough knowledge of the evolving technologies of cameras and the complex chemical science involved in developing pictures taken with them. Although some of the men (and a small number of women) who practised this craft worked at points for the few large photographic firms, such as William Notman in Montreal, Ottawa, and Halifax or William James Topley in Ottawa, they were mostly small-scale commercial operators, often itinerant, who served many individual and institutional clients.[13] The Canadian Pacific Railway, for example, contracted with many freelance photographers to provide pictures, and in 1892 organized its own photography department. A decade later, it hired its first staff photographer.[14] The Canadian Department of the Interior likewise hired freelancers to produce pictures of new immigrants.[15] Some local photographers became *flaneurs*, roaming the cities for images that they could market commercially, perhaps to newspapers and magazines.[16] Gradually, especially once Kodaks were on the market, a growing number of amateurs began buying cameras and taking their own pictures for non-commercial purposes. Some coalesced into local camera clubs.[17]

The earliest commercial photographers were a new kind of craftworker, sometimes with backgrounds in art or mechanical work. Outside the handful of large firms, which hired staff with varied skills, they were most often self-employed and typically fell into a lower middle class of artisans and shopkeepers, rather than working-class wage-earners. They brought together a blend of technical competence, business sense, and artistic inspiration in a complex relationship between their freelance sale of images and their engagement with particular subjects, including working people. Among amateurs, the cost of camera equipment kept most workers from participating. Yet the story of one female camp cook in British Columbia who poured the huge sum of $35 into a camera in 1899 suggests that some workers were prepared to make sacrifices in order to become shutterbugs.[18]

Photographs

Photography was deeply rooted in the scientific and technological experiments of the industrial-capitalist age, but it was also deeply shaped by artistic conventions. Thanks in large part to the technical limitations that required subjects to be perfectly still while the camera was recording an image, the first twenty years of picture taking were dominated by portraits, taken for the most part in studios and modelled on the long-standing traditions of painted portraits. Customers were

Excise officer from a distillery, 1868. McCord Museum, I-30178.1

Young miners in North Wellington, BC. Archives of Ontatio, F 1405–15–127, MSR 8361, file 48, photo 1079

encouraged to strike formal poses and were placed in theatrical tableaux of various kinds to establish the appropriate mood and to affirm their social status.[19] The beautifully structured images of men and women of the upper classes were icons of their power and authority, and were often sold in multiple copies as *cartes-de-visite* to be collected in albums. Yet, the cheaper end of the business, especially the production of tintypes, served some proletarians, who wanted images of themselves to adorn their homes or to send back to family. They dressed in their finest outfits or perhaps in a clean version of their work clothes, alongside tools and props of their trade, using the occasion to celebrate their occupational identity, much as they did in labour parades in the late nineteenth century.[20] Portraits established in the popular imagination what a photograph was most often supposed to be, and would cast a long shadow over picture-taking long after the technical constraints on movement in front of the lens had passed.[21]

Group portraits emerged in the late nineteenth century as a variant with special meaning for wage-earners. Some local craft unions arranged for formal pictures of their members before the annual Labour Day parade.[22] Employers also often contracted with local photographers to take a picture of their whole workforce, usually gathered in their work clothes on the job or on the back steps or front lawn of the enterprise. By the 1920s, these were often long panorama pictures, including scores of workers. They were evidently intended to promote social integration and company loyalty.[23]

The other strong influence from the fine arts was a fascination with landscapes. From the earliest days, commercial photographers lugged their cumbersome equipment out of doors to take shots of "picturesque" urban, rural, or wilderness landscapes, with an emphasis on the quaint, exotic, and sublime.[24] There was a rapidly growing market for copies of these "views" in bourgeois households, particularly, by the 1870s, in two-dimensional "stereoscopes" and eventually as picture postcards.[25] The railway companies, notably the Canadian Pacific Railway, also commissioned landscape photographs to promote travel.[26] The new camera clubs had a special fascination with this kind of "pictorialism," as they struggled to turn out photos that could be considered art.[27] If people appeared in these images, they were incidental, merely part of the total landscape (and had to be instructed not to move so as not to create a blurry image). Some of those "views" nonetheless drew on long-standing artistic fascination with handicrafts, seafaring labour, and rural work, including the exotic loggers and miners who toiled

Workers at Greening Wire Company, Hamilton, 1890s. McMaster University, School of Labour Studies Collection

on the periphery of settlement. So, inadvertently, some workers found their way into commercially produced scenic photographs, typically in stilted poses while they waited in suspended motion for the shutter to close, rather than natural or impromptu activity.[28]

Toronto's O'Keefe Brewery in the 1920s. LAC, PA-068062

The scientific patina that accompanied the camera also brought the photographer out of his studio to take up contracts to "document" various features of Canadian social and economic development. Businesses often wanted pictures of their production processes, such as the Grand Trunk's building of the Victoria Bridge in Montreal in 1858 and Quebec's iron mining operations, both as a record and as publicity.[29] Government agencies, such as the Geological Survey of Canada, wanted pictures of natural resources.[30] In both cases, workers might well appear, as they did in other landscapes, but they were not the objects of the investigations. They generally remained small figures, without distinctive features, merely giving the dominant elements of the pictures some proportion. As this practice of industrial documentation extended into the early twentieth century, the workers who appeared were more commonly presented as extensions of the machinery they operated. They might stop to look at the camera, but more often they kept on producing. They rarely smiled or looked pleased to have their pictures taken.[31] Eventually, the "scientific managers" of the 1910s and 1920s turned to still photography and motion-picture film in the form of personnel management and "motion studies" as a mechanism for monitoring the workers' performance on the job.[32]

The Canadian state too turned to photography as part of its efforts to promote economic development and to regulate the population more effectively. Many workers appeared in these pictures. They were caught up in the new institutions of surveillance and discipline that proliferated in the second half of the nineteenth century – the new prisons, reformatories, poorhouses, asylums, schools, and clinics. Often using the portrait form (in this context often known as mug shots, and sometimes appearing on "wanted" posters), photographers were commissioned to document criminals, immigrants, the diseased, juvenile delinquents, "lunatics," and many more, all of whom were assumed to be passive subjects to be put under a scrutinizing gaze. Such photographs were routinely and repetitively generated images that could be analysed for their "evidential force," and formed part of a large array of technical and bureaucratic practices, which were in turn linked to the new theories and methodologies of emerging social-scientific professions – notably sociology, anthropology, criminology, psychology, and public health. More professional police forces also began to incorporate photos of crime scenes as legal evidence to be used in court. In the heat of the First World War, the Canadian government paid photographers to document the war experience, as a clear effort to shape public perceptions of that bloody catastrophe as a noble, heroic endeavour. In all these ways, photography thus came to be integrated into modern modes of governance.[33]

In parallel with the United States's Jacob Riis or Lewis Hine, a few photographers also did work for non-governmental reform agencies, which made some use of photographic evidence in "social documentary."[34] Just before the First World War, for example, J.S. Woodsworth incorporated photos into his study of "slum" life in Winnipeg, Medical Officer of Health Charles Hastings did the same in his study of "The Ward" in Toronto, and the Methodist and Presbyterian investigators who set out to produce preliminary social surveys of several Canadian

Children in Toronto's infamous "Ward." Archives of Ontario, ACC 6355 S8973

cities used snapshots in their pamphlets and posters. These images were presented, alongside tables of statistics, as hard "evidence" of the impact of poverty on workers' lives and the need for intervention to help them.[35]

In the 1930s Canada had no equivalent of the phalanx of photographers working for the US Farm Security Administration, who produced

Winnipeg tinsmiths on Labour Day around 1915.
Provincial Archives of Manitoba, N1643

self-styled "documentary" work of working people – Dorothea Lange and Walker Evans, among many others – and the parallel group in New York's Photo League.[36] Nor was there any large project of systematic photographic documentation to compare with Mass Observation in Britain in the late 1930s.[37] In contrast to several other industrial countries, the networks of left-wing activists in Canada did not seem to spawn collectives of radical worker-photographers who set out to use their images as weapons in the class struggle.[38]

There were many photographers, however, who found outlets for their work in magazines and newspapers. At the turn of the century,

Toronto May Day parade, 1934. City of Toronto Archives, *Globe and Mail* 33197

local photographers regularly produced images of community events and organizations including portraits of unionists and shots of labour parades, some of which might end up in the local newspaper.[39] The 1920s and 1930s saw a quantitative leap in the production of photographs as newspapers and magazines began to hire photographers to provide more visual documents to accompany print stories. These so-called photojournalists had a penchant for the sensational, and turned their gaze on many parts of working-class experience, including unemployed protests and the strikes of the 1930s and 1940s that brought the modern labour movement into being.[40]

In postwar Canada, professional photographers became much more confident that their work was art, to be featured in gallery exhibitions and coffee-table books. Some assembled collections of photographs

Hamilton telephone operator and friends, c. 1914. McMaster University, School of Labour Studies Collection

that presented the ordinary lives of working people. Following a path blazed by the US documentary photographers of the 1930s, these picture-takers sought to convey a respectful sense of quiet dignity, without any overt moralistic critique or political agenda.[41] By the 1980s, a small number of photographers with more definite political commitments were producing images that highlighted workers organizing and fighting back. They identified with social movements, including workers' movements, as part of an international practice of guerilla camera work. In some cases their work was sponsored by unions or other community groups.[42]

Alongside this public, generally commercial photographic production ran a much more private stream of picture-taking. The arrival of the easier-to-use Kodak camera at the end of the nineteenth century and the release of the cheap Brownie version in 1900 (only $1) encouraged thousands of Canadians (including some workers) to take their own pictures, quickly known as snapshots. The lack of flash attachments limited picture taking to the out-of-doors, but, even later, the subject matter tended to be limited to family activities, especially celebratory occasions such as birthdays and weddings, outings to the beach, and other moments of informal fun, not the sadness, misery, or suffering of daily life. The images produced were heavily influenced by the tradition of portraiture, and tended to convey proud respectability, but also a playful, theatrical frolicking that ridiculed the pomposity of formal portraits. For workers these were statements about their values and aspirations.[43]

Uses

Photographs had private and public uses. Studio portraits might sit on a dresser, but probably ended up in photo albums, the household repositories of memory. That, of course, was where the most prized family snapshots also ended up (the rest were probably stored in drawers or shoeboxes). The work of maintaining these albums was often in the hands of wives and mothers. The growing number of studies of family snapshots generally have had little to say about how workers in particular used this form of picture-taking.[44] Probably only a minority of working-class families could afford cameras and the costs of developing film, but among them there is every reason to believe that the albums were carefully preserved as records of good times.

Institutional uses of photographs often involved publication of some kind. Companies that commissioned photos of their buildings, their production processes, and their products incorporated them in annual reports, product catalogues, and other company publications intended for general publicity about the company. They also made them available to business and trade periodicals for special articles.[45] By the 1920s the range of these corporately sponsored images occasionally extended to close-ups of workers to be included in company magazines for employees, which proliferated in the late 1930s, with the goal of encouraging worker loyalty and discouraging unionization. In the United States Lewis Hine had turned his creative energies towards similar portraiture under corporate sponsorship, including the famous Empire State Building photos. This kind of imagery would also preoccupy work done by the National Film Board's Still Photography Division to boost workers' morale and productivity during the Second World War. Corporations also included photographs in their advertising, but it seems that they did not often use workers in those images.[46]

In the nineteenth century, photographic images could be included in publications only if they were converted to engravings or lithographs. By the end of the century, a process for making "half-tone" images took hold, and many magazines included them, though most advertisers avoided photographs until the 1920s.[47] Mass-market newspapers also slowly began to incorporate photos, expanding their use in the 1930s, sometimes in photo-essays on particular themes. They were following the lead of the hugely popular new US photo magazines of that decade, *Life* and *Look*.[48] Images of workers in various settings produced by photojournalists thus began to circulate widely and frequently.

Reform-minded photographers also incorporated some images into their publications, lantern-slide shows, and exhibitions, increasingly as part of some state-sponsored program, notably child-saving, housing reform, and public health.[49] Meanwhile, since the turn of the century, unions had hired local photographers to take the dignified group pictures, often around Labour Day, intended for union members or for mounting in union halls. Like other newspaper publishers, however, early-twentieth-century labour journalists had made extremely limited use of photos in their publications. As a new labour movement had taken shape in the 1930s and 1940s, however, periodicals aimed at union members included many more photographic images, often drawing on the new work of photojournalism. These have not been systematically studied in Canada, but in the United States it is clear that the images tended to be carefully selected to promote sober, restrained, respectable unionism – portraits of labour leaders, static group portraits, shots of meetings and conventions, but few of picket-line confrontations.[50]

In general then, although photographs had been in circulation since the 1840s, the mass-production of photographic images came much more slowly. Indeed, in the early twentieth century, many working people may have had more exposure to moving images in movie theatres than to still images in the daily newspapers they read. The images of workers themselves may have been largely limited to specialized publications for readers interested in business or social reform. The saturation of media with photography really only began between the World Wars and expanded enormously in the second half of the twentieth century.

The Record

Canadian workers have thus appeared in many different kinds of photographs taken for widely different purposes. In some, they were

United Electrical Workers Hamilton executive. McMaster University, School of Labour Studies Collection

merely incidental to the landscape or mechanical processes that were at the centre of the picture-taker's project. In others, they were made subjects of more direct, intense scrutiny by crusading individuals with some kind social engineering in mind. In others, they got special attention from company-sponsored photographers whose camera work was intended to shape a loyal, dutiful consciousness in the workforce. In still others, images of workers provided colour for sensationalist journalistic reporting. All those forms of photographic practice originated outside the working class and constructed the images of workers based on agendas from the middle or upper classes. Yet workers could find photography a tool in pursuit of their own goals. Studio portraits allowed many to display small icons of respectability, and snapshots enabled growing numbers to celebrate the bonds of familial solidarity that sustained them.

The gaps in the photographic record of working-class Canada are also important. The volume and diversity of images is much more limited before 1900, and only gradually expands in the early decades of the twentieth century, before the flood that begins in the 1930s. Throughout that history, the domestic sphere, and the work carried on there, got little attention. People of colour, especially African-Canadians and Asians, were much less likely to catch the camera's eye than whites. Indeed, the photographic record of Canadian workers is preponderantly an extended document of whiteness.

In totality, then, photographs of Canadian workers across time fall far short of providing a complete documentary record of working-class experience and construct diverse, contradictory narratives about that experience.

Photography and Hegemony

Another large set of questions remains about how photography functioned as a hegemonic mechanism to reinforce or challenge workers' positions within Canadian society. If photography was a mode of communication, what are the messages it has communicated about working-class Canada over a century and a half?

Photography needs to be appreciated as a significant force within the dynamics of class, race, and gender since the middle of the nineteenth century. Photographic imagery has had hegemonic power that has both helped to rationalize working-class subordination within Canadian society and the oppression of women and visible minorities within that class, and to encourage working-class compliance. Photographs have constructed working people as a number of social types, which convey powerful meanings about class relationships in industrial-capitalist society. Many of the photos featuring workingmen on the job give them the qualities of crude, degraded *beasts*, roughly clad, enveloped in grime and foul air, overshadowed by machinery. Their social subordination is manifest. Many of those taken by urban social reformers made their working-class subjects into *victims*, often apparently helpless women and children framed within sordid slum households, in need of middle-class intervention to save them. Some of those images were

Dofasco workers, Hamilton, 1930s. McMaster University, School of Labour Studies Collection, LS372

aimed at the risks they posed to public health, and constructed working people as a *menace*. The institutional photography that was built into police, charity, and child-saving work conveyed the same message of danger. Photojournalists who captured moments of violence, such as strikers' picket lines or angry demonstrations, added to that fear of workers. Other photographic images projected more positive meanings. For the photographers who contributed images to company magazines, workers could be presented as *heroes*, proud, loyal, highly valued producers. For the few socialists who used a camera, that heroism could extend to their determination to fight for a better world. For many workers themselves, photographs in the form of portraits, individual and group, made them into *citizens*, objects of the respectability and social equality that they believed they deserved.

Photography then could be a significant force in shaping hegemonic notions of social relations, especially rationalizing class, gender, and racial subordination, and in engendering working-class compliance. It continues to play a vital role in shaping a dominant collective memory of "the way we were," in the recent and distant past. Yet it has always been a fluid medium, open to multiple interpretations, and increasingly available to those who would challenge inequities. From their early use of tintypes to establish respectability, to the portraits of union leadership in labour magazines to establish a determined commitment to collective struggle, to the snapshots of beaming children at a backyard barbeque to affirm family solidarity, workers found ways to make the hegemonic force of photography work for them.

Notes

1 Gregory S. Kealey, *Toronto Workers Respond to Industrial Capitalism, 1867–1892* (Toronto: University of Toronto Press 1980); Bryan D. Palmer, *Working-Class Experience: Rethinking the History of Canadian Labour, 1800–1991* (Toronto: McClelland and Stewart 1992); Bettina Bradbury, *Working Families: Age, Gender, and Daily Survival in Industrializing Montreal* (Toronto: Oxford University Press 1993); Paul Craven, ed., *Labouring Lives: Work and Workers in Nineteenth-Century Ontario* (Toronto: University of Toronto Press 1995); John Belshaw, *Colonization and Community: The Vancouver Island Coalfield and the Making of the British Columbian Working Class* (Montreal and Kingston: McGill-Queen's University Press 2002); Craig Heron, *Lunch-Bucket Lives: Remaking the Workers' City* (Toronto: Between the Lines 2015).

2 Ralph Greenhill and Andrew Birrell, *Canadian Photography: 1839–1920* (Toronto: Coach House Press 1979); Stanley G. Triggs, *William Notman: The Stamp of a Studio* (Toronto: Coach House Press 1985); Jim Burant, "Pre-Confederation Photography in Halifax, Nova Scotia," *JCAH* 4, no.1 (Spring 1977), 25–44; J. Russell Harper, "Dageurreotypists and Portrait Takers in Saint John," *Dalhousie* Review 36, no. 3 (1955), 259–70; Nicole Cloutier, "Les disciples de Daguerre à Québec, 1839–1855," *JCAH* 5, no. 1 (1980), 33–7; Lilly Koltun, "Pre-Confederation Photography in Toronto," *HOP* 2, no. 3 (July 1978), 249–63; David Mattison, "The Claudets of British Columbia: Melting, Assaying, and Photographing All Day," *HOP* 14, no. 2 (April–June 1990), 135–53; David Mattison, "Richard Maynard: Photographer of

Victoria, B.C.," *HOP* 9, no. 2 (April–June 1985), 109–29; Claire Weissman Wilks, *The Magic Box: The Eccentric Genius of Hannah Maynard* (Toronto: Exile Editions 1980).

3 For some rare examples, penned by Canadian archivists, see J. Robert Davison, "Turning a Blind Eye: The Historian's Use of Photographs," *BC Studies* 52 (Winter 1981–2), 16–35; David Mattison, "In Visioning the City: Urban History Techniques through Historical Photographs," *UHR* 13, no. 1 (June 1984), 43–52; Lorraine O'Donnell, "Towards Total Archives: The Form and Meaning of Photographic Records," *Archivaria* 38 (Fall 1994), 105–18; see also David D. Perlmutter, "Visual History Methods: Problems, Prospects, Applications," *Historical Methods* 27, no. 4 (Fall 1984), 167–84; Elspeth Brown, "Reading the Visual Record," in Ardis Cameron, ed., *Looking for America: The Visual Production of Nation and People* (Malden, MA: Blackwell 2005), 362–70.

4 See, for example, Robert Harney and Harold Troper, *Immigrants: Portraits of the Urban Experience, 1890–1930* (Toronto: Van Nostrand Reinhold 1975); Roger Hall and Gordon Dodds, *A Pictorial History of Ontario* (Edmonton: Hurtig 1978); Roger Hall and Gordon Dodds, *Canada: A History in Photographs* (Edmonton: Hurtig 1981); Craig Heron, Shea Hoffmitz, Wayne Roberts, and Robert Storey, *All That Our Hands Have Done: A Pictorial History of the Hamilton Workers* (Oakville, ON: Mosaic Press 1981); Bill Gillespie, *A Class Act: An Illustrated History of the Labour Movement in Newfoundland and Labrador* (St John's: Newfoundland and Labrador Federation of Labour 1986); Doug Smith, *Let Us Rise!: An Illustrated History of the Manitoba Labour Movement* (Vancouver: New Star Books 1985); Working Lives Collective, *Working Lives: Vancouver, 1886–1986* (Vancouver: New Star Books 1985); Edward Cavell, *Sometimes a Great Nation: A Photo Album of Canada, 1850–1925* (Banff: Altitude Publishing 1984); Mark Kingwell, and Christopher Moore, *Canada, Our Century: 100 Voices, 500 Visions* (Toronto: Doubleday Canada 1999); Lionel Koffler, *Quebec, 1850–1950* (Richmond Hill, ON: Firefly Books 2005).

5 Raphael Samuel, *Theatres of Memory, Volume 1: Past and Present in Contemporary Culture* (London: Verso 1994), 313–77. Canada's *Material History Review* (renamed the *Material Culture Review* in 2006) showed virtually no interest in photographs.

6 For example, Peter Robertson, *Relentless Verity: Canadian Military Photographers since 1885* (Toronto: University of Toronto Press 1973); Triggs, *William Notman*; Nancy Marrelli, *Montreal Photo Album: Photographs from Montreal Archives* (Montreal: Véhicule Press 1993); Henri Robideau, *Flapjacks and Photographs: A History of Matti Gunterman, Camp Cook and Photographer*

(Vancouver: Polestar Book Publishers 1995); Frances Rooney, *Working Light: The Wandering Life of Photographer Edith S. Watson* (Ottawa: Carleton University Press 1996); Keith McLaren, *Light on the Water: Early Photography of Coastal British Columbia* (Vancouver and Seattle: Douglas and McIntyre and University of Washington Press 1998); Faith Moonsang, *First Son: Portraits of C.D. Hoy* (Vancouver: Presentation House Gallery/ Arsenal Pulp Press 1999); M. Brook Taylor, *A Camera on the Banks: Frederick William Wallace and the Fishermen of Nova Scotia* (Fredericton: Goose Lane Editions 2006); Benjamin H.D. Buchloh, and Robert Wilkie, eds., *Mining Photographs and Other Pictures, 1948–1968: A Selection from the Negative Archives of Shedden Studio, Glace Bay, Cape Breton* (Halifax and Sydney: Press of the Nova Scotia College of Art and Design and University College of Cape Breton Press 1983).

7 The most insightful recent collection on photographic history is Carol Payne and Andrea Kunard, eds., *The Cultural Work of Photography in Canada* (Montreal and Kingston: McGill-Queen's University Press 2011).

8 Carol J. Williams, *Framing the West: Race, Gender, and the Photographic Frontier in the Pacific Northwest* (New York: Oxford University Press 2003); Daniel Francis, *Copying People: Photographing British Columbia First Nations, 1860–1940* (Saskatoon and Calgary: Fifth House 1996); Brock V. Silversides, *The Face-Pullers: Photographing Native Canadians, 1871–1939* (Saskatoon: Fifth House 1994); Payne and Kunard, eds., *Cultural Work.*

9 Allan Sekula, "Photography between Capital and Labour," in Buchloh and Wilkie, eds., *Mining Photographs*, 193–268.

10 Graham Clarke, *The Photograph* (New York: Oxford University Press 1997); Allan Trachtenberg, *Reading American Photographs: Images as History, Mathew Brady to Walker Evans* (New York: Hill and Wang 1989); Susan Sontag, *On Photography* (New York: Farrar, Straus, and Giroux 1977); Roland Barthes, *Camera Lucida: Reflections on Photography* (New York: Hill and Wang 1981); Naomi Rosenblum, *A World History of Photography* (New York: Abbeville Press 1997); Payne and Kunard, eds., *Cultural Work*; John Tagg, *The Burden of Representation: Essays on Photographies and Histories* (Minneapolis: University of Minnesota Press 1993); Geoffrey Batchen, *Burning with Desire: The Conception of Photography* (Cambridge, MA: MIT Press 1997).

11 Rosenblum, *World History*; Greenhill and Birrell, *Canadian Photography.*

12 Reese V. Jenkins, *Images and Enterprise: Technology and the American Photographic Industry, 1839 to 1925* (Baltimore: Johns Hopkins University Press 1975); Greenhill and Birrell, *Canadian Photography*; Lilly Koltun, ed., *Private Realms of Light: Amateur Photography in Canada, 1839–1940*

(Markham, ON: Fitzhenry and Whiteside 1984); Eaton S. Lothrop, Jr., "The Brownie Camera," *History of Photography* 2, no. 1 (January 1978), 1–10.

13 Greenhill and Birrell, *Canadian Photography*; Burant, "Pre-Confederation Photography"; Koltun, "Pre-Confederation Photography"; Triggs, *William Notman*; Roger Hall, Gordon Dodds, and Stanley Triggs, *The World of William Notman: The Nineteenth Century Through a Master Lens* (Toronto: McClelland and Stewart 1993); Mattison, "Richard Maynard"; Mattison, "Claudets"; Andrew Rodger, "William James Topley: Reflections on a Capital Photographer," Library and Archives Canada, https://en.wikipedia.org/wiki/William_James_Topley; Cloutier, "Les disciples de Daguerre"; Colleen Skidmore, "Women Workers in Notman's Studio": "Young Ladies of the Printing Room," *HOP* 20, no. 2 (Summer 1996), 122–8; Diana Pederson and Martha Phemister, "Women and Photography in Ontario, 1839–1929: A Case Study of the Interaction of Gender and Technology," in Marianne Gosztonyi Ainley, ed. *Despite the Odds: Essays on Canadian Women and Science* (Montreal: Véhicule Press 1990), 88–111; Wilks, *Magic Box*; Rooney, *Working Light*.

14 Jonathan Hanna, Robert C. Kennell, and Carol Lacourte, *Portraits of Canada: Photographic Treasures of the CPR* (Calgary: Fifth House 2006).

15 Rodger, "William James Topley."

16 Doug Smith and Michael Olito, *The Best Possible Face: L.B. Foote's Winnipeg* (Winnipeg: Turnstone Press 1985); Christopher Hume, "Introduction," in *William James' Toronto Views: Lantern Slides from 1906 to 1939* (Toronto: James Lorimer 1999); Vincenzo Pietropaolo, "William James: Toronto's First Photojournalist," in John Lorinc et al., eds., *The Ward: The Life and Loss of Toronto's First Immigrant Neighbourhood* (Toronto: Coach House Press 2015), 123–7.

17 Koltun, ed., *Private Realms of Light*; Colin Ford, ed., *The Story of Popular Photography* (London: Century 1989).

18 Robideau, *Flapjacks and Photographs*; Susan Close, *Framing Identity: Social Practices of Photography in Canada (1880–1920)* (Winnipeg: Arbeiter Ring Publishing 2007).

19 Jana Bara, "Through the Frosty Lens: William Notman and His Studio Props, 1861–1876," *HOP* 12, no. 1 (January–March 1988), 232–30.

20 Michael L. Carlebach, *Working Stiffs: Occupational Portraits in the Age of the Tintype* (Washington: Smithsonian Institution 2002); Harry R. Rubenstein, "With Hammer in Hand: Working-Class Occupational Portraits," in Howard B. Rock, Paul A. Gilje, and Robert Asher, eds., *American Artisans: Crafting Social Identity, 1750–1850* (Baltimore: Johns Hopkins University Press 1995), 176–98; Richard Steven Street, *Everyone Had Cameras:*

Photography and Farmworkers in California, 1850–2000 (Minneapolis: University of Minnesota Press 2008); Greenhill and Birrell, *Canadian Photography*, plate 5; Hall and Dodds, *Canada*, 16; Craig Heron and Steve Penfold, *The Workers' Festival: A History of Labour Day in Canada* (Toronto: University of Toronto Press 2005).

21 Shannon Thomas Perich, *The Changing Face of Portrait Photography: From Daguerreotype to Digital* (National Museum of American History in association with The Smithsonian Institution Scholarly Press, Washington, DC, 2011).

22 Heron and Penfold, *Workers' Festival*, 40, 52–3, 55, 58, 63.

23 There are numerous examples of these workplace group portraits sprinkled through published histories of labour; see, for example, Heron et al., *All That Our Hands Have Done*, 3, 7, 25, 27, 42, 96; Heron, *Lunch-Bucket Lives*, 258, 259, 260, 299; Judith Hoegg Ryan, *Coal in Our Blood: 200 Years of Coal Mining in Nova Scotia's Pictou Mining* (Halifax: Formac Publishing 1992), vi–vii, xiii, 9, 11, 13, 26, 43, 53, 68, 104, 125; Gillespie, *Class Act*, 32, 79; Smith, *Let Us Rise*, 39, 45; Working Lives Collective, *Working Lives*, 24. See also Josh Sapau, *The Big Picture: America in Panorama* (New York: Princeton Architectural Press 2013).

24 Trachtenberg, *Reading American Photographs*, 119–63; Peter B. Hales, *Silver Cities: The Photography of American Urbanization, 1839–1915* (Philadelphia: Temple University Press 1984).

25 William Culp Darrah, *The World of Stereographs* (Gettysburg, PA: Darrah 1977); Allen Anderson and Betty Tomlinson, *Greetings from Canada: An Album of Unique Canadian Postcards from the Edwardian Era, 1900–1916* (Toronto: Macmillan 1978); Hal Morgan and Andreas Brown, *Prairie Fires and Paper Moons* (Boston: D.R. Godine 1981).

26 Hanna et al., *Portraits of Canada*.

27 Lilly Koltun, "Art Ascendant," in Koltun, ed., *Private Realms of Light*, 32–71.

28 Greenhill and Birrell, *Canadian Photography*, 52; Gillespie, *Class Act*, 23, 31; Working Lives Collective, *Working Lives*, 8, 38; Koltun, ed., *Private Realms of Light*, 128, 158, 183, 223; McLaren, *Light on the Water*, 28, 35, 39, 48, 79, 108, 118, 119, 124, 127; Taylor, *Camera on the Banks*, 17, 18, 20, 25, 34, 35, 45, 50, 58–9; Jill Delaney, "John Vanderpant's Canada," in Payne and Kunard, eds., *Cultural Work*, 57–69.

29 Greenhill and Birrell, *Canadian Photography*, plates 17, 18; Triggs, *William Notman*, 38–43, 78; Robert G. Wilson, "William Notman's Stereo Perspective: The Victoria Bridge," *HOP* 20, no. 2 (Summer 1996), 108–12; Rooney, *Working Light*.

30 E. Hall, *Early Canada: A Collection of Historical Photographs by Officers of the Geological Survey of Canada* (Ottawa: Queen's Printer 1967); R.G. Blackadar,

On the Frontier: Photographs by the Geological Survey of Canada (Ottawa: Geological Survey of Canada 1982); Birrell, *Into the Silent Land: Survey Photography in the Canadian West* (Ottawa: Information Canada 1975).

31 Heron et al., *All That Our Hands Have Done*; Gillespie, *Class Act*, 51, 57, 70; Smith, *Let Us Rise*, 98, 100, 101; Working Lives Collective, *Working Lives*, 14, 43, 44, 50, 52, 54, 56, 60, 185; David Nye, *Image Worlds: Corporate Identities at General Electric, 1890–1940* (Cambridge, MA: MIT Press 1985).

32 Elspeth H. Brown, *The Corporate Eye: Photography and the Rationalization of American Commercial Culture, 1884–1929* (Baltimore: Johns Hopkins University Press 2005), 65–118; Elspeth H. Brown, "Welfare Capitalism and Photography: N.C.R. and the Visual Production of a Global Model Factory," *HOP* 32, no. 2 (Summer 2008), 137–51; Richard Lindstrom, "'They All Believe They Are Undiscovered Mary Pickfords': Workers, Photography and Scientific Management," *Technology and Culture* 41 (October 2000), 725–51.

33 Jonathan Finn, *Capturing the Criminal Image: From Mugshot to Surveillance Society* (Minneapolis: University of Minnesota Press 2009); Rachel Hall, *Wanted: The Outlaw in American Visual Culture* (Charlottesville, Virginia: University of Virginia Press 2009); Martin Kemp, "'A Perfect and Faithful Record': Mind and Body in Medical Photography Before 1900," in Ann Thomas, ed., *Beauty of Another Order: Photography in Science* (Ottawa: Yale University Press in association with National Gallery of Canada 1997, 120–49; Sarah Bassnett, "Picturing Filth and Disorder: Photography and Urban Governance in Canada," *HOP* 28, no. 2 (Summer 2004), 149–64; Stephen Bulger, "Arthur Goss: Documenting Hardship," in Lorinc et al., eds., *The* Ward, 104–11; Brian S. Osborne, "Constructing the State, Managing the Corporation, Transforming the Individual: Photography, Immigration, and the Canadian National Railways, 1925-30," in Joan M. Schwartz and James R. Ryan, eds., *Picturing Place: Photography and the Geographical Imagination* (London: I.B. Tauris 2003), 162–91; Tagg, *Burden of Representation*; Peter Robertson, "Canadian Photojournalism During the First World War," *HOP* 2, no. 1 (January 1978), 37–52.

34 Jacob A. Riis, *How the Other Half Lives: Studies among the Tenements of New York* (New York: Dover Publications 1971 [1890]); Maren Stange, *Symbols of Ideal Life: Social Documentary Photography in America, 1890–1950* (Cambridge: Cambridge University Press 1989). On a somewhat earlier use of photography to document working-class life in London, England, see Angela Vanhaelen, "*Street Life in London* and the Organization of Labour," *HOP* 26, no. 3 (Autumn 2002), 191–204.

35 J.S. Woodsworth, *My Neighbour: A Study of City Conditions, A Plea for Social Service* (Toronto: University of Toronto Press 1972 [1911]); Bassnett,

"Picturing Filth and Disorder"; Alan Hunt, "Measuring Morals: The Beginning of the Social Survey Movement in Canada, 1913–1917," *HS/SH* 35, no. 69 (May 2002), 171–94.

36 Carl Fleischhauer and Beverly W. Branan, eds., *Documenting America, 1935–1943* (Berkeley: University of California Press 1988); Pierre Borhan, *Dorothea Lange: The Heart and Mind of a Photographer* (Boston: Little, Brown and Company 2002); Trachtenberg, *Reading American Photographs*, 231–85; Mason Klein and Catherine Evans, *The Radical Camera: New York's Photo League, 1936–1951* (New Haven: Yale University Press 2011). The Still Division of the National Film Board never had the scope and freedom to develop a style that might parallel US developments. Carol Payne, *The Official Eye: The National Film Board's Still Photography Division and the Image of Canada, 1941–1971* (Montreal and Kingston: McGill-Queen's University Press 2013); Renate Wickens-Feldman, "The National Film Board of Canada's Still Photography Division: The Griersonian Legacy," *HOP* 20, no. 3 (Autumn 1996), 271–7.

37 Humphrey Spender, *Worktown: Mass-Observation by Camera* (London: Royal College of Art 1975); Lucy Curzon, "Another Place in Time: Documenting Blackpool for Mass Observation in the 1930s," *HOP* 35, no. 3 (August 2011), 313–26.

38 Leah Ollman, *Camera as Weapon: Worker Photography between the Wars* (San Diego: Museum of Photographic Arts 1991); Jorge Ribalta, ed., *The Worker Photography Movement (1926–1939): Essays and Documents* (Madrid: Museo Nacional Centro de Arte Reina Sophia 2011).

39 Heron and Penfold, *Workers' Festival*.

40 Hall and Dodds, *Canada*, 172–5, 184–5; Hall and Dodds, *Picture History of Ontario*, 199, 201; Heron et al., *All That Our Hands Have Done*, 133, 162, 168–80; Smith, *Let Us Rise*, 78, 79, 81, 83, 90; Working Lives Collective, *Working Lives*, 174, 176, 178, 180. On photojournalism, see Michael L. Carlebach, *The Origins of Photojournalism in America* (Washington, DC: Smithsonian Institution Press 1992); Michael L. Carlebach, *American Photojournalism Comes of Age* (Washington, DC: Smithsonian Institution Press 1997); Claude Cookman, *American Photojournalism: Motivations and Meanings* (Evanston, IL: Northwestern University Press 2009).

41 See, for example, James Lorimer and Myfanwy Phillips, *Working People: Life in a Downtown Neighbourhood* (Toronto: James Lewis and Samuel 1971); John Paskievich, *A Place Not Our Own: North End Winnipeg* (Winnipeg: Queenston House 1978); Lawrence Chrismas, *Alberta Miners: A Tribute* (Calgary: Cambria Publishing 1993).

42 For example, Vincenzo Pietropaolo, *Celebration of Resistance: Ontario's Days of Action* (Toronto: Between the Lines 1999); Vincenzo Pietropaolo,

Canadians at Work (Toronto: Canadian Auto Workers 2000); Vincenzo Pietropaolo, *Not Paved with Gold: Italian-Canadian Immigrants in the 1970s* (Toronto: Between the Lines 2006); John Maclennan, *The Spirit of Our Movement: Celebrating Toronto Labour in the 21st Century* (Toronto: Toronto and York Region Labour Council 2011); Antigoni Memou, *Photography and Social Movements: From the Globalization of the Movement (1968) to the Movement Against Globalization (2001)* (Manchester: Manchester University Press 2013).

43 Eaton S. Lothrop, Jr., "The Brownie Camera," *HOP* 2, no. 1 (January 1978), 1–10; Sarah Greenough and Diane Waggoner, with Sarah Kennel and Matthew S. Witkovsky, *The Art of the American Snapshot, 1888–1978* (Washington: National Gallery of Art 2007); Ford, ed., *Story of Popular Photography*; Brian Coe and Paul Gates, *The Snapshot Photograph: The Rise of Popular Photography* (London: Ash and Grant 1977); Julia Hirsch, *Family Photographs: Content, Meaning, and Effect* (New York: Oxford University Press 1981); Jo Spence and Patricia Holland, eds., *Family Snapshots: The Meanings of Domestic Photography* (London: Virago 1991); Martha Langford, *Suspended Conversations: The Afterlife of Memory in Photographic Albums* (Montreal and Kingston: McGill-Queen's University Press 2001); Close, *Framing Identity*; Braden Cannon, "The Photographs of Allan Godby and Charles Lee: Photographic Practice in a Canadian Mining Community," *HOP* 36, no. 4 (September 2012), 439–50.

44 Barbara Levine and Stephanie Snyder, eds., *Snapshot Chronicles: Inventing the American Photo Album* (New York: Princeton Architectural Press 2006); Deborah Chamber, "Family as Place: Family Photograph Albums and the Domestication of Public and Private Space," in Schwartz and Ryan, eds., *Picturing Place*, 96–114: Hirsch, *Family Photographs*; Spence and Holland, eds., *Family Snaps.*

45 See, for example, the images in Buchloh and Wilkie, eds., *Mining Photographs and Other Pictures.*

46 Brown, *Corporate Eye*, 119–58; Lewis W. Hine, *Men At Work: Photographic Studies of Modern Men and Machines* (New York: Dover Publications 1977 [1932]); Hanna et al., *Portraits of Canada*, 25, 192; Rosemary Donegan, "Karsh's Working Man: Industrial Tensions and Cold War Anxieties," in Dieter Vorsteher and Janet Yates, eds., *Yousuf Karsh: Heroes of Light and Shadows* (Don Mills, ON: Stoddart 2001), 153–61; Yousuf Karsh, *Industrial Images* (Windsor: Art Gallery of Windsor 2007); Carol Quirke, *Eyes on Labor: News Photography and America's Working Class* (New York: Oxford University Press 2012); Payne, *Official Eye*, 79–106.

47 Christopher R. Harris, "The Halftone and American Magazine Reproduction, 1880–1900," *HOP* 17, no. 1 (Spring 1993), 77–80; Brown, *Corporate Eye*, 159–216.

48 Wendy Kozol, Life's *American Family and Nation in Postwar Photojournalism* (Philadelphia: Temple University Press 1994).

49 Stange, *Symbols of Ideal Life.*

50 Quirke, *Eyes on Labor.*

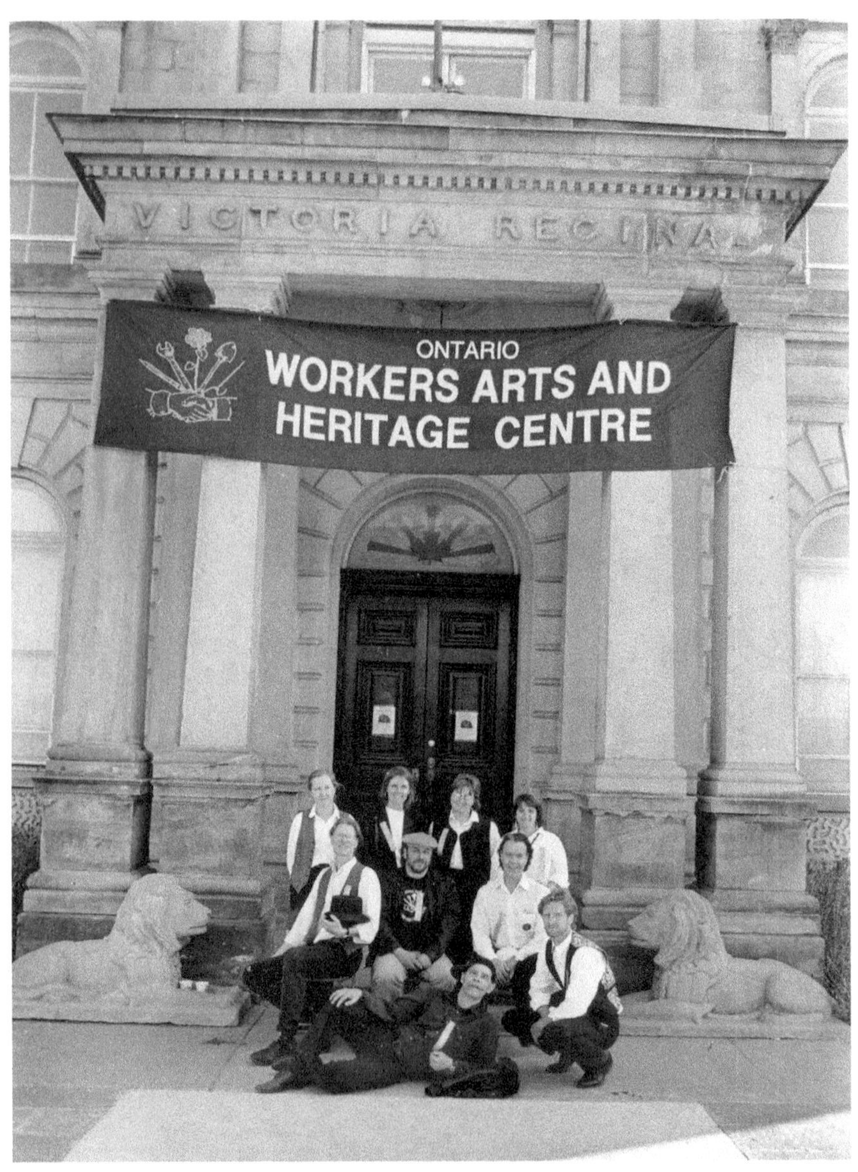
VICTORIA REGINA
ONTARIO
WORKERS ARTS AND
HERITAGE CENTRE

Chapter Fourteen

The Labour Historian and Public History

Historians of the working class in Canada have seldom been comfortable in an ivory tower. Lurking within even the most dedicated scholars in the field is the popular educator who wants to participate in a wider dissemination of knowledge than academic channels normally allow. Their goals combine their training and their social and political commitments. They want more people, especially working people, to share their understanding of the past and to be able to use that knowledge creatively and effectively in confronting the challenges of modern capitalist society. For some, this is part of the struggle to reconcile their own working-class backgrounds and their new middle-class professional jobs. Many also get inspiration from their involvement in social movements outside the university[1] and from the "History Workshop" movement in Britain.[2] Whatever the reason, labour historians find their way into non-academic settings to give lectures, teach courses or workshops,[3] and write short popular accounts of workers' history.[4]

These opportunities have generally been limited for people whose professional lives are so strictly defined by university and college teaching and the circuit of academic conferences – especially in a country with less well developed programs in workers' education than those offered through the Workers Educational Association in Britain or the long-established labour studies programs in the United States.[5] Yet, during the 1980s, labour historians found growing numbers of people outside academia who shared their interest in the workers' past. More teachers were trying to introduce this story into their classrooms.[6] Archivists and

Workers Arts and Heritage Centre board, 1995.
Author's collection, Cees Van Gemerden

librarians were more eager to preserve the records of this experience.[7] Artists, musicians, and playwrights were not only making workers and their history a theme in their art, but also creating projects to encourage working-class artistic expression.[8] Unionists and union staff were slowly developing enough interest in workers' history to recognize that it was not being well enough preserved.[9] Gradually these distinct strands began to coalesce into coalitions to organize public programs to preserve and celebrate workers' history and culture. Labour historians often played major roles in pulling together these new projects as part of their search for a new definition of the intellectual's social role that breached the walls around academia more effectively.

What follows here are my own reflections on collaborative work with a variety of people, for the most part from outside academic life, in several different projects in workers' history in southern Ontario in the 1980s and 1990s.[10] These comments are intended both to highlight the challenges facing labour historians in this kind of engagement outside the academy and to suggest possible ways to negotiate them. The emphasis on problems in this discussion should not overshadow the enormous personal rewards that this work brings – the ongoing, humbling process of learning, the new scope for creativity, the deep attachments among co-workers, the warmth of appreciative audiences. It has always been worth the effort.

Workers' Heritage

Launching new programs in workers' history brought the various participants in this new movement into the rapidly expanding realm of historical reconstruction known as "public history." This term is now used to refer to a diverse range of public programming undertaken through museums, historic sites, historical societies, architectural conservancy associations, and government agencies, all run with a mixture of government and private funding. It can take the form of monuments and plaques, restored buildings, exhibitions and displays, speeches and lectures, films and videos, special events, festivals, pageants, and other celebrations – all intended to preserve and interpret particular elements of the past as embodiments of shared values and aspirations – our "heritage." Public-history projects have multiplied rapidly in Canada since the early 1970s – a doubling of the number of museums, for example, from about 1,000 in 1972 to over 2,000 by the early 1990s (some 600 of them in Ontario).[11] For the most part, the dominant modes of cultivating public memory have been highly selective in their form and content, and have conveyed implicit (and sometimes overt) elitist lessons about hierarchy, social and civic harmony, ideological consensus, and cultural cohesion. Public history, for example, has fed the well-cultivated myths of Ontario society as one steeped in benign paternalism, popular deference, and other manifestations of deeply rooted conservatism. Until the 1980s, only a few museums, historical societies, or historic sites acknowledged that workers were part of the national, provincial, or local "heritage." Most simply ignored workers' past in their programming.[12]

The 1970s and 1980s did see some soul-searching in heritage institutions and some effort to recognize greater diversity in the past. The strongest pressures came from the blossoming "multiculturalism" of ethnic groups not drawn from the British Isles[13] and, to a lesser extent, from the diffusion of feminist critiques throughout the culture generally.[14] The emergence of new state funding to support the history of women and ethnic and racial groups helped to make them a higher priority in heritage planning. As the staff in some of these institutions became more professionalized and more sensitive to the new developments in Canadian social history, some workers' history ultimately found its way inside as well. A few large museums (especially in Western Canada) and a growing number of local museums have made serious efforts to address working-class experience.[15] Yet, these new initiatives remained limited: they rarely involved consultation with the labour movement, and, across the broad canvass of mainstream heritage programming, workers still remained invisible or marginalized.

In response, the clusters of labour historians and others interested in workers' history and culture consciously appropriated the term "heritage" and declared that the neglect of "workers' heritage" had to stop. They meant that not only did workers have a right to pass on to their children the collective memory of their particular history, but also that all Canadians should know about workers' contribution to the larger society. In the face of widespread indifference in mainstream heritage institutions, much of the new public programming of workers' heritage was organized outside the established institutional frameworks. Distinct organizations were formed that drew together a variety of people and groups. Labour historians have worked with the local labour movement in Vancouver, Winnipeg, Sudbury, Toronto, Hamilton, Sydney, and New Waterford to develop walking tours of working-class history.[16] Ottawa and Kingston had active workers' heritage committees connected to the local labour councils.[17] Since 1980 the Écomusée du

Fier Monde in Montreal has been constantly evolving into a fascinating community-based project in the preservation of working-class history.[18] And new projects keep emerging.[19] Most of the comments that follow are based on my work with what is probably the most ambitious of these projects to date – the Ontario Workers Arts and Heritage Centre, a collaboration begun in 1988 among representatives of organized labour, artists and curators, teachers, archivists, community activists, and academics. After many years of planning and fund-raising, the Centre was able to open a permanent headquarters in the historic Customs House in Hamilton in November 1996, where it now runs an extensive range of programming.[20]

For labour historians, these new projects in workers' public history involve extending their professional skills as scholars and teachers.[21] They apply their accumulated knowledge about the conditions of working-class life, workers' strategies of coping, and their struggles to change their world, or use their research skills to dig deeper into a specific subject.[22] They also recognize the need to communicate to the less well-informed, just as in their undergraduate classrooms or their talks to labour audiences. From its earliest nineteenth-century forms, the museum was always seen as an educational tool that parallelled other forms of cultural diffusion such as public schools, and, however much museum practices have changed, the didactic, educational role remains predominant. Yet, for the historian, in many ways, the move into public history has meant stepping onto a stage where the script and stage directions are much less familiar. A few historians have worked sporadically with local history societies and museums, and some have begun to teach courses in public history to undergraduate and graduate students. But most university-based historians have never done this kind of work, nor been trained to undertake it. Moreover, it is not highly valued within the academic reward system of tenure and promotion, nor supported by most agencies of scholarly funding.[23]

The historian who crosses the great divide between academic and public history will first be shocked at the devastation that a decade of government budget-slashing has accomplished in the cultural sector. Starved of public funds, administrators of museums and other public-history institutions are scrambling to organize volunteer labour, to raise funds from the community, and to compete for extremely limited "partnerships" in the private sector to run their programs. They may also have to shape their programming to fit the priorities of state bureaucracies – towards multiculturalism, for example, rather than class-based history.

In this context, it is not surprising that workers' heritage projects have had to rely heavily on financial support from unions.

Above and beyond these constraints, the labour historian who enters public history is confronted with at least four other major adjustments: competing for attention with other voices of historical interpretation; learning to work with artefacts; finding new ways to communicate ideas; and coping with diverse audiences. These are dilemmas for any historian but particular challenges for the labour historian.

Competing Interpretations

Any historian drawn into public history is probably first forced to confront the fact that he or she has no monopoly on historical interpretation within the project team. In fact, a new humility will no doubt be necessary in agreeing to work with non-academics who are glad to have his or her expertise on board, but may not accept the historian's right to set the agenda for the project.[24] As many as three other kinds of historical interpretation and communication compete with academic history (and can have much larger audiences).

The first comes from what is often termed the "heritage community" – a loose assortment of people who run local museums, historical societies, and historic sites. In most provinces their interests are promoted by some kind of province-wide historical society of "history buffs," as well as the more professionally oriented Canadian Museums Association and its provincial counterparts.[25] Most of these people have little or no training in academic history (though, since the 1970s, a small but growing percentage may have both history degrees and some professional training in museology or archives studies).[26] Most are volunteers who devote a great deal of time to preserving local heritage, especially old buildings, cemeteries, and the remnants of pioneer life.

The work of these local history enthusiasts is heavily empirical. They amass artefacts and great quantities of information about people and events in a community, which they often publish far outside the orbit of university presses. But their empiricism masks some unmistakable assumptions. As some critics have argued, the heritage community tends to have a nostalgic, relatively uncritical view of the past – one that emphasizes harmony and such solid virtues as hard work and determination and one that assumes the past is closed and shut off from the present. For them, touching the past through public history should be a feel-good experience, a retreat from the disruptions of modernism into a simpler, less troubling world. The rapid proliferation of all these heritage projects after 1970 suggests that many white, Anglo-Celtic, middle-class, and middle-aged Canadians were looking for a cultural anchor in the face of the devastation of familiar urban landscapes, a rapidly changing population mix, rising social conflict, and a steady erosion of local control.[27]

Within this heritage community, an important competitor to workers' heritage is the industrial museum, usually run by the enterprise that worked on the site, such as Redpath Sugar in Toronto, Hiram Walker in Windsor, and, until 1997, Seagram in Waterloo. Here the machinery and technical processes of production loom large in the public programming. So do the products made there and the popular culture within which they circulated, including product advertising (Toronto's Bata Shoe Museum is a striking example). These are invariably up-beat places, celebrating the "progress" represented in industrial transformation and presenting a sanitized version of the past. Workers generally appear as embodiments of technical expertise or as machine tenders. If the social relations of the workplace are acknowledged, they are presented in a glow of "we-were-all-one-happy-family" corporate paternalism. None of the serious accidents or diseases of the workplace, the harsh indignities inflicted by supervisors, the paltry wages, the sexist and racist hiring policies, or the flashes of bitter labour-management conflict – all of which labour historians have documented repeatedly – find their way into the exhibitions. Even where local communities undertake to revive this industrial history in an old mill or plant, the same emphasis may prevail.[28] There have been important exceptions, such as the handful of miners' museums in Canada.[29]

In practice, labour historians may find most of the heritage community more of an impediment (or at least a silent or indifferent onlooker) than a direct competitor in programming workers' heritage. With the exception of the heritage work in a few single-industry towns, especially mining communities, workers have not often figured in the reconstructed past in local museums and historical societies. The buildings that heritage groups thought were worth preserving were either the earliest "pioneer" structures (including military fortifications), or the grand public buildings and lavish homes of the wealthy.[30] The events or social institutions worth remembering were almost never strikes, unions, socialist parties, or anything else smacking of conflict and confrontation. Until the early 1990s, the government-run Ontario Heritage Foundation had only one commemorative plaque devoted to workers' protest out of more than one thousand across the province – and the one group of workers remembered was the "Tolpuddle Martyrs," British labour organizers who had been exiled in the 1830s.[31]

Not surprisingly, the labour movement has had little contact with the heritage community. Occasionally local heritage activists turned their pens to chronicling local labour history, but more often that writing came from inside the "House of Labour" itself.[32] For the most part, the Canadian labour movement had no interest in a plunge back into sepia-toned nostalgia.[33] In fact, until the 1980s, the labour movement's interest in its own history was limited. Outside the national Canadian Labour College, few unions included labour history in their education programs, and few sponsored the writing of their own histories.[34] In part, it was the gradual retirement of a whole generation of labour activists who originally got involved in the 1930s and 1940s that prompted a renewed interest in labour history and labour biography.[35] In part too, that turn resulted from the greater availability of academic labour historians willing to work with labour. In large part, though, a slowly emerging historical consciousness reflected a growing concern among unionists about the attacks on unions and their hard-won gains.[36]

When labour leaders began to articulate the need for heritage preservation, they certainly did not use the antimodernist arguments that still animate so much of the rank and file in the heritage community. A central thrust of the labour movement's participation in workers' heritage projects is to make the past relevant to the current situation of working people. Unionists look to the past for validation of their contemporary concerns and for the threads of a tradition of resistance and struggle. That too can be a selective use of the past, focusing on organized workers and on successful confrontations, rather than the full range of working-class experience. Specifically, they tend to put their financial resources behind history projects that focus on their own unions or branches of the labour movement. Women, people of colour, the homeless, the unorganized generally lack that kind of sponsorship. So, while labour historians may find the older heritage community ignoring them, they may also find that the public history desired by the labour movement may engage only part of their expertise and interests.

Whether in a community museum or a labour hall, this kind of public history also involves a great deal more commemoration and mythmaking than most academics are accustomed to. Many may identify strongly with their subjects (business historians and biographers are often particularly committed), but hard-boiled social and cultural historians may squirm uncomfortably in this new "public" arena. This is particularly true when exhibit themes directly address the labour movement. There is scope here for critical history, but it is constrained by the inevitable expectation of the organizers or sponsors of exhibitions that "we did great things together in the past." So far it has been fairly easy to inject criticisms of sexism and racism within working-class experience, largely because activists within working-class communities are raising those issues today. Other subjects must be treated gently or avoided, however – bureaucratization, communism, or battles between unions within the "House of Labour," for example. This dilemma is deepened by the need for union money, as other sources of funding disappear. There is no need, however, for labour historians to be simply uncritical tools of narrow union agendas. It is possible to find ways to encourage current union members to consider their own history in a different light. Historians can use their critical lenses to play an active role in helping to shape popular "myths" among working people, to strengthen an appreciation of the diversity of working-class experience.

The second form of historical reconstruction that academic historians will find themselves up against is the mass media, which, independent of any official mandate, regularly infuse popular consciousness with their versions of history (or project those produced elsewhere). Newspapers have considerable impact here, as do mass-produced novels and popular histories (such as those produced by Pierre Berton or Heather Robertson). But, these days, these media have much less impact than historical films, television mini-series, or the whole cable channel devoted to "History." Film and video have taken on an immensely powerful role in influencing perceptions of the past.[37] Some workers' history has been finding its way into these visual media over the past fifteen to twenty years, and some film-makers certainly see themselves as loosely part of the workers' heritage movement. Films dealing with workers may be fictional works, non-fiction documentaries, or a hybrid known as "docudrama."[38] Recently, for example, television viewers in Ontario have had access to a CBC drama on children in Cape Breton coal mines (*Pit Ponies*), a documentary on the 1946 steelworkers' strike in Hamilton (*Defying the Law*), and another on the lives of workers in Toronto's Inglis plant (*Working Days*). They have also had the chance to see a major feature film about a Cape Breton mining community (*Margaret's Museum*).[39]

For labour historians, the problem is that even documentaries follow cinematic conventions that are different from the historian's craft.

These visual reconstructions are most often produced by film-makers with little or no historical training, who typically consult with historians but still write their scripts independently. Nuancing of interpretation almost inevitably succumbs to the emphasis on narrative or character development. The conventions of film-making also put a premium on high-quality visuals and tight editing. So academic historians may find themselves battling with film-makers over historical accuracy and interpretation.[40] Given the power of the visual in contemporary culture, this is a medium that we can expect will continue to be influential in conveying historical messages to large audiences (although films about working-class experience are hard to fund and will probably remain small in number).[41] It is a medium that labour historians must be prepared to struggle with to get their expertise respected and integrated, even if the price may be frustration.

Historians have had to compete with a third form of constructing history that is much less public but undoubtedly has a much wider basis in the working class. That is the oral culture that passes on the memory of local events, colourful people, or daily routines, usually in the form of story-telling. These versions of the past are communicated over the family dinner table, the backyard fence, the cafeteria table at work, the beer glasses in a tavern, and countless other informal settings. Generally they have few public outlets, although they may be part of the public culture of after-dinner speeches or occasionally may carry over into the local print and broadcast media (relatively little is passed on through ballads or other popular music as in earlier societies). The historical experience of women is largely relegated to these channels.[42]

This kind of popular memory is not necessarily a static view of the past, and can bring a critical perspective – say, a parent's memory of a son's death in a war that contains little of the heroism of official renditions on Remembrance Day.[43] Researchers engaged in oral history of workers may actually discover a deep contempt for other sources of historical reconstruction ("they don't really understand what happened"). Of course, popular story-telling can be problematic for the historian. The stories tend to be narrowly focused on the most immediate personal relationships within families, neighbourhoods, and workplaces, rather than on broader social dynamics. Indeed, they are often seen consciously as a transmission belt of memories to the next generation within kinship circles or within a particular workplace. They can be full of stoicism in the face of adversity, but, overall, optimistic, as befits a process intended to promote dignity and respect. The popularly related stories of the Great Depression of the 1930s, for example, are generally about survival in the face of chronic economic insecurity (rather than unrelenting defiance through strikes or demonstrations).[44] Nor are these memories innocent or pristine. Memories change – not just through erosion but also through unconscious revision (since such stories almost invariably involve reflection on the ever-changing contemporary world). In fact, popular memory is imbedded in that complex ideological amalgam known as "common sense." Story-telling may not have much direct connection to academic or popular writing on history, but it is filtered through a variety of dominant social, cultural, and political discourses – in schools, the mass media, and public commemoration, in particular. The rhetoric and imagery of the Cold War, for example, shaped popular memories of labour struggles in crucial ways. Sometimes, moreover, the collective working-class memories of a community can been compressed and reintegrated into a more expansive, though factually less certain, tale with the status of "legend."[45] Many Canadian labour historians have grappled with these limitations in their academic scholarship, and, therefore, can bring a sensitivity to the use of oral history.[46] In public-history work, they will feel more pressure to respect the process of story-telling, but they can nonetheless interrogate and contextualize the content as carefully as any other sources. This can be a major challenge when the story-teller is a respected, elderly worker.[47]

Bringing workers' stories into public history work can be simply the vacuum cleaner approach of the oral historian – accumulating information as the raw material for exhibitions, just as academic historians gather oral evidence for their scholarly writing. But that process and the resulting product are generally controlled by the interviewer and may simply take the familiar academic shape. We are typically too insensitive to notice and appreciate the particular cultural form of the working-class story – its narrative structure, its cadences, its ethical power. In workers' heritage programming, the challenge is to recognize that the mode of story-telling (rather than the didactic text panel) is central to the way in which most workers understand the past. The use of video-taped interviews within exhibitions and of elderly workers as tour guides can help. It is also important to recognize that humour is a central force in working-class story-telling, rather than the earnest preachiness or melodrama that middle-class writers tend to adopt in their accounts of working-class life. If the labour historian working in public history has no sense of humour, or at least irony, he or she is doomed.

The Workers Arts and Heritage Centre also used personal reminiscences as the basis for two of its published walking tours, which included oral cassettes with recorded voices to be used in a tape recorder during the tour. A 1997 display on women in northern-Ontario mining communities used transcribed interviews as text, and a 1998 exhibition on Ontario autoworkers presented the actual voices of Studebaker workers. But, on the whole, the Centre's exhibitions have reflected the academic's more abstract conceptualization of the past and have not been structured around story-telling. We still have much to learn about how to link our analytical insights to this popular mode of communication, especially through first-person narrative.[48]

The Centre has discovered, however, that story-telling makes superb theatre. Several times after late 1996, WAHC staged *CuFu*, a one-man show performed by Charlie Chiarelli, a professional story-teller-turned-actor, who grew up in the Italian neighbourhood around the Centre. The performance was a brilliant pastiche of personal stories that brought to life more powerfully than any text panel the nature of Hamilton's postwar immigrant working-class experience. It has been extremely popular with audiences.[49]

Academically trained labour historians, then, must manoeuvre among these competing claims to historical interpretation by heritage enthusiasts, film-makers, and community story-tellers. They soon discover the need to work out a fine balance between their claims to professional expertise and their respect for the insights and perspectives of other kinds of practitioners. Frequently they will find that they have the most critical voice in the project team and will have to negotiate recurrent tendencies to commemorate and glorify – a difficult but not impossible task. Fortunately there are many people employed in public history who share this concern.[50]

Confronting the Artefact

Once labour historians have come to terms with the competing methods and goals of "doing" history, they are confronted with a second major adjustment – the importance of the artefact as both a source of interpretation and a medium of communication with the past. For the most part, other than those studying native peoples, few academic historians make use of artefacts in their research. They may glean some insights from material-culture researchers, but most remain firmly rooted in archival paper.[51] It is therefore a new research challenge to set off in search of objects to be used in an exhibition and to interpret history through them.[52] Furthermore, historians are not accustomed to foregrounding their primary sources. They usually bury most of them in their footnotes, dropping only the juiciest tidbits into their texts. In contrast, public history usually assumes that visitors will get much of the message from their own direct appreciation of objects from the past. Our written analysis on a text panel or an exhibition catalogue may have much less immediate impact than the material objects themselves.

For historians of the working class, this reliance on the artefact poses particular problems. Just as workers left behind relatively few pieces of paper for us to sift through in researching our books, so too most of their material culture has not been well preserved. Museums and historical societies have seldom been as interested as we might like in the tools of working-class housewives and wage-earners, the clothing workers wore, and the objects they surrounded themselves with on a daily basis. What they have may be poorly or inaccurately identified.[53] That neglect is not surprising since documenting the material culture of working-class life is extremely difficult.[54] Where can museum staff turn for descriptions of a worker's kitchen or bedroom, a factory lunchroom, a local tavern, or even the inside of a union hall? Fortunately, for the twentieth century at least, many answers lie in the memories of elderly workers. Along with the historian's careful research in newspapers, public-health reports, social surveys, and so on, interviews can help to clarify what to look for. Often, it turns out that much of this material culture is still to be found on the walls and shelves and in the basements and attics of many working-class families. The challenge is to get people to bring forth objects that they have rarely thought of as having any historical value outside their own family history. A bigger dilemma is how to portray the world of work in gargantuan workplaces – such as the open-hearth department of a steel mill or the assembly line of an auto plant. No one makes much effort to save large industrial machinery. Owners often sell it off for scrap.[55]

For the labour-historian-turned-public-historian, the material culture of the formal organizations of the working class ought to be more accessible. But the banners, placards, floats, charters, photographs, pins, ribbons, regalia, posters, commemorative booklets, union labels, and so much more have not been well looked after over the years. Much was intended to be ephemeral (including the colourful floats, costumes, and effigies from labour parades), and much was pitched out or passed into private hands as unions dissolved or officers changed. Unions are busy organizations with limited time, money, or inclination to devote to careful preservation of their artefacts. Recent efforts to locate this kind of material in southern-Ontario union offices for a WAHC exhibition on labour parades was depressingly unrewarding. More efforts to promote preservation within unions and labour centrals will be necessary.

Public historians interested in workers' heritage have wisely responded to the challenge of bringing working-class history back to life by extending their programming out beyond the walls of heritage institutions to use working-class neighbourhoods as living artefacts and as an active resource for portraying workers' heritage. The results have been impressive, if limited so far. Walking tours, community-sponsored exhibitions, installations, workshops, commemorative events, and so on have made it possible to use the architectural heritage of these older neighbourhoods and the oral traditions still alive and well within them to bring to life an earlier period of working-class history (though obviously this tends to be limited to the twentieth-century experience). At this point, academic historians may well find themselves drawn to fascinating new historiographical questions about spatial dimensions of history and the uses of memory that can enrich their scholarship immensely.[56]

Unfortunately, the ability to use these neighbourhoods as an "ecomuseum" is increasingly constrained by four new forces that have emerged over the past thirty years in many larger cities: the devastation of so-called urban renewal projects, the dispersion of so many of these older working-class communities to the suburbs, the colonizing of the older neighbourhoods by middle-class renovators (or new working-class immigrants), and the steady, long-term de-industrialization of so many old industrial areas, which has often led to the abandonment and eventual destruction of both workers' housing and important old industrial buildings. The demolition of Toronto's Inglis factory was a striking case in point.[57] The heritage agencies with power to designate historically significant buildings rarely raise a ruckus about industrial heritage, despite the fact that community life may have revolved around these sites for decades. Hardly any factories or mills have been preserved as heritage sites, and those that have tend to be nineteenth-century mills situated in picturesque river valleys.[58]

So, for all these reasons, labour historians will find themselves in a scramble for artefacts. As in our scholarly endeavours, we may find ourselves heavily dependent on sources generated outside the working class – temperance literature, public-health posters, or commercial advertising aimed at working-class housewives, for example. Above all, however, we are drawn to photographs. The most common visual display of working-class history is a photographic exhibition. There are, of course, a multitude of problems with seeing these as the unfiltered windows on the workers' past. Most of the photos taken at the time and almost all those that have survived were produced by people outside the working class who found workers quaint, exotic, pathetic, heroic, or, in the case of professional studio photographers, simply respectable customers. Many historians have used photographs in their books and articles far too uncritically – as merely illustrations, without questioning the assumptions and conventions that lay behind the photographer's eye. In heritage work, labour historians can bring that sensitivity to the use of photographs in heritage presentation and can try to encourage visitors to examine the biases in this kind of artefact. They don't always do so.[59]

Modes of Communicating

The third adjustment that historians have to make in moving into public history is to the new modes of communication that we must learn to work with (and for which they are generally completely untrained). They typically get far less room to put their thoughts into writing in public history than in academic work. They may get the chance to contribute to a catalogue or handout, but the space is limited, and the prose must be sparse. They are exhorted not to write out their books on the wall, since visitors to heritage installations have little tolerance for excessive wordiness.[60]

Most of their written contributions to public history are short paragraphs mounted on text panels alongside or embedded within a display. Far more of their analysis must be communicated visually (or perhaps orally) through the selection and presentation of artefacts, the arrangement of space within the exhibition, and the use of lighting and sound. Museum installations are also increasingly interactive, involving hands-on contact with displays and access to CD-ROMS, interactive videos, and motion-activated lighting and sound. Historians' expertise rarely extends to these media. As an American museum administrator has suggested, "An exhibition or a historic site is much more than the written text of labels and conveys much more complex information through spatial relationships, visual images, real things, and social interactions in a three-dimensional environment that is social, multisensory, and largely self-directed."[61]

Preparing this public-history material involves forms of teamwork that contrast sharply with the individualism of most academic scholarship. In some cases, historians have to work with museologically trained staff and professional designers. Many museums and historical societies, however, cannot afford such professionalism, and the historian and the local heritage enthusiasts have to make their own judgments. In this process they may fall back on the unquestioned formalities of the museums in their youth, with little understanding of new developments in museology.

Academics, nonetheless, generally do have a lot of experience in trying to communicate ideas in a learning process, and have been getting a lot more experimental in classroom techniques. Feminist influences on pedagogy[62] have been at the forefront of a wave of new concern to take account of students' social backgrounds in curriculum development, to engage them more actively in the learning process (with debates, role playing, or dramatizations), to stimulate small-group teamwork in classroom discussion, and to encourage projects that connect with the world beyond the university (e.g., with oral-history projects). Many labour historians have learned that helping students understand what workers faced in the past, how they managed to survive, and how they rallied to change their world requires a good deal more than giving them information. They encourage them to look critically at primary historical sources and at the way history is written. They send them off to conduct interviews with seniors. All of these developments in university teaching can be good experience to bring to bear on public history.

There are counter-pressures, however. What historians discover soon after their plunge into public history is that heritage presentations are competing with lavish "theme-park" approaches to public culture for patrons' attention and tourist dollars – a trend that, regrettably, turns the past into a contained, definable commodity to be consumed in leisure time, outside the "real" world of modern society.[63] There is a growing assumption that museums have always been too earnest and that they cannot compete for the public's leisure time unless they become some kind of entertainment. The drying-up of stable state funding at all levels for heritage projects means that non-profit heritage institutions are desperate to attract admission fees (and to promote gift-shop sales). And the theme parks have set the pace in terms of expensive interactive technology and entertaining exhibits. Ultimately, few heritage institutions beyond such giants as the Royal Ontario Museum or the National

Museum of Civilization can ever hope to compete head to head with Canada's Wonderland. There is unlikely to be a marked shift in cultural consumerism towards small heritage projects and institutions.

Historians of the working class may find this pressure to inject excitement into exhibitions particularly daunting since they have no experience in turning their research into entertainment (beyond classroom showmanship), they may have so few artefacts or images to work with, and, typically, the tight finances of their heritage projects prevent the use of expensive interactive toys. At WAHC, several exhibitions ended up as flat displays attached to walls, with only limited three-dimensionality and even more limited interactivity. Yet smaller projects can still make an impact if imaginatively conceived. It is possible to have active exhibitions about working-class history without CD-ROMs or interactive videos. Visitors can be "entertained" by doing as much as by watching. Keeping the exhibits as accessible and hands-on as possible is a starting point. Labour historians are well aware of the importance of manual labour in the working-class home or the paid workplace, and can use their knowledge of labour processes to help make visitor-friendly tools (original or reproductions) central to displays about the household, the factory, or the construction site. Dioramas of particular work settings need not be fenced off with ropes or plexi-glass and can allow visitors to examine or try their hand at washing clothes by hand, shaping wood with a plane, or whatever.[64] In a stab at a different mode of presentation, I designed a large board game to demonstrate the pre-welfare-state family economy for a working-class kitchen in the 1930s, which, I am told, many children and adults found as engaging as any computer simulation. Theatre and music can also enhance exhibitions (Jackie Washington, a well-known Hamilton African-Canadian blues musician who grew up in the working-class North End, has performed several times at WAHC, for example). In the process of conceptualizing, labour historians invariably find themselves stretched in creative new directions by their interaction with the designers and artists who have been hired to make the exhibitions visually compelling.

Audiences

The fourth adjustment that academic historians have to make is to different audiences. Many aspire to write their books for a wide, educated readership and succeed to varying degrees. In reality, their scholarly production most often reaches few beyond the specialists in the field who share their fascination with the subject, a slightly wider circle of graduate students, and, if they are lucky, some undergraduates who are compelled to read their work. In contrast, public history assumes from the start that the potential audience is wide, diverse, and unspecialized, ranging from the half-interested school children herded through local museums, to vacationing tourists (with or without children) checking out local attractions, to seniors seeking the nostalgia of past experience, to citizens seriously interested in deepening their knowledge of history and culture. One researcher found local museums in Ontario aiming at the comprehension level of a thirteen-year old,[65] but, in reality, it is risky to assume a single homogeneous audience. The diversity of audiences confronts the historian with the need to find a level of interpretation and a mode of communication that takes into account the ignorance and misconceptions, as well as the deep reservoirs of knowledge about a subject, that visitors might bring with them.

In the case of workers' heritage, there are two special problems. The first is that museums are not particularly popular with most working people. Or, perhaps more fairly, workers tend to prefer to spend their time in other ways. There are plenty of workers who are fascinated with history and participate in local history societies and heritage events, but they tend to be exceptional and most often elderly. Like most of us, workers' first contact with museums was probably on compulsory school trips, where many must have found the serious, didactic tone of the grand halls filled with glass cases to be an extension of the class biases they were facing in their classrooms. Most did not find anything much relevant to their own lives in the institutions they were compelled to visit and had little inclination to come back. It is ironic that, while the Workers Arts and Heritage Centre chose to locate in Hamilton as a city with a rich working-class history, workers did not arrive spontaneously at our doors in large numbers. In July 1997, when a huge summer festival drew thousands of people to a waterfront park about half a mile away, perhaps a hundred walked up the hill to see the Centre's highly relevant exhibition on the social uses of the harbour entitled "The People and the Bay." Avoiding the word "museum" in favour of "arts and heritage centre" has not helped much since the word "heritage" still has official connotations and is not one that many working people use (at least not in this way).

The labour historian will probably also find that few workers want to fill their leisure hours immersed in the grim reality of slum life or exploitation in the workplace that runs through so much of the social history that we write. In their leisure time, they might understandably prefer not to confront experiences that are not so far from their own daily lives – jobs that are still unrewarding or unfulfilling, economic insecurity in their own families, general feelings of powerlessness, and so on. Why should we expect people to spend a Sunday afternoon getting depressed about their lot when they can find more fun almost anywhere else? What they seem to respond to best are the suggestions in exhibitions that workers were active agents in the past – that a wage-earner could take pride in his or her production, that a housewife strategized creatively against poverty, that a group of workers fought back against low wages, that a well-known local politician supported working people's struggles, and so on. Labour historians therefore may find themselves tailoring their contributions to public history to tone down the bleak and discouraging parts of workers' heritage.

One promising way to try bridging the gulf between a heritage centre and its working-class audiences is to involve working people themselves in the planning, development, and organization of an exhibition, so that a heritage display is not simply a professional product seeking a passive audience. The Écomusée in Montreal has pioneered this work in Canada and has had considerable success.[66] WAHC has had several exhibitions to which specific unions have been convinced to contribute, although involving members in the planning and production has proved difficult to organize. Two projects integrated unionists: members of two CUPE locals in Hamilton collaborated with artist Jim Miller on a project called "Making Time," and a group of retired Studebaker workers helped create an exhibition on their working lives in the Hamilton plant. Three projects did grow out of other bases in the community – residents of Hamilton's North End contributed to the walking-tour project known as "The Workers' City," a local centre for immigrant women worked with a number of local artists, and a group of high-school history students developed a small exhibition known as "Working Family Treasures" aimed at displaying the story behind some familiar object in an elderly relative's household.[67] The Centre's limited experience with this kind of community-based exhibition suggests that there are rich rewards but also large practical problems. Working people have to be convinced that their histories have any relevance, and also have to be encouraged to shed their deference to professional direction. They may too easily assume that the existence of the Centre means that we will organize the project for them.

Labour historians and their collaborators in workers' public history may soon discover, moreover, that they have to confront some conventional assumptions about historical exhibitions among working people. Even the key supporters of workers' heritage inside the labour movement have surprisingly old-fashioned notions about what they want in their museum. To a great extent, they seem to expect a fairly traditional exhibition with formal glass cases, only this time they want to see them filled with labour memorabilia. They are delighted with the grand architecture of the old Custom House that WAHC inhabits – in spite of all the museological debates about avoiding the museum as "temple."[68] It is not hard to see that these assumptions among working people are based not only on their limited contact with museums, but also on their deep concern about respectability. Just as they believe that union photographs should be carefully posed portraits, and public occasions should maintain a basic decorum,[69] so too, museums or heritage centres devoted to workers' history should be proper, respectable places – even if that means being formal and stuffy.

Ultimately, the labour historian and his or her collaborators in workers' heritage projects may want to question the very notion of an "audience." Perhaps the greatest conceptual hurdle to get over is that heritage programming should be a cultural package ready and waiting to be appreciated by visitors (much as we imagine our books in relation to our readership). In practice, WAHC has learned that after a splashy opening night, an exhibition may have little life unless it connects with ongoing community activism. Off-the-street visits may be minimal, but group visits from schools, unions, seniors' organizations, and so on are always more successful. The Centre is also attracting growing numbers of labour, arts, women's, and other community groups who are eager to use the space for meetings, events, and celebrations. The exhibitions then tend to be appreciated as historical or artistic links with the present, rather than merely abstracted cultural products waiting for an audience. Labour historians can also bring their sensitivity to the flow of working-class life to suggest many ways to carry programming outside central locations (like Hamilton's Custom House) into shopping malls, unemployment offices, community centers, union halls, churches, and a variety of locations where working people regularly gather.[70]

The public history of working-class experience can be enlightening ("I didn't know that happened!"), challenging ("How could people be treated so badly?"), reassuring ("We've done some great things together!"), or ennobling ("They really were the salt of the earth!").

Yet it should also be at least somewhat empowering – the knowledge or inspiration working people get from "workers' heritage" should give them some critical tools for assessing and confronting their present situations. As labour historians have discovered in their classrooms and their own research projects, the link between the past and the present can be a powerful force.[71]

None of these comments should be interpreted as a suggestion that labour historians involved in public history have to abandon their intellectual integrity to some kind of pop-culture pablum. People want us involved in these projects for what we do best – researching and interpreting the past. We are simply developing a new role for the "public intellectual," which has traditionally included intervention into the formation of public opinion and can now take on new dimensions. The difficult learning curve for us is how and where to communicate our knowledge beyond the classroom, the academic conference, and the scholarly publication. If we are prepared to work collectively and respectfully with other non-academic practitioners of historical reconstruction, to learn new visual and oral modes of communicating, and to reorient our thinking away from creating a cultural product for cultural consumption towards a more dynamic development of public history programs within the daily lives of working people, then we can be extremely effective in helping to make workers' heritage a fuller part of Canada's cultural legacy. In the process we will help to build a more democratic culture.

Notes

1 For reflections by one such labour historian, see Michael Piva, "Labour Historians and Unions: Assessing the Interaction," *L/LT* 27 (Spring 1991), 209–11. The emergence of a new generation of labour historians is traced in Gregory S. Kealey, "Writing about Labour," in John Schultz, ed., *Writing about Canada: A Handbook for Modern Canadian History* (Scarborough: Prentice-Hall Canada 1990), 145–74. For reflections on the difficulties of reconciling a working-class background with intellectual work, see Richard Hoggart, *The Uses of Literacy* (London: Penguin 1957); Richard Sennett and Jonathan Cobb, *The Hidden Injuries of Class* (New York: Vintage Books 1972); Janet Zandy, ed., *Liberating Memory: Our Work and Our Working-Class Consciousness* (New Brunswick, NJ: Rutgers University Press 1995).

2 History Workshop began in 1966 in Ruskin College at Oxford University. It involved a new, more participatory approach to adult education for

working-class students, in which they researched and wrote their own history within a framework of collective support and critique. In 1975 a new journal, *History Workshop*, appeared, and a large conference was convened at Ruskin each year. This new approach to history also brought into being many local working-class history groups known as "history workshops." In addition to the journal itself, see Raphael Samuel, "History Workshop, 1966–80," in Samuel, ed., *People's History and Socialist Theory* (London: Routledge and Kegan Paul 1981), 410–17.

3 Probably the most high-profile example has been the Labour College of Canada, which has included academically trained labour historians in its teaching staff for many years. See Max Swerdlow, *Brother Max: Labour Organizer and Educator* (St John's: Canadian Committee on Labour History 1990); Piva, "Labour Historians and Unions"; John Bullen, "Rewarding Your Enemies, Punishing Your Friends: The Labour College Strike of 1983," *L/LT* 27 (Spring 1991), 163–74.

4 For example, Ian McKay, *The Craft Transformed: An Essay on the Carpenters of Halifax, 1885–1985* (Halifax: Holdfast Press 1985); Craig Heron, Shea Hoffmitz, Wayne Roberts, Robert Storey, *All That Our Hands Have Done: A Pictorial History of the Hamilton Workers* (Oakville: Mosaic Press 1981); Working Lives Collective, *Working Lives: Vancouver, 1886–1986* (Vancouver: New Star Books 1985); Mercedes Steedman, Peter Suschnigg, Dieter Buse, eds., *Hard Lessons: The Mine Mill Union in the Canadian Labour Movement* (Toronto: Dundurn Press 1995); Wayne Lewchuk and the CAW Local 525 Retirees, *Working and Motoring in a Steeltown: The History of CAW Local 525: 1948–1998* (Hamilton: Ontario Workers Arts and Heritage Centre 1998).

5 See Bruce Spencer, "Industrial Studies for Trade Unionists," *L/LT* 30 (Fall 1992), 261–75; Elaine Bernard, "Labour Programmes: A Challenging Partnership," *L/LT* 27 (Spring 1991), 199–209; Joel Denker, *Unions and Universities: The Rise of the New Labour Leader* (Montclair, NJ: Allanheld Osmun 1981). Since the late 1970s, several Canadian universities (Athabaska, Brock, Manitoba, McMaster, Saskatchewan, Simon Fraser, Windsor, York, among others) have belatedly begun offering Labour Studies programs. On the decline of the Workers Educational Association in Canada, see Ian Radforth and Joan Sangster, "'A Link between Labour and Learning': The Workers Educational Association in Ontario, 1917–1951," *L/LT* 8/9 (Autumn 1981/Spring 1982), 41–78.

6 See Myer Siemiatycki and Gail Benick, *Labour Studies in the Classroom: An Introduction* (Toronto: Toronto Board of Education 1984); Peter Seixas, "Teaching Working Class History in B.C.," *L/LT* 27 (Spring 1991), 195–9; Myra Novogrodsky, "Putting Workers' History into the Schools," *Worklines*,

Spring 1994, 8. Novogrodsky was hired by the Toronto Board of Education as its Women's Studies and Labour Studies Co-ordinator, and later headed its Equity Studies department.

7 See *Archivaria*'s "Special Issue on Documenting Labour," 27 (Winter 1988–9); and the Association of Canadian Archivists, *Labour Archives Bulletin.*

8 The most important forms were the Mayworks Festival, which began in Toronto in 1986 and emerged in a few other Canadian cities in subsequent years, and the Artist and the Workplace Program, sponsored by the Ontario Arts Council. See Catherine McLeod, *Mayworks: Ten Good Years* (Toronto: Mayworks 1996); Karl Beveridge, "Working Partners: The Arts and the Labour Movement," in Steedman et al., eds., *Hard Lessons*, 251–68; "Programme Links Unions and Artists," *Worklines*, Spring 1994, 10–11; and Karl Beveridge and Jude Johnston, *Making Our Mark: Labour Arts and Heritage in Ontario* (Toronto: Between the Lines 1999). Rosemary Donegan has curated several exhibitions with work and workers as the central theme; see, in particular, *Spadina Avenue* (Vancouver and Toronto: Douglas and McIntyre 1985); and *Industrial Images/Images industrielles* (Hamilton: Art Gallery of Hamilton 1989).

9 See, in particular, D'Arcy Martin, "The Ontario Workers' Museum" (initial discussion draft prepared for the Arts and Labour Subcommittee, Ontario Federation of Labour, 7 June 1988).

10 These include a photographic history project through the McMaster Labour Studies Program, presentations to three Ontario Museum Association conferences (one of which I co-chaired), a term on the Toronto Board of Education's Labour Education Committee, a curriculum development project for that board using historical photographs, three historical presentations at plaque unveilings for the Ontario Heritage Foundation (on whose board I was vice-chair for three years), guest lectures to teachers' conferences, labour-arts events, historical societies, and unions, and twelve years on the board of the Ontario Workers Arts and Heritage Centre, as administrator, lobbyist, fundraiser, historical advisor, curator, and much more.

11 J. Lynne Teather, "Museum-Making in Canada (to 1972)," *Muse*, Summer/Fall 1992, 29; Greg Baeker, Margaret May, and Mary Tivy, "Ontario Museums in the 1990s," *Muse*, Summer/Fall 1992, 120.

12 Mary Tivy, "Museums, Visitors, and the Reconstruction of the Past in Ontario," *MHR* 37 (Spring 1993), 35–51; Chris Miller-Marti, "Local Museums and the Creation of 'The Past,'" *Muse*, Summer 1987, 36–9; Lovat Dickson, *The Museum Makers: The Story of the Royal Ontario Museum* (Toronto: Royal Ontario Museum 1986); C.J. Taylor, *Negotiating the Past:*

The Making of Canada's National Historical Parks and Sites (Montreal and Kingston: McGill-Queen's University Press 1990); Daniel Francis, *National Dreams: Myth, Memory, and Canadian History* (Vancouver: Arsenal Pulp Press 1997); Michael Wallace, "Visiting the Past: History Museums in the United States," in Susan Porter Benson, Stephen Brier, and Roy Rosenzweig, eds., *Presenting the Past: Essays on History and the Public* (Philadelphia: Temple University Press 1986), 137–61; Michael Bommes and Patrick Wright, "'Charms of Residence': The Public and the Past," in Richard Johnson et al., eds., *Making Histories: Studies in History-Writing and Politics* (London: Hutchinson 1982), 252–302.

13 See, for example, "The Ukrainian Cultural Heritage Village," *Muse*, Summer 1987, 8; Laurence Grant (with Mary Smith and Pat Zimmer), "Cultural Pluralism in Three Ontario Community Museums," *Muse*, Winter 1992, 54–6; Sandra Morton Weizman, "Multiculturalism in Museums: *A Coat of Many Colours*, A Case Study," *Muse*, Spring 1992, 60–2.

14 For critiques of the treatment of women in public history, see Sharon Reilly, "Setting an Agenda for Women in Museums: The Presentation of Women in Museum Exhibits and Collections," *Muse*, Spring 1989, 47–51; Jane R. Glaser and Artemis A. Zenetou, eds., *Gender Perspectives: Essays on Women in Museums* (Washington: Smithsonian Institution Press 1994); and Thomas Dublin, Nancy Grey Osterud, and Joy Parr, eds., "Special Issue on Public History," *Gender and History* 6, no. 3 (November 1994), including Laurence Grant's discussion of developing an exhibition on the history of women at the Windsor Community Museum. See also Tina Bates and Helen Knibb, "The Museum as a Teaching Resource for Women's History," in Bettina Bradbury et al., eds., *Teaching Women's History: Challenges and Solutions* (Athabasca: Athabasca University Press 1995), 245–54.

15 In January 1983 the Ontario Museum Association sponsored a large conference on the history of work, "Industrious in Their Habits: Rediscovering the World of Work," but the long-term impact on the Ontario heritage community seems to have been negligible. There is no consistent inventory of exhibitions relating to working-class history in Canada. The Manitoba Museum of Man and Nature has had a series of a exhibitions, beginning with "Concerning Work" in 1982 (which travelled across the country) and including a display on "Winnipeg 1919"; see Alan F.J. Artibise and Wendelina A. Fraser, "Concerning Work: Change in the Work Process in Canada, 1850–2000," *Muse*, Summer 1984, 34–6. The Vancouver Museum organized a large exhibit on "Making a Living, Making a Life" in 1992. In Ontario, the Woodlands Cultural Centre in Brantford presented an exhibition on native iron workers entitled "Skywalkers" in 1987, the

Welland Museum has presented several exhibits on workers' lives, and the Windsor Community Museum opened an exhibition on autoworkers and auto production in 1998. Women's work was featured in exhibits in Welland, Brant County, Chatham-Kent, Peterborough, and Raleigh. Miners' history has had plenty of ongoing attention at the Miners' Museum in Glace Bay, NS, and the Cumberland Museum in Cumberland, BC, among others. The Beaton Institute at the University College of Cape Breton has undertaken a many-faceted "Steel Project," which included the production of a video on the history of steelworkers and steel-making. For a review of similar and even more widespread developments in the United States, see Mike Wallace, "Razor Ribbons, History Museums, and Civic Salvation," *RHR* 57 (Fall 1993), 221–41.

16 Peter Steven, "Time Tripping: Cross Country Check-Up on Labour History Tours," *Our Times*, September–October 1996, 24–8.

17 Peter Boyle, "Project Highlights Kingston Workers," *Worklines*, Spring 1994, 7; Ken Clavette, "Giving a Voice to Ottawa's Disappearing Industrial Workers – Preserving Our Heritage: An Oral History Project," *Worklines*, Fall 1996/Winter 1997, 17–19.

18 "L'Écomusée de la maison du fier monde," *Muse*, Winter 1991, 8–9; "Innovation Marks Montreal Museum," *Worklines*, Spring 1994, 9.

19 In the United States, this kind of collaboration has resulted in the publication of a glossy, well-illustrated magazine, *Labor's Heritage*, by the AFL-CIO's George Meany Centre.

20 The evolution of the Centre since 1994 and the range of its activities can be traced through the pages of its newsletter, *Worklines*, which is published twice a year. See also the first annual report issued in November 1997.

21 Hervé Gagnon explores some of these issues in "Education and the History Museum: Change or Tradition?" *Muse*, Summer 1989, 54–7.

22 In two WAHC exhibitions that I worked on, for example, I simply incorporated my previous scholarship, but a third required a great deal of new research.

23 In 1988 the Ontario Heritage Policy Review's *Summary of Public Submissions* (Toronto 1988) included only six people (out of 247 presenters) who gave a university address. I was virtually the only academic historian to show up at its large public meeting at Toronto's Harbourfront to discuss the issues (my invitation to this event resulted from some work I had done with the Ontario Museum Association a few years earlier). At the same time, it must be said that the discussion at that meeting proceeded as though university history departments did not exist. On this heritage review, see Baeker, May, and Tivy, "Ontario Museums,"

122–3. For discussions of the importance of contact between academic historians and public history, see Thierry Ruddel, "The Museum's Need for a Critical Conscience: A Role for Universities," *Muse*, November 1989, 52–3; Adrienne D. Hood, "The Practice of [American] History: A Canadian Curator's Perspective," *JAH* 81, no. 1 (December 1994), 1011–19; and Hood, "Toward Collaboration? Museums, Universities and Material Culture Studies in *Canada*," ibid., 85, no.1 (February 1998), 37–40; Alan Brinkley, "Historians and Their Publics," ibid., 81, no. 1 December 1994), 1027–30.

24 For a strong statement of independence from a "city historian," see Cary Carson, "City Museums as Historians," *JUH* 18, no. 2 (February 1992), 183–91.

25 There may also be state heritage agencies. The Ontario Heritage Foundation, for example, was charged with a modest, ambiguous role of heritage programming, mostly maintaining a network of historical plaques, providing funds for other heritage and archaeological activities, and operating a string of stately rural mansions as local museums and the historic Elgin–Winter Garden Theatre in Toronto.

26 The Ontario Museum Association began offering certificate courses in "museum studies" in 1979; Baeker, May, and Tivy, "Ontario Museums," 121. See also Hood, "Toward Collaboration?"

27 Mary Tivy, "Museums, Visitors, and the Reconstruction of the Past in Ontario," *MHR* 37 (Spring 1993), 35–51; Jean Friesen, "Introduction: Heritage Futures," *PF* 15, no. 2 (Fall 1990), 194. The antimodernist impulse is also explored brilliantly in Ian McKay, "Tartanism Triumphant: The Construction of Scottishness in Nova Scotia, 1933–1954," *Acadiensis* 21, no. 2 (Spring 1992), 5–47; and *The Quest of the Folk: Antimodernism and Cultural Selection in Twentieth-Century Nova Scotia* (Montreal and Kingston: McGill University Press 1994). See also T.J. Jackson Leers, *No Place of Grace: Anti-Modernism and the Transformation of American Culture, 1880–1920* (New York: Pantheon Books 1981).

28 For descriptions of Canadian examples, see *The Seagram Museum* (Erin, ON: Stoddart 1992); Janet Homewood, "The Canadian Railway Museum," *Muse*, Spring 1991, 10–11; Jean Mackintosh, "The Albemi Valley Museum," *Muse*, Summer/Fall 1991, 14–15; Kris Anderson, "The British Columbia Forest Museum," *Muse*, Spring 1992, 8; Michelle Audet, "La Musée minéralogique et minier de Thetford Mines," *Muse*, November 1997, 52–3. For critical discussions of industrial museums in Britain and North America, see Bob West, "The Making of the English Working Past: A Critical View of the lronbridge Gorge Museum," in Robert Lumley, ed., *The Museum Time-Machine: Putting Cultures on Display* (London: Routledge 1988), 36–62; Tony Bennet, "Museums and 'The People,'" in *Museum Time-Machine*, 63–85; Wallace, "Visiting the Past."

29 See, for example, "Miners' Museum," *Muse*, Autumn 1983, 4–5.

30 See, for example, Stephen Barber, "Conserving Winnipeg's Built Heritage, 1974–1985," *PF* 15, no. 2 (Fall 1990), 301–27. For a discussion of the biases of the "preservationist" movement in the United States, see Michael Wallace, "Reflections on the History of Historic Preservation," in Benson, Brier, and Rosenzweig, eds., *Presenting the Past*, 165–99; on the British experience, see Bommes and Wright, "Charms of Residence."

31 Mary Ellen Perkins, comp., *A Guide to Provincial Plaques in Ontario* (Toronto: Ontario Heritage Foundation 1989). During the 1990s, OHF plaques were unveiled in honour of Hamilton's labour MLA Allan Studholme, the 1872 printers' strike in Toronto, and the Nine-Hour movement in Hamilton. *Worklines*, Fall 1995, 5–7. The lack of interest in workers' heritage was evident in the fact that WAHC had been open for eighteen months before Hamilton's local history society held a meeting there, and that apparently none of the members had previously visited the Centre on their own.

32 For example, Thomas Melville Bailey, *They Knew What They Wanted: A History of Local 18, United Brotherhood of Carpenters and Joiners of America, Hamilton, Ontario, Canada* (Hamilton 1983). Labour's home-grown historians included Morden Lazarus in Ontario, who wrote *Years of Hard Labour: An Account of the Canadian Workingman, His Organizations, and Tribulations Over a Period of More Than a Hundred Years* (Don Mills: Ontario Federation of Labour 1974); *Up from the Ranks* (Don Mills: Ontario Federation of Labour 1977); and *The Long Winding Road: Canadian Labour in Politics* (Vancouver: Boag Foundation 1977); also Edward E. Seymour, whose *Illustrated History of Canadian Labour, 1800–1974* (Ottawa: Canadian Labour Congress 1976) sold thousands of copies in labour-education courses throughout the labour movement. Sometimes unions turned to academically trained people for this work – Eugene Forsey, Paul Phillips, Greg Kealey, or Ian McKay, for example.

33 In the "Popular Front" period of the late 1930s, the Communist Party of Canada resurrected some popular history to give some roots to their contemporary struggles against fascism. In this vein, the party's leading intellectual, Stanley Ryerson, produced *1837: The Birth of Canadian Democracy* (Toronto: F. White 1937). In the early 1950s the party also sponsored a project in workers' history to be entitled "With Our Own Hands," under the editorship of Margaret Fairley. It was never completed. See Gregory S. Kealey, *Workers and Canadian History* (Montreal and Kingston: McGill-Queen's University Press 1995), 52; David Kimmel and Gregory S. Kealey, "With Our Own Hands: Margaret Fairley and the 'Real Makers' of Canada," *L/LT* 31 (Spring 1993), 253–85.

34 See, for example, A.L. Hepworth, "Education Activities of Congress Affiliates," *Canadian Labour*, November 1960, 25–7. On the Canadian Labour College, see Swerdlow, *Brother Max*. At a workshop of the Canadian Committee on Labour History in 1990, New Brunswick unionist Raymond Leger argued that "the labour movement in general has not used labour history as an educational tool as it should have"; see "The New Brunswick Experience," *L/LT* 27 (Spring 1991), 211–12. For a discussion of the limited interest in local workers' history among some American unions, see James R. Green, "Workers, Unions, and the Politics of Public History," *PH* 11, no. 4 (Fall 1989), 15–19.

35 Labour biographies began to blossom in the 1970s and 1980s; see, for example, John Davidson and John Deverall, *Joe Davidson* (Toronto: James Lorimer 1978); Rick Salutin, *Kent Rowley, The Organizer: A Canadian Union Life* (Toronto: James Lorimer 1980); Howard While, *A Hard Man to Beat: The Story of Bill While, Labour Leader, Historian, Shipyard Worker, Raconteur* (Vancouver: Pulp Press 1983); Gerald Fortin and Boyce Richardson, *Life of the Party* (Montreal: Véhicule Press 1984); George MacEachern, *George MacEachern: An Autobiography*, ed. David Frank and Don MacGillivray (Sydney: University College of Cape Breton Press 1987); Jack Scott, *A Communist Life: Jack Scott and the Canadian Workers' Movement, 1927–1985*, ed. Bryan D. Palmer (St John's: Committee on Canadian Labour History 1988); Milan (Mike) Bosnich, *One Man's War: Reflections on a Rough Diamond* (Toronto: Lugus Productions 1989); Swerdlow, *Brother Max*; Nicholas Fillmore, *Maritime Radical: The Life and Times of Roscoe Fillmore* (Toronto: Between the Lines 1992); Susan Crean, *Grace Hartman: A Woman for Her Time* (Vancouver: New Star Books 1995); Doug Smith, *Cold Warrior: C.S. Jackson and the United Electrical Workers* (St John's: Canadian Committee on Labour History 1997); Frank Colantonio, *From the Ground Up: An Italian Immigrant's Story* (Toronto: Between the Lines 1997).

36 The changing context for unions in Canada is discussed in Leo Panitch and Donald Swartz, *The Assault on Trade Union Freedoms: From Wage Controls to Social Contract* (Toronto: Garamond Press 1993).

37 The interaction of working-class audiences and feature films is explored in Peter Stead, *Film and the Working Class: The Feature Film in British and American Society* (London: Routledge 1989).

38 The development of the docudrama is traced in Eric Breitbart, "The Painted Mirror: Historical Re-creation from the Panorama to the Docudrama," in Benson, Brier, and Rosenzweig, eds., *Presenting the Past*, 105–17.

39 For a guide to American (and a few Canadian) films about workers, see Tom Zaniello, *Working Stiffs, Union Maids, Reds, and Riffraff: An Organized*

Guide to Films about Labor (Ithaca: ILPR Press/Cornell University Press 1996).

40 The best-known recent example of tension between documentary film-makers and academic historians in Canada is addressed in David J. Bercuson and S.F. Wise, eds., *The Valour and the Horror Revisited* (Montreal and Kingston: McGill-Queen's University Press 1994). For a revealing interview with American film-maker Ken Burns, who has made several historical documentaries, see "The Movie-Maker as Historian: Conversations with Ken Burns," *JAH* 81, no. 2 (December 1994), 1031–50.

41 Norflicks Productions set out to organize a major series of thirty-nine hour-long documentary films for television, under the rubric of "The People's History of Canada: Working People's Contributions to Canadian Life." The first, *Defying the Law,* is an excellent presentation of the 1946 steel strike in Hamilton. The company assembled an advisory board of academics, unionists, and cultural workers.

42 The Center on History-Making in America found through surveys that respondents to the question "Where do you turn for information about the past?" listed, in order of frequency, "books; family members or relatives; primary sources, such as letters or archival material; professionals including scholars and teachers; and television." In subsequent interviews, "grandparents were seen as the most trustworthy sources for information about family and human experiences, while teachers as well as TV were perceived as biased." Barbara Franco, "The Communication Conundrum: What Is the Message? Who Is Listening?" *JAH* 81, no. 1 (June 1994), 157.

43 John Bodnar explores this difference in *Remaking America: Public Memory, Commemoration, and Patriotism in the Twentieth Century* (Princeton: Princeton University Press 1992).

44 See, for example, W. Peter Archibald, "Distress, Dissent, and Alienation: Hamilton Workers in the Great Depression," *UHR* 21, no. 1 (October 1992), 3–32.

45 Larry Peterson develops this fascinating perspective on working-class memory in "Workers' Memory as Legend and Myth: Reconstructing Labor Conflicts at Pullman" (paper presented to the North American Labor History Conference, Detroit 1996).

46 See, in particular, Joan Sangster, "Telling our Stories: Feminist Debates and the Use of Oral History," *Women's History Review* 3, no. 1 (1994), 5–28.

47 Popular Memory Group, "Popular Memory: Theory, Politics, Method," in Johnston et al., ed., *Making Histories*, 205–52; David Lowenthal, *The Past Is a Foreign Country* (Cambridge: Cambridge University Press 1985), 193–210.

48 For descriptions of two successful exhibitions based on oral history, see Judith Coake and Susan Pointe, "Voices from Memory: A Community-Made Exhibition," *Muse*, August 1997, 45–7; Roberta Kremer, "Spoken Memories: The Use of Oral History in Exhibitions," *Muse*, December 1998, 36–9.

49 For a discussion of the many uses of museum theatre, see Sherry Anne Chapman, "Forward Through the Past: Reminiscence Theatre and Museums," *Muse*, December 1998, 12–14.

50 On this dialogue, see, for example, Edward T. Linenthal, "Committing History in Public," *JAH* 81, no. 1 (December 1994), 986–91.

51 Joy Parr has been a significant exception; see her "Shopping for a Good Stove: A Parable about Gender, Design, and the Market," in Parr, ed., *A Diversity of Women: Ontario, 1945–1980* (Toronto: University of Toronto Press 1995), 75–97.

52 Most museums have a permanent collection of artifacts around which they structure their exhibitions. WAHC chose not to build up such a collection, but rather to remain an "interpretive centre," gathering material for exhibitions as needed.

53 Mary Tivy, "The Quality of Research Is Definitely Strained: Collections Research in Ontario Community Museums," *MHB* 27 (Spring 1988), 61–8.

54 For one stimulating study, see Lizabeth A. Cohen, "Embellishing a Life of Labor: An Interpretation of the Material Culture of American Working-Class Homes, 1885–1915," in Dirk Hoerder, ed., *Labor Migration in the Atlantic Economies: The European and North American Working Classes during the Period of Industrialization* (Westport, CT: Greenwood Press 1985), 321–52. Some work on working-class housing in Canada is also suggestive; see Richard MacKinnon, "Company Housing in Wabana, Bell Island, Newfoundland," *MHB* 14 (Spring 1982), 67–71 ; "Tompkinsville, Cape Breton Island: Co-operativism and Vernacular Architecture," *MHR* 44 (Fall 1996), 45–63; and "Making a House a Home: Company Housing in Cape Breton Island,"*MHR* 47 (Spring 1998), 46–56; JoAnn Latremouille, *Pride of Home: The Working Class Housing Tradition in Nova Scotia, 1749–1949* (Halifax: Lancelot Press 1986). Domestic technology is discussed in Suzanne Marchand, "L'impact des innovations technologiques sur la vie quotidienne des Québécoises du debut du XXe siècle (1910–1940)," *MHB* 28 (Fall 1988), 1–14; Parr, "Shopping for a Good Stove."

55 For a survey of industrial history in Canada, see Louise Trottier, "Preserving Canada's Industrial Heritage: Studies and Achievements, 1987–1992," *Machines* (Summer 1993), 9–15; on the challenges in preserving industrial heritage, see John Weiler, *Our Working Past: Conserving Industrial Relics for Recreation and Tourism* (n.p. 1982); Thomas E. Leary, "Shadows in

the Cave: Industrial Ecology and Museum Practice," *Public Historian* 11, no. 4 (Fall 1989), 39–60; and Laurence F. Gross, "Problems in Exhibiting Labor in Museums and a Technological Fix," *Technology and Culture,* 1993, 392–400. One of the more successful industrial-history projects in the United States is at the Youngstown Historical Centre of Industry and Labor in Ohio; see Curtis Miner, "Review of 'By the Sweat of Their Brows': Forging the Steel Valley," *JAH* 80, no. 1 (December 1993), 1019–24.

56 See Robert Kristofferson, "The Past Is at Our Feet: The Workers' City Project in Hamilton, Ontario," *L/LT* 41 (Spring 1998), 181–97; Delores Hayden, *The Power of Place: Urban Landscapes as Public History* (Cambridge, MA: MIT Press 1995); Binette, "L'Écomusée de la Maison du Fier Monde"; Wilma Wood, "The Cowichan and Chemains Valleys Ecomuseum: The Ecomuseum Concept as a Successful Planning Tool for Government and the Governed," *Muse,* 1991, 10–11; R. Peter Heron, "Museums: Cultural Institutions and Islands of Hope," *Muse,* Autumn 1990, 53–6; Koke and Pointe, "Voices from Memory."

57 See David Sobel and Susan Meurer, *Working at Inglis: The Life and Death of a Canadian Factory* (Toronto: James Lorimer 1994). In 1992 the Bostonian Society made this process of working-class dislocation the subject of an engaging exhibition; see James R. Green, "Review of 'The Last Tenement: Confronting Community and Urban Renewal in Boston's West End,'" *JAH* 80, no. 1 (December 1993), 1025–30.

58 The Canadian Society for Industrial Heritage was founded only in 1990. For a review of recent developments, see Trottier, "Preserving Canada's Industrial Heritage." For examples of efforts to preserve local industrial heritage in four American industrial centres, see Brian O'Donnell, "Memory and Hope: Four Local Museums in the Mill Towns of the Industrial Northeast," *Technology and Culture* 37, no. 4 (October 1996), 817–27.

59 For stimulating discussion of the biases of photographs of workers, see Allan Sekula, "Photography between Capital and Labour," in Benjamin H.D. Buchloh and Robert Wilkie, eds., *Mining Photographs and Other Pictures, 1948–1968: Photographs by Leslie Shedden, A Selection from the Negative Archives of Shedden Studio, Glace Bay, Cape Breton* (Halifax and Sydney: Press of the Nova Scotia College of Art and Design 1983), 193–268; Eric Margolis, "Mining Photographs: Unearthing the Meanings of Historical Photos," *RHR* 40 (Spring 1988), 33–48; Alan Trachtenberg, *Reading American Photographs: Images as History, Mathew Brady to Walker Evans* (New York: Hill and Wang 1989); Lawrence W. Levine, "The Historian and the Icon: Photography and the History of the American People in the 1930s and 1940s," in Carl Fleischhauer and

Beverly W. Brannan, eds., *Documenting America, 1935–1943* (Berkeley: University of California Press 1988), 15–42; Alan Trachtenberg, "From Image to Story: Reading the File," in *Documenting America*, 43–73 ; Ken Cruikshank and Nancy B. Bouchier, "'The Pictures Are Great but the Text Is a Bit of a Downer': Ways of Seeing and the Challenge of Exhibiting Critical History," *CHR* 80, no. 1 (March 1999), 96–113 .

60 Some museums that have attempted to keep up with the social history produced in academia have gone overboard in producing lengthy, nuanced text panels, which do become fairly dense "books on the wall."

61 Franco, "Communication Conundrum," 158.

62 See Bradbury et al., *Teaching Women's History.*

63 Lowenthal, *The Past Is a Foreign Country.*

64 It must be said that WAHC has yet to make full use of this possibility. Morever, it has real limitations for mass-production work processes.

65 Tivy, "Quality of Research," 66.

66 The Power of Place group has been quite active as well; see Hayden, *Power of Place.*

67 Kristofferson, "The Past Is at Our Feet"; Robert Yates, "It's About Time: A Review of 'Making Time,'" *Worklines*, Spring/Summer 1997, 3–4; Renee Johnston, "Spinning Yarns: Stories of Women's Work in North End Hamilton," *Worklines*, Fall/Winter 1997–8, 7–8; Shawn Shoesmith, "Working Family Treasures," *Worklines*, Spring/Summer 1998, 10.

68 Duncan Cameron, "The Museum, Temple or Forum," *Curator* 14, no. 1 (1971), 11–24.

69 Rumour has it that there are CAW members who have never forgiven Bob White for allowing himself to be shown on national television, in the NFB film *Final Offer*, using disreputable four-letter words, despite the fact that most of them use the same spicy vocabulary every day.

70 For discussions of some of these dilemmas in programming community history, see Linda Stopes, "Oral History and Community Involvement: The Baltimore Neighbourhood Heritage Project," in Benson, Brier, and Rosenzweig, eds., *Presenting the Past*, 249–63; Jeremy Brecher, "A Report on Doing History from Below: The Brass Workers' History Project," ibid., 267–77; James Green, "Engaging in People's History: The Massachusetts History Workshop," ibid., 339–59.

71 For parallel reflections, see John E. Fleming, "African-American Museums, History, and the American Ideal," *JAH* 81, no. 1 (December 1994), 1021–6.

Chapter Fifteen

The Relevance of Class

In May 1945 a young Canadian couple exchanged wedding vows and began a half-century of life together. Harold, age twenty-three, was still in his Royal Canadian Air Force uniform, but would soon be donning the work clothes of a manual worker in a series of relatively low-skill jobs. Marg, age twenty-one, gave up her position as a telephone operator and started to set up the family household before Harold was finally released from the Air Force. Over the next few years they helped launch the Baby Boom by having two sons, whom they raised in a small house perched on the outer edge of suburban Toronto. Once the boys were both in school in the late 1950s, Marg returned to the paid workforce, and spent some twenty years as a secretary. Like a declining majority of Canadians in the postwar period, Harold, Marg, and the boys were Anglo-Canadian, English speaking, Canadian-born, and white. They were also working class.

That last label is undoubtedly the most controversial. It has slipped out of common usage in the writing of a good deal of history in recent years. Using class as a category of historical analysis has faced either outright hostility or, more often, benign neglect among those more preoccupied with gender and race as social, cultural, and political identities. The purpose of the following discussion is to use the lives of these four Canadians as a small window on how class worked historically in Canada and to establish its relentless relevance for the writing of our history.

To begin, we need to step out onto a minefield of theoretical contention that Harold, Marg, and at least one of the boys would have found

Scarborough home. Author's collection

mystifying and probably pointless. Class as a category of historical analysis defies easy definition.[1] In the 1950s and again in the 1980s and 1990s, it was intellectually fashionable to deny that it existed in any significant way, but, even between those points, there was a great deal of intellectual and political contestation over how we would know class when we stumbled over it in the past or present. In the 1970s and 1980s many Canadian social historians kept their ears attuned to the raging debates over the concept that blew up in other parts of the English-speaking world, particularly in Britain.[2] At that point, for most scholars, there was a broadly shared assumption that the starting point was the world of waged work within capitalist society, that is, the "material" or the "economic." When, for example, a number of capitalists opened factories, mines, or fast-food outlets and set out to recruit a workforce, and when large numbers of people made themselves available as wage-earners in those enterprises, they collectively began the process of creating class experiences – on both sides of the divide and in relation to other more independent middling social groups. Their interactions – both contestations and accommodations – regularly destabilized and reconstituted material situations. These processes became known as the "structural" component of class identity, the part that many poststructuralist thinkers have so decisively rejected as "crude reductionism" or "economism."[3]

Harold and Marg might not have been so dismissive. They could easily have explained to sceptics exactly what the pressures and constraints of material structures meant. Leaving the family farm with only a grade 9 education and no marketable skills, Harold's job prospects and earning ability were restricted. Marg's background in a shopkeeping family and a grade 11 education constrained her employment opportunities to lower-end clerical work at best. These were limited jobs, not expanding careers. What they earned restricted the family's living standards. They lived most of their married lives in a small, five-room frame house, rarely bought new furniture, ate simple meals, rarely went out to restaurants or movies, relied on older, used cars, had no money for expensive dental work, limited their summer vacations to a visit to Marg's mother's cottage and later to short, inexpensive family camping expeditions, and worried constantly about debt. By the end of the 1950s, in fact, they found they could not survive on Harold's wages alone, and, like thousands of other Canadian working-class housewives at that point, Marg went out to work full time (as employers finally rejected the long-standing taboo on hiring married women). Even with two pay cheques coming in, penny-pinching was a way of life. Only in the 1970s, when both boys had moved out and established independent households, did Harold and Marg's living standards begin to improve to any great extent.[4]

Indeed, Marg could also have explained how, in the face of ever-present economic vulnerability, she managed the family household as effectively as possible to sustain what historians have come to call a family economy. Economical shopping to stretch wages, along with family labour to avoid cash outlays, were still crucial in the 1950s and 1960s.[5] As a small investment strategy, Harold and Marg also bought two acres of land with no water or sewer connections and a half-finished house, which they spent many years fixing up (in a suburban neighbourhood where such owner-built houses were numerous).[6] Eventually, they made small sums by selling off four lots for new housing, and, many years later, in the late 1980s, sold the remaining land for a substantial sum. Many working-class families had similar survival strategies in this period, much as they had done for generations in Canada in response to the economic uncertainty of their material situation.[7]

All that said, there has never been a clear theoretical consensus about what various scholars and writers have actually meant by "structure." Broadly speaking, they drew on two largely unacknowledged (and generally unfortunate) literary images. Liberal writers within the social sciences tended to use geological metaphors of "stratification" made up of "layers" or "strata." In the structural-functionalist social science of the 1950s and 1960s, classes were simply objective categories of occupation and income in which people found themselves as a result of their individual capabilities, and which existed in a nonconflictual balance with each other that guaranteed social cohesion and integration. Relations among these groups were merely a question of status. Studying social class in this way was largely to describe and label – for example, to identify "lifestyles" or to locate inequality or poverty lines – rather than to analyse how these categories got created and filled with particular people. The most important question seemed to be charting individual movement between occupational groups, or "social mobility," especially in the middling groups.[8]

Further to the left, the imagery of "structures" often became more architectural than geological. Some orthodox Marxist writing seemed to conceive of the so-called material "base" as a mindless block of bricks and mortar and heavy machinery, though more commonly the focus of attention was the relations of production between owners and wage-earners in and around all that technology. In either case, the "base" was assumed to be analytically distinct from a "superstructure" of institutions, cultures, ideas, ideologies, and languages.[9] That perspective, however, tended to be the conceptual landscape of theorists, rather than empirically oriented historians, far more of whom got their intellectual inspiration from much more dynamic currents of subtler Marxist thought that emerged in the second half of the twentieth century, especially what has become known as Anglo-Marxism.[10] Those writers helped many historians to understand that the architectural metaphor does not work, and that the base-superstructure distinction is deeply problematic. The functioning of a factory or a mine or a fast-food outlet rested on the relationships of human beings, as worked out every day on the job, informally and institutionally; but was also shaped from outside by laws and regulatory apparatuses of various kinds and by a host of cultural influences. The material or the economic does not exist in some analytical space completely apart from the discourses of culture and politics, nor does it necessarily take precedence in some kind of hierarchy of causation – simply because the material, the cultural, and the political are so tightly interrelated and mutually constituted.[11] In particular, studies of the state in its many dimensions have emphasized the relative autonomy of its policies, programs, and practices and its critical impact on economic activity, not in a simple, servile relationship to the material realm.[12] Through international comparisons, we have also learned how differently the social relations of production can develop in different regions and countries, depending on the timing of industrialization, the particular forms of industrial development, the extent of managerial and technological innovation, different pools of labour, different traditions of labour organizing, and, in particular, divergent state policies. This was why so many of us talked about class formation as not universal, but as contingent and specific, and why there has been such a great emphasis on narrowly focused local studies of class experience.[13]

What made all this seem "structural" was how much of it appeared to be beyond much individual control, involving large numbers of people simultaneously in broadly similar processes of seemingly inescapable subordination. The relentlessness is perhaps best symbolized by two clocks – one beside the bed and the other at the entrance to the workplace. I invite any sceptics to ride Toronto's Bloor-Danforth subway line any weekday morning between 6:00 and 8:00 a.m. to see the stamp of that structural reality in the tired faces of working-class commuters moving between those two clocks.

Much of even the more sensitive, sophisticated research and writing on class and class formation in history, however, suffered from a severe myopia about gender, which has always added crucial additional dimensions to any notion of "structure." The working class was not simply made up of male wage-earners, but also included other unwaged members of the family households out of which those wage-earners emerged each day – women, children, the elderly, and the disabled. The family and all the relationships and practices within it therefore had to be a major focus of analytical attention alongside the world of production. Girls and women faced systematic restrictions on the range of their social options, both in the family home, where they were expected to take responsibility for most domestic tasks, and in the broader public world of employment and citizenship. Compelling discourses about gender roles and identities, and about rigidly distinct public and private spheres, justified these inequities, including male labour leaders' tendency to construct the working class as masculine.[14]

Similarly, theorists of ethnicity and race have reminded us that the life experiences of all wage-earners and their families also took shape within additional limitations and pressures resulting from their position within particular ethnic and racial relationships. Occupational hierarchies in almost all Canadian enterprises included ethnic and racial distinctions that grew out of segmented labour markets and invariably put the white, anglo-Celtic workers at the top and various other European, Asian, African, and First Nations groups in less skilled, less well-paying jobs further down the occupational scale. Potent discourses of racial ordering sustained those practices of discrimination, nurtured by Canada's place as a white-settler dominion within a far-flung, multiracial empire. "Race" was thus closely connected to nationality and citizenship.[15]

Writers and scholars now tend to argue that these three forces worked together, simultaneously, to produce distinctive experiences, for example, for a male Italian-Canadian construction worker, a female black Caribbean-born domestic worker, or a white anglo-Celtic female secretary like Marg. Bringing together this "holy trinity" of social history obviously injects more complexity and diversity into class analysis, and it draws our attention to many more sites of experience – at home, in neighbourhoods, in community organizations, in schools, in health clinics, and so on – but it does not make class disappear. It simply requires more sensitivity in investigating how these social forces interacted.[16]

The "structure" of the class experience, then, has meant the regularized patterns of engagement with the means of production, the divisions of labour within patriarchy, and the racial distinctions in particular societies.[17] Most importantly, structure has meant dynamic relationships – between the broad social classes, genders, and racial and ethnic groups, and among people within those categories. Inevitably, it meant that those structural patterns were never fixed for all time, but were constantly shifting and changing, being reconstructed and reformed. Those who insist that fragmentation, instability, and fluidity are hallmarks of our turn-of-the-millennium globalized, postmodern society have underestimated how much has always been in flux since the first flickering of capitalist modernity in the mid-nineteenth century in British North America. There was never a moment of one single lurch into a homogeneously modern experience. Class formation was always a project under construction, and class "location" was frequently fluid as people moved (or were pushed) between occupational possibilities.[18]

Of course, as the class experience kept moving under the workers' feet over the past century and a half, what has been at work has been the uneven accumulation of wealth and the unequal distribution of power and authority, in which more powerful social classes and the power blocs within which they participated pursued their own best interests.[19] Power is central to any sustainable conception of class. But power did not flow only from a single, centralized source. Capitalists did not dictate all working-class behaviour in any mechanistic way, and, despite plenty of evidence of strike-breaking and red-baiting, state policy has seldom relied principally on overt coercion. Workers' responses were conditioned through a vast number of decentralized forces, some of them within state institutions, others elsewhere. In this sense, the post-modern/poststructural critique of what is taken to be old-fashioned Marxism is right to draw our attention to the diffusion of power to many sites.[20] Although Harold and Margaret had a strong sense of who the rich and powerful were, epitomized in household discussions about the flamboyant Canadian industrialist E.P. Taylor, those were distant, relatively unknown people. They had a sharper sense of difference from the variety of interventionist middle-class people they more regularly encountered in inherently disciplinary settings – the company managers, doctors, school teachers, clergymen, government bureaucrats, and others who had a direct or indirect role in controlling and regulating their lives. These middle-class professionals were in fact the custodians and propagators of the regulatory discourses that promoted the self-disciplined body and mind.[21] Harold and Marg might have resented the ways that the members of these other classes impinged on their lives, but they also generally worried about their own inadequacy and inferiority alongside such people. These were not merely individual reactions, but formed broad patterns across many working-class communities.[22]

In fact, the deepest scholarly and theoretical controversies have entered in when we ask what people thought about their structural circumstances, and how they responded to them. On the one hand, it would certainly be unwise to assume that living within structural pressures and constraints had no impact on how members of particular classes conceived of themselves and their material situation. Strong dispositions, widely shared by people in diverse situations, emerged from living within those regular, routinized contexts.[23] Yet, on the other hand, it would also be an exaggeration to argue that consciousness or awareness of their lives was completely determined in this way, that their structural situation led straightforwardly to any obvious, predictable way of thinking and acting, whether compliance or resistance. Indeed, one of the most significant breakthroughs in recent writing of social history has been the recognition that consciousness of the class experience cannot be a simple read off class location as a direct reflection of material conditions. There has to be theoretical space to allow for the historical subjects, individually and collectively, to engage in some independent reflection and assessment, to exercise some degree of agency, albeit within the narrative limitations of the language through which it is expressed. Harold and Marg, like others in their situation, processed the economic constraints on their lives through familiar cultural lenses. To use a slippery concept, we can say that this is how people have "experienced" their structured social existence. Moreover, the meaning that people like them drew from their social experience could vary, particularly because there were always many different discourses at work attempting to ascribe that meaning and to encourage particular behaviour or action. Some of those flowed through institutionalized channels like the mass media or the education system, or even the labour movement, while others operated through informal modes and practices of communication on the job, in the neighbourhood, or around the kitchen table. They might mutually reinforce a compelling social vision, but the divergences among them could create plenty of discursive cacophony. People like Harold and Marg then understood the world around them through a complex kind of awareness that was shaped by the structured patterns of their daily life, the information, ideas, and language available to make sense of them, and their own willingness and ability to accept, reject, or adapt those understandings.[24]

It is worth noting in passing that most of the sound and fury has raged over working-class consciousness (or the lack of it), but class awareness has varied among the major social classes depending on the power and resources (or "capacities") at their disposal.[25] Class-consciousness has always been particularly vigorous at the top and in the middle of the social scale. Ironically, given all the scholarly attention, workers have always constituted the loosest, least coherent, least unified of the social classes, the one least able to express its own sense of itself. New patterns of labour-market recruitment regularly brought people into wage-earning from pre-industrial backgrounds or, like Harold and Marg, from experiences outside wage-earning. They brought with them values and practices rooted in those previous class locations that persisted in the new proletarian context.[26] Workers brought together as the raw material of a working class generally had to learn over time to cooperate, and could be highly vulnerable to constructions of their experience from elsewhere.

Labour historians (including me) have put a preponderance of their scholarly energy into documenting one particular set of discourses and practices, those involved in mobilizing working people around their distinct class interests. It is now clear that a united, coherent working class was not sitting ready-made, but had to be constructed through a painstaking process of argument and conversion and difficult mobilization. We now have a rich history (and historiography) of unions and political organizations that articulated those goals from a variety of ideological perspectives. We certainly still need to know about the organized, the militant, and the radical and their impact; but we have been somewhat less successful in situating their efforts within the broader landscape of working-class life. In fact, unionization in Canada was consistently attacked and marginalized until the Second World War, and since then has seldom risen much over a third of the gainfully employed. And even among those, there were reluctant conscripts like Harold who had no strong attachments to the most familiar forms of working-class solidarity. The crises of labour movements in the western world since the 1970s have also compelled some reflection on how workers allow right-wing, anti-union politicians such as Ronald Reagan, Margaret Thatcher, or Mike Harris to become hegemonic politically.

One answer has come from the largely discredited notion of workers' "false consciousness."[27] Others drew on the idea of hegemony developed by Antonio Gramsci,[28] or various theories of language laid out by Michel Foucault and other postmodern writers responsible for the cultural or linguistic "turn" in the writing of social history, which has brought an insistence on the primacy of language itself in creating human subjects.[29] Whatever the theoretical inspiration, the central question remains what, if any, relationship exists between cultural and political discourses and the social, material, or "structural" condition of historical subjects. The postmodern approach has been to deny any connection. Others, myself included, agree that there is no direct, inevitable reflection of the material in the cultural, but see the necessity of looking closely at the interaction. Most writing inspired by the linguistic turn has looked to the texts of particular discourses and not to their reception. It is important to appreciate that this is a negotiated process, through which members of subordinate groups engage in some kind of weighing and evaluation in the light of their material existence and the kinds of awareness that their experience has produced. They listen and accept, comply and ignore, confront and reject, mix and integrate the discursive elements swirling around them. In the process they nonetheless construct a class identity that distinguishes them from the middle and upper classes. To make this clearer, let me turn more specifically to the discursive universe of Harold and Marg between the 1940s and the 1970s. In particular, I want to consider the major cultural cross-currents that have most often been proposed as the death-knells of class awareness in postwar North America. So I descend from the rugged, wind swept peaks of theoretical disputation to the carefully trimmed lawns of working-class suburbia.

Harold and Marg never talked about themselves as members of a working class – indeed rarely used the word "class." They were not prone to thinking in such abstract sociological terminology.[30] But they did refer to themselves as "working people," often in a slightly self-deprecating comparison with middle-class people ("just working people"). They were trying to signal a general like-mindedness with others similar to themselves and a difference from others – a prickly defence of hard work and manual labour (and a suspicion of idleness);[31] a reliance on collective mutual support and care; a pride in self-help, self-sufficiency, and independence; a hard-headed preference for the utilitarian, concrete, and practical – the "sensible" and "down-to-earth" – over the abstract or theoretical; a greater comfort with the local and familiar than the exotic or strange; a sense of propriety but also an informality, lack of pretension, genuineness, and simplicity; a preference for emotional intensity over "refined" restraint or aestheticism; and a relentless fixation on the value and cost of everything. When the older boy struck up a friendship with the son of the local bank manager, he was gently admonished that his new friend had "false values." Much of this framework of thinking carried over from the world of small-scale family farming and shopkeeping out of which they came, but it was recast in a context of life-long wage-earning. They drew on what was more like folklore about the value and rewards of hard work and the merits of those who toiled – hoary old chestnuts in Canadian popular culture. And, although mainstream culture said less and less about such worthiness, they continued to extract from such popular myths a pride and dignity distinct from people who were not "working people."[32]

The circuits of that folk wisdom were among workmates and neighbours, but even more among kin. In fact, in a familiar pattern from their own childhoods, the most important solidarities for Marg and Harold were with their extended families, even though they did not necessarily live nearby.[33] They got loans, jobs, help with manual labour and child care, and general moral support, and they reciprocated.[34] They also visited and socialized with kin more often than friends or neighbours, and exchanged gifts with many of them at birthdays and Christmas. Kin were also an important audience for Harold and Marg's performances of respectability. These were networks of social solidarity that, for all their potentially oppressive patriarchal dynamics, rejected competitive individualism and could thrive on life-long loyalty, mutual support, and warm emotional attachments. And these were solidarities that the womenfolk were expected to nurture as part of their domestic responsibilities.[35]

Yet that was not the whole story of class identity in their lives. Implicitly, Harold and Marg were also part of a broader working-class experience. They were newcomers to the working class in the 1940s, but they were beneficiaries of the major working-class mobilizations of that decade.[36] They built their new life together on the victories of those great wartime and postwar confrontations. Once Harold started at the public utilities commission in the early 1950s, he was a member of a local of the International Brotherhood of Electrical Workers. He had no enthusiasm for the union, rarely went to its meetings or read its monthly magazine, stayed home during its only strike, and expressed no affinities with the broader labour movement. Yet, like so many other male wage-earners in the postwar period, he and his family reaped the benefits of collective working-class organization in the workplace that many more male breadwinners now enjoyed – regular wage increases, modest promotion opportunities (in his case from metre-reader to service man), a benefit plan, more leisure time in the form of forty-hour weeks and regular paid holidays and vacations,[37] and, most important in his Depression-era consciousness, good job security.

He and Marg and the boys also felt the effects of the reconstruction of politics in the 1940s in response to major working-class mobilizations that had brought into mainstream government policy the Keynesian ideas of full employment.[38] Harold was never unemployed after the early 1950s and never drew unemployment insurance. Expanded state intervention also brought many new jobs, and Harold found secure public-sector employment with a public utilities commission that was providing service to the huge number of new homes spreading through suburbia, often with help from new state housing programs. Marg's paid work as a medical secretary was possible because of the large-scale increase in public support for health care that brought many more people into doctors' offices. The new state social expenditures also brought better roads, which facilitated commuting to work, shopping, socializing, holidaying, and better schools, which enabled both the boys to get to university. They would also take advantage of major state programs to promote more social security – the monthly baby-bonus cheque that Marg always looked forward to, the Veterans' Land Act that allowed them to purchase their house and two acres of land, the health insurance, and pension plans – all of which amounted to small but definitely significant enhancements of their quality of life.[39] Harold and Marg would never have tried to articulate a clear vision of their social rights in postwar society, but implicitly they built their dreams and aspirations within that new hard-won consensus that working people had a new right to a decent standard of living.[40] It is important to add, however, that the dominant political narratives that were used in the 1950s to explain this new world of enhanced social security did not highlight the agitation of workers and their allies a decade earlier that lay behind it. In fact, class-based narratives were vanishing as the Cold War settled in.[41] So other discourses became more readily available to working people like Harold and Marg to try to comprehend and act on their social situations.

One of those involved gender. The 1950s has become known as a period of powerful re-assertion of rigid gender norms within traditionally structured heterosexual families, symbolized by such media icons as Ward and June Cleaver and Jim and Margaret Anderson (*Father Knows Best* was a family favourite).[42] Both Harold and Marg certainly wove into their consciousness some sharp-edged gender expectations. Harold saw himself as a workingman in the full meaning of the term. He expected to go out to work for wages and to have specific gendered tasks around the household – garden and yard maintenance, car repairs, upkeep on the house, and so on. The stove and washing machine were a mystery to him until Marg was dying of cancer in the 1990s, and he played only a marginal role in socializing his sons.[43] He was committed to breadwinning for his family and would rather have been able to earn a "living wage" that would have kept his wife out of the labour market,[44] but at the same time he was uncomfortable with many of the responsibilities of patriarchy and often needed prodding or nagging to bring him out of a kind of boyish resistance to domestic burdens and tensions – much like many other men in his class. He participated in a rougher homosocial celebration of that boyishness among his blue-collar workmates – swearing, joking, roughhousing, storytelling, and what not – of which the rest of the family was only dimly aware, though he never joined them in a tavern or other after-work activities.[45]

For her part, Marg was a strong, dominant figure in the family, who kept a firm control over family life, but she struggled to do that within the expectations of rigid gender identities. She accepted full responsibility for all domestic labour and took great pride in her gleaming, well-ordered household and cooking skills.[46] She constantly pushed Harold to be the strong breadwinner husband that she expected,[47] and watched over the boys for any deviations from the narrow path to manliness (even though expecting them to help with housework). Yet, in practice, she struggled with a much more complex view of her own femininity. While trying persistently to meet current standards of youthful beauty and attractiveness (through intermittent regimes of diet and exercise), she juggled the demanding double-day of paid secretarial work and unpaid domestic responsibilities, partly because the family needed extra income, but also, as she told the boys, because she wanted more to her life than the family household could offer.[48] She had started work in the early 1940s when the rapidly expanding occupational possibilities for women in the wartime economy had opened up visions of wider possibilities. Now she basked in the respectability of working in doctors' offices, despite the scorn she must have felt from the popular media that questioned the worthiness of working mothers.[49] She also enjoyed the greater leverage her income gave her in the family's financial decision-making. She often expressed a deep frustration at the unfairness of her crushing responsibilities, but the language of second-wave middle-class feminism in the 1960s and 1970s never resonated with her – indeed, it frightened her – and working in non-union jobs, she never had access to the emerging labour feminism of the 1970s.[50] She continued to believe that, for working people, a well-ordered family structured around familiar gender roles was the basis of security, success, and happiness. She saw her central role as a working-class wife and mother as an important process of holding everything together, to keep it all from flying apart. Doing so could nourish her self-esteem and pride, but she lived with considerable stress and disappointment.[51]

Many writers then and since have situated these still rigid gender identities spatially – in the treeless mud of former farmlands where the suburbs were springing up in the 1950s. A lot of popular discourse at the time (and since) claimed that these new residential zones were social levellers, where everyone became middle class. As several sociologists in the United States and at least one in Canada discovered in that period, however, most suburbs had distinct class complexions, and many of the familiar patterns of working-class family life were simply transferred to these new locations.[52] Harold and Marg's neighbourhood was no exception. Yet the suburb brought a new way of life for a man who had grown up on a farm and a woman raised in a big city. Theirs was not as intimate and close-knit a community as many workers had known in older downtown working-class neighbourhoods with their corner shops, cafes, taverns, clubs, halls and so on.[53] Life here relied centrally on the family car. Harold and Marg rarely walked anywhere. They drove some distance to their jobs in the suburbs, and on weekends wheeled into relatively impersonal suburban shopping centres, also often far from home. People they worked with and lived near similarly drove off in all directions. What people in the new postwar working-class suburbs created spatially through their housing choices was thus new in working-class history. Their sense of "community" was now far more sprawling and loose. It gave far less opportunity for associating together and for sharing common experience on a daily basis on doorsteps and street corners. It probably made the family a more central feature of their lives.

We are often told that in the postwar period religion also became a powerful force in the cultural landscape of North Americans. For Harold and Marg, religious belief and practice were indeed important. Theologically, they were attached to a moderate version of an "old-time" evangelical Protestantism that historians have been telling us recently had long been common among many working people.[54] The socially mixed United and Presbyterian church congregations they joined were less significant as social spaces than as spiritual filling stations and sites for public rituals of respectability every Sunday morning (except in the summer, when God was apparently on holiday).[55] For Marg in particular, these were intense moments of weekly spiritual renewal. In their daily lives, their religious precepts became arguably the most compelling discourse available to them to give meaning to their social situation. It certainly encouraged resignation to fate and hope for divine intervention to improve their lives or to explain their misfortunes. Yet it also structured their thinking in other significant ways. On the one hand, it gave them a set of clear moral precepts and a strong code of "thou-shalt-nots" to govern personal behaviour, which encouraged sharp judgments about individual moral worth and an easy condemnation of laziness or other moral failings. Among working people struggling for decency and respectability, this could be a significant force in distinguishing them from classes above them, but also from those neighbours in the owner-built suburbs who seemed more dissolute or degenerate. Yet, on the other hand, their Protestant faith also provided a ready vocabulary, a rich imagery, and a treasure trove of Biblical references for understanding and evaluating the world. It gave them a strong sense of the equality of all humans before God and a brotherhood of man. It was in fact the core of their sense of democracy. When the chair of the Board of Elders, a local businessman, stood up in their church to lambaste those who dropped too little onto the collection plate, Harold and Marg spluttered that the man did not understand working people and that Jesus had driven the money-changers from the temple. They promptly searched out and found a more compatible congregation.[56]

Religion, of course, is closely connected to ethnic and racial identity, which, we are often told, became enhanced in postwar Canada – the era of blossoming francophone nationalism, multiculturalism, and white Anglo-Canadian reaction. Harold and Marg would probably never have admitted to having an ethnic identity beyond "Canadian." They both had Scottish roots, but limited attachment to British cultural symbols and an unrelenting scorn for the monarchy, which they saw as pretentious and undemocratic. The suburb where they settled was solidly white and Anglo-Celtic, and the immediate school district included only one African-Canadian and two Japanese-Canadian families.[57] Like their working-class Anglo-Canadian neighbours, Harold and Marg were acutely conscious of ethnic and racial difference, and slotted people into rigid categories with predictable behaviour, particularly personal and public morality. In the 1950s, they accepted Hollywood's version of First Nations people and the minstrel-show image of blacks. Although they nominally opposed discriminatory policies and occasionally socialized with non-white friends, they expected ethnic and racial minorities to lose their distinctiveness, and had no tolerance for those who fought back, including French-Canadians. As the American civil rights struggles unfolded in the 1960s, they scoffed that they did not understand what all the fuss was about,[58] but the growing population of Caribbean blacks in Toronto also made them increasingly uneasy. Race and ethnicity then were tightly woven into their sense of themselves in a complex fashion that labour historians will recognize from many studies – a democratic, egalitarian, if sometimes patronizing inclusiveness among those who seemed to pose little threat, and a harsh distancing from those whose cultures appeared to challenge white, Anglo-Canadian privilege.[59]

Harold and Marg tended to root their sense of ethnic entitlement in a vague notion of their citizenship. If asked, they would no doubt have expressed a strong awareness of their civil rights, particularly personal liberty, in contrast to what they were told about Communist tyranny,[60] and expected the police and courts to treat them fairly. In practice, however, they never turned to those institutions for any kind of real support. They also knew they had political rights and voted in virtually every election. In the 1950s, they were loosely Diefenbaker Conservatives. For them, that silver-tongued Tory wrapped together a Cold War anti-communism, a strong "unhyphenated" Canadian nationalism, a suspicion of French-Canadian pretensions, and an anti-elitist populism. They would probably have agreed with songster Bob Bossin that Diefenbaker "always had a hand for the working man."[61] Those were not secure political moorings, however, and by the 1970s, as public social protest swirled around them, they seemed to lean more often to the NDP.[62] That was a practical rather than an ideological shift, however, and did not last into their later life.

Politics generally held little appeal to them beyond a kind of short-term entertainment value, and they certainly never joined a political party. They often denounced politicians as fundamentally untrustworthy and politics as corrupt.[63] In fact, overall, they had limited faith in the state to help them much, and were more likely to complain about taxes or restrictions on personal liberties. I would argue that a profound detachment from politics and the state characterized much of the postwar working class in Canada, in sharp contrast to a more engaged middle class.[64] It would certainly be hard to claim that, for Harold and Marg, appeals to their identities as citizens were a powerful force in their daily lives. Perhaps symbolically, they never flew a Canadian flag.

A stronger claim has been made about the impact of mass culture on working people in the postwar period. Marg and Harold kept some distance from much of this, for the practical reason that they had little to spend on commercialized pleasures.[65] In any case, they tended to prefer participatory popular culture such as singing and occasionally square dancing. But from the late 1950s on, a television set took pride of place in their living room and was on for some part of almost every evening. Out of that flickering screen beamed a myriad of messages about the way the world allegedly worked. The impact on this family, however, was limited and fractured by age and gender. The boys were TV addicts. But Harold was always more detached, except during Saturday's "Hockey Night in Canada," and Marg preferred wholesome, earnest sitcoms and dramas that reinforced the core values in her approach to life. They favoured the folksier CTV news over the snootier CBC broadcasts. In general, they both looked for what was familiar and reassuring. Little of what they watched, however, gave them much of a glimpse of their own lives, since television scripts in that period were almost invariably sanitized stories of middle-class Americans. It was spectatorship on a different world.[66]

Through much of the media, the life of such middle-class people was also being held up as a goal worth aspiring to. Why not push your children up the social ladder into the middle class? A powerful ideology of social mobility through meritocracy suffused Canadian society in the 1950s and 1960s. Families like this one were told repeatedly that higher educational credentials would bring greater occupational choices and social status, and in Ontario the vastly expanded space in universities and colleges, especially in the Toronto area, made this look possible. Four-fifths of the boys' generation in Canada never made it to post-secondary education, but, with sharp memories of their own difficult youth and truncated schooling in the hard times of the 1930s, Harold and, especially, Marg wanted to give their own boys a better chance.

Since Harold was permanently employed and Marg was working full-time as the secondary income-earner, the family could afford to delay having income from the boys. Like a sizeable minority of Canada's working-class parents, they poured their hopes for family betterment into the next generation.[67]

The results were mixed at best. To the profound disappointment of Harold and Marg, the younger boy lasted less than a year in an engineering program and became an electrician instead. The older boy went through post-graduate training and ended up in a professional career. His parents greeted his apparent success with gushing pride but also growing unease. They worried about the unfamiliar ideas he embraced and his new-found atheism. They were shocked at his plunge into the youth counter-culture – his long hair, "sloppy" clothing, communal living, and petulant radicalism. They must have felt betrayed that their son had become so distant, hostile, and apparently ungrateful. Once he eventually found full-time work, they were mystified by the content and rhythms of his job, which seemed to include a lot of unsupervised pencil-pushing. For Harold and Marg, formal schooling was palpably the most deeply felt dividing line between themselves and middle-class Canadians, and now the line ran right through the middle of their family. In many ways, they felt they had lost a son to processes they could not fully understand.[68]

Marg and Harold certainly did not abandon hope that their own lives could be better, and, with shorter working hours and relatively more disposable income once Marg was working full time, they were susceptible to appeals to find fulfilment and identity in the world beyond work.[69] Some postwar social scientists were convinced that workers like Harold and Marg had simply been integrated more tightly into capitalist society through easier access to consumer goods and thus suffered "bourgeoisification" or "embourgeoisement."[70] Were they? For this couple, consumerism was not a simple phenomenon. On the one hand, their purchases were necessarily limited by tight budgets (and a resistance to running up debt). They were also invariably practical. Buying their house was a hard-headed decision to find affordable housing and to make some extra money from the land around it – not a flight to some suburban utopia.[71] Beyond the house, the car was their most important possession. Yet it too met a practical need – there was no public transit to their part of the suburbs until the 1970s, and their whole way of life had to be organized around automobility. Indeed, the car was arguably enabling working people like Harold and Marg to redefine public space and to appropriate more of it.[72] These major purchases, along with the refrigerator[73] and deep freezer, were simply basic efforts to make life a little easier and more comfortable. And Marg knew that it was her extra earnings that made it all possible. On the other hand, Marg was a dedicated, almost compulsive shopper – she loved the experience. Without a driver's licence, she dragged Harold and the boys off on frequent consumerist expeditions through the cheaper department stores in suburban shopping centres (K-Mart, Woolco, Zellers, etc.). But the pleasure was not merely in the looking and buying. Shopping had a larger purpose. For Marg, it was a careful process of finding bargains on small goods that would enhance the family's comfort and respectability. She was enormously proud of her ability to use her shopping skills to put a good face on the family. Her triumph was to put together products of her shrewd shopping expedition into a display – the costumes and stage set of respectability. This was her "text"; she inscribed her aspirations in the material culture – the textures, colours, surfaces, and objects – of the family household.[74]

So Harold and Marg lived through the three decades after the Second World War actively engaged with powerful discourses that, according to much historical and theoretical writing, should have channelled their consciousness away from class-based identities. Yet, as I have tried to suggest, that would be a simplistic reading of their consciousness and behaviour. They constructed an understanding of their social situation and a set of behavioural practices from elements of their upbringing in farm houses and urban shops, from the variety of cultural forces around them, but also from the regular need to make ends meet. They justified and rationalized their behaviour within the discursive frameworks available to them, but that involved negotiation of all that received wisdom in the specific context of their lives and a process of sifting, adjusting, absorbing, and rejecting, often in confusion and with contradictory consequences. Their understanding of the world, in all its fragmented, incomplete, and muddled dimensions, was constantly woven and re-woven in ways that connected with the daily realities of surviving through wage labour. In the process they not only shaped distinctively working-class forms of gender, suburbanism, religion, ethnicity, citizenship, popular culture, meritocracy, and consumerism; but also wove all of those into a distinctively working-class identity. If we are to come close to understanding the making of working-class Canada in the postwar period, we will need to pay attention to how working people drew on these cultural resources around them to fashion something new and distinctive.

For Harold and Marg the core of that identity was working-class respectability. What they wanted above all was to achieve the public affirmation of their success in combatting the economic vulnerability that resulted from their subordination and the demoralizing effects of having to accept limited earnings from employers who demeaned their skills. Their class struggle was to maintain a level of decency in the face of still tight material constraints. In these circumstances, respectability was not simply an attitude – it was a practice. In fact, for Marg, respectability was a collective performance, one that involved orchestrating all family members into active, dramatic compliance.

Harold and Marg never walked a picket line or marched in a demonstration. They never went to a union picnic or marched in a Labour Day parade. They never took out membership in a radical organization or attended any meetings or events of such groups. They therefore stood outside the mainstream of most writing in labour history. But, if we scale down our preconceived expectations of collective class accomplishments, they were nonetheless, in the broadest sense, part of a class *for itself*, expressing one form (and certainly not *the only* form) of class consciousness. They were somewhat deferential, but not passive or easily manipulated. In their own ways, they were unquestionably engaged in a class-based struggle for existence, which they shared with countless thousands of other Canadians in the postwar period. They did not wage this struggle alone. Unions or political parties remained unfamiliar, distant, and unappreciated as vehicles of their interests and concerns (as they quietly took for granted the benefits of Harold's union membership); but from their respective backgrounds they knew they could trust family and kin as crucial collective resources for their immediate, local, and narrowly conceived battles for security and dignity.

In fact, they are exemplars of something more generalized within the working class – what I like to call working-class realism. It was not a fixed political position and certainly not a synonym for conservatism, but rather a propensity among workers during the past 150 years to evaluate what is possible and realizable in any given context and to act on that understanding, an evaluation often proceeding from similar places in the same period across the working class. At historic moments such as 1886, 1919, or 1946, the scope of "realistic" possibilities could expand dramatically.[75] At others they contracted just as abruptly. The difference between those moments was how workers evaluated their changing social circumstances through the cultural and discursive lenses available to them. In the case of Harold and Marg, the context of full employment and Keynesian state policies in the three decades after the war gave them a new terrain on which to make a decent life for themselves, but their responses fit patterns running back to the Montreal families of the 1870s.[76]

And what about the boys? What happened to them? Their adult lives diverged sharply, one closer to their parents' working-class experience, the other moving into a middle-class professional niche. Like many professionals in the public sector, the older boy was nonetheless unionized and walked picket lines for his own union twice.[77] Yet his conception of class came increasingly from research and writing on the history of working-class Canada. As he stands before you today, honoured that his labours on these subjects garnered him sufficient respect to be elevated to head an organization of Canadian historians, he remains convinced, from personal experience, intellectual formation, and political awareness, that class analysis in Canadian history, and in the present, is more important than ever.

But we have to do it right. We have to retain an important component of the materialism that always inspired class analysis. But we also have to incorporate the many complexities and complications that all the rethinking of class has brought about. If we do, unassuming people like Harold and Marg will find their rightful place in history.

Notes

1 There has, of course, been a much longer history to the term than I am acknowledging here. See Raymond Williams, *Keywords: A Vocabulary of Culture and Society* (London: Fontana 1986), 57–9.

2 For example, see Gregory S. Kealey, "Labour and Working-Class History in Canada: Prospects for the 1980s," *L/LT* 7 (1981), 67–94. This marked a departure from Canadian historians' general indifference to the concept. See S.R. Meeling, "The Concept of Social Class and the Interpretation of Canadian History," *CHR* 46, no. 3 (September 1965), 201–18. For a review of the British debates, see Geoff Eley and Keith Nield, *The Future of Class in History: What's Left of the Social?* (Ann Arbor: University of Michigan Press 2007).

3 The three most influential books in critiquing "materialism" were Gareth Stedman Jones, *Languages of Class: Studies in English Working-Class History, 1832–1982* (Cambridge: Cambridge University Press 1983); Joan Scott, *Gender and the Politics of History* (New York: Columbia University Press 1988); and Patrick Joyce, *Visions of the People: Industrial England and the*

Question of Class, 1848–1914 (Cambridge: Cambridge University Press 1991). See also Patrick Joyce, ed., *Class* (Oxford: Oxford University Press 1995); and John R. Hall, ed., *Reworking Class* (Ithaca, NY: Cornell University Press 1997).

4 Marg was on the leading edge of married women returning to full-time employment. Between 1951 and 1961, the proportion of married women in Ontario working for pay rose from one in ten to one in five. By the mid-1960s, half the provinces' female workforce was married. Joan Sangster, "Doing Two Jobs: The Wage-Earning Mother, 1945–70," in Joy Parr, ed., *A Diversity of Women: Ontario, 1945–1980* (Toronto: University of Toronto Press 1995), 99–100; Veronica Strong-Boag, "Home Dreams: Women and the Suburban Experiment in Canada, 1945–60," *CHR* 72, no. 4 (December 1991), 479–81.

5 The backyard vegetable garden lasted only a few summers, probably as a result of the low cost of fresh food in those decades.

6 S.D. Clark noted that in Toronto's suburbs of the early 1950s, "taking over the countryside in this early phase of movement of population from the city was most successfully accomplished by people in impoverished circumstances prepared to accept whatever the country had to offer them in preference to what was available to them in the city." The east end of the Township of Scarborough, where Harold and Marg settled, welcomed many such people. S.D. Clark, *The Suburban Society* (Toronto: University of Toronto Press 1966), 23–46 (quotation at 29). Working-class suburbs in the period are also discussed in Strong-Boag, "Home Dreams," 484–8; Pierre Vallieres, *The White Niggers of America* (Toronto: McClelland and Stewart 1971), 78–120. On the general phenomenon of owner-building, see Richard Harris, *Creeping Conformity: How Canada Became Suburban, 1900–1960* (Toronto: University of Toronto Press 2004), 148–52.

7 Harris, *Creeping Conformity*; Clark, *Suburban Society*; Lizabeth Cohen, *A Consumers' Republic: The Politics of Mass Consumption in Postwar America* (New York: Alfred A. Knopf 2003), 200–12. Doug Owram is undoubtedly right to see all this as a search for security after the disruptions of depression and war. See Doug Owram, "Canadian Domesticity in the Postwar Era," in Peter Neary and J.L. Granatstein, eds., *The Veterans' Charter and Post–World War II Canada* (Montreal and Kingston: McGill-Queen's University Press 1998), 205–23. See also Magda Fahrni, *Household Politics: Montreal Families and Postwar Reconstruction* (Toronto: University of Toronto Press 2005). The older patterns are discussed in Bettina Bradbury, *Working Families: Gender, Age, and Daily Survival in Industrializing Montreal* (Toronto: Oxford University Press 1993).

8 Rosemary Crompton, *Class and Stratification: An Introduction to Current Debates*, 2nd ed. (London: Polity Press 1998). There was a Marxist variant that pursued the infinite complexities of mapping the class "positions" or "locations" of various groups within capitalist society, notably Eric Olin Wright, *Classes* (London: Verso, 1985). For a more freewheeling approach to class as status, see Paul Fussell, *Class: A Guide Through the American Status System* (New York: Simon and Schuster 1992).

9 For the clearest statement, see G.A. Cohen, *Karl Marx's Theory of History: A Defence* (Princeton: Princeton University Press 1978). That mode of thinking led some Marxist writers and scholars to focus primarily on the top-down restructuring of capitalist industry and its internal management. In particular, see Harry Braverman, *Labor and Monopoly Capitalism* (New York: Monthly Review Press 1974).

10 Harvey J. Kaye, *The British Marxist Historians* (London: Polity Press 1984); Eley and Nield, *Future of Class*, 19–43; Bryan D. Palmer, *E.P. Thompson: Objections and Oppositions* (London: Verso 1994).

11 Karl Polanyi made this point more than half a century ago in *The Great Transformation: The Political and Economic Transformation of Our Times* (Boston: Beacon Hill Press 1957). More recently, the commanding figure in arguing against a base-superstructure model or a separation of structure and agency was E.P. Thompson. In his early work Anthony Giddens also advanced a parallel notion of "structuration" that integrated the two. See also Ellen Meiksins Wood, *Democracy against Capitalism: Renewing Historical Materialism* (Cambridge: Cambridge University Press 1995); Raymond Williams, "Base and Superstructure in Marxist Cultural Theory," *NLR* 82 (November/December 1973), 3–16; William H. Sewell, Jr, "Toward a Post-Materialist Rhetoric for Labor History," in Lenard R. Berlanstein, ed., *Rethinking Labor History: Essays on Discourse and Class Analysis* (Urbana: University of Illinois Press 1993), 15–38.

12 Ralph Miliband, *The State in Capitalist Society* (London: Quartet Books 1984); Bob Jessop, *The Capitalist State: Marxist Theories and Methods* (New York: New York University Press 1982); Leo Panitch, "The Role and Nature of the Canadian State," in Leo Panitch, ed., *The Canadian State: Political Economy and Political Power* (Toronto: University of Toronto Press, 1977), 3–77; Ian McKay, "The Liberal Order Framework: A Prospectus for a Reconnaissance of Canadian History," *CHR* 81, no. 4 (December 2000), 617–45.

13 In particular, see Ira Katznelson and Aristide R. Zolberg, eds., *Working-Class Formation: Nineteenth-Century Patterns in Western Europe and the United States* (Princeton: Princeton University Press 1986).

14 Joan Scott, *Gender and the Politics of History* (New York: Columbia University Press 1999); Joy Parr, "Gender History and Historical Practice," in Joy Parr and Mark Rosenfeld, eds., *Gender and History in Canada* (Toronto: Copp Clark 1996), 8–27; Ava Baron, ed., *Work Engendered: Toward a New History of American Labor* (Ithaca, NY: Cornell University Press 1991); Alice Kessler-Harris, *Gendering Labor History* (Urbana: University of Illinois Press 2007); Laura L. Frader and Sonya O. Rose, "Introduction: Gender and the Reconstruction of European Working Class History," in Laura L. Frader and Sonya O. Rose, eds., *Gender and Class in Modern Europe* (Ithaca, NY: Cornell University Press 1996), 1–33; Meg Luxton, *More Than a Labour of Love: Three Generations of Women's Work in the Home* (Toronto: Women's Press 1980).

15 Donald Avery, *Reluctant Host: Canada's Response to Immigrant Workers, 1896–1994* (Toronto: McClelland and Stewart 1995); Constance Backhouse, *Colour-Coded: A Legal History of Racism in Canada, 1900–1950* (Toronto: University of Toronto Press 1999); Franca Iacovetta with Paula Draper and Robert Ventresca, eds., *A Nation of Immigrants: Women, Workers, and Communities in Canadian History, 1840s–1960s* (Toronto: University of Toronto Press 1998).

16 In particular, see Joy Parr, *The Gender of Breadwinners: Women, Men, and Change in Two Industrial Towns, 1880–1950* (Toronto: University of Toronto Press, 1990); Ruth Frager, "Labour History and the Interlocking Hierarchies of Class, Ethnicity, and Gender: A Canadian Perspective," *IRSH* 44 (1999), 217–47; Pamela Sugiman, "Privilege and Oppression: The Configuration of Race, Gender, and Class in Southern Ontario Auto Plants, 1939 to 1949," *L/LT* 47 (Spring 2001), 83–113; Kathleen Canning, "Gender: Meanings, Methods, and Metanarratives," in *Gender History in Practice: Historical Perspectives on Bodies, Class, and Citizenship* (Ithaca: Cornell University Press 2006), 3–62; Sonya O. Rose, "Class Formation and the Quintessential Worker," in *Reworking Class*, 133–66.

17 Neville Kirk also uses this broader construct of structure in "Decline and Fall, Resilience and Regeneration: A Review Essay on Social Class," *ILWCH* 57 (Spring 2000), 88–102.

18 "On the Job in Canada," in this volume; Gregory S. Kealey, "The Structure of Canadian Working-Class History," in *Workers and Canadian History*, 329–44.

19 Jamie Brownlee, *Ruling Canada: Corporate Cohesion and Democracy* (Halifax, NS: Fernwood Publishing 2005); Stanley Aronowitz, *How Class Works: Power and Social Movement* (New Haven, CT: Yale University Press 2003); Michael Zweig, *The Working Class Majority: America's Best Kept Secret* (Ithaca, NY: ILR Press 2000); Ian McKay, "Canada as a

Long Liberal Revolution: On Writing the History of Actually Existing Canadian Liberalism, 1840s–1940s," in Jean-François Constant and Michel Ducharme, eds., *Liberalism and Hegemony: Debating the Canadian Liberal Revolution* (Toronto: University of Toronto Press 2009), 347–452.

20 Mitchell Dean, *Governmentality: Power and Rule in Modern Society* (London: Sage Publications 1999).

21 As many scholars have been reminding us, coping with these structural pressures constantly engaged the human body – in physical labour, childbirth, levels of health and nutrition, accidents, sexuality, and much more. Kathleen Canning, "The Body as Method? Reflections on the Place of the Body in Gender History," in *Gender History in Practice*, 168–89; Ava Baron, "Masculinity, the Embodied Male Worker, and the Historian's Gaze," *ILWCH* 69 (Spring 2000), 143–60.

22 They were palpably nervous having to entertain the parents of the older boy's first partner, a university professor and his stay-at-home wife. On this general working-class sense of failure alongside the more educated, see Richard Sennett and Jonathan Cobb, *The Hidden Injuries of Class* (New York: Vintage Books 1973); also James Lorimer and Myfanwy Phillips, *Working People: Life in a Downtown City Neighbourhood* (Toronto: James Lewis and Samuel 1971), 46.

23 One influential theorist labels such "durable, transposable dispositions" as the "habitus" that shaped much behaviour. Pierre Bourdieu, *Outline of a Theory of Practice* (Cambridge: University of Cambridge Press 1977); and "What Makes a Social Class? On the Theoretical and Practical Existence of Groups," *Berkeley Journal of Sociology* 32 (1987), 1–17.

24 E.P. Thompson, *The Making of the English Working Class* (London: Penguin 1968), 9–15; William H. Sewell, Jr, "How Classes Are Made: Critical Reflections on E.P. Thompson's Theory of Working-Class Formation," in Harvey J. Kaye and Keith McClelland, eds., *E.P. Thompson: Critical Perspectives* (Philadelphia: Temple University Press 1990), 59–66; Marc W. Steinberg, "Talkin' Class: Discourse, Ideology, and Their Roles in Class Conflict," in Scott W. McNall, Rhonda F. Levine, and Rick Fantasia, eds., *Bringing Class Back In: Contemporary and Historical Perspectives* (Boulder, CO: Westview Press 1991), 261–84; and "Culturally Speaking: Finding a Commons between Post-Structuralism and the Thompsonian Perspective," *SH* 21, no. 2 (May 1996), 193–214; Canning, *Gender History in Practice*, 72–7, 101–20; Eley and Nield, *Future of Class*. In an effort to break the simplistic assumption that awareness of working-class self-interest leads straightforwardly to collective organization in support of those interests, Ira Katzelson has tried to elaborate a more sophisticated

analytical framework of "levels" of awareness, which, however, do not fundamentally abandon the close association of material situation and political expression. Ira Katzneson, "Working-Class Formation: Constructing Cases and Comparisons," in *Working-Class Formation*, 3–41. Even one of the severest critics of postmodernist history, Neville Kirk, has admitted that "language and systems of discourse play active roles in the creation of aspects of social reality, rather than being mere expressions and reflections of a totally given, or preexisting external reality." See Neville Kirk, "History, Language, Ideas, and Post-Modernism: A Materialist View," *SH* 19, no. 2 (May 1994), 233.

25 Goran Therborn, "Why Some Classes Are More Successful Than Others," *NLR* 138 (1983), 37–55.

26 Like others in his position, Harold kept alive a faint hope of starting his own business; but, after a bank manager rejected his application for a loan to start a trucking company with his brother in the 1950s, he never actively pursued such an independent option.

27 This argument rested on two kinds of explanations. One focused on the narrow, exclusive self-interest of better-off workers, who cut themselves off from the less skilled – a "labour aristocracy" in the nineteenth century and a white-supremacist occupational elite in the twentieth. The other put more emphasis on ideological failings of "reformist" labour leaders. Such a perspective suffered from both unfortunate condescension toward working people (who appeared as either charlatans or dupes) and an impossible standard of comparison – no working class has ever reached the purity of class consciousness expected of them.

28 This Italian Marxist of the 1920s argued that the class domination and subordination could not be explained simply by the exercise of direct coercion, but required the cultivation of "consent" to the system of subordination, that is the production through many cultural institutions and processes of hegemonic understandings of capitalist societies that were accepted by the subordinated as apparently intuitive "common sense." Antonio Gramsci, *Prison Notebooks* (New York: Columbia University Press 1992); Jackson Lears, "The Concept of Cultural Hegemony: Problems and Possibilities," *AHR* 90, no. 3 (June 1985), 567–93; Constant and Ducharme, eds., *Liberalism and Hegemony*.

29 Paul Rabinow and Nikolas Rose, eds., *The Essential Foucault: Selections from Essential Works of Foucault, 1954–84* (New York: New Press 2003).

30 Harold and Marg had little time or interest in printed text beyond the daily newspaper, one or two women's magazines, and the Bible. Magazines from union and church were largely ignored.

31 Even though Marg spent her paid workdays seated at a desk, engaged in relatively clean office work, she came home to a great deal of hard manual toil.

32 Bryan D. Palmer, *A Culture in Conflict: Skilled Workers and Industrial Capitalism in Hamilton, Ontario, 1860–1914* (Montreal and Kingston: McGill-Queen's University Press 1979), 97–122; Gregory S. Kealey and Bryan D. Palmer, *Dreaming of What Might Be: The Knights of Labor in Ontario, 1880–1900* (Toronto: New Hogtown Press 1987); Lorimer and Phillips, *Working People*, 106–17; Michele Lamont, *The Dignity of Working Men: Morality and the Boundaries of Race, Class, and Immigration* (Cambridge, MA: Harvard University Press 2000); Wally Seccombe and D.W. Livingstone, *"Down to Earth People": Beyond Class Reductionism and Postmodernism* (Aurora: Garamond Press 2000), 47–8.

33 As S.D. Clark made clear in his study of Toronto's suburbs of the 1950s, the more remote and under-serviced, such as Harold and Marg chose, filled up overwhelmingly with younger couples under age 35. In their case, older kin therefore remained either in the city or in rural areas. Clark, *Suburban Society*, 82–90.

34 Harold got his first job driving a coal truck from an uncle who owned a small firm, and later had help getting his public-utilities job from Marg's uncle, a suburban politician. Both boys got summer jobs from uncles or family friends, and, after the younger boy dropped out of university, Marg's cousin shepherded him into an electrical apprenticeship. They got cast-off furniture from kin. They also reached out for help from kin – Marg's grandmother provided a mortgage for their first house; Harold regularly borrowed tools from this father and got his brother to help dig a well and fix a disabled car; and Marg talked to her mother every day about any number of domestic problems and sent the boys to stay with her twice for extended periods when Marg was seriously ill; and eventually Marg moved her mother into their household in her old age.

35 We have been told about similar kin solidarities among new immigrant groups in this same period, but the experience of this Anglo-Canadian family suggests that we should be paying far more attention to family and kin in our understanding of working-class behaviour in postwar Canada more generally. Franca Iacovetta, *Such Hardworking People: Italian Immigrants in Postwar Toronto* (Montreal and Kingston: McGill-Queen's University Press 1992); John R. Gillis, *A World of Their Own Making: Myth, Ritual, and the Quest for Family Values* (Cambridge, MA: Harvard University Press 1996); Leslie Bella, *The Christmas Imperative: Leisure, Family, and Women's Work* (Halifax, NS: Fernwood Publishing 1992);

Micaela di Leonardo, "The Female World of Cards and Holidays: Women, Families, and the Work of Kinship," *Signs* 12, no. 3 (Spring 1987), 440–53. The importance of kin networks was noted in Canadian, American, and British studies of working-class life undertaken in this period. Lorimer and Phillips, *Working People*, 45; Berger, *Working-Class Suburb*, 67–8, 72; William M. Dobriner, *Class in Suburbia* (Englewood Cliffs, NJ: Prentice-Hall 1963), 106–7; Mirra Komarovsky, *Blue-Collar Marriage* (New Haven, CT: Yale University Press 1987 [1962]), 36–7, 208–15, 236–79; Lilian Breslow Rubin, *Worlds of Pain: Life in the Working-Class Family* (New York: Basic Books 1976), 197; Michael Young and Peter Wilmott, *Family and Kinship in East London* (London: Routledge and Kegan Paul 1957).

36 Peter S. McInnis, *Harnessing Labour Confrontation: Shaping the Postwar Settlement in Canada, 1943–1950* (Toronto: University of Toronto Press 2002); Judy Fudge and Eric Tucker, *Labour before the Law: The Regulation of Workers' Collective Action in Canada, 1900–1948* (Toronto: Oxford University Press 2001), 263–301; Bryan D. Palmer, *Working-Class Experience: Rethinking the History of Canadian Labor, 1800–1991* (Toronto: McClelland and Stewart 1992), 278–90.

37 In the early 1940s, Harold had been required to work Saturday mornings, like most other blue-collar workers. By the 1970s, he was able to use the overtime provisions of the collective agreement to work up a month's extra holiday time, in addition to the month he was already entitled to.

38 David A. Wolfe, "The Rise and Demise of the Keynesian Era in Canada: Economic Policy, 1930–1982," in Michael S. Cross and Gregory S. Kealey, eds., *Readings in Canadian Social History, Vol. 5: Modern Canada, 1930–1980s* (Toronto: McClelland and Stewart 1984); Robert M. Campbell, *Grand Illusions: The Politics of the Keynesian Experience in Canada, 1945–1975* (Toronto: Broadview Press 1987).

39 Dennis Guest, *The Emergence of Social Security in Canada* (Vancouver: University of British Columbia Press 1980); James Struthers, "Family Allowances, Old-Age Security, and the Construction of Entitlement in the Canadian State, 1943–51," in Neary and Granastein, eds., *Veterans Charter*, 179–204; Dominque Marshall, *The Social Origins of the Welfare State: Quebec Families, Compulsory Education and Family Allowances, 1940–1955* (Waterloo: Wilfrid Laurier University Press 2006); Richard Harris and Tricia Shulist, "Canada's Reluctant Housing Program: The Veterans' Land Act, 1942–1975," *CHR* 82, no. 2 (June 2001), 253–82.

40 S.D. Clark was thus too hasty in claiming that new suburbanites wanted "a home, not a new social world." Clark, *Suburban Society*, 110. The home was the centrepiece of new aspirations for a better life. Magda Fahrni

perceptively calls this a search for "economic citizenship"; see *Household Politics*, 119–23.

41 Reg Whitaker and Gary Marcuse, *Cold War Canada: The Making of a National Insecurity State, 1945–57* (Toronto: University of Toronto Press 1994).

42 Strong-Boag, "Home Dreams"; Owram, "Canadian Domesticity"; Valerie J. Korinek, *Roughing It in the Suburbs: Reading Chatelaine Magazine in the Fifties and Sixties* (Toronto: University of Toronto Press 2000).

43 Blue-collar men interviewed in the United States in the 1960s and 1970s had similar attitudes to housework. See Komarovsky, *Blue-Collar Marriage*, 50–6; Rubin, *Worlds of Pain*, 10. See also Luxton, *More Than a Labour of Love*, 180. Harold was nonetheless prepared to do dishes regularly and sometimes made brown-bag lunches for himself and the boys.

44 Joan Sangster found many women she interviewed faced similar resistance to their wage-earning from their husbands. Sangster, "Doing Two Jobs," 120–l.

45 I have explored some of the issues of working-class masculinities in "Boys Will Be Boys: Working-Class Masculinities in the Age of Mass Production," *ILWCH* 69 (Spring 2006), 6–34; and "The Boys and Their Booze: Masculinities and Public Drinking in Working-Class Hamilton, 1890–1946," *CHR* 86, no. 3 (September 2005), 411–52. On the homosocial life of married working-class men in this period, see Komarovsky, *Blue-Collar Marriage*, 28–32. See also Thomas W. Dunk, *It's a Working Man's Town: Male Working-Class Culture in Northwestern Ontario* (Montreal and Kingston: McGill-Queen's University Press 1991).

46 In her interviews with working-class housewives in the early 1960s, Mirra Komarovsky found considerable satisfaction with the domestic role. *Blue-Collar Marriage*, 56–60. Compared to an early-twentieth-first-century household, Marg's work at home was still relatively labour intensive. For food preparation, the family's only electric domestic technology before 1970 included a stove, refrigerator, toaster, and deep freezer, for cleaning a vacuum cleaner and floor polisher, and for laundry a wringer washing machine and electric iron. Domestic technologies in postwar households are explored in Joy Parr, *Domestic Goods: The Material, the Moral and the Economic in the Postwar Years* (Toronto: University of Toronto Press 1999). The "labour-saving" technologies did not necessarily mean less work for housewives, since expectations of good housekeeping rose dramatically in the same period. See Luxton, *More Than a Labour of Love*, 117–59; Ruth Schwartz Cowan, *More Work for Mother: The Ironies of Technology from the Open Hearth to the Microwave* (New York: Basic Books 1983). When she started full-time work, Marg insisted that part of her income had to cover the cost of having a cleaning woman in once a week.

47 Marg even insisted that Harold barbeque the steaks as a symbol of postwar masculinity – a task he neither liked nor excelled at. On that practice more generally, see Christopher Dummitt, "Finding a Place for Father: Selling the Barbeque in Postwar Canada," *JCHA* 9 (1998), 209–23.

48 See also Rubin, *Worlds of Pain*, 169. Marg had opportunities not available to married women living in many Canadian resource towns. See Luxton, *More Than a Labour of Love*, for a discussion of women in a Manitoba mining town.

49 Sangster, "Doing Two Jobs," 102–7, 120–5.

50 As Strong-Boag notes, feminists tended to be preoccupied with issues of paid work and had little positive to say about the domestic labour that women like Marg took so seriously. Strong Boag, "Their Side of the Story," 66–9. On labour-based feminism, see Meg Luxton, "Feminism as a Class Act: Working-Class Feminism and the Women's Movement in Canada," *L/LT* 48 (Fall 2001), 63–88.

51 For similar, though more tragic stories of working-class wives and mothers in this period, see Vallières, *White Niggers*, 80–5; Carolyn Steedman, *Landscape for a Good Woman: A Story of Two Lives* (London: Virago Press 1986). For the persistence of many of these gender dynamics in working-class households into the 1980s and 1990s, see Meg Luxton and June Corman, *Getting By in Hard Times: Gendered Labour at Home and on the Job* (Toronto: University of Toronto Press 2001).

52 Berger, *Working-Class Suburb*; Dobriner, *Class in Suburbia*; Herbert J. Gans, *The Levittowners: Ways of Life and Politics in a New Suburban Community* (New York: Vintage 1967); Clark, *Suburban Society*.

53 For example, see Lorimer and Phillips, *Working People*.

54 Nancy Christie and Michael Gauvreau, "The World of the Common People Is Filled with Religious Fervour," in G.A. Rawlyk, ed., *Aspects of the Canadian Evangelical Experience* (Montreal and Kingston: McGill-Queen's University Press, 1997), 337–50; Eric Crouse, "'They Left Us Pretty Much as We Were': American Saloon/Factory Evangelists and Canadian Working Men in the Early Twentieth Century," Canadian Society of Church History, *Historical Papers* 1999, 51–7; Norman Knowles, "'Christ in the Crowsnest': Religion and the Anglo-Canadian Working Class in the Crowsnest Pass, 1898–1918," in Michael Behiels and Marcel Martel, ed., *Nation, Ideas, and Identities: Essays in Honour of Ramsay Cook* (Don Mills, ON: Oxford University Press 1997), 57–71; Melissa Turkstra, "Working-Class Churches in Early Twentieth-Century Hamilton: Fostering a Distinctive Working-Class Identity and Culture," *HS/SH* 41, no. 82 (November 2009), 459–504.

55 Beyond a few years in a "Couples Club," Harold and Marg were not joiners within their congregations. They sent the boys to Sunday School (where Marg taught for a while) and later to a teenage church group.

56 The democratic thrust of their Protestant faith also made them harsh critics of Catholicism, which they saw as priest-ridden authoritarianism. For the role of religion in black working-class consciousness in the United States, see bell hooks, *Where We Stand: Class Matters* (New York: Routledge 2000), 38–49.

57 Three-quarters of residents of the suburban township (later borough) in which they lived in 1961 were Canadian born, and the same proportion claimed British ethnicity. Clark, *Suburban Society*, 100.

58 Marg was particularly scornful of the mother in the neighbourhood's only black family, who had begun writing articles about Anglo-Canadian racism. "We never did anything to her," she insisted.

59 For example, see Allen Seager, "Class, Ethnicity, and Politics in the Alberta Coalfields, 1905–1945," in Dirk Hoerder, ed., *"Struggle a Hard Battle": Essays on Working-Class Immigrants* (Dekalb: Northern Illinois University Press 1986), 204–24; Carmela Patrias, "Relief Strike: Immigrant Workers and the Great Depression in Crowland, Ontario, 1930–1935," in *Nation of Immigrants*, 322–58; Gillian Creese, "Class, Ethnicity, and Conflict: The Case of Chinese and Japanese Immigrants, 1880–1923," in Rennie Warburton and David Coburn, ed., *Workers, Capital, and the State in British Columbia: Selected Papers* (Vancouver: University of British Columbia Press 1988), 55–85; Maria Kefalas, *Working-Class Heroes: Protecting Home, Community, and Nation in a Chicago Neighborhood* (Berkeley: University of California Press 2003), 27–43.

60 Whitaker and Marcuse, *Cold War Canada*. In the 1980s, Marg would still look visibly frightened at the prospect of visiting a Communist country like Cuba.

61 Peter Stursberg, *Diefenbaker: Leadership Gained, 1956–62* (Toronto: University of Toronto Press 1975); Denis Smith, *Rogue Tory: The Life and Legend of John G. Diefenbaker* (Toronto: Mcfarlane, Walter, and Ross 1995). The lyrics of "Dief Will Be the Chief Again" are available at www.stringband.net. Harold and Marg were Canadian counterparts to the much-studied British working-class Tories of the same period. In particular, see Robert McKenzie and Allan Silver, *Angels in Marble: Working Class Conservatives in Urban England* (Chicago: University of Chicago Press 1968); Eric A. Nordlinger, *The Working-Class Tories: Authority, Deference and Stable Democracy* (London: MacGibbon and Kee 1967).

62 Across the country the rising support for the party brought provincial NDP victories in Manitoba, Saskatchewan, British Columbia, and

official-opposition status in Ontario. Desmond Morton, *The New Democrats, 1961–1986: The Politics of Change* (Toronto: Copp Clark 1986).

63 David Halle found similar views among New Jersey blue-collar workers in the 1970s. *America's Working Man*, 191–201. Many social scientists explored the apparent weakness of class voting in Canada. For example, see Jon H. Pammett, "Class Voting and Class Consciousness in Canada," *CRSA* 24, no. 2 (May 1987), 269–90.

64 For example, see Lorimer and Phillips, *Working People*, 75–117. Hence, the voting patterns of people like Harold and Marg are not good indicators of class awareness, since they did not expect electoral politics, or much else about the workings of government, to have much to do with confronting the major issues in their daily lives.

65 They did give the boys access to commercialized youth culture by buying them cheap transistor radios and a record player.

66 Paul Rutherford, *When Television Was Young: Primetime Canada, 1952–1967* (Toronto: University of Toronto Press 1990); Eric Barnouw, *Tube of Plenty: The Evolution of American Television* (New York: Oxford University Press 1990); Gerard Jones, *Honey, I'm Home! Sitcoms: The Selling of the American Dream* (New York: St Martin's Press 1992); Berger, *Working-Class Suburb*, 74–6. There was even a Sunday evening ritual of eating dinner while watching such family-oriented television as "Disneyland."

67 Neil Guppy and Scott Davies, *Education in Canada: Recent Trends and Future Challenges* (Ottawa: Statistics Canada 1998), 88; Paul Axelrod, *Scholars and Dollars: Politics, Economics, and the Universities of Ontario, 1945–1980* (Toronto: University of Toronto Press 1982); Doug Owram, *Born at the Right Time: A History of the Baby Boom Generation* (Toronto: University of Toronto Press 1996). On working-class interest in the educational advancement of the next generation, see also Berger, *Working-Class Suburb*, 15–27.

68 Sennett and Cobb explore these ambivalent feelings among American working-class parents in *Hidden Injuries of Class*. See also Michael D. Yates, *In and Out of the Working Class* (Winnipeg: Arbeiter Ring Publishing 2009).

69 Cohen, *Consumers' Republic*, 152–5.

70 Herbert Marcuse, *One-Dimensional Man: Studies in the Ideology of Advanced Industrial Society* (Boston: Beacon Press 1964); John H. Goldthorpe, *The Affluent Worker in the Class Structure* (London: Cambridge University Press 1969); David Lockwood, *The Blackcoated Worker: A Study in Class Consciousness* (London: Unwin 1966). More recently, postmodern critics of class have generally made consumerism central to their alternative perspective. For example, see John R. Hall, "The Reworking of Class Analysis," in *Reworking Class*, 5.

71 S.D. Clark found this practical need for affordable housing was the main motivating force behind the move to the suburbs. *Suburban Society*, 47–81.

72 See James J. Flink, *The Automobile Age* (Cambridge, MA: Massachusetts Institute of Technology Press 1990); Clay McShane, *Down the Asphalt Path: The Automobile and the American City* (New York: Columbia University Press 1994); *Steve Penfold, The Donut: A Canadian History* (Toronto: University of Toronto Press 2008).

73 The refrigerator was purchased in the 1950s when getting ice blocks for the ice box became difficult in the outer suburbs.

74 See Joy Parr, "Household Choices as Politics and Pleasure in 1950s Canada," *ILWCH* 55 (Spring 1999), 112–28. Class differences in consumption are also explored in Cohen, *Consumers' Republic*; and Pierre Bourdieu, *Distinction: A Social Critique of the Judgement of Taste* (Cambridge, MA: Harvard University Press 1984).

75 See Kealey and *Dreaming of What Might Be*; Craig Heron, ed., *The Workers' Revolt in Canada, 1917–1925* (Toronto: University of Toronto Press, 1998).

76 As revealed in Bradbury, *Working Families.*

77 There were also personal challenges in adapting to a middle-class way of life. bell hooks explores some of these issues in *Where We Stand*, as do Jake Ryan and Charles Sackrey in *Strangers in Paradise: Academics from the Working Class* (Boston: South End Press, 1984), and Yates in *In and Out of the Working Class.*

www.ingramcontent.com/pod-product-compliance
Lightning Source LLC
LaVergne TN
LVHW020430080826
844660LV00034B/1376

* 9 7 8 1 4 8 7 5 2 2 5 1 3 *